LIFESCAPES

Why does landscape matter to us? We rarely articulate the often highly individual ways it can do so. Drawing on eight remarkable unpublished diaries, Jeremy Burchardt demonstrates that responses to landscape in modern Britain were powerfully affected by personal circumstances, especially those experienced in childhood and youth. Four major patterns are identified: 'Adherers' valued landscape for its continuity, 'Withdrawers' for the refuge it provides from perceived threats, 'Restorers' for its sustaining of core value systems, and 'Explorers' for its opportunities for self-discovery and development. *Lifescapes* sets out a new approach to landscape history based on comparative biography and deep contextualization, which has far-reaching implications. It foregrounds family structures and relationships and the psychological dynamics they generate. These, it is argued, were usually a more decisive presence in landscape encounters than wider cultural patterns and forces. Seen in this way, landscape can be understood as a mirror reflecting our innermost selves and the psychosocial influences shaping our development. This is a compelling and original study of the relationship between individual lives and landscapes.

JEREMY BURCHARDT is Associate Professor in Rural History at the University of Reading. He is Principal Investigator of the Arts & Humanities Research Council research network 'Changing Landscapes, Changing Lives' and was P. H. Ditchfield Fellow at the Museum of English Rural Life, 2019–20. His previous publications include *The Allotment Movement in England, 1793–1873* (2002) and *Paradise Lost: Rural Idyll and Social Change since 1800* (2002).

Series Editors

Deborah Cohen, *Northwestern University*
Margot Finn, *University College London*
Peter Mandler, *University of Cambridge*

'Modern British Histories' publishes original research monographs drawn from the full spectrum of a large and lively community of modern historians of Britain. Its goal is to keep metropolitan and national histories of Britain fresh and vital in an intellectual atmosphere increasingly attuned to, and enriched by, the transnational, the international and the comparative. It will include books that focus on British histories within the UK and that tackle the subject of Britain and the world inside and outside the boundaries of formal empire from 1750 to the present. An indicative – not exclusive – list of approaches and topics that the series welcomes includes material culture studies, modern intellectual history, gender, race and class histories, histories of modern science and histories of British capitalism within a global framework. Open and wide-ranging, the series will publish books by authoritative scholars, at all stages of their career, with something genuinely new to say.

A complete list of titles in the series can be found at: www.cambridge.org/modernbritishhistories

LIFESCAPES

The Experience of Landscape in Britain, 1870–1960

JEREMY BURCHARDT

University of Reading

CAMBRIDGE
UNIVERSITY PRESS

Shaftesbury Road, Cambridge CB2 8EA, United Kingdom

One Liberty Plaza, 20th Floor, New York, NY 10006, USA

477 Williamstown Road, Port Melbourne, VIC 3207, Australia

314–321, 3rd Floor, Plot 3, Splendor Forum, Jasola District Centre,
New Delhi – 110025, India

103 Penang Road, #05–06/07, Visioncrest Commercial, Singapore 238467

Cambridge University Press is part of Cambridge University Press & Assessment,
a department of the University of Cambridge.

We share the University's mission to contribute to society through the pursuit
of education, learning and research at the highest international levels of excellence.

www.cambridge.org
Information on this title: www.cambridge.org/9781009199872

DOI: 10.1017/9781009199858

First published 2023

Printed in the United Kingdom by CPI Group Ltd, Croydon CR0 4YY

A catalogue record for this publication is available from the British Library.

Library of Congress Cataloging-in-Publication Data
Names: Burchardt, Jeremy, 1969– author.
Title: Lifescapes : the experience of landscape in Britain, 1870–1960 / Jeremy Burchardt.
Description: Cambridge ; New York, NY : Cambridge University Press, 2023. | Series:
Modern British histories | Includes bibliographical references and index.
Identifiers: LCCN 2022034113 (print) | LCCN 2022034114 (ebook) | ISBN 9781009199872
(hardback) | ISBN 9781009199858 (epub)
Subjects: LCSH: Landscapes – Great Britain – History. | Landscapes – Social aspects – Great
Britain. | Country life – Great Britain. | Great Britain – Rural conditions. | Great Britain –
Historical geography. | British – Diaries. | English diaries.
Classification: LCC GF551 .B87 2023 (print) | LCC GF551 (ebook) | DDC 304.2094109/04–
dc23/eng20221209
LC record available at https://lccn.loc.gov/2022034113
LC ebook record available at https://lccn.loc.gov/2022034114

ISBN 978-1-009-19987-2 Hardback

'O! The one life within us and abroad'
S. T. Coleridge

CONTENTS

FIGURES

A NOTE ON THE SUBTITLE

Lifescapes began as an investigation of landscape experience in England. But personal landscapes do not map neatly onto national boundaries. Many of the most compelling landscape experiences of the eight diarists selected for study took place in Scotland or Wales. This is therefore a book about landscape experience 'in Britain' but not about 'British landscape experiences'.

PREFACE

Landscapes, and perhaps especially rural landscapes, can affect people profoundly. Moreover, they can do so in deeply personal and often enduring ways. Yet the private meanings that landscape holds for us often go unarticulated and leave few traces in the historical record. Probably for this reason, they have hitherto received little attention from historians. The aim of *Lifescapes* is to develop a methodology that will open up this deep history of landscape and to apply it in the specific historical context of late nineteenth- and early twentieth-century England. The methodology can best be described as comparative landscape biography and it is deployed here in relation to the experiences of eight contrasting individuals, in the hope of bringing a much wider history into view.

Landscapes are not just the backdrop to life: through the meanings and significance we attribute to them, and the encounters we experience in them, they can be vital to our well-being and even, as the lives reconstructed in this book demonstrate, to our emotional equilibrium and development. Our relationship with landscape is a mirror of our lives in which both short-term circumstances and long-term structural features are reflected. More particularly, aspects of ourselves – thwarted hopes, longings and needs – that do not find expression or fulfilment in our everyday lives are often projected onto and can sometimes even be partially satisfied through landscape. Hence paying close attention to the roles landscape played in people's lives in the past illuminates the human constraints and limitations imposed on them by the societies in which they lived. To study the experience of landscape is also to study the human condition and the adequacy with which different forms of society are adapted to it.

As this perhaps suggests, this book is not a conventional history. It is at once more particular and more universal in its methods and aims than most histories – more particular because it seeks to reconstruct an aspect of its subjects' lives (i.e. the significance of rural landscapes to them) in painstaking biographical detail, and more universal because it does so with a view to identifying aspects of our relationship to landscape that are not necessarily specific to the times or places under study. This sits uneasily with the traditional historiographical preference for 'splitting' rather than 'lumping' – emphasizing the contrasts rather than the commonalities between different historical events and circumstances. Nor, despite appearances, should this book really be classified under the heading of biography or life writing. It shares with biography a commitment to the – ultimately of course unattainable – ideal of comprehensive knowledge and understanding of the life under study and to its representation in chronological order. But whereas biography is typically descriptive, my aim is analytical. The individual lives presented here are studied with a view to what they can tell us about the wider implications of one particular facet of them – the affective significance of rural landscapes. Nor should this book be considered an example of prosopography or group biography because the individuals studied do not form part of a group. Indeed, in order to maximize the range and diversity of the study, they were on purpose selected to be as different from each other as possible, except in the centrality of rural landscapes to their lives. My aims are closer to those of analytical collective biographies such as James Hinton's humane and enlightening *Nine Wartime Lives* (2010) and *Seven Lives from Mass Observation* (2016), but my premises and methods are very different. *Nine Wartime Lives* is principally focussed on a short period of its subjects' lives (the Second World War), while *Seven Lives from Mass Observation* is a slim volume confined to brief albeit captivating overviews. The core methodological principle of *Lifescapes*, by contrast, is in-depth contextualization. Only, I maintain, by reconstructing as many aspects as possible of the life of the individual concerned can the full implications and bearings of the role of landscape in their lives be understood. Similarly, I argue that our experience of landscape is shaped as much or more by long-term factors, often operating at a lifelong scale, as it is by immediate circumstances. These change, if they do at all, only very slowly, so a long-span approach is essential. These methodological considerations, and the need to achieve a sufficiently broad basis for comparison, explain the length of the book.

In some respects the questions this book asks and the conclusions it reaches belong as much to psychology as to history or life writing. Nevertheless it is motivated by very different interests and concerns than contemporary experimental psychology, and it adopts radically different methods. While experimental psychology is admirably rigorous, the price to be paid for this is that it often stops well short of addressing the more complex aspects of human motivation and behaviour that Freudian and other psychoanalytical approaches seek to explain. Conversely, psychoanalytical theories lack empirical verification and are difficult to retrofit to the messy complexity and incompleteness of historical evidence. Psychoanalytical influences can doubtless be discerned in this book behind the scenes but I have not felt constrained (nor do I have the expertise) to impose a specific psychoanalytical framework on the evidence. Perhaps, indeed, the approach I have taken is closer methodologically to that of a novelist than to that of most historians, biographers or psychologists. Certainly I have sought, insofar as it lies in me, to bring a novelist's sensibility, interests, flexibility and interpretative freedom to bear on my reading of the source material. This, it seems to me, is a legitimate and indeed logical response to the widespread recognition among historians, and within the humanities more generally, of the inherent and inescapable sub-jectivity of historical interpretation. Although non-historical disciplines such as the natural sciences may be able to avoid this through the experimental method, even the most influential historical and sociological models such as those formulated by Marx, Weber or Foucault remain contentious and unveri-fiable. Where my approach differs sharply from a novelist's is that I have accepted the historian's fundamental discipline of subordination to the evi-dence. I have invented nothing, tried to avoid suppressing anything and have taken as the litmus test of my interpretations how fully they account for all the evidence of which I am aware.

Just as this book is distinctive and, I hope, innovative in its methodology and disciplinary orientation, so it is in its understanding of landscape. Two approaches have dominated landscape history: the material and the cultural. Each has generated a rich and diverse literature. Within landscape history, the best-known and most influential examples of the first are W. G. Hoskins' *The Making of the English Landscape* (1955) and Oliver Rackham's *The History of the Countryside* (1986). Fascinating and rewarding as the material approach to landscape history can be, however, it tells us little about the wider significance of landscape. Here the cultural approach, exemplified by works like Simon Schama's *Landscape and Memory* (1995), David Matless' *Landscape and Englishness* (1998) and Paul Readman's *Storied Ground* (2018), is more reveal-ing. Indeed, across a broad swathe of the arts and humanities, the cultural approach to the study of landscape has become overwhelmingly dominant. It is underpinned by broader interpretative and methodological shifts within dis-ciplines such as social and cultural history and historical geography, notably the so-called linguistic or cultural turn, which emphasizes the role of large-scale cultural formations or 'discourses' in shaping or even determining the ways of perceiving, thinking, feeling, uttering and acting available to people in any particular cultural context. The cultural approach construes our relation-ship to landscape in terms of larger cultural constructs such as national identity, regionalism, modernity, the rural idyll and so forth. This has yielded important insights into the shifting cultural co-ordinates of landscape and the way these relate to policy and, more doubtfully, the economy (as in Martin Wiener's 1981 study *English Culture and the Decline of the Industrial Spirit*). What is less clear is how much it tells us about the actual experience of being in the landscape. The cultural approach draws mainly on texts produced by writers, artists, scholars and policymakers, and it is not at all clear that these are representative of the way less-prominent and less-privileged people experi-enced the countryside. How far were cultural discourses about national

identity, modernity, planning or whatever in the minds of non-elite people
when they were out and about exploring rural England? Did the value such
people set on the countryside derive from their exposure to discourses of this
kind? The evidence presented in this book suggests that cultural formations
had some influence on the role rural landscapes played in everyday lives,
especially for people with literary interests. However, even for these people,
distinctive personal influences, notably childhood experiences and family,
residential and employment circumstances, affected the way they related to
the countryside and the significance it held for them far more deeply than
discursive ones. This directly challenges, at least in relation to landscape,
a generation of historiographical assumptions that culture determines experience. Rather, this book maintains, a close, long-run, in-depth biographical
reading of the evidence suggests that the affective significance landscape held
for people was predominantly shaped by the often highly personal circumstances and situations of their lives, especially those encountered in childhood.
Moreover, it might reasonably be argued that it is primarily for this affective
significance to millions of people that the countryside should matter to social
historians, rather than for the more speculative consequences that have been
attributed to its cultural representation.

Closer, perhaps, to the understanding of landscape advanced in this book
is what has become known as the 'new nature writing'. Some of the best
examples of this, such as Nan Shepherd's *The Living Mountain* (written in the
1940s, published 1977), are not in fact especially new, but it is only recently,
through the work of writers like Richard Mabey, Roger Deakin, Kathleen
Jamie, Robert Macfarlane and Helen Macdonald, that the new nature writing
has emerged as a distinct genre. It is difficult to summarize so diverse a body
of work but one feature that it has in common, and which links it closely to
the perspective of this book, is that it is centrally concerned with the experience of landscape (and of rural landscapes withal). Moreover, it typically
seeks to explicate this through a close, biographical focus on what happens
when someone is in or moves through a particular landscape. In many
respects *Lifescapes* is a historian's counterpart to the new nature writing.
However, I am also seeking to extend it in different directions. As a primarily
autobiographical, even confessional genre, new nature writing at its best is
able to render responses to nature and the countryside with remarkable
fidelity. I hope to replicate this in the setting of comparative biography,
a challenging undertaking given that biographers, unlike autobiographers,
do not have direct access to their subjects' inner experiences. The new nature
writing is characteristically immediate in another sense too – as a record of
experience, it is primarily concerned with the present or recent past rather
than with more extended personal histories. Even though they prompt
authorial thoughts that range far and wide through myth and prehistory,
for example, the walks and voyages described in Macfarlane's *The Old Ways*

(2012) themselves play out over a matter of days and weeks. The new nature writing rarely connects the responses it registers with such close attention over the long arc of a lifetime, nor with enduring dispositions, character traits and emotional structures. There are exceptions: works such as Mabey's *Nature Cure* (2005) and Macdonald's *H Is for Hawk* (2014) do relate encounters with nature to deep personal experience over an extended time period and show how the two can exist in a dynamic relationship with each other. Yet even these unfold primarily over a period of two or three years, admittedly with some extended retrospect, so cannot follow the ongoing and developing connections between lives and landscapes over long timescales in the ways I have tried to in *Lifescapes*. There are also significant differences in aims, method and style between the often anecdotal, reflective, literary, first-person mode of the new nature writing and the analytical, comparative, evidence-based, third-person mode in which *Lifescapes* is written. Wide as these differences are, however, they represent complementary and, it seems to me, equally valid ways of exploring a vast and, until recently, almost unmapped region of human experience.

* * *

Acknowledgements do not usually begin with anti-thanks, but it would be unfair not to mention the Research Excellence Framework – inspired by Gradgrind, named by Bounderby – without which this book would have been finished several years sooner.

During the archival research on which the book is based I also incurred many debts that it is a pleasure to acknowledge – too many to do more than list the archivists, librarians and researchers who helped me. My thanks, then, to Laheba Alam, Julie Atkins, Matthew Blake, Margaret Bonney, Caroline Bourne, Paul Brassley, Liz Bregazzi, Cedric Brown, Charlie Carpenter, Michael Carter, John Cave, Paul Chatfield, James Collett-White, Ben Daubney, Sarah Davis, Jane de Gruchy, Ollie Douglas, John Draisey, Christopher Duggan, Sian Edwards, Rosie Everritt, Catherine Eyre, Rob Eyre, Mark Freeman, Mark Frost, Caroline Furey, Bridget Gillard, Alice Grayson, Liz Green, Clare Griffiths, Darran Gwynne, Josephine Halloran, Jaime Harris-Hughes, Jane Humphrey, Yohji Iwamoto, Julie Lamara, Margaret Lambert, Frances Lansley, Ryan Lavelle, Jane Lewis, David Luck, Andrew Lusted, Peter Mandler, Sally Mason, Elizabeth Matthew, Harriet Moffet, Peter Monteith, Lindsay Moreton, Sally Morgan, Ami Naramor, Andrew Nash, Sue Neville, Margaret O'Sullivan, Helen Parish, Michael Powell, John Prest, Amy Proctor, Jayavel Radhakrishnan, Maggie Ramsden, Paul Readman, Fran Ricketts, Gillian Roberts, David Rymill, David Sissons, Jim and Pat Smart, Louise Smith, Lianne Smith, Robert Snape, Peter Sowden, Mike Squires, Michael Stephens, Alex Swanston, Melanie Tebbutt, Jennifer

Thorp, Deborah Tritton, Jacqui Turner, Matthew Watson, Susan Watt, Emily West, Jonathan Westaway, Robin Whittaker, Maxine Willett, Alison Woodward, Matthew Worley, Donna Yamani and Integra Software Services Pvt Ltd, Pondicherry (for Figure 2.1).

There are also some deeper debts that require fuller acknowledgement. Without Liz Friend-Smith's commitment and perceptive editorial input this project would not have seen the light of day in its current form. My colleagues in the Department of History at the University of Reading provided an encouraging and supportive working environment over the many years during which this book was written. John Attfield generously gave me permission to use the diaries of his mother, Sadie Attfield (née Barmes), as the basis for Chapter 9 and offered valuable comments on the draft version of that chapter. Susan Clifford helped me with customary precision and speed in the crucial task of identifying suitable diaries for analysis. Paul Salveson drew my attention to the John Johnston diaries. Hannah Newton made careful, thought-provoking comments on Chapter 5, as did Paddy Bullard on the preface. I am especially grateful to Keith Snell for his perceptive insights and observations on several of the chapters and to Philip Conford, Rachael Jones and Nicola Whyte, who read and commented on the book with exemplary care. Rachael kindly drew my attention to the Dickinson bankruptcy, which has a crucial bearing on Chapter 6. I would also like to thank Cambridge University Press' two anonymous readers. Perhaps every author wonders whether anyone outside their own circle will understand what they are trying to say, and I will never forget the gratitude I felt when I read their reports, which showed that at least two people had.

Words cannot do justice to my deepest and most personal debts. My father Andrew's love and support has been a constant presence during the writing of this book and throughout my life. The biographical approach that underpins *Lifescapes* reflects my grandmother Arne's unfailing interest in and care for individual lives, historical and contemporary. The contributions of my sister, Tania, my son, Michael, and my daughter, Rachael, have been no less appreciated for being mainly behind the scenes. Judith, my wife, was an invaluable and ever-patient sounding board and constructive critic on the walks during which I worked out the structure and many of the ideas and interpretations of what follows, which is informed by values we share.

Lifescapes is dedicated to the memory of Edward and to Margaret Morris. Their farm in Saxelbye, Leicestershire, was my second home in childhood, where, many years ago, the seed this book grew from was sown.

~

Introduction

A few miles west of the Thames-side village of Streatley, the Ridgeway, hallowed by time and legend, turns north and climbs gently towards the scarp of the Berkshire Downs. In season the air is filled with the sound of skylarks, but there are few signs of human habitation – by the standards of southern England, this is remote country. The turf swells and dips in vast unhurried undulations like a majestic procession of giant ocean waves. In summer it can be hot and dry here, for the chalk bedrock that gives the landscape its classic contours also sucks the moisture out of it. By the side of the track, a kind soul has provided a water tap and trough. Next to this is a stone dedicated to the memory of a local general practitioner, Dr Basil Phillips. It bears the simple inscription 'He was a countryman.'

I know nothing of Dr Phillips beyond this, but those who cared about him evidently felt that his love of the countryside had been of central importance in his life. So too in a different way was it for the woman I spoke to years ago at Glendurgan Garden on the shores of the Helford River in Cornwall. Gazing over the luxuriant palms, bamboos and camellias to the royal blue sea, framed between verdant hills, we exchanged remarks about the compelling beauty of the scene before us. I explained that as a rural historian I was interested in the relationship between people and landscape. She told me that her family had been coming to the Helford since she was a child, that they were deeply attached to it and that one of them (I forget which) had fixed her mind on the memory of the view now before us to mitigate a long and demanding labour.

One further indication of the themes with which this book is concerned will perhaps suffice. On 7 March 1913, 'W. N. P. Barbellion' (Bruce Cummings) made the following entry in his diary:

> Have been feeling very 'down' of late, but yesterday I saw a fine Scots Fir by the roadside – tall, erect, as straight as a Parthenon pillar. The sight of it restored my courage. It had a tonic effect. Quite unconsciously I pulled my shoulders back and walked ahead with renewed vows never to flinch again. It is a noble tree. It has strength as a giant, and a giant's height, and yet kindly withal, the branches drooping down graciously towards you – like a kind giant extending its hands to a child.[1]

---

[1] W. N. P. Barbellion, *The Journal of a Disappointed Man* (London, 1919), 111.

1

As these examples intimate, rural landscapes, or elements of them, have for a long time had a powerful affective influence on many English people.[2] The aim of this study is to understand why. The method I have adopted is, as far as I am aware, one that has never previously been attempted: a comparative in-depth assessment of the significance of rural landscapes to several individuals across their entire lifespans.[3] Indeed, to the best of my knowledge this has not previously been attempted even for one person, mainly, perhaps, because historians have been more inclined to see landscape in material or cultural rather than, as here, in psycho-social terms.[4] They may also have doubted whether sources exist that would allow us to reconstruct the relationship between lives and landscapes in such detail. Possibly also the scale of research apparently required has seemed daunting. Nevertheless, I hope to show that suitable sources do exist, that the research required, while certainly time-consuming, is not impossibly so, and that the in-depth psycho-social approach to landscape history advocated here can yield rich rewards.[5]

Sources and Timeframe

The book is based on eight remarkable manuscript diaries, in each of which the countryside and the writer's relationship with it figures prominently. None of the diaries was written for publication or has yet been published.[6] All the

---

[2] Although, as subsequent chapters will underline, not uniquely to English people or landscapes.

[3] Due to the uneven distribution of source material, however, I have been able to achieve this more fully and satisfactorily in some chapters than others.

[4] My understanding of landscape is closer to Shelley Egoz's view that it is 'at once the relationship between humans and their surroundings, and the confluence of physical subsistence and psychological necessities'. Shelley Egoz, 'Landscape and Identity in the Century of the Migrant', in Peter Howard, Ian Thompson, Emma Waterton and Mick Atha (eds.), *The Routledge Companion to Landscape Studies*. 2nd ed. (London, 2018), 329–40, at 330.

[5] Rural sociologists and geographers have for some time recognized the heuristic value of a biographical approach – for example, to unravel the complex motivations informing migration decisions. See Keith Halfacree, 'Moving to the Countryside ... And Staying: Lives beyond Representations', *Sociologia Ruralis* 52 (2012), 92–114. More recently some historians have advocated a 'biographical turn', an approach *Lifescapes* broadly endorses and exemplifies. See Hans Renders, Binne de Haan and Jonne Harmsma (eds.), *The Biographical Turn: Lives in History* (London, 2016), 2; James Hinton, *Seven Lives from Mass Observation: Britain in the Late Twentieth Century* (Oxford, 2016); and, in relation to landscape, Jonathan Finch, 'Historic Landscapes', in Peter Howard, Ian Thompson, Emma Waterton and Mick Atha (eds.), *The Routledge Companion to Landscape Studies*. 2nd ed. (London, 2018), 166–75, at 173. See also Nicola Whyte's illuminating work on landscape and life course in an early modern context – for example, 'Landscape, Memory and Custom: Parish Identities c.1550–1700', *Social History*, 32 (2007), 166–86.

[6] Selective editions of several of them, notably the Hallam, Johnston and Catley diaries, are, however, surely warranted.

diaries are exceptionally long-run, several extending to more than sixty and one to more than eighty volumes, this latter comprising something like 5 million words. Each offers an extraordinary window not only on the external circumstances of the writer's life, but also on their innermost thoughts and feelings, making it possible to reconstruct the intricate connections between these and the landscapes where (and often in relation to which) they were lived out in unprecedented detail – hence the book's title, *Lifescapes*.

When I began research for this study, my aim was to explain the rise in the popularity of the countryside since the late nineteenth century. It seemed to make sense to begin in about 1870, as the establishment of several prominent preservationist and pro-rural organizations around this time suggested the countryside was becoming rapidly more popular, and to end it in 1945, since the Second World War has often been seen as a high-water mark of English ruralism. A secondary reason for stopping short in the mid-twentieth century was the difficulty of finding good source material for the late twentieth century – suitable diaries from this period do not yet seem to have found their way into public repositories. During the course of research, however, I became dissatisfied with the somewhat teleological question of why the countryside *became* more popular. Partly this was because the premise that rural landscapes were less cherished before circa 1870 has not yet been systematically examined by historians and so remains an assumption. But I was also concerned that the one-sided emphasis on identifying and explaining change would detract from what increasingly seemed the more important and interesting questions of how people experienced rural landscapes and why these landscapes sometimes mattered so much to them. By the time I began writing, therefore, I had reformulated my principal research questions in this less loaded way. I have retained the original timeframe because the shift in focus occurred after I had completed most of the research, but there is no longer a strong intellectual rationale for it other than the problem of sources and practical constraints on research time and book length.

The Diarists

Diaries are among the most revealing but also most complex and potentially misleading of historical sources. To reap their abundant harvest, a historian must pay close attention to methodology, assess the diaries in question carefully in the light of this, and keep in mind the nature and limitations of the source material – the aims of the first chapter of this book, paving the way for the eight biographical chapters that follow. These mainly proceed chronologically but where the emphasis falls more on continuity than change, I have sometimes adopted a thematic approach. Throughout I have tried to bring out the distinctiveness of each diarist's relationship to rural landscapes. Yet many of the elements that, combined, make up this distinctiveness were shared with other diarists, more with some than others. One of the principal difficulties in writing this book has been how to indicate these commonalities without detracting from the uniqueness of each diarist's ruralism. The solution I have adopted is to group the diarists into four pairs; the two diarists comprising each pair seem to me to share something important with each other in the way they related to rural landscapes that they do not share to the same extent with the other diarists.

The first of these groupings, consisting of the guidebook writer Beatrix Cresswell and the railway lathe operator William Hallam, I have designated 'Adherers', since they valued rural landscapes above all as guarantors of continuity with a cherished past (Chapters 2 and 3). The second pair, the would-be artist Katherine Spear Smith and the déclassé weaver Violet Dickinson, can best be described as 'Withdrawers': their lives were marked by a pattern of progressive retreat into the countryside as each attempted to escape from oppressive external and internal circumstances (Chapters 4 and 5). The Bolton general practitioner John Johnston and the Dudley probation officer Bert Bissell (Chapters 6 and 7) were 'Restorers' for whom rural landscapes were a catalyst for personal and ethical regeneration. The final pair, the London County Council clerk Sadie Barmes and the Bristol bookshop worker Fred Catley, were passionate 'Explorers', venturing out eagerly into the countryside in search of new impressions, sensations and ideas.

None of these men and women made their living in a direct sense (at least not at the outset) from the countryside. The subject of the significance of rural landscapes to those who earned their living from them, such as farmers and farmworkers, is a fascinating one that deserves to be researched in depth.[7] But it is a different one, and in this book I want to keep the focus on those who had an essentially non-instrumental relationship to rural landscapes. It was these people who, in a period of sharply contracting agricultural employment, were mainly responsible for the popularity of the countryside as a place to visit and enjoy.

Elite and Popular Ruralism in Modern England

The prominence of ruralism within the English tradition has been a subject of enduring interest to scholars since the publication of Raymond Williams' *The Country and the City* in 1973.[8] Williams demonstrated that ruralism formed a kind of shared cultural language pervading English literature from the sixteenth century through to the twentieth. John Barrell showed that the same could be said of an important strand of eighteenth- and nineteenth-century

---

[7] Jeremy Burchardt, 'Farm Diaries', in Paddy Bullard (ed.), *A History of English Georgic Writing* (Cambridge, 2022), 79–98, dips a toe in the water.

[8] Raymond Williams, *The Country and the City* (London, 1973).

English painting, while scholars including Georgina Boyes and David Jacques have extended this perspective to other art forms such as music and landscape gardening.[9] From the mid-nineteenth century English politicians and business-men increasingly professed ruralist sensibilities too. The pronounced ruralism of the English cultural, political and economic elite has attracted much attention from historians, as in Martin Wiener's influential *English Culture and the Decline of the Industrial Spirit*.[10] Many studies of the role of nature and rural landscapes in the works of writers like Wordsworth, Keats, the Brontës, Hardy, Meredith and Lawrence have been written, not to mention Georgian and First World War poetry, while the pastoralism of composers like Vaughan Williams, Butterworth, Finzi and, in certain respects, Elgar is also well known. The same applies to artists and art critics: nature and landscape are central to scholarly assessment of nineteenth-century figures such as Constable, Turner, Palmer, Ruskin and the Pre-Raphaelites, while Alexandra Harris has recently reminded us how intensely preoccupied early twentieth-century 'Romantic Moderns' like John Piper, Stanley Spencer and Graham Sutherland continued to be with the countryside.[11] Scholars have also considered the ruralism of politicians such as Stanley Baldwin and, in his own pugnacious fashion, Lloyd George, and the argument that there was a systematic pro-rural bias in nineteenth- and twentieth-century English politics is well worn.[12] There have been fewer studies of individual businessmen that assess their affinity for the countryside, but in aggregate this too is familiar territory – the proclivity of successful businessmen to buy country estates and wrap themselves in the trappings of rural gentility has been the subject of exhaustive studies by (among others) Lawrence and Jeanne Stone, F. M. L. Thompson and W. D. Rubinstein.[13] While there is certainly more to learn about why varieties of ruralism appealed so strongly to the English elite in the nineteenth and early twentieth centuries, historians could hardly be accused of neglecting the issue.

Until the late 1980s, the same could not have been said of popular ruralism. Since then, there have been several significant studies, notably Helen Walker's

---

[9] John Barrell, *The Dark Side of the Landscape: The Rural Poor in English Painting, 1730–1840* (Cambridge, 1983); Georgina Boyes, *The Imagined Village: Culture, Ideology, and the English Folk Revival* (New York, 1993); David Jacques, *Georgian Gardens: The Reign of Nature* (London, 1983).

[10] Martin Wiener, *English Culture and the Decline of the Industrial Spirit* (Cambridge, 1981).

[11] Alexandra Harris, *Romantic Moderns: English Writers, Artists and the Imagination from Virginia Woolf to John Piper* (London, 2010).

[12] See, for example, Howard Newby, *Green and Pleasant Land? Social Change in Rural England* (Hounslow, 1979).

[13] Lawrence Stone and Jeanne C. Fawtier Stone, *An Open Elite: England, 1540–1880* (Oxford, 1986); Francis Michael Longstreth Thompson, *Gentrification and the Enterprise Culture: Britain 1780–1980* (Oxford, 2001); W. D. Rubinstein, 'New Men of Wealth and the Purchase of Land in Nineteenth-Century Britain', *Past & Present* 92 (1981), 125–47.

unpublished thesis (1987), Harvey Taylor's *A Claim on the Countryside* (1997), and some of Alun Howkins' works (especially sections of *The Death of Rural England*, 2003).[14] It is worth recapitulating the most telling evidence, as it demonstrates that the eight diarists who are the principal subjects of this book were far from alone in caring about the countryside. On the contrary, even on the most conservative estimates, hundreds of thousands of people were enthusiastic participants in outdoor leisure by the 1930s, and probably from well before this.[15] An article in the 1931 handbook of the Manchester Federation of Ramblers claimed, for example, that '[d]uring some fine summer week-ends, there are approximately 10,000 ramblers and fresh-air seekers of either sex somewhere in the Derbyshire highlands'.[16] Equally large numbers of ramblers could be found in the south: when the celebrated broadcaster S. P. B. Mais printed a 'pink railway leaflet' advertising a guided walk to Chanctonbury Ring to see the sunrise, the Southern Railway ran four special trains from London to Steyning station, although unfortunately it began to rain and the sun failed to appear.[17] Ticket sales provide another way of estimating the number of people visiting the countryside: by the early twentieth century, half a million people travelled by train to the Lake District every year.[18]

As early as 1913 the Cooperative Holiday Association had 18 rural centres at which, in that year, 16,000 guest weeks were spent; its offshoot the Holiday Fellowship provided 5,241 guest weeks at its centres in 1919 and had 36 local groups by the mid-1920s.[19] The Youth Hostels Association was formed in 1930 and grew extraordinarily rapidly: by 1939 it already had 83,417 members. The Cyclists Touring Club had 60,449 members as early as 1900, although the rural element was not always as central to cycling as it was to the rural holiday and overnight organizations or to rambling.[20] Figures for the membership of

---

[14] Harvey Taylor, *A Claim on the Countryside: A History of the British Outdoor Movement* (Edinburgh, 1997); Helen J. Walker, 'The Outdoor Movement in England and Wales, 1900–1939' (University of Sussex, PhD, 1987); Alun Howkins, *The Death of Rural England: A Social History of the Countryside since 1900* (London, 2003).

[15] Walker, 'The Outdoor Movement', 347. Warren estimates there were half a million ramblers in the 1930s: A. Warren, 'Sport, Youth, and Gender in Britain, 1880–1940', in Clyde Binfield and John Stevenson (eds.), *Sport, Culture, and Politics* (Sheffield, 1993), 66. Olive Morgan found more than half the girls in her sample enjoyed rambling: quoted in Claire Langhamer, *Women's Leisure in England 1920–1960* (Manchester, 2000), 77.

[16] Taylor, *A Claim on the Countryside*, 229.

[17] Peter Brandon, *The Discovery of Sussex* (Andover, 2010), 173. This echoes one of the best-known literary renderings of popular ruralism: Leonard Bast's anticlimactic night walk to see a rural sunrise in E. M. Forster's *Howard's End* (London, 1910).

[18] Paul Readman, *Storied Ground: Landscape and the Shaping of English National Identity* (Cambridge, 2018), 95.

[19] Walker, 'The Outdoor Movement', 153, 55, 68; Robert Snape, 'The Co-operative Holidays Association and the Cultural Formation of Countryside Leisure Practice', *Leisure Studies* 23 (2004), 143–58.

[20] Walker, 'The Outdoor Movement', 228, 54.

rambling organizations are elusive because the movement was so decentralized. More than 300 local organizations were affiliated to the newly constituted Ramblers' Association by 1935; typical of the smaller local clubs may have been the Glenfield Rambling Club (Kilmarnock), with a membership of about 800.[21]

It was also in this period that rural preservationism emerged as a significant force. The National Trust was founded in 1895 and the Council for the Preservation of Rural England (CPRE) in 1926, the latter a partnership of twenty constituent bodies.[22] The formation of these two major national organizations was the culmination of a long period of growth in preservationism. The Commons Preservation Society had been formed as early as 1865. The Kyrle Society, dedicated to the protection of open spaces, footpaths and rural amenities, was established the following year, the Lake District Defence Society in 1883, the Selborne League (for nature conservation) in 1885 and the Society for the Promotion of Nature Reserves in 1912, to mention only the most prominent.[23] It was only after the Second World War that the National Trust and the CPRE became mass membership organizations, partly due to a change in strategy, but the proliferation of preservationist groups and their high political profile reflects a much wider interest in the countryside.[24]

Another indication of the strength of popular interest in the English countryside in the first half of the twentieth century was a boom in the publication of countryside books. Perhaps the most successful of the distinctively rural publishers was Batsford Books. About four hundred thousand books in their British Heritage series had been sold by 1949. Batsford employed the highly regarded illustrator Brian Cook to design their book covers from 1932; in total Cook produced dust jackets for seven series comprising more than eighty predominantly rural books for the company over the next twenty-three years.[25] Even more successful was Methuen's H. V. Morton, thirty-two editions of whose *In Search of England* had been published by 1944.[26] Series such as Arthur Mee's 'The King's England' were enormously popular and this was also the heyday of the predominantly rural regional novel genre, with authors

---

[21] Taylor, *A Claim on the Countryside*, 251, 31.

[22] John K. Walton, 'The National Trust Centenary: Official and Unofficial Histories', *Local Historian*, 26 (1996), 80–8.

[23] On preservationism, see Philip Lowe, 'The Rural Idyll Defended: From Preservation to Conservation', in Gordon E. Mingay (ed.), *The Rural Idyll* (London, 1989), 113–31. See also John Ranlett, '"Checking Nature's Desecration": Late-Victorian Environmental Organization', *Victorian Studies* 26 (1983), 197–222; David Matless, *Landscape and Englishness* (London, 1998), 25–100; Paul Readman, 'Landscape Preservation, "Advertising Disfigurement" and English National Identity, c.1890–1914', *Rural History* 12 (2001), 61–83.

[24] Readman, *Storied Ground*, 12–13.

[25] Catherine Brace, 'Publishing and Publishers: Towards an Historical Geography of Countryside Writing, c.1930–1950', *Area* 33, (2001), 293.

[26] Matless, *Landscape and Englishness*, 65.

like Mary Webb and Sheila Kaye-Smith so popular that they even inspired a best-selling parody, Stella Gibbons' *Cold Comfort Farm* (1932).[27] Many rural-themed magazines and journals had large circulations too, notably *Country Life* (1897) and *The Countryman* (1927). The new medium of radio was quick to tap into the popular appetite for rural-themed material – the BBC commissioned Mais to create a well-received series entitled *This Unknown Island* in 1932, in which he travelled to seventeen different parts of Britain and spent a week in each.[28] Artists who specialized in rural landscapes such as Paul Nash, Eric Ravilious and Rowland Hilder were cherished by the public: it has been estimated that as many as 13 million plates of Hilder's Flowers of the Countryside series were printed.[29] In both world wars, the government exploited popular ruralism in its recruitment and propaganda campaigns, employing artists like Frank Styche and Frank Newbould in the expectation that their lush pastoral vision of England would resonate with the public.[30] This tactic was satirized in an often-reproduced cartoon by *Punch* in which the Everyman figure of 'Mr William Smith', persuaded to enlist to 'preserve his native soil inviolate', returns from military service in 1919 to find that his pristine village has become a polluted industrial town.[31] The desire not only to visit and view but to live in the countryside was certainly becoming more widespread in the interwar years, especially in the Home Counties: the population of rural Berkshire, for example, increased by more than 50 per cent between 1901 and 1951, despite a steep fall in agricultural employment.[32] Stanley Baldwin's claim that 'the sight of a plough team coming over the brow of a hill' was 'the one eternal sight of England' may have been a hyperbolic exercise in wishful thinking, but it did not belie his carefully cultivated image as a common-sense moderate: such sentiments chimed with attitudes that had become mainstream and conventional.

There is, then, ample evidence of widespread public interest in, and enthusiasm for, the countryside by the interwar years. But while our knowledge of what might be termed the macro-history of popular ruralism is now quite extensive, especially with regard to the institutional, political and cultural history of the outdoor movement, we know much less about its

---

[27] Keith D. M. Snell (ed.), *The Regional Novel in Britain and Ireland, 1800–1990* (Cambridge, 1998); Keith D. M. Snell, *The Bibliography of Regional Fiction in Britain and Ireland, 1800–2000* (London, 2017).

[28] Maisie Robson, *An Unrepentant Englishman: The Life of S. P. B. Mais, Ambassador of the Countryside* (Rotherham, 2005), 87–8.

[29] Rowland Hilder, *Rowland Hilder Country* (London, 1987), 15–16.

[30] David Monger, 'Soldiers, Propaganda and Ideas of Home and Community in First World War Britain', *Cultural & Social History* 8 (2011), 338–42.

[31] Matless, *Landscape and Englishness*, 24–5.

[32] Jeremy Burchardt, 'Historicizing Counterurbanization: In-migration and the Reconstruction of Rural Space in Berkshire (U.K.), 1901–51', *Journal of Historical Geography* 38 (2012), 155–66.

micro-history – how the countryside fitted into the lived reality of people's lives. This is partly because, under the influence of the 'cultural turn' of the 1980s, many historians assumed that experience, if it was a valid category of historical analysis at all, was produced by wider cultural structures ('discourses'). Much emphasis was placed on the so-called rural idyll – shorthand for an idealized, chocolate-box view of the countryside, purged of conflict and suffering, and allegedly the dominant frame through which the countryside was seen at all social levels.[33] It was usually argued, or implied, that the rural idyll reflected the values, interests, concerns and sensibilities of high-cultural opinion-formers, notably writers and artists, often closely linked to the political and economic elite, and that these values then percolated down to the rest of the population. Prevalent though it has been in the scholarship of the past few decades, however, the rural idyll paradigm is overdue for revision. In the present context, its most problematic feature is its dismissiveness: the implication, on the one hand, that those outside the cultural elite were incapable of independent personal response to landscape and, on the other, that most of what people valued in the countryside was a delusion.[34] Setting this high-handed view aside, the truth of the matter is that the lived experience of popular ruralism is still largely a closed book to us. Many even of the most basic questions remain unanswered, not so much for lack of evidence as because we have not asked them. When, for example, did people go out into the country? How strong an influence was the weather, or was the timing of rural expeditions determined largely by when people were free from other commitments (such as work)? Were outings mainly planned in advance, or sometimes responses to short-term circumstances such as the unexpected arrival of friends or a domestic row? How did major life events such as marriage, the birth of children, moving house, losing a job, illnesses and bereavements affect the way in which people related to rural landscapes? Or were longer-term influences like disposition, habits and family traditions more decisive? How did people get to the countryside and what did they do when they were there? Were rural expeditions usually solitary encounters with nature, as the stereotype of Romantic individualism would have it, or more often collective? Was rural England, as a leisure landscape, the preserve of young hikers and cyclists, or visited by older people, children and family groups too? Similarly, how gender and class-inflected was ruralism – did men and women, working-class and middle-class, look for different things, perhaps

---

[33] Including by myself: Jeremy Burchardt, *Paradise Lost: Rural Idyll and Social Change in England, 1800–2000* (London, 2002).

[34] For further reasons to consign the rural idyll paradigm to the dustbin of history, see Jeremy Burchardt, 'The Rural Idyll: A Critique', in Verity Elson and Rosemary Shirley (eds.), *Creating the Countryside: The Rural Idyll Past and Present* (London, 2017), 64–73, and Matless, *Landscape and Englishness*, 16–17.

in different places and different ways, in the countryside?[35] Were there important contrasts in the kinds of landscape – mountains, moors, woods, farmland – to which people responded? How did ruralism relate to other facets of people's lives – politics, religion and social and cultural networks, for example? Most of all, what did people seek and what did they find in the countryside – what did it mean to them and how did it affect them?

Because historians have not hitherto undertaken a close micro-historical assessment of popular ruralism of this kind, it seems to me that the full significance of the subject, and in particular the depth of meaning many people found in rural landscapes, has not yet been recognized. Even *A Claim on the Countryside*, a work of exceptional originality and scholarship, has little to offer in this respect. Taylor suggests that the appeal of the countryside was 'simple' and 'uncomplicated', implying that it does not need to be analysed, or even perhaps that it is a primary affect beyond analysis.[36] However, as I hope to demonstrate, the reasons that drew people to the countryside were often much more interesting and less obvious than this.

Defining the Field

The diarists whose lives this book considers used a range of terms to describe their interest in the countryside, usually in an unstudied, unselfconscious, and inconsistent way. Among their preferred words were 'country', 'countryside', 'nature', 'rural' and, occasionally, 'landscape', often in adjectival phrases such as 'country pleasures' or 'natural beauties'. I have followed this eclectic use of language, except where a diarist's use of one term rather than another seemed to have a significance that warranted discussion. Of course, each of these words has an interesting etymological history. The first English instance of 'country-side' cited in the *Oxford English Dictionary* is from *Tom Brown's Schooldays* in 1857, although the hyphenated form had been in common use for several decades previously. It is thought that the original sense was relational: a particular place or area lay on the country side of somewhere else (as opposed to the town side, hill side, river side or whatever).[37] 'Nature', according to Raymond Williams' *Keywords*, is 'perhaps the most complicated word in the [English] language'.[38] My concern, however, is with the place of the

---

[35] Kerri Andrews' pioneering *Wanderers: A History of Women Walking* (London, 2020) unfortunately came to my attention too late to inform this study.

[36] Taylor, *A Claim on the Countryside*. 'It was generally uncomplicated motives that generated the mass outdoor movement of the 1920s and 1930s' (266); 'An uncomplicated enjoyment of walking in the hills can be traced back into the eighteenth century' (58). See also page 86: early walking was 'overwhelmingly simple and natural'.

[37] 'Country-'Side, N.', *Oxford English Dictionary* (Oxford, 2018). www.oed.com/view/Entry/43098?redirectedFrom=countryside&amp.

[38] Raymond Williams, *Keywords* (Oxford, 2014), 164.

countryside in the wider context of these diarists' lives, rather than in the language available to them to describe this place, or the ancestry of this language. Adoption and use interest me more than the alluring but doubtful quest for ultimate origins, which often seems to me to explain less than it purports to, in the same way that many economic historians regard uptake as more significant than invention per se.

Nevertheless, a few brief observations about the key terms informing this study, my understanding of their relationship to each other and how I have used them seem in order. Of these, 'popular ruralism' perhaps requires most explanation. *Lifescapes* is premised on the need for a study of popular ruralism but in contrasting this with elite ruralism, I do not mean to imply the existence of a sharp divide between the two. That would be no more probable than the top-down reductionism of the rural idyll literature. At least as used here, popular ruralism denotes an approach rather than a distinct group of people or unified social phenomenon. The defining features of this approach are, firstly, an openness to the possibility that the ways people related to landscape may have owed as much or more to circumstances bearing quite personally on their own lives as to wider cultural influences, and hence, secondly, a commitment to looking directly at the evidence about the role of landscape in people's lives, rather than assuming we can infer it from cultural representations circulating more generally. These methodological principles are informed by a view of history that sees people who lived in the past as interesting and worthy of study in their own right, rather than for their influence and prestige alone, or even as involuntary representatives of some larger category or group to which we have assigned them. The careful attention this book gives to the apparently quotidian details of largely unknown, uncelebrated lives is intended as an assertion that every life, illustrious or obscure, equally deserves and, sources permitting, equally rewards historical contemplation.[39]

A second word that features frequently in this study is 'countryside', a term which some scholars, wary of its subjective connotations, seek to avoid, preferring to deploy apparently more objective concepts such as 'nature' or 'the natural world'. Yet, at least in an English setting, this tendency to reduce the countryside to nature, or to use the two interchangeably, seems to me unhelpful. In some cultural contexts, such as North America or Australia, it may be viable to construe popular engagement with rural landscapes as a subset of the wider history of the relationship between humanity and the natural world. Certainly the concept of 'wilderness' has a compelling cultural history of its own in relation, in particular, to the United States. However, most

---

[39] My intentions in this regard are similar to those expressed in Hinton, *Seven Lives*, 161. 'Uncelebrated' is a relative term: Bissell has been admirably celebrated in his own Dudley and Methodist communities, while Harry Cocks and Paul Salveson have written perceptively about the 'Eagle Street College' of which Johnston was a member.

scholars would agree with Thoreau that it is 'vain to dream of a wilderness distant from ourselves'.[40] There is no true wilderness in the sense of a landscape unmodified by man. The crucial difference between the English and North American contexts, then, is not so much the presence or absence of wilderness, but that it has been easier to think in terms of wilderness in the New World. In England, however, not only is there no wilderness but there has not for many centuries been any extensive tract of land that it has been possible to think of as wilderness (Dartmoor may be the nearest exception). For this reason and perhaps others, human elements have rarely been excluded from popular conceptions of or preferences in rural landscapes in England. Cottages and farms, churches and castles, bridges, windmills, hedgerows, drystone walls and even roads have all been cherished components of the English rural landscape at times. Nature, or what is perceived as natural, is indubitably essential to popular conceptions of the English countryside but there is another essential element too – the imprint of human activity, softened by time. It is no accident that the name of England's most successful voluntary organization incorporates both: The National Trust for the Conservation of Places of *Historic Interest or Natural Beauty* (my emphasis). This yields a useful working definition of the English countryside: the countryside = nature + history.[41] The English countryside can then be seen as a 'middle landscape', standing between and potentially mediating the polarized opposition of the human and the natural. This is a theme that recurs, with variations, in many of the ensuing chapters.

Another word that I have used extensively is 'landscape'. In the eighteenth century this was primarily an artistic term applied to paintings and then to the country-house gardens inspired by them. 'Landscape' therefore carried connotations of a distanced observer separated from the land he or she was looking at. A now well-established critique of this purely visual way of apprehending land argues that the 'gaze' of the detached observer is intrinsically proprietorial and domineering. Over the past few decades scholars have worked hard to develop a more open, non-hierarchical and multisensory conception of landscape. This understanding of landscape is sometimes better suited to my purposes than the word 'countryside', which retains associations with a particular kind of English landscape – the classic patchwork of pasture and arable, woods and hills – that does not always reflect those to which the

---

[40] Quoted in Simon Schama, *Landscape and Memory* (London, 1996), 578.

[41] This is more specific than but consistent with the European Landscape Convention's generic definition of landscape as 'an area, as perceived by people, whose character is the result of the action and interaction of natural and/or human factors'. *European Landscape Convention* (2000), cited in Mick Atha, Peter Howard, and Emma Waterton, 'Introduction. Ways of Knowing and Being with Landscapes: A Beginning', in Howard et al. (eds.), *The Routledge Companion to Landscape Studies*, xxi. Compare also Readman, *Storied Ground*, especially 3–4, 8–9.

eight diarists responded. 'Landscape', by contrast, has become a more universal term, used by scholars all over the world. A further advantage of 'landscape', as it is now understood, is that it avoids a sharp distinction between rural and urban. This is a study of popular ruralism, but for all eight of the diarists, most of the time at least, the boundary between rural and urban was blurred and permeable. In each case their most intense, compelling and deeply felt landscape responses were concentrated towards the rural end of the spectrum but they drew the line between rural and urban in different places and, for several of them, where this line was changed over time. In writing this study, I have increasingly found 'landscape' a valuable word for its flexibility and capacity to sidestep reductive dualisms such as the town–country dichotomy and, notwithstanding its infrequency in my source material, have made much use of it.

I am also, however, seeking to extend our understanding of landscape in new ways, through developing a 'deep history' of it.[42] Depth and breadth are the two principal axes of scholarship and my intention in arguing for a deep history is to complement rather than supplant the 'broad' approach to landscape history predominant hitherto. Indeed, much of the most innovative and stimulating landscape history writing of recent years has been 'broad' in this sense: alongside Schama, Matless and Readman's contributions, I am thinking of works like Bunce's *The Countryside Ideal* (1994), Tilley's *A Phenomenology of Landscape* (1994), Ingold's *The Perception of the Environment* (2000), Williamson's *The Transformation of Rural England* (2002) and Watkins' *Trees, Woods and Forests* (2014). Nor do I mean to imply that the approach this book advocates is the only valid form a deep landscape history could take. There are other ways of 'doing' landscape history that could, with equal reason, lay claim to the term. What I have in mind here, particularly, are microhistories of landscape and community like Barry Reay's *Microhistories*. Some of the best of these are regrettably unpublished doctoral theses, such as M. H. Ferguson's remarkable 'Land-Use, Settlement and Society in the Bagshot Sands Region, 1840–1940' (University of Reading, PhD, 1980). These are 'deep' in the sense that the structural factors bearing on the development of a particular community are exhaustively explored – the geological, climatic, economic, social, political and cultural aspects, and their interactions with each other – aiming at its most ambitious to achieve a kind of 'total' history in a local context.[43]

---

[42] 'Deep history' in my usage of the term connotes depth of human experience, so is at a wide remove from the sociobiological 'deep history' advocated by Daniel Lord Smail and other neurohistorians, although eventually perhaps scientific progress may bring about a convergence.

[43] 'Total' history may be an illusory goal but the best community micro-histories remain exceptionally rewarding.

Yet, admirable and enriching as the community micro-histories approach can be, it leaves a vast realm of what landscape means to us, perhaps the most important one, almost untouched. If we are to enter this largely unarticulated, hidden realm we need to go deeper still, into the myriad entanglements and reciprocities between lives and landscapes as experienced at the individual level. Of course, for every gain in depth there is a corresponding loss of breadth, in the same way that the greater a telescope's magnification, the more restricted its field of view. Schama looks at an entire culture, Readman at a nation, Reay at a neighbourhood and this book at eight individuals. But although seen in high resolution, the deep history I advocate should not be mistaken for a subjectivist, 'inner' history. On the contrary, the method depends on the fullest possible reconstruction of the external circumstances of the individual's life to show how these shaped, and to some extent were reciprocally shaped by, inner responses to landscape in an ongoing open-ended dialectic.[44]

As this suggests, a deep history of landscape must be highly particular and specific. But like any history it must also reach for wider conclusions. I have sought to minimize the tension between these aims by keeping the biographical chapters predominantly in the first register and displacing systematic comparison and generalization to the Conclusion. This therefore has to carry much of the analytical weight of the book and is split into three correspondingly substantial parts. The first seeks to explain popular ruralism, examining its origins, the analytical value of the adherer–withdrawer–restorer–explorer framework and summarizing other rewards and satisfactions yielded by the diarists' landscape encounters and experiences. The second part draws revisionist conclusions about the characteristics of popular ruralism, focussing on walking as a mode of landscape experience, private and social landscapes, vision and the tourist gaze, the relationships between town and country and the human and the natural, and the intersections of ruralism, gender, class and age. The third and final part considers the wider implications of *Lifescapes*, questioning a number of interpretative strategies and axioms prevalent within social history since the 1980s and assessing the contemporary bearings of the deep history of landscape that the chapters which now follow seek to develop.

---

[44] This is congruent with Ingold's influential conception of landscapes as congealed 'taskscapes' (the pattern of interconnected activities unfolding in a given spatial context over time), although methodologically the deep history I advocate is far removed from Ingold's macrocosmic approach. Tim Ingold, *The Perception of the Environment: Essays on Livelihood, Dwelling and Skill* (London, 2000).

Diaries, Life Writing and Popular Ruralism

Reading Diaries

There are many ways to read diaries. Traditionally, historians have quarried them for evidence about events or individuals regarded as of special significance. So numerous editions and studies of diaries and memoirs have been written by prominent politicians: the Greville, Shaftesbury, Stanley and Gladstone diaries, for example. Diaries written by writers and artists such as Fanny Burney, Benjamin Haydon, Lewis Carroll and Arnold Bennett have also attracted much attention. Such diaries are used principally for what might be termed their objective content, as a source of factual information about events, people and places. However, over the past few decades historians, notably those researching disadvantaged or oppressed groups such as women and slaves, have attended increasingly to the subjective content of diaries – the perceptions, motivations and experiences of the diarists themselves. *Lifescapes* takes a similar approach.

Studies of or based on diaries have not always had a good reception from historians. This partly reflects a more general conflict of purpose between biographical and historical writing. Biographical writing, including most studies of diaries, has traditionally been concerned with the singular and the particular, aiming to provide a readable and convincing account of an individual life. For most historians, this is of little intrinsic value: the aim of history as an academic discipline is to construct overarching narratives and interpretations, to generalize as far as the often very complex and multifaceted evidence allows.

In the past few years, however, a new approach to the study of diaries has emerged. This aims to bridge the gap between the particularity of biography and the historian's urge to generalize by adopting a systematically comparative approach. An early example was Stavenuiter's analysis of fifteen diaries and other personal documents written by elderly people in the nineteenth-century Netherlands.[1] More recently, historians have sought to achieve more precise, fine-grained biographical comparison through book-length research. James Hinton's Mass Observation–based studies of selfhood, identities and

---

[1] Monique Stavenuiter, 'A Cracked Mirror: Images and Self-Images of Elderly Men and Women in the Netherlands in the 19th-Century', *Journal of Social History* 29 (1995), 357–73.

citizenship during the Second World War are notable recent examples.[2] *Lifescapes* stands in this tradition and seeks to develop it further through examining a particular dimension of the lives considered, the affective significance of landscape, at a lifetime scale.

A question of crucial significance to historians using life writing sources is how – to quote one of the pioneers of diaries scholarship, Robert Fothergill – the reader can 'make a mental distinction between the first-person narrator who speaks in the diary and the historical personage who held the pen'.[3] Many life writing scholars would argue that it is impossible to reach the 'historical personage', and that our task as critical readers is simply to expose the discursive tropes through which the narrator constructs their identity.

To dismiss the individual represented in a diary as a wholly illusory ideological construct, however, seems an exaggeratedly totalizing view to me. I am more sympathetic to the sensitive, empathetic, alert but respectful reading techniques advocated by some feminist scholars (although I see no reason to restrict this approach to diaries written by women). Huff, for example, argues that we should read diaries as 'friendly explorers', a view close to my own.[4] Like an explorer, when we begin to read a diary we do not know what we will find, nor even necessarily what we should be looking for. The significance of what we see may not be obvious at first glance. A diary, like any other historical source, provides clues which the historian must assemble, using clues provided by other sources wherever available, into a pattern of coherent meaning. Diaries and other kinds of life writing are not, any more than any historical source ever could be, definitive 'maps of the soul' – the interpretative map always has to be made by the historian. If the historian is a careful, sensitive reader and is able to relate the diary as fully as possible to other texts and contexts, the map will be richer, more detailed and more convincing.

Alert reading requires the historian to read with questions in mind. One of the most critical questions for a historian using life writing sources is why the source was written. There will be different answers in the case of different individuals. Several of the diarists considered in this book asked themselves the question and in most cases they were unable to answer it. Baffled by his own persistence, Johnston exclaimed:

> Of what earthly use is it for me to keep on filling up book after book in this way with my monotonous and uninteresting scribbling?[5]

---

[2] James Hinton, *Nine Wartime Lives* (Oxford, 2010). See also *Seven Lives*, which surveys a longer span of its subjects' lives, but in less depth.

[3] Robert A. Fothergill, *Private Chronicles: A Study of English Diaries* (London, 1974), 48.

[4] Cynthia Anne Huff, 'Reading As Re-vision: Approaches to Reading Manuscript Diaries', *Biography* 23 (2000), 504–23. Compare Hinton, *Seven Lives*: 'It is through a process of empathetic engagement that I have tried to enter into the experience of these seven people.'

[5] Bolton Archives History Centre (BAHC), ZJO 1/20 (Johnston diary, 14 Mar. 1892). Compare Cresswell, quoting Ellen Terry: '"A diary is a document useful to the person

Since each of them sustained their diary more or less continuously over several decades, this suggests a strong unconscious motive or motives. In one case, Hallam's, it seems likely that writing a diary served related functions to one of his other major commitments – writing down inscriptions. Both had the effect of preserving memory and hence guarding against the loss of the past. There are many other reasons, however, for keeping a diary and it would probably be a mistake to assume that the preservation of memory was the major motive for each of the other seven diarists considered here. Equally important, for example, may have been the opportunity to reflect on the day's events.[6]

Another question we need to ask when reading diaries is when the entries were made. Were they written on the same day as the events described? If so, when? Was each entry written in a single session, or were they, as in Johnston's case, sometimes interrupted and then resumed? Many diarists appear to have written up their entries just before going to bed, allowing them both to record all the events of the day and to take stock before going to sleep, and for many diarists this seems to have become a perhaps comforting routine. However in a few exceptional cases, including one discussed in this book, entries were written at the very moment the diarist was experiencing the events being recorded. Diarists vary greatly in how conscientious they are, both with respect to the regularity and length of entries and how soon after the events described they were written up. Spear Smith frequently left gaps of weeks or even months in her diary, which she sometimes filled up in summary form afterwards. She was careful to acknowledge this: 'I am writing this long after I had left Fittleworth, so I ought not to head it Monday 6th.'[7] Catley was equally open, if less conscience-stricken: 'I confess, being some days behind with my journal, I remember very little about today.'[8] Cresswell, by contrast, rarely missed a day. Diarists are not necessarily constant in this respect: Hallam was certainly not unusual in keeping his diary more conscientiously before he had children than afterwards.

We also need to be alert to the practice, which Bellanca persuasively claims is almost universal among long-standing diary keepers, of re-reading old diaries and revising entries.[9] Luckily, in the case of handwritten diaries like those on

---

who keeps it – dull to the contemporary who reads it, invaluable, centuries afterwards, to the student who treasures it." Ellen Terry – Story of my Life. I'm not sure that my diary responds to this definition.' Beatrix Cresswell, *Diaries*, 1909, endpapers.

[6] Philippe Lejeune, *On Diary* (Honolulu, 2009), 194–6. Alongside the preservation of memory and reflection, Lejeune highlights self-expression and the sheer pleasure of writing as principal motivations for diary writing.

[7] Hampshire RO [HRO], 19M99/1/2a (Katherine Spear Smith, diaries, 6 Aug. 1906 [written afterwards]). See also, for example, HRO, 19M99/1/1 (Smith diaries, Aug. 1902).

[8] Bristol RO, 41419/22 (Catley diaries, 12 Oct. 1932).

[9] Mary Ellen Bellanca, *Daybooks of Discovery: Nature Diaries in Britain, 1770–1870* (Charlottesville, 2007), 31–4. See also Lejeune, *On Diary*, 324–6.

which this book is based, it is usually easy to see where an entry has been revised. It is not always easy to tell when it was revised, although some very scrupulous diarists date the revision, and sometimes there are other textual clues.[10] On the whole, the shorter the interval between the date to which an entry refers and the time of writing the better, because it is likely to provide a more detailed and accurate account of events, reported speech and the felt flux of daily life. Retrospective entries and additions can have their own advantages, however. As time passes, significant, lasting experiences often stand out more clearly from ephemeral ones, and reflection may have enabled the writer to become aware of feelings of which he or she was unconscious at the time.

When reading a diary, we must also ask ourselves what the diarist does *not* write about.[11] All diaries contain omissions, intentional or otherwise. Most omitted events, thoughts and feelings were probably simply considered insufficiently important by the diarist to merit recording, or, especially in the case of post-dated entries, had slipped the diarist's memory. However, there are many other reasons for omissions. Some subjects may have been considered unsuitable or unseemly; for most of the diarists I have looked at, sex is the most obvious major example, although Catley and, very circumspectly, Dickinson, did describe sexual experiences in their diaries. Events or issues that gave rise to unpleasant emotions such as fear and shame were doubtless also often omitted by diarists, although one use of a diary can be therapeutic and some diarists actively sought to work through fears and difficulties by writing them down. Some omissions were certainly due to lack of space, especially in diaries, like most of Cresswell's, written in preformatted printed diaries. Equally, lack of time must often have limited the fullness of diary entries. Some matters that might be of great interest to a historian probably went unmentioned because they were so obvious to the diarist that it did not occur to him/her to explain them.

It may seem odd to ask who a diary was written for, since the usual assumption is that a diary is a private matter, the 'book of the self', written for the diarist's own sake rather than for anyone else. But that is not necessarily true. Diaries written for publication are a special case and constitute an almost negligible fraction of all diaries, although they have attracted disproportionate scholarly attention. However, many diaries that were not written with publication in mind were nevertheless written with half an eye to being read by others. Dorothy Wordsworth, for example, kept her diary partly as a source of poetic material for her brother William and their friend Coleridge.

---

[10] Smith, for example, appended to an entry originally made on 16 April 1906 information she had subsequently discovered: 'Note: The Black bees are Anthophora pilipes and the ones with white spots, their cuckoos, Melecta armata. KSS March 1909.' HRO, 19M99/2/4 (Smith nature notebooks, 16 Apr. 1906).

[11] Compare Hinton, *Seven Lives*, 5.

Many diarists occasionally read excerpts from their diaries to family members or friends, and some did so regularly. Some diarists, especially children, kept a diary because someone else had asked or required them to do so; such diaries were often inspected. Even where the diarist evidently neither expected nor wanted anyone else to read the diary, as with Spear Smith's commonplace book, inscribed 'for my eyes only', the question of whether the diarist had an audience in mind as they wrote is a real one. It has been argued that even the most private of diarists writes with an imagined reader looking over their shoulder. Certainly all diarists are in some degree self-conscious, since the act of writing, of rendering thoughts, feelings and events into words, requires conscious choices (what to include, what to exclude, what form of words to use) that interpose a degree of separation between experience and expression. But not all diarists are equally self-conscious. Just as with contemporary and retrospective entries, it is not so much a question of one kind of diary being more valuable than another, as that different kinds of diary tell the reader different things. Highly wrought, literary diaries written with publication in mind may tell the reader much about how the writer wanted to be seen by contemporaries or posterity, and sometimes about how they saw themselves. This is invaluable to those researching the historical formation and expression of selfhood and identity, a major preoccupation of recent life writing scholarship. However, such diaries are likely to foreground events and sentiments that promote their authors' constructed narratives of selfhood while downplaying or suppressing other elements.

Of course, just as all diarists are to some degree self-conscious, it is also true, although often forgotten, that all diarists are in some degree unselfconscious: that is, no diarist has perfect knowledge of themselves. Diarists, like the rest of us, are only in varying degrees aware of their feelings, motives and personal characteristics, and this partial awareness means that the sometimes strenuous attempts diarists make to determine posterity's perception of them is doomed to failure. But not to complete failure, because the more energetically a diarist seeks to shape their own image, the less material that points in a different direction, or is irrelevant to this purpose, is likely to survive the writing filter. Thus while the diarist may not succeed in coercing the reader into accepting their own self-image, they may limit, sometimes drastically so, the availability of material from which a fuller and deeper understanding might be developed. While one way of reading a diary may be as a 'friendly explorer', there is another sense in which reading a diary is a struggle between the diarist, seeking to impose their desired self-image on the reader, and the reader, seeking to question, subvert or extend this image.

The distinction between published and unpublished diaries deserves comment in this connection. As with almost everything else about life writing, it is less absolute than it seems.[12] The status of diaries can change: many once-unpublished

---

[12] On the advantages of unpublished diaries, see Harriet Blodgett, *Centuries of Female Days: Englishwomen's Private Diaries* (New Brunswick, 1988). See also Lejeune, *On Diary*, 30–1.

diaries have subsequently been published, sometimes against their authors' wishes. Conversely, some diaries written for publication remain unpublished. Published diaries are often excerpts from longer originals, which may no longer survive. The few diaries not written for publication that have subsequently been published in full, like Gladstone's, were almost invariably written by major public figures. Unpublished diaries not written for publication are much the most valuable for a study of popular ruralism because, on the one hand, a less severe writing filter has usually been applied, and, more importantly, the best such diaries are far longer than comparable published diaries, yielding a vastly greater depth of evidence.

Selecting Diaries for Study

Finding suitable diaries proved difficult. The deep history methodology I intended to adopt required diaries that were unpublished and not apparently written for publication, included a long run (preferably twenty years or more) of near-continuous entries, and that provided, on the one hand, a detailed description of everyday events and activities and, on the other, rich evidence of the diarist's thoughts and feelings, in relation both to rural landscapes and to other aspects of their life.

I did reject a few otherwise eligible diaries because the diarist had a similar class, gender and regional background to one I had already studied – the most important case being Theodora Roscoe, who as an upper middle-class woman from southern England was too similar in background to Spear Smith to warrant inclusion.[13] Apart from this, the only diaries I was able to identify that met these criteria are the eight on which this book is based.

There is one celebrated collection of twentieth-century life writing (including many diaries) that I have purposely avoided: the Mass Observation archive. Mass Observation has many attractions for historians. It is well documented and there is a degree of standardization in sources such as the directives and diaries that facilitates comparison. Nevertheless, Mass Observation has its limitations too. It is heavily focussed on the Second World War, and although some of the diaries extend into the 1950s or beyond, none continues for forty years or more, as do several of the diaries used for this study. It is often difficult or impossible to locate evidence relating to the life of Mass Observation diarists before and after the period covered by their diaries. Although the richness and variety of the Mass Observation archive and associated material is extraordinary, those who chose to contribute to Mass Observation were in some ways a distinctive and unusual group. They were self-selecting and seem to have been better educated, more 'progressive' politically and intellectually and more

---

[13] Centre for Buckinghamshire Studies, D 115 (Roscoe Manuscripts).

likely to be drawn from the ranks of the white-collar and professional middle class than the rest of the population.[14] Of course diarists are inherently likely to be more self-conscious and literary than other people, so some of these biases may be impossible to avoid entirely. Nevertheless, despite the proliferation of revealing studies based on the Mass Observation archive, there is a sense that social and cultural historians of twentieth-century England have been over-reliant on it. There are, after all, literally thousands of other diaries from this period in public repositories which have scarcely been touched by historians. Beyond this, an unknown but surely orders-of-magnitude larger number remain in private hands (one of which has been used in this study). More systematic exploration of this vast resource is surely warranted.[15]

For the reasons given above, people who write diaries are unlikely to be typical of the wider population. Typicality, however, is an elusive historical concept. In an important sense no individual can ever be 'typical' since everyone is different, often in unexpected ways. As E. P. Thompson warned long ago, there is no such thing as an 'average' worker.[16] The rationale for adopting a micro-historical approach is not to pursue such a mythical being but to reveal connections and processes that a cruder mesh might miss. These connections and processes *may* then turn out to have a wider historical currency. That can only be established by further study.[17]

This suggests that achieving typicality is neither feasible nor necessary. More important is to select diaries of diverse provenance so as to identify varieties and contrasts. Subject to the criteria given above, I have therefore tried to achieve a degree of balance with respect to gender, class, region, urban/rural residence and time period (on ethnicity, see later in this chapter). This proved easiest in relation to gender: four of the diarists are female, four male. The diaries are reasonably well spread chronologically: their authors were born respectively in 1852, 1861, 1868, 1885, 1886, 1902, 1907 and 1911. It would have been preferable to include diarists born in the 1870s and 1890s but, without reducing the spread in more critical respects, suitable diaries could not be found. Some degree of balance has been achieved with respect to region, although again this is not entirely satisfactory, and classification is difficult since several of the diarists made inter-regional moves. When their diaries began, two were living in London, two in the south, two in the south-west, one in the Midlands and one in the north. The underrepresentation of the north is particularly regrettable in

---

[14] This may be less true of Mass Observation's second incarnation, the Mass Observation Project (1981 onwards): Hinton, *Seven Lives*, 163.

[15] A growing number of unpublished diaries – more than nine thousand at the time of writing – are now available for public consultation at the Great Diary Project, Bishopsgate Institute, London. https://www.thegreatdiaryproject.co.uk [accessed 10 Dec. 2018].

[16] Edward Palmer Thompson, *The Making of the English Working Class* (London, 1963), 233–7.

[17] Hinton, *Seven Lives*, 6.

view of the comparative historiographical neglect it has suffered, but unfortunately suitable northern diaries proved elusive. This was exacerbated by funding restrictions that made it more difficult to investigate northern archives than those closer to the University of Reading, from where the study was carried out. It is to be hoped that further research on popular ruralism will prioritize northern and perhaps also Midlands sensibilities and experiences.

Just as the diarists moved between regions, they also moved between town and country, except for Barmes, who lived in urban areas throughout her life. Few non-agriculturalists seem to have spent their whole lives in the countryside, and none of the diarists did so.[18] It would have been interesting to assess whether such a person evinced as strong an attachment to the countryside as diarists who, like Hallam and Johnston, were brought up in rural areas but were subsequently forced to leave them in search of employment.

Between them, the eight diarists spanned a complete range of settlement types from isolated cottages and farms to hamlets, villages, market and factory towns, provincial cities and outer and inner London. Unsurprisingly, however, it proved more difficult to achieve a satisfactory range with respect to class. Of the eight diarists, one was unambiguously working class, three lower middle class (the daughter of a small shopkeeper, a bookshop employee, a probation officer), three were from professional backgrounds (the daughter of a civil engineer, a clergyman's daughter who became a guidebook writer, a general practitioner) and one was downwardly mobile upper middle class (an art dealer's daughter who became a smallholder). There is plainly an underrepresentation of the working class and an overrepresentation of the professional middle class. Again, this was driven by the availability of suitable diaries. When gender is taken into account, the class skew becomes even more pronounced: of the four female diarists, one was lower middle class, two had professional backgrounds and the fourth was upper middle class. The rarity of diaries written by working-class women, especially in the nineteenth century, presumably reflects a lack of time, space and materials for writing as well as educational disadvantage.

The most notable omission from this study is that none of the diaries I was able to find was written by a person of colour (POC). This reflects not only Britain's changing ethnic composition, but also the underrepresentation of POC life writing in archival collections and significant (and ongoing) barriers to accessing the countryside for POC.[19] Ethnicity is to the fore in the chapter on Sadie Barmes, who was Jewish, but there is a need for much further research on ethnicity and the experience of landscape in Britain. For this and earlier

---

[18] Colin Pooley and Jean Turnbull, *Migration and Mobility in Britain since the Eighteenth Century* (London, 1998), 145.

[19] Sarah Neal and Julian Agyeman (eds.), *The New Countryside? Ethnicity, Nation and Exclusion in Contemporary Britain* (Bristol, 2006).

periods, however, a different methodology than the one used here will almost certainly be required, given the apparent unavailability of source material.

One other bias in relation to the diaries chosen for analysis should be mentioned: all but one have been deposited in public archives. How some diaries but not others come into the public domain is a question that deserves more thought than historians appear to have given it, although Huff has some interesting reflections on the subject.[20] It is probably no accident that four of the diarists never married and only two had children, one of whom was the diarist whose diary remains in private hands. Diaries written by parents with surviving offspring are doubtless more likely to remain with the family. Further research, sources permitting, on ruralists who went on to have children would be interesting.

In addition to the eight unpublished diaries on which *Lifescapes* is primarily based, I have also drawn freely on other life writing sources where available, including autobiographical fragments, letters, handwritten notes, sketches and paintings (especially important for diarists with artistic interests such as Spear Smith and Dickinson), extra-textual objects like pressed flowers, newspaper cuttings and locks of hair, and printed works where these exist, notably in the case of Cresswell, who wrote several guidebooks for the Homeland Association.[21] It is important to emphasize that this is not a study of diaries, nor even of diarists; rather, it is a study of popular experience of the countryside, using diaries as its principal source.

The primary weakness of diaries and other autobiographical sources is that they are necessarily written from a single standpoint – the diarist's own. I have used biographical material such as memoirs and letters written by relatives, friends and acquaintances and, in some cases, local history investigation on the ground to gain a wider range of perspectives. A second intrinsic limitation of diaries is that there is always a 'dark period' before the diary begins. Fortunately the diaries I have used for this study all contain some retrospective autobiographical material, sometimes, as with Johnston and Hallam, in the form of a memoir of the author's life up to the commencement of the diary. In other cases, as with Dickinson, biographical material written by others can help to fill in the earlier part of their lives. Thirdly, all diaries necessarily end, if in a few instances only just, before the diarist's life does. In the case of Spear

---

[20] Huff, 'Reading as Re-vision', 508–9.

[21] On extra-textual items in diaries, see Lejeune, *On Diary*, 39–40. Bellanca notes the interplay between diaries and published work (Bellanca, *Daybooks*, 35). This is more apparent in the case of the diarists she studies, all of whom are well known and most of whom were professional writers. However, despite their obscurity, several of the diarists considered in this book were in fact published writers, although in most cases only to the extent of a few letters or poems in magazines. In these instances, as with Bellanca's diarists, it is often apparent that observations initially recorded in diaries were subsequently worked up into published poems or, in Cresswell's case, guidebook descriptions.

Smith, Hallam, Cresswell, Dickinson and Bissell, the diaries run to within a year or two of the diarist's death, so the gap is small. For the other three diarists, the situation is less satisfactory. I have been able to use biographical evidence provided by a family member to fill out Barmes's later life but I have very little evidence for Catley after the diaries end, and for Johnston almost none at all. This is one of the occupational hazards of studying the lives of uncelebrated people: they fade in and out of history, and even for relatively recent lives many of the basic details may already be unrecoverable.

The opposite problem, that of having too much information, can oddly also be a difficulty when working with very long-run, extremely detailed unpublished diaries.[22] A rough estimate suggests the diaries and related primary sources on which this study is based extend to something like 20 million words. I have read every word of the shorter ones like Barmes's but, for the very long diaries such as Cresswell's and Johnston's, I have had to sample, although intensively. Another historian reading the same diaries would doubtless reach other conclusions in some respects, partly through reading different entries although probably more because they would bring contrasting prior knowledge and perspectives to bear.[23]

---

[22] See Jake Hodder, 'On Absence and Abundance: Biography As Method in Archival Research', *Area* 49 (2017), 452–9.

[23] Compare Hinton, *Seven Lives*, 161: 'Other historians . . . will no doubt find in these lives material to illustrate interpretations of the period quite different from those I sketched out in Chapter 2.'

Adherers

Beatrix Cresswell and William Hallam were, on the face of it, different in just about every possible way. She was the daughter of an Anglican clergyman, while he was the son of a groom. She was a woman of independent means who lived in a genteel cathedral city, while he was a factory worker inhabiting a rapidly growing railway town. Yet there were profound similarities (as well as some contrasts) in the role that rural landscapes played in their lives. For both, the countryside was a fundamental source of stability and security – a carrier and guarantor of childhood memories, experiences and structures of feeling to which they adhered with passionate commitment.

2

Beatrix Cresswell

Exeter Antiquarian

'I feel that devoutly doing what one ought to do may be rewarded by doing what one likes to do!' Beatrix Cresswell confided to her diary on 23 October 1903.[1] This nicely captures the dialectic between duty and pleasure, constraint and self-assertion, that structured her life. The daughter of an Anglican clergyman, she remained steadfastly anchored in the traditions and values in which she had been brought up. Yet for most of her adult life she made few concessions to the overt demands and expectations of others, determinedly shaping the external circumstances of her life, insofar as they were amenable to human agency, to her own will. After her mother's death Beatrix moved to a house she had previously identified as the one she would like to live in above all others, in the best of locations in the best of towns. She made her decision with little regard to employment or earnings considerations and none to the wishes of relatives or friends. Similarly, she cobbled together a precarious income by undertaking commissioned or, occasionally, speculative work that interested her, mainly writing of various kinds but also genealogical and archival research. She was the only one of the diarists studied in this book who earned her living primarily by her pen (or rather, in this case, typewriter), although the Madras Railway shares inherited from her parents helped eke out her income.

Most of Beatrix's writing was about, or at least closely related to, the countryside. Rural landscapes were of professional as well as personal interest to her, in contrast to the other seven diarists studied in this book, with the partial exception of Dickinson. Her ruralism was distinctive also in its geographical scale: it was closely focussed on a single county (Devon - see Figure 2.1). Other diarists responded to the countryside at more local or wider scales. For Spear Smith, it was particular commons, woods and even individual trees and bushes that mattered, while Catley identified with the West Country as a whole rather than one specific county, although he also cared deeply about geomorphologically defined tracts of country such as the Chew valley or the Mendips. For most of the other diarists, the location of the countryside they found themselves in does not seem to have been especially important: it was

[1] Devon Heritage Centre, DRO 4686M/F40 (Beatrix Cresswell Diary, 23 Oct. 1903).

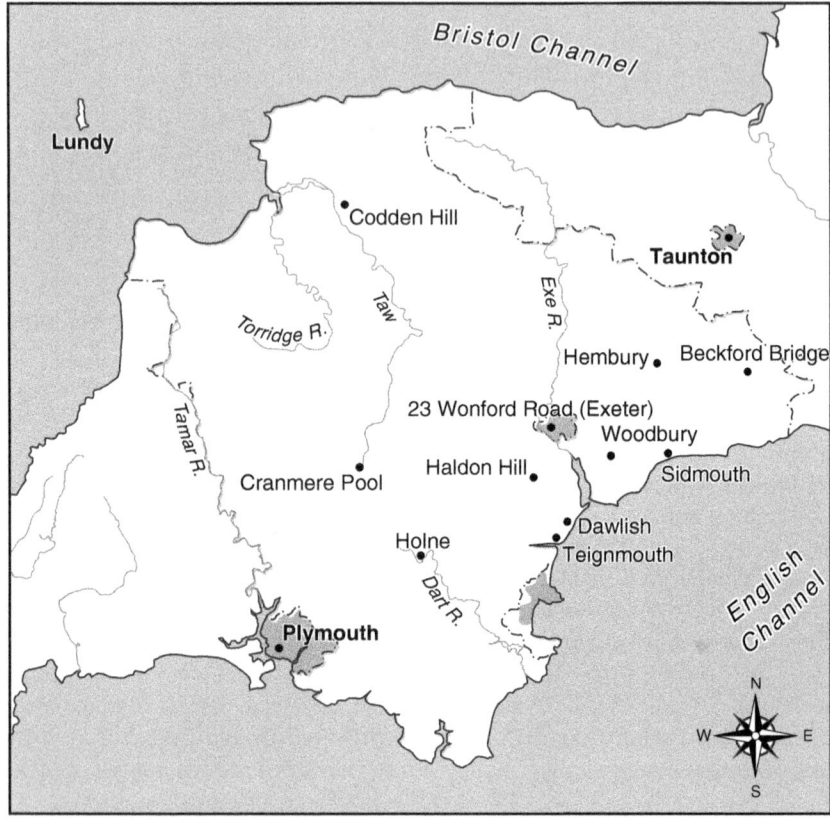

Figure 2.1   Beatrix Cresswell's Devon

the qualities they perceived in the landscape itself that appealed (or failed to appeal), rather than its spatial co-ordinates. The closest parallel with Cresswell in terms of the spatial scale of his ruralism is Hallam. While his loyalty was primarily to the village where he grew up (Lockinge) and its rural environs, he also developed a wider interest in and commitment to the county to which Lockinge belonged, Berkshire.[2]

Despite the fact that he was a working-class man while she was a genteel middle-class woman, William's ruralism also resembled Beatrix's in other core respects. Both had a profoundly historical apprehension of rural landscapes, both cherished the past and had reservations about aspects of the present, both expressed this through Conservative political convictions and to both the

---

[2] On the rise of the county as a unit of identity, see Nicholas Mansfield, *English Farmworkers and Local Patriotism, 1900–1930* (London, 2001).

architecture and territorial divisions of the Church of England were fundamental and essential elements of the rural landscape. It is interesting to note
that both were born in the 1860s: if we accept that the third quarter of the
century was an 'age of equipoise', as W. L. Burn claimed, and that the 1870s
and 1880s were a turning point in English social history, it could be argued that
this generation was subject to more rapid and disruptive change than previous
or subsequent cohorts.[3] Writing in 1923, Beatrix empathized with her elderly
visitor Jessie Clark: 'Decidedly Victorian, tho' attempting to adapt herself to
lower times', a remark that she could equally have applied to herself.[4]

The main source for Beatrix's life is her diaries, forty-two volumes of which
are preserved at the Devon Heritage Centre in Exeter. These span her last
forty-three years, from 1898 to 1940, with the exception of 1900, in which year
she kept no diary. Many of the volumes include ancillary material such as
newspaper cuttings, letters from family and friends, playbills and, occasionally,
non-textual items such as leaves and pressed flowers. Between 1920 and 1924
Beatrix kept a nature notebook, and there is also a commonplace book dating
from 1874, although this consists mostly of Greek and Latin exercises. She
wrote numerous guidebooks for the Homeland Handbooks series and
a number of other antiquarian books and pamphlets, mainly concerned with
Devon churches and local history. In addition there are a few short stories and
ephemeral pieces in contemporary magazines such as *Cycling*, *The Queen* and
The Monthly Packet. She also wrote several novels and other tales but these do
not survive.[5] Other than this, the most valuable source is the diaries her father,
Richard, kept until his death in 1882. Further evidence can be gleaned from the
census and other sources of biographical information, such as the obituary in
Devon and Cornwall Notes and Queries.

How should we approach this extensive source material? Beatrix's diaries
are remarkably complete. Only a few days are blank, mainly during periods of
illness. On the whole the entries appear to have been written up on the day in
question, although a few are clearly retrospective. During the First World War
diaries of Beatrix's preferred kind often only became available several months
into the year in question. However, Beatrix explains that she has copied the
entries for these months into the relevant diaries from paper notes made at the
time. Beyond minor textual corrections perhaps, there is no reason to believe
she edited the entries in doing so.

All in all, the diaries can be regarded as contemporary or very-near-
contemporary sources. A much more problematic issue is the form in which
they were written. Beatrix preferred to use pocket appointment diaries with

---

[3] William L. Burn, *The Age of Equipoise* (New York, 1964), 30–1. Jose Harris, *Private Lives,
Public Spirit: Britain 1870–1914* (Oxford, 1995), 252.

[4] Cresswell, Diary, 26 Jul. 1923.

[5] She sent most of them to the rubbish dump: Cresswell, Diary, 26 Feb. 1916.

limited space for each entry. This and the elliptical, often ironic, style in which she writes means that the diaries provide less rich insight into inner thoughts and feelings than more expansive diaries such as Johnston's or Spear Smith's. However, the sheer volume of material helps to compensate for this – there are so many entries and words that distinctive patterns, turns of phrase, responses and predilections inevitably emerge. In addition, some of the publications, especially Beatrix's account of her visit to Oberammergau in 1890 and her Homeland guide to Dartmoor, contain valuable extended accounts that can yield a fuller, more nuanced understanding.

Richard Cresswell's diaries shed valuable light on Beatrix's childhood. They are mainly concerned with his daily activities and interests and Beatrix features, as one would expect given the gender, class and period provenance, only occasionally. However, they offer valuable insights into the many ways in which Beatrix followed, but sometimes also chose not to follow, in her father's footsteps. Despite their infrequency, the entries mentioning Beatrix are often very revealing, not least because they allow us to see her through someone else's eyes.

The main difficulty to which the sources give rise is simply filling the gap between 1882, when Richard's diaries cease due to his death, and 1898, when Beatrix's begin. There are some helpful back-references in Beatrix's diaries, although these are not always easy to interpret or contextualize. The most useful material is in Beatrix's published work. *A Retrospect: Life at Oberammergau in 1890* (1900) is a direct, detailed, vivid account of her extended sojourn in the celebrated Bavarian village in the year in question. However, it tells us little about her life before or afterwards. *Dartmoor* (1898) incorporates two compelling narratives about childhood and youth experiences in relation to the moor, although the lack of context generates interpretative ambiguity. There are also several magazine articles from the late 1890s that provide suggestive indications about what Beatrix may have been thinking, feeling and doing at the time, but as most of these are fictional, they need to be interpreted with care. Beyond this, the census and baptism and burial records allow us to reconstruct a bare outline of the life histories of the other members of Beatrix's immediate and extended family during her lifetime and, where relevant, before she was born.

***

Richard Cresswell, although ordained in the Church of England, never became a beneficed clergyman. He was a curate at Salcombe Regis in Devon for a few years and continued to stand in for incumbents on an ad hoc basis thereafter, but his main occupation and source of income was tutoring boys in Latin and ancient Greek. This left him free to arrange his time as he chose and he spent much of it on his interests and pastimes. He is a classic example of the Victorian clergyman-naturalist, assembling a large collection of fungi, seaweed and algae that Beatrix later secured for the Royal Albert Memorial Museum in Exeter. For most of her childhood the family lived at Lugehay House in Teignmouth, and her father often took walks along the sea wall or over nearby Haldon Hill in search of specimens to examine under his microscope. Richard was a keen gardener, kept detailed weather records, sketched (especially trees and cliffs) and enjoyed discussing the theological controversies of the day with clerical friends. He emerges from his diaries as an affectionate, modest-natured husband and father. The volumes that pertain to Beatrix's early childhood begin with height measurements for the children. As a baby, Beatrix evidently kept her parents awake quite a bit at night, but Richard seems to have taken this in good part: 'she is a very good little girl and gives very little trouble' (1864).[6] This echoes his attitude to his eldest child, Richard Henry, later that year, at a time of parental anxiety about money and health: 'A letter from RH but he writes daily and very kindly. He is a dear good boy. He does not yet seem to understand the position of affairs.'[7]

Richard's diaries evince similar affection for his daughters Christiana (born 1849) and Anastasia (born 1855). On 31 December 1877 he '[t]hought much of Chrissy and her journey and her plans . . . I hope all may go well with her', while an entry for 31 May 1876 records that Stasia was a 'dear good girl'.[8] He was devoted to his wife, Fanny, noting on the occasion of their thirty-seventh wedding anniversary that they had had 'many happy years together, at least I can speak for myself'.[9] As so often, we know less about the wife than the husband. None of her letters or other writing appears to have survived. She was born Frances Creighton in Hooghly, Bengal, 1822; was living with her mother, the widow of an army officer, in Hawkhurst, Kent, in 1841; and married Richard two years later. The diaries suggest that Fanny worked hard in the house – when he was unwell, Richard was often concerned that she was overburdened, although they had a cook and a housemaid.[10]

Beatrix was born on 14 January 1862, very much the youngest child of the family – even Stasia was seven years older. Like many youngest daughters at the time, she stayed longer at home than her siblings, and ultimately the responsibility for looking after her mother fell to her. Chrissy was living in London by her twenty-first birthday, while Stasia seems to have left Lugehay House in her mid-twenties or earlier. Beatrix, however, continued to live with and, latterly, to care for Fanny until her death in 1904, by which time Beatrix was forty-two.

However, there were also potentially more positive aspects of being the youngest in the family. She was, according to her father, 'everybody's pet',

---

[6] Richard Cresswell, Diary, 18 Apr. 1864.
[7] Richard Henry was seventeen at the time. Richard Cresswell, Diary, 27 Nov. 1864.
[8] Richard Cresswell, Diary, 31 Dec. 1877 and 31 May 1876.
[9] Richard Cresswell, Diary, 14 Dec. 1880.
[10] Richard Cresswell, Diary, 1 Jan. 1865.

being 'a good deal spoilt by everybody, most of all perhaps by her sisters', while her good looks 'win her the favours of strangers continually'.[11] Richard was in the habit of recording how she spent her birthday each year, and the entries for the late 1860s run along the same lines. A typical example is that for 1868: 'the little maid passed a very happy day, at least if having her own way, and every kind of moderate indulgence could make her happy'.[12] At this age her favourite occupations seem to have been playing with her dolls, having friends round to tea and, increasingly, reading.[13] When the weather permitted, she 'had out her hammock and book' in the garden, although as a teenager she also delighted in the 'gaiety, hospitality and happiness' of the parties at Bitton House, across the road, and elsewhere in the area.[14]

As her father was at home so much, Beatrix spent much time with him, especially as she grew older. He nursed her when she was ill, played tunes for her dolls to dance to and helped her with the museum she was making.[15] She seems to have felt very much at ease with him: 'Beatrix sat with me a long time sewing and doing a bit of Greek, I fancy she likes taking refuge with me, she has pretty much her own way when she is here, and talks as she fancies.'[16] By 1875, they had begun regular lessons each morning: 'B's lessons. I sometimes think that hearing her little lessons is as pleasant as any part of the day. Perhaps she is not quite of the same mind about saying them.'[17]

Despite Richard's characteristic disinclination to impute his own feelings to others, there is good reason to believe Beatrix enjoyed these sessions, if not necessarily the preparation for them. She learnt well and later in life frequently incorporated ancient Greek phrases in her diary entries. Her father does not seem to have pressed her too hard: she had holidays over Christmas and at other festive periods and was allowed to sleep in late and miss her lessons when she had been to one of her many parties.[18] She often accompanied him on his walks, worked with him in the garden and came to meet him at the station when he returned from visiting his mother in London.[19] She was evidently

[11] Richard Cresswell, Diary, 1 Jan. 1867, 1 Jan. 1868 and 1 Jan. 1866.
[12] Richard Cresswell, Diary, 14 Jan. 1868. Even eleven years later, when Beatrix was seventeen, she had not only many presents but also 'a good deal of indulgence' for her birthday. Richard Cresswell, Diary, 14 Jan. 1879.
[13] Richard Cresswell, Diary, 14 Jan. 1871 and 14 Jan. 1875.
[14] Richard Cresswell, Diary, 4 Feb. 1882 and 17 and 18 Aug. 1882; Beatrix F. Cresswell, *Teignmouth: Its History and Its Surroundings* (London, 1906), 47.
[15] Richard Cresswell, Diary, 20 May 1869, 14 Jan. 1875 and 1 Mar. 1878.
[16] Richard Cresswell, Diary, 31 Dec. 1872.
[17] Richard Cresswell, Diary, 11 Jun. 1875 and 16 Mar. 1876.
[18] Richard Cresswell, Diary, 19 Dec. 1877, 18 Aug. 1880.
[19] Walks: Richard Cresswell, Diary, 3 and 28 Feb. and 2 Mar. 1876; 24 Feb. 1878; 25 Feb. and 12 Nov. 1880. Gardening: 30 Oct. 1875, 24 Sep. 1879 and 10 Sep. 1881. Meeting at the station: 15 Feb. 1872.

devoted to him and in later life took great pleasure in being told that she was exactly like him: 'Am I? I love to be told so.'[20]

Richard's sudden death in 1882, at the age of only sixty-six, was a devastating blow. Even fifty-six years later, Beatrix felt haunted by 'the dreadful time of Papa's death' and on its anniversary wrote of 'the dismals of this hateful day'.[21] Although she was to suffer many other bereavements in the course of her life, none echoed down the years like this. Why did it have such a profound effect? We can only speculate but, apart from the loss of a beloved parent, it also signified, perhaps, the end of a happy, protected childhood, plunging her suddenly and with very little preparation into a cold adult world. We have no diaries from the period but Richard's death must have precipitated an immediate and severe financial crisis. The Cresswells were barely able to cover their expenses as it was, and Richard's tutoring seems to have been their main source of income. Given the closeness of the marriage and her financial dependence on him, Fanny may well have been prostrated by the unexpected catastrophe too, which would hardly have helped Beatrix. It is unclear how far the older sisters were in a position to steady the ship. Chrissy had married a London journalist, John Jennings, two years before and the family seem to have felt that she had lowered herself in doing so. There are indications that contact was broken off – years later Beatrix castigated herself for 'a certain pride of intention "to have nothing to do with the Jennings"'.[22] Stasia was no longer living at home either and by the late 1890s her relationship with Beatrix had broken down, largely, it would seem, because Beatrix regarded her as utterly feckless. The diaries make clear that the origins of the estrangement lay in a temperamental incompatibility which the crisis arising from Richard's death can hardly have failed to exacerbate.

We know little about Beatrix's life for the next six years but, at some point, for unknown reasons, she went to Canada. She was at the Niagara Falls on 4 July 1883, which puts her departure within fifteen months of her father's death, so it seems likely there was a connection.[23] Leaving home would have eased the pressure on the Lugehay House finances a little but, depending on how straitened the family's circumstances were, this might not have been enough. What Beatrix really needed was to earn money and it may be that she had been offered an opportunity to do so in Canada.

By the mid-1880s, however, she seems to have been back in England. She spent much time with two elderly spinsters, Mary and Lucy Gardiner, great friends of Fanny's, and gradually 'slipped into the happy position of a sort of

[20] Cresswell, Diary, 13 Feb. 1905.
[21] Cresswell, Diary, 13 and 14 Apr. 1938.
[22] Cresswell, Diary, 9 Oct. 1915.
[23] Cresswell, Diary, 4 Jul. 1925.

favoured child of the house'.[24] The Gardiners were eager admirers of the Oberammergau Passion Play, which they had witnessed for the first time in 1872 and again in 1880.[25] Much to her delight, they offered to take Beatrix with them to Oberammergau in the next 'Spieljahr', 1890. Beatrix's account, written ten years later, eloquently conveys the excitement and intensity of the experience. Her first sight of the pine-clad, sometimes snow-capped mountains of the Tyrol was 'like getting inside a picture'. As they trundled closer to the village, Beatrix asked if she might get out and walk:

> Stepping down seemed to give me a sense of the new and undiscovered, a fresh world opening before me as my feet trod the mountain road. Oh, the delight of walking after days of being cooped up in the train – the freshness of the country after cities and hotels! There were new flowers on either side of the road: meadow-sweet with long white tassels, a yellow daisy, large blue centaureas, harebells, lovely sweet butterfly orchids, and yellow monkshood ...
>
> When the hill top was gained, and the slow stell-wagen came up, I begged to be allowed to walk the rest of the way ... Miss Lucy had no objection, and the stell-wagen rattled off ... leaving me to the delights of this new lovely land.
>
> And thus I entered the 'Heilige Thal', as it is always best for pilgrims to reach their Mecca – on foot.[26]

Reality lived up to expectations. They stayed in the village for much of that summer and Beatrix saw the play several times. However, what she revelled in most was her complete independence. She was free to explore the mountain valley as and when she wished, either on her own or accompanied by the two much younger sons of the man with whom she and Miss Lucy were staying. She climbed the Kofelberg and gazed transfixed at her 'first sight of eternal snows in the white tipped ranges that fringed the far far distance, peeping over the shoulder of nearer blue hills'.[27] She rejoiced in the abundant flowers, meadows, rocks and woods – everything was so 'deliciously new that I cared little where I went or what I did'.[28] But this 'epoch of complete delight' was brought to an end by the arrival of another friend of Miss Lucy's, bringing three girls in tow 'with whom it was of course understood I should in future share my walks and experiences'.[29] This was a characteristic reaction: although

---

[24] Beatrix F. Cresswell, *A Retrospect: Life at Oberammergau in 1890* (Exeter, 1900), 2.

[25] So Beatrix tells us – but the decennial Passion Play, interrupted by the Franco-Prussian War, was held over from 1870 only to the following year; '1872' is presumably therefore an error for 1871.

[26] Cresswell, *A Retrospect*, 3.

[27] Cresswell, *A Retrospect*, 22.

[28] Cresswell, *A Retrospect*, 33.

[29] Cresswell, *A Retrospect*, 41.

gregarious at other times, when in the countryside Beatrix preferred to be on her own.

Why did Oberammergau make such an indelible impression on Beatrix? For many reasons. Not only did it offer freedom, independence and excitement at a time of her life when she was much in need of these things, but it did so in a setting of the utmost natural beauty. All these elements fused in her mind with the way of life of the villagers, which corresponded in her eyes to an ideal vision of religious community in the countryside: 'It was as if the whole valley were some vast Cathedral, and those living there the ministers therein. Occupied during secular hours with their daily work, assembling periodically to conduct a service in God's honour [i.e. the Passion Play], in which all, from the infant to the old man, could take part ... simply and naturally.'[30]

Beatrix always found it deeply appealing when her constitutive attachments to religion and rurality resonated with each other in this way, and she was drawn to the possibility of conflating the two.[31] This is vividly apparent in the account of the Bradley Woods Preacher's Pit, where secret Presbyterian prayer meetings were held after the Reformation, which she later included in her Homeland guide to Newton Abbot (1908). The pit figures in her description as a microcosm of the 'vast Cathedral' of the Ammergau that had affected her so profoundly in her youth:

> [I]t is a very wonderful place, full of suggestions to those who know its history. Nature has cushioned the stones with the softest moss, fallen trees serve as benches, the boughs close overhead to make the roof, and the birds, accompanied by some distant ripple of the stream, sing as choir. It is still the temple of Nature, where she teaches divine truths to such as will listen.[32]

Later in life she was intrigued by 'blue-doming', the view that outdoor communion with God was as valid a form of worship as church attendance. But the whole tenor of her Anglicanism, grounded in orthodoxy and respect for traditional forms, spoke against this. So, although she looked, she would not leap:

> An ideally lovely day. Early church (glad later I had gone) and so beautiful that I walked back by the river. After breakfast ... [a] most lovely run, over Woodbury, the distances wonderful, green valleys reaching up to blue hills ...

---

[30] Cresswell, A Retrospect, 59.

[31] On the nexus between religion and rurality, see Elizabeth Baigent, '"God's Earth Will Be Sacred": Religion, Theology, and the Open Space Movement in Victorian England', Rural History 22 (2011), 31–58.

[32] Beatrix Cresswell, Newton Abbot (Devon) and Its Neighbouring Villages, Including Chudleigh (London, 1908), 23. See also Beatrix Cresswell, A Book of Devonshire Parsons (London, 1932), 118–19.

> I should not have liked to skip church for 'Blue dome-ing', but having
> been to church the blue dome was a great pleasure.[33]

* * *

Given what a powerful and multilayered response Oberammergau had evoked
in Beatrix, it is hardly surprising that the towns and cities they visited on their
journey back to England proved an anticlimax: 'nothing I saw afterwards has
so vivid, so loving a hold on my memory as Oberammergau, last seen through
a mist of blinding tears'.[34] She consoled herself, however, with the thought
that 'the mountains on which we rambled are unchangeable'.[35] She felt this
not only about mountains but other elements of the rural landscape: years
later she observed in her diary that '[t]he country never changes except when
it is built on'.[36] To someone whose attachments ran so deep, the perceived
unchanging permanence of the countryside was one of the fundamental
sources of its appeal.

By the time she went to Oberammergau, Beatrix had begun to write for
publication. Among her earliest published pieces were three short stories for
The Monthly Packet. A story entitled 'Which was the fairest' is a latter-day
reworking of the Judgement of Paris, in which the heroine, Mysie, is (like
Beatrix) the youngest of three sisters. The oldest sister becomes engaged and
the middle sister excels in the classics tripos at Girton College, but Mysie
stays at home, apparently doing nothing. Unbeknownst to anyone, however,
she has been making quilts to raise money for a fountain to be placed in an
East End churchyard garden, intended to brighten the lives of the working
class. The story ends with the handsome young curate Leonard's discovery of
Mysie's secret.[37] 'The veiled sphinx' recounts the desperate lengths to which
an ancient Egyptian girl of peerless wisdom has to go in order to open her
husband's eyes to her worth. 'Stolen honours' again features Mysie, this time
as the unacknowledged author of a prize-winning essay on Shakespeare,
misattributed to a boorish young man of the family's acquaintance until
the story's resolution.

The obvious theme shared by these three stories is neglected worth in
a young woman. It is difficult not to read a biographical meaning into this.
While Beatrix may have been 'everyone's pet' as a child, she was fifteen years
younger than her brother, thirteen years younger than Chrissy and seven
years younger even than Stasia. When her sister-in-law Margaret died in

---

[33] Cresswell, Diary, 9 Jun. 1929.
[34] Cresswell, *A Retrospect*, 59.
[35] Cresswell, *A Retrospect*, 62.
[36] Cresswell, Diary, 28 Mar. 1928.
[37] Beatrix F. Cresswell, 'Which Was the Fairest', *The Monthly Packet*, 96, 1 Dec. 1888, 246.

1923, Beatrix wrote that she would 'miss her very much. She was nice to me when I was a miserable kiddie snubbed by everyone'.[38] While her siblings may have indulged her, at least when she was younger, they doubtless had their own concerns and interests to which Beatrix was peripheral. The centre of gravity in Lugehay House, at least until Stasia left home, must have been with the older children. They may have had kind intentions but it seems possible Beatrix felt patronized or even ignored.

The emphasis in the first story on educational disadvantage is also interesting. Richard Henry went to Oxford, even though in his father's opinion his grasp of classics was not altogether secure. Beatrix was a quick learner, well versed in Greek, and although not really intellectually minded, may have felt that she had been denied educational opportunities to which her abilities entitled her.

Another theme, present to some degree in all three stories, is of a young woman being compelled to hide her light under a bushel. Beatrix certainly felt this herself to some extent, though whether it was religious or gender expectations that constrained her, or possibly a sense that it would be unbecoming to take the shine off her sisters' achievements, is unclear. She sometimes copied quotations into her diary; one such is revealing in this respect: '"Modesty consists in hiding from the world that merit of which you yourself are conscious." John Taylor Coleridge – written when a schoolboy – it was said facetiously – but – how true!'[39]

One direction in which Beatrix attempted to extend her talents at this time was writing for children. *The Royal Progress of King Pepito* was published in 1889 and had some success, although Beatrix plausibly attributed this to the illustrations by Kate Greenaway rather than to the text.[40] This was followed by *Alexis and His Flowers*, which, despite its stilted dialogue, warrants further consideration because it sheds light on Beatrix's character and its relationship to her ruralist commitments.

As Beatrix had been, Alexis is an isolated child without playfellows his own age. He lives with his great uncle, a kind, affectionate clergyman-botanist who, however, dies part way through the book. Alexis takes comfort in flowers, cherishing their 'quaint old-fashioned names' and the 'old legends and customs' associated with them he had learnt from his great-uncle: '"Violets blossoming too profusely in the autumn portend an epidemic the next year," said Winter, gravely.'[41]

---

[38] Cresswell, Diary, 27 Jan. 1923.

[39] Cresswell, Diary, 1909, memorandum.

[40] It is unclear how Beatrix came to collaborate with Greenaway. Perhaps the point of contact was Beatrix's artist cousin Etta.

[41] Beatrix F. Cresswell, *Alexis and His Flowers: Flower Lore for Boys and Girls* (London, 1891), 12, 34. The Rector clearly has affinities with Richard Cresswell, in whose diaries flower and weather lore also feature. Richard Cresswell, Diary, 1 Jan. 1872.

This predilection for 'old legends' is equally manifest in Beatrix's diaries. It reflects her reverence for the past but also a surprising agnosticism towards superstition and readiness to suspend rational judgement. On 10 February 1910, she feared bad luck might ensue from her maid Mary breaking a mirror, while in December 1917 she seriously entertained a rumour that Lord Kitchener was not dead but for reasons unknown hiding, seriously injured, in the Orkneys.[42] She found ghost stories 'very fascinating', disliked sleeping in a room with a window opening onto a churchyard and seems to have believed that the dead appear in our dreams at their own behest.[43]

With respect to Beatrix's ruralism, however, the most significant feature of *Alexis* is simply that it underlines how much flowers, especially wild ones, mattered to her. The plethora of colourful flowers in the Alpine pastures had been an inextricable part of her delight in Oberammergau and she continued to record sightings of wildflowers frequently throughout her life, with no slackening of interest even in her last years. Characteristically, however, she never explains what they meant to her. It is possible that, like Spear Smith, she saw in them a reflection of herself, but this is not convincing. Beatrix did not anthropomorphize flowers nor project herself into them. While she was regarded as beautiful in childhood, there is no sign she cared much about this in her adult life: she was far too busy doing things to have much time to bother about her appearance. Nor does the passive gentleness associated with flowers (and with which Beatrix endows Alexis) correspond to her energetic, determined, forthright character.

The attributes of flowers to which Beatrix most obviously responded were, in the first place, their beauty, brightness and colour. Several of the other diarists, male as well as female, shared this feeling, notably Dickinson, Spear Smith, Catley and Johnston. Secondly, and more distinctively, Beatrix rejoiced in abundant, overflowing drifts of wildflowers, gathering armfuls of them almost beyond her capacity to carry. This correlates with and perhaps gave expression to her own enthusiastic, even excessive, character. Thirdly, the familiarity of the wildflowers she mentions was important. Although she was a competent botanist (albeit that her bluestocking friend Miss Ruddock knew 'more of the smaller and less showy plants than I do'), the range of flowers regularly recorded in the diary is unexpectedly restricted: mainly snowdrops, daffodils, primroses, 'snapjack' (Greater Stitchwort) and a few others. In contrast to the nature diarists Bellanca investigated, Beatrix had little interest in rarity, except when she found herself in an exotic location like the remote island of Lundy, where it seemed pleasingly appropriate to find a rare figwort.[44] Her pleasure in familiar flowers was related to the delight with which she

[42] Cresswell, Diary, 10 Feb. 1910 and 30 Dec. 1917.
[43] Cresswell, Diary, 1 Jun. 1906, 18 Apr. 1910 and 31 Oct. 1939.
[44] Cresswell, Diary, 9 Jul. 1923.

recorded their annual return in her diary. This was a form of homecoming, a reunion with old friends, to whom, as ever, she held fast.

As with so much else in her life, Beatrix's love of flowers was in part inherited from her father. But in this instance, the respects in which she chose to depart from his example are equally significant. He, on the whole, was more interested in garden flowers while she responded most enthusiastically to those she found growing in the wild, perhaps reflecting the contrast between his modest orderliness and her impulsive freedom. If he brought back anything from a walk, it was likely to be a fungus or perhaps algae, in which he had a scientific interest, collecting them systematically and examining them under his microscope. Her interest was aesthetic rather than scientific and she paid little heed to plants other than flowers except, occasionally, for trees.

Beatrix often brought flowers home, on occasion even expressing a 'need' for them. On 27 January 1906, she bought a pot of daffodils after returning from a long, unsuccessful foray in search of catkins: 'sheer extravagance but one must have some flowers'.[45] It seems to have mattered to her, as it did to Catley, to bring flowers into the house, part of an intriguing dialectic between the wild and the civilized that ran through her life. This 'need' for flowers, however, should not be overplayed in her case. She rarely mentioned them once they were indoors, nor does she seem to have minded too much where they went: 'To Idestone for flowers for the Museum table. Good fun gathering for the table. Really lovely evening – hills looking beautiful.'[46]

Indeed, as this entry implies, it seems likely that the gathering was more important to Beatrix than the use to which the flowers were eventually put. Flower gathering had become a widespread cultural practice by the early twentieth century, one that deserves fuller historical investigation. But historians perhaps too readily assume that, by placing something in its cultural context, they have explained it. Beatrix would probably not have collected flowers if it had not been an established cultural practice, but many of her peers, equally exposed to flower gathering, showed no particular inclination towards it. If they wanted flowers they bought them or grew them in their gardens. Why, in contrast, did Beatrix embrace it so enthusiastically?

Part of the reason was probably physiological. Beatrix's abundant vitality poured itself far more naturally into action than thought or words. Verbally she was never effusive, noting ruefully that her literary productions were 'always on the short side' and finding the larger pages of her 1937 diary 'more than I want to fill'.[47] Although she greatly respected her brother, she

[45] Cresswell, Diary, 27 Jan. 1906.
[46] Cresswell, Diary, 30 Apr. 1920. The museum in question was the Royal Albert Memorial Museum, where Beatrix worked during World War I. See also 15 Aug. 1920.
[47] Cresswell, Diary, 28 May 1933 and 4 Jan. 1937.

chafed in his company since all he wanted to do was lie on the sofa and read.[48] She wanted to be out and doing, and flower gathering was a satisfying expression of this – constantly moving, constantly active. It also helped to give a point to her rural walks and rides. She greatly enjoyed these but, like many people, preferred her excursions to have a purpose, even if much of her pleasure came from being out in the countryside rather than from her ostensible object. There was, then, a willed element to Beatrix's love of flowers, fond of them though she genuinely was. The activity of gathering them, emanating in part from somatic processes and in part from her need for a sense of purpose, was, by contrast, integral to her identity, assuring her of and confirming her sense of selfhood.

Alexis and His Flowers and *The Royal Progress of King Pepito* suggest that Beatrix was seeking to fashion herself into a children's writer in the late 1880s and early 1890s. This was one of a number of false starts at the time. There is a sense, in these years, of Beatrix trying to find her path in life and not quite succeeding. She ventured into rural crafts and had a spinning wheel at the Arts and Crafts Exhibition in Torquay in 1894. Then for a while she ran a tea shop, but closed this with relief in 1899. By this time she was passionately absorbed in a little cottage in the backwoods that she rented and sometimes slept the night in, prevailing on friends and relatives to visit whenever she could. This gave way in the early years of the new century to a mania for picture postcards, which she exchanged with other collectors across the globe. None of these obsessions lasted for long. Beatrix did not lack self-discipline, but she was a creature of enthusiasms and depended more than most on 'inspiration' (a favourite word) for motivation. Perhaps this had its origins in her childhood, when, as her father's diary records, she was frequently 'indulged' and may have become used to having her own way.

One of the passions that took hold of Beatrix at this time, however, proved more durable and consequential: cycling. The safety bicycle, of which John Kemp Starley's 'Rover' (1885) was the first commercially successful example, revolutionized cycling, making it easier, safer, cheaper and more amenable to women and leading to the cycling craze of the 1890s. Beatrix seems to have been comparatively late to the party, beginning to ride, it would appear, only in the second half of the decade, probably in 1896.[49] Perhaps there was an autobiographical element to her 1898 short story 'The Humiliation of Helen Travers', which recounts the conversion of the initially disdainful protagonist to the cycling cause.[50] As this suggests, however, she was quick to combine her

---

[48] Cresswell, Diary, 6 Sep. 1918.

[49] The flyleaf of her 1898 diary records miles ridden in the two previous years as 3,337¾ and 1,000 respectively. The much lower figure for 1896 suggests she may have begun cycling part way through the year. It is suspiciously rounded, presumably an estimate. If she was prepared to enter an estimate for 1896, it would have been odd not to enter estimates for previous years too, had she been cycling then.

[50] Beatrix F. Cresswell, 'The Humiliation of Helen Travers', *Cycling* 395 13 Aug. 1898, 103.

new interest with her existing literary bent, publishing a string of short ephemeral tales in *Cycling* over the next few years. Indeed *Cycling* remained a valuable and reliable source of income, albeit on a small scale, well into the 1920s.

Beatrix flung herself into her new passion with characteristic energy. She cycled 4,067 miles in 1898, including an extended tour of rural Ireland in late summer. The mileage for each ride was recorded in a special Lett's 'Cyclist's Diary'. In this first year, the entries were rather sparse, consisting mainly of routes and distances, but they later expanded. Without realizing it at first, she had 'got into the habit of journalizing', a habit that she was henceforth to maintain every year (except, for some reason, 1900) for the rest of her life.[51] Her discovery of cycling also had important consequences for her relationship with the countryside. It enabled her to combine her energetic, active nature and desire for fast movement with her love of flowers and the rural. She enjoyed walking, but it was, until she was past middle age, rather too slow and passive for her. Moreover, cycling allowed her to explore a much wider territory than she could have done on foot. The indications are that, now she had a bicycle, she went out into the countryside much more frequently than she did before.

Cycling in late Victorian Devon was not for the fainthearted. The lanes were dusty in the summer but much worse was the sometimes virtually impassable mud of winter. The hills, numerous in Devon, were often too steep to be ridden up given the cycling technology of the day. On the whole, however, while she detested mud, Beatrix revelled in the challenges of terrain and weather:

> Over Haldon through the snow! Across G[reat] Haldon and over Chudleigh Bank. Deep drifts at the Saddle Back. This was 18 miles – but I had to carry the machine over the snow (carried it 1¾ miles).[52]

Battling against the wind could also be exhilarating:

> To Sandygate. Pushed about in the wind. Marsh Marigold. Lovely.[53]

Like many good cyclists, she found it frustrating to have to 'crawl' along with less proficient companions ('M[argaret] rides fearfully feebly') and preferred to ride on her own:

> To Mamhead in the morning. A charming ride must be alone.[54]

---

[51] Cresswell, Diary, 31 Dec. 1907.

[52] Cresswell, Diary, 26 Feb. 1898. Compare her exultation in the 'tremendous and unsparing' gradients of Tiverton Deanery, 11 and 26 Aug. 1905.

[53] Cresswell, Diary, 4 May 1898. She was, however, not above getting on a train when faced with a strong headwind if she needed to get somewhere.

[54] Cresswell, Diary, 15 and 20 Apr. 1898; 2 Mar. 1899.

Her preference for doing things on her own went deeper than this, however. It is reflected in many other aspects of her life. In contrast to Catley, she preferred to walk on her own. It was 'lovely all alone on the moors' on 25 September 1928, while a visit to a hundred-acre bluebell wood with friends prompted the comment 'I sh[oul]d have liked to be there alone!'[55] She enjoyed identifying and exploring new paths for herself.[56] In later years, when visiting churches had become one of her principal interests, she noted that she liked those she had to discover for herself best, and found it frustrating to have a companion with her.[57] When doing something she cared about, she wanted to do it her own way, and found the presence of others at best distracting, often a constraint. While she enjoyed socializing and looked forward to visits from friends and relatives, she was usually relieved when they left, often starting the following day's diary entry with the celebratory exclamation 'O beata solitudo'.[58]

Beatrix's frequent changes of direction between the late 1880s and the early 1900s may partly have reflected what seems to have been a period of considerable emotional turbulence. There are indications she had a relationship with someone she refers to as 'H.': on 17 May 1912, at Chideock, she notes that it is sixteen years (i.e. 1896) since she was there with 'H. and Mrs W.' and felt disinclined to climb Golden Cap again. She does not elaborate but, in context, the natural inference is that she wished to avoid recapitulating or overlaying intense emotions associated with her previous visit. Fingle Bridge on Dartmoor evoked strong feelings for the same reason:

> I don't think I have been here since H. and I were there fishing!! A place full of memories. I made a sketch and felt a glamour [sic] of 'the days that are no more'. It is just as well to revisit such scenes with those who know nothing of the past.[59]

Beyond this, all we know of the relationship with H. is that it was highly charged and left behind powerful memories of a kind Beatrix did not wish to share.

Feelings also seem to have been running high at Lugehay House during and beyond this period. Another retrospective diary entry records that 'The Teignmouth existence concluded with dischord [sic] that passed from 1896 to 1899 or indeed 1901.'[60] We know that Beatrix was involved with H. in 1896, but H.'s invisibility in Beatrix's early diaries suggests that the relationship may have been over by 1898. A diary entry for 17 March 1904 prompts an

---

[55] Cresswell, Diary, 25 Sep. 1928 and 27 May 1934.
[56] Cresswell, Diary, 25 Mar. 1913.
[57] Cresswell, Diary, 4 Apr. 1908 and 18 Mar. 1903.
[58] 'O blessed solitude'. Cresswell, Diary, 18 Sep. 1911, 23 Jan. 1915 and 26 Jul. 1929.
[59] Cresswell, Diary, 31 Jul. 1909. See also 15 May 1915 (Widecombe a 'place of "memories"').
[60] Cresswell, Diary, 12 Mar. 1904.

alternative explanation. Beatrix notes that, following her mother's death, she has been able to pay 'those beasts in Teignmouth'. The 'beasts' appear to have been tradesmen – the Cresswells led a hand-to-mouth financial existence and relied on credit, which, it would appear, was beginning to run out locally by this time.

This explanation is not entirely persuasive either, however, since it was only in 1901 that Beatrix and Fanny left Teignmouth, whereas Beatrix implies that the 'dischord' had at least ameliorated by 1899. More probable is that the discord was precipitated by the tragedy of Chrissy's death, which also took place in 1896. She was only forty-seven and left three young orphans behind. It seems likely that this widened the rift between her younger sisters. Had Stasia perhaps adopted a more tolerant attitude to Chrissy's marriage? Was there conflict over what to do about the children? At all events, by 1901 Stasia was living with Etta Cresswell at the other end of the country, at Nunholm Farm in Dumfriesshire, and was barely on speaking terms with Beatrix.[61]

Despite these challenging emotional circumstances, Beatrix continued to extend her range of interests and activities. In the long run, the most important development proved to be the commencement of what she referred to as her 'Deaneries' (1 November 1899). This was a hugely ambitious project to visit and describe every parish church in all twenty-four of the Diocese of Exeter's Anglican deaneries (which fortuitously coincided almost perfectly with the administrative county of Devon), anticipating Pevsner's Buildings of England series, albeit at the scale of a single county. It was to be the major work of Beatrix's life, occupying much of her time for the next quarter century. Only two of the twenty-four volumes were published (Beatrix presented the type-script originals to the City of Exeter in 1925) but, despite this, the Deaneries proved deeply rewarding once she was fully immersed in them, from 1902 onwards. The project combined four of her central commitments: ecclesiastical, historical, natural and territorial. She referred to her 'church-hunting' expeditions, with a characteristic touch of irony, as 'gëorgoepiscopal' rides and rambles.[62] The word was taken from Coleridge and is quoted in Beatrix's guide to the Quantocks, where she parses it as 'farm and church'.[63] Coleridge's reference was to Virgil's Georgics, a practical survey of country life and one of the cornerstones of rural literature. While Beatrix's Deaneries were

---

[61] Cresswell, Diary, 6 Dec. 1902. Etta was Stasia and her siblings' cousin.

[62] On hunting metaphors and English ruralism, see Donna Landry, *The Invention of the Countryside: Hunting, Walking, and Ecology in English Literature, 1671–1831* (Basingstoke, 2001).

[63] Beatrix F. Cresswell, *The Quantock Hills: Their Combes and Villages* (London, 1904), 42–3. For the original reference, see Mrs Henry Sandford, *Tom Poole and His Friends*. Vol. 2 (London, 1888), 196.

concerned with just one element of rural life, the research took her this way and that, criss-crossing the Devon countryside:

> A splendid day gëorgoepiscoping . . . Most lovely riding, though very hilly. A charming day.[64]

The ecclesiastical aspect of the Deaneries is perhaps the most obvious. All Beatrix's most serious work was connected with the church in some way. Although she often greatly enjoyed researching them, she regarded her Homeland Handbooks as comparatively ephemeral money earners, still more so her short pieces in *Cycling* and other magazines. She attended church regularly, listening on the wireless in old age when unable to get there in person. Although she generally eschewed outright expressions of emotion or religiosity, in keeping with prevalent English establishment mores at this time, she seems to have regarded her Deaneries research as a form of religious observance:

> Reading a life of Dr Neale. It is most interesting to find that . . . he too felt that sense of being at church, when in a church studying it. He would have understood the spiritualism of church hunting – he knew it.[65]

Despite this, it is difficult to believe that the inspiration behind the Deaneries was primarily spiritual. Although she held a lot inside herself, Beatrix was not really a spiritual person. She writes about a vast range of subjects in her diaries and the depth and strength of her feelings is often acutely apparent, but she hardly ever mentions prayer or God. Presumably she prayed in church, possibly also at bedtime, but she does not say so. Her silence with respect to God almost seems like avoidance. Her practical, task-orientated, down-to-earth nature hardly lent itself to the contemplation of ineffable ideas such as transubstantiation or the Trinity. Yet the church as an institution, tradition and home was so fundamental to her sense of identity that it would have been anathema to her to question its underlying premises. She was not the kind of person to cut off the branch on which she was sitting. It is, indeed, this nexus between the church and her identity that more plausibly accounts for the ecclesiastical aspect of the Deaneries project. It was a way of continuing, affirming and remaining within the happy securities of her childhood. As with so many of the things that mattered most to her, it was directly connected with her father.

From this point of view, the Deaneries project was fundamentally a work of preservation, even memorialization. The historical aspect of it was almost as

---

[64] Cresswell, Diary, 21 Jun. 1904.

[65] Cresswell, Diary, 30 Oct. 1907. 'Dr Neale' must be the Anglo-Catholic ecclesiologist John Mason Neale. See Susan Drain, 'Neale, John Mason (1818–1866)', *Oxford Dictionary of National Biography*, Oxford, 2004. Online ed., Jan. 2014 [www.oxforddnb.com/view/article/19824, accessed 11 Sept. 2016].

important as the ecclesiastical. Beatrix much preferred the older churches – after moving to Exeter, she worshipped by choice at St Mary Arches, the city's best-preserved Norman church and one of the oldest buildings in the county. Visiting newer churches was rather a chore:

> Finished the churches in Torquay – such a crowd of modern churches is very dull.[66]

It is telling that Beatrix took pains to copy inscriptions in the churches she visited.[67] Again, this was a preoccupation she shared with Hallam. Many inscriptions, especially on floor slabs and external walls, were subject to erosion and liable to become illegible. Yet the point of 'setting in stone' is to make something permanent. Copying inscriptions was an act of resistance to the ravages of time, born of a determination that the past should not be effaced nor the chain of connection between the living and the dead broken.

The relevance of the natural environment to explaining the deep satisfaction Beatrix derived from the Deaneries project is perhaps less obvious, but should not be overlooked. It took her out into the countryside again and again and her diaries are replete with references to her delight in weather, landscape, flowers, birds and lambs on these occasions. There was certainly a sense of the journey being as important as the arrival. Rather as with flower gathering, church hunting, in addition to its other rewards, gave Beatrix a rationale for rural excursions. With her strong sense of duty and belief in work before pleasure, she stood to gain more than most from an ulterior purpose for things she enjoyed. She was inclined to regard country walks or rides undertaken purely for their own sake as 'frivolous', although she was often willing to set theory cheerfully at defiance, especially when 'inspired' by sunny weather.[68]

The fourth pillar on which Beatrix's Deaneries stood was the territorial. By the time she began the project, she was already deeply invested emotionally in Devon. This was congruent with, and at some level must have been an expression of, her attachment to her childhood verities. The Deaneries project both expressed her profound rootedness in the county and deepened it further. On returning home from London on 4 June 1914, she rejoiced to be back in 'Glorious Devon'.[69] Devon was more beautiful, in her eyes, than other counties such as Oxfordshire, which she visited in 1934, or Greece, extolled by her niece Clarice.[70] During an extended visit to Florence in 1925, she confided to her diary that though she felt 'horribly ungrateful' to her friend Mary Alban, who

[66] Cresswell, Diary, 12 May 1903.

[67] Cresswell, Diary, 26 and 27 Jan., 23 May and 3 Oct. 1903; 26 Mar. 1909.

[68] Cresswell, Diary, 4 Mar. 1911.

[69] Cresswell, Diary, 4 Jun. 1914. The phrase 'Glorious Devon', popularized by Sir Edward German's eponymous song of 1905, subsequently became the centrepiece of a phenomenally successful Great Western Railway marketing campaign.

[70] Cresswell, Diary, 10 May 1934 and 12 May 1924.

had invited her there to give a prestigious lecture: 'I can't help counting the days to my return. My <u>heart's</u> in Devon.'[71]

The Deaneries project took Beatrix to every single one of Devon's 543 parishes, many of which had two or even three Anglican churches.[72] She visited almost all these churches twice or more, since after completing her initial survey in 1912, she spent the next thirteen years thoroughly revising each of the twenty-four volumes. As she virtually always cycled or walked, often travelling along minor byways between one parish and the next, she came to know Devon comprehensively, in extraordinary depth and detail. The Deaneries endowed her with a gratifying standing in the county's local history and archaeological community, provided a richly satisfying outlet for her energies and gave her an absorbing purpose. 'Don't want to do anything else!', she expostulated as early as October 1902.[73] For nearly quarter of a century, she had 'Deaneries on the brain' the best part of the time.[74]

But although archaeology, as Beatrix called it, was engrossing it was not remunerative – 'the very D. when it gets into one's bones', as she lamented in 1905.[75] Her finances, like her father's, were always precarious and she could not afford to spend all her time on the Deaneries. For many years, what kept her afloat financially was her association with the Homeland Association. Founded by the publisher, preservationist and patriot Prescott Row, this aimed to 'show that every district of these islands possesses scenery of beauty and even of peculiar distinction, often, moreover, hallowed by inspiring memories'.[76] Beatrix eventually wrote eleven guides for Homeland (one co-authored), published initially between 1898 (*Dartmoor*) and 1909 (*Bideford*). The guides were popular and went through numerous editions, so as with the Deaneries, the process of revision kept Beatrix employed, and in this case remunerated, until well into the 1920s. She enjoyed writing them, lightweight though they were in her eyes, and they allowed her to combine her ruralist interests with earning a living.

It was no accident that the first of Beatrix's Homeland Handbooks was *Dartmoor*. Her deepest topographical attachment was always to Devon as a whole, and no single place within the county or outside it mattered to her as intensely as, for example, Raikes Wood to Johnston or the Chew valley to Catley. Dartmoor nevertheless was laden with meaning for Beatrix. She returned there throughout her life – 'I feel I <u>must</u> get into Dartmoor', she

[71] Cresswell, Diary, 4 Nov. 1925.
[72] Cresswell, Diary, 21 Feb. 1903.
[73] Cresswell, Diary, 29 Oct. 1902.
[74] Cresswell, Diary, 7 Nov. 1903 and 17 Sep. 1904.
[75] Cresswell, Diary, 17 Feb. 1905.
[76] 'The Publisher's Address to the Reader', in Cresswell, *Dartmoor with Its Surroundings* (20th edition, London, 1925; first published 1898), 6. On Prescott Row, see 'Mr. Prescott Row.' *Times* [London] 18 Jan. 1929: 14. *The Times Digital Archive*. Web. 11 Sep. 2016.

wrote after a 'splendid' ride over it in May 1918.[77] Her guide to it, although conventional enough in places, is more revealing than might be expected. Always confident of being liked, she quickly establishes a genial, confiding relationship with the reader:

> Perhaps you left the throbbing heart of England, the most populous city in the world, this morning; and a journey of not many hours has brought you into the loneliest and wildest part of the country, so untameable, so unchangeable, that the dweller of bygone days, did he return, would probably find but little alteration in the lapse of centuries.[78]

The cultural influences here are readily apparent: the perception of Dartmoor as wild, primitive and untameable was already well established by 1898.[79] Eden Phillpotts' Dartmoor novels, the first of which was published the same year, present the moor in similar terms.[80] But within this repertoire, it is not accidental that Beatrix places particular emphasis on the moor's unchangeable character. A profound need for the things she loved to be permanent runs like a leitmotif through her writing, interests and commitments. In this context, it is of central significance that the moor was closely associated with her father. In one of two deeply personal anecdotes in *Dartmoor*, Beatrix explains that her father used to take her to see the 'Blue Hills' nearly every day, and promised that one day when she was old enough they should go there together, a promise, we are told, duly fulfilled, 'and begetting that love of the Moor which never perishes'.[81] Although she never expressed it in these terms, Beatrix swung between two Devonian poles: Dartmoor, the pole of wilderness, and Exeter, the pole of civilization. The innermost sanctum of Dartmoor – wilderness within wilderness – was Cranmere Pool:

> Cranmere Pool is perhaps the heart of Devon, the source of those rivers which are the life giving streams of the county.[82]

Yet in a second anecdote, Beatrix describes the Pool as the 'dreariest, most untameable spot in England'. Left alone on the adjacent moor while her unnamed companion searches for their route, she is overwhelmed by desolation and feels an urge to run away. The profound securities Dartmoor so vitally carried for her enabled Beatrix to find greater freedom there than anywhere

---

[77] Cresswell, Diary, 9 May 1918.

[78] Cresswell, *Dartmoor*, 10.

[79] Tim Fulford, 'The Materialization of the Lyric and the Romantic Construction of Place: Bards and Beasts on Dartmoor', *Romanticism* 22 (2016), 1.

[80] William John Keith, *Regions of the Imagination: The Development of British Rural Fiction* (Toronto, 1988), 109–15. Beatrix appreciated Phillpotts' descriptions of the moor. Cresswell, Diary, 11 May 1922. Arthur Conan-Doyle's *The Hound of the Baskervilles* was published only in 1902, four years after Beatrix's *Dartmoor*.

[81] Cresswell, *Dartmoor*, 8.

[82] Cresswell, *Dartmoor*, 54.

else, but perhaps also intensified her awareness of what it would be like to be deprived of them, lost in boundless solitude.[83]

She enjoyed researching and writing *Dartmoor* and was gratified by its favourable reception. As she needed the money too, it is unsurprising that she responded enthusiastically to the offer from Homeland to write volumes on Teignmouth, Dawlish and Taunton over the next three years. Meanwhile, a major change had taken place in her domestic life: she and her mother moved from Lugehay House, her home of thirty-nine years, to 10 Barton Terrace, Dawlish, in 1901.[84] Whether the Cresswells chose Dawlish because Beatrix was intending to write about the area, or vice versa, is uncertain. It is equally unclear why they moved at all. Possibly, as we have seen, the family had run out of credit in Teignmouth. Aside from escaping their creditors, the move to Barton Terrace probably saved money because the house was much smaller. In any case, in some way or other the move seems finally to have resolved the discord of the previous five years.

While at Dawlish, Beatrix finished the Homeland volumes both about the town itself and about Taunton. She celebrated the completion of the Taunton volume in her habitual manner by going out that afternoon for a long walk over Haldon to the Belvedere, twenty miles or more.[85] Clouds, however, were gathering on the metaphorical horizon. Fanny's health was deteriorating and in November she had a series of violent seizures, described by her daughter as heart attacks.[86] This was the start of what was to prove one of the most difficult periods of Beatrix's life (not to mention Fanny's, but this can only be inferred from the diary). The invalid showed little improvement and by the end of the month Beatrix was already champing at the bit to get out and do more church hunting:

> This is not a very lively kind of existence!! Thank goodness this 'Drear November' is over.[87]

But Beatrix's troubles were only just beginning. She was trapped in the classic situation of the youngest daughter, left alone to care for an ageing parent in an era when the relevant statutory social services simply did not exist. With her brother in London and estranged sister far away in the north, assistance from her family was minimal. Despite the emphasis in some recent research on religious and charitable provision, the Cresswells received no help from these sources

---

[83] This episode is analysed more fully in Jeremy Burchardt, '"Far away and close to home": Children's toponyms and imagined geographies, c.1870–c.1950', *Journal of Historical Geography* 69 (2020), 68–79.

[84] Cresswell, Diary, 26 Mar. 1901.

[85] Cresswell, Diary, 28 Apr. 1902. Compare Diary, 7 Apr. 1923, when she went for an afternoon walk having finished the first volume of her history of Shobrooke in the morning, 4 Oct. 1918, when she would like to have gone on a walk after finishing a major archival task at the Museum, and 23 Aug. 1924.

[86] Cresswell, Diary, 24 Nov. 1902.

[87] Cresswell, Diary, 29 Nov. 1902.

either. As her mother's condition deteriorated, it became ever more difficult to leave her even for a short time and Beatrix often spent the night in her room:

> Existence is certainly most deadly dull at present.[88]

She began the New Year characteristically by quoting folklore:

> 'New Year, forth looking out of Janus' gate
> Doth promise hope of new delight'
>   The above line has been running in my head all day – let's hope it's a good omen.[89]

For all her energy and determination to do what she wanted, there was an aleatory streak in Beatrix, related to her willingness to entertain superstition. This gap in her sense of agency was especially pronounced in relation to her literary fiction: she seems to have felt it was entirely 'on the knees of the Gods' (as she expressed it) whether a novel or play was accepted for publication.[90] More subtly, her sense of what the future might bring in other ways was pervaded by the same attitude. To a certain extent, this reflected genuine limitations on her freedom of action. Powerful emotional, familial, social, religious and financial constraints prevented Beatrix from leaving her mother at this time. But although Beatrix's situation in 1903 undoubtedly intensified it, her tendency to regard the future as *au fond* outside her power to predict or influence runs through her diaries from beginning to end. Perhaps it was related to her reliance on 'inspiration', a capricious force over which she had no conscious control, to provide motivation.

A good example of her sense of powerlessness at this time is her private response to an invitation from Etta to stay with her in Dumfries over Easter. 'Toujours yearnings', Beatrix wrote in her diary – words that were to recur frequently henceforth. She longed to get away, almost anywhere, but could not see how to do so.[91] Her low spirits were not helped by the wet and windy weather in the first few months of the year:

> Yesterday was so lovely, and Mama so much better that I hoped for a week of fine weather and freedom. Today it rains again, Mama has collapsed once more, and I am suffering from 'general debility'. Under the circumstances, it may as well rain . . . I am beginning to think humanity very courageous in even wanting to prepare for the future![92]

[88] Cresswell, Diary, 10 and 8 Dec. 1902.
[89] Beatrix Cresswell, Devon Heritage Centre, DRO 4686M/F79. Beatrix Cresswell Nature notebook, 1 Jan. 1920.
[90] See, for example, Diary, 13 Feb. 1903: 'I do wonder whether that egg will hatch', in reference to a play she had just submitted to a publisher.
[91] Cresswell, Diary, 3 Jan. 1903. See also Diary, 5 and 25 Mar. 1903.
[92] Cresswell, Diary, 9 Mar. 1903.

Beatrix was about as unsuited to the situation she found herself in as could well be imagined. What was required was someone restrained, patient and sedentary, whereas Beatrix was strong-willed, impulsive and highly energetic. It is perhaps not surprising that frustration and even a hint of resentment show through in her diary entries at times. Her main relief was rides in the nearby countryside, snatched from her all-too-brief intervals of freedom:

> Mama has the jaundice again! She seems very poorly. I got a ride up the valley this afternoon and picked some primroses. It was very nice getting them, and being in the lanes.[93]

Fanny seems to have made a temporary recovery in the spring and Beatrix was able to get out more. This encouraged her to accept Homeland's invitation to write a guide to the Quantocks and allowed her to complete Ipplepen Deanery.[94] However, her mother's health took a turn for the worse in the summer and, on medical advice, the Cresswells agreed to employ a nurse. The day she arrived, 17 July, Fanny had a 'fearful attack on her heart', so severe that Beatrix thought she was going to die.[95] A week later, Fanny was still 'very feeble' and the strain was telling on her daughter:

> This is a most dreary sort of existence – and one can't help wondering 'how long?' An unanswerable question, though evidently there is no hope of her ultimate recovery.[96]

The arrival of the nurse did, however, at least make it possible for Beatrix to escape occasionally for a few hours:

> Thanks to making some rearrangement of hours with nurse, I got up on Haldon. I have really longed to be there many times. The heather is lovely. I gathered a lot and sent some to Clarice.[97]

By early August the first draft of the Quantocks book was finished as far as it could be without another visit.[98] Initially this seemed quite out of the question, but in early September Dr Little advised Beatrix she might leave her mother for a night or two:

> Here am I actually at Williton ... A most lovely day. Hills looking beautiful.[99]

---

[93] Cresswell, Diary, 4 Mar. 1903. See also Diary, 10–12 Mar., 21 Apr. and 9 and 23 May 1903.
[94] Cresswell, Diary, 7 Apr. and 29 May 1903.
[95] Cresswell, Diary, 17 Jul. 1903.
[96] Cresswell, Diary, 25 Jul. 1903.
[97] Cresswell, Diary, 29 Jul. 1903. Margaret and Clarice visited in mid-August, enabling Beatrix to go out for another walk. Diary, 14 Aug. 1903.
[98] Cresswell, Diary, 3 Aug. 1903.
[99] Cresswell, Diary, 7 Sep. 1903.

Four days after returning home, she had completed the book and sent it off to Homeland. The two days she had spent in the Quantocks had been an exhilarating release but this seems to have alienated her even further from Fanny:

> When I sit with her I feel as if we had become suddenly separated by year upon year. She seems so aged sometimes, as if she were my grandmother rather than mother. We don't seem to meet on the same plane of existence.[100]

The next few months were well-nigh unendurable. If Beatrix was ill suited to nursing, her mother was no model patient either. She was fractious and demanding, asking for something every few minutes, and prone to dire prognostications.[101] One Thursday morning she announced she would die the following Tuesday.[102] Beatrix held out from one rural excursion to the next. On 30 October, she got to East Budleigh:

> It was very nice seeing the Otter again – I don't know why I love it so – it is a very favourite river of mine.[103]

On 10 November, she received a letter from Prescott Row, asking when her revisions to *Dartmoor* would be complete. She had not yet been able to start them. By the following evening, despite finishing Aylesbeare Deanery, she was in the 'deepest blues', having spent a 'purgatorial' afternoon with her mother:

> Sick nursing seems to me to remove the last rays of our affection for an old and very <u>harty</u> [*sic*] invalid! What wouldn't I give to get away![104]

Six days later she managed to get to Dartmoor. It was a kind of coming up for air:

> Started literally at dawn by first train for Newton – rode to Ashburton where I found a puncture! Left the cycle and walked to Holne, Buckfastleigh and back, a splendid 10 miles. Holne ch[urch] extremely interesting. Moors looking lovely ... Very cold on the moor – but so pleased to see the Dart at Holne, it was quite too lovely. Wish I could be in these parts a week!![105]

But as the year drew to a close, there were signs that Beatrix was nearing the end of her tether. For months, a half-acknowledged wish for her mother's death had been hovering beneath the surface in her diary and this now came into the open.[106] Morbid thoughts gained the upper hand:

[100] Cresswell, Diary, 12 Sep. 1903.
[101] Cresswell, Diary, 29 and 30 Sep. 1903.
[102] Cresswell, Diary, 8 Oct. 1903.
[103] Cresswell, Diary, 30 Oct. 1903.
[104] Cresswell, Diary, 11 Nov. 1903.
[105] Cresswell, Diary, 17 Nov. 1903.
[106] The first veiled hint of this is on 13 July. On 7 December, Beatrix for the first time expressed an explicit wish that 'since things are hopeless ... this year will see the end'. Cresswell, Diary, 7 Dec. 1903.

> I have been drawing a weird picture of a skeleton going upstairs. He seemed in the summer to sit on the doorstep huddled up – now he is standing on the stairs waiting to go into Mama's room. I have had a headache all day.[107]

Beatrix's powerful yearning for freedom was in severe and apparently irreconcilable conflict with the remnants of filial affection and duty. It is hardly surprising she had a headache. But for good or ill, six weeks later her trials were over. As so often, Beatrix expressed herself elliptically, resorting to a quotation in ancient Greek:

> τε τελος ται. 6.30 am. R.I.P.[108]

Her brother Richard came down from London overnight. Beatrix was deeply grateful: '[f]elt once more as if I had someone to depend on'.[109] Fanny was buried on 3 February and Richard stayed until the 12th. When she parted from him at St David's station, Beatrix felt '[v]ery much left all alone'.[110] But her thoughts had already been turning towards the future. For months, she had been dreaming of a move to Exeter, where she would be able to pursue her antiquarian interests much more effectively, and she had even identified a bungalow that would suit her. The entire entry for 2 February, the second day after her mother's death, consists of the following:

> I can have my dear little house.[111]

Figure 2.2   Beatrix's 'dear little house', 23 Wonford Road

---

[107] Cresswell, Diary, 18 Dec. 1903. See also 2 Jan. 1904, when she went out to sketch the 'weird wild scene' of a trawler wrecked at Langstone Point during the night.
[108] 'The end shall be.' Cresswell, Diary, 31 Jan. 1904.
[109] Cresswell, Diary, 1 Feb. 1904.
[110] Cresswell, Diary, 3 and 12 Feb. 1904.
[111] Cresswell, Diary, 2 Feb. 1904.

The decision to move to Exeter was one of the most important of Beatrix's life. Fundamentally, it was a centripetal move. It can best be understood in relation to the dialectic between centre and periphery, authority and freedom, culture and nature that structured her life. Exeter, Devon's county town, was the capital of the territory Beatrix had chosen as her own. It was also the seat of the diocese, so in moving to it Beatrix was also moving to the local centre of the Anglican Church to which she adhered so closely her whole life. With its library, archives, museum and university college, Exeter offered cultural riches far beyond anything either Dawlish or Teignmouth could match; it was obviously the place Beatrix had to go if she was to fulfil the capacity she perhaps sensed in herself to join the ranks of the county's leading antiquarians and local historians. Beatrix's passionate commitment to authority and tradition, incarnated for her by the monarchy and the Church of England, led her to revere such places as Windsor and Canterbury.[112] Exeter was the Devonian equivalent.

For all this, relocating to Exeter was not necessarily an anti-rural move. A crucial part of Exeter's appeal was that it was a small, historic town, intimately related to the countryside in which it was set. Beatrix could see her beloved Haldon from the garden of the 'little house' and was distressed, years later, when the neighbours put up a high fence that blocked her view.[113] Conversely, it pleased her when she could look back to Exeter from out in the countryside, as when she stayed with friends at Holcombe Burnell in July 1909:

> Across the valley Exeter – I can see the Cath[edral] and St Leonard's – almost like looking home. Tonight the lights are so pretty.[114]

Town and country are states of mind, not stable spatial categories. Exeter, like most other towns, had many rural enclaves within it, and Beatrix frequently resorted to these when she was unable, for reasons of time or otherwise, to reach the 'deep' countryside outside the city. One of her favourite walks was along the ship canal, a good place for flowers and insects in summer. But her favourite local excursion was to Countess Weir:

> A good morning's work over Shobrooke. Then the call of the wild proved too much for me. I found the wild in the fields beyond Countess Weir where I had a thermos tea above the river, hardly anyone thereabouts: most delicious. Came home with Marsh Marigolds.

---

[112] Cresswell, Diary, 9 Jul. 1931 and 25 May 1914.
[113] Cresswell, Diary, 27 Jul. 1934.
[114] Cresswell, Diary, 3 Jul. 1909.

Cuckoo, swallows, butterflies, all the ingredients of summer at once, and
very warm. A glorious day.[115]

Perhaps the most revealing sign of how much the connection between
Exeter and its rural hinterland mattered to Beatrix, however, is her delight in
wildflowers brought from the country into the city. She frequently mentioned
this in her diary, especially when the flowers in question were the first of their
kind she had seen in Exeter that year:

Saw two girls in town wearing bunches of snowdrops and primroses in
from the country for market day.[116]

She was sad when William Burnett, long-time street flower-seller in Exeter,
died in 1934, and folded a newspaper obituary into her diary. He was evidently
a man after her own heart:

A flower-seller from boyhood, he never sold a garden flower; all were
culled from the moors, woods, fields and the sea-shore. Every day after
dinner he would set out for the country, tramping everywhere, and never
using a conveyance. He probably knew more nooks and crannies where
flowers may be found earlier than anywhere else than any other West-
country man.[117]

Beatrix's love of Exeter gives the lie to the frequent assumption that
ruralism is essentially an expression of anti-urbanism. It is true that she
detested modern industrial towns such as Kidderminster ('most unattract-
ive') and south London ('[o]ne always wonders ... why anyone lives
here').[118] But she very rarely encountered such places, and it is difficult
to believe that her ruralism can have been in reaction to them. If
anything, it was the other way round: her love of the country, which
she was so accustomed to being in, made her less tolerant of the contrasting attributes of big cities. This became more pronounced as she got
older:

An ideally lovely day ... We went by devious primrose paths to Hembury
Fort, and had the common above the camp all to ourselves. It was most
delightful, with the utter stillness of the country.[119]

---

[115] Cresswell, Diary, 21 Apr. 1924.
[116] Devon Heritage Centre, DRO 4686M/F79 (Beatrix Cresswell Nature notebook, 7 Jan.
1921). The second flower name is difficult to construe in the original: 'primroses' seems
likely from orthography and context. Other references to wildflowers in the city include
Nature notebook, 30 Jan. 1920, 3 Feb. 1920, 4 Mar. 1920, 18 Jan. 1923 and 15 Jan. 1924,
and Diary, 3 Feb. 1910, 16 Jan. 1923, 24 Jan. 1929 and 14 Mar. 1938.
[117] Insert in Cresswell, Diary, 1934 [original source unprovenanced]. See also Cresswell,
Diary, 23 Jan. 1934.
[118] Cresswell, Diary, 14 May 1936 and 22 May 1914.
[119] Cresswell, Diary, 2 Apr. 1923.

In contrast, the constant din of London made her feel unwell:

> In the afternoon I developed a prize headache ... I find the streets here
> very noisy, no cessation of sounds.[120]

Beatrix moved into her new home, 23 Wonford Road, on 16 March 1904. 'Vita Nuova', she headed her diary entry for that day.[121] There was much courage, tinged perhaps with ruthlessness, in her determination to put the past behind her. Declaring boldly that 'I intend to enjoy myself – vive la joie!', she threw herself into the new life energetically.[122] 'What a day!!' she wrote on 9 May, before recounting a breathless whirl of social activities, concluding that it had been '[m]ost awfully jolly, and how unlike life in Dawlish.'[123] On 16 June, she resumed church hunting, went on an exciting trip to Prague in September, and began a new 'tale', the first for a long time, on 11 December.[124] Even Methuen's rejection of her novel in February failed to dent her spirits. Looking back on the previous year in March 1905, she felt her relocation to Exeter had been:

> the best move I ever made in my life ... The twelve months here resulted
> in a life full of interests, heaps of friends.[125]

Characteristic of the buoyant freedom she felt at this time was her decision to take a long holiday in Italy with Clarice. Without children of her own, but strongly attached to Richard, Beatrix felt a special interest in her niece. There was also some affinity of character. While Richard was quiet and scholarly, Clarice shared her aunt's energy and sociability. There were predictable difficulties in the teenage years, which Beatrix did her best to mediate. Clarice also had her aunt's determination to do things her own way, but as time was to reveal, in an exaggerated, headstrong form, and without the deep attachments and good sense that balanced Beatrix's impulsiveness. Both seem to have enjoyed the holiday. Beatrix admired the 'most lovely wonderful scenery' as they passed through the Alps en route to Turin, but the highlight to the trip was perhaps Vesuvius, 'with a mantle of snow by day and streams of fire at night – awesomely marvellous'.[126]

Nevertheless, Beatrix was, as ever, pleased to return home to Devon. She lost no time in reconnecting with her familiar touchstones: spring was at its height and the day after getting back she went on a delightful 'spin' on her

---

[120] Cresswell, Diary, 9 Jan. 1913.
[121] Cresswell, Diary, 16 Mar. 1904. 'Vita Nuova' means 'new life' in Italian.
[122] Cresswell, Diary, 21 Apr. 1904.
[123] Cresswell, Diary, 9 May 1904.
[124] Cresswell, Diary, 16 Jun., 27 Sep. and 11 Dec. 1904.
[125] Cresswell, Diary, 17 Feb. and 16 Mar. 1905.
[126] Cresswell, Diary, 13 and 24 Mar. 1906.

bike, 'everything looking so pretty'.[127] Clarice wrote to say that she found Kensington rather 'drossy' after Italy but Beatrix would have none of it:

> I'm glad to say there's no drossiness here. Devon and Exeter will never lose their charm for me.[128]

A fortnight later she recommenced church hunting with a most enjoyable eighteen-mile ride to Silverton:

> I felt so glad to have begun the Deaneries once more – quite as if the Reins of Existence were properly resumed at last.[129]

Later that month, one of her friends got married and another was engaged, prompting the reflection:

> 'I, even I only am left' – to single blessedness!! Still, I am inclined to think it is blessedness. Under present circumstances. Certainly independence – with all its attendant benefits.[130]

As this suggests, Beatrix was ambivalent about marriage. She enjoyed male company and there were occasional hints of dalliances.[131] The year before, she had wondered whether she was an 'awful fool' for thinking there was a hidden meaning behind the meetings Mr and Mrs Reed seemed anxious to set up between her and their son Harbottle: '[t]hey want me to join the Badminton Club he belongs to!'.[132] The Reeds came round to tea on 6 February, leaving Beatrix in a state of suspense: 'what will the next move be?'.[133] Alas, it was not quite what she expected: on 19 April, Mrs Reed informed her that they were leaving Exeter for good.[134] But it seems unlikely that Beatrix would have been willing to relinquish her independence anyway. A long country walk and a pertinent poem had clarified her feelings:

> A most lovely day. Took a long walk over hill and dale in the morning – very muddy nothing here seems to dry – but I do like being in the wild even without a bicycle . . . Have read [illegible], a quaint pretty poem of the 'sixties:
>
> > Oh life was sweet and beautiful
> > Its pretty pleasures all my own
> > Oh life of life was very full
> > And every minute lived alone.

---

[127] Cresswell, Diary, 4 May 1906.
[128] Cresswell, Diary, 7 May 1906.
[129] Cresswell, Diary, 18 May 1906.
[130] Cresswell, Diary, 30 May 1906.
[131] She greatly enjoyed hunting for mace stands in Exeter Cathedral with Mr Warren, resplendent in uniform, in March 1919, for example: 'it was so nice being with a nice man!'. Cresswell, Diary, 17–21 Mar. 1919.
[132] Cresswell, Diary, 24 Jan. 1905.
[133] Cresswell, Diary, 6 Feb. 1905.
[134] Cresswell, Diary, 19 Apr. 1905.

Them's my sentiments! The lady's state before marriage! A sort of warning for me?[135]

This was well judged. Beatrix had a rich, fulfilling life and found restrictions imposed by others unendurably irksome, as her mother's last illness had only too compellingly demonstrated. Marriage on any terms, let alone those of Edwardian middle-class gentility, was probably not for her. In contrast to the superficially similar case of Spear Smith, there are no indications in Beatrix's diaries of a desire for children, suppressed or otherwise, and not a hint of repining in her later years that she had chosen to remain single and childless.

It is telling that, in contemplating her relationship with Harbottle Reed, Beatrix's mind passed directly from her enjoyment of being in the wild to 'the lady's state before marriage'. She frequently refers to the Devon countryside, especially the more remote parts of it, as 'the wilds'. Evidently the countryside symbolized freedom for her. But it was more than a symbol: being in the countryside gave Beatrix a *real* experience of freedom. She could go where she wanted, do what she wanted, unconstrained by the demands of other people. When she was somewhere really remote, she was free even from reminders of the existence of such demands. This was perhaps why it pleased her so much to have a wood or common 'all to myself'.[136]

In the light of this, it is unsurprising that Beatrix's longing for 'the wilds' was often at its highest pitch when she had friends or relatives staying with her for protracted periods, as in August 1907. On the 23rd, Beatrix confessed her frustrations to her diary:

> It's very wrong to find one's family so oppressive! I hope they don't find out. I certainly get more and more wedded to blissful solitude.[137]

The following day was '[a] lovely day – the sort of day one longs to spend entirely in the wilds'.[138] Margaret and Clarice left on the 26th and four days later she was '[o]ff at 9 a.m. for the wilds', staying the night at a farm in Lamerton on the fringes of Dartmoor.[139] It was similar when Richard visited in September 1918, but she felt more able to leave him to his own devices:

> R.H.C. lies on the sofa and reads the Greek Testament. Lovely aft[ternoon] – the call of the wild irresistible, so to Wonford lanes where I got 1lb of blackberries.[140]

---

[135] Cresswell, Diary, 8 Feb. 1905.
[136] Cresswell, Diary, 2 Jun. 1920.
[137] Cresswell, Diary, 23 Aug. 1907.
[138] Cresswell, Diary, 24 Aug. 1907. Compare 17 Jun. 1916, when 'glorious' weather made Beatrix want to be 'over the hills and far away'.
[139] Cresswell, Diary, 30 Aug. 1907.
[140] Cresswell, Diary, 6 Sep. 1918.

Beatrix's urge to get out into the wilds could be powerful and compelling, especially when the weather was 'inspiring'. Wednesday, 13 July 1910, was:

One of those days –

A gift of God, a perfect day
Wherein no man shall work but play
Wherein it is enough for me
Not to be doing but to be –

Out to Woodbury after breakfast: to the common where I sprawled in the heather … A really glorious day when one has revelled in sunshine, flowers and being out of doors.[141]

It was again the exhilarating summery weather that drew Beatrix out into the countryside on 14 May 1925:

Summer is y-comen in – with a rush. One of those days when one must get into the wilds. Got on with Deanery all the morn – into city … and took a bus to Pinhoe – and so up to Cheynegate where I had tea in a blue bell wood, and listened to cuckoos. Most lovely.[142]

For all her reliance on 'inspiration', Beatrix believed strongly in work before play. Always, for her, freedom existed within and even depended upon the structure of familial and religious authority in which she had been brought up. Even on days like this, she often worked in the morning and went out only in the afternoon.[143] There were many occasions when she would have liked to 'go a-roamin' but did not do so because other demands precluded it.[144] Conversely, there were other occasions, especially later in life, when she threw up her work entirely for the day, as on 11 August 1939, when her younger friend Evelyn took her for a 'spin' over Haldon, and 'neither socks nor letters [got] done'.[145]

Beatrix took great delight in motoring. Her first ride in a car was on 9 May 1907. She thought it 'very lovely, but the pace rather terrific'.[146] Cars became an important supplement to her other modes of exploring the countryside – on foot, by bike, train and bus. After learning to ride, cycling remained her mode of choice for decades. It gave her almost complete freedom to go when and where she wanted and to be on her own. As she got older, however, first walking and then driving began to assume greater significance.

[141] Cresswell, Diary, 13 Jul. 1910.
[142] Cresswell, Diary, 14 May 1925. Compare 2 Aug. 1913, when the weather was again '[t]oo fine to stay in'.
[143] Compare Cresswell, Diary, 28 Jul. 1922.
[144] Cresswell, Nature notebook, 7 Oct. 1920.
[145] Cresswell, Diary, 11 Aug. 1939.
[146] Cresswell, Diary, 9 May 1907. On the pleasures of travelling at speed through the countryside, see Rosemary Shirley, *Rural Modernity, Everyday Life and Visual Culture* (Manchester, 2016), 38–41.

By the second half of the 1920s she seems no longer to have had the physical appetite for long cycle rides and more often walked. For longer excursions, she was now dependent on someone taking her out for a 'spin' – usually Evelyn or Mr Munro. The comfort and convenience of cars suited her well and she always enjoyed the sensation of moving rapidly through the landscape. The drawback, however, was that she was no longer in control of when she went out, and entries like that for 3 September 1928 become more frequent: '[t]he sort of day one longs for someone to come and take one out for a spin'.[147] She also had to put up with sometimes unwelcome company.

Beatrix's satisfaction with life in her first few years in Exeter was briefly interrupted by a contretemps with her maid Annie, who had come with her from Dawlish:

> I have been horrified, disgusted and generally annoyed by finding that Annie had a man sleep in the house on Sunday night! It is too detestable to find that anyone one has trusted will do such a thing . . . I am determined to keep this place respectable, much as I dislike 'respectability'.[148]

Annie refused to relinquish her man, secretly allowing him in on other occasions, and Beatrix reluctantly came to the conclusion she would have to give her notice: 'I mean to be "Missus" in my own house!'[149]

In due course, however, Beatrix found another long-term, live-in servant, one who was to become central to her life for the best part of three decades: Mary Kitto. Mary was not without her drawbacks as a servant: she was prone to emotional collapses, could not be relied on to keep the house in order while Beatrix was away, and seems to have had a weakness for drink (on one occasion Beatrix returned to find that a 'fearfully repentant' Mary had finished all her sloe gin).[150]

Despite or perhaps partly because of this, the relationship became a close one. For all her failings, Mary was devotedly loyal and Beatrix appreciated her ladylike manners. She became more a companion than a servant. They talked about friends and common interests and Beatrix valued her frequent letters when they were apart. Mary brought out a tender, responsible side in Beatrix that was not otherwise much in evidence in her relationships with people (though it was with her dog Lavvie, and Lavvie's various feline successors). Perhaps it was easier for Beatrix to sustain intimate relationships at close quarters on an unequal basis, as with servants or animals: they, on the whole, had to fit round her rather than vice versa.

The first decade of the twentieth century was the apogee of Beatrix's work for Homeland. Following the books on Dartmoor, Teignmouth, Dawlish, Taunton and the Quantocks came *Newton Abbot* and *The North*

[147] Cresswell, Diary, 3 Sep. 1928.
[148] Cresswell, Diary, 2 Jul. 1907.
[149] Cresswell, Diary, 3 Sep. 1907.
[150] Cresswell, Diary, 22 Jan. 1913.

Cornish Coast (both 1908) and *Barnstaple, Bideford* and *Bude* (all 1909). After *Dartmoor*, Beatrix forbore from including intimate anecdotes in her published work, but there are, nevertheless, valuable insights that can be gleaned into the meanings landscape held for her from the later Homeland guidebooks. As might be expected, one of the most prominent themes is her forthright ruralism. In *Teignmouth*, she counters claims that the district lacks interest by asserting that she herself would 'never find any spot uninteresting where all nature lay before me "under the open sky"', while the preface to *Newton Abbot* mounts a more historicized defence of the value of the rural:

> Our English villages, all over the country, have characteristics not to be found in any other country in Europe. Nowhere do we see such pictur-esque groupings of cottage architecture, with glowing gardens of old-fashioned flowers, as in England. The English village, too, has retained the aspect of feudal life; the cottage, the manor house, church, and parsonage are in close proximity, close friendship, depending upon one another just as they did hundreds of years ago. Germany is visited for its old medieval towns, Italy for its art treasures; and those who would see what is best in rural life should come to England. And some of the loveliest rural scenery in England will be found in the neighbourhood of Newton Abbot.[151]

Beatrix returns to this theme in the last paragraph of the book, which expresses the same sense of the affective dependence of urban landscapes on their rural settings so apparent in her love of Exeter:

> For it is the country life that charms at Newton Abbot, where the country-side, smiling down upon the town, makes the town itself attractive.[152]

For all her ruralism, Beatrix barely mentions agriculture in her Homeland guides. Her diaries reveal that she was sympathetic to farming, often express-ing concern about the effect of inclement weather on the harvest, but it was marginal to her experience of landscape and she may have assumed it would be of little interest to guidebook readers. By contrast, both *Dawlish* and *Newton Abbot* draw attention to cottage industries: the Taxod embroidery at Holcombe and Aller Vale pottery around Kingskerswell.[153] Beatrix appreci-ated art needlework, completing many banners, tablecloths and the like for sundry churches, and had dabbled in rural crafts in her younger days. Like many at the time, she seems to have felt that there was an intrinsic

---

[151] Cresswell, *Teignmouth* (London, 1901), 7; Cresswell, *Newton Abbot* (London, 1908), preface.

[152] Cresswell, *Newton Abbot*, 66.

[153] Beatrix F. Cresswell, *Dawlish and the Estuary of the Exe (South-West)* (London, 1902), 36; Cresswell, *Newton Abbot*, 28.

affinity between the countryside and cultural production.[154] This aestheticized understanding of rural life was congruent with her love of flowers, which is abundantly manifest in the Homeland books:

> [T]hose who recall the appreciation of the cottager for 'crazy patchwork' will understand the silks, spangles, and gilding of 'Taxod' reach the very hearts of the workers. It reminds one of the cottage gardens with their profusion of gay flowers, creepers reaching to the top of the thatch, the background of the green hills covered with orchards – for Holcombe valley is bespread with orchard lawns. May is the month in which to see it, when all around is a mass of rosy blossom, and the wild white narcissus, 'butter and eggs', flower under the trees.[155]

On the whole, Beatrix's Homeland guides render landscape conventionally, drawing the reader's attention to picturesque views, pastoral scenes and literary associations.[156] However, these often have more distinctive personal inflections. The vividness of her response to colour is frequently apparent:

> Denbury is a village of delightful colourings; grey walls, grey thatch or slate roofs, splashed with great patches of orange lichen, and wild yellow wallflowers, that grow in every possible cranny.[157]

The imprint of her 'gëorgoepiscopal rambles', and the inseparable intertwining of ecclesiastical, historical, natural and territorial elements that made them what they were, can also be felt:

> The villages that lie up the Teign valley beyond Chudleigh form a group of some of the most interesting parishes in Devon ... each church is a little treasure house of art and antiquity; and these gems are set in some of the loveliest rural scenery imaginable. All through the year this is Nature's garden, but fairest in the spring, when the banks are thick with primroses, periwinkles, and wood anemones, and the bluebells sway in sheets of azure under the bushes.[158]

Beatrix is at pains to emphasize that beauty is due not only to nature but to the shaping influence of history, observing, for example, that the beautiful

---

[154] Cresswell, *Newton Abbot*, 30. See also Jeremy Burchardt, '"A New Rural Civilisation": Village Halls, Community and Citizenship', in Paul Brassley, Jeremy Burchardt and Lynne Thompson (eds.), *The English Countryside between the Wars: Regeneration or Decline?* (Woodbridge, 2006); Jeremy Burchardt, 'State and Society in the English Countryside: The Rural Community Movement 1918–39', *Rural History* 23 (2012), 87–8.

[155] Cresswell, *Dawlish*, 36–8. Other manifestations of Beatrix's love of flowers in the Homeland guides can be found in Cresswell, *Teignmouth*, 98 and 118–9; Cresswell, *Dawlish*, 48; Beatrix Cresswell, *Bude and Its Borderland* (London, 1909), 42.

[156] Cresswell, *Dawlish*, 20, 50; Cresswell, *Newton Abbot*, 50.

[157] Cresswell, *Newton Abbot*, 34.

[158] Cresswell, *Newton Abbot*, 52.

wooded slopes above Luscombe Castle were not 'forest primeval', but planted by the great-grandfather of the present owner.[159] If a veiled political defence of the aristocracy is implicit in this, she also dwells more democratically on the contribution of the 'British Celt, the Saxon Churl, [and] the English labourer' to the long making of the landscape, as they trod out the pathways leading to 'field and copse and farmstead'.[160] The way in which rural landscapes linked past and present, the natural and the human affected her profoundly:

> From the ascending road that winds through the park the river soon becomes visible, a blue streak at the foot of the valley. Standing thus, the chapel is just below; close by are the house and gardens; beyond, meadows, orchard, thatched roof and sloping hill – a spot where we are made to feel that:
>
> > 'The past and present here unite
> > Beneath Time's flowing tide.'[161]

This perspective reaches its apogee in *The Quantock Hills*, where Beatrix rejoices in the Luttrells' continuous ownership of East Quantoxhead House 'through all the vicissitudes of history' since the Conquest, celebrates the 'marks of successive historical epochs' discernible at Stogursey, and gives readers a panoramic view of 'page after page' of English history 'written here on the green countryside' from the top of Cothelstone Beacon.[162]

History, for Beatrix, flowed seamlessly into myth. The Arthurian legends appealed to her powerfully and in *The North Coast of Cornwall* she opined that local tradition was too strong to leave any room for doubt about Arthur's existence.[163] Tintagel Castle, seen from Bude, looked 'like some vision of the land of Faerie'. There was, she thought, 'nothing like it, perhaps, in all England' for its combination of natural magnificence and poetical romance.[164] Her fascination with ghosts and the supernatural are also in evidence in the Homeland guides, notably in relation to the gruesome murders attributed to the 'mad monk' of Lidwell, a ruined chapel on the slopes of Haldon, familiar to her from childhood.[165] With her acute sense of the rich mythological and

---

[159] Cresswell, *Dawlish*, 21. This perspective became commonplace in the mid-twentieth century, finding its way, for example, into the Scott Report of 1942. Great Britain Committee on Land Utilization in Rural Areas, *Report of the Committee on Land Utilisation in Rural Areas*. Vol. 6378 (London, 1942), 4, 9–10.

[160] Cresswell, *Dawlish*, 48. Compare Robert Macfarlane, *The Old Ways: A Journey on Foot* (London, 2012), especially 35–56.

[161] Cresswell, *Teignmouth*, 105 (Haccombe). The quotation is from Henry Wadsworth Longfellow's 'A Gleam of Sunshine' (1866).

[162] Cresswell, *The Quantock Hills*, 68, 56, 9–11.

[163] Beatrix Cresswell, *The North Coast of Cornwall from Constantine Bay to Crackington Haven* (London, 1908), 89.

[164] Cresswell, *Bude*, 63.

[165] Cresswell, *Teignmouth*, 82.

historical layering of landscape, it is unsurprising that Beatrix evinced a staunchly preservationist sensibility, although she does not seem to have joined any explicitly preservationist organizations.[166]

Haldon emerges from the earlier Homeland volumes, written when she still lived at its foot, as a powerful presence, 'a beautiful expanse of wild country, in summer a sheet of colour from the heather and gorse, with bog and copse and dark fir plantations breaking the view in endless variety'.[167] Interestingly, in the light of her *annus horribilis* in 1903, when she so often yearned to escape there, she attributes restorative properties to Haldon:

> [F]or true it is:
>
>> 'If you're hipped, out of spirits or ill,
>> Better by far than a potion or pill
>> Is a summer-day's run upon Haldon Hill.'[168]

Beatrix was always enthused by 'wild country', wherever she found it. Her generally rather low-key account of *Bude and Its Borderland* rises to eloquence when it reaches the 'wild and striking' scene at Crackington Haven.[169] Likewise with Watersmeet in Devon:

> Such spots are indescribable. A spur of woodland is thrust into the gorge, on one side is the broad stream of the East Lyn, on the other Combe Park Water comes tearing down, in spring no inconsiderable waterfall. The features of the rivers are characteristic of every 'meeting of the waters,' one stream that dashes turbulently into the bosom of a stiller, calmer river, the two contrasting natures blending into one perfect whole.[170]

This epitomizes the paradoxical but harmonious intermingling of exhilarating wildness and 'utter stillness' that Beatrix found in the countryside, a contrast that reflected fundamental antimonies in her own nature.

Despite her affinity for wilderness and Devon's maritime traditions, the sea had surprisingly little appeal for Beatrix. Partly this seems to have been because she could feel its power only too well:

> Standing on the edge of Stepper Point and looking along the grand coast scenery, we may admire, but there must be awe mixed with our admiration. Only the dwellers inland regard the sea as a holiday playfellow. To

---

[166] Cresswell, *Teignmouth*, preface; Cresswell, *The Quantock Hills*, preface; Beatrix Cresswell, *Barnstaple, and the Beauties of North Devon* (London, 1909), 1.

[167] Cresswell, *Teignmouth*, 80.

[168] Cresswell, *Dawlish*, 39. The quotation is from Richard Harris D. Barham, 'The Monk of Haldon: A Legend of South Devon', *Temple Bar: A London Magazine* 20 (1867).

[169] Cresswell, *Bude*, 59.

[170] Cresswell, *Barnstaple*, 48.

those who know its powers, terror, rather than pleasure, is suggested by
those jagged rocks and the deep, clear water.[171]

Perhaps the nub of the matter was that seascapes, unlike landscapes, had no
legible history. However wild they might be, landscapes such as Haldon and
Dartmoor were palimpsests upon which historical events and personal memories had been written and rewritten. They were carriers and even guarantors
of the deep human affections and loyalties that were so central to Beatrix's life.
Within the wildness, she found home. The sea, by contrast, constantly in
motion, erased the traces of the past almost before they had been created. It
offered a very different kind of wildness, cold and impersonal. On the whole,
Beatrix turned her back on it.[172]

The Homeland guides are also interesting for the light they shed on the
nexus between landscape and Beatrix's sense of identity. Her devotion to
Devon is less apparent in the guides than in her diaries, probably because
her remit required her to extoll each of the areas she wrote about, be they in
Devon, Cornwall or Somerset. Nevertheless, her county patriotism can be read
between the lines at times:

> Of the three Wells, Abbotskerswell is prettiest: an ideal Devonshire village
> of thatched cottages and flowery gardens, all embedded in orchard lawns,
> and clustering in a deep hollow, steep of ascent or descent, whichever way
> we take.[173]

Conversely, there are derogatory comments about Cornwall and Somerset
in the privacy of the diaries. The former, Beatrix tells us, 'never does attract
me', while she judged the Quantocks, despite their reputation, not so wild as
her own less celebrated Haldon.[174]

In the main, despite the avowed intention of the Homeland series to foster
a patriotic love of the nation's landscapes, Beatrix's guides project only a muted
sense of Englishness. Kenn is described as 'a typically English village . . . with its
rustic inn and the busy forge where the chink of hammer and anvil ring over
the green'.[175] Cornwall, it is suggested, does not quite belong in England, and
this may be relevant to Beatrix's coolness towards the county, although West
Country rivalry is probably a more pertinent consideration.[176] But although
the Englishness of the landscapes she was writing about was rarely in the

---

[171] Beatrix Cresswell, *The North Cornwall Coast* (London, 1908), 35. See also *Bude*, 30 and
36.
[172] She recognized the grandeur of the Cornish coast but disliked it. Cresswell, *Bude*, 29–30
and Diary, 15 Mar. 1912.
[173] Cresswell, *Newton Abbot*, 30.
[174] Cresswell, Diary, 26 Aug. 1919 and 12 Jun. 1903.
[175] Cresswell, *Dawlish*, 72.
[176] Cresswell, *The North Cornish Coast*, 9.

forefront of her mind, it did matter to her at some level. The most telling evidence of this is an account of a night walk along the north Devon coast:

> But before we quit this coast we must manage to take one walk upon it in the evening; the ramble may be in any direction we please, but preferably one that will lead us up a fair height, and the hour, if the evenings are light, must not be too early. For we come not for scenery, but for lighthouses. All along the coast they flash and gleam, from Harty Point to the Severn sea. If it is clear we shall see them like winking stars on the Welsh shore and up towards the Bristol channel. At either end of Lundy they glitter, and close to us at Bull Point on one side and Braunton Burrows on the other. All through the night they gleam unwearied, the tireless guardians of England's coast.[177]

The link between Englishness, landscape and protection here is interesting, and it appears elsewhere in Beatrix's work.[178] Again, it seems possible that her early experiences as the youngest child in a large, established family are relevant. She sought security as well as freedom, recurrently expressing a perceived need to have 'someone to depend on'.[179] The authority structures of family, church and monarchy to which she adhered so firmly were pivotal in this regard. Each had its spatial correlates, arranged like Russian dolls, one contained in the next: home, Exeter, Devon, England.[180] Although England was well in the background as a physical and emotional presence most of the time, its role as a kind of long stop in this security structure was nevertheless significant.

Beatrix's impressive authorial productivity in 1908–9 was part of a virtuous circle of growing happiness and confidence. Her end-of-year summary for 1908 concluded that it had been 'a very pleasant year, especially in literary success, the one thing worth living for'.[181] In 1911 she gave her debut paper at the Devonshire Association, which was to become an important forum for her, allowing her to mingle with the county's leading local historians and archaeologists.[182] It was a year of 'progress and success socially'.[183] The following year was a momentous one because it saw the completion of the first draft of the Deaneries, although she immediately set about revising them.[184] She continued to expand her social and professional horizons in

---

[177] Cresswell, *Barnstaple*, 39.
[178] Cresswell, *Bude*, 63.
[179] Cresswell, Diary, 15 Dec. 1902, 1 and 18 Feb. 1904 and 31 Dec. 1935.
[180] Compare the inscription the Oxfordshire farm labourer Mont Abbot requested for his gravestone: 'Old Mont, Enstone, Oxon, England'. Sheila Stewart, *Lifting the Latch: The Life of Mont Abbott – Oxfordshire Farm Boy, Labourer and Shepherd* (Oxford, 1987).
[181] Cresswell, Diary, 31 Dec. 1931.
[182] Cresswell, Diary, 26 Jul. 1911.
[183] Cresswell, Diary, 31 Dec. 1911.
[184] Cresswell, Diary, 31 Dec. 1912.

1913, giving a well-attended public lecture on the history of the bishops of Exeter.[185] Although she felt she had not done as much work as she should have, largely because of her busy social engagements, she judged it 'a happy and successful year'.[186]

The outbreak of war in 1914 did little to disrupt the rising trajectory of Beatrix's life. Although her initial enthusiasm soon faded, the closest the war came personally was when her cousin once removed Frank Cresswell was killed near Arras on 18 May 1916. She does not seem to have known him well, but felt 'dreadfully sorry' for his mother, and was repelled by Stasia's heartless reaction, which left her wondering 'if she feels anything, or enters into others' feelings'.[187] Beatrix was more deeply affected by the death of her old friend Gertrude Harris in November 1914 and the suicide of her niece Frances in October 1915, neither due to the war.[188] There was little change in her day-to-day activities. Her work at the museum left her plenty of free time and she spent much of it, as before, cycling across rural Devon, working sometimes on the revisions to her Deaneries, sometimes updating one or other of her Homeland Handbooks.[189] This took her frequently out into 'the wilds', where as before she rejoiced in the beauty of springtime flowers and blossom, sketched and paddled during the summer, and foraged or admired leaf colour in the autumn.[190] Visits to and from her brother in Kensington continued, Beatrix doing her best to mediate between the parents and their truculent daughter.[191] Professionally, the most satisfying achievements of the war years were completing the revisions to the Shirwell and Okehampton Deaneries, the publication of a transcription of the Edwardian church inventories of Devon and a lecture series on Exeter churches to the girls of Miss Jago's school.[192]

Although the war remained far away, it did affect Beatrix's mood. In looking back over 1917 she felt that it had been 'a year full of anxieties, which I have felt even if they have not come very near me', although it had been successful personally.[193] Weary both of her tedious museum work and the seemingly never-ending conflict, she inscribed the start of her 1918 diary with a quotation from Cowper:

> O for a lodge in some vast wilderness,
> Some boundless contiguity of shade,

[185] Cresswell, Diary, 20 Dec. 1913.
[186] Cresswell, Diary, 31 Dec. 1913.
[187] Cresswell, Diary, 5 and 7 Aug. and 31 Dec. 1914; 25 Jan. 1915; 27 May 1916.
[188] Cresswell, Diary, 2 Nov. 1914 and 8 Oct. 1915.
[189] Cresswell, Diary, 26 Jun. 1911.
[190] Cresswell, Diary, 8 Feb., 15 and 26 May 1915, 9 Aug. 1916, 11 Oct. 1914 and 4 Oct. 1915.
[191] Cresswell, Diary, 3 Feb. 1915.
[192] Cresswell, Diary, 25 Nov. 1915, 30 Dec. 1916 and 4 Oct. 1916. Beatrix Cresswell, *The Edwardian Inventories for the City and County of Exeter* (London, 1916).
[193] Cresswell, Diary, 31 Dec. 1917.

> Where rumours of oppression and deceit
> Of unsuccessful or successful war,
> Might never reach me more![194]

However, a more acute and pressing trouble was renewed (albeit unspecified) difficulty with Mary. On 6 March there were 'domestic storms, cataclysms, thunder etc etc – most exhausting'.[195] Unwilling to turn Mary out, not least because she had no other home, Beatrix's thoughts turned to escape:

> I long for a day in the country, but I don't know when it will come off.[196]

As usual, however, it was not long before Beatrix found a way to put her wishes into practice. Six days later she was on her way to Posbury:

> Daffodils by the stream – walked on to Oldridge, and back home – a long way but very delightful. So remote that one might almost find the desirable 'Lodge in the wilderness' in that direction.[197]

But domestic trials continued. Mary was 'decidedly squiffy again' on 30 March, taking herself ostentatiously up to bed on Beatrix's return from the cathedral, leaving her ready to 'sit down and cry . . . with distress and perplexity'.[198] April saw some improvement but the installation of electric lighting in early May turned the house upside down again. Beatrix fled to Dartmoor:

> A glorious day. Early ch[urch] then off to the moors! . . . Gorse simply lovely everywhere. Rode back. After Tedburn the road is vile: cut up with timber traffic, and like riding on a nutmeg grater. But I really have had a splendid day.[199]

The situation with Mary seems to have stabilized in the summer, and the autumn passed pleasantly with visits to Hembury Hill and Sidmouth, much blackberrying and commissioned archival work.[200]

Military affairs barely feature in Beatrix's diary during these months, to the point where one wonders whether one of the reasons she found Armistice Day 'indescribable, almost unbelievable' is because the war had ceased to be a prominent part of her life some time ago.[201] Among the few ripples peace brought was polling day, but in accordance with her convictions she did not vote (nor would she have done in 1922 had she not 'yielded to masculine

---

[194] Cresswell, Diary, 1918, front-papers. The quotation is from William Cowper, *The Task, Book II, The Timepiece*, ll. 1–5 (1785).
[195] Cresswell, Diary, 6 Mar. 1918.
[196] Cresswell, Diary, 11 and 12 Mar. 1918.
[197] Cresswell, Diary, 18 Mar. 1918.
[198] Cresswell, Diary, 30 Mar. 1918.
[199] Cresswell, Diary, 9 May 1918.
[200] Cresswell, Diary, 26 Sep., 17 Oct., 13 and 26 Aug., 6 and 26 Sep. 1918.
[201] Cresswell, Diary, 11 Nov. 1918.

pressure').[202] She had stopped working at the museum in March and this gave her more time to work on her Deaneries, which she made full use of in 1919. As ever, she relished being out in the Devon countryside:

> The bluebells in the copses are marvellous – a shimmering sheet of blue. Walked back from Axminster. A lovely day – the country is really wonderful.[203]

The following day was equally idyllic:

> [A] glorious walk up breezy hills with cowslip meadows. Home by Beckford Bridge, a real old packhorse bridge. Got out of the way – but it hardly mattered – everywhere was so lovely. All the churches I wanted to do here are done.[204]

Beatrix's rural excursions had always been associated with freedom, enjoyment and a release from duty and responsibility. With the war over, Mary more settled and the revisions to the Deaneries progressing well, she seems to have felt in carefree spirits, and her intoxication with nature and the countryside was more apparent than ever. One sign of this was her decision to start keeping a nature notebook in 1920. She maintained this intermittently until 1924. The entries closely resemble those in her diaries with the non-wildlife elements stripped out. As with the nature diaries studied by Bellanca, there are many 'first seens', although in keeping with Beatrix's affinity for the familiar, these are almost exclusively the cyclical return of well-known flowers and birds in spring, rather than lifetime 'first seens'.[205] Nor was she anxious to police the boundary between the wild and the domesticated: she celebrated 'dear little lambs' as a sign of spring as readily as she did catkins, primroses and swallows. A prominent feature of the nature notebook, more so even than the diaries, is its fascination with seasonal and weather lore:

> 'If St Paul be fine and clear
> It betides a happy year'
> A lovely day, hope it will prove a good omen.[206]

As this example indicates, there were close links between such lore and the church calendar, which Beatrix knew intimately and observed closely. Like the springtime 'first seens', and indeed the practice of keeping a diary itself, these encoded and validated a cyclical and hence ultimately static, rather than linear and progressive, concept of time. This ministered to Beatrix's deep need to

[202] Cresswell, Diary, 14 Dec. 1918 and 15 Nov. 1922. The Representation of the People Act (1918) had enfranchised most women aged over thirty.
[203] Cresswell, Diary, 19 May 1919.
[204] Cresswell, Diary, 20 May 1919.
[205] Bellanca, *Daybooks*, 60.
[206] Cresswell, Nature notebook, 25 Jan. 1920.

hold on to the way of life in which she had been brought up and to the family and church traditions that were so central to it.[207]

Perhaps the highpoint of 1920, at least with respect to carefree enjoyment of the countryside, was the long walk she took from Barnstaple on 2 June:

> To Bishops Tawton. By the river path all the way. Cofton work done. Had bread – cheese – beer at the 'Chichester Arms', then up Codden Hill – simply glorious. Sat there ever so long like Little Bo Peep – with 9 sheep for company – a world all singing soaring larks and sunshine. Now that everybody rushes round in motorbuses one has these lovely places to oneself. Descent into Landkey, further than it looked. Got tea there. Then back to Barnum [Barnstaple] by wood path and a lovely quarry pond. Never on the high road all day.[208]

This is perhaps the fullest expression of a primordial, Edenic quality implicit in many of Beatrix's accounts of her best days in rural Devon. Such days allowed the capacity for joy in her nature to express itself untrammelled by the restrictions and impediments of daily life, principally occasioned by inter-action with other people. It is not accidental that these glorious days were almost invariably solitary. The 'company' of the sheep and larks is equally integral, however. Beatrix wanted to be affectively at one with the world, if it were possible to be so on her own terms.

Glowing accounts of gëorgoepiscopal and other rural rambles recur in Beatrix's diaries over the next two years. She could find '[n]o space ... to record the wonderful beauty of Haldon on this autumn afternoon' in her nature notebook on 2 October 1920 but was more eloquent the following April at Fleming in Cornwall:

> Cherry orchard simply lovely, like fairy land. More dainty and graceful than apple. It is absolutely beautiful looking over the Tamar and Hamoaze. Bitter cold light.[209]

Sufficiently frequent visits to Dartmoor remained de rigueur, and she was there for several days in May 1922:

> Returned via Ashburton – the views up towards Dartmoor grand, looking stupendous in the grey light. Lovely by the Dart.[210]

The major event of 1922, however, was Beatrix's journey to the Lake District, where she 'buried the hatchet' with Stasia, Etta and their compan-ion Scottie, who were now living there.[211] Afterwards she was very glad to

[207] Compare Duncan Forbes, *The Liberal Anglican Idea of History* (Cambridge, 1952).
[208] Cresswell, *Diary*, 2 Jun. 1920.
[209] Cresswell, Nature notebook, 19 Apr. 1921.
[210] Cresswell, Diary, 11 May 1922.
[211] Cresswell, Diary, 15 Jun. and 30 Dec. 1922.

have done so, although she found the experience of '3 females all talking at once, and 5 days yapping at the same time' very disconcerting.[212] She admired the grandeur of the fells, but Beatrix rarely embraced non-Devonian land-scapes wholeheartedly: she longed for 'the geniality of the west' (although Exeter was barely further west than the Lakes), and noted that the hills were 'scarcely "mountains"'. Her feelings are summed up in her response to meeting an ex-Devonian clergyman one day: 'Mr Panton erstwhile of St Edmunds Exeter – feels an exile – so should I if I had to live here.'[213]

The following year, 1923, was 'most successful as regards work', and indeed earnings.[214] The diary for this year includes a list of work done, among which was a history of Shobrooke (typescript), revisions to Homeland's Brixham guide, two short pieces for *The Queen*, genealogical research on various pedigrees and wills and archival work for the county librarian, all of which Beatrix was paid for. She also completed a transcription of the first volume of the Kenn parish registers, a history of Heavitree for the parish magazine, some notes on Devon churches and the typing of the Plympton, Hartland and Woodleigh volumes of the Deaneries.[215] However, it was also, as she noted, a year of deaths: 'someone one liked every month'.[216] Henceforth, there were to be few years in which she escaped the death of a close friend or relative.

She went up to Kensington in February 1924, finding her brother aged and Clarice 'quite the boss'.[217] Beatrix never felt comfortable there and was relieved to decamp to Waddon in south London, where Prescott Row lived. Here she felt much more at home.[218] She had become gradually closer to Row over the years: he had proved not only a financial lifeline but a staunch and affectionate friend. Folded into her diary for this year is a note from him, dated 14 February and humorously addressed 'My only Valentine'.[219] Row was, as Beatrix knew, a devoted husband but, having foresworn marriage, she appreciated decorous gallantry from the right kind of man. Although he was no older than her, she called him 'Daddy' and he seems indeed to have become a father figure, someone she looked to for sustenance, protection and even love.[220]

Beatrix's finances were more precarious in 1924 than the previous year. As her outgoings had not changed materially, this was probably because commis-sioned work seems to have been harder to come by. This was to change in 1925, one of the most eventful of her life (a 'year of happenings', as she wrote

[212] Cresswell, Diary, 26 Jun. 1922.
[213] Cresswell, Diary, 26 Jun. 1922.
[214] Cresswell, Diary, 31 Dec. 1923.
[215] Cresswell, Diary, 1923, endpapers.
[216] Cresswell, Diary, 31 Dec. 1923.
[217] Cresswell, Diary, 2 Feb. 1924.
[218] Cresswell, Diary, 16 Feb. 1924.
[219] Cresswell, Diary, 1924, enclosure.
[220] Cresswell, Diary, 16 Feb. 1924.

retrospectively). It began badly, with her brother's death in March, the most serious blow Beatrix had sustained for many years. Professionally and financially, however, 1925 was a triumph. Mary Alban had invited her to Florence to give a lecture on R. D. Blackmore to the English expatriate community there. Blackmore was the son of a Devonshire parson and his best-known novel was set on Exmoor, so this was much to Beatrix's taste. The lecture was a great success and Beatrix repeated it in Exeter later in the year. Another notable achievement, 'one of my best efforts' in her own eyes, was to secure her father's precious botanical collection for the museum. It had become available after her brother's death. The most momentous event, however, was the final completion and binding of her Deaneries:

> The Deanery is bound!! Went a long and lovely, but very hot scramble walk from the 3 Horseshoes to Star Barton, and back by Whitestone lanes. Got many flowers (more than I expected) – the rain has freshed everything. Came home and found the Deanery on my desk – Jubilate Deo![221]

A few days afterwards, she exhibited the bound volumes to her neighbour and intermittent employer, the county librarian Mr Tapley Soper, a delightful and highly satisfactory occasion.[222] This was followed later in the month by a grand celebratory tea party for all her friends, also a great success.[223]

The triumphs of 1925 were the culmination of Beatrix's professional life. Ironically, however, 1925 also marked the beginning of a long downhill slope. Never again was she to revel in her strength or accomplish so much as she did that year. Richard's death seems to have affected her more deeply than perhaps she realized at the time: for decades he had been a 'buttress' to her but now she had to stand on her own.[224] The main problem, however, was that the greatest achievement of 1925, the completion of the Deaneries, contained the seeds of destruction. The Deaneries had been her life's great work and, now it was finished, Beatrix recognized that she felt a sense of 'Othello's occupation gone'.[225] Rarely thereafter did she recapture the same energy she had had before. Next July she spent a few days on Dartmoor in connection with a paper she was giving at Belstone Women's Institute. It was 'most lovely' by the River Lyd but she failed to find the Staghorn Moss she was searching for:

> Some day I must try again, but I fear my Dartmoor days are over. Could hardly drag myself to Sowton (2 miles). I feel I can hardly walk at all.[226]

[221] Cresswell, Diary, 4 Jul. 1925. The Three Horseshoes was a public house near Cowley, north of Exeter. She must have known that the bound Deaneries would shortly be returned, so this walk may have had something of a celebratory character.
[222] Cresswell, Diary, 13 Jul. 1925.
[223] Cresswell, Diary, 30 Jul. 1925.
[224] Cresswell, Diary, 18 Feb. 1904.
[225] Cresswell, Diary, 31 Dec. 1925.
[226] Cresswell, Diary, 28 Jul. 1926.

Given all that Dartmoor signified for her, this was quite a renunciation –
a farewell to youth, vigour and passions that had animated her for decades.

Although she managed to earn fifty-eight pounds in 1926, looking back on it
she felt it had not been a nice year: she had not felt well throughout. Physically,
she was perhaps a little better in 1927 and did some useful work revising the
Newquay Homeland guide. But she was shaken by her kitten Rosie's death in
June and Stasia's the month after. Beatrix was shocked to discover that her
spendthrift sister had sold the family jewels ('a dismal matter over which
I c[oul]d howl').[227] There was some softening – on the day of Stasia's burial,
Beatrix expressed a wish that 'with all her failures and faults, and I fear they
were many', she had 'tried to keep nearer to her in thought'.[228] Rosie's death hit
her harder, even prompting a rare poem ('My Rosie'), written on a blank page
at the back of the 1927 diary.[229] Beatrix's tender feelings flowed most readily
towards small creatures such as kittens and dogs. She often writes of 'dear little
lambs' while swallows are 'little dears'.[230] The same sentiment could extend to
inanimate objects, especially if, like bicycles and typewriters, they functioned
as extensions of her body. She nicknamed what seems to have been her first
bicycle 'Flying Wheel' and felt something akin to guilt when she replaced it
with 'Chainless'.[231] For her typewriter, she even composed an epitaph, albeit in
typically ironic vein:

> SACRED TO THE MEMORY OF
> A BAR LOCK TYPE WRITER AGED 20 WHICH
> STRUCK WORK FEBRUARY 1927 ON THE DEATH
> OF THE EARL OF DEVON: EARNING MONEY FOR
> ITS POSSESSOR TO THE LAST
> Corona Four, go and do thou likewise.[232]

While obviously not restricted to the countryside, this feeling did contribute
to Beatrix's ruralism, since the small animals that primarily elicited it were
usually to be found in rural settings, while bicycle and typewriter were tools
that enabled her, respectively, to explore the countryside and generate an
income from it. It was partly, of course, because she found it difficult to sustain
close relationships with people that Beatrix poured her abundant affections
into little animals and things. But there is also a hint of self-identification about
it, and as with so much else this goes back to her earliest experiences as very
much the littlest one of the family.

---

[227] Cresswell, Diary, 26 Oct. 1926.
[228] Cresswell, Diary, 10 Jul. 1927.
[229] Cresswell, Diary, 1927, endpapers.
[230] Cresswell, Nature notebook, 31 Jan. 1921; Cresswell, Diary, 12 Apr. 1916. See also Nature
notebook, 7 Apr. 1923 and Diary, 11 Jan. 1909 and 26 Jul. 1929.
[231] Cresswell, Diary, 7 Mar. 1898.
[232] DRO 4686M/F82, 'Beatrix Cresswell. Newspaper cuttings, etc, 1920s–1940s'.

It was Beatrix's own health that failed in 1928: she came down with bronchitis on 1 March and for the next six weeks, diary entries are few and far between. The illness was very serious and she was not expected to live. The one unanticipated compensation was the great kindness of her Exeter friends. She walked into town for the first time on 14 May and found 'getting along . . . quite a difficult process, everyone stops to say how glad they are to see me out again'.[233] It took a long time for her to recover her strength and for months she was dependent on friends with cars to take her out 'for a spin'.[234] Her end-of-year summary is compelling and worth quoting in full:

> So ends 1928. A desultory year, and a rather odd one. I suppose no one reaches the brink of that river for the first time without having a queer feeling afterwards – one seems to have touched on the unknown. That wonderful display of kindness and friendship has been amazing. Had it not been for Mr Maverick [one of her genealogical clients] I sh[oul]d have earnt next to nothing, and the loss of bodily strength is trying – moreover I feel that I must not give way to laziness, but try and be more energetic.
>
> Clarice is useless – Etta feeble and far away, and I know she and I are better friends when apart. There is no one to depend on but Mary – and in many ways I have to uphold her. But I don't know what I sh[oul]d do without her devotion and friendship.
>
> The future is on the knees of the Gods.[235]

Barely had life resumed a semblance of normality than Beatrix was prostrated by another crushing blow: the death of 'Daddy' Row on 15 January 1929. This hurt her more than anything since her own father's death and she was puzzled by the force of her reaction:

> I feel more upset than can be expressed – dear, dear Daddy . . . I have spent the day in wreath making and tears. Mary most sympathetic: I could hardly feel more overwhelmed if the death were in the house.[236]

Though she seems not to have been aware of it, some of Beatrix's feelings towards her father had clearly become attached to Prescott Row, over and above the latter's undoubted warmth, kindness and generosity. His death recapitulated her father's and was therefore in some degree a reliving of that earlier shattering bereavement.

As before, landscape could do little to assuage the root cause of the trouble, but a trip to Orcombe Point near Exmouth ten days later, a beautiful run over Woodbury Common, left Beatrix feeling 'much freshened up' after so much

[233] Cresswell, Diary, 14 May 1928.
[234] Cresswell, Diary, 23 Jun. 1928.
[235] Cresswell, Diary, 31 Dec. 1928.
[236] Cresswell, Diary, 16 Jan. 1929.

misery.[237] Returning from another excursion to Newton Abbot a few days later, she was cheered by seeing:

> Lambs, fluffy catkins, and one delicious bit of ploughing, the gulls following the plough.[238]

But these were flickers of light in the prevailing darkness. The spring passed dismally: she felt unwell and bereft of energy. Her diary entries from this period resemble those from 1903:

> Existence is dull and uninteresting – I have the 'blues' badly . . . My doll is not even stuffed with sawdust: I think there is no stuffing in her.[239]

At last, on 23 June, life stirred again: 'I have conceived an idea for a new Magnum Opus, and feel much inspired.'[240] Revealingly, this turned out to be *A Book of Devonshire Parsons*. Short of a biography, which she may have felt was unwarranted given her father's comparative obscurity, the connection with him could hardly be closer. The frontispiece was a drawing of the Parson and Clerk Rocks, which he had drawn while his daughter sat with him fifty-seven years before, and the quotation from Oliver Goldsmith on the title page, praising as it does the man who was priest, husbandman and father all in one, fitted Richard, with his enthusiasm for growing things, to perfection.[241] That it was this book which eventually restored to Beatrix her customary 'inspiration' after months of grieving for Row underlines the connection between the two deaths. *Devonshire Parsons* allowed Beatrix to draw on the deep knowledge she had acquired of the county's rural parishes and their incumbents through decades of research for the Deaneries and Homeland Handbooks. She included material on clerical heroes about whom she had written before and whom she admired for their social conscience, literary prowess or both, among them Hawker of Morwenstowe, Charles Kingsley and R. D. Blackmore. This was her most serious and sustained literary undertaking since completing the Deaneries four years earlier but it was on a much smaller scale and she had finished it by early December:

> My paper ship S.S. Opus launched! May it have a prosperous voyage, safe harbourage and a profitable cargo. There was a dear little new moon this even to which I commended her.[242]

---

[237] Cresswell, Diary, 26 Jan. 1929.

[238] Cresswell, Diary, 5 Feb. 1929.

[239] Cresswell, Diary, 21 Mar. 1929. See also 2 Jun. 1929: 'I wish I felt more inspired for writing . . . I do nothing – what is worse I don't want to do anything.'

[240] Cresswell, Diary, 23 Jun. 1929.

[241] Richard Cresswell, Diary, 31 Dec. 1872; Cresswell, *A Book of Devonshire Parsons*, frontispiece and title page.

[242] Cresswell, Diary, 4 Dec. 1929.

Alas, less than a fortnight later the ship was back in port, unceremoni-ously returned by Methuen.[243] It was as well that Beatrix had other sources of income, principally, in this period, genealogical research com-missioned by her wealthy American benefactor Mr Maverick, to whom, as ever to those who showed her kindness, she was deeply grateful.[244] However, she persisted with her 'opus' and eventually persuaded Heath Cranton to publish it in 1932.

It was in a sense unfortunate that Beatrix had completed her new magnum opus so quickly. Really what she needed was a replacement for the Deaneries but, by the start of 1930, she was back where she had been a year ago in this respect. At some level it seems likely that she simply did not have the energy, and perhaps did not believe she would have the time, to commence another project on the same scale. This left her at the mercy of small projects that, with the exception of *Devonshire Parsons*, did not engage her interests deeply. In 1930 she published *A Short History of the Worshipful Company of Weavers, Fullers and Shearmen of the City and County of Exeter*, which she had been working on intermittently for some years, but which she had never really found absorbing. On 7 August 1926, for example, she had gone out cycling because the weather was 'too lovely for "Weavers" in a library'.[245]

Such progress towards recovery that Beatrix had been able to make was dashed by another wounding bereavement, this time her friend Mary Alban.[246] Beatrix had known her for years – they used to go out on flower-gathering walks in the fields round Exeter, to Sowton and else-where, and it had been Mary who invited her to Italy in 1925 for what proved to be one of her greatest and most memorable successes. Beatrix seems to have invested ever-growing affection in Mary over the years, as other friends and relatives died or proved unreliable. As always, Beatrix was best able to sustain a warm relationship with an equal at a distance. All in all, the friendship with Mary was one of the closest she had left and she felt the loss acutely. She was staying with Mrs Row in Croydon when she heard the news, and a few days later went to Stoke Poges church, which she had to herself for three hours:

> Read the Elegy under the spreading yew tree and quite broke down thinking of Mary. It is a lovely place, all roses, and the old ch[urch] most interesting.[247]

[243] Cresswell, Diary, 17 Dec. 1929.
[244] Cresswell, Diary, 31 Dec. 1929.
[245] Cresswell, Diary, 7 Aug. 1926.
[246] Cresswell, Diary, 4 Jul. 1931.
[247] Cresswell, Diary, 9 Jul. 1931. The reference is to Thomas Gray's *Elegy Written in a Country Churchyard*, composed in Stoke Poges churchyard.

Later in the day she went on to Windsor, which strengthened as much as Stoke Poges had consoled her. The castle stood 'like a rock' and she felt that 'Windsor, Eton, the Thames are the heart of England.'[248]

A similar pattern repeated over the next three years. In early 1933, inspiration came to her again in the form of a tale about a prehistoric man she referred to as 'Homunculus'. She became quite engrossed in it, quoting in explanation E. F. Benson's aphorism that '[n]obody could write a line unless he thought that he was embarked on a work of genius'.[249] Genius or otherwise, however, she had finished the book by early June. At a loose end again, and afflicted by painful feet, she already felt she was 'getting to the end of [her] tether' by the end of the month.[250] She was uneasy about Homunculus, aware that it was too short, but resigned to the fact that 'my work won't expand'.[251] The Devonshire Association meeting at Ilfracombe in early July provided some relief. Her room had an 'ideal view' and she enjoyed the sunsets: 'I don't think I have ever seen a <u>pink</u> sea before.'[252] In August she made one of her increasingly frequent visits to Sidmouth, where she enjoyed the lovely weather and watched 'the semi-nude savages getting sunburnt' (she had never had much time for the working class).[253] She gave successful papers at Whipton and Colyton, and although chronically short of cash, felt that there was 'life in the old dog yet'.[254]

Despite persistent attempts to find a publisher, however, in March 1934 Homunculus came 'home to roost' for the last time. It was to be an unsatisfactory year. Beatrix had had a protracted chest infection in late January and when she recovered she felt 'no inspiration' for the commissioned genealogical work that was now her main source of income.[255] She found herself 'longing for a spin' by early March but until a holiday in Sussex two months' later there was little to cheer her. While no match, in her eyes, for Devon, the landscape and ancient towns pleased her. There were primroses, albeit also too many houses, along the line on the way down from London, and Rye and Winchelsea a ('haunt of ancient peace')

---

[248] Cresswell, Diary, 9 Jul. 1931. Compare *Salter's Guide to the Thames*. Thirteenth ed. (Oxford, 1910), 1: the Thames Valley was 'the real centre of English life and of English history', cited in Readman, *Storied Ground*, 271.

[249] Cresswell, Diary, 2 Apr. 1933.

[250] Cresswell, Diary, 30 Jun. 1933.

[251] Cresswell, Diary, 1 Jun. 1933.

[252] Cresswell, Diary, 1 and 2 Jul. 1933.

[253] Cresswell, Diary, 2 Aug. 1933. Compare Diary, 17 Jan. 1903 ('poor people always want to pay in kind').

[254] Cresswell, Diary, 19 Apr., 26 Oct. and 9 Jul. 1933.

[255] Cresswell, Diary, 26 Jan. and 28 Feb. 1934.

met with unreserved approbation. Best of all, however, was Bodiam Castle:

> I am so glad to have been there. It is perfectly lovely, so stately and dignified and the moat with the waterlilies perfect. Cuckoo, swallows – flowery lanes to get there – and utter peace on arrival.[256]

However, all things considered she was glad to be home again. On the journey back from Paddington she noticed how different the landscape of the more arable south-east was from that of the West Country:

> The land of elms very different from the land of oaks. I don't think I have ever realized the effect of foliage on landscape before.[257]

The pleasure Beatrix took both in going away and in coming back on this occasion was highly characteristic. There was a powerful dialectic at work in her between home and away-from-home, parallel in some ways to the pull of contraries she experienced between town and country, centre and periphery. The depth and strength of her attachment to home is beyond doubt. 'Home – all well' is inscribed at the head of countless entries in her diaries, an almost audible sigh of relief. Despite this, there was as strong a movement away from as towards home in Beatrix's life. She spent a quite extraordinary proportion of her time away from home – including her sometimes very lengthy holidays, perhaps as much as a third. 'I feel as if I paid visits home and stayed away', she wrote in the midst of one particularly extreme period of intermittency.[258] Of course there were practical reasons for this, connected with her Deaneries and Homeland research, but had she wanted to spend less time away (especially overnight), she could easily have done so in a relatively small area like Devon.

Some light is shed on this paradoxical dynamic by the discomfort and anxiety being at home often involved for Beatrix. She had never found it easy to live with anyone else on an equal footing, and even with servants it was difficult. Mary Kitto's intermittently obstreperous behaviour could well be interpreted as a classic example of an asymmetric power struggle, with Mary forced to use covert methods such as emotional collapse and even perhaps alcoholic intemperance in order to stand her ground against the economically, socially and legally more powerful Beatrix. But Beatrix did not find it easy to stand on her own either. In going out, as she recurrently and almost incessantly did, to stay in rectories or with friends in their homes, but only occasionally in the more impersonal boarding houses and hotels, she may have been seeking a home-from-home in the Devon countryside, allowing her to have the comforts and some of the security of the real home without the burdens that

---

[256] Cresswell, Diary, 3 May 1934.
[257] Cresswell, Diary, 10 May 1934.
[258] Cresswell, Diary, 27 Jul. 1907.

unavoidably came with it. Hence she luxuriated in the 'delightful rectory atmosphere' of Shute vicarage on 15 May 1919, and the following day at Stockland wrote yet more effusively that: 'in this place I seem to forget the existence of anywhere else – feel no anxieties'.[259]

Meanwhile, however, Beatrix's relationship with her closest surviving relative was deteriorating fast. In June, Clarice, now living in Italy, wrote that she specially wanted to see Beatrix, while in her aunt's view postponing her visit to Exeter as long as possible. When she did eventually appear, Beatrix found her remote and different, while a subsequent letter was dismissed as 'the usual Italian gush'. Clarice's disparagement of England was detestable and her adulation of Mussolini left Beatrix cold.[260] Looking back on the year on 31 December, Beatrix's main concern was that it had been such a bad one for work, with little inspiration and not much doing – she had earned only fourteen pounds.[261]

Beatrix's shaky efforts to get back on her feet were dealt a hammer blow by Mary's unexpected death in August 1935.[262] She missed her dreadfully. Even Dartmoor at its best was of no avail:

> Real wild moors. No one about. Gorse and heather beautiful. I have had the darkest 'blues' all day. Glad I return tomorrow.[263]

Two days later she confided to her diary that:

> I feel as if my literary efforts had ended. Things are at a standstill and I don't seem to want them to move on.[264]

Stoically, Beatrix attempted to reassemble her life. Clarice was no help: Beatrix caustically observed that she 'sends many instructions as to "how to do it", as long as she is not asked for personal help in the doing'.[265] More to the point was the arrival of the new maid, Minnie, who proved very capable, so much so that, despite her high wages, she was, in Beatrix's view, more economical than Mary. She was also spirited, cheerful and kind. But she was much younger than Beatrix, inclined to throw things away, and entirely lacked the long memory and depth of connections that Beatrix had shared with Mary. Beatrix's end-of-year summary was understandably bleak:

> This has been an upsetting year, and I feel it has taken a lot out of me. I do wish I had someone to fall back on.[266]

---

[259] Cresswell, Diary, 15 and 16 May 1919.
[260] Cresswell, Diary, 9 Sep. 1937 and 8 and 28 Aug. and 4 Oct. 1934.
[261] Cresswell, Diary, 31 Dec. 1934.
[262] Cresswell, Diary, 28 Aug. 1935.
[263] Cresswell, Diary, 13 Sep. 1935.
[264] Cresswell, Diary, 15 Sep. 1935.
[265] Cresswell, Diary, 9 Oct. 1935.
[266] Cresswell, Diary, 31 Dec. 1935.

As had happened so many times since 1925, Beatrix was just beginning to feel a bit better when something else went wrong. This time it was a literal, physical blow: she was crossing Bedford Circus in Exeter when she was 'knocked down smash' by a cyclist.[267] She had to have a clot removed from her leg as a result, and was in considerable pain for the next fortnight.[268] This, however, was an injury that time could heal and distraction alleviate. A coach tour to Worcester and Lichfield in May lifted her spirits: she enjoyed the Malvern Hills, a view of Tewkesbury Abbey and a walk through a bluebell wood, but above all the fact that everything was 'so refreshingly different'.[269] A few weeks afterwards, the underlying situation had reasserted itself, and Beatrix was feeling that life was 'all uphill' again. But a more ambitious tour to the River Wye in August gave her a greater boost, even a glimmer of hope for the future:

> I do hope now that things will cease happening and I may get a little repose. I feel ever so much better for the long 'bus run – it was all so new and interesting. I sh[oul]d like to see Monmouth and Chepstow again – must try what the spring will do.[270]

The spring, however, did not oblige, or at least not in the way Beatrix had envisaged. She had increasing trouble with her legs, to the point where she found it difficult even to get to church and had to take a taxi, an unthinkable luxury to one of her frugal habits, when she wanted to go to the cathedral. Country walks, let alone gëorgoepiscopal rambles, were now to a large extent a thing of the past.

Yet there were compensations, or at least consolations. She bought a wireless, and though its batteries gave endless trouble, she was able to listen to church services when she could not attend in person. In fine weather she spent much time on the veranda, quietly enjoying the sunshine. The greatest pleasure, however, was being taken for a spin. The loyal Evelyn Worthington often took her out to Woodbury and sometimes to more distant Hembury. For a change she was sometimes able to go with Mr Munro, as on 11 September when he drove her up the Exe valley: '[v][ery] pretty, all green and shady by the river'.[271] But for all her enjoyment of these 'spins', they left her entirely at the mercy of her friends' kindness, nor did they give her anywhere near the same degree of immersion in the rural that her rides and walks had once done. Although she does seem to have adjusted her expectations in line with the new realities, it is unsurprising that Beatrix concluded 1937 with the pithy observation 'I do wish I had not become such a crock.'[272]

---

[267] Cresswell, Diary, 20 Feb. 1936.
[268] Cresswell, Diary, 24 Feb. and 4 Mar. 1936.
[269] Cresswell, Diary, 11 and 12 May 1936.
[270] Cresswell, Diary, 30 Aug. 1936.
[271] Cresswell, Diary, 11 Sep. 1937.
[272] Cresswell, Diary, 31 Dec. 1937.

The best feature of the first part of 1938 was Sidmouth, which she visited four times in as many months. 'I certainly like Sidmouth, there must be some magnetism that takes me there', Beatrix surmised. The attraction was, in part, not far to seek. The journey was a beautiful one, over gorse-and-heath-clad commons, long enough to be interesting but not so long as to become uncomfortable. It lay on Beatrix's side of the city so it was easily accessible, and, when she was feeling well enough, she could reach it by bus as well as in someone else's car. The town itself was genteel and sedate, with good hotels and boarding houses where she could sit quietly enjoying the view of esplanade, cliffs, countryside and sea. There were also two less obvious attractions. In her eyes, it was a place that 'never alters'; and to the north-east it was sheltered by the high ground of Salcombe Regis, her father's old parish.[273]

Sidmouth did Beatrix good. On 18 March, for example, she woke up feeling 'lazy and stupid, disinclined for anything'. But she 'screwed up some energy' and got on the bus:

> I think I c[oul]d enjoy motoring on a broomstick! There were Marsh Marigolds at Clyst St Mary. Furze gorgeous and golden in the sun over Woodbury. Sidmouth bright sunshine, pretty sea . . . Felt all the better and brighter for my outing.[274]

Later in the spring, Beatrix spent a fortnight in Sidmouth, enjoying the sunshine, flowers, sea views and unspoilt countryside:

> I do not think I want to live here, but I do like being here. Sorry to be going off tomorrow – but I feel much better for this fortnight of idleness.[275]

Bolstered by her holiday, she felt 'inspired' to work at her history of Umberleigh, working at it for the next three months with a semblance of her old enthusiasm.[276] June saw her at the Devonshire Association in Barnstaple. She 'revelled' in 'so much male society', which she thought was 'good for one's brains':

> I have enjoyed this meeting very much, everyone has been so kind, and I have been so much in it. But it must be my last. I am such a tottering old woman, and must look so decrepit.[277]

Beatrix was certainly not free of anxieties over the next few months. Apart from her difficulty walking, she was shocked to learn that Minnie was intending to get married. They got over this earthquake, however, and the greater one of her subsequent pregnancy and confinement – from whatever combination

---

[273] Cresswell, Diary, 28 Jul. 1905; 23 Feb. 1928.
[274] Cresswell, Diary, 18 Mar. 1938.
[275] Cresswell, Diary, 6 Apr. 1938.
[276] Cresswell, Diary, 30 Apr., 3 Jul. and 3 Sep. 1938.
[277] Cresswell, Diary, 25 Jun. 1938.

of loyalty and prudence, Minnie decided to stay, although of course there was a brief interruption of normal service while she was in the lying-in hospital. Despite these worries and disruptions, there was also unclouded enjoyment at times, most often when Evelyn 'blew in' to take her out for a spin:

> [W]e went a glorious run – meadows all buttercups, horse chestnuts splendid . . . over Gittisham Common to Sidmouth, where we had tea at the Bedford.[278]

Four days later they had an even more beautiful drive:

> Evelyn took us up to Hembury. Most lovely drive, and H. looking its best – it is always at its best in Rhododendron time – the slopes on either side the paths all blue bells – a misty sweep like a blue carpet laid down. Heard cuckoo for first time – it was wonderful up there, so utterly peaceful. E[velyn] and P[eggy] went off for a bit and I sat on the lawn – even the birds seemed quiet, it was just a world of flowers.[279]

For once in these years of increasing dependency, Beatrix was on her own among the flowers and birds in the countryside again. Something else is here too – serenity of a completeness she had rarely experienced in her younger days.[280] She owed this partly to her age, disposition and sensibilities, but also to the specific assemblage of landscape elements (quiet, solitude, flowers and it would seem sunshine) that happened to be present on this occasion.

Neither public nor private circumstances favoured Beatrix at this juncture, however. For all Minnie's loyalty, it was really too much for her to look after the baby while in full-time paid employment. She began to hint darkly about moving to a cottage in Crediton with her husband and baby, leaving Beatrix stranded. Meanwhile the world teetered on the brink of a precipice. When war broke out, Beatrix felt the same mix of patriotic elation and gloom she had done in August 1914. 'Why can't nations live and let live?' she protested on 8 October, unconsciously adapting a favourite phrase of her brother's – but the same evening she sat up late to hear H. V. Morton's paean to heroic English virtues on the radio and was too excited to sleep.[281]

By mid-November, she had developed a cough that would not go. It developed into bronchitis in December and Beatrix's end-of-year summary was understandably downbeat: '[t]he last day of one of the most unpleasant years History has to record – a strain from end to end'. The one redeeming feature was Evelyn, 'the good angel of us all', who came on an almost daily basis.[282]

---

[278] Cresswell, Diary, 23 May 1939.
[279] Cresswell, Diary, 27 May 1939. Peggy, who was visiting Beatrix, was the daughter of Prescott Row.
[280] Compare Cresswell, Diary, 20 Sep. 1939.
[281] Cresswell, Diary, 8 Oct. 1939.
[282] Cresswell, Diary, 31 Dec. 1939.

But the exceptionally cold January of 1940 was not propitious for Beatrix's health. The last entry in the diary is for the 31st:

> Min has been away on her own affairs in Crediton. Evelyn came, kind of her to do so. She does not at all like my cough.[283]

Well she might not. In only another sixteen days, Beatrix was dead. Evelyn apart, most of her friends and family had predeceased her, and Clarice, her executor, was still in Rome, quite unable to fulfil her legal or personal obligations. There was a short obituary in *Devon and Cornwall Notes & Queries* but the eyes of the public were elsewhere in the dark days of 1940, and it is hard to avoid the conclusion that one of Devon's most ardent, prolific and devoted antiquarians passed into the night with less acknowledgement and recognition than she deserved.[284]

* * *

Vital and vigorous though she was, Beatrix was not generally of a reflective disposition. Indeed, for all the energy and range of her writing, in some ways she was not even very articulate, at least emotionally. There is a sense of something held in: no close relationships with equals, no passionate causes, the ultra-concise diary entries and ironic tone. Perhaps being out in the countryside, especially when absorbed, as she often was, in the beauty of the landscape, allowed reflection to happen at an unconscious level. Quiet hillsides like Codden Hill, Woodbury and Hembury, bright with flowers or birdsong, seem to have been most conducive to this. But she was also powerfully drawn to 'the wilds', epitomized by Dartmoor. As her account of the terrifying sense of isolation that overcame her near Cranmere Pool suggests, this seems to have enabled her to encounter aspects of her being that were repressed, suppressed or otherwise did not find ready expression in her day-to-day life. More certainly, her ruralism was the principal outlet for her urge to be free, especially powerful in her case because she felt such a strong need to do things her own way. Freedom always existed for her, however, within and in relation to larger structures of authority and security. She found both in the countryside: the parish churches she devoted so much of her adult life to visiting represented the anchoring traditions in which she had been brought up, and their rural setting her delight in going where she wanted and doing as she pleased within these structures. This parallels the dual function of the countryside in providing both an escape from home when frictions with relatives or servants became too much, but also an alternative 'home-from-home' in the rectories and friends' houses where she so often stayed. Above all, however, the countryside

---

[283] Cresswell, Diary, 31 Jan. 1940.
[284] 'Miss Beatrix Cresswell', *Devon and Cornwall Notes & Queries*, 1940, 49–51, in DRO 4686M/F82, 'Beatrix Cresswell. Newspaper cuttings, etc, 1920s–1940s'.

offered Beatrix a shelter from and antidote to change, to which her deep attachments left her severely exposed. It was an existential necessity for her that the continuity between past and present should remain unbroken, and the countryside was in her eyes the embodiment of this continuity. While urbanization, secularization, franchise reform and the decline of the aristocracy resonated with some of these needs, all had their origins in Beatrix's childhood and youth. They were, at root, a product of her character, the long-term psychological influences bearing on it as she grew up and the traumatic effect of her father's early death.

3

William Henry Hallam

Swindon Turner

'I seem a person of contradictions', William Hallam confided to his diary on 3 May 1925, 'my employment the most modern, my hobby the old. My only reading either topographical or antiquarian books or detective novels.'[1] Certainly Hallam's was a complex character, yet the contradictions lay perhaps more in his circumstances than in himself. In many respects he was a classic victim of the seismic upheavals of modernization and industrialization, forced to work for almost his whole adult life in a vast, sprawling factory while remaining passionately attached to the countryside of his childhood.

The Diaries

The main source for Hallam's life is his remarkable diaries – eighty-two volumes spanning sixty-seven years from 1886 to 1952 – at a rough estimate something like 5 million words. There is only one major gap, between 16 November 1894 and 1 March 1897, the period in which he got married and his first child was born. Such a long-run, virtually complete diary sequence is exceptional, especially given Hallam's working-class background. Furthermore, he was an unusually consistent diarist, rarely missing a day, and although the entries are typically short, they achieve a rewarding balance between factual reportage and inward thoughts, feelings and experiences. As so often, the physical form of the diaries is important: most of Hallam's were written in pre-printed volumes with a limited space for each entry.[2]

---

[1] Hallam Diaries, Berkshire Record Office (hereafter BRO) D/EX 1415/30, 3 May 1925. In keeping with my aim of writing as a 'friendly explorer', in the chapters concerned with them I use the diarists' first names, with the exception of Hallam and Johnston, who addressed their close friends by surname.

[2] For an interesting discussion of the influence of the physical form of diaries on their composition, see Huff, 'Reading As Re-vision', 517–18. Huff suggests that the extra-textual material included in many women's diaries can carry important meanings. Hallam's diaries contain little extra-textual material but his occasional rather wobbly ink sketches do express meanings that words could not convey. The first entry for 1886 is embellished with a crude green man, encapsulating Hallam's immersion in rural tradition. The 1889 title page has flowers, leaves, a tree and insects; on the left, a sickle, scythe and spade; and on the right what appear to be industrial tools. Here we have a figurative expression of the

This encouraged concise daily entries; although he quite often exceeded the space provided, the width of the margins and other unprinted spaces meant that he could only squeeze in a few extra lines by doing so. In some years, he bought a general-purpose lined notebook and this allowed him to write more expansively, but, perhaps because he had by now acquired the habit, he generally maintained his regular daily entries.

Although diaries can no more be 'objective', in the sense of neutral and comprehensive, than the human beings who write them, Hallam's diaries do have much to commend them as a record of events. While there are a few retrospective entries like that for 6 October 1886 ('Very wet in the evening. I . . . wrote up my diary which I had left for a week'), the detail, precision and freshness of most of the entries suggests that they were written on the day in question, often, it would seem, as with many regular diarists, just before going to bed.[3] It seems only to have been when his routine was disrupted, notably by night work, that he failed to do so.[4] In common with most diarists, Hallam re-read his diaries, but there are few deletions or changes to the original.[5] All in all, it seems unlikely that retrospect or faulty memory played much part in what has come down to us.

Why Hallam began to write diaries is difficult to say. As with many diarists, he was puzzled about this himself. On 27 May 1939 he wrote, 'Today I celebrate my 71st birthday . . . It must be over 50 years since I started keeping these notes. Why I did begin and why I continue to do so I can't explain – it's all been a humdrum existence.'[6] However, the impulse was evidently a strong one. He had apparently kept a diary as a child, although this is now lost, but 'When I left school and went to Swindon, I troubled no more about a diary, as it was a monotonous life, until the middle, about, of 1886, when I happened to buy as a note book, a Renshaw's Diary, and then thought I would start from that day and again chronicle my daily experience.'[7] By this time diary writing was a well-established cultural practice, although perhaps less so among the working class (on one occasion Hallam observed that he did not imagine there were more than a handful of other diarists writing in Swindon contemporaneously with him). In many respects, however, he was a natural diarist. He was

---

split between Hallam's rural origins and industrial occupation; the predominance of naturalistic images leaves the reader in little doubt where his loyalties lay. Hallam Diaries, BRO D/EX 1415/1.

[3] Hallam Diaries, BRO D/EX 1415/1, 6 Oct. 1886. For a few entries there is direct evidence that they were written on the day in question, as on 13 September 1891: 'lay down in the afternoon . . . and wrote up this diary'.

[4] Hallam Diaries, BRO D/EX 1415/2, 30 Aug. 1891.

[5] 'I have just finished reading some of the back of this diary.' Hallam Diaries, BRO D/EX 1415/2, 7 Oct. 1894.

[6] Hallam Diaries, BRO D/EX 1415/45, 27 May 1939.

[7] Hallam Diaries, BRO D/EX 1415/1, Preface.

passionately devoted to recording and preserving the history of Lockinge, Berkshire and the countryside and it is hardly surprising that he felt an impulse to record the events of his own life in the same way. Indeed, in his mind there was an intrinsic connection between diary writing and rurality. He concluded the preface to the first volume of his diaries thus:

> How I wish I had a place in the country, for manifold are the chances there (for anyone who has any inclination at all for observation) for chronicling.[8]

As will become apparent, however, the lack of a 'place in the country' did not prevent him from writing a 'chronicle' that is as rich a record of the nexus between self and landscape as any we have.

Childhood and Youth

Hallam was born in the Berkshire village of East Lockinge on 27 May 1868, the sixth child and third son of John Hallam, stud groom to Lord Wantage. His childhood seems to have been a happy one, perhaps unusually so, and he formed affectionate, enduring relationships with his siblings. George, the brother closest to him in age, was a bosom companion and although he spent less time with his sisters, he visited Eliza several times while living in London and wrote frequently to his sisters in India and New Zealand. The death of his eldest brother grieved him: John, he wrote afterwards in his diary, had been 'one of the most harmless and inoffensive men that ever lived'.[9] He was fond of his father, although in later life this was tempered by a critical awareness of his impetuosity. It was his mother, Sarah, whom he loved and respected most, but he was not one to wear his heart on his sleeve and his (retrospective) entry for 15 November 1884 reads only 'Today my dear mother died aged 51.'[10] Later he wrote, with reference to the family's frequent moves in the years before he was born, 'I often think what a time my poor mother must have had, never settled anywhere long together and a family of young children to look after.'[11] The most painful evidence of his devotion to his mother ('such a careful thrifty woman'), however, is the contrast he repeatedly drew between her and his father's second wife ('an extravagant, selfish woman ... slack in judgement').[12] 'Mrs Hallam', as she is called in the diaries, doubtless had many faults, but her usurpation of his mother's place was plainly the taproot of her son-in-law's vehement hostility.

Hallam's father had been born and brought up in Clifton, Nottinghamshire, where his family had lived for generations. He worked for Sir Juckes Granville

---

[8] Hallam Diaries, BRO D/EX 1415/1, Preface.
[9] Hallam Diaries, BRO D/EX 1415/25, 6 Oct. 1918.
[10] Hallam Diaries, BRO D/EX 1415/1, 15 Nov. 1884.
[11] Hallam Diaries, BRO D/EX 1415/24, 18 Dec. 1916.
[12] Ibid.

Juckes-Clifton as a boy and then, at the age of eighteen, started at Welbeck Abbey under Captain Ellis (later Lord Howard de Walden). Ellis was a diplomat and solider, and John accompanied him with the 11th Hussars to the Crimea, where he was quartered in Scutari. Later travels with Ellis took John to Malta, Gibraltar, Norway, Denmark, Sweden and Ireland, where he spent many years. Subsequently he entered the service of Charles Craufurd Fraser VC, Colonel of the 11th Hussars. However, when the regiment was sent to India in 1866, John left Colonel Fraser to work for Colonel Robert Loyd-Lindsay (created Lord Wantage in 1885).[13] Lindsay's wife, Harriet, was the daughter of Lord Overstone and, on their marriage in 1859, Overstone's extensive Berkshire estates had been settled on the young couple, who took up residence at Lockinge House, where they continued to live for the rest of their lives.[14] John and Sarah did so too until their respective deaths in 1916 and 1884. The period from 1866 to 1884, covering the whole of William's childhood, must have seemed a strange contrast to the parents and older children with what had gone before: residential stability in a quiet English village in exchange for one exotic foreign location after another.

These early years in Lockinge were truly formative in Hallam's life. It was in some respects a typical English village, with a mainly agricultural population of 330 in 1881, falling to 261 in 1891 and remaining at about this level until after the First World War.[15] Wantage was only two miles to the north-west but had a population of under 4,000; the nearest large town was Swindon, seventeen miles away. Lockinge lay well off the main road from Wantage to Reading and the nearest railway station was Wantage Road, a three-mile walk across the fields. The village was therefore relatively isolated without being remote. However, although in size, social structure and topography it hardly differed from hundreds of other English villages, the management of the Lockinge estate became increasingly distinctive. The estate, which included almost all the land in the parishes of West Lockinge, East Lockinge and Ardington, ran up onto the downs and was predominantly arable in the mid-nineteenth century. The agricultural depression of circa 1879 to circa 1894 hit downland parishes hard: corn was especially vulnerable to foreign competition and wet weather. Many of Lord Wantage's tenants found themselves in difficulties; there was the prospect of land going out of cultivation and the labourers on the estate losing their livelihoods. However, Wantage was an unusual man with strong Tory Anglican

---

[13] Ibid.

[14] Roger T. Stearn, 'Lindsay, Robert James Loyd-, Baron Wantage (1832–1901)', *Oxford Dictionary of National Biography*, Oxford, 2004; online ed. May 2008 [www .oxforddnb.com/view/article/34544, accessed 13 Mar. 2011].

[15] 1881 Census of England and Wales, Population Tables 2, Table 4, 'Area, Houses, and Population of Civil Parishes in the Several Registration Sub-districts in 1871 and 1881'; 1891 Census of England and Wales, Population Tables 2, Table 2, 'Area and Population in Registration Districts and Sub-districts and in Civil Parishes'.

convictions and a fervent belief in social unity. He was also, after inheriting his father-in-law's estates and investments in 1883, one of the richest men in England. He decided to draw on this wealth to preserve the social fabric of the Lockinge estate. He gave rent rebates to tenant farmers and, when this proved insufficient, took the land in hand himself, so that by 1893 he was farming 4,427 acres on his own account.[16] He planted copses and shelter belts and constructed wind pumps, water pipes and cattle troughs on the chalklands between the downs and the villages. This allowed unprofitable land once used to graze sheep and grow corn to be converted to good-quality pasture on which cattle and horses could be raised. At the same time it provided much employment on the estate, boosted further by associated projects such as the construction of new roads onto the downs and extensive estate workshops.[17]

These measures were unusual enough to attract the attention of the Liberal *Daily News*, which sent its reporter George Millin to investigate. Millin's article appeared under the title 'Arcadia Realised' on 25 September 1891 and gives a fascinating picture of the estate at the height of Wantage's great paternalist experiment:

> Seen in early summer especially [Ardington and Lockinge] strike one as quite a little rural paradise. The estate is beautifully timbered; the cottages with their ornamental eaves and pointed gables, their fanciful chimney-stacks and pretty porches overgrown with ivy and roses, their grassy slopes and lawns and flower-beds, all present innumerable points of view with which the artist would be enraptured. Every villager has, or may have, his allotment. There is an admirable reading room and a public house in charge of a salaried manager who has no interest whatever in pushing the sale of drink, but who is especially required to provide soup in winter, and tea and coffee and other non-intoxicants at all times. There is a first-rate co-operative store . . . at which the people can get all the necessaries of life, clothes, grocery, bread, meat, and provisions, on profit-sharing terms . . . In addition to all this, over a hundred villagers are employed in [work]shops fitted with all kinds of the latest machinery and the best appliances . . . There are two churches and an excellent school. In short, it is a little self-contained world in which nobody is idle, nobody is in absolute want, in which there is no squalor or hunger, while in the midst of it all is the great house of Lockinge, the beautiful home of Lord and Lady Wantage, always ready to play the part of benevolent friends to all who need their help, and . . . sincerely desirous of promoting the happiness and well-being of their people.[18]

[16] Michael Ashley Havinden, *Estate Villages Revisited: A Second, Up-dated Edition of a Study of the Oxfordshire (Formerly Berkshire) Villages of Ardington and Lockinge* (Reading, 1999), 77.
[17] Havinden, *Estate Villages Revisited*, 92–3, 114.
[18] The *Daily News* reports, which also covered a number of other villages, were later published as George Francis Millin, *Life in Our Villages. By the Special Commissioner of the 'Daily News'. Being a Series of Letters Written to That Paper in the Autumn of 1891*

Hallam's diaries confirm that the village school, which he attended from the age of three to sixteen, provided an admirable educational foundation. He observed that the schoolmistress, Elizabeth Loe, was 'an intelligent and well read woman', and his first extant diary, commenced two years after he left school, shows that he was already a keen reader and fluent writer.[19]

Despite all the attractive features of 'this delightful Berkshire colony', however, Millin's final verdict was that 'the whole thing is radically rotten and bad' because 'Lord Wantage has done for the people, in the true spirit of benevolent Toryism, what the people ought to be able to do for themselves'. He quoted a local woman who told him that '[T]hey [the inhabitants] all votes Lord Wantage's way, of course. It wouldn't do for 'em to go agin 'im.' He might have added that there was no chapel on the estate and that Wantage warned his employees not to join the National Agricultural Labourers Union. The price the villagers of Ardington and Lockinge paid for their economic security was political and social subservience.[20]

Millin's reservations notwithstanding, Hallam's experience of growing up in this distinctive environment evidently fell little short of 'Arcadia Realised', and there can be little doubt that it had a profound and lasting influence on his perceptions of the countryside. The family lived right at the centre of the estate, in one of the outbuildings adjoining Lockinge House. John was responsible for the welfare of the estate's horses, including feeding, exercise, veterinary care, breeding, maintaining the stud books and supervising the stable hands. The Lockinge Shire Horse Stud was among the most famous in the country, comprising ninety-nine pedigree horses in 1901, worth £11,580; John's position as stud groom was an important and trusted one.[21] This helps to account for the proprietorial confidence with which his son called on Wantage's patronage when he needed it and the familiarity with which he is referred to as 'L.W.' in the diaries. The counterpart, however, was William's unshakeable devotion to the Loyd-Lindsays and everything connected with them. Lord Wantage's death in 1901 affected Hallam deeply and he noted its anniversary in his diary, along with his own father's.[22]

It was through Wantage's auspices that Hallam obtained a five-year apprenticeship at the Great Western Railway (GWR) works in Swindon. But he 'was home sick all the time' and after another six months at Swindon got a job at S. Z. di Ferranti's electrical engineering works in London (February 1890).[23]

(London, 1891). On reading rooms, see Carole King, 'The Rise and Decline of Village Reading Rooms', *Rural History* 20 (2009), 163–86.

[19] Hallam Diaries, BRO D/EX 1415/18, 18 May 1911.

[20] However, wages on the estate were no higher than elsewhere in rural Berkshire and after a few years the profit-sharing scheme ceased to pay bonuses as the agricultural depression ate into the profitability of the estate.

[21] Havinden, *Estate Villages Revisited*, 250.

[22] Hallam Diaries, BRO D/EX 1415/5, 19 May and 10 Jun. 1902.

[23] Hallam Diaries, BRO D/EX 1415/1, Preface.

It is unclear how, if at all, Hallam felt that the move would help with his homesickness, although Eliza lived just over a mile away from his own Westbourne Park lodgings.[24] It may well have been that his unhappiness at the GWR works, which at its peak in the 1920s was among the largest factories in the world, employing fourteen thousand people, was such that anything seemed better. However, employment in London proved precarious. He was given notice to leave from Ferranti's on 13 February 1891 and struggled to find a new job, trying about twenty places over the next few days before finding work in Deptford – only to find himself suspended within a few weeks.[25]

This time employment proved even more difficult to come by ('here's May come and still out of a job') and on 2 May he took the drastic step of asking Lord Wantage to find him a place at Crewe railway works far away in the north, which would effectively have meant severing his ties with Lockinge. When news came on the 18th that there would be a vacancy at Swindon in a few days, he did not hesitate and started back 'inside' again on the 26th, remaining there for the rest of his working life.[26]

Swindon

Hallam's day-to-day existence in Swindon conformed surprisingly closely to some of the classic tropes of industrial working-class life:

> Wife got up when I did at 20 past 5 to begin washing. They have put up a new hooter this last week which makes a more infernal row than the other.[27]

Not only did the day begin early, but it often ended late. Hallam was frequently on overtime until 8.00 or 9.00pm, after which he would come home, have supper and tumble into bed. Next morning he would be up again by 5.30am and go straight off to work, although the Saturday shift usually began later. As church occupied much of Sunday morning, this left very little time for anything else. Overtime appears to have been compulsory when imposed by the GWR management and Hallam detested it ('today we commenced blasted overtime again'), although even worse was night work, which could last for a week or more but was fortunately less common.[28] As a turner,

---

[24] Hallam Diaries, BRO D/EX 1415/2, 14 Apr. 1891.

[25] Hallam Diaries, BRO D/EX 1415/2, 9 Apr. 1891.

[26] Hallam Diaries, BRO D/EX 1415/2, 2 and 18 May 1891. 'Inside' was the name by which the Works was known in Swindon: see Rosa Matheson, *Railway Voices: 'Inside' Swindon Works* (Stroud, 2008).

[27] Hallam Diaries, BRO D/EX 1415/15, 13 Jul. 1909. The hooter was a dominant feature of Swindon life for decades and came to be held in much affection locally – as ever, Hallam was evidently out of sympathy with his neighbours and workmates in this respect. Matheson, *Railway Voices*, 85–93.

[28] Hallam Diaries, BRO D/EX 1415/2, 19 Jun. 1897; BRO D/EX 1415/26, Aug. 1919; BRO D/EX 1415/28, Dec. 1921.

Figure 3.1 William Hallam aged twenty-five. By this time he was living in Swindon but not yet married.
Reproduced by kind permission of the Berkshire Record Office (BRO D/EX 1415/71/1)

he had to use dangerous machinery and heavy equipment and parts.[29] He sustained several serious injuries, lacerating his right thumb on a lathe in 1891, almost breaking his arm in 1915 and injuring his shoulder so badly in

---

[29] The Works was notoriously dangerous: it had its own artificial limbs department, which had issued four thousand limbs by the 1930s. Matheson, *Railway Voices*, 97–100.

1929 that he was off work for more than twenty-two weeks, costing him more than £50 in lost earnings.[30]

The diaries contain remarkably little information about what Hallam actually did at work, in sharp contrast to the rich accounts of leisure and family. In the main his experience of work seems to have been thoroughly negative. Apart from his injuries, the overtime and the night shifts, work was often physically exhausting, especially in the summer heat:

> Hotter than ever today. 77 deg. Felt very thankful when 9 o'clock came at night, when I felt fairly knocked up.[31]

Not that winter was much better:

> I have a terrible cold coming on through working in that cold new shop.[32]

He seems to have had little interest either in the work itself or in his workmates, and he disliked having to pay a subscription to the Amalgamated Society of Engineers (ASE).[33] He longed for the holidays and hated coming back after them: the work went 'beastly <u>dead</u>' and he felt 'wretchedly miserable'.[34] Returning from the long lay-off after his shoulder injury was even worse:

> I quite dreaded getting up this morning in the cold and dark to go to work; but needs must and I did. My arm awful painful with the cold.[35]

Although Hallam could hardly be said to enjoy his job, working for the GWR gave him the domestic stability and reliable income he craved. Compared to what he would have earned as a labourer in Lockinge, had that been on offer, the pay in Swindon was good. Financial security mattered a great deal to him, not least because he was the family's sole breadwinner. He made a note of his weekly earnings most Fridays and at the end of every year totted up his savings, which through great care and economy gradually accumulated. In 1920 the Lockinge farmer James Gibbs died, leaving assets worth £158, and Hallam noted with some wonder: 'Little did I think when I was a youngster at Lockinge

---

[30] Hallam Diaries, BRO D/EX 1415/2, 7 Dec. 1891, 1415/24, 21 Sep. 1915 and 1415/34, 7 Feb. 1930.

[31] Hallam Diaries, BRO D/EX 1415/2, 19 Jun. 1891. See also Hallam Diaries, BRO D/EX 1415/18, 29 May 1911.

[32] Hallam diaries, BRO D/EX 1415/28, 3 Dec. 1921.

[33] Hallam's fierce individualism held him aloof from the camaraderie and friendship to which, Matheson claims, most interviews with works employees testify. Matheson, *Railway Voices*, 33, 155.

[34] Hallam Diaries, BRO D/EX 1415/2, 19 Apr. 1892. See also BRO D/EX 1415/2, 8 Jul. 1891, BRO D/EX 1415/5, 20 Jul. 1902 and BRO D/EX 1415/15, 12 Jul. 1909.

[35] Hallam Diaries, BRO D/EX 1415/34, 10 Feb. 1930. The miseries of Swindon night work, overtime, accidents, the factory hooter, heat and cold and compulsory overtime are confirmed in Alfred Williams, *Life in a Railway Factory* (London, 1915), chapters 8, 13, 15, 16, 18.

and he the big farmer in the village that one day I should be able to buy him up.'[36] The reward for Hallam's decades of unhappy labour was financial peace of mind and modest prosperity. Yet, although he never was in fact laid off at Swindon, the shadow of unemployment always loomed:

> Such a slaughter in the Works again. 810 notices of discharge given out this day. Everybody nearly in our Shop had the nerves, I know I did for no one felt safe. 21 had notice in our shop. I felt quite ill with suspense but thank God I am safe so far. Our children came in from play crying through being upset by other children crying whose fathers had notice. Some heart-breaking cases amongst them married men with large families and no prospect of work before them.[37]

By contrast, Lockinge remained a haven and he continued to visit frequently, especially while he was courting the domestic servant Sophie Hawkins, whom he met in 1891. Hallam's diary charts how quickly the relationship developed into the central one of his adult life. 'I did feel it when we parted', he wrote on 19 July. By December he could 'hardly live from her'. It was more than three years before they were in a position to marry but Hallam's ardour remained undimmed:

> After all my bad luck in London, out of work etc how it has all turned out for vg best in only meeting with Sophie. One thing though I am certain of I never loved till I saw her.[38]

Depth of attachment to people and places was the fundamental feature of Hallam's character. Accounting for this is probably beyond the range of historical explanation, especially given the loss of his childhood diaries, but part of the answer may lie in his relationship with his mother. There are many indications that he had been very close to her, as youngest children often are. Sarah's death when he was only sixteen must have been devastating and it seems likely that there was a connection between this and his subsequent devotion to Sophie, insofar as the gap left by one much-loved person can ever be filled by another. The corollary of Hallam's deep affections, however, was a profound antipathy to change and fear of loss. Sophie met his need for love but whether Hallam's relationship with her mitigated these fears or simply increased his exposure to loss is less clear.

The three children, Marjorie, Dorothy and Muriel, were born in 1896, 1897 and 1900. They went to school, grew up and in due course married and formed households of their own. Marjorie and Dorothy stayed close to home while Muriel emigrated to Canada and married E. Harvey Marvin of the Toronto stockbrokers Marvin and Fleming. By this time the First World War had come

---

[36] Hallam Diaries, BRO D/EX 1415/26, 1920.
[37] Hallam Diaries, BRO D/EX 1415/15, 22 Jul. 1909. See Matheson, *Railway Voices*, 41–2.
[38] Hallam Diaries, BRO D/EX 1415/2, passim.

and gone without greatly disturbing the even tenor of Hallam's ways. The Works shifted into war production and, perhaps because of this, there seems to have been no question of military service. Overtime increased and Hallam invested in war bonds but, in most respects, his life carried on much as it had before 1914. By the time the Second World War broke out, he had already retired. The events that really mattered in his life were more personal. He missed Muriel, 'out there in Toronto', and Marvin and Fleming's declaration of bankruptcy in June 1931 caused distress and anxiety in the Hallam household.[39] Much worse was to come in January 1936, however. Sophie broke her thigh in a fall after being taken ill a day or two previously. She was admitted to hospital and operated on the following day. Her husband's usual reticence gave way entirely:

> [W]ent in to see my dear wife who was just coming round and oh my God how bad she looked I could have broken my heart.[40]

He could think of little else, praying fervently at church the following Sunday that she might live. For weeks she remained critically ill and it was not till early March that she was finally out of danger. Hallam's diary entry for the 10th, the day they brought her home, exudes the battered elation of a personal Dunkirk: the most vital thing improbably preserved from a shattering defeat. Shattering it certainly was, since Sophie never recovered the use of her injured leg and was effectively wheelchair-bound thereafter. Gradually they reassembled their lives and, despite Sophie's disability and the limitations it imposed, this appears to have been a period of contentment for them both. He was willing and able to do most of the housework, shopping and cooking, and took her out on short local walks or across to the Town Gardens, where the two passed many quiet hours enjoying the flowers and open air. However, it was not to last: she died on 28 March 1946. Hallam held his grief in check but it can be read between the lines:

> My loganberry has never bloomed so prolific before. How pleased dear Wife would have felt.[41]

He outlived her for ten years in which he had to endure loneliness and deteriorating health. However, he remained in close contact with his daughters and in his last years his grandchildren, his garden and his enduring interest in the countryside and all things connected with it gave him pleasure and provided some sense of purpose. He continued keeping his diary until 1952 and seems to have abandoned it only when he no longer had the strength and energy to keep it going.

---

[39] Hallam Diaries, BRO D/EX 1415/35/6, 18 Jun. 1931.
[40] Hallam Diaries, BRO D/EX 1415/41, 14 Jan. 1936.
[41] Hallam Diaries, BRO D/EX 1415/59, 28 Aug. 1936.

Character, Opinions and Beliefs

Hallam was a man of strong character and firm opinions, fiercely independent and individualistic. After he left school he continued to read widely, eventually acquiring sufficient knowledge of the history, topography and archaeology of Lockinge and Berkshire that he could correspond on an equal basis with figures such as P. H. Ditchfield, the doyen of Berkshire antiquarians, a remarkable achievement for a self-educated man of humble origins.[42] This educational distinction and the modest material comfort he eventually attained were both hard won and it is perhaps unsurprising that he could be unsparing in his criticism of those who fell short of his exacting moral and intellectual standards. Quite typical was his account of a paper given by a fellow member of the Field Club during an outing on 30 June 1906:

> Went to Wotton Bassett ... here Mr Coleman met us and [we went] first to the church where he read a rambling paper on that edifice which contains nothing of note except the rood loft stairs.[43]

Similarly scathing judgements recur throughout the diaries. W. G. B. Murdoch's *From Edinburgh to India and Burmah* was a 'rotten book and his pictures as rotten as his writing', his sister-in-law's children were 'a perfect plague', while he thought a curate who blundered in summarizing the Parable of the Unjust Steward 'ought to study more'.[44] Harsher still was his verdict on the death of Swindon's station master, a man evidently known to him: 'No doubt he was drunk and fell off the engine.'[45]

Yet he was generous in his praise where he perceived merit:

> I am afraid my poor sister out there [in New Zealand] is in a very very bad state ... Her only joy is in her husband who is without doubt one of the best husbands who ever lived. There is not one in a thousand like him. His whole life has, since his marriage, been full of sacrifices even to leaving his country and all his friends for his wife's sake. I could never be what he is.[46]

In the light of Hallam's dedication to his own wife, this was commendation indeed.

Nor was he one to jump on a popular bandwagon; indeed, he was more likely to take the opposite tack. Recalling a disgraced former rector of Lockinge, he observed: 'Doubtless he was the biggest scamp that ever occupied

---

[42] Reverend P. H. Ditchfield (1854–1930) was co-editor of three volumes of the *Victoria County History of Berkshire* and secretary (later president) of the Berkshire Archaeological Society for thirty-eight years.

[43] Hallam Diaries, BRO D/EX 1415/10, 30 Jun. 1906.

[44] Hallam Diaries, BRO D/EX 1415/15, 21 and 29 Jul. 1909; BRO D/EX 1415/20, 4 Aug. 1912.

[45] Hallam Diaries, BRO D/EX 1415/2, 6 Mar. 1897.

[46] Hallam Diaries, BRO D/EX 1415/5, 8 Sep. 1902.

this pulpit but this sermon [on Ephesians 5:16] was I think the <u>best</u> I have ever heard from it, but who should judge him, who can say he <u>tried</u> to live upright but was too weak.'[47]

Hallam's independence of character contributed to his political views. When he lived in Lockinge, he professed himself a radical. This set him apart from most of the estate's inhabitants: as Millin had found, '[T]hey all votes Lord Wantage's way.' Even nonconformity was barely tolerated: on 6 April 1890 Hallam, out for a walk with Lex and Victor Whittle, met '3 or 4 of the Lockinge chaps going to Hendred to upset an open air meeting'. This notwithstanding, there was in fact at least one other radical in Lockinge – Hallam's friend George Brown – but the two apparently quarrelled about Irish Home Rule every time they met.[48] Hallam seems to have been constitutionally unable to agree with those around him, at least about political matters. This independence of mind, verging on cantankerousness, probably helps to explain the sharp change in his political views after he arrived in Swindon. Here, Liberalism and radicalism were much more prevalent. Within a few years Hallam had become a strong Conservative with an intensity sufficient to disturb his wife's sleep:

> Last night my wife was moaning and crying in her sleep and I woke her up to know what was the matter and she said she was dreaming I had a pistol and was going to shoot her because Mitchel [*sic*] Banks hadn't got in.[49]

But Hallam's Conservatism was not just a reaction against the political values of many of those around him in Swindon. It also reflected his loyalty to Lockinge and, now that he was no longer under his aegis, Lord Wantage. In other respects, too, it went hand in hand with his developing outlook, values and convictions. Above all, Conservatism as Hallam understood it was about retaining the link with the past. He deeply deplored the demise of old families, houses, traditions and ways of life; indeed, so strong were his feelings about this in adult life that it is difficult to see how he could have been anything other than a Conservative politically. Loyalty was one of the hallmarks of his character, and with loyalty went gratitude, in the first instance to Lord Wantage, and by extension to other wealthy benefactors, present and past:

> I went to Newbury this morning ... I then spent an hour in St Nicholas Church looking well at every window and before I came out knelt down and said a prayer for the soul of John Winchcombe for founding such a noble building. I thought it very thoughtful that a window is put up to his memory.[50]

---

[47] Hallam Diaries, BRO D/EX 1415/30, 25 Oct. 1925.
[48] Given Hallam's later views, one would imagine that he opposed Home Rule.
[49] Sir Reginald Mitchell Banks was the (victorious) Conservative parliamentary candidate for Swindon. Hallam Diaries, BRO D/EX 1415/28, 20 Oct. 1922.
[50] Hallam Diaries, BRO D/EX 1415/15, 6 Jul. 1909.

The lack of gratitude for such beneficence he perceived in socialists provoked his ire:

> We had an excursion of the Field Club to Ramsbury this afternoon by motor car. I took the wife ... Although we had only permit to look round the grounds of Ramsbury Manor Lady Burdett met us and was most kind and gracious – one of the real aristocrats – and took us indoors and told us we were free to look over every room we wished to – (how many of these so called socialists would have said the same of their house).[51]

Hallam's independent spirit also contributed to his Conservatism. He rarely asked for anyone's sympathy and, while his diary entries are sometimes acerbic, there is little trace of self-pity. His many accidents at work, some of which must have been acutely painful, are reported in a plain, matter-of-fact way, as are other injuries, illnesses and mishaps. Equally, he expected to fend for himself and his family financially. He kept a careful record of income and expenditure, lived frugally, joined the Hearts of Oak Friendly Society to guard against the effects of illness and injury, and contributed to the Amalgamated Society of Engineers' pension scheme. Perhaps for these reasons, he seems to have believed in self-help rather than state welfare or redistribution.

His Conservatism, however, was far from conventional. He was, for example, an outspoken opponent of the Boer War:

> Peace – at last no one was more pleased with the finish than I was, yet some of the jingoes must come jeering at me ... I told them all I glory in the attitude I have taken all along, with regard to this damndable [sic] capitalistic war.[52]

A few days later Hallam went down to St Paul's church (Swindon) for a thanksgiving service:

> I would not have gone however if I had known for it was more a Thanksgiving for Victory than for Peace ... It is disgusting now to hear all these sort of people talking about the blessings of Peace when for 2 years and 7 months they have not opened their mouths a moment to any peace but rather have urged on the hell hounds of war.[53]

Although Hallam did not oppose the First World War, he was certainly alive to its horror:

> This terrible war seems to get worse and no signs of any finish to it.[54]

> Dreamt I was out on the battlefields in France and saw awful sights.[55]

[51] Hallam Diaries, BRO D/EX 1415/30, 6 Sep. 1924.
[52] Hallam Diaries, BRO D/EX 1415/5, 2 Jun. 1902.
[53] Hallam Diaries, BRO D/EX 1415/5, 8 Jun. 1902.
[54] Hallam Diaries, BRO D/EX 1415/24, 18 Jun. 1915.
[55] Hallam Diaries, BRO D/EX 1415/24, 12 Mar. 1916.

At the end of the war, it was peace rather than victory he celebrated, and he did so in a characteristic way by planting an apple tree in his garden.

Hallam's attitude to war was congruent with many of his other values and commitments. His preference for quiet walking, cycling, rowing, sitting or lying in the countryside, parks or his garden was not the sign of a militaristic disposition. Equally striking is his indifference to sport, games or indeed any form of competition (except perhaps politics). This is remarkable at a time when sports such as football and horse racing enjoyed a mass following among working-class men, while it was almost impossible to escape whist and other card and board games. All this Hallam disdained. He was patriotic but his patriotism intensified as it became more local and his strongest commitment of this kind was certainly to Lockinge rather than the nation. Moreover, this patriotism was almost purely positive in that it expressed a deep love of familiar things from the past, rather than antipathy towards incarnations of 'the other'.

Hallam's attitude to capitalism is a little more difficult to read. There is no mistaking the anger in his denunciation of 'this damndable capitalistic war'. Yet in some respects he was a model petit-bourgeois, saving assiduously, carefully watching the value of his savings, dreaming of buying an attractive property in the countryside, determined to remain financially independent, opposed to strikes and municipal enterprise.[56] Even here, however, there was some consistency. What Hallam cared most about was the unbroken chain of connection with the rural past. In this sense, and in his High Churchmanship, he was more an old-fashioned Tory than a modern Conservative. The expansionist, imperialist, restlessly modernizing dynamic within capitalism was corrosive of the landscape, social structure and way of life of pre-industrial England that he so much wanted to preserve. He disliked the trend of the times and self-consciously rejected some of the most iconic signifiers of modernity:

> Shall never have a wireless installed here.[57]

> [in despair after a day of rain at the seaside, August 1935] ... went to a picture house, the 2nd time only I think I've been in one ... In wet, cold weather seaside places are the God-dam limit for visitors with bed and breakfast.[58]

However, if capitalism was bad, socialism was worse since it threatened not merely to corrode, but systematically to dismantle the things he cared about.

---

[56] He was not, however, a miser. He spent freely on things that mattered to him, like the *Victoria County History of Berkshire*, and immediately offered his daughter the large sum of £100 when Marvin and Fleming failed.

[57] Hallam Diaries, BRO D/EX 1415/30, 9 Sep. 1924.

[58] However, Hallam did record on 22 August that year that he 'swept our bedroom carpets, landing and stairs and 2 sitting room Carpets this morning with our Goblin Vacuum Cleaner', evidently a new and somewhat exciting purchase. Hallam Diaries, BRO D/EX 1415/41, 30 Aug. 1935.

Hallam's attitude to religion was more straightforward. From the outset, he appears to have been a High Church Anglican. It always pleased him to find ritual and, especially, incense in use at a church. However, he showed no inclination towards Catholicism. It seems likely that his High Churchmanship owed much to Lord Wantage, a notably devout Anglican. It also harmonized with his love of the past, harking back to the pre-Reformation church without disavowing the specifically English character of Anglicanism. Quite where God fitted into Hallam's worldview is more difficult to say. On the whole, he seems to have corresponded fairly closely to a greater Lord Wantage in the sky. Hallam had little hesitation in invoking his help in difficult times but did not think it necessary to pay him much attention otherwise.[59] Although he went to church most Sundays, sometimes twice, throughout the period covered by the diaries he displayed few signs of guilt when he chose, for example, to go for a walk instead. Perhaps, as the youngest in a large but close-knit family, Hallam felt a conviction that love, whether from his parents, Lord Wantage or God, was his inalienable right.

As this implies, religion was bound up with Hallam's very powerful feelings about home, continuity and childhood. Together, these underpinned his sense that there was a benign order in the universe. It is unsurprising, then, that going to church could, at its best, harmonize and order Hallam's sense of things:

> To St Paul's at XI. It was a beautiful sunny day and I was late and as I went into Church I felt quite an elevation of soul. The congregation were all in their fine summer clothes, singing the Introit 'Father of Heaven whose love profound' and the Incense rising from the midst of the white clothed servers.[60]

Although transcendent experiences like this were in their nature rare, the routine and rituals of churchgoing seem to have fostered calmness and peace of mind quite reliably. On the rare occasions when church failed to produce such results, Hallam was disappointed, as on 28 June 1931, when he 'came out of church feeling no benefit at all only annoyance' after a poor sermon made worse by distracting giggles from the row behind.

Hallam's faith was tested by the succession of losses that he, like many people, suffered in adult life: the deaths of Lord Wantage (1901) and his father (1916), his growing isolation from Lockinge, Muriel's departure to Toronto (1924) and the failure of her husband's business (1931). The heaviest blow was Sophie's disability (1936) and this does seem to have dented his religious fervour:

> Another new book [diary volume] commenced. As I get older I think at beginning each one – shall I live to finish it. Up at ¼ past 7. Got breakfast

[59] Hallam Diaries, BRO D/EX 1415/2, 1 Mar. 1891.
[60] Hallam Diaries, BRO D/EX 1415/21, 25 May 1913.

as usual. Dot [Dorothy] came down and helped her mother up and dressed. I intended going to Ch[rist] Ch[urch] at XI but it came on to rain so I didn't go – a poor excuse admittedly, but I am afraid my candle of faith is burning very low at times these days – the wick wants snuffing.[61]

Nevertheless Hallam continued to go to church, perhaps as much for the comfort brought by the familiar routine as due to enduring belief.

Hallam's Ruralism

Hallam's religious and political convictions, and his character more generally, shaped and reflected his ruralism, which was central to his life.[62] The country-side provided the backdrop for his childhood and youth and the setting for many of his most cherished pastimes and interests. He walked and cycled along its paths and lanes, swam, rowed, fished and skated on its ponds and lakes and gathered berries and mushrooms from the woods and fields. He admired its grand houses and medieval churches but also its vernacular architecture – cottages, barns and farmsteads. He was fascinated by its folklore and customs and read avidly about its history. Every aspect of the life of the countryside interested him: even after moving to Swindon he was mindful of the fortunes of agriculture and he would talk at length to rural craftsmen about their work. He went out into the countryside almost whenever he could, absorbing the beauty of the landscape and studying its diverse features with a historian's and an archaeologist's eye. While it was the human aspects of the countryside that appealed to him most (geology failed to stir him), he valued its wildlife too: animals, birds, flowers and, especially, trees. He hoped in the end to retire to a cottage in the country. The countryside and its life touched almost every aspect of his being, practical, social, intellectual, emotional, even existential. The rest of this chapter considers the varied dimensions of Hallam's ruralism, seeking to explore its functions and to understand why the countryside played so large a role in his life.

Walking

As with most of the other diarists considered in this book, walking was central to Hallam's interest in the countryside. Throughout the period covered by the diaries – that is to say between the ages of eighteen and eighty-four – he was a frequent walker, although when he was older he no longer covered such long distances and was more likely to walk close to home. In July 1891, to take an example from the years before his marriage, he went on eight walks, and in

---

[61] Hallam Diaries, BRO D/EX 1415/45, 13 Nov. 1938.
[62] As it was to Hallam's better-known Works contemporary, Alfred Williams. Matheson, *Railway Voices*, 37.

June 1897 on ten. The births of his children meant fewer opportunities for walks: in July 1897, just after Dorothy's birth, he went on only a single walk, and that an unavoidable one from Wantage Road to Lockinge.[63] When the children were a little older, the Hallams began to walk as a family, typically several times a month except in late autumn and winter. In May 1903 five walks are recorded in the diary, two of them with the Field Club, one with Hallam's friend Hudson and two with the family.[64]

As a working man for most of his life, Hallam was constrained in when he could go out. After his marriage, weekend and holiday afternoons were usually the best opportunity once domestic tasks and cooking were done.[65] One such occasion was Christmas Day 1918:

> We had roast turkey for dinner which was as tender and cooked as well as any turkey served up on any table in the country. Cold and dry. So we went for a walk in the afternoon for our digestions [*sic*] sake.[66]

Going for a walk after church on Sunday was also a regular habit. Probably the fresh air and activity provided relief after having to sit still for two or even three hours during the service.[67] In a similar way, he sometimes went out after he had been cooped up inside most of the day doing something, as on 13 April 1900, when he spent several hours cataloguing newly arrived coins then went for a walk in the afternoon.[68] Other circumstances could also induce the Hallams to go out when they might not otherwise have done. When Sophie's father was staying with them in August 1915, for example, they seem to have been under some constraint until he went to bed, after which they went for a walk, presumably in order to be able to talk.[69]

Unsurprisingly, Hallam was much more likely to go out in good weather. Rain, however, appears to have been more likely to prevent a walk than sunshine was to prompt it. He was a methodical man who often formed his plans several days in advance and if he had, as on 10 May 1939, decided to do the spring cleaning, a 'perfect English summer day' was not enough to persuade him to change them.[70] In general, the impression the diaries give is that Hallam's rural interests and activities responded more to his medium- and

---

[63] Hallam Diary, BRO D/EX 1415/2.

[64] Hallam Diary, BRO D/EX 1415/6.

[65] For example on 20 Jun. 1891, 25 Jul. 1891, 24 Apr. 1892, 23 Sept. 1894, 31 May 1903, 5 Aug. 1912, 4 Jun. 1916, 5 Aug. 1916, 25 Dec. 1918, 6 Jul. 1919, 10 May 1925, 27 May 1928, 21 and 28 Jun. 1931, 25 Mar. 1933.

[66] Hallam Diaries, BRO D/EX 1415/25, 25 Dec. 1918.

[67] See, for example, 6 Apr. 1890, 31 May 1891, 7, 21 and 28 Jun. 1891, 6 and 20 Sep. 1891, 11 Oct. 1891, 22 May 1892.

[68] Hallam Diaries, BRO D/EX 1415/3, 13 Apr. 1900.

[69] Hallam Diaries, BRO D/EX 1415/24, 1 Aug. 1915.

[70] Hallam Diaries, BRO D/EX 1415/45, 10 May 1939. See also, for example, 1 May 1911, when Hallam bought a book, paid a subscription, went to the Bath Road reading room

long-term needs, values and commitments than to day-to-day events and circumstances.

When he was young, Hallam frequently covered long distances on foot. On 22 April 1886 he left work at 1pm, washed, dressed and at 2pm set off for Lockinge, 'where I arrived about 9 very tired'.[71] This was a walk of more than twenty miles. Four days later he went on a seventeen-mile walk over the Downs with his brother George and Lex Whittle.[72] Prior to his marriage, if he was at Lockinge for more than a day or two, Hallam almost always went out for a long walk over the Downs. Thereafter his walks were usually with Sophie and, until they left home, the children, so he rarely covered such distances. As he got older he found he no longer had as much stamina as when he was younger: after a walk from Challow to Charney and back on 2 June 1917 he 'felt much more tired than I used to with walking' (he was then aged forty-nine).[73]

Many of Hallam's shorter walks and some of his longer ones had a practical purpose: indeed, for most of his life this was his principal means of transport. He never owned a car and did not ride a bicycle until he was twenty-three. Even after this, once his initial burst of enthusiasm had passed, he rode relatively rarely.[74] However, even non-discretionary walks undertaken purely to reach a particular destination could offer aesthetic, intellectual, emotional and, on occasion, spiritual rewards. He particularly loved the familiar walk from Wantage Road station to Lockinge. It signified coming home and passed through attractive countryside, the two aspects reinforcing each other:

> Went into work till 12, and then went home by the ¼ to 2 train. George [his brother] and George Whittle met me at the station, and we walked home across the meadows.[75]

The inclusion of the otherwise redundant words 'across the meadows' suggests that the rural aspect of the walk was an essential part of Hallam's experience of it.[76] On another occasion Hallam had gone to Denchworth in the mistaken expectation that he would find a pre-Reformation bell there. The first part of the journey was by train but he had to go the rest of the way on foot. However, although this was a walk from necessity rather than choice, and ended in

and planted a row of potatoes rather than go for country walk, although it was 'an ideal May Day'.

[71] Hallam Diary, BRO D/EX 1415/1, 22 Apr. 1886.

[72] Hallam Diary, BRO D/EX 1415/1, 26 Apr. 1886.

[73] Hallam Diary, BRO D/EX 1415/25, 2 Jun. 1917.

[74] Hallam's means of accessing the countryside did change over time. After moving to Swindon he increasingly used a combination of train and walking to reach rural places of interest. As he got older he took buses and, at least once, a coach tour. In his retirement his elder daughters or their husbands took him on rural car trips.

[75] Hallam Diary, BRO D/EX 1415/1, 18 Sep. 1886.

[76] See also Hallam Diary, BRO D/EX 1415/2, 25 Jun. 1897: 'Went home – I quite enjoyed the walk from Wantage Road.'

disappointment, his verdict was 'as the walk was enjoyable I reckon the fare paid for that'.[77]

Social Amenity

One of the primary affordances of the countryside for Hallam was that it provided a space for conducting relationships. He walked frequently with friends, especially in his youth. Walking and, to a lesser extent, cycling, riding in a trap and rowing, gave opportunities to talk, do things together and share experiences. Although he was not a teetotaller, Hallam rarely drank and in this respect walks may have been a substitute for the pub. It is difficult to know what subjects were discussed on these occasions. With his Lockinge friends the Whittle brothers, there may not have been much talk: Hallam's accounts of their walks suggest the focus was on exploration, finding birds' nests, gathering berries and the like. With other friends, there was probably more conversation. When he went for a walk 'round Whittles, Kitford and etc' with Brown, politics doubtless featured largely.[78] Similarly, it seems likely that the vexed question of where he should live was the main topic on (and may even have occasioned) the long walk he took round Maida Vale and Willesden with 'A. T.'; shortly after returning, Hallam gave his landlord notice.[79]

The crucial role that walks played in the formation and development of Hallam's relationships is apparent in many respects. Indeed, it would be no exaggeration to say that, at least in his younger days, walking was the main vector of his friendships. For example, between 4 and 7 April 1890, while he was at home over Easter, he went walking with the Whittles every day. After he met Sophie in 1891, most of his walks were with her, initially sometimes accompanied by her friend Rhoda. A prominent feature of these walks was gathering berries and mushrooms.[80] Here again, an ostensibly practical activity also offered more subtle rewards: companionship, shared labour, seeking and finding and perhaps a sense of nature's bounty, as on 22 September 1894 when he and Sophie found 'such a quantity of blackberries' on the riverbank near Padworth.[81] Reaching the countryside on foot from Swindon took more determination but walks to outlying villages like Rodbourne, Moredon, Stratton and Chisledon remained a pivotal social mode. He also went on cycle rides with his friend Austin, as on 12 September 1891, when they cycled to Marlborough. Hallam, still a novice, found it hard work: 'never sweat so in

[77] Hallam Diary, BRO D/EX 1415/2, 24 Apr. 1897.
[78] Hallam Diaries, BRO D/EX 1415/1A, 21 Jul. 1889.
[79] Hallam Diaries, BRO D/EX 1415/2, 15 Mar. 1891.
[80] Hallam Diaries, BRO D/EX 1415/1, 23 Jul. 1886 and 1415/2, 13 Jul. 1891.
[81] Hallam Diaries, BRO D/EX 1415/1, 23 Jul. 1886; 1415/2, 13 Jul. 1891 and 22 Sep. 1894.

all my life'. Undeterred, the two rode to Wootton Bassett three days afterwards and later that autumn to Aldbourne.[82]

The countryside was never more valuable to Hallam as a space for developing relationships than when he was courting Sophie. Again, this was partly due to the lack of alternatives. It seems unlikely that the family home was large enough to sit comfortably and talk in, and even if it had been it would not have offered the young couple much privacy. Nor did Lockinge provide much in the way of covered public spaces where Hallam and Sophie could be together. Reading rooms were often restricted to men, although it is unclear whether this was so in Lockinge, few respectable women wanted to be seen in a pub, and there was of course no cinema, music hall or assembly rooms.[83] It was not only for want of anywhere better that Hallam and Sophie chose to spend so much time outdoors, however. As when he walked up on the Downs with the Whittles, there is no mistaking the exhilarating sense of freedom and shared experience Hallam and Sophie gained from their walks together. Indeed, they went out on foot together almost whenever they could during their courtship. The two first spoke on 4 May 1891 and had already begun to walk out before Hallam went back to Swindon on 26 May. The day before, Hallam noted in his diary:

> A miserable wet day as could be which made me very wild as I had been looking forward to a walk with S[ophie] and my last Sunday too.[84]

However, he went back to Lockinge whenever he could at weekends and on 13 June walked down to Ardington with Sophie and Rhoda. He then took them for a row, staying out with Sophie until 9.30. The next day he went for a walk with Sophie in the morning, then took the two young women rowing again. Sophie accompanied him part of the way to Wantage Road on his way back. He took his holiday that year in Lockinge, arriving on 9 July in the evening and going straight out for a walk with Sophie. He went walking with her again on the 11th and on the 12th 'went up on the downs with her for 3 hours, and I asked her if I might give her an engagement ring and she said yes'. The next day he went mushrooming with Sophie and Rhoda, and on the 16th in the evening again went out for a walk with Sophie, as he did on the 17th and on the 19th (twice). Sometimes Hallam went round to have tea with Sophie, and he caught glimpses of her at church, but apart from this walks were really the only way he saw her. Often when he came home to Lockinge at weekends during this period, he and Sophie would take two or more walks a day. For example on 26 September he went for a walk with her after tea and then again from 9 till 10.

---

[82] Hallam Diaries, BRO D/EX 1415/2, 14 Jun., 12 and 15 Sep. and 31 Oct. 1891; 6 Nov. 1892.

[83] David Beckingham, 'Gender, Space, and Drunkenness: Liverpool's Licensed Premises, 1860–1914', *Annals of the Association of American Geographers* 102 (2012), 647–66, at 649.

[84] Hallam Diaries, BRO D/EX 1415/2, 25 May 1891.

The following day they went out for a walk until church, then again afterwards, and she accompanied Hallam part of the way to Wantage Road. Similarly he went out twice with her on Saturday, 17 October, and twice again the next day; including a long afternoon walk up to 'the folly' and back. They were prepared to brave winter and bad weather. On 5 December, although it was 'very wet going up from [the] station', they went out twice and the next day went on a long walk to the local landmark Scutchamer Knob, a prehistoric barrow high up on the Downs.[85] By this time they had evidently settled into a routine of going out for long walks together:

> At 2 Sophie came out and we went on our usual walk up on the Downs . . .
> Got back at 5. After church went out together again for a while and also at
> 9 for the last night.[86]

It cannot have been an accident that Sophie came from Lockinge or that the surrounding landscape was the setting for so much of Hallam's courtship of her. He felt this to be his countryside and walking it with her brought together two things that he loved.

Walking also played an important role in Hallam's family life after his marriage, allowing him to teach his children about nature and to pursue his varied rural interests. A favourite expedition was across the fields to Westlecote:

> [A]fter tea we went out along by Westlecote and sat on the grass an hour.
> I went into that lime kiln where Passmore . . . discovered his Roman villa
> and found 13 good fossils. I also notice the sand martins had been building
> in great numbers in the face of the quarry.[87]

He showed these sand martin holes to his children on another expedition to Westlecote on 16 August the same year.

Hallam's interests chimed well with the 'nature study' the children were taught at school. On Sunday, 10 July 1906, the whole family went out for a 'delightful nature study ramble, the children said, across Wroughton fields'. The next evening Hallam mounted a dragonfly for the children to take to their school museum.[88] Sophie also took the children out for walks, sometimes with friends' children. After the children had left home Hallam and Sophie continued to go on walks with each other, often across the fields to Wroughton or up to Kings Hill. After Sophie became wheelchair-bound their walks were necessarily shorter and the rustic but local Ladder Lane became a favourite.

In 1931 Marjorie and her husband, Bob Manning, bought a Morris Minor. Thereafter Bob sometimes took Hallam out on car trips through the countryside.

[85] Hallam Diaries, BRO D/EX 1415/2, passim.
[86] Hallam Diaries, BRO D/EX 1415/2, 24 Jan. 1892.
[87] Hallam Diaries, BRO D/EX 1415/5, 13 Jul. 1902.
[88] Hallam Diaries, BRO D/EX 1415/10, 10 and 11 Jun. 1906.

The first such trip was to Wanborough and back, on 12 June that year.[89] The Mannings' car became particularly valuable to the Hallams after Sophie lost the use of her legs. On 17 July 1945, for example, Marjorie took Sophie round Broad Hinton and Wootton Bassett in the car while Hallam stayed at home.[90]

Aesthetic and Intellectual Rewards

The countryside offered a rich array of social affordances to Hallam. Despite an emotional and expressive restraint typical of many working-class diarists, however, he was also sensitive to its beauty. He responded strongly to trees, especially when in blossom or just coming into leaf:

> A beautiful day again and the trees beautiful with foliage. The loveliest bit of green leaf is along by St Mark's Church, when the limes are just out, looking a delicate green, as they do just now.[91]

Water often pleased him, contributing to a calm, contemplative mood:

> The village [Ashton Keynes] is certainly pretty, with the water and bridges adding to the charm . . . [92]

> This evening as we are not on overtime I had a ride to Lyddington and walked up on to the Castle where we had a lay down enjoying the fresh air. It was beautiful up there. Coate Reservoir lay under the sun shining like a sheet of glass.[93]

As this suggests, Hallam enjoyed views and often sought them out:

> This morning walked to Uphill . . . We went across to the tower close by and ascended it to have the view.[94]

> Hudson and his daughter came up to tea and supper. It was wonderfully clear in the early evening so much so that Hudson said he thought we must be able to see Malvern Hills and he and I went specially along by the Hospital to see but we could not. He has seen them 3 or 4 times in 30 years.[95]

Often however his appreciation of the rural landscape was general and encompassing rather than focused on a specific element:

---

[89] Hallam Diaries, BRO D/EX 1415/35, 12 Jun. 1931.
[90] Hallam Diaries, BRO D/EX 1415/54, 17 Jul. 1945.
[91] Hallam Diaries, BRO D/EX 1415/5, 26 May 1902, BRO D/EX 1415/3, 20 Apr. 1900, BRO D/EX 1415/6, 4 May 1903, BRO D/EX 1415/30, 15 May 1925, BRO D/EX 1415/32, 19 and 30 May 1928, BRO D/EX 1415/59, 28 Aug. 1948.
[92] Hallam Diaries, BRO D/EX 1415/5, 21 Jun. 1902.
[93] Hallam Diaries, BRO D/EX 1415/2, 8 Jun. 1892. See also ibid., 30 Apr. 1892.
[94] Hallam Diaries, BRO D/EX 1415/41, 27 Aug. 1935.
[95] Hallam Diaries, BRO D/EX 1415/5, 29 Jun. 1902.

The country looks perfect.[96]

This afternoon D[orothy], Bob [son-in-law] and Zoe [granddaughter] came to tea then we all went for a walk across Westlecote Fields. Beautiful out in the county [sic] and met hardly a soul.[97]

While Lockinge and its countryside held unique meaning for him, his apprehension of beauty in rural landscapes was not dependent on personal identification with them:

Padworth is such a nice country better than Lockinge.[98]

I had a most silly dream last night. I dreamt I and my father and our children went to see some Eskimo relations ... the scenery in Greenland was beautiful and we stayed up late there and ... were just encamping [for the night] when I woke up and found myself in bed to my great relief.[99]

He was especially open to aesthetic impressions when on excursions or holiday. On such occasions his diary can convey a tangible sense of escape from the drabness of Swindon into a brighter world:

Day off from work. Went to Longleat by charabanc with wife and Field Club. I had never been beyond Beckhampton so all new country. Scenery quite fine beyond Devizes – almost like Devon some of the lanes. At Potterne a grand old ½ timber house.[100]

Arriving at Longleat, Hallam was entranced with the gardens and the superb view of the house. Tea was followed by a walk round the lake which was set in 'a wooded glade full of the scent of azalea and the colour of the rhododendrons'. In wrapping up his account of this memorable day, Hallam laid aside his wonted scepticism:

[W]e had had a perfect day. Not a cloud all day and if we get over every other difficulty in life like this one – not much to grumble about.[101]

Hallam's aesthetic sensibility was catholic with regard to rural landscape, encompassing views, hills, fields, streams, trees and many other elements. The distinction between the natural and the constructed meant little to him. What mattered was whether the object of his gaze harmonized with his sense of what properly belonged to a traditional, organically developing countryside, of which villages and market towns were part:

Today went to Malmesbury and saw the grand old abbey. How I should like to have seen it in its splendour and I thought how is it, that God to whose praise and glory it was built, how is it he suffered it to be destroyed

---

[96] Hallam Diaries, BRO D/EX 1415/35, 6 Jun. 1931.
[97] Hallam Diaries, BRO D/EX 1415/32, 13 May 1928.
[98] Hallam Diaries, BRO D/EX 1415/2, 22 Sep. 1894.
[99] Hallam Diaries, BRO D/EX 1415/12, 29 Apr. 1907.
[100] Hallam Diaries, BRO D/EX 1415/30, 6 Jun. 1925.
[101] Ibid.

so. The doorway was grand on the south side simply splendid. Also the
Norman arches [here Hallam drew a little sketch of intersecting arches]
and arcades. Plenty of jackdaws about it.[102]

Up to Kewstoke – a most interesting little church with a very fine Norman
doorway on S and an equally fine stone pulpit.[103]

Other constructed elements of the landscape that elicited Hallam's approba-
tion included hill forts (Liddington, Worlebury), chalk figures (Uffington,
Hackpen), parks and landscape gardens (Swindon's Town Gardens, Grove
Park in Weston-super-Mare, Corsham Court), country houses (Ufton Court,
Longleat), cottages (Potterne, Kintbury Cross), barns (Great Coxwell), bridges
(Ashton Keynes) and reservoirs (Coate).

He also drew much intellectual sustenance from the countryside, finding
a rich diversity of interests and subjects to study in it: everything from insects
to painting. 'Whoever thought there was so much in blackbeetles', he mused on
finishing Fabre's book on the subject.[104] He was passionate about collecting
and recording almost everything to do with the rural past: fossils and flints,
memorial and bell inscriptions, the genealogies of Berkshire landed families
and the country houses with which they were associated. He observed and
thought carefully about changing agricultural practices and the making of the
Berkshire landscape – in some respects he was a landscape historian ahead of
his time. He deepened his knowledge of these subjects through extensive
reading, which he kept up throughout his adult life.[105] His rural interests
also provided the subject-matter for his exchanges with scholars like
Ditchfield and Charles Edward Keyser, Ditchfield's precursor as president of
the Berkshire Archaeological Society.[106]

Existential Landscapes

As well as offering social, aesthetic and intellectual rewards, the countryside
fulfilled what might be described as existential needs for Hallam. Most obviously, it provided relief from the anxieties, tedium and misery associated with
work, to which it was in many respects the antithesis. Here there was no one to
tell Hallam what to do, no threats, no dangerous, noisy machinery and no
hordes of people unsympathetic to his values and background. It is interesting
that, especially in his early days at Swindon, he often went on long trips taking

---

[102] Hallam Diaries, BRO D/EX 1415/2, 23 Apr. 1892.
[103] Hallam Diaries, BRO D/EX 1415/41, 28 Aug. 1935.
[104] He probably read the translation by Margaret Roberts, published by Macmillan the
previous year: Jean-Henri Fabre and E. Merrifield, *Insect Life: Souvenirs of a Naturalist*
(London, 1901).
[105] Hallam Diaries, BRO D/EX 1415/18, 11 May 1911. See also D/EX 1415/20 25 Aug. 1912,
D/EX 1415/30 12 Feb. 1925, D/EX 1415/48 30 Jun. 1942 and D/EX 1415/59 14 Aug. 1948.
[106] See, for example, Hallam Diaries, BRO D/EX 1415/28, 3 Dec. 1921.

him far out into the surrounding countryside: to Malmesbury, Marlborough, Hungerford, Aldbourne or Avebury, and of course to Lockinge. He very rarely went to large towns although Reading, Oxford and even London were all comparatively accessible.

Freedom

Hallam seems to have had a preference for walking or cycling through downland. Lockinge itself lay below the downs and walking to the north, east or west would have taken Hallam through the Vale of the White Horse so it is significant that when in Lockinge he almost always chose to go 'up on the downs'. Many of these walks took him to conspicuous viewpoints such as White Horse Hill, Churn Hill or Scutchamer Knob. Even when in Swindon, several miles from the hills, Hallam sought out downland. In the first three months after buying his new bicycle, for example, he went on five long cycle rides, four of which took him up onto the Downs. It was harder to reach the hills on foot from Swindon but Bassett Down was within striking distance and a favourite destination. Walks or rides out to the downs and other hills tended to elicit more enthusiastic comment in the diary: a 'fine ride' from Wroughton to Avebury, Marlborough, Ogbourne, Coate and back to Swindon; 'beautiful' up by Liddington Castle; 'we walked up on top of Hillsborough a beautiful elevation'.[107] Part of the appeal of hills and downs may have been that, consciously or otherwise, they reminded him of his 'own' country round Lockinge, yet the diaries also convey a sense of freedom and exhilaration in being lifted up above the world amidst the fresh air and far-ranging views. The contrast with flat, grimy, built-up Swindon again seems relevant here.

Exploration and Discovery

If the countryside, or aspects of it, could offer freedom, it could also offer scope for exploration and discovery. This is especially apparent in Hallam's compelling accounts of the long expeditions he undertook through the Lockinge countryside in his youth, usually accompanied by one or more friends. What comes through is a vivid sense of immersion in a profoundly known landscape – known through work, exploration, long familiarity and a de facto sense of ownership. Walking up and down, this way and that, across this landscape over many years, Hallam made it his own. Seemingly ordinary places then acquired a meaning and resonance – a luminosity – exceeding their ostensible significance. This can only be indicated by quotation *in extenso*. Two examples must suffice. The first is an expedition on 5 April 1890, while Hallam was 'at home' on a week's vacation:

> Got up at 7. After breakfast I and Lex Whittle went up to Porter's Farm – Betterton for the butter. I had not been up there I think for years, not since

---

[107] Hallam Diaries, BRO D/EX 1415/2, 8 Jun. 1892.

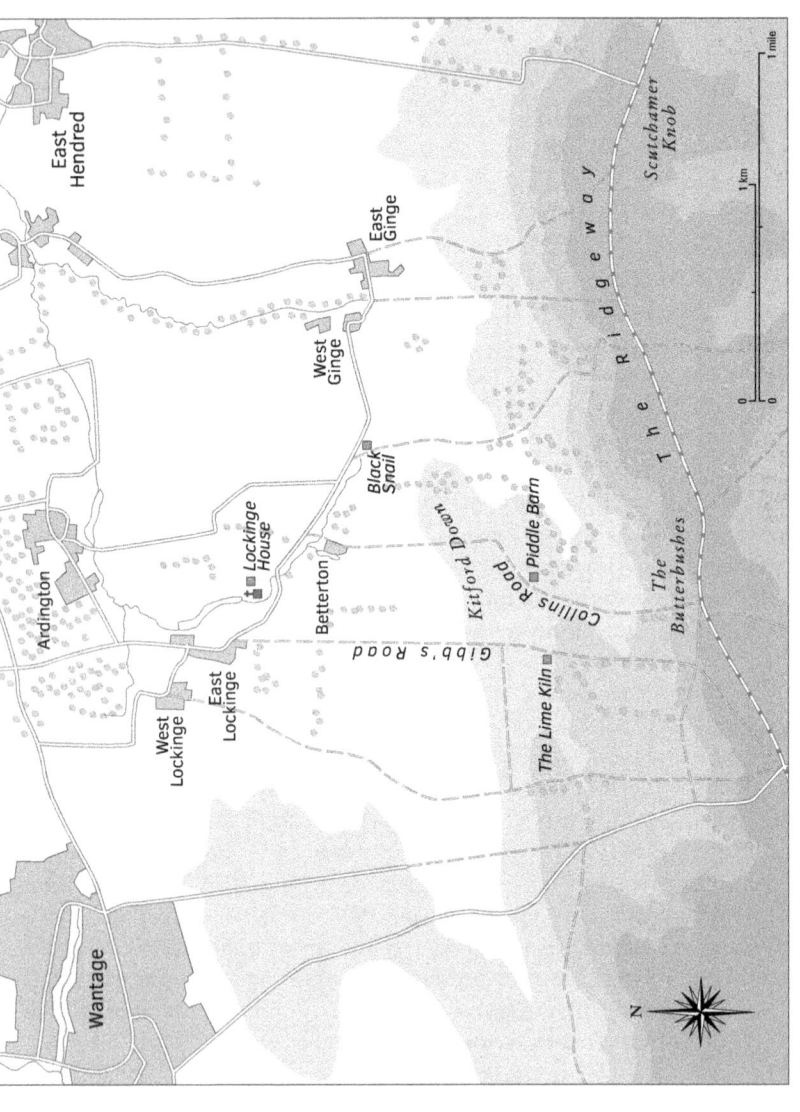

Figure 3.2 The Lockinge countryside

I was a school boy and fetched it regularly. We had a few shots at some birds going up with L's revolver but did not kill any. [inserted:] I am very glad. Coming back through the 'Close' we looked for duck's nests but found none. Up at Collins (where L went for eggs) we noticed the ruinous structure at Betterton House. This is bought now by Lord Wantage and so another old Berkshire family is wiped out. The Collin's [sic] have lived here now for 380 years. A brass plate records their entry here in the reign of Henry VII. The brass is in the house. I afterwards went up to Mrs C and got a sitting of Eggs and took up the Lodge to sit a hen on. After dinner (as we had leave) L., V. and I went all up Collin's Close. Up the Lower Close we saw several sportive trouts ... Further up we found a blackbird's nest with 4 eggs. In that part of the Close which is opposite Collin's Kitchen Garden the vegetation is very rank and here I should think a likely place to view a Jack O Lantern [sic]. It is very marshy and in places impenetrable. If we had had our likenesses taken here, any one at London would have thought we were out in the jungle. A water rat or two plunged in from the side we were on and took refuge on the opposite bank in the various holes with which they have honeycombed the bank. The smell from all this rank vegetation is very offensive. In fact we could quite seem to taste it as we breathed. Various birds the Jenny Wren, Golden Crested Wren, Long Tailed Tit and others chirruped about us. In an openish space out in the Sun, we suddenly came onto 4 snakes basking. They all wriggled off and one taking to the water quickly swam further up the stream. We kept on up the right hand bank of the stream till we came to Upper Betterton Farm where the first springs of all bubble out of the Chalk Marl. Just up here are 4 houses which stand in a hollow which is always known as Black Snail. Up here we had a bit of a hunt after a wren. We then walked back by the opposite side of the stream. All the upper part is cultivated with water cresses, a man named Aldworth makes his living at it. He lives at Hendred. Coming back, just by Betterton Pillars, down the road, is a tree planted by HRH Princess Louise 1880. It looks very weakly though and has never grown any I think. Straight down this close to the horse trough was the walk and drive to Betterton. It has every appearance of an ancient avenue ... After tea we had a walk down to the bottom of the avenue and back as it is best to get as much fresh air as possible now.

This passage reveals a great deal about the nature and sources of Hallam's ruralism. In the first place, it is almost entirely written in the first person plural. The route Hallam and the Whittles took, the wildlife they saw, even the smells they smelt, are all presented as collective experiences. Perhaps this relates to the claims scholars such as Regina Gagnier have made about the intersubjectivity of working-class identities, although in other respects Hallam's was very much an individual, even isolated, consciousness.[108] Secondly, Hallam's account

[108] R. Gagnier, *Subjectivities: A History of Self-Representation in Britain, 1832–1920* (Oxford, 1991).

shows that his experience of the countryside took place on at least three levels: the directly experienced present, recollection of childhood and knowledge of history. Each of these three levels is vividly present to him. The first comes through in the immediacy with which the events of the day are rendered: the offensive smell, the four snakes wriggling off. The second is especially apparent in connection with the visit to Betterton for the butter: 'I had not been up there I think for years, not since I was a school boy and fetched it regularly.' There is a sense here of a place or practice which is known deeply and has become part of the texture of Hallam's life because it has been visited or done *repeatedly*. The third level of meaning is the historical awareness:

> Up at Collins (where L went for eggs) we noticed the ruinous structure at Betterton House. This is bought now by Lord Wantage and so another old Berkshire family is wiped out. The Collin's [*sic*] have lived here now for 380 years. A brass plate records their entry here in the reign of Henry VII. The brass is in the house.[109]

Here the three levels are interwoven: Hallam and Lex notice the ruin on their walk, which gives rise to the observation that Lord Wantage has now bought it, which in turn calls to Hallam's mind that a brass plate recalling the antiquity of the connection between the Collins family and Betterton is located in the house. Presumably Hallam knows this because he saw it on at least one occasion when he came to fetch butter in his childhood. So the public history is part of Hallam's personal life and the severing of the connection between Collins and Betterton severs him from his own past too.

The passage also sheds light on Hallam's attitude to animals. Donna Landry has argued that hunting was the principal paradigm through which pre-modern attitudes to wild animals was filtered. Furthermore, Landry suggests, working people, especially in the countryside, continued to relate to wildlife principally in this way long after the Romantics had developed a new, more sentimental relationship to animals.[110] As someone who grew up among farm labourers and craftsmen, the son of an estate worker, Hallam might be expected to manifest the older sensibility. To a certain extent he does: he and Lex, later joined by Lex's brother Victor, shoot at some birds, search for duck's nests, notice several 'sportive' trout, and have 'a bit of a hunt after a wren'. This was hardly serious hunting, however: they did not catch, still less kill, any of the animals encountered on their walk. The water rats (probably water voles), golden-crested wren, long-tailed tit and four snakes seem to have been observed as interesting natural phenomena rather than prey. Hallam's inter-polation that he is 'very glad' he did not succeed in killing any birds with Lex's revolver is interesting in this connection. It is unclear what kind of birds they

---

[109] Hallam Diaries, BRO D/EX 1415/1A, 5 Apr. 1890.
[110] Landry, *The Invention of the Countryside*, 80–6.

shot at – if game birds then Hallam's gladness might have been on the grounds that he would have been guilty of poaching from his patron Lord Wantage had he succeeded in killing them. However, it seems unlikely that Hallam and Lex would have risked poaching in broad daylight so close to Lockinge House. A more probable explanation is that he did not want to kill the birds. Indeed, for a countryman Hallam makes strikingly few references to killing animals in his diaries. Although a keen fisherman in his youth, he had little interest in hunting or shooting and does not seem to have owned a gun.[111] Kindness to animals was a telling virtue in his eyes: the principal good quality he attributed to his father in the informal diary-entry obituary he wrote for him was that he was 'one of the most humane of men to animals and human beings'.[112] On the other hand, Hallam was not sentimental about animals and never kept a pet.

Returning to the Collins' Close account, it is worth underlining the remarkable vividness with which Hallam reprises his sensory experience of the countryside. He not only apprehends the landscape visually but smells and even tastes the rank vegetation and hears the little birds chirruping. This full absorption transports Hallam far away from the everyday urban world he normally resided in at this stage of his life. The scrub he ventures into is 'very marshy and in places impenetrable', a place where mysterious phenomena such as the Jack O' Lantern (*ignis fatuus*) might be expected, and as wild as the jungle. The irony here is that this is literally Hallam's home turf and it is his very familiarity with it that allows him to discover in it so untamed a space.

In the same passage we see Hallam the landscape historian, noting that Upper Betterton Farm is sited where the first springs bubble out of the chalk marl; Hallam the folklorist, recording that the hollow where the four houses stand is always known as Black Snail; Hallam the observer of rural industries, describing the cultivation of watercress, and Hallam the explorer, venturing into almost impenetrable thickets and down little-known paths.

The second passage worth quoting at length is for 15 July 1902. Again Hallam was at Lockinge:

> This morning I went a drive to Wantage and after getting back I had a walk up in the cemetery. Bless me, what a lot is being buried there in these few years and to think I knew all of them well, some there not so old as I am. After dinner I went up on the Downs. I went first across Kitford to the Pond which is going to rack and ruin. Here some splendid specimens of blue dragonflies, the males greatly predominating. I then went on up Gibbs' Road, as we called it years ago. The old ashen tree is still standing but in a very rotten state all its nourishment is through its bark for all the

[111] An exception that perhaps proves the rule: 'I got up at 7.30 and killed a stray cat that had been prowling about here all day yesterday and would come back after I had carried it outside about a dozen times.' He had evidently gone to some lengths to avoid killing the cat.

[112] Hallam Diaries, BRO D/EX 1415/24, 18 Dec. 1916.

interior has been rotting away and to make it worse some mischievous devils have lit a fire in it. This tree the oldest men have told me was a landmark ever since they remember. The locality for a 100 years has been known as 'Up by Ashen Tree'. When I got to the Lime Kiln I went down into it to get some coprolites for I never met with such fine specimens as are to be found here. I stayed some time talking to the lime burner, who calls these things 'Thunderbolts'. [Digression about old Dick Miles the previous lime burner]. Then up onto the Downs as far as the Ridgeway. I spent about an hour in a chalk pit looking for fossils but found none . . . I came back down Collins road, the Butterbushes, and the Jew's Harp and past Piddle Barn. In all this district where the Downs' land stretch into the villages the farms for centuries have been laid out in long narrow strips running from north to south. This plan was so as to give each farmer a fair share of the down land which is no good but for sheep feeding. Each farmer then dug chalk up on the hills, and made a road from his farmstead in the villages, up on to the downs so there still exist a great number of chalk roads all running parallel. In Lockinge alone there were Whitefield's Road, Collins' Road, Gibbs Road and Brown's Road. These roads cross a dip in the Downs and here each farmer made himself a barn and cattle shelter and cart house and also dug a dew pond to catch water so when on the top of the downs you can see all along a row of farm buildings each in the same position.[113]

Here we have a similar mix of personal retrospect, observation of nature, folklore and landscape history, but in this case Hallam is alone, which perhaps encourages more extended reflection. What comes through particularly clearly in this second passage is that the retrospect and history are the counterpart of an acute sensitivity to change and to the loss of cherished things. 'Bless me, what a lot is being buried there in these few years and to think I knew all of them well.' Whether Hallam was conscious of it or not, something of the feeling his visit to the cemetery induced seems to have carried through into his subsequent walk, expressing itself initially in a brooding preoccupation with change and decay – the pond going to rack and ruin, the old ashen tree very rotten – and eliciting one of his most characteristic and deep-seated responses, his determination to preserve the past by recording it. From this point of view, it is the details that matter, hence the predominantly antiquarian turn of his interest in the past. Conversely, there is little more reprehensible than endangering the link between past and present, which is why the men who lit the fire in the tree are 'mischievous devils'.

A striking feature of the two quoted passages, especially the second, is their naming of places, which has an almost incantatory quality: Collins' Close, Black Snail, Betterton Pillars, Kitford, Up by Ashen Tree, the Lime Kiln, the Butterbushes, the Jew's Harp, Piddle Barn and then the roads: Whitefield's, Collins', Gibbs and Brown's. There is magic in naming, and here Hallam seems

[113] Hallam Diaries, BRO D/EX 1415/5, 15 Jul. 1902.

not to be merely recording but invoking the co-ordinates of his world, wrapping them round him so as to express and confirm his identification with the Lockinge landscape.

Remembrance

Recording, remembering and restoring was central to Hallam's life and the place of the countryside within it. He was fascinated by rural customs and traditions, filling two notebooks with Berkshire folklore and recording details of Ardington Feast, the final Christmas performance of the Lockinge mummers, dancing round the maypole and beating the bounds in his *History of the Parish of East Lockinge, Berks.*[114] Field Club excursions provided him with rich material, which he often entered into the diary:

> We met our guides Mr Rogers and Mr Pearson and ... walked to Pagan Hill where I saw the only second May Pole I ever saw in my life. The other was at Aldermaston. This one is painted in blue and white bands and they were just digging it up as the bottom was got rotten. A little further along we saw the new one on tressles [sic] which is to be put up in its place. Next to Renwick where by the Pool Mr Pearson told us of the mock mayor festivities then up through Runwick Woods to the Tumulus and a long walk through the trees to the Castle Bungalow; on the way he showed us the Butter Beech, the king of the Forest under which the price of butter was regulated by the farmers of this district. After tea we climbed Painswick Beacon and had a lecture on its history and next walked to Painswick and was fortunate to hear there beautiful bells ringing in peal – known all over the world. Also saw the yew trees which are said to number 99 and the 100 will never grow.[115]

The most striking expression of Hallam's determination that the thread of continuity between past and present should not be broken was his commitment, even as a young man, to copying inscriptions. This need not have been distinctively rural, but in his case it largely was. He began, as ever, with Lockinge:

> Wrote to George and copied down some inscriptions from the Churchyard and also in the Church.[116]

Thereafter he invested much time and effort to transcribing Berkshire churchyard inscriptions. At Uffington, for example, he copied down ninety-eight inscriptions on his second visit but noted that 'a lot more remains to be done'.[117] Partly because of his loyalty to Berkshire and partly for practical

---

[114] Berkshire sayings, folklore and dialect words BRO D/EX 1415/67; Further examples of Berkshire beliefs, BRO D/EX 1415/68; *History of the Parish of East Lockinge, Berks* (1900). See also Havinden, *Estate Villages Revisited*, 102–3.

[115] Hallam Diaries, BRO D/EX 1415/18, 3 Jun. 1911.

[116] Hallam Diaries, BRO D/EX 1415/2, 18 May 1891.

[117] Among numerous other references to the transcription of Berkshire churchyard inscriptions in the diaries see D/EX 1415/5, 19 May 1902; D/EX 1415/20, 3 and 16 Aug. 1912; D/

reasons, Hallam did not copy inscriptions when outside his native county, but he felt strongly that someone should:

> These inscriptions [at Lydiard Tregoze] should be copied down while they are still legible but I do not feel sufficiently interested in Wiltshire to take the job on.[118]

Few things roused his ire more than to see inscriptions put at risk:

> I was disgusted to see in the churchyard several white marble and other slabs which had been taken down out of the old church and now all but obliterated by the weather.[119]

Unlike Cresswell, as well as recording inscriptions, Hallam also cut them:

> I went with F Whittle on to [Lockinge] Church Tower where I cut my name. Mine is there now about 18 times. I also cut my brother George's there.[120]

Inscriptions, even in a non-funerary context, carry strong connotations of memorialization and it is interesting that Hallam cut George's name as well as his own. A second striking association between inscriptions and the memory of someone Hallam loved occurs in the diary entry for 19 May 1902:

> I went down to Ardington to see Lord Wantage's grave as I had not seen it yet. It is marked by a plain oak cross and as I stood at the foot of his grave, I could not but take off my cap and pray: 'Jesu, pitying Saviour Blest/Grant him Thy Eternal Rest.'
> Copied down several inscriptions before leaving.[121]

Over and above his general concern with historical continuity, Hallam's dedication to recording grave inscriptions surely relates to a fear of mortality or, perhaps more accurately, a determined effort to keep it at bay.[122] Whether the mortality in question was his own is less clear. The eighteen-odd cuttings of his name might suggest it was and of course diary writing is also (among other things) a form of self-memorialization. Despite serious accidents at work and the deaths of many of those closest to him, however, Hallam's diaries do not suggest an unusual preoccupation with his own mortality.

EX 1415/26, 16 Aug. 1919; D/EX 1415/28, 24 Jun. 1922; D/EX 1415/37, 7 Mar. 1933; D/ EX 1415/45, 18 May 1939.

[118] Hallam Diaries, BRO D/EX 1415/5, 24 May 1902; see also BRO D/EX 1415/41, 27 Aug. 1935 (Uphill).

[119] Hallam Diaries, BRO D/EX 1415/15, 9 Jul. 1909.

[120] Hallam Diaries, BRO D/EX 1415/1, 22 Jul. 1886.

[121] Hallam Diaries, BRO D/EX 1415/5, 19 May 1902.

[122] Compare Schama's understanding of landscape as a consolation for mortality. Schama, *Landscape and Memory*, 15.

The far more urgent and pressing problem for him was his need to hold on to the people and things he loved, and his tragic awareness that he was ultimately powerless to do so.

Given his deep-seated need for continuity and exposure to loss, it is unsurprising that Hallam venerated those who restored the past. Above all this was true of the restoration of country houses, an act of piety that brought together his love of rural tradition with his gratitude to the aristocracy:

> This afternoon I had a treat for Miss Sharp invited me up to Ufton Court to tea and have a look over the House and I went all over it, the Hall is now restored and quite grand and the entrance porch all cleaned of its mucky paint and the timbers and door all of their natural black oak colour. Lucky it is to have had such a tenant.[123]

> ... we also went over Moor hall just outside Stroud a house built in 1682 by a descendent of Sir Thomas More ... Mr Pearson told us 10 years ago it was a ruin almost and would have fallen down by now but these people took it in hand and lovingly restored it and now it will last another 400 years.[124]

> [T]hen another treat – we went over the Manor House which Harold Brakespeare has rescued from decay and restored it beautifully ... a very enjoyable outing.[125]

Nature

Although the history, architecture and traditions of the countryside lay closer to his heart, Hallam always took an interest in wildlife. He observed mammals, birds, fish, reptiles and insects, noting, for example, on 3 August 1902 that he had caught the biggest tiger moth he had ever seen.[126] He read natural history books – 'rare and vanishing birds of England' and the like – ordered a pack of 'nature' playing cards, and was pleased when he saw a glow worm for the first time. He recorded unusual wildlife phenomena, such as the shooting of a white rook with pink eyes at Lockinge in 1902 and the abundance of sparrows in Swindon despite their decline elsewhere.[127] Bird calls and songs seem to have appealed to him especially: the croaking of a pair of ravens; two owls hooting to each other in the night 'somewhere over Kings Hill way'; a blackbird 'whistling like to burst himself' from the finial of a gable in Bath Road.[128]

---

[123] Hallam Diaries, BRO D/EX 1415/15, 7 Jul. 1909.

[124] Hallam Diaries, BRO D/EX 1415/18, 3 Jun. 1911, Field Club trip to Stroud and Painswick.

[125] Hallam Diaries, BRO D/EX 1415/32, 19 May 1928, Field Club trip to Corsham.

[126] Hallam Diaries, BRO D/EX 1415/5, 3 Aug. 1902.

[127] Hallam Diaries, BRO D/EX 1415/5, 19 May 1902, BRO D/EX 1415/10, 10 Jun. 1906.

[128] Hallam Diaries, BRO D/EX 1415/25, 9 Jul. 1919, 1415/30, 5 Jun. 1925, 1415/35, 20 Jun. 1931.

Above all, however, Hallam cherished the cuckoo, habitually recording when he heard its call and where it appeared to be coming from:

> I heard the cuckoo this morning at 5.30 . . . and also again at 8.30 . . . It was over in King's Hill.[129]

He and Sophie often went for walks on purpose to hear the cuckoo, especially when it had so far eluded them that year.[130] Kings Hill and Ladder Lane were the most promising nearby locations, but it was better if possible to go further out into the countryside, perhaps to Wroughton fields or along the canal, where Hallam heard and saw no fewer than four pairs on 22 June 1902.[131] Sometimes hearing the cuckoo in the morning at home seems to have prompted them to go out in search of it again later, as on 28 May 1916:

> Up at 5 and heard the cuckoo while I was in our kitchen . . . [A]fter tea wife and I went for a walk round by the Old Mill Stream and Westlecote. Cuckoo on all the time.[132]

Listening for the cuckoo, especially for its first call, was by this time a well-established British tradition. That, however, is only to say it was available as a cultural practice; it does not explain why Hallam and his wife were among those who chose to adopt it. Nor does it explain the depth of feeling that they came to attach to hearing the cuckoo. One element was simply familiarity: listening for the cuckoo together over so many years gave it the status of a family tradition. This seems to have been even more important once Sophie became disabled: it was something they could still do together on terms of equality and it recalled happier times before she lost the use of her leg. There was more to it than that, however. The call of the cuckoo was an echo of the countryside, visiting them in their urban exile. It was surely for this reason that it particularly gladdened Hallam to hear it indoors – even when the walls of the urban prison seemed highest, the cuckoo's call could still reach him.[133] When, because of their advancing years and later Sophie's disability, they could no longer go so far out into the country, they could still walk down Ladder Lane and hope that the cuckoo would bring the countryside to them.[134]

The cuckoo represented nature's calendar as well as the sound of the countryside. One aspect of Hallam's alienation as an industrial worker was the artificial rhythm the factory enforced on him, symbolized by the loathsome

---

[129] Hallam Diaries, BRO D/EX 1415/5, 22 and 29 May 1902, BRO D/EX 1415/6, 19 May 1903, BRO D/EX 1415/30, 11 May 1925.

[130] Hallam Diaries, BRO D/EX 1415/30, 10 May 1935; Hallam Diaries, BRO D/EX 1415/18, 7 May 1911.

[131] Hallam Diaries, BRO D/EX 1415/5, 22 Jun. 1902.

[132] Hallam Diaries, BRO D/EX 1415/24, 28 May 1916.

[133] Hallam Diaries, BRO D/EX 1415/18, 23 May 1911.

[134] Hallam Diaries, BRO D/EX 1415/45, 30 May 1939, BRO D/EX 1415/48, 7 Jun. 1942.

hooter. He hated his subjection to works time and got up as late as he could, often having to run to work to avoid losing pay. It is hard to imagine a better example of the oppressive experiences Edward Thompson described in 'Time, Work-Discipline and Industrial Capitalism', the reservations of some scholars notwithstanding.[135] Given his preference for staying longer in bed when he wanted to, his pleasure in stretching out on the ground in the sunshine and the alternating pattern of energetic activity and 'thoro' lazy day[s]' he adopted when on holiday, it seems reasonable to assume that Hallam was by disposition and inclination more attuned to task-time than clock-time and that, left to himself, he would have adopted the less regular habits Thompson claims prevailed before the Industrial Revolution.[136] Part of the appeal of the cuckoo's call may have been that it signified this gentler, more natural ordering of time.

Home

Still more important to Hallam than the connection to nature was his powerful feeling about home. As in Cresswell's strikingly analogous case, this was quadripartite and concentric, although the elements involved and the weightings attached to them differed. For Hallam, Lockinge was at the core; arranged around it in circles of decreasing intensity were the Lockinge countryside, Berkshire and England. The first three played an active role in his everyday life but his national patriotism only manifested itself under special circumstances, such as when Britain was under military attack. On 24 September 1916, for example, he was 'overjoyed to see 2 Zepps had been fetched down' near Victoria Road in Swindon.[137] He mourned the death of King George V in 1936 and was dismayed at what he perceived as the electorate's ingratitude to Churchill in 1945.[138] But he was far from belligerent and showed no hostility to or prejudice against people from other countries. National patriotism contributed significantly to his home feeling but in a diffuse, mainly latent way.

A correlate of Hallam's home feeling was his more generalized orientation towards and identification with the countryside. This was especially apparent in his enduring dream of retiring to a cottage in the country (not, in his imagination, usually located specifically in Berkshire). He was an early example of the counter-urbanizing impulse, often regarded as a late twentieth-century phenomenon:

> Before tea I went up to Ufton Court with my wife's father. I always go up here, just once, whenever at Padworth, to see Ufton Court, as it takes my fancy so, and if I had money would be just the place I would live in ...

---

[135] Edward Thompson, 'Time, Work-Discipline, and Industrial Capitalism', *Past & Present*, 38 (1967), 56–97. Ingold, *The Perception of the Environment*, 323–38.
[136] Hallam Diaries, BRO D/EX 1415/10, 10 Jun. 1906.
[137] Hallam Diaries, BRO D/EX 1415/24, 24 Sep. 1916.
[138] Hallam Diaries, BRO D/EX 1415/41, 20 Jan. 1936.

> Coming back I noticed Inkpen Beacon, and Kintbury X and an old Tudor house just by it, that would suit me.[139]

The difficulty, of course, was that he did not have that kind of money. But something more modest might not be out of reach:

> If it please God to give me health and strength and work for another 12 years I shall begin to think of retiring if I can get my superannuation from the ASE and get hold of a cheap old country cottage with a good garden.[140]

Hallam's ruralist sensibilities and interests formed a mutually supporting pattern. His yearning for rural retirement was fuelled by accounts in *Country Life*, which he read in the Swindon Mechanics Institute, of the restoration of dilapidated old cottages into 'nice residence[s]', and by other prompts that signified rurality for him such as fine weather and the cuckoo's call:

> I heard the cuckoo this morning when I was getting up. I was so pleased the first time Ive [sic] heard him this year. A most glorious day today. It makes me long to be living in an old cottage in the country.[141]

This powerful and persistent vision of an idyllic life in the country, free of work, grime and Swindon, has a spiritual quality, dreamlike and otherworldly, and may indeed have owed something to religion as well as to Lockinge and childhood. Certainly Eden, Lockinge, gardens, purity and beauty were bound up in his mind:

> The hottest day I reckon we have had since the 10th of July last year when I had that jaunt up to Lockinge. I thought it would be or it was like a morning in the Garden of Eden when a thick mist went up and watered the garden. It was as wet as a rain.[142]

Sophie saw things rather differently:

> [On a visit to wife's niece, Hatfield Peverell] This house is a terrible shanty. Only lath and plaster and timber beyond all repair . . . My wife said to me the first night 'I should think this will cure you of your damned silly idea of buying an old house in the country, to retire to, when you have finished work.'[143]

Hallam remained quite impervious to this wifely scepticism. Yet he never did retire to his cottage in the country, even after Sophie's death. Why must be a matter of speculation, but perhaps he was caught in one of the

[139] Hallam Diaries, BRO D/EX 1415/5, 27 Jul. 1902.
[140] Hallam Diaries, BRO D/EX 1415/18, 29 May 1911. However, the rapid post-1945 increase in rural property prices made Hallam's dream less affordable. Hallam Diaries, BRO D/EX 1415/54, 24 Jul. 1945.
[141] Hallam Diaries, BRO D/EX 1415/25, 26 Jan. 1917, D/EX 1415/26, 28 and 29 Aug. 1919. See also Hallam Diaries, BRO D/EX 1415/31, 2 and 14 Jan. 1927.
[142] Hallam Diaries, BRO D/EX 1415/30, 14 May 1925.
[143] Hallam Diaries, BRO D/EX 1415/30, 20 Sep. 1924.

characteristic traps of the modern urban–rural relationship. There were deeply felt needs that urban life, as then constituted, failed to fulfil, yet he was too thoroughly enmeshed in it to break out. The comfortable, convenient home, the easy access to the reading room, shops, medical care and other facilities and, above all, the sheer familiarity stood in his way. Not until the late twentieth century did cars and mains utilities reduce the opportunity cost of rural life.

Re-evaluating Swindon

Hallam's relationship to Swindon was also changing, however. In his younger days he had disliked the town almost as much as the Works: it might be where he lived, but it was not home. Yet 'home' is a complex, mutable congeries of ideas and feelings. For Hallam, it signified above all the place where his feelings were centred, where his deepest attachments were located, in the present and in his recollection of them. But willy-nilly, the longer he lived in Swindon, the more the centre of gravity of his feelings shifted from Lockinge to Swindon. This was perhaps especially so after Lord Wantage and his father died. But the crucial vector was surely Sophie, who was deeply associated with both Lockinge and Swindon. He first met her in Lockinge; she had worked for Lord Wantage; and he courted her on countless walks this way and that over his Lockinge 'country'. Yet it was in Swindon that they made their home, living together in 60 Kent Road for forty-nine years. This was where their children were born and grew up, and where Sophie and William grew old after the children had gone. It was where Sophie broke her thigh, and where Hallam cared for her for ten more years until she died. Inevitably and insensibly, Swindon became home.

Hallam's attitude to Swindon changed only very gradually and perhaps unconsciously. Faint beginnings of a sense of identification are apparent in 1906, when he took his brother George and 'an amateur geologist friend' on a grand tour of Swindon quarries and showed them 'all the antiquities in the town'.[144] A visit from George again prompted a walking tour in September 1912. Hallam describes the sights of modern Swindon in some detail and although there is an ironic distance there is also a hint of pride:

> Then we went down the steps and along the canal to Kingshill Bridge and along the path to the Subway to show this to my brother, as it will soon be closed and a good thing too for the morals of the Town. This Subway I reckon one of the sights of Swindon. Then along Bruce St down over the canal branch, which is not a canal now as there is no water in it. Next we went up Ferndale road which is the longest street in Swindon and along Cricklade road to the County Ground to see those new Gates which have just been put down by the Town Council and

[144] Hallam Diaries, BRO D/EX 1415/10, 16 Jun. 1906.

which I don't consider ornamental at all and dear at the money they
have cost.[145]

By July 1919 Swindon is more definitely 'my town', although Hallam is still
ashamed of it:

We heard from the men coming in to work this morning that a mob of
riff-raffs burnt down the new flagpole at the Town Hall last night. Why –
no one knows ... I felt ashamed of my town.[146]

A wet holiday in Weston-super-Mare in August 1935 revealed that a real and
significant change had taken place in his feelings, although it was now more
than five decades since he had started at the Works. Not only were the Hallams
pleased to fall in with a Mr and Mrs Butlin, also from Swindon, but Hallam
confessed that as the rain came down he 'sat in a shelter in the Winter Gardens
wishing I was home in Swindon'.[147] Nor was this a momentary impulse: on
3 September he noted in his diary that he was 'glad to be home and do as
I like'.[148] Confirmation that Swindon had now definitively become 'home'
came when Hallam, remarkably for a working man, gave a radio talk on the
derivation of Swindon place names for the BBC.[149] If Swindon had a past that
was worth caring about, its place in Hallam's personal pecking order was
assured.

It is easy to see that, given his long residence there with Sophie, Swindon
in a sense had to become home. But how did Hallam reconcile this with his
deep love of the countryside and antipathy to the urban? The diaries show
that, progressively over many years, he found 'rural' elements within or
adjoining Swindon and that these enabled him to achieve a practical reconciliation, even if he never renounced his long-held dream of retiring to
a cottage in the country. These rural elements fell into four main categories.
First was Swindon's urban fringe. Kent Road was close to the southern edge
of Swindon, so even a short walk brought the Hallams out into the countryside. Particularly important to them were Wroughton and Westlecote fields,
favourite destinations for picnics and nature rambles, Kings Hill, whence
owls could be heard hooting, and Ladder Lane, where Hallam often took
Sophie to listen for the cuckoo in their last years together. While these areas
might not have seemed especially rural in comparison to the 'deep' countryside around Lockinge, or the freedom of the downs, they brought the
sights, sounds and smells of the country almost within touching distance of

---

[145]   Hallam Diaries, BRO D/EX 1415/20, 1 Sep. 1912.
[146]   Hallam Diaries, BRO D/EX 1415/25, 22 Jul. 1919. According to Matheson, however,
        respectability was central to working-class life in early twentieth-century Swindon.
        Matheson, *Railway Voices*, 18.
[147]   Hallam Diaries, BRO D/EX 1415/41, 30 Aug. 1935.
[148]   Hallam Diaries, BRO D/EX 1415/41, 3 Sep. 1935.
[149]   Hallam Diaries, BRO D/EX 1415/48, 18 Jun. 1942.

Swindon and were cherished for that. They were also still actively farmed and Hallam often noted the state of the harvest and the implications of the weather for it:

> I and wife sat out on our lawn all the afternoon, it was a perfect day. After tea we went a walk across the Wroughton Fields. I've never seen heavier crops of grass than there is now.[150]

Indeed, he seems to have taken an increasing interest in farming as he got older. He was less able to go out on long walks and spent more time in Swindon, so perhaps noticing good and bad farming weather, and the state of the crops when he saw them, helped to maintain the contact with Lockinge, the countryside and his childhood.[151]

Secondly, urban Swindon incorporated relics of the countryside such as the site of the old Pest House he discovered behind Goddard Avenue in 1924, or Southbrook Farm, where he happened to find himself in May 1939:

> This house must be I judge 250 years old of stone and stone tiled. 2 or 3 families live in it now for no land attaches to it now in fact it isn't a farm for all the land is built over.[152]

Thirdly, there was their own garden at 60 Kent Road. As the years passed, Hallam was increasingly disposed to sit in the garden rather than go out when it was warm:

> A perfect English summer day . . . This afternoon sat out in deck chair all the time till tea time reading and sleeping and smoking.[153]

Working in the garden became more important to him too. The diary records when he planted a row of potatoes, sprouts or beans, and when he chopped firewood to save on the cost of coal.[154] As with noticing the state of the harvest, it seems likely that this provided a point of contact with the agricultural world of his childhood.

Finally, and perhaps most important of all, was the Town Gardens, a favourite outing for Hallam and Sophie in the warmer months.[155] They took great

---

[150] Hallam Diaries, BRO D/EX 1415/35, 21 and 28 Jun. 1931.

[151] Hallam Diaries, BRO D/EX 1415/24, 20 Aug. 1915, 1415/41, 31 Mar. 1936, 1415/59, 7 Aug. 1948, 1415/63, 16 Sep. 1951.

[152] Hallam Diaries, BRO D/EX 1415/30, 4 Oct. 1924, 1415/45, 17 May 1939.

[153] Hallam Diaries, BRO D/EX 1415/48, 20 Jun. 1942. See also BRO D/EX 1415/37, 12 Mar. 1933, 1415/41, 24 Aug. 1935, 1415/48, 7 and 31 Jun. 1942, 1415/54, 8 and 17 Jul. 1945. On 'English' weather, see Chapter 7.

[154] Hallam Diaries, BRO D/EX 1415/18, 1 May 1911; see also BRO D/EX 1415/41, 14 Mar. 1936.

[155] Hallam Diaries, BRO D/EX 1415/20, 4 Aug. 1912, 1415/24, 5 Aug. 1916, 1415/63, 23 Sep. 1951.

pleasure in the beautiful flowers, usually staying for an hour or two, but occasionally, when time allowed and the sun shone, for most of the day:

> Bank holiday. We cut a basket of sandwiches and took books and went up in Town Gardens from 11 to 4. Had a sun bath and read Islands of the Vale.[156]

After Sophie's accident they could no longer walk in the Westlecot or Wroughton fields and the Town Gardens became an even more prominent feature of their lives:

> Whit Sunday. No church, but did the next best thing – took wife out in her chair up in the Town Gardens. We sat up there 2 hours – no cooking to do so no hurry.[157]

It seems clear that the Town Gardens, Hallam's own garden and the countryside played analogous, albeit not wholly interchangeable, functions in his later years. An excerpt from his diary entry for 11 July 1919, during their Ilfracombe holiday, illustrates this well:

> Weather still as grand as ever. Wife and I went up on top of the Torrs this afternoon and sat there all the afternoon and had our tea there.[158]

One could quite easily substitute 'the Town Gardens' for 'the Torrs' in this sentence without substantially changing the nature of the activity or experience. Equally, there is a family likeness between the 'mass of white blossom' of Hallam's loganberries (30 May 1928), the 'wooded glade full of the scent of azalea and the colour of rhododendrons' at Longleat (6 June 1925) and the Town Gardens 'now looking at its best' (7 June 1925).[159] Garden, park and countryside each offered natural beauty and tranquillity, and this was conducive to restful contemplation and quiet companionship.

As this suggests, the growing satisfaction Hallam took in the quasi-rural elements he found in and on the fringes of Swindon was facilitated by age-related changes in the role the countryside played in his life. When he was younger his ruralism took active, physical forms. He went on long, tiring walks and cycle rides, clambered up rocks, pushed his way through undergrowth, collected flints and fossils, and came home sweaty and mud-bespattered. He knew the countryside through his body. As he grew older, he knew it more

[156] Hallam Diaries, BRO D/EX 1415/28, 5 Jun. 1922. See also 1415/18, 6 May 1911, 1415/59, 30 Aug. 1948, 1415/60, 6 Aug. 1949. Eleanor G. Hayden's *Islands of the Vale* (London, 1908) concerned village life in the Vale of the White Horse, encompassing Lockinge.
[157] Hallam Diaries, BRO D/EX 1415/45, 28 May 1939. See also BRO D/EX 1415/45, 21 May 1939 and 1415/54, 3 and 13 Jul. 1945.
[158] Hallam Diaries, BRO D/EX 1415/25, 11 Jul. 1919.
[159] Hallam Diaries, BRO D/EX 1415/32, 30 May 1928; 1415/30, 6 Jun. 1925; 1415/30, 7 Jun. 1925.

passively, with his senses rather than by the movement of his body through the landscape. He absorbed the beauty of the view from a cliff-top seat, the call of the cuckoo gladdened his heart, the scent of azaleas delighted him, or he simply sat in the garden enjoying the warm sunshine. These quieter modes of engaging with landscape were not limited to the 'urban countryside' but they were compatible with it to a greater extent than was the more dynamic ruralism of his younger days.

Through these various means, then, much of what he had once so cherished in Lockinge Hallam eventually found ways of transplanting to or reconstructing in Swindon, achieving a considerable degree of integration and stability in the latter part of his life there. Over and above this, he was now financially secure and seems no longer to have had much fear of losing his job. He had built up a fine collection of mainly antiquarian, archaeological and topographical books, and was a respected figure in Berkshire and Wiltshire local history circles. Especially before Sophie's illness cast a shadow over their lives, there was much to bring him contentment in these later years in Swindon:

> I meant going down to the Reading Room and Lib[rary] tonight but I was so comfortable in my sitting room with a good fire, armchair, pipe and paper I never went out.[160]

> I was left to my own company and we never fell out.[161]

> Today I sat in a comfortable chair, reading an interesting book vol 5 of Newbury District Field Club, a mellow pipe, not a soul about, with 1000£ [sic] invested in 'antibilious' stock, I thought – what more does a fellow want.[162]

* * *

The '"antibilious" stock' notwithstanding, for most of his adult life Hallam was an unambiguously alienated proletarian in the purest Marxist sense. He hated his work, which was dangerous, insecure, coercive, tiring, tedious and often uncomfortable, but his efforts to find more congenial employment proved unavailing. He hated the town to which he had moved in order to obtain work almost as much – he was anti-industrial and anti-urban to his fingertips. Acute as was his alienation from the GWR Works and (for decades at least) from Swindon, however, it was neither the original nor the most powerful source of his ruralism, all the main elements of which can be traced back to his childhood and youth. It was then that he came to know the landscape around Lockinge in such intimate depth, then that he developed his fascination with rural history,

---

[160] Hallam Diaries, BRO D/EX 1415/31, 20 Jan. 1927.
[161] Hallam Diaries, BRO D/EX 1415/32, 29 May 1928.
[162] Hallam Diaries, BRO D/EX 1415/32, 30 May 1928.

archaeology, folklore and craft traditions and then that his abiding loyalties to his family, Lord Wantage, the village and to Berkshire were woven together. Undoubtedly this happy childhood laid the groundwork for his adult ruralism. Nevertheless not everyone who has a happy childhood develops a passionate interest in and commitment to the environment in which they grew up. What was different about Hallam? The force that animated his love of the countryside above all was a profound antipathy to change and a fear of loss. It was the depth of his attachments that made this fear so powerful, and to some extent it may be an inescapable part of the deeply lived human life. Why Hallam's attachments ran so deep is difficult to say, although it seems likely that the early death of his mother is part of the explanation. The upshot, however, was that maintaining continuities and connections was crucial to him. This helps to explain the particular character of his ruralism. What mattered to him about the countryside was not whether it was 'natural' or 'artificial' but the ongoing continuity of life, human and non-human, in a known and lived-in landscape. In many respects his outlook and the way he related to landscape exemplify Ingold's 'dwelling perspective', whereby landscape is understood temporally as an ongoing process to which human activity is integral.[163] Not for Hallam the pernicious belief that we are alien from or outside nature, rather than part of and acting within it – the way he engaged with, acted in and felt and thought about landscape was wholly contrary to purified constructions of this kind.

* * *

In view of Hallam's deep concern with continuity from one generation to the next, it seems appropriate to turn, at the end of this chapter, to his children and grandchildren. They picked up the baton of his attachment to the countryside and carried it forward. Dorothy got herself a bicycle and rode off to visit archaeological sites like Avebury (6 May 1911) and Wayland's Smithy (9 September 1915); Marjorie, when living in Stert, chose to stay in a rambling thatched farmhouse that approximated very closely to her father's dream of 'an old cottage in the country' (14 January 1927); and Muriel wrote to tell him that she had been on holiday 'out in the Wilds, 250 miles from Toronto' (23 August 1948).[164] The family tradition of ruralism even went down to the next generation. On 1 August 1949 a letter from Hallam's grandson arrived, proudly announcing that he had milked a cow and fed fowls on a farm at Bude in Cornwall.[165] His grandfather must have been pleased.

---

[163] Ingold, *The Perception of the Environment*.
[164] Hallam Diaries, BRO D/EX 1415/18, 6 May 1911; 1415/24, 9 Sep. 1915; 1415/31, 14 Jan. 1927; 1415/59, 23 Aug. 1948.
[165] Hallam Diaries, BRO D/EX 1415/60, 1 Aug. 1949.

Withdrawers

While Cresswell and Hallam held on to a precious past, Spear Smith and Dickinson fled from an intimidating present. The pattern of progressive withdrawal from London ever deeper into the countryside is a marked one and the vital role of rural landscapes in providing a refuge is unmistakable in the two women's lives. However, Spear Smith and Dickinson were trying to escape from different things and the countryside helped them in different ways, with different consequences. Dickinson fled not least from her own relatives, although it was rarely long before one or other of them turned up on her doorstep, whereas Spear Smith withdrew into rather than seeking to break out of the inner circle of her family.

4

Katherine Spear Smith

Hampshire Artist

Uniquely among the subjects of this book, Katherine Spear Smith spent most of her early years abroad. She was born in India on 20 September 1884, just over a year after her brother, Alic. Her father, Walter, worked as a consultant engineer in the Public Works Department of the Indian Civil Service, a tolerably senior position. Kate, her mother, was of genteel birth; several of her numerous sisters married clergymen. The family took great pride in the Spear name, which had been handed down for five generations in commemoration of Joseph Spear, an officer in Rodney and Nelson's navy. He was at Cape St Vincent (1780), the Saintes (1782) and the Toulon Blockade (1810–11). Commanding the sloop *Goree* he fought a fierce action against a superior force of two French brigs off Marie-Galante in the West Indies in the most fêted traditions of the Royal Navy (1808), following which he was appointed Post-Captain.[1] It was probably because of this connection that the Smiths were so attached to the sea, although this also reflected their broadly conventional, perhaps slightly conservative upper middle-class outlook.[2] Walter used to bring home 'The Story of the Sea' to Katherine every week. She made model ships and devised a coat of arms for herself featuring a spear and warship, signing herself 'Admiral Spear'.[3] Other than this, the family's values were Romantic, Ruskinian and Protestant, roughly in that order.

Katherine differed from the other diarists not only in spending her early childhood abroad: she was also the only one who never worked for her living, and had the shortest life, dying at the age of thirty-six. Like Cresswell, Dickinson and Bissell, she did not marry. She was an unusually private person: although she was a trained artist, it would seem that none of her paintings was publicly exhibited and, despite her significance as a naturalist, at least in a local context, only one short letter was ever published. This was in *British Birds*

---

[1] Joseph Spear (16 Jan. 2016). In *Wikipedia, The Free Encyclopedia*. https://en.wikipedia.org /w/index.php?title=Joseph_Spear&oldid=700162348 [accessed 17 Feb. 2016].

[2] On the sea and English identity, see Readman, *Storied Ground*, 25.

[3] New College Archives [NCA], PA SMA 1/5 (Smith Diary: 8 Jan. 1898: 'painted portholes on my ship'; 'father brought me home "The Story of the Sea". He always does, every week'; on 2 Apr. 1898 Katherine tried to make a wooden yacht).

when she identified a scarlet grosbeak at Titchfield.[4] As this perhaps suggests, she was primarily interested in nature, although the countryside in a wider sense did matter to her. In this, she has something in common with Bissell, although she acquired a far more extensive knowledge of natural history than he did. She was also much more interested in picturesque landscapes, including their built elements, than he was, reflecting her artistic training. Cottages and farm buildings appealed to her: she described Titchfield as 'a very picturesque old-world village', while nearby Catherington was 'old and very pretty'.[5]

The sources for Katherine's life are rich but discontinuous. Her diaries are thoughtful and expressive but also intermittent, in places retrospective and do not cover the last six years of her life. Her extensive nature notebooks contain much biographical material, just as the diaries contain much natural history – a good example of the tendency of different forms of life writing, and indeed other related genres that would not normally be regarded as biographical, to converge. There are also several sketches and watercolours, some poems and short stories and an extensive collection of letters. Most of this is in the Hampshire Record Office but the letters, a diary fragment and some other material are in New College archives, Oxford. The letters are mainly between Katherine and Alic but there are also several other pairings including letters from Walter to Kate and between Kate and her children. On the whole the letters tend to be more ephemeral than the diaries and notebooks but they provide valuable biographical context and in some of her later letters to Alic, Katherine opens her inmost thoughts. Between them these sources make it possible to gain insight into many aspects of Katherine's life, although most of her childhood remains a blank and we know less than we might about her daily life in London since the notebooks and letters (less so the diaries) are skewed towards the holidays.

It is tempting to approach the notebooks as a 'nature diary', in the sense identified by Bellanca.[6] Among the nature diaries she discusses are two that connect closely to Katherine's notebooks: Edith Holden's and Margaret Shaw's. All three women were quite unknown outside a small circle in their lifetimes and their work was unpublished. Shaw was born two years after Katherine; Holden was a little older but also died in 1920. Each wrote extensive, detailed nature notes and made beautiful paintings and drawings of plants and animals, combining attentive empirical detail with a Romantic sensibility.[7] Holden and Shaw, however, attempted to purge their meticulously worked and highly polished diaries of all disruptive personal and even locational

---

[4] *British Birds* 7(6) (1 Nov. 1913), 179.
[5] Hampshire Record Office (hereafter HRO), 19M99/1/3a (Smith Diary, 1911, undated); NCA, PA SMA 1/29 (Letter from Katherine Smith to Alic Smith, 13 Sep. 1916).
[6] Bellanca, *Daybooks*.
[7] Sarah Edwards, 'Edith Holden: An Extraordinary Lady? The Vexed Debate about the "Diary of a Nobody"', *Life Writing* 2 (2005), 43.

information, creating a perfect escapist art form that seals nature hermetically from the world.[8] Katherine's nature notebooks, conversely, are fragmentary and unfinished, replete with thoughts, feelings, short narratives and references to people and places.[9] These differences may diminish them as works of art but enhance their value for understanding her experience of nature and the countryside.

Other than the date she was born, almost the first thing we know about Katherine is that when she was five, the family briefly returned to England, probably in connection with the start of Alic's formal education at Woodlands School in South Woodford, London (1889–93). While at Woodlands, Alic lived with Aunt Annie in nearby Wanstead. Walter sailed for India again from Liverpool on board the SS *Niagara* on 10 October 1889 but Kate and presumably Katherine remained in England until at least June 1890. By March 1891, however, mother and daughter were back in India, living in Dalhousie, about two hundred miles north-west of Simla, where Alic had been born. In 1894 Alic began to attend Dulwich College in south London while Walter obtained an appointment as secretary (chief administrative officer) of King's College London, enabling the family to live together in one place.[10] From then onwards the whole family lived permanently in England, initially at Belvedere in Dulwich Grove.

Beyond these sketchy outlines we know little about Katherine's early childhood. She hardly ever refers to India in her subsequent writing. A rare exception is in an undated diary entry describing her rapturous response to seeing Lake Windermere for the first time: 'I had never seen anything so lovely as the mountains and lakes (except the Himalayas in India).' Katherine was a cautious girl and adhered closely to the established canon of Romantic taste in which she had been brought up. The brackets seem almost grudging, as if she wanted to forget or disavow India.

Perhaps Katherine had been somewhat lonely without Alic after she and her mother returned to the Punjab in 1890/1. Not unusually in the context of the time, her parents seem to have regarded their first duty as being towards each other; the children, while held in great affection, were expected to take second place, an order of priorities exemplified by the decision that Kate should live

---

[8] While the form, artistic value and cultural significance of Holden and, to a lesser extent, Shaw's nature journals have been much discussed, less attention has been paid to their purpose and function.

[9] Bellanca argues that 'locality, locality, locality emerges as a most prominent theme' in the journals she studied. In Katherine's notebooks and diaries, although place certainly matters, this is telescoped down to the scale of her garden and a few punctuation marks such as the copse, the common or the river, in contrast to the wider parochial scale Bellanca seems to have had in mind. Bellanca, *Daybooks*, 9.

[10] Walter became the secretary of King's College in 1895. Email from Lianne Smith, Archives Services Manager, King's College, London, 30 Oct. 2015.

with her husband in India rather than with her seven-year-old son in England. Walter wrote frequently to his wife when they were apart – when he was in the Punjab his work often took him away from home on civil engineering projects such as inspecting and repairing canals. The letters are mainly concerned with his professional affairs, people he met, religion and his relationship with Kate – the children do not feature prominently. Back in England the parents often chose to be together while the children went to visit one or other of their numerous aunts and uncles. In August 1895 Katherine was staying with her mother's brother Uncle Willie and his wife Aunt Charlotte in Birkenhead, under instructions from Kate to 'be good and not give any trouble' while her parents were in Edinburgh.[11] In April 1897 both children were in Gosport with 'Aunt Lalla' and her husband, Reverend M. J. Wilby. Two months later the parents went to visit relatives in Weston-super-Mare, leaving the children at home, Alic being tasked 'to very carefully wind up the dining room clock on Sunday morning'.[12] In September, it was the children's turn to go to Weston while the parents went off on a cycling tour to Hindhead in Surrey ('You have no idea how Mother has taken to bicycling, she thinks nothing of hills now.').[13] This pattern continued throughout Alic and Katherine's childhood and youth.

Walter's letters to his children were few and far between. When he did write, it was usually to both children at once. More often, he sent his love via his wife, who wrote more frequently to her 'darling chicks', albeit rarely at length. This is not to imply that Katherine was uninfluenced by her father. Quite the contrary – his hobby of landscape painting and interest in rural scenery (he was an enthusiastic walker) became central to her life.[14] But although he seems to have been very fond of her, he evidently regarded her as peripheral to the serious adult matters that occupied his attention. Kate was devoted to her children but Walter seems to have been the emotional centre of her life. Furthermore, as Katherine grew up, her sensibilities and interests diverged from her mother's. Kate's letters are mundane and bustling, full of practical concerns and domestic details. She was preoccupied with the health of the innumerable aunts, alterations to clothing, shopping, travel arrangements and recipes. Her daughter was of a very different cast of mind, intellectual and high-minded. Katherine's letters, diary entries and notebooks express her varying responses to rural landscapes, her close observation of nature and her aesthetic, moral and religious hopes and doubts.

[11] NCA, PA SMA 1/5 (Letter from Kate Smith to Katherine Spear Smith, 17 Aug. 1895).
[12] NCA, PA SMA 1/5 (Letter from Kate Smith to Katherine Spear and Alic Halford Smith, 4 Jun. 1897).
[13] NCA, PA SMA 1/5 (Letter from Kate Smith to Katherine Spear and Alic Halford Smith, 5 Sep. 1897).
[14] Enthusiastic walking: see, for example, NCA, PA SMA 1/5 (Letter from Kate Smith to Katherine Spear, 1902: 'Father has gone out for his usual long walk').

Emotionally, then, there was a gap that, increasingly, Katherine's parents could not fill. This seems to have been the principal cause of her exceptional closeness to her brother. The children were similar in age and it seems likely that they were thrown together a great deal in their early childhood in India. Katherine was barely five when Alic went to school in England and she can have seen little of him over the next four years; they wrote to each other but this can hardly have compensated for the lost companionship. The experience of separation and reunion deepened and intensified their relationship. Although there is no reason to believe Aunt Annie was unkind, Alic must have missed his family at times during his South Woodford years, while Katherine, younger and with fewer memories, seems to have constructed a perhaps idealized image of her absent brother.

An entry in Katherine's diary for 14 July 1906 elucidates the development of her relationship with Alic and how this connected to her sense of identity:

> I have been reading Dorothy Wordsworth's Journal, and have been inspired to follow her example; though I can never never keep such a simple and beautiful Journal as she did. Her descriptions of nature are so beautiful and deeply felt; and somehow I seem to have the same kind of feelings for nature which she had. Her life was so pure and simple (I should do well to follow her example!) and she had a brother, the poet Wordsworth, of whom she was entirely fond; I too have a brother. I love her like a sister.[15]

Katherine was no doubt aware of another parallel: the Wordsworths' exceptional closeness had arisen partly from an enforced separation in late childhood.[16] It seems unlikely, however, that she recognized the more troubling implications of her identification with Dorothy, whose relationship with William brought her sorrow as well as joy and was almost certainly the main reason she never married. It has often been argued that the costs and benefits of the relationship were unequally shared: she gave William literary inspiration, encouragement and devotion but William's marriage to Mary Hutchinson deprived Dorothy of her unique role, while she remained emotionally fettered to him.[17] Like Dorothy, Katherine never married – but neither did Alic.

In contrast to some interpretations of the Wordsworths' relationship, then, there is little sense of unequal emotional returns between Katherine and Alic but this does not mean that such close sibling bonds, for all the joy they brought, were unproblematic. A short story Katherine wrote when she was

---

[15] HRO, 19M99/1/2a (Smith Diary, 14 Jul. 1906).

[16] Stephen Gill, 'Wordsworth, William (1770–1850)', *Oxford Dictionary of National Biography*, Oxford, 2004; online ed., May 2010 [www.oxforddnb.com/view/article/29973, accessed 11 Feb. 2016].

[17] For a persuasive counterview, see Lucy Newlyn, *William and Dorothy Wordsworth: All in Each Other* (Oxford, 2013).

about fourteen sheds some light on this. The story concerns two children, Constance aged fourteen and Donald aged fifteen. Constance clearly represents Katherine, and Donald Alic. The two children have had no parents for some reason since the age of seven and are utterly devoted to each other and quite inseparable. Constance is very sensitive to landscape and sketches. Con and Don (as they call each other) are looked after by an unsympathetic aunt, but fortunately a kind old sea captain of their acquaintance invites them to go on a voyage to America with him. The captain has two children, Leonard and Hilda, both about the same age as Con. The voyage begins, there is a terrible storm but this is followed by a beautiful sunset. Con obtains permission for them to go back on deck after tea. Her delight in the sunset causes her to look radiant herself; Leonard (who, our author is at pains to inform us, is very 'hansom') gazes rapturously at her. The author then appears to feel a little guilty about forgetting Don and Hilda, but she assures us that they were an equally comely couple. Here the story more or less comes to an end.

On the face of it, the tale of Con and Don is a perhaps quite typical early-teenage wish-fulfilment story, showing, as do two or three slight pencil sketches now in the Hampshire Record Office, that Katherine, just like other girls, dreamt of a handsome lover. But there are some more distinctive undercurrents: her sense of herself as peculiarly responsive to natural beauty, the significance that sketching had for her and, above all, her exceptionally close relationship with Alic. This is really the most interesting aspect of the story. Not only do 'Con' and 'Don' rhyme but 'C' and 'D' are, of course, adjacent letters of the alphabet. It is difficult to imagine a more emphatic statement of identity short of outright merger. In this respect Katherine seems a good candidate for the relational sense of self that some feminist critics have argued is characteristic of female identities as constructed in life writing, although as we shall see this is only part of the picture in Katherine's case. It would seem that the only way Katherine could imagine marrying is if Alic got married as part of the same package; indeed, in this story there is a perfect pairing where the brother marries the sister's sister-in-law. In a sense, then, the marriage confirms and cements the sibling bond in that the Alic character is now not only brother, but also brother-in-law to the sister. The most telling aspect, however, is that the story stops short before arriving at its implicit endpoint – the marriage of the four central characters. It is difficult to avoid the conclusion that even a form of marriage that redoubled her relationship with Alic was psychologically unacceptable to Katherine. Perhaps the same was true for him too.

Thanks to a diary kept on a few scraps of paper between January and April 1898, we know a little about Katherine's home life in her mid-teens. On the whole the picture that emerges is one of placid professional middle-class domesticity. Katherine spends much of her time reading – a bit of Dickens and some of Lamb's *Tales from Shakespeare*, but her real love is adventure stories.

She and Alic take the *Boy's Own Paper* and Katherine relishes in particular the pieces by Gordon Stables.[18] Their nanny, Miss Porter, reads Jules Verne's *Round the World in Eighty Days* to them. The *Girl's Own Paper* arrives but at this age boyish adventure is more to Katherine's taste – above all Rider Haggard, whose *The People of the Mist* is a 'most glorious, exciting book – I liked it awfully' (three years later, however, she chose *Pride and Prejudice* for her birthday present). Katherine paints, begins violin lessons and attempts to ride a bicycle. Her parents take the children to the Natural History Museum and to Dulwich Picture Gallery. Aunts and cousins visit; they go to church and to Jones and Higgins' sale. There are as yet few signs of a consistent interest in nature or the countryside although Katherine is receptive to the beauty of the stars on a clear winter's night.

By April 1900 the family had moved the short distance to 63 Alleyn Park, also in Dulwich. Katherine began to keep a diary again on 12 August 1901, although she was never especially disciplined about this and some entries were written retrospectively. 'I am a very bad one at keeping a diary, and have missed two months', she confessed in February 1902. On 19 September 1901 she recorded that the family had decided that she should give up the violin: a small thing in itself but presaging the dialectical pattern of hope and resignation that was to become a dominant feature of her adult life. 'I am sorry in a small degree, but glad in a greater', she observed. In contrast to her earlier diary, Katherine's interest in natural history is apparent, initially in the form of a shell collection.[19] There was nothing unusual about this; indeed, as Lynn Barber observes 'there was hardly a middle-class drawing-room in the country that did not contain an aquarium, a fern-case, a butterfly cabinet, a seaweed album, a shell collection, or some other evidence of a taste for natural history'.[20]

---

[18] Gordon Stables wrote boys' adventure stories, often about the sea. He was a pioneer of caravanning, a nature lover and an active supporter of the Sea Birds Protection Society. All of this would have appealed to Katherine. G. S. Woods, 'Stables, William Gordon (1837x40–1910)', rev. Guy Arnold, *Oxford Dictionary of National Biography*, Oxford, 2004 [www.oxforddnb.com/view/article/36229, accessed 11 Feb. 2016].

[19] On 18 September 1901 Katherine bought a book about shells that she had been looking a long time for; in February 1902 she had quinsy and Mr Blatherwick, the doctor's assistant, happened to see her shell collection – they had 'quite a nice talk on Natural History'. HRO, 19M99 1/1 (Smith Diary).

[20] Lynn Barber, *The Heyday of Natural History 1820–1870* (London, 1980), 13. Barber's claim is a little overstated, although admittedly Kate Smith had a fern collection: NCA, PA SMA 1 5 (Letter from Kate Smith to Katherine Spear Smith, 11 Jun. 1901), as did Catley: BRO 41419/3 (Fred Catley Diary, 23 Apr. 1926). It should also be acknowledged that Barber is referring to the mid-nineteenth century. The scholarly consensus seems to be that by 1900 amateur natural history was on the wane, although further research on the early twentieth century might call this into question. However, the Smith family may in this respect as in some others have been rather conservative.

As might be expected, in her late teens Katherine was showing many signs of a developing individuality and self-consciousness. Apart from the diary and the new interest in natural history, she began to write poetry. Thirty of her poems survive, written when Katherine was between the ages of seventeen and twenty-one. Although they are unlikely to attract the attention of literary critics, they are of considerable interest for the light they shed on her character, sense of identity and structure of feeling, and the ways these are refracted through and to some extent shaped by her absorption in nature and rurality. The poems draw on Romantic and High Victorian models, echoing Wordsworth, Coleridge, Shelley, Arnold and Tennyson. In archetypically Romantic vein, every poem is premised on the assumption that nature is the gateway to spiritual understanding. Katherine's high-mindedness and the way in which her sense of identity was held within a very particular, even in some respects determining, cultural construction are plainly apparent.

The manifest position from which the poems are written is idealistic. In a poem with the arch-Romantic title 'Imagination', Katherine wishes for 'A soul, with thoughts for wings' that 'soars up to heaven high' and hopes to find 'Immortal splendours in high halls of thought'. In another poem she tentatively proposes that a 'maid' who lived near the 'influence sweet' of 'woods and hills, and flowers dear' would 'have a heart as pure and bright/ As mountain streams, or crystal light'. Such idealism was a deep-seated part of Katherine's character, central to her sense of herself, and is certainly to be respected and in some ways admired. It soon becomes clear in the poems, however, that the 'high halls of thought' are defined against a rejected worldly 'other':

> We leave the world, and fly from all mankind
> We fly from worldly pomp and all that's naught.[21]

Because she loves nature and approaches it with becoming humility, Katherine believes that she can hear:

> A voice that reaches me at last
> Speaks of the sunset in the sky
> And all the mysteries that lie
>
> Within the realm of nature sweet[22]

But worldly others are excluded from these profound spiritual truths:

> For nature will not teach the proud,
> But puts before their eyes a cloud
> They do not see, and do not hear
> The glories that to me are dear.[23]

[21] HRO, 19M99 4/15 (Smith Poems: *Imagination*, n.d. [1901]).
[22] HRO, 19M99 4/15 (Smith Poems: 'The Lonely Road Winds Round the Hill', Aug. 1905).
[23] Ibid.

She reserves her fiercest condemnation for 'women of this later age' who:

> . . .vainly strive to reach the crown
> The earthly crown not meant for you[24]

Rejecting the world comes at a price – a high one, potentially, in Katherine's case. The way in which she constructs her identity here – using the fact that she is not a career woman to prove that she possesses the precious 'spiritual' qualities she most values – has a crucial bearing on subsequent developments in her life and did not bode well for her future prospects should she change her mind and attempt to enter the public sphere.[25]

Another penalty that Katherine was liable to incur if she followed her injunction to turn her back on the world was loneliness.[26] The poems are profoundly ambivalent, even contradictory, on this point. Solitude is a pervasive theme but Katherine insists that she is not in fact lonely:

> Ah Solitude, how beautiful thou art.
> I love thee more than pomp and show of worlds
> Yet not alone I roam, for nature's heart
> Is here to keep me company alone.[27]

'In a Wood at Evening' explains that Katherine finds her friends among the little things of nature but this is not altogether convincing. There is a persistent emphasis on dreams of 'things divinely fair' or 'long past' in the poems and it is difficult to see why dreams of elsewhere should recur so frequently if the present were as wholly satisfactory as Katherine maintains. Moreover, there is a persistent undertone of sadness in the language of the poems. In 'Solitude', for all nature's company, the breezes sigh and shadows flit across the lees. 'I Stood Alone in the Valley' projects a Wordsworthian sense of lost childhood happiness:

> I looked back at the smiling vale
> And thought of life, of all my life,
> In youth all sunshine it had been,
> But shadows o'er my mountains came

---

[24] HRO, 19M99 4/15 (Smith Poems: To 'Some' Women, n.d.).

[25] Amanda Vickery influentially argued that the concept of 'separate spheres' is of limited utility for understanding the reality (as opposed to ideological representations) of women's lives in nineteenth-century England. Amanda Vickery, 'Historiographical Review: Golden Age to Separate Spheres? A Review of the Categories and Chronology of English Women's History', *Historical Journal* 36 (1993), 383–414. If so, Katherine Spear Smith must have been unusual among women of her time in the remarkable extent to which she remained in the private sphere of family life. However, as will become apparent, the barriers that impeded her from entering the public sphere were only in part a consequence of her gender.

[26] On the modern history of loneliness, see K. D. M. Snell, 'The Rise of Living Alone and Loneliness in History', *Social History* 42 (2017), 2–28.

[27] HRO, 19M99 4/15 (Smith Poems: Solitude, May, 1901).

> And made it drear and sad to me.
> But it had gone, and I had come
> To nature to be comforted.[28]

Whether nature's comfort had wholly banished the shadows is open to doubt, as the final stanza of 'The Lonely Road', one of Katherine's last surviving poems, indicates:

> This beauty sinks into my heart
> The dream becomes of me a part;
> The whispers of the dying day
> Help me along my lonely way.[29]

It would not be worth placing too much emphasis on these poems, which in many respects reflect typical late-teenage concerns and anxieties for a girl of Katherine's time and class, were it not for the fact that so many of the themes and emotional conjunctures emergent in them are powerfully apparent in Katherine's later life and in the profound but deeply ambivalent role that nature and the countryside played in it. The question, ultimately, is how far nature provided Katherine with comfort, sustenance and perhaps even liberation, and how far it served to reinforce or validate emotional structures that trapped her in an emotional cul-de-sac. This darker possibility peeps through the closing stanza of 'Approaching Autumn' (August 1905), which presumably unwittingly hints that 'nature' in Katherine's understanding of it has been recruited to the forces of emotional repression:

> Oh, gladness here it is to sit;
> Though still a thought of sadness steals
> Into the joy – that speaketh low
> Of brighter days that are o'er-past.
> But yet this wood of nature holds
> A charm, as of a quiet mind;
> And with a steady hand she soothes
> Quick beatings of a heart, to rest.[30]

There are, however, as yet few indications of thoughts of sadness in Katherine's diaries for this period. Much more apparent is her increasing range of interests. The family went to Seaford for a holiday in April 1902 and for the first time Katherine's diary shows a thoughtful, analytical interest in landscape:

> Seaford is not really a pretty place, but it has many good points. The sea is lovely, and of a good colour, then there are downs. There is a down on the east of the town, on the top of a high white chalk cliff. From the top you can see the sea and white cliffs stretching to Beachy Head; and on looking inland, you see the Sussex downs stretching for miles, and fading into

[28] HRO, 19M99 4/15 (Smith Poems: 'I Stood Alone in the Valley', Oct. 1902).
[29] HRO, 19M99 4/15 (Smith Poems: 'The Lonely Road Winds Round the Hill', Aug. 1905).
[30] HRO, 19M99 4/15 (Smith Poems: 'Approaching Autumn', Aug. 1905).

misty blue on the horizon, they lie asleep, bare of trees, with clouds and sunshine chasing each other across their grassy slopes.[31]

The lyrical yearning towards misty blue horizons suggests that landscape could prompt 'quick beatings of a heart' as easily as it could still them for Katherine, as it could for several of the other diarists.

After the family returned from Seaford Katherine began to attend Lambeth School of Art. She had been painting in oils, emulating her father's watercolours, since at least January 1898, when Kate had constructed a 'studio' out of crates for her.[32] At about the same time she started art school, Katherine began singing lessons. These took place at home in Dulwich, as her teacher lived in Crystal Palace which, Katherine explained, was 'too great a hill for me to walk'.[33]

An entry in Katherine's diary for June 1902 echoes the poems in placing her love of nature at the core of her emerging sense of identity:

> I am also a great lover of nature; people say I have no friends, but I have the whole of Nature for my friends. What infinite beauty, wonder, and greatness there is in Nature; the more you think of it and observe it, the more you are lost in the great glory of it, and of its Maker. If you observe Nature, love it, and feel it, it raises high thoughts and ideas and feelings; much higher than those poor people who walk through life without seeing and feeling it – but stop – I must go no farther, for I shall be talking of what I do not know. Let it suffice, that I am a lover of Nature, and try to be a Naturalist in my little way.[34]

In August the Smiths spent seventeen days in the Lake District, taking the train to Windermere, sailing up the lake to Ambleside and staying the night at the Red Lion in Grasmere. It was almost a pilgrimage for a family so steeped in the literature and ethos of English Romanticism, and as might be expected they visited iconic sites such as Dove Cottage, Southey's tomb at Crosthwaite and Ruskin's favourite English viewpoint, Friar's Crag. Katherine responded intensely to the landscape:

> As we neared the head of the Lake [Windermere], the mountains became higher and higher; the sun was setting and firing great clouds which rested on the mountains summits with gold, great gorges and clefts in the mountains looked dark and menacing. It was lovely, as you gazed at the head of the Lake, and at the mountains rising up in grandeur, you felt there must be some beautiful, enchanted land beyond, that the mountains were enchanted

---

[31] HRO, 19M99 1/1 (Smith Diary, 11 Apr. 1902).
[32] NCA, PA SMA 1/5 (Smith Diary, 25–27 Jan. 1898).
[33] HRO, 19M99 1/1 (Smith Diary, 11 Apr. 1902).
[34] HRO, 19M99/1/1 (Smith Diary, 1 Jun. 1902). The phrase 'lover of nature' was an established one, used, for example, in Edward Jesse, *Gleanings in Natural History: With Local Recollections* (1832), which encouraged readers to keep natural history diaries. See Bellanca, *Daybooks*, 88.

themselves and there dwelt knights and ladies, castles and dragons and everything else pertaining to the romance of the golden days.[35]

As at Seaford, beauty lies in the distance, in an 'enchanted land beyond'. It is unsurprising that at the age of seventeen Katherine projected her hopes into a latent future. Whether these vivid experiences of landscape helped Katherine by stirring up powerful but dormant longings, or held her back by providing a dreamy substitute for the living realization of these hopes, is less clear. What can be said is that encounters of this kind with rural landscapes were becoming an increasingly important and enriching source of self-discovery, as Katherine's response to Derwentwater, where they went next, indicates:

> It is a most beautiful lake, the mountains rise up majestically all around, not only round it, but wherever there is a break in the near mountains, you see mountains stretching away beyond and fading into the distance. The fairy-like enchanted distance, where one's imagination loves to wander, and make up tales and romances of the happy land beyond.
>
> At the head of Derwentwater are gathered many very high mountains, and a gorge passes through them, called Borrowdale. At the other end Skiddaw rises in all its majestic solitude.
>
> Our house was ... just under Skiddaw, and I learnt to love that mountain dearly. I have watched it when sunshine and clouds were chasing each other over it, like smiles and frowns over a great giant's brow, at other times when it seemed to rouse itself in anger, when the clouds looked threatening and dark as they hid its summit. And again often in the evening, when gentle sunset clouds rested on its head, it seemed so peaceful and quiet and tranquil.[36]

In October Alic went up to Oxford, the start of what was to become an important association with New College. Katherine missed him very much but, as before, separation only seemed to strengthen the bond between the two siblings. She had 'lovely long letters' from him – he had been greatly enjoying Ruskin's *Modern Painters* and undertook to read it with her in the vacation. Fortunately from Katherine's perspective the term was only a short one and on 14 December she confided to her diary:

> One thing I am looking forward to very much is – Alic is coming home on Tuesday!!![37]

---

[35] HRO, 19M99/1/1 (Smith Diary, Aug. 1902 [written Oct. 1902]).

[36] HRO, 19M99/1/1 (Smith Diary, Aug. 1902 [written Oct. 1902]). Skiddaw in the late nineteenth century was 'still probably the most popular mountain in the Lakes': Readman, *Storied Ground*, 121.

[37] HRO, 19M99/1/1 (Smith Diary, 14 Dec. 1902). Alic expressed similar impatience in his letters during periods of lengthy separation: 'I am looking forward to Friday very much, as I am getting rather tired of your being away.' NCA, PA SMA 1/10/5 (Letter from Alic Smith to Katherine Spear Smith, 25 Jul. 1909).

The following Easter Alic and Katherine spent at Weston, going out almost every day to explore the local woods. She had recently joined the Selborne Society, a characteristic late Victorian hybrid between natural history, preservation and recreation concerns.[38] She took her new duties 'to protect wild birds & flowers etc: & to promote the study of Natural History' seriously. They harmonized with her interest in art – at Weston, she made two pencil sketches of trees, attempting to put into practice Ruskin's recommendations in *The Elements of Drawing*.[39] It was also around this time that she began to keep a nature notebook, possibly inspired by the Selborne Society's magazine *Nature Notes*, which she was now receiving monthly. She was delighted to see a nuthatch for the first time.[40]

That summer the family rented a cottage at Lee-on-Solent for the season. Katherine soon began to explore the surrounding countryside, especially the common, where she walked on at least ten of the first seventeen days of April.[41] As a fully paid-up Selbornian, she applied herself diligently to improving her knowledge of nature, noting on 17 April that she had discovered from her bird book that some eggs she had found in a nest on the common belonged to a mistle thrush. Her prose, informed by a painter's eye, reflects her deepening aesthetic and emotional responses to nature and landscape:

> In the evening I watched some pairs of Herring gulls at sea; struggling against the wind, turning and swooping back, hovering and flying low, and then gently rising on the waves. It is a beautiful sight to watch gulls flying, and to see the turn and the flash of their wings in the sun, and their slow gliding and sailing high up in the blue sky; and to watch their steady flight home-wards, when the sun is setting and throwing a long path of glory across the quiet breathing sea.[42]

Katherine never achieved, nor did she perhaps desire, the objectifying distance Dorinda Outram describes as the essential attribute of the professional naturalist.[43] On the contrary, she got as close to nature as she could, and her nature notes are infused with what could be perceived as anthropomorphizing emotion. She empathizes tenderly with little things, small birds and insects especially. Undoubtedly this reflects an aspect of Katherine's own identity as a youngest child, and one who was very much perceived as such by her family ('My dear little daughter', as her mother addressed her in a letter sent to Weston [emphasis in original]).[44] She is concerned for the linnets, greenfinches and

---

[38] On the Selborne Society, see Ranlett, 'Checking Nature's Desecration'.

[39] HRO, 19M99/1/1 (Smith Diary, Apr. 1903).

[40] NCA, PA SMA 1 2 (Letter from Katherine Smith to Kate Smith, 10 Apr. 1902).

[41] HRO, 19M99/2/1 (Smith Nature Notebooks, Apr. 1904).

[42] HRO, 19M99/2/1 (Smith Nature Notebooks, 3 Aug. 1904).

[43] Dorinda Outram, 'New Spaces in Natural History', in N. Jardine et al. (eds.), *Cultures of Natural History* (Cambridge, 1996), 249–65.

[44] NCA, PA SMA 1 5 (Letter from Kate Smith to Katherine Spear Smith, 14 Apr. [1901?]).

sparrows that come down to the shore to drink because 'poor little things they could not bathe, as some people were sitting just by the pools'.[45] Equally, she rejoiced in the return of migrant swallows as if they were kindred spirits:

> I saw more Swallows today, at least 6 were wheeling about over the Common; it was so beautiful to see them again; I welcome them with delight.[46]

Empathizing with nature, regarding it as her friend, and committed to a Wordsworthian understanding of it as holy and ultimately benign, Katherine struggled to accommodate its harsher manifestations. On 1 September she came face to face with one of these:

> I was walking down the road by myself, when I saw some object in the road . . . I went nearer, a woman passed by, and a weasel ran into the hedge from the middle of the road, leaving something behind; this I saw was a huge toad, it gave a few leaps onto some grass near, but it seemed rather weak; when all was quiet again the weasel popped out of the hedge, and stood on its hind legs and looked quickly all round, seeing me it went back into the hedge; I kept perfectly quiet, and it came out again, and ran to the place where it had left the toad . . . it saw the toad in the grass, pounced upon it, shook it, and carried it off into the hedge . . . I could not bear to see the poor toad carried off in that way, but I could do no good, and I think the toad was hurt already.

The episode evidently disturbed her. On the last leaf of the notebook is a rough pencil draft for part of the entry, the only instance of this in the notebooks:

> The weasel seized the toad in its mouth, shook it, and carried it off through the hedge. I am unable to say if it ate the toad made a meal of the toad.

The process of revision progressively obscures the uncongenial reality: from the explicit 'ate', to the slightly softer 'made a meal of' to the final version, which draws a veil over the event at the point where the toad is 'carried off'.[47]

After the long summer vacation, Katherine found it hard to uproot herself from Lee: 'I can't bear coming back to London and leaving all the birds and beautiful country and sea behind.'[48] However, there was one major compensation: she began studying landscape painting at King's College Ladies Department Art School. Sometimes she was able to escape to the countryside for a few hours: there was one particularly enjoyable walk with Walter from Chalfont Road to Chorleywood in Hertfordshire on 22 October 1904. The autumn colours were magnificent and she found the

---

[45] HRO, 19M99/2/1 (Smith Nature Notebooks, 3 Aug. 1904).
[46] HRO, 19M99/2/4 (Smith Nature Notebooks, 12 Apr. 1906).
[47] HRO, 19M99/2/1 (Smith Nature Notebooks, 1 Sep. 1904).
[48] HRO, 19M99/2/1 (Smith Nature Notebooks, 29 Sep. 1904).

picturesque old-fashioned cottages, village green and manor house at Chenies very appealing.[49]

The Smiths were at Lee again over Christmas. On Boxing Day the season of goodwill was rudely shattered for Katherine when she saw some men shoot a seagull. Her wounded response bears witness to the closeness of her identification with nature and to the delicate vulnerability that was the basis for this:

> [T]he poor bird was just in front of me, it struggled a little, and one wing went under the water, the men picked it up and threw it into the boat, and rowed away. I could not bear to see it killed; why did they take that beautiful innocent life? And as the man took hold of it, and it uttered a cry, he laughed!![50]

On 29 March 1905 the family returned to Lee but to a different house, Priory Cottage, which they continued to rent for holiday use until December the following year. From Katherine's point of view, the most important feature of the new house was its 'very good hedges', in which a pair of thrushes nested.[51] Katherine's interest in the habits of common garden birds like these is characteristic. She was always pleased to see an unfamiliar bird and the conventional tropes of nature diaries identified by Bellanca such as the first-seen and the catalogue list are present in her nature notes but in a comparatively muted form.[52] Many more pages are devoted to close, respectful observation of the behaviour of common birds, the colour and form of plants and the effects of light on land and seascapes. Careful, detailed observation was part of the ethos of the Victorian field naturalist, influenced by Paleyan natural theology – nature in all its manifestations was understood as having been created expressly by God, so it was de rigueur to pay reverent attention to every last detail.[53] The Smith family's devotion to Ruskin, who also preached the virtues of minute, painstaking attention to the facts of nature (in contrast to the Romantic emphasis on its meaning), no doubt also influenced Katherine. But neither Paley nor Ruskin explain Katherine's particular empathy for the ordinary and the self-effacing, her preferential attention to that which others might pass over as unworthy of notice. A good example is her description of a skylark's flight. Although she is far from indifferent to the celebrated beauty of the bird's song, she chooses to focus instead on a precise account of its movements:

> I went into the fields near the sea; the larks are singing exquisitely now;
> I watched several; they rise from the ground and commense [*sic*] singing;

[49] HRO, 19M99/2/1 (Smith Nature Notebooks, 22 Oct. 1904).

[50] HRO, 19M99/2/1 (Smith Nature Notebooks, 26 Dec. 1904).

[51] HRO, 19M99/2/3a (Smith Nature Notebooks, undated entry, 1905).

[52] The third element Bellanca identifies as a defining trope of the nature diary, the daily weather record, is absent in Katherine's nature notes. Bellanca, *Daybooks*, 30.

[53] Barber, *The Heyday of Natural History*, 21.

they mount up into the sky in a straight line, with short pauses in ~~mounti~~ ascending; quivering their wings, then clapping them close to their sides. When they have mounted to a great height, they fly along horizontally across the sky, round and backwards and forwards. Then they descend in a straight line, or nearly so; they come down at a great rate sometimes, but always alight gently on their feet, with out-stretched wings. The moment they touch the ground their song ceases. When on the ground they walk, and run.[54]

So unmistakably do the nature notebooks register the sensitivity with which Katherine's feelings vibrated in sympathy to the minutiae of nature that it would be easy to overlook the exhilaration and joy her country walks also sometimes brought her. This was perhaps especially so when she had Alic for company, as on 12 April:

It has been a most glorious day ... I went for a walk with my brother, along the cliff and under-cliff, towards Hill-head. When we first came to the sea, a mist hung over it and we could not see the island [i.e. the Isle of Wight]; gradually the clouds broke and the mist melted, and we could see the island and horizon; the sea was a most exquisite blue, with a golden spit of sand and pebbles running out into it; the sea was lovely all morning, changing colour every instant, with bands and currents of blue green, or grey, etc.[55]

Before Lee, Katherine had shown few signs of attachment to particular places (topophilia, to use Yi Fu Tuan's neologism).[56] She had hitherto lived a somewhat peripatetic life: from the Punjab to Weston-super-Mare, back to the Punjab, then two different addresses in Dulwich, with interludes in Birkenhead, Gosport and Weston. Several of the other diarists considered in this book developed powerful attachments to the places where they grew up (Hallam and Lockinge; Johnston and Annan; Cresswell and Devon) but this does not seem to have been the case for Katherine.[57] The Smiths were a thoroughly English family and Dalhousie can never have seemed unambiguously like home, not least because Alic was in England from 1889 onwards and Walter was often away for work reasons. Nor is there much evidence that Katherine was especially attached to the area around Dulwich. Lee was different in several respects: Katherine seems to have felt free, and indeed eager, to go for frequent walks on her own; the area offered rich possibilities for nature

[54] HRO, 19M99/2/3a (Smith Nature Notebooks, 5 Apr. 1905).
[55] HRO, 19M99/2/3a (Smith Nature Notebooks, 12 Apr. 1905).
[56] Yi-Fu Tuan, *Topophilia: A Study of Environmental Perception, Attitudes, and Values* (New York, 1990).
[57] Historians and, until recently, geographers have not made much use of the concept of place attachment. For an overview of the psychological literature, see Lynne C. Manzo and Patrick Devine-Wright (eds.), *Place Attachment: Advances in Theory, Methods and Applications* (Abingdon, 2021).

study; the rural Hampshire landscape was, to her eyes, far more beautiful than the cityscapes of London; and she was close to the sea, always significant to the Smiths.

As Linda Maynard has shown, landscapes visited repeatedly in childhood or youth can become invested with deep-seated meaning.[58] This was certainly the case for Katherine in relation to Lee. However, there are many different ways in which landscapes can carry individual meaning. It is instructive to compare Katherine's love for the countryside around Lee with Hallam's for the Lockinge downs. Hallam's love for Lockinge was that of the embedded native – it was spatially and temporally multi-layered, a folding together of geology, wildlife, archaeology, history, folklore, farming practice, craft traditions and the events of his own life. Hallam's Lockinge was pre-eminently a social landscape, dwelt in and co-created by its people. Katherine's Lee, conversely, was a private landscape, shared perhaps with Alic but otherwise only with the birds, flowers and trees. People feature only as an intrusion:

> Suddenly, as we were sitting there, a nightingale burst into song in a bush not more than three yards from us; it was in the middle of the bush, but we could see it trembling and shaking with its song; it seemed to sing with all its heart and might, and was so occupied that it did not fly away, when two men on bicycles passed close to the bush (which was near the road), and then two heavy carts.[59]

Because the family has no roots in the area, Katherine neither knows these people nor anything about them. However, she is also cut off by character and class. While she was far too modest to be a snob, the social imperative to avoid mixing with working people was powerful:

> In the afternoon (it being a Saturday), mother and father and I went in a steam-boat down the river to Greenwich. The boat was horribly crowded, with common people; but the river was very interesting and picturesque.[60]

Since the landscape has no social dimension for Katherine, nor does it have any meaningful history, except such as is sufficient to endow the older farm buildings with an artistically 'picturesque' quality.

But the private, inward-looking character of Katherine's topophilia does not mean that it mattered any less to her than Hallam's more richly textured love for

---

[58] Linda Maynard, '"Dream Lives": Fraternal Uses of Spaces of Childhood to Express Separation and Loss during Wartime', paper given at Spaces and Places of Childhood and Youth conference, University of Reading, 24 Sep. 2015.

[59] HRO, 19M99/2/3a (Smith Nature Notebooks, 12 Apr. 1905).

[60] HRO, 19M99/1/2a (Smith Diary, 14 Jul. 1906). Compare the family's dismay at the orange-eating crowds atop Snowdon – '[W]e were so disgusted, we came back by the same train (only staying on the summit about 15 minutes!)': Smith Diary, Aug. 1906, undated entry.

the Lockinge downs did to him. On the contrary, the special tenderness for little things that was at the core of her responsiveness to nature left Katherine acutely exposed to loss, as when her beloved common was converted into golf links:

> [W]e went for a walk on the Common in the evening. The grass is growing on the Golf Links again, so it does not look quite so bad; but it can never be the same again to me. My copse looked as beautiful as ever from the outside, except where there had been left some bundles of cut-down gorse; but when we went into the copse, how sad I became; for someone had cut down many of the beautiful oak trees, and hewed and hacked about some of the undergrowth, and completely destroyed a most lovely wild rose tree, which I remembered was so beautiful last year! and my dear old oak tree that lent over the bank, and whose trunk had been covered with soft green moss, that was cut down too! But a little Chiffchaff was singing to reassure me, – in the same tree on which it had sung last year – that my wood might be beautiful again, when the young trees grew up, and the bracken, and bramble, and rose gently covered the desecrated ground. But its song was a little mournful, still, for things that had been, and were no more.[61]

On 26 August Katherine fell ill with rheumatic fever. As on previous and subsequent occasions, she made little of her illness, painful and protracted though it proved to be – she was singularly lacking in self-importance and may not have thought it warranted much notice. However, it was far more serious than she evidently realized – rheumatic fever can cause permanent damage to the heart valves, especially when it is recurrent.[62] As it was, it was not until 25 September that she felt sufficiently well to come downstairs. She took pleasure in watching two coal tits, a species she had never seen before, in the fir trees on one side of the garden.[63] Back in London, she noted at the start of a new volume of her diary that living where she did led her to appreciate the countryside all the more when she was in it. As spring gave way to summer, the family's thoughts were dominated by anxiety about whether Alic would 'get his First'; there was great relief and celebration when Alic's telegram arrived, bearing good news, on 26 July.[64] Meanwhile, Katherine had been preparing for an important development in her own life: she was going to join 'a sketching class held by Mr Cole' at Fittleworth in Sussex on 3 August.

Rex Vicat Cole, son of the distinguished landscape painter George Vicat Cole and an accomplished landscapist himself, was a key figure in Edwardian

[61] HRO, 19M99/2/3a (Smith Nature Notebooks, 9 Jul. 1905). On golf course landscapes, see Clare Griffiths, '"A Good Walk Spoiled"? Golfers and the Experience of Landscape during the Late Nineteenth Century', in Chad Bryant, Arthur Burns and Paul Readman (eds.), *Walking Histories, 1800–1914* (London, 2016), 195–217.
[62] HRO, 19M99/2/3a (Smith Nature Notebooks, 25 Sep. 1905).
[63] HRO, 19M99/2/3a (Smith Nature Notebooks, 25 Sep. 1905).
[64] HRO, 19M99/1/2a (Smith Diary, 26 Jul. 1906).

art education, teaching in the women's department of King's College London from 1894 to 1910.[65] Art schools at this time were often linked to residential sketching classes led by well-known painters. Cole had a studio at New Hall Farm, near Bolton Abbey in the West Riding, but this was a long way from London, and in 1906 he decided to lease Brinkwells, a secluded cottage set among sweet chestnut woods about a mile and a half north of Fittleworth, with a view to turning it into a studio.[66]

The location was an obvious and apt one. Fittleworth had strong family connections: two of his three sisters lived in cottages in the woods and both his father and grandfather had painted in the area.[67] Turner had visited Sussex frequently, publishing *Views in Sussex* in 1817 and painting some of his most celebrated landscapes at Petworth. Constable also knew Sussex well and thought the hanging woods above Arundel, not far from Fittleworth, 'beyond everything beautiful'. John Linnell, Copley Fielding and Henry George Hine were among the other Victorian artists who contributed to Sussex's growing reputation, such that, by the 1880s, in Peter Brandon's words, 'artists descended on Sussex in crowds', a claim supported by Peter Howard's statistical analysis of landscapes exhibited at the Royal Academy Summer Exhibition, which shows that, by 1900, 10 per cent of these land- scapes were of Sussex scenes.[68] This was part of a wider 'discovery of Sussex' between circa 1880 and 1939.[69] The vogue for the county was driven partly by a powerful desire to escape from 'darkest London' in late Victorian and Edwardian times. Unlike neighbouring Surrey, which had been popular with artists and writers at an earlier period, Sussex was far enough away not to be directly affected by London's remorseless expansion but was still close enough to be easily accessible by train. Writers such as Sheila Kaye-Smith and Eleanor Farjeon represented the county as singularly resistant to modernity, a place where ancient folk customs and vernacular traditions survived unblemished.[70]

[65] Tim Barringer, 'Cole, Reginald George Vicat [Rex] (1870–1940)', in *Oxford Dictionary of National Biography* (Oxford, 2004) [www.oxforddnb.com/view/article/53160, accessed 15 Nov. 2015].

[66] Carol Fitzgerald and Brian W. Harvey, *Elgar, Vicat Cole and the Ghosts of Brinkwells* (Chichester, 2007), 43.

[67] Fitzgerald and Harvey, *Elgar, Vicat Cole and the Ghosts of Brinkwells*, 90.

[68] Brandon, *The Discovery of Sussex*, 201 (Turner), 204 (Constable), 202–3 (Linnell), 205–6 (Fielding, Hine), 204 (quotation). Peter Howard, *Landscapes: The Artists' Vision* (London, 1991), 148. This represented a rise from 6 per cent in 1850; the county peaked at 14 per cent in the late 1920s.

[69] Brandon, *The Discovery of Sussex*.

[70] See, for example, Sheila Kaye-Smith's *Sussex Gorse* (1916), in which Boarzell Heath symbolizes the enduring power of the primitive, and Eleanor Farjeon's *Elsie Piddock Skips in Her Sleep* (1937). The rise of regional fiction is discussed in Keith, *Regions of the Imagination*.

Fittleworth itself was a microcosm of many of the aspects that made Sussex so appealing to artists and tourists at this time. The village was set at the foot of the South Downs, on the River Arun, among beautiful, extensive woods. Rivers and woods had attracted artists since the Picturesque movement of the late eighteenth century. Downland was a more recent artistic taste, stimulated in part by an interest in the primitive and in simpler, more abstract landscapes.[71] The village itself was noted for its picturesque cottages and vernacular buildings at a time when a rising preservationist consciousness and reaction against modernity were fostering great interest. The Swan Inn has a parlour the panels of which were decorated with paintings, given in lieu of payment, by artists who had stayed there.

Accompanied by her mother as far as Victoria Station, Katherine travelled down to Fittleworth on 4 August, excited but not without trepidation. She lodged with several other art students in Brookview Cottage, 'the quaintest old place'. Her minutely detailed, almost photographic description emphasizes the antiquity and vernacular features of the cottage and its 'rambling', picturesque garden, which seems to have been laid out in the cottage garden style then coming into vogue.[72] Away from home on her own for the first time (except to visit relatives), in an excitingly unfamiliar place, aged twenty-one, Katherine seems to have been transported to a plane of heightened, intensified experience, where the sensations of months were compressed into moments. In the morning she went for a walk by the beautiful river along banks bright with meadowsweet and purple loosestrife. Characteristically her gaze was drawn to the Downs, blue and misty in the distance. In the evening she followed a path up to the common. She retraces her route both in her nature notebook, written then and there on the common, and in her diary. It was evidently a metaphorical as well as a literal path, a Pilgrim's Progress leading up to the Romantic heights she dreamt of:

> Evening. It is very beautiful here, on the Common. From the house where I am staying a winding path through a silver birch copse leads to a gate on the hill, and lets you out on to the Common. It is very high up here, and I can see away into the distance, to where the beautiful Downs are sleeping, the shadows of the clouds resting on their gently rounded sides; they look mysterious and dream-like in the distance ... Running down the hill, on one side of the Common is a belt of Fir Trees, the wind is sweeping through them, and sounds to me like far-off waves.[73]

This was the only entry Katherine made in her nature notebook while she was at Fittleworth that summer. She had not yet tried to paint anything at this

---

[71] Howard, *Landscapes*, 173, 76.
[72] NCA, PA SMA 1 2 (Letter from Katherine Smith to Kate Smith, 4 Aug. 1906).
[73] HRO, 19M99/2/4 (Smith Nature Notebooks, 4 Aug. 1906).

point, which may be significant, as her diary, written up 'long after', suggests that doing so did not prove entirely straightforward:

> I managed to practically finish four pictures, and began a fifth; and having the satisfaction of Mr Cole's saying I had improved very much in the three weeks I was there; but sometimes I can't help feeling despondent about my painting, and thinking I shall never be able to paint really well; but I must not give way to melancholy thoughts, I know it is wrong; and shall try to go on steadily and see what can be done with patience![74]

Nor were the social aspects of the sketching class altogether satisfactory. On the second day, a Miss Hawksley arrived. Katherine's comments are untypically cutting:

> She was about forty, very fussy and very satisfied with her own powers of painting; she painted in water-colours, and very badly! She had been abroad all the winter, painting in the Isle of Capri. She talked a great deal about what she had seen etc.[75]

It would seem that Miss Hawksley was one of those ambitious career women who 'vainly strive to reach the crown', deplored in Katherine's poem 'To "Some" Women'. It is hardly surprising that Katherine, quiet, sensitive and modest as she was, recoiled from someone evidently cut from cruder cloth. Whether it was Miss Hawksley's crassness or her artistic self-assurance that most troubled Katherine is less clear.

In the end, it was something of a relief to come home. After the initial excitement had subsided, she seems to have felt a little lonely at Fittleworth. No-one saw her off at the station but Alic met her at Victoria and she was quickly reabsorbed into the bosom of her family. She had little time to mull over her experiences, since the following day (24 August 1906) Kate, Alic and Katherine took the midnight train from Paddington to Chester for a holiday in North Wales, iconic territory for Romantic travellers like the Smiths. They admired the Conway valley and Swallow Falls before arriving at Capel Curig, where they stayed for seventeen days. Katherine did not do much painting. If anything, her confidence seems to have been damaged by Vicat Cole's sketching class:

> It was a glorious walk along the Bangor road, the mountains were very wild, and at sunset, the light streamed in a great beam of red or gold between a pass in the mountains, bathing the foot of one in a golden mist; a mountain torrent rushed at one's feet. I tried to paint it but did not feel equal to finishing it.[76]

[74] HRO, 19M99/1/2a (Smith Diary, 6 Aug. 1906 [written later]).
[75] HRO, 19M99/1/2a (Smith Diary, 6 Aug. 1906 [written later]).
[76] HRO, 19M99/1/2a (Smith Diary, 24 Aug. 1906 [written later]).

The mountains of Snowdonia elicited a strikingly different response from Katherine than had Skiddaw four years earlier. She had 'learnt to love that mountain [Skiddaw] dearly' but felt rebuffed by the Welsh peaks:

> I came prepared to love these mountains dearly, but they seemed to disdain my love, rising up stern and bare, all sufficient in themselves, and wrapped in an impenetrable sublimity. I remember one day, it was cold and had been raining, and the sun did not shine; I walked up and down the road by myself, looking at the mountains and the torrent, when a little robin came and perched in a bare tree beside me and sang his sweet mellow song, and it warmed my heart. – But the mountains were very beautiful, and the clouds seemed to love them, and rest on their peaks.[77]

Why was Snowdon stern and bare whereas Skiddaw had been peaceful, quiet and tranquil? The weather may have played a part but they had clouds as well as sunshine in the Lakes, while they were lucky enough to ascend Snowdon on a day when the summit was clear. Nor can vegetation explain much: the two mountains are and were equally treeless above their lowest slopes. It was Katherine's feelings, rather than the mountains, that had changed. At seventeen, the world lay all before her, and when she gazed at the Cumbrian lakes and mountains she saw hopeful prospects stretching far ahead. At twenty-one she was attempting to realize some of those prospects and, as her reflections on Fittleworth suggest, this was proving a more daunting proposition than she had anticipated.

Katherine's language in this passage prompts further questions. It is highly gendered: although the mountains are not explicitly masculine, Katherine figures them in tropes that correspond to a particularly severe, patriarchal version of Romantic masculinity. Compare, for example, Coleridge's 'Hymn before Sunrise, in the Vale of Chamouny', in which he addresses Mont Blanc as 'sovran . . . dread and silent Mount', with 'bald awful head'. Coleridge, however, is exhilarated by the mountain and the poem comes close to conflating peak, poet and divinity.[78] Katherine too sees in the mountains an emphatic expression of selfhood, albeit one from which she is excluded. This Romantic, archetypically male version of the self as unitary, self-sufficient, stable and enduring is one that feminist life writing scholars such as Gagnier have been at pains to debunk.[79] They argue that it is a mythical construct and that it simply does not correspond to most women's sense of self, which is putatively relational, multiple and contingent. The privileging and normalizing of this middle-class, masculine version of the self serves, according to this analysis, to marginalize and delegitimize the experiences and identities of subordinate groups such as women and the working class. Was the disdain Katherine

---

[77] Ibid.
[78] Ironically Coleridge had seen the mountain only in his imagination.
[79] Gagnier, *Subjectivities*.

attributed to the Welsh mountains really a figurative expression of what she perceived as the failure of her identity to measure up to what, did she but know it, was an alien cultural imposition? Did she feel this particularly acutely in the summer of 1906 because she was, for the first time, attempting to break into a masculine public sphere in which a heroic unitary self was de rigueur?[80]

This is, up to a point, a persuasive interpretation. The Smiths, as we have seen, were deeply imbued with Romanticism and in some respects this seems to have worked better for Walter and Alic than for Katherine. Kate's primary interests lay elsewhere, in the familial, domestic sphere. Although she seems to have been happy enough to go on walks and cycle rides or gaze at paintings with the rest of the family, her letters indicate that these things were far from central to her concerns. This may have insulated her from the effects of the family's gendered performance of Romantic tourism. While father and son climbed Skiddaw and tramped twenty-four miles over the hills, Katherine went for seven-mile walks and 'got a good many nice beetles'.[81] Walter and Alic climbed Snowdon on foot while Katherine and Kate went up by train.[82] This pattern is recurrent. Unless there was a chronic health problem not mentioned in her diaries, notebooks or letters, there seems no physical reason why she should not, at the age of seventeen, have been able to walk as far as her father and brother.

What is less clear is whether the root cause of Katherine's difficulties was lack of belief in her ability to reach the summit of her chosen vocation, or the fact that she felt obliged to climb it in the first place. It is telling, and a pointer towards the ornithological withdrawal of the future, that it was a little bird that brought her relief in Snowdonia. Interestingly, she assumed the robin was male, despite the fact that, in this species, both sexes sing. This suggests that while a particular version of Romantic masculinity may have been oppressive for Katherine, she also sought and found comfort and encouragement from masculine sources, a pattern that is certainly apparent in her relationship with Alic. Indeed, the fundamental contrast in the Snowdon passage is not between male and female, since both mountain (implicitly) and bird (explicitly) are male, but between great and small. It was Katherine's deep-seated modesty and lack of self-importance, characteristics influenced but far from determined by her gender, that precluded a heroic assertion of herself as a Romantic artist on the Coleridgean model, rather than her gender per se.

---

[80] Whether Katherine's exposure to Ruskin's ideas contributed to her doubts about her ability to become a painter is unclear. Marsh demonstrates that many young female painters found Ruskin encouraging and inspiring, but this was mainly through personal contact, in contrast to his more negative published pronouncements. Jan Marsh, '"Resolve to Be a Great Paintress": Women Artists in Relation to John Ruskin as Critic and Patron', *Nineteenth Century Contexts* 18 (1994), 177–85.

[81] HRO, 19M99/1/1 (Smith Diary, Aug. 1902 [written Oct. 1902]).

[82] HRO, 19M99/1/2a (Smith Diary, Aug. 1906 [written later]).

Whatever the cause, the Welsh mountains crystallized and enabled Katherine to express a sense of confinement and oppression, of being prevented from being herself:

> [W]e had a beautiful drive home, the sun setting and shedding beams of light in the Llanberis pass was glorious; and yet I did not quite like it, the pass is so narrow and deep, and I felt so enclosed by the huge stern walls of mountain. I would always rather be on the <u>top</u> of hills or downs, with a great space of sky and air around me, than in a valley enclosed by walls of rock.[83]

After coming back from Wales, the family spent some time at Lee. However, that December the Smiths moved from Kensington to the aptly named Park View House in Rickmansworth, twenty miles north-west of London. Now that he had got his job in Whitehall, Alic had moved back in with the family and perhaps the house in Kensington was too small. Moving to the outer suburbs on the fringe of the countryside was a widespread pattern among the London upper-middle class at this time and is both a marker of the family's social success and an indicator that their values were broadly mainstream. However, the family's commitment to ruralism was stronger than most and the move to Rickmansworth was to prove only the first step in a ruralist trajectory. Katherine's feelings were mixed. On the one hand, she was thrilled to be living in 'real country . . . valleys and rivers, and hills clothed in woods, splendid trees everywhere, and fields and lanes'. She made a studio for herself up at the top of the house and revelled in the bird life. Indeed, it seems likely that Walter and Kate chose Rickmansworth, and Park View House in particular, largely with Katherine in mind. On the other hand, now that they were living in the country, it no longer seemed necessary to continue to rent the house at Lee. This represented a familiar pattern of loss for Katherine: 'I loved that little house and garden, and the open sea and cliff, and my little bird friends; but that is all over now too.'[84]

Despite the doubts she had experienced at Fittleworth, Katherine continued to apply herself diligently to her artistic studies. The annual exhibition of the students' paintings in January proved to be a highlight:

> I am glad to say David Murray spoke favourably of my pictures, and said a thing that was very true, and clever of him to find out – 'Here, I see, we have a Lover of Nature.' Later on Mr Cole awarded me the scholarship to go to Fittleworth this summer for 4 weeks. Alic gave me Ruskin's 'Modern Painters' in a nice pocket edition, in which after my name he put (L.N.) which meant 'Lover of Nature', as I think he was pleased David Murray liked my pictures.[85]

---

[83] HRO, 19M99/1/2a (Smith Diary, Aug. 1906 [written later]). Compare HRO, 19M99/1/3a (Smith Diary, 11 Jul. 1909): 'what a joy it was to be beside the free wide sea again!').

[84] HRO, 19M99/1/2a (Smith Diary, Aug. 1906 [written later]).

[85] HRO, 19M99/1/2a (Smith Diary, 1907, undated).

Murray was a well-known Scottish landscape painter and one of the 'visitors' (inspectors) for the ladies' art department. His praise, and the award of the scholarship that followed, must have been especially encouraging to Katherine given her uncertainty about the value of her work. Perhaps more striking, however, is what the episode reveals about how central 'Nature' had become to her sense of identity. Alic, more attuned than his parents to his sister's inner life and hopes, understood this and his affirmation must have further reinforced Katherine's inclination to construe her identity in this way.

The Smiths took advantage of their new location in 'real country' by going on walks in the nearby Chilterns. One such walk in the summer of 1907 proved especially memorable. Katherine, her mother and 'Uncle Tom' took the train to Chorleywood, then walked to Chenies and on to Chalfont Road station.[86] They had lunch in a beech wood, asked their way of an old miller and were told by him that there was a ruined church in an adjacent wood. They went into the wood ('most enchanting and mysterious') and eventually found the elusive church in a little enclosure of firs:

> It was indeed a little church, but so old and beautiful, before Norman I should think, it had no roof, and was over-grown with ivy, which seemed as if it would fain keep the little church a secret to itself, and the sweet tall flowers and long grasses were helping to hide it too. Indeed it was a lovely spot, and productive of much thought.[87]

We read ourselves into the landscape: it was not only the little church which would 'fain keep ... a secret to itself'. One wonders whether among the thoughts it gave rise to in Katherine was an inclination to believe that the loveliness and beauty of the little church depended on its seclusion.

On 6 July Katherine went down to Fittleworth for a second time to take up Vicat Cole's scholarship. Again this proved a mixed experience. She was, if anything, even more responsive to the beauty of the surroundings:

> It always gave me intense joy to look at the Downs, ever fresh and lovely, ever changing like the sea, with every mood of the sky. I saw many a wonderful effect on them, especially when a storm swept across or along them, then sometimes I held my breath, and all seemed a dream![88]

---

[86] This may have been the T. Pemberton given on the family tree as the husband of Marion, a younger sister of Kate's.

[87] Ibid.

[88] HRO, 19M99/1/2a (Smith Diary, 6 Jul. 1907).

Figure 4.1   Katherine's painting of the South Downs from Fittleworth
Reproduced by kind permission of the Hampshire Record Office (HRO 19M99/3/1)

But as in North Wales, the deeper the impression the landscape made on her, the less she felt able to give expression to it:

> It is useless to try and describe any of the effects, I should have done that at the time, and then even, it would have been no good, such things are <u>felt</u>, and remembered, stored up in the 'chambers beautiful' of one's mind, but difficult indeed to write in words! And I found them more difficult still to paint![89]

However, Katherine seems to have been feeling for a way out of this impasse. Whereas she felt sternly rejected by the peaks of Snowdonia, at Fittleworth this year a countervailing impulse allowed her to experience nature once again as friendly and supportive rather than hostile and challenging:

> I think I must have been discouraged, although Mr Cole gave me every encouragement – but I felt every thing to be so beautiful, and the effort to express them in paint so difficult, so inadequate, that I felt sometimes I could only go to Nature without any presumptuous attempt to represent her; ~~and lay~~ to go to her with nothing but an open loving heart, ready and

[89] Ibid.

eager to receive whatever ~~she~~ she had to bestow! And how glorious was the gift![90]

Whether this 'glorious gift' was an adequate compensation for the abandonment of her ambition to become a successful painter is one of the central questions raised by the remaining years of Katherine's life.

In summer 1907, however, her feelings on this point were still in flux. Shortly after arriving at Fittleworth, she walked up to the belt of pines that led to the common and wrote a long letter to Alic, explaining that she thought it was not perhaps her vocation to paint and that something else, designing perhaps, might be more suitable. Later she regretted sending the letter: at the end of the three weeks, Vicat Cole invited her to stay on longer so that she could finish a large canvas of a ditch bright with meadowsweet and purple loosestrife, but Kate would not allow this, convinced that her daughter had been miserable and homesick while away.[91]

The following Easter the Smiths went down to Salcombe for a short holiday, taking in Weston, Torquay and assorted relatives on the way. Katherine revelled in the dramatic cliff scenery of Bolt Head and the unfamiliar seabirds and plants of the area. Her nature notebook is replete with detailed observations and sonorous scientific names: Cochlearia Danica, Ruscus Aculeatus, Phylloscopus Trochilis, Saxicola Oenanthe.[92] Her growing confidence as a field naturalist, and mastery of the technical vocabulary required, is apparent. There is no mention of painting.

The close of the 1907–8 academic session brought her studies at the ladies' art department to an end.[93] She obtained her certificate in landscape and later in the summer went down to Fittleworth again for the last time. There are no diary entries and the nature notebook, beyond some vividly observed descriptions of the flight and calls of nightjars on the common, gives few clues to Katherine's state of mind. However, a letter from Alic suggests that, for the third year in a row, Fittleworth proved a mixed blessing: 'I was so sorry to hear from Mother about all your trouble, at Fittleworth; I hope you will have a better time this week.'[94]

She was still an active member of the Selborne Society, attending meetings and reading a biography of the doyenne of popular naturalists, Mrs Brightwen, an erstwhile vice-president of the Selbornians.[95] She provided Katherine, in quest still for her true path in life, with another possible model for her identity.

---

[90] Ibid. Deletions in original.
[91] Ibid.
[92] Danish scurvy grass, butcher's broom, willow warbler and wheatear respectively.
[93] HRO, 19M99/5/8/15 (Certificate of Attendance at King's College Art School, 1907–8).
[94] NCA, PA SMA 1/10/5 (Letter from Alic Smith to Smith undated [1908]).
[95] On Mrs Brightwen, see W. Brightwen and E. Gosse, *Eliza Brightwen: The Life and Thoughts of a Naturalist* (London, 1909).

Mrs Brightwen, Katherine noted in her diary, 'filled her hours' by getting up at
5 in the morning, studying nature in her garden and then giving up the rest of
the day to doing good to others and ministering to the poor. 'And yet she was
delicate and a great sufferer.'[96]

Rickmansworth provided ample scope for a dedicated Selbornian. During
the winter, Katherine hung out coconuts and fat in the garden for the tits and
hoped to attract nuthatches by putting out two nest boxes. She went on
frequent walks and one day was startled to see a flash of blue, and then another,
skim across a pond: kingfishers. Convinced they had a nest in the bank, she
went home to fetch her binoculars but was dismayed to find half-a-dozen boys
tearing round the pond and scrambling up the banks. Overcoming her habitual
shyness, she persuaded them to go away. The next day she found two boys
birds-nesting among the hedges on the way to Loudwater and got them to
promise not to take any eggs from the nests of unusual birds, for which she
undertook to compensate them, a revealing example of how the apparently
incompatible priorities of rural working-class children and an upper middle-
class lady could be reconciled through the transfer of cash.[97]

Being able to get out into the countryside more easily and frequently seems
to have worked well for Katherine, judging by the lively, cheerful entries in her
nature notebooks. The coming of spring gave her particular pleasure:

> At last the cold bitter winds have gone, and the snow and frost are all
> melted; there is a delightful feeling of spring in the air, and all the birds are
> singing ceaselessly. The thrushes [sic] notes are now quite perfect, and the
> blackbird sings his mellow flute-like notes; the missel-thrush is very
> loquacious, and the Chaffinch is bubbling over with his song and courts
> his mate. Robins are now in pairs and sing sweetly. The wren seems very
> rejoiced at the change in the weather and utters his praise loudly.[98]

The Chiltern beech woods feature prominently in the nature notebooks for this
period. On a long walk from Great Missenden to Wendover in early May,
Katherine plunged up to her knees in beech leaves as she walked down an eroded
path. Looking back she saw the blue sky between the stems of the beeches and
above the vivid green of the young leaves. She had even found herself a copse,
a successor to the little wood that had meant so much to her at Lee. Evidently
a kind of peace had come to her in the rural environment of Rickmansworth:

> It was very sweet and still in the copse, with the sunlight colouring the last
> years bramble leaves, and the swelling buds of the trees; the fresh green
> leaves of the blue-bells were covering the ground and Dogs Mercury was
> in flower; then the mellow notes of a blackbird floated on the air, and

---

[96] HRO, 19M99/1/3a (Smith Diaries, 5 Jul. 1909).

[97] HRO, 19M99/2/7 (Smith Nature Notebooks, 26 and 27 Mar. 1909).

[98] HRO, 19M99/2/7 (Smith Nature Notebooks, 19 Mar.) The entry is prefaced by
a quotation from Wordsworth: 'It is the first mild day of Spring.'

a robin sang sweetly beside me, and a Missel Thrush began his song in a distant copse. I lent against a tree and looked at the pale spring sky and the tree tops against it, and thought how beautiful it all was.[99]

Perhaps the most notable event in Katherine's life at this time, however, was that she got a dog – an affectionate cocker spaniel called Di. Both Di and Billi, Katherine's cat, missed her while she was on a painting excursion to the popular artists' colony of Walberswick on the Suffolk coast (11–17 July 1909). Alic wrote a warm, amused letter, reassuring Katherine that her pets, although pining for her, were nevertheless eating and in good health. But Alic's humour had an ulterior purpose: the painting had not gone well, ostensibly because it had rained and Katherine had been poorly. She only managed to complete two sketches. The pattern is unmistakeable: every time Katherine went away to paint she 'did not feel up to much painting' and came back dejected. Increasingly, however, she seems to have been able to separate her feelings about painting from those about nature, aided by her growing technical proficiency as a naturalist and perhaps by the promptings she had experienced at Fittleworth two years before to approach nature with 'nothing but an open loving heart'. Alic wrote in reply to a now-lost letter of hers that he was 'glad you have got some comfort from the birds, if not from painting'.[100]

Walberswick was evidently intended as a substitute for Fittleworth and even if the painting (or at least Katherine's assessment of it) was no more successful, the emotional aftermath certainly was, although how far this was due to the greater strength Katherine was now able to draw from nature and how far to the fact that in Walberswick her fragile artistic self-confidence was less exposed to corrosive contact from art students like Miss Hawksley is difficult to say. Three years previously Katherine had carried the doubts generated at Fittleworth with her to North Wales. In summer 1909 the Smiths likewise departed for a lengthy holiday, this time in the Highlands, almost immediately after Katherine returned from Walberswick. However, this holiday, as Katherine noted in an undated addendum to her diary, 'was a very happy time, and the memory of the glorious scenery is now one of my most treasured and beautiful possessions'.

They went up on the Great Central through Sheffield, which predictably did not appeal to Katherine, and then along the Settle and Carlisle line through the Yorkshire Dales, whose wild quiet loneliness entranced her. From Glasgow they proceeded by steamer down the Clyde, through the Crinan Canal and then up Loch Linnhe to Fort William. The scenery grew increasingly impressive, gleams of light breaking through the misty mountains of Morven and, in

[99] HRO, 19M99/2/7 (Smith Nature Notebooks, 27 Mar. 1909).
[100] NCA, PA SMA 1/10/5 (Letter from Alic Smith to Katherine Spear Smith, 14 Jul. 1909). Alic's letter is consistent with the evidence of the nature notebooks, which record the 'graceful and swift' flight of common terns fishing over the sea. HRO, 19M99/2/7 (Smith Nature Notebooks, 12 Jul. 1909).

the gathering dusk, the grim peaks of Glencoe rising up awfully above Ballachulish. Back on dry land, the Smiths explored Glen Nevis, Katherine taking particular pleasure in the flowers – bog asphodel, spotted orchis, cotton grass, bog myrtle and the rare and beautiful Grass of Parnassus ('I found it beside a river: it is the most lovely flower'). She picked a Grass of Parnassus bud, put it in water and it opened in the night, almost certainly the model for one of her most delicate and accomplished drawings.

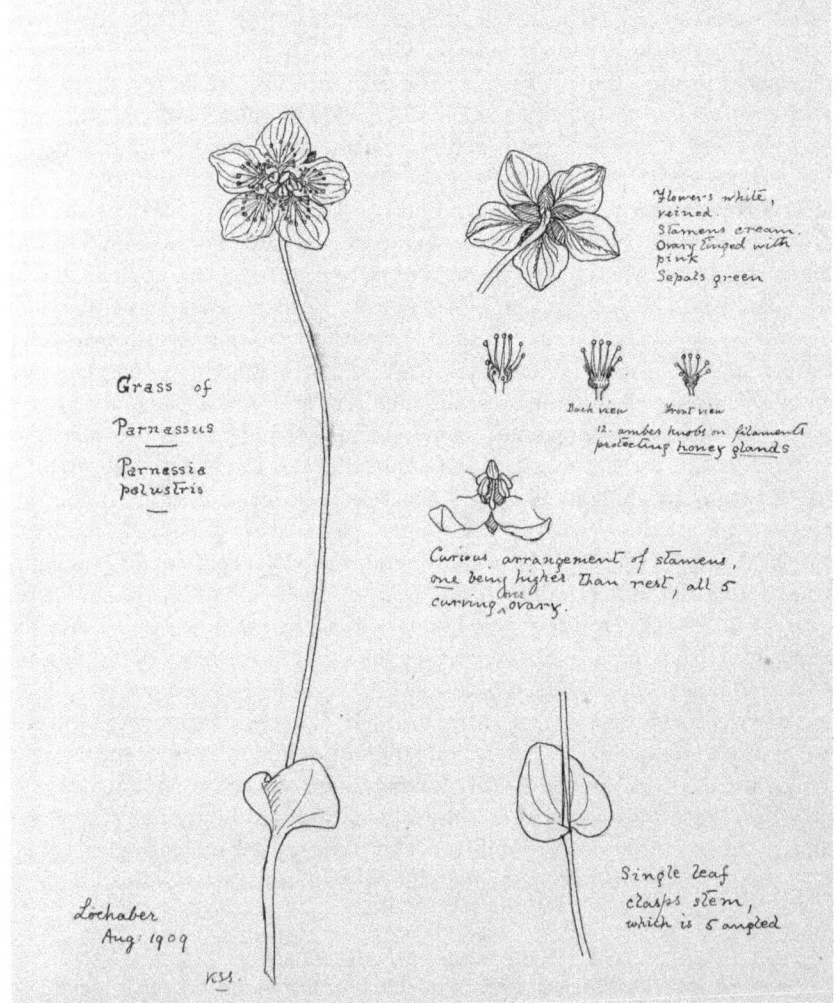

Figure 4.2   Katherine's drawing of the Grass of Parnassus from Glen Nevis
Reproduced by kind permission of the Hampshire Record Office (HRO 19M99/1/3)

It is evident from the botanical details and annotations that Katherine made this drawing in the spirit of a naturalist rather than an artist. Paradoxically, casting art aside seems to have liberated her powers of artistic self-expression.

The following day (8 August), the Smiths went to the English church in Fort William. At this point in her life, religion does not seem to have affected Katherine especially strongly but she was interested to see a number of clan chiefs, nearly all young men in Highland dress, which she thought gave them a very becoming and aristocratic demeanour. Her family, doubtless influenced by Walter Scott, were drawn to the Romantic vision of the Highlands and Katherine also enjoyed the bagpipe competition, Highland dancing and caber-throwing at the Lochaber Gathering on the 24th. They visited Glenfinnan to see where Bonnie Prince Charlie raised his standard, and other fêted West Highland landscapes such as Glencoe and Loch Coruisk.

It was, however, the environs of Fort William that impressed Katherine most. One day they took a steamer along Loch Lochy.[101] Standing at the taffrail, or perhaps on the roof of the cabin, Katherine gazed at the steamer's wake, extending mesmerically across the calm waters of the loch. It took her into dreamland again:

> The reflections were the most wonderful I have seen, the hills & rocks & trees were all faithfully represented as in a crystal mirror; the steamer made no ripple each side, only behind a white wake and spreading from it long undulating lines which had the effect of concave and convex mirrors, where the hills were still clearly reflected, but in distortion; so that at one point they met and enclosed a piece of blue sky which looked like another lake below the surface of the one we were on! We felt like 'Alice Through the Looking Glass', gazing into another world but just like our own.[102]

At times during this holiday Katherine's soul seemed to feed on beauty. One stormy Friday she walked up the road beside Loch Linnhe, watching the shadows and sunlight flitting across the hills. Down the Great Glen she saw 'a vision of beauty': the mountains were intensely blue, some in shadow, and a misty rain was passing over them. As she gazed, the sun shone out in the mist and the whole valley was filled with rainbow colours, 'all misty and full of glorious light'.[103]

Literally and metaphorically, the highpoint of the holiday was Ben Nevis. In keeping with the family's gendered Romanticism, Walter and Alic climbed to the summit while Katherine and Kate stayed down below.[104] This, however, did

---

[101] Probably the well-known Great Glen steamer *Gondolier*.
[102] HRO, 19M99/1/3a (Smith Diaries, 17 Aug. 1909).
[103] HRO, 19M99/1/3a (Smith Diaries, 20 Aug. 1909).
[104] HRO, 19M99/1/3a (Smith Diaries, 23 Aug. 1909). Alic had arrived from London on the 21st.

nothing to reduce the powerful impression the mountain made on the youngest Smith:

> The train suddenly turned a corner, and there was a sight to take one's breath away! the sun was shining full on Ben Nevis and the red screes of the mountain beyond it, in great slashes of glorious red, and all round were deep pure blue shadows, and a mist just sliding across the lower part of the mountain. To describe it, is beyond me, but the effect was exalted and glorious in the extreme![105]

A second encounter with the Ben just over a week later was more intimate. The Smiths had followed a little road leading into the hills and come to a beautiful secluded moor, covered with heather, moss, boulders and little streams. Rising up grandly behind this was the summit of Ben Nevis, dark and blue and wild. Here, Katherine felt, was the true spirit of the mountains and moors: 'a glorious freedom & wildness, an intimate relation between cloud & earth, sunshine & mist & rainbow, the sound of torrents, & the feeling of wide spaces!'[106]

This 'glorious freedom & wildness', the liberation of spirit prompted by the encounter with wide open spaces, appears to be a characteristic modern response to rural landscapes. Keith Thomas draws attention to it in *Man and the Natural World* and Taylor also sees it as a central element in the outdoor movement.[107] It has often been linked with alienation in the classical Marxist sense:

> I'm a rambler, I'm a rambler from Manchester way
> I get all me pleasure the hard moorland way
> I may be a wage slave on Monday
> But I am a free man on Sunday[108]

No oppressive factory owner was, however, extracting surplus value from Katherine. Indeed, the problem was if anything that she had too little rather than too much to do. The freedom that she yearned for, especially at this time in her life, cannot have been from material constraints, for there were none. One might go further and suggest that she suffered from no significant external constraints of any kind at all. Her family had shown that they were willing to encourage and support her, emotionally and financially, in her chosen career as an artist and there is every indication that they would have been willing to do so had she preferred a different path. When she seemed drawn to music, they

---

[105] HRO, 19M99/1/3a (Smith Diaries, 10 Aug. 1909). Katherine shows herself a true Romantic in claiming not to be able to express what she has just described vividly.

[106] HRO, 19M99/1/3a (Smith Diaries, 18 Aug. 1909).

[107] Keith Thomas, *Man and the Natural World: Changing Attitudes in England 1500–1800* (Harmondsworth, 1984), 267; Taylor, *A Claim on the Countryside*.

[108] Ewan MacColl, 'Manchester Rambler'. Lyrics: https://mudcat.org/@displaysong.cfm?SongID=3843 [accessed 21 Nov. 2018].

arranged singing lessons for her, and when she developed a serious interest in natural history, they moved to the countryside, in part at least so she would better be able to pursue this. Nor are there any indications that Katherine was signifi-cantly held back by overt social constraints. Her paintings were praised by her teachers, among them two leading contemporary artists, one of whom awarded her a scholarship towards the cost of her studies and entreated her to stay on longer at his sketching class to finish a canvas. Katherine showed no sign of wanting to pursue any vocation other than art or music but, had she done so, she would have found that social attitudes to women's employment were becoming more favourable. Even the rather conservative *Girl's Own Paper*, which Katherine took in her teens, accepted the need for fulfilling work for middle-class women prior to marriage, while attitudes to female employment in more progressive magazines such as *Queen* were very positive by 1900.[109] The constraints on Katherine were real and serious but they were internal rather than external.

Some light on the nature of these constraints may be shed by the timing of Katherine's yearning for freedom. It was above all in her mid-twenties that she exulted in the liberation of mountain vistas and open spaces. These do not feature in her poems, written in her late teens and early twenties, in which the words 'free' and 'freedom' are conspicuous by their absence. Nor do the entries in Katherine's diary and notebooks written in her late twenties and thirties evince the passionate embrace of freedom that she expressed repeatedly between 1906 and 1909. We must look to Katherine's situation and to the events in her life if we are to understand her energetic and distinctive responses to landscape at this time. The nub of the matter seems to have been that she was caught between the hammer of her expectations and the anvil of her doubts. She felt that she ought or even needed to achieve something notable, preferably in the artistic field, but the harder she tried to do so, the more she was undermined by her doubts that she was capable of this. The 'glorious freedom' she embraced so eagerly in the mountains corresponded to an exhilarating escape from this constraint and to a life-affirming belief in the value and capacity of her true self. The difficulty, for Katherine and for anyone who takes an interest in her, lies in gauging whether it was her expectations or her doubts that were the root cause of her difficulties.

One way out of the dilemma, hinted at in the all-embracing binaries of earth and sky, sun and rain in Katherine's celebration of Ben Nevis, was to dissolve the distinction between herself and the landscape. Part of Katherine yearned for this, but such a dissolution involves the annihilation of the self, perhaps

---

[109] Kristine Moruzi and Michelle Smith, '"Learning What Real Work ... Means" : Ambivalent Attitudes towards Employment in the *Girl's Own Paper*', *Victorian Periodicals Review* 43 (2010), 433; Arlene Young, 'Ladies and Professionalism: The Evolution of the Idea of Work in the *Queen*, 1861–1900', *Victorian Periodicals Review* 40 (2007), 189–215.

even a death wish. One of her last diary entries before leaving the Highlands carries these Keatsian overtones:

> 27th August. In the evening we went up on the moor, and following a track we saw a wild valley with mountains all round rising up darkly from it, where were a few white cottages. From the moor we could see the mountains of the Glen we had visited in the afternoon, & from where we stood, the Loch between was hidden & it looked as if the moor stretched on & on to these dark blue peaks, across which a beam of the sun was mistily shining. The dark wide spaces of this moorland covered with heather in full bloom, & scattered over with rocks & mossy peat streams, are indescribably lovely; with the fresh wind blowing on one's face & the faint scent of the aromatic sweet gale or bog myrtle. Here I should have liked to have stayed & watched the night come down on to the dark peaks standing stationary all around & the white mists wrapping them in their cold embrace!![110]

We know little about Katherine's life in the following year, 1910, because she did not keep a diary, nor did she send or receive many letters. There are, however, a few entries in the nature notebooks. These suggest that for most of the year she continued her quiet existence at Rickmansworth, putting out food for the birds, trying to coax the nuthatches into using her nestboxes and walking in the Chilterns, often with Di. On one of these walks she came across a beautiful sight: a plant of wild arum was growing in the shade of a beech tree, its delicate, half-transparent hood, upright rod of purply-brown flowers and green arrow-shaped leaves forming a lovely picture, delicate, subdued and harmonizing perfectly with the surrounding beech leaves. She found several more arum plants but none that looked like this one, as they were among grass. Reflecting on this afterwards, she concluded that it was the background of dead leaves that had brought out the beauty in the usually ordinary-looking arum: 'How often does a certain environment or background, bring out a beautiful character!' Perhaps, as so often in her responses to nature and landscape, Katherine had herself partly in mind. If so, this suggests a dawning realization that her personality might only be able to come into its own in certain environments – quiet, peaceful, non-pressurizing ones for example.[111]

On the whole, this seems to have been a period of contentment and stability in Katherine's life. The entries in her nature notebooks are vivid and precise, stylistically reminiscent (perhaps not accidentally) of Dorothy Wordsworth:

> November 17th Had a severe frost in the night; the day was fine with sunshine. In the Park, I noticed an Ash Tree had shed its leaves in the night, and they were lying thick just beneath it. Several cows were eating these Ash leaves; they were still a good deal green, so I suppose the cows enjoyed them.

[110] HRO, 19M99/1/3a (Smith Diaries, 27 Aug. 1909).
[111] HRO, 19M99/2/7 (Smith Nature Notebooks, 18 May 1910).

The beech trees seem almost the last trees to shed their leaves; there are many on still, also on Silver birch. After a frost, when there is no wind, the leaves fall rustling down straight from the trees.[112]

In April the following year, the Smiths went down to Lee again after an absence of four years. Katherine's prose breathes her delight in rediscovering familiar haunts:

> Went to the copse near Melville Farm, where there used to be primroses; found them all out, and the ground covered with anemones also. Found one blue-bell in flower; wood spurge out. The Elm bushes & boles were in tiny leaf.[113]

The following day Katherine revisited her beloved copse on the common and rejoiced to find it 'almost unchanged', the beautiful holly trees standing just the same.[114] Evidently the scars caused by the construction of the golf course had healed more quickly than she anticipated. It was doubtless in part because of the great success of this return to Lee that Walter made the momentous decision to buy an old Georgian house, Titchfield Lodge, in the eponymous village, only four miles from Lee. The plan was that the family would live there permanently when he retired, a further step in the Smiths' counter-urban migration away from London, and, in the meantime, they would come down for the holidays. They arrived for the first time on 27 July 1911. Katherine wrote enthusiastically about the high red brick wall that surrounded the large garden full of fruit trees. It was a remarkably hot summer, but she was unable to enjoy it as only a few days after arriving she fell ill with another bout of rheumatic fever and was in bed for six weeks. Even in late September she was still unable to go out for walks, but was sufficiently recovered to distinguish the calls of the male and female brown (tawny) owl and a hoarse yell that she plausibly took to be that of a barn owl.[115]

That autumn proved to be exceptional for leaf colour. Back in Rickmansworth, Katherine went out frequently, partly no doubt making up for the weeks she had been cooped up in bed over the summer. She made exquisite botanical drawings of two wild service trees in the park and revelled in the play of light and shadow on the richly tinted landscape:

> The clouds were magnificent this morning, great towering autumn clouds, with long straight bases, that let the sunlight roll over the landscape, touching the autumn trees to pale flame (for they are mostly yellows left) in front of a rich dark background.[116]

---

[112] HRO, 19M99/2/7 (Smith Nature Notebooks, 17 Nov. 1910).

[113] HRO, 19M99/2/7 (Smith Nature Notebooks, 18 Apr. 1911). The last sentence echoes Browning's 'Home Thoughts from Abroad', appropriately enough since this was indeed a kind of homecoming.

[114] HRO, 19M99/2/7 (Smith Nature Notebooks, 19 Apr. 1911).

[115] HRO, 19M99/2/9 (Smith Nature Notebooks, 25 Sep. 1911).

[116] HRO, 19M99/2/7 (Smith Nature Notebooks, 25 Oct. 1911).

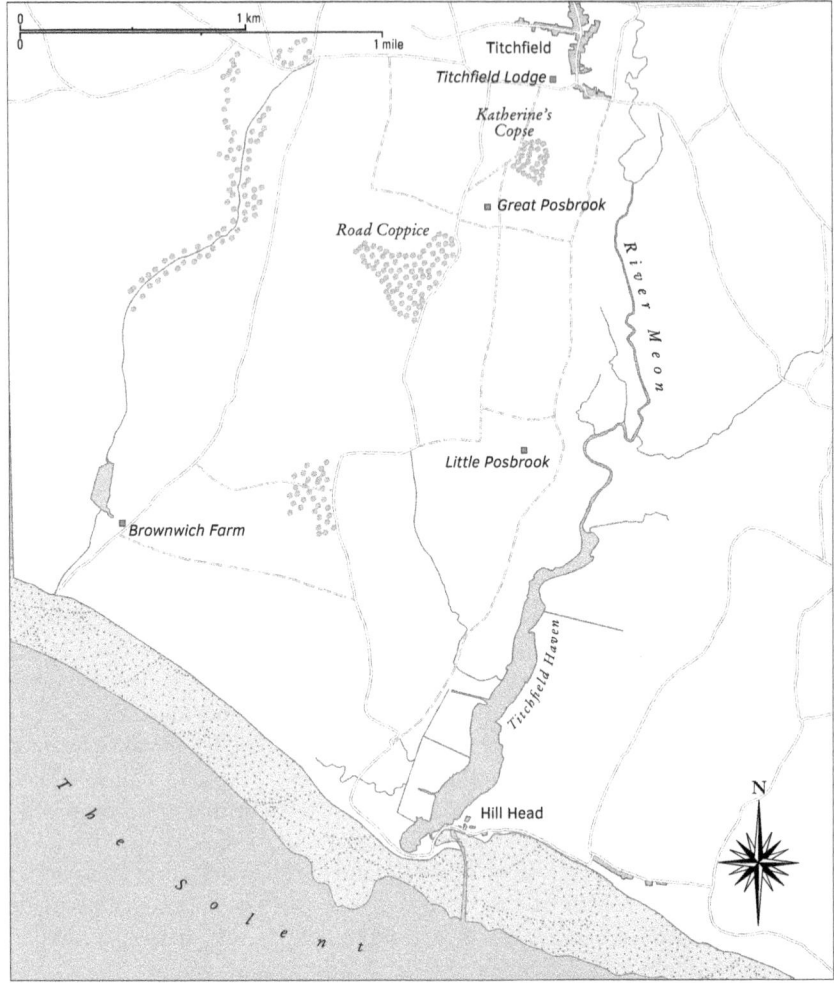

Figure 4.3 Titchfield Lodge, Katherine's copse and the sea
Redrawn by The Maps Archive from OS County Series 1:10560, 2nd Revision, 1909 ©
Crown Copyright and Landmark Information Group Limited 2022. All rights reserved.

The Smiths returned to Titchfield Lodge for Christmas and again over the
Easter vacation in 1912. On 19 April Katherine noticed a pair of long-tailed tits
fluttering around a holly bush close to the copse across the field. One had a soft
white feather in its beak. With characteristic patience, she stood perfectly still
until one of the birds flew into the bush and out again. When both birds had
gone, she went into the bush and found the nest, a dome covered with grey
lichen and cobwebs. It was complete apart from the inner lining of feathers.

She took care to touch neither nest nor bush, 'so I hope they won't mind!'[117] Others, however, showed no such solicitude. Returning to the nest two days later, Katherine was horrified to discover that:

> [S]omeone had torn it out of the Holly tree, and it was scattered on the ground, torn to bits, one mass of feathers!! How brutal and wicked some people are! I was much overcome; such sweet little birds they were.[118]

This is of a piece with her pained response to the shooting of the seagull on Boxing Day 1904. There may, however, be another element at work too. Katherine had been interested in nests for several years, often recording their locations in her nature notebooks and sometimes actively setting out to find them. This now seems to have become more frequent, and the accounts of watching for and finding birds' nests longer and more emotionally charged.[119] At twenty-seven, she was well past the age at which most women married and had children and her thirtieth birthday cannot have seemed far off. Given her already close identification with little birds, wilfully destroying a nest may in this context have seemed even more wantonly hurtful.[120]

Perhaps this was a harbinger of the spiritual crisis that engulfed her in June, and which seems to have lasted off and on until at least October 1914. It seems to have begun with further doubts about her direction in life. On 4 June 1912 she made up her mind to give more time to music, berating herself for shamefully neglecting her singing and piano practice. She wrote to a Mrs George about lessons but acknowledged despondently to her diary that 'My mind is so changeable, I vacillate between wanting to paint and wanting to play and sing and natural history etc and it is most trying!'[121] Three days later things were worse. She had been singing German Lieder ('I think I ought to learn German') but this had agitated her and she decided to go out for a walk with Di.

The crisis initially manifested itself in the form of acute religious doubts. This in itself is a measure of its severity. While Walter's letters to Kate from India dwell at times on religious themes, neither the church nor God had formed an especially prominent part of Katherine's upbringing. Before 1912 religion is barely mentioned in her diaries, nature notebooks or letters.[122] Her sudden plunge into religious turmoil suggests a sharp break in her emotional life: an urgent inner

---

[117] HRO, 19M99/2/9 (Smith Nature Notebooks, 19 Apr. 1912).

[118] HRO, 19M99/2/9 (Smith Nature Notebooks, 21 Apr. 1912).

[119] Nature notebooks references to nests: 6 Jun. 1913 (three nests); 8 Jun. 1913; 12 Jun. 1913 (two nests); 10 Apr. 1914; 19 Apr. 1914; 19 Jun. 1915. HRO, 19M99/2/6a and 19M99/2/7 (Smith Nature Notebooks, 1913–15).

[120] Bellanca notes that Dorothy Wordsworth also identified closely with little birds. Bellanca, *Daybooks*, 134.

[121] HRO, 19M99/1/3a (Smith Diaries, 4 Jun. 1912).

[122] Like the canonical nature diarists Bellanca considers, Katherine's diaries and notebooks express profound respect and reverence for nature but do not, any more than Cresswell's, theologize it. Bellanca, *Daybooks*, 19.

exigency that neither art nor nature sufficed to meet. On returning from her walk, which had considerably soothed her, she confided to her diary that she had often been very troubled 'lately'. She attributed this to 'the war going on within every man between good and evil', a formulation that she had found in F. D. Maurice's *The Kingdom of Christ*, which she had been reading in bed till late the previous night.[123] She too, she explained, was seeking to be freed from 'this awful bondage of sin', feeling 'more and more how awful it is'. The lengthy passage in her diary becomes increasingly insistent and desperate in tone, replete with biblical capitalization and archaisms. The depth of Katherine's misery and the fragility of her dutiful determination to look on the bright side are only too apparent:

> But oh! I do see a glimpse of glory now and then, when I struggle out of the darkness and depression, and I see dimly that the Kingdom of Christ which I am seeking to enter, is a spiritual kingdom, and that with it, nothing earthly is to be compared! Oh God, give me light, and grant that that Light may dwell in me; and I do know and believe that Light to be Jesus Christ Himself.[124]

Alas for Katherine, there is little indication that much light dwelt in her for some time to come. There is a gap of more than two years in her diaries from June 1912 to September 1914, and when the diaries resume (in the new form of a 'commonplace book', modelled on a suggestion in one of Charles Kingsley's letters) they almost immediately turn to a retrospective assessment of the inner crisis through which Katherine had passed. We can, however, glean something from her nature notebooks. As was now their custom, the Smiths spent most of the summer at Titchfield in 1912. It is unclear whether they were there over Christmas. If so, it cannot have been for long as on 14 January Katherine was walking near Loudwater Hill, north of Rickmansworth, when she saw a kestrel rise up with a bird in its talons, perhaps a starling or thrush, she thought. Gripped by pain of a different kind herself, Katherine's empathy was acute: 'The poor bird screamed out when the Kestrel pounced upon it, but was silent after.'[125]

In March the Smiths went down to Titchfield but again Katherine was ill, this time fortunately only for a week. She did at least have the invalid's compensation of rebounding high spirits when she recovered, relishing a walk to the copse across the field: 'It was a most lovely warm spring day today, one could almost feel things growing.'[126] Just over a month later the

---

[123] F. D. Maurice, *The Kingdom of Christ* (1906).

[124] HRO, 19M99/1/3a (Smith Diaries, 7 Jun. 1912).

[125] HRO, 19M99/2/7 (Smith Nature Notebooks, 13 Jan. 1913). It seems more likely that the predator was a sparrowhawk, since the kestrel, similar in flight profile, feeds mainly on rodents and would find it difficult to catch a bird as large as a starling.

[126] HRO, 19M99/2/9 (Smith Nature Notebooks, 22 Apr. 1913). See also NCA, PA SMA 1/29 (Letter from Katherine Smith to Alic Smith, 22 Apr. 1913), which expresses the same sentiment.

whole family was at Howtown (on Ullswater in the Lake District) for a short holiday. Katherine enjoyed the beautiful moors, woods, flowers and, especially, the unfamiliar birds: redstarts, wood warblers, tree pipits and a curlew. Difficult as this phase of her life was, she was still capable of taking her old delight in nature. On 6 June she saw a redstart in the corner of a meadow near an old wall. Convinced it must have a nest nearby, she watched the bird until it went into a hole in the wall, of which she took careful note. Getting to the place was far from easy because she was separated from it by a high wall and a brook but she realized she could circumvent these by climbing up the hillside and getting onto a track. From here she had to clamber over a gate, skirt along the wall and then climb up onto a stone in order to peer into the hole. There at last she found the nest, moss lined with feathers; the hen redstart did not move a muscle as Katherine gently touched her with a stick.[127] Not content with this, Katherine set off up the hill in search of more nests and soon spotted a pair of wheatears that seemed to fly repeatedly to a patch of scree on the mountainside. They went into a hole among the stones and parsley ferns. Marking it by eye, Katherine scrambled up and soon found the nest, under some stones and half hidden by a small foxglove. It was too dark to see into but on the 8th she returned and had the satisfaction of seeing the mother wheatear feeding her three young. She also mentions the nests of house martins, chaffinches, a common sandpiper and a meadow pipit in her nature notes while they were in Howtown.

What are we to make of this? Her remarkably active and determined quest for the redstart and wheatear nests is not the mark of someone plunged into deepest gloom nor whose hopes have been entirely extinguished. At the same time, such headlong pertinacity and physical exertion was decidedly out of character. Nor was searching for nests nearly as prominent a feature of any of her other holidays. On balance it seems likely that Katherine's behaviour while in Howtown sprang at least in part from emotional pressures, which may have been partly unconscious, relating to her age and situation. With no hint of a prospective spouse on the horizon, in practice her freedom to choose whether to have children was rapidly being taken away from her.

Summer 1913 was again spent mainly at Titchfield. There are few entries in the nature notebooks but on 13 August Katherine spotted an unusual bird perching on a stem. It was brilliant scarlet and on looking it up in Saunders' *Manual* she concluded that it could only be a male scarlet grosbeak.[128] This was an exciting discovery and led to what appears to be Katherine's only publication, if such it can be called – a letter in the November 1913 volume

---

[127] This was to check that the bird was not a young one – the light was poor and Katherine could not see.

[128] The guide Katherine consulted was presumably Howards Saunders, *An Illustrated Manual of British Birds* (London, 1889).

of *British Birds*.[129] Meanwhile, Titchfield seems to have been becoming more important to the family: they went down there for a weekend that month and were there again over Christmas, into the New Year and for Easter. The place suited Katherine to perfection: peace and seclusion, proximity to the sea and her old haunt at Lee, woods and marshes and a rich variety of birdlife. In a surprisingly short time, Titchfield became a more satisfying and complete home to her than any other she had had. While this could not entirely insulate her from the inner tribulations that continued to afflict her, it was soothing and Katherine's letters from Titchfield show that at least at times she was in blithe spirits there:

> Today sitting at my window I saw a flock of House Martins have arrived on their southward migration – they settle on the roof just above my west window, & then fly off together, with their pretty rattling notes. It is a delight to watch them, their flight is so lovely & graceful: they come sailing up almost into my face & swoop up to the roof; & then with a whir are all off again. It is like being in the air with them, & such a lovely feeling, of buoyancy & lightness.[130]

In late July the Smiths travelled up to Barden in the West Riding of Yorkshire, on the face of it a surprising exception to the family's preference for archetypical Romantic landscapes. However, Barden was only a stone's throw from Rex Vicat Cole's studio at New Hall Farm, so Katherine would have known the area by repute. As so often, the excitement and lift of spirits prompted by arriving in a new place register clearly:

> This is a most lovely place, with moors all round: the surroundings all seem mountainous, stone walls & bracken & mountain flowers, & such lovely hairbells [sic], but no heather. The moors are splendid & quite wild in parts, & have lovely long swelling lines but different from the Downs, more mountainous. The river is fine, & wide, & there is a most beautiful old stone bridge spanning it at Barden. The ruins of Barden Towers are quite in keeping, straight bleak walls of stone.[131]

At Titchfield later that summer, Katherine began a commonplace book, in which she would record 'anything which interested me, just for my own eye alone'. One of the first entries concerned Venus, which she had seen one

---

[129] 'Probable Scarlet Grosbeak in Hampshire', *British Birds* 7 (1913), 179. Bellanca points out that although the journals she studied were not themselves written for publication, they all connect in some way with published writing by the authors or their intimates. With the exiguous exception of the *British Birds* letter, this was not true for Spear Smith, suggesting we should be careful about reading across from canonical diarists, who were almost certainly atypical in this respect. Bellanca, *Daybooks*, 35.

[130] NCA, PA SMA 1/29 (Letter from Katherine Smith to Alic Smith, 8 Sep. 1914) (spelling as in the original).

[131] NCA, PA SMA 1/29 (Letter from Katherine Smith to Alic Smith, 22 Apr. 1913).

evening shining in a calm space of clear green sky surrounded by grey clouds. This led her to think of Wordsworth's lines:

> Fair as a star when only one
> Is shining in the sky[132]

A long discussion with Alic ensued, during which they agreed that people (such as an unnamed interlocutor of Katherine's) who disdained Wordsworth's use of plain language in the poem could not possibly appreciate it and had a crude notion of poetry. This very satisfying talk left her in an optimistic, confident mood and soon afterwards she wrote a long analysis of the emotional difficulties that had beset her over the previous two years. She claimed she was very happy now and that 'the old dark depression' had gone and seldom returned. When it did she could 'throw it off' by prayer. She bewailed what she now saw as the underlying cause of her unhappiness:

> For how many years I have planned my life, and thought in my own strength I could do great things – that I could paint or play and sing and many other things; but all my plans failed as long as I thought of myself, and I felt I was a wretched failure. But at last I hope I have learnt the lesson, that I myself am nothing, and can do nothing apart from God ... So I have surrendered myself to Jesus, I have given my will to Him, and I shall plan no more or worry but leave all to Him.[133]

It is probably not coincidental that this epiphany, if that is what it was, occurred around 20 September 1914, since:

> This was my thirtieth birthday, and I think I shall remember it! Such awful strife in the world, but oh, thank God I have at last peace in myself, through Him: and I thank Him for the way He has led me all these years.[134]

Subsequent entries in the commonplace book seek to shore up and embed this perspective. On 17 October Katherine copied out 'some passages that help me' from Gertrude Page's *Where the Strange Roads Go Down*, which she had just finished.[135] One of these concerns a tempter who offers joy, sweetness and 'the kingdom of love' in exchange for 'all those high-flown notions of honour and right which only break your life, and give you nothing in return'. In another passage, the heroine, Joe, realizes that she has been wrong to seek personal happiness and must conquer herself.[136]

---

[132] William Wordsworth, 'She Dwelt among Untrodden Ways'. This is surely another of Katherine's many projections of her own identity. As is so often the case, her idealism was not without a tinge of narcissism.

[133] HRO, 19M99/1/5/2 (Smith, 'A Common-Place Book', Sep. 1914).

[134] HRO, 19M99/1/5/6 (Smith, 'A Common-Place Book', Sep. 1914).

[135] Gertrude Page, *Where the Strange Roads Go Down*, 3rd ed. (London, 1913).

[136] HRO, 19M99/1/5/7 (Smith, 'A Common-Place Book', Oct. 1914).

Commenting on these extracts, Katherine asserts that only as we lose ourselves do we find ourselves, and explains that she has given herself up to God's will entirely: 'I dedicate myself to Christ – and what peace it is!' However, this unfortunately was not the end of the story since:

> [N]ow comes the practical question – how to act and what to do for Him. And now it has come to me today, – that we need some 'ideal' to work for, some good in view, which through our own peculiar circumstances it seems that God has appointed for us.

This quickly led Katherine right back into the dilemma she believed she had escaped from, and the next few lines are telling:

> ~~Now so far I have not been able to put a practical ideal before me, something to work for. I cannot be a missionary, nor~~
> Here I formulated a plan, and an earthly goal to work for – but I have cut it out since, as I do not think it is for us to plan, but God, Who has a work for everyone, and will lead us on step by step, as we are ready. I think the thing to do is leave off worrying about self, and to leave all to Him, and think of others, and do His Will as we see it.[137]

The difficulty lay in the last four words. Substituting God's will for her own was all very well, but how was she to know what God wanted, any more than she knew what she wanted herself?

To all appearances, then, Katherine's sudden embrace of religion seems like a desperate bolt-hole rather than a real solution to her difficulties. There is something strained and unconvincing in the long, strident paragraphs in which she maintains she has found peace through God and in her repeated claims that she is now 'very happy'.[138] It has the air of a willed insistence that her difficulties are behind her, rather than a genuine resolution. Nor does the extreme self-abnegation Katherine enjoins upon herself seem a very promising basis for happiness. Yet the evidence of the diaries, notebooks and letters is unequivocal: after October 1914 there are no further references to 'dark depression', Katherine's spirits were much lighter and at times over the next six years she was exceptionally happy. What had happened? One clue, perhaps, is that Katherine's determination to 'leave all to Him' echoes her impulse to 'go to Nature ... with nothing but an open loving heart' seven years earlier in Fittleworth. Something seems to have been prompting her from within to give up her artistic ambitions. In the first iteration she associated this with nature; the second time round, in need of stronger medicine, she drew on religion.

---

[137] HRO, 19M99/1/5/8-9 (Smith, 'A Common-Place Book', Oct. 1914). The deletion is in the original. With this entry, the commonplace book comes to an end. Perhaps, having decided she had resolved her difficulties, Katherine no longer wished to think about them.

[138] See, for example, HRO, 19M99/1/5/5 (Smith, 'A Common-Place Book', Sep. 1914).

While she seems to have been quite unconscious of any subterfuge, it seems clear that nature and God, respectively, were acting as emotional bridges over which she could cross to escape from the impasse in which she was trapped. After October 1914 God is rarely mentioned in her nature notebooks or letters.

Katherine liked the idea of becoming an artist and it is unsurprising that forgoing it was very painful. It seemed to offer a solution to both of the fundamental questions she had been wrestling with: who should she be and what should she do? For years she had been experimenting with different inflections of her identity – adopting a persona as an artist would not only provide a gratifying foundation for this but also earn the endorsement and approval of her family, whose Romantic ethos it would perfectly embody. Moreover it appeared to provide an answer to the related question of her purpose in life. Since there was no immediate or probable prospect of marriage, and since she was not expected to work for a living, Katherine needed to find something else to do. Art seemed to solve that problem too.

For all this, she was not necessarily mistaken in giving it up. Trying to become a recognized artist had made her miserable and had turned painting, previously a pleasure, into a millstone round her neck. Although the vision of herself as an admired artist was an alluring one, in the end it was oppressive since it was incompatible with a more fundamental aspect of her personality: her modesty and lack of self-importance. This was the more so because of the Smiths' elevated, Ruskinian conception of the aesthetic and moral value of art. Unlike Miss Hawksley, Katherine was deeply averse to pushing herself forward or asserting her artistic persona in public. Relinquishing her dream of becoming an artist, then, freed Katherine from the oppression of feeling she needed to become something she never could be. It allowed her to follow her real inclinations, wants and preferences rather than continuing the attempt to impersonate an idealized, illusory version of herself. In this respect, it was truly liberating. However, it did not necessarily equip her with a purpose in life, except perhaps in a Miltonic 'they also serve who only stand and wait' sense. Would this suffice in the longer term? Nor is the impact of Katherine's self-abnegation on her feelings about marriage and children obvious. When she surrendered to Jesus, was she giving this up too? Many of her responses to landscape and nature in the years prior to and during her spiritual crisis suggest that a suppressed yearning for marriage and children was part of her unhappiness. Given the scale, intensity and timing of the crisis and its resolution, it seems likely that Katherine accepted she would not marry or have children at the same time as she abandoned her artistic hopes. This was probably an enormous relief in a day-to-day sense but whether, had she lived longer, more complex pressures would have reasserted themselves remains an open question.

Sometime before this, probably in 1913, the family had moved back from Rickmansworth to Kensington, perhaps because they were now spending so much time at Titchfield that they no longer felt they needed a main residence in the country. Kensington was also more convenient for Alic, now working at the Scottish Office (Walter by this stage seems to have been less desk-bound). As was to be expected given how much she had cherished her walks in the Chilterns, the prospect of moving back to London filled Katherine with dismay. In her new-found spirit of smiling through suffering, however, shortly after returning to Kensington she assured her diary that:

> It is wonderful how good God is to us, and to me who thought it would be so dreadful to live in a town – but now I am very happy.[139]

Such protestations notwithstanding, she was extremely glad to return to Titchfield just before Christmas. The beauty of the grass and trees in the winter sunshine 'almost took one's breath away' after the murky dullness of London. Once again, Titchfield seems to have soothed her and she wrote a calm and contemplative letter to Alic on 6 January 1915, evidently in response to some remarks he had made earlier:

> I had a lovely walk this morning, & as I can think so much better in the open air, I thought of all you said about goodness, & it all became much clearer – (if I get away from so many books etc – things are much easier to see), & I felt much more than ever before, the meaning of those beautiful lines of Wordsworth's in 'Tintern Abbey' about 'a sense of something far more deeply interfused . . . .' – you know all the lines. I can't explain, but the feeling takes you out of yourself & you feel so free; & it is so comforting to feel, at this time especially, that all good things & the soul can never die.[140]

This carries more conviction than the overstrained commonplace book entries of the previous autumn, not least because it is calmer and less strenuous. Having fought her way through the crisis, Katherine was now reaching the sunny uplands. Her next letter to Alic, dated Titchfield, 19 April, continues the mood and subject:

> I have been doing a pen & ink sketch, & have others in view; & have taken to reading Wordsworth again with great enjoyment. It is curious how free one feels when one has done a drawing or is doing it! As I sat sketching, in the sun by the wood leading to Bronwich Farm, the birds sang so beautifully: – the Willow Wrens are all here now, but not the Nightingale.[141]

The experience of freedom Katherine describes will probably be familiar to anyone who has ever been wholly absorbed in an attentive task requiring complete concentration, and bears a close resemblance to the feeling of

---

[139] HRO, 19M99/1/5/6 (Smith, 'A Common-Place Book', Oct. 1914).
[140] NCA, PA SMA 1/29 (Letter from Katherine Smith to Alic Smith, 6 Jan. 1915).
[141] NCA, PA SMA 1/29 (Letter from Katherine Smith to Alic Smith, 19 Apr. 1915).

being taken out of yourself mentioned in her previous letter to Alic. It is also significant that the sense of freedom she describes in the second letter arose in the context of sketching. In the past, art had more often been a source of anxiety and dismay and there are many references to unsatisfactory, uncompleted or unattempted paintings. These intimations that Katherine had turned a corner are amplified by similarly untroubled references to sketching and painting in subsequent letters.[142]

Despite occasional mentions of 'this awful war', hitherto it had not impinged on her very much. Her letters to Alic barely mention the fighting, although sometimes she adds a one-line postscript to the effect that the news from Russia seems good, that it is very sad another submarine has been lost, or whatever, rather as if on finishing the letter it occurs to her that she ought to have said something about the war. This is hardly surprising as none of the people she most cared about were directly affected. Neither Alic nor Walter seems to have considered volunteering, Alic presumably because the government wanted him in the Scottish Office, Walter because, in his late fifties, he was beyond the age at which men were expected to do so. In September, however, the war came closer:

> When I wrote to you last, we had not seen about poor Cheeseman; mother & I were very upset; I ~~am~~ so sorry, & it is very sad for you & how terrible for his family – was his sister very fond of him?
>
> Oh Alic, how dreadful this War is – it does seem so wicked – I know God is good, but surely this is to show us how awful evil is. For it must be evil that causes all this terrible pain; – & you may have had to go, & oh, I could not bear it.[143]

Notwithstanding these clouds on the horizon, the indications are that Katherine was finding increasing fulfilment in her personal life. Returning to Titchfield on 31 March 1916 brought a burst of joy.[144] 'It is glorious to be in the country again!' she exulted in her nature notebook, while to Alic she wrote:

> It is beautiful in the country, it is like new life to be in it again! . . . I miss you very much and wish you were here to feel the freshness & beauty.[145]

---

[142] As she no longer kept a diary after abandoning the commonplace book, Katherine's letters and her intermittent nature notebooks are the most valuable sources for the last years of her life. For cheerful references to drawing or painting, see NCA, PA SMA 1/29 (Letter from Katherine Smith to Alic Smith, 25 Aug. 1915).

[143] NCA, PA SMA 1/29 (Letter from Katherine Smith to Alic Smith, 17 Sep. 1915).

[144] Since she had also been at Titchfield for a weekend in November and again over Christmas and into the New Year, her exhilaration cannot be attributed to an unusually long absence.

[145] HRO, 19M99/2/9 (Smith Nature Notebooks, 1 Apr. 1916); NCA, PA SMA 1/29 (Letter from Katherine Smith to Alic Smith, 31 Mar. 1916).

Nor did this joy prove fleeting. Throughout April, Katherine's nature notebook and letters glow with delight and eagerness to get out into the country. Easter morning was unforgettable:

> 23rd Easter Day. I woke very early in the morning, to see the sun shining on the green field out of my window, and glowing on the trees. The birds were singing exquisitely, and then I heard the Cuckoo for the first time this year, like a 'wandering voice'. For a long time he sang with the accompaniment of the other birds. I shall never forget the glorious golden morning, and the golden voice of the cuckoo; it was very beautiful.[146]

Alic went back to London on the 24th but this failed to damp Katherine's spirits. Even though it was dull and cold she went to the nearby copse to pick flowers, declaring afterwards in her nature notebook that there was nothing so lovely as an English copse full of primroses in spring. The weather the following day was 'glorious' and she and Aunt Edith, who had come to stay, walked along the banks of the Meon down to the sea.[147] The river reflected golden kingcups and the daisies in the green grass on the meadows reminded her of stars.[148] Wednesday began perfectly with a nightingale singing below her bedroom window, an eagerly anticipated sound.[149] It turned out 'Another real English Spring day, when it is good to be alive'.[150] In the evening she went down to the nearby copse to pick primroses for sending back to London:

> It was a glorious sight, the low sun shining in the trees and bushes, and the floor all carpeted with sweet flowers, primroses, blue violets, white and rosy anemones, and blue bells; and looking closer, were barren strawberry flowers nestled in the grass. It was beautiful, stooping low among them, the fresh sweet scents, and soft colours and the lovely forms of leaves and flowers, one seemed in some forgotten world, or heavenly land, where all was good and beauty and truth, and I thought of Wordsworth and how 'the meanest flower that grows can give thoughts that do often lie too deep for tears'.
>   Then through the soft spring air came the call of the cuckoo.[151]

Her cup was overflowing: as she wrote that evening in her nature notebook 'I was quite intoxicated with the Spring today, and the day passed like a lovely dream.'[152]

---

[146] HRO, 19M99/2/9 (Smith Nature Notebooks, 23 Apr. 1916).

[147] This may have been Edith Paige-Cox, the wife of Kate's cousin W. L. Paige-Cox.

[148] NCA, PA SMA 1/29 (Letter from Katherine Smith to Alic Smith, 25 Apr. 1916).

[149] See the postscript to her letter of the previous day expressing her conviction that nightingales were already singing in the bushes by the sea but observing that she had not yet heard them at Titchfield. NCA, PA SMA 1/29 (Letter from Katherine Smith to Alic Smith, 25 Apr. 1916).

[150] The 'Englishness' of weather is considered in Chapter 7.

[151] HRO, 19M99/2/9 (Smith Nature Notebooks, 26 Apr. 1916).

[152] Ibid.

Katherine's rendering of her experience in the copse provides a fascinating glimpse into the complex ways in which cultural representations, sensory experience, moods and the long arc of our own personal narratives of hope and disappointment can interact with and shape each other. She brought many things with her into the copse. Of these, the first that came into play was the buoyant, optimistic mood she had been in all day.[153] That meant that, rather than being blocked by gloomy or preoccupying thoughts, the gateways of sensation were open. This so, the sensations of light, colour, form and touch (the warm air against her cheek) were direct and unmediated. The cuckoo's call is more complicated: quite probably the rich, soft sound would have pleased her ear even had she not known whence it came, but her background being what it was, in hearing it she also heard its cultural resonances. A bulkier item of cultural baggage, of course, was Wordsworth. Why did the *Immortality Ode* come into her mind at this moment? On consideration, it is perhaps hardly surprising. The themes of the Ode – loss, resignation, acceptance and finally the attainment of a deeper joy the other side of sadness – resonated compellingly with Katherine's most profound experiences of the previous few years. It would seem that the spiritual elevation induced in her by the sights, scents and sounds of the copse had opened up and flowed into these deep experiences, which in turn brought the poem into her mind.

Katherine was spending more and more of her time at Titchfield, usually with her parents; Alic visited frequently. She was there throughout August and September, taking great interest in bird migration. The effects of the war continued to be minimal in practical terms. The Smiths started to keep chickens and it was difficult to get workmen to do odd jobs because of the scarcity of labour but otherwise life continued much as usual.[154] However, in Katherine's eyes there was a connection between the war and her deepening joy in landscape and nature:

> The world seems very sad at present, doesn't it ... Do you know that somehow or other because of all this sacrifice, the world seems also very beautiful, as if there was something very precious in it.[155]

Perhaps something of this feeling is apparent in her deep sense of loss at the felling of a row of elms outside the Lodge in February 1917:

> There was a fearful blow awaiting us, though fortunately I had heard about it the day before – all the beautiful Elm trees in the road in front have been

---

[153] On mood, see Ben Highmore, 'Feeling Our Way: Mood and Cultural Studies', *Communication and Critical/Cultural Studies* 10 (2013), 427–38. I would, however, emphasize the antecedent influences (the resolution of her spiritual crisis, her happiness at Titchfield, relationship with Alic, the warm spring sunshine, etc.) that had wrought this mood in Katherine, rather than regarding mood as an autonomous variable in itself.

[154] NCA, PA SMA 1/29 (Letter from Katherine Smith to Alic Smith, 19 Apr. 1915).

[155] NCA, PA SMA 1/29 (Letter from Katherine Smith to Alic Smith, 13 Sep. 1916).

cut down utterly! It is really awful, and the blank is terrible. If I had only known before they did it, I should have appealed to have some at least left. One snapped off in a great gale we had here in the Autumn, and they may have been frightened, but most were quite sound, and very stately and beautiful. Our house seems to have lost half its stateliness, and seems shorn and forlorn. This Spring will not see the reddening of the Elm trees buds, nor the stars look through their net of innumerable twigs; and this much beauty has passed forever from the earth. I feel a great sadness whenever I look in the direction where the trees were, and though the sunset reddens in a broad expanse of sky, the sun will never again make a glorious light and shade between their stately trunks.[156]

Many trees were cut down during the First World War due to the immense demand for pit props, trench timber and railway sleepers, in the context of disrupted supplies from the Baltic. According to Joshua West 50 per cent of productive forests were felled in Britain between 1914 and 1918 and hedgerow trees did not escape either.[157] This enormous loss of trees had a significant emotional impact and remains an unwritten chapter in the psycho-geography of the British landscape.[158] Katherine was by no means alone in her experience, although of course every loss is felt personally and individually, nor is it clear how far her particular trees were felled as a contribution to the war effort and how far because they were regarded as dangerous.

There is, however, an even wider context. The language and sentiments of Katherine's lament for her 'beautiful Elm trees' are strikingly reminiscent of Hopkins' 'Binsey Poplars', which although composed in 1879 was first published in 1918, a year after the entry in Katherine's nature notebook. It is highly unlikely that Katherine saw a manuscript copy of the poem, so the close identification with the trees and corresponding threat of 'unselving' when they are cut down that pervades both accounts must reflect a shared 'structure of feeling' (to borrow Raymond Williams' term) rather than influence.[159] It arises, on the one hand, from an intense projection of feelings into the landscape, or specific objects (such as trees) within it, and on the other, from the experience of being powerless to defend them. The structure of feeling predates Hopkins: something similar is present, searingly at times, in John Clare's poetry and in Dorothy Wordsworth's journals.[160] It may be that

---

[156] HRO, 19M99/2/11 (Smith Nature Notebooks, 23 Feb. 1917).

[157] A. Joshua West, 'Forests and National Security: British and American Forestry Policy in the Wake of World War I', *Environmental History* 8 (2003), 271.

[158] See, for example, Lewis Grassic Gibbon, *A Scots Quair* (London, 1937), 116.

[159] For the publication history of 'Binsey Poplars', see www.bodleian.ox.ac.uk/news/2013/binsey-poplars. For Williams' use of 'structure of feeling', see, for example, Williams, *The Country and the City*, 170.

[160] See, for example, Clare's great anti-enclosure poem 'Remembrances'. Dorothy Wordsworth lamented the 'sad ravages' made in the Loughrigg woods in her Grasmere journal, 4 March 1802: Dorothy Wordsworth, *Journals of Dorothy Wordsworth* (Oxford, 1971), 97.

comparatively powerless groups such as rural workers and women felt it especially early or acutely, although 'Binsey Poplars' suggests that by the late nineteenth century anyone was potentially exposed to it. During the twentieth century it seems to have become quite widespread, energizing rural preservationism and prompting legislative measures such as Tree Preservation Orders.

Katherine appears to have been at Titchfield for most of the first four months of 1917 but March and April were bitterly cold and although she appreciated the beauty of a heavy snowfall followed by blue sky and sunshine on 1 April, the protracted winter weather was tiresome and deprived her of much of the pleasure she usually derived from the return of spring.[161] Walter suggested that she was 'hankering after' a change and in a letter to Alic she even wrote that she was looking forward to coming to see him in London, 'for after all I am fond of London in many ways, & would not always like to be buried here!'[162] A contributory factor seems to have been that the war was beginning to affect the Smiths' home life to a greater extent. There was no gardener and no-one to look after the poultry.[163] Walter and Alic were away in London, so it fell to Katherine and her mother to manage both the garden, now planted with potatoes, and the numerous chickens, which left little time for enjoying the country even when the weather did improve.[164] An undated letter from Kate indicates that Katherine did go up to London later in the spring, while in June mother and daughter went on holiday to Minehead, taking in Porlock and Porlock Weir.[165] They were back at Titchfield later in the summer and again in February and April 1918, Katherine's nature notes showing her continuing interest in bird migration and the seasonal changes in birdsong.

In October 1918 the Smiths went to Minchinhampton in Gloucestershire for a fortnight. It was the first time Katherine had been in the Cotswolds and her nature notes evince her customary pleasure in discovering a new landscape. They also show that she had developed an analytical interest in landscape that encompassed built as well as natural elements:

> This Common is a nearly flat table-land, or platform, from which wonderful views are seen all round, of little valleys & dales, with steep hills some-times covered with woods, or with fields bisected by stone-walls; & little stone villages & towns clustered in the valleys, or creeping up the hillsides, & again solitary stone farm-houses, surrounded by a few trees & stone-barns, & then fields.[166]

---

[161] HRO, 19M99/2/11 (Smith Nature Notebooks, 1 Apr. 1917).

[162] NCA, PA SMA 1/5 (Letter, Walter Smith to Smith, 25 Jun. 1917); PA SMA 1/29 (Letter, Katherine Spear Smith to Alic Smith, 13 Apr. 1917).

[163] HRO, 19M99/2/11 (Smith Nature Notebooks, Feb. 1917).

[164] NCA, PA SMA 1/29 (Letter, Katherine Spear Smith to Alic Smith, 26 Apr. 1917).

[165] NCA, PA SMA 1/5 (Letter, Walter Smith to Katherine Spear Smith, 25 Jun. 1917).

[166] HRO, 19M99/2/6a (Smith Nature Notebooks, 12 Oct. 1918).

She was a little disappointed by the paucity of birds on the common and by the mediocre weather but made the best of it by studying the remaining flowers and, when the sun came out, the luxuriant autumn colours and the blue mist in the valleys. While there is no hint of the radiant joy of April 1916, the nature notebook entries for this holiday suggest that Katherine was in a calm, stable frame of mind, reaching out to new interests and alive to beauty wherever she could find it.[167]

January 1919 marked a significant change in the Smiths' lives, albeit one that represented the fulfilment of a long-held plan: they moved to Titchfield permanently. For Katherine this was, perhaps, less of a change than for the other three, since she had been spending so much time in Hampshire anyway. Initially, in any case, she was in no position to enjoy it, since she was laid up in bed for most of the month, it would seem with a recurrence of rheumatic fever. The illness was painful, especially in her legs, but she bore it with her usual quietness, although she did miss Alic's company.[168] The hardest thing was perhaps being unable to go outside for so long. It helped a little that Kate had moved her dressing table to one side, enabling her daughter to see out more easily. Better still was a bunch of early spring flowers from the garden, primroses, polyanthus and snowdrops:

> [T]hey smell & look so very sweet & fresh, I wish I could paint the fresh
> earth-spirit-awaking of them, & send it to you! I will try to later on, when
> I can get up. I think there is a wonderful spirit in flowers, (I mean
> a different spirit in each) that it would be lovely to catch & paint wouldn't
> it?[169]

When she eventually recovered, she went to London for a few days with Kate. The return journey, however, through the chaos of post-war disruption and the railway strike, resembled a lurid nightmare. Kate was barely fit to travel due to a chest infection. At Waterloo, as they were saying goodbye to Alic, a throng of soldiers crowded into their compartment, filling it with cigarette smoke. They got into another compartment at Farnborough but more passengers poured in shortly afterwards at Basingstoke, including a gassed soldier and a 'rabid socialist' who talked incessantly. At Eastleigh they had to wait nearly four hours for a train because of the strike. There were no fires in the waiting rooms and they were waylaid by a penniless, half-starved boy who told them, coughing and sneezing, that he had influenza. Terrified of catching the Spanish Flu, they rushed off to dose themselves with 'Bactoral' but compassion won out and they returned to give the boy a shilling for some hot Bovril. It was nearly 7pm by the time they arrived home at Titchfield. Even here their troubles were

---

[167] HRO, 19M99/2/6a (Smith Nature Notebooks, 7–16 Oct. 1918).
[168] NCA, PA SMA 1/29 (Letter, Katherine Spear Smith to Alic Smith, 16 Jan. 1919).
[169] Ibid.

not over, as Aunt Flo and Aunt Meta were both seriously ill and required nursing, while Walter was gruff, agitated and not in perfect health himself. In the circumstances, it is remarkable that Katherine's letter to Alic was so spirited. She did, however, feel his absence acutely:

> We were so sorry to leave you dear, & you were so good to us all the time.
> I do so wish we all lived together again; why have these separations to be?
> It seems you must not be perfectly happy in this world.[170]

Certainly there was not much happiness for Katherine over the next few weeks as she succumbed to a 'chill' brought on, she believed, by the long, cold wait at Eastleigh.[171] By 23 February, she was at last well enough to go out and was gladdened to hear the skylarks singing beautifully over the field opposite the house.[172] It was another cold March but on 4 April it felt quite spring-like at last and:

> I heard & then saw the first Chiff-chaff! I rather think there were two. It
> was beautiful to welcome the dear little birds again.[173]

Evidently Katherine's close identification with small birds remained as strong as ever.

No letters to, from or about Katherine appear to survive for the rest of 1919 so, since she was no longer keeping a diary, the only source is her nature notebook. She seems to have been at Titchfield the whole time at least through to late November, except for a brief period at the end of April and in early May. During spring and early summer her entries are mainly concerned with which birds were singing and breeding, where their nests were and how they reared their young. Later in the summer the focus shifts to which birds are still in song and to the early signs of autumn migration. In late autumn and early winter there are fewer entries, probably because there was less to record and Katherine did not go out so much, but she noted when different species of bird began to sing again after their mute period during the summer. As in the previous year, the indications are that, while there may have been few moments of great exhilaration, her life had taken on an even tenor and she was calm and content.[174]

Katherine resumed her nature notes on 1 January 1920; they continue till 14 May. On the face of it, the entries are very similar to those she made in the two previous years. She mentions the weather, birds singing, flowers coming into bloom, butterflies, bats and bees. It is true that she uses more abbreviations and that the entries are perhaps a little less frequent than sometimes in

---

[170] NCA, PA SMA 1/29 (Letter, Katherine Spear Smith to Alic Smith, 27 Feb. 1919).
[171] HRO, 19M99/2/11 (Smith Nature Notebooks, 1919 [undated]).
[172] Ibid., 23 Feb. 1919.
[173] Ibid., 4 Apr. 1919.
[174] Ibid., 5 Apr. to 24 Nov. 1919.

the past but it would take an alert reader to infer what was in fact the case – she was seriously ill. The symptoms were those of a severe respiratory illness, but it seems likely that the underlying cause was heart failure brought on by her recurrent attacks of rheumatic fever. We know little about the progression of the disease in 1920 but a letter from Alic to Kate dated 8 March reveals that it was already a cause of deep concern to the family. Alic wrote from New College, Oxford: he had been offered a Fellowship the previous year and had decided to accept, resigning his position at the Scottish Office. His letter reports at length on a conversation he had had with a Dr Haldane. Alic was concerned about a recent test that had shown abnormalities in the composition of Katherine's blood. According to Dr Haldane, this was a normal adjustment to reduced oxygen availability, found also in people living at high altitudes – it was an encouraging sign that Katherine had adapted well to her illness rather than a cause for concern. He advised that the oxygen machine the Smiths had acquired for her need only be used during severe attacks of breathlessness.[175]

Despite Dr Haldane's suave assurances, it must have been extremely unpleasant and very frightening for Katherine when she was acutely short of breath. She continued, however, to observe and record nature in the same way as before. There is no hint of self-pity or, indeed, any direct reference to her illness at all. It would seem that she had better days, and on some of these Alic took her down to the sea in a trailer.[176] One such occasion was on 24 March:

> Went down to sea and back by Hill-head in trailer; lovely! Reeds still pale buff. Several swans out in the sea. Greater Stitchwort out in fl[ower]: in the hedge rows. Gorse in fl[ower]: Daffodils wonderfull [sic] in gardens at H. h.[Hillhead].[177]

Alic took her down to the sea again on 30 March and 6 and 17 April. Katherine's old delight in the spring was evident on all three occasions, despite the state of her health, and continued into early May. The 30th of March was a 'Lovely morn, sun and sea looked glorious . . . Field Speedwell <u>very</u> blue, wide open in sun'. On 6 April it was the sea she particularly appreciated: 'most beautiful, very calm & pale & glittering with sun in places, very misty, distance seemed far away'. On the 17th she heard the cuckoo first thing when she woke and at intervals all day. Going down to the sea in the trailer was 'most lovely'.

---

[175] NCA, PA SMA 1/11 (Letter, Alic Halford Smith to Kate Smith, 8 Mar. 1920).

[176] This seems to have been either a bicycle or a hand trailer. It is first mentioned in the nature notebooks in 1911, almost immediately after the Smiths arrived at Titchfield. Katherine used it occasionally to go down to the sea, which it was felt was rather far for her to walk (although sometimes she did). Whether this reflected the family's gendered assumptions about physical capacity or a genuine limitation, arising perhaps from Katherine's recurrent attacks of rheumatic fever, is difficult to ascertain. HRO, 19M99/2/9 (Smith Nature Notebooks, 7 Aug. 1911).

[177] HRO, 19M99/2/2a (Smith Nature Notebooks, 24 Mar. 1920).

On 1 May 'the first thing I heard was the scream of <u>Swifts</u>' and on the 10th a linnet sang 'so sweetly' on the top bough of the apple tree in the garden.[178]

The rest is silence. On 4 October Alic wrote to his mother again from New College:

> I have put the flowers in water; they look very beautiful. I hope to go to the cemetery with them early tomorrow morning.[179]

Katherine had died at Titchfield on 24 September, aged only thirty-six.[180] There is no direct evidence of the effect on her family, although a letter from Walter to his wife three years later expresses his conviction that she had gone to a place of perfect happiness and would be parted from them only for a time.[181] Almost immediately, however, the Smiths sold Titchfield Lodge and moved to Oxford. The house was indelibly associated with Katherine: both her deep love for the place and her long illness, suffering and death. Perhaps it was simply too painful for Walter, Kate and Alic to remain there. In any case, Titchfield had always really been for Katherine more than anyone else: now she was no longer alive, the house had lost its point. Nevertheless, the abrupt decision to sell it represented a drastic change in the family's plans. For at least nine years the Smith parents had intended Titchfield Lodge to be their permanent home after Walter retired, while Alic made his way in the world elsewhere. In rebasing at Oxford, the family was drawing in on itself in the same way an injured snail pulls back into its shell. The move proved permanent for all three and must have been intended to be so from the start, since they chose to bury Katherine in Oxford rather than Hampshire or London: evidently they wanted her close to them in death, as she always had been in life. Probably it was Alic who suffered most in the long run. Although highly successful in his career, rising to become vice-chancellor, he was never popular with the other dons, who seem to have regarded him as aloof and detached.[182] It is impossible to know why he made so few friends, or indeed why he did not marry, but the loss of such a devoted and deeply loved sister at so young an age can hardly have been anything other than devastating. Walter no doubt spoke for all of them when he wrote to Kate: 'The remembrance of our darling Kathy will always be with us.'[183]

* * *

[178] HRO, 19M99/2/2a (Smith Nature Notebooks, 30 Mar., 6 and 17 Apr., 1 and 10 May 1920).

[179] NCA, PA SMA 1/11 (Letter, Alic Halford Smith to Kate Smith, 4 Oct. 1920).

[180] Death Certificate, 25 Sep. 1920.

[181] NCA, PA SMA 1/ 4 (Letter, Walter Smith to Kate Smith, 1 Jan. 1923).

[182] 'Mr. A. H. Smith', *The Times* (London), Monday, 14 Jul. 1958, 10. Alic shared his sister's love of art and the statue of Lazarus he commissioned from Jacob Epstein still stands in New College Chapel. Lazarus, brought back to life by Jesus, may have had poignant significance for him (a suggestion I owe to Rachael Jones).

[183] NCA, PA SMA 1/ 4 (Letter, Walter Smith to Kate Smith, 1 Jan. 1923).

Katherine's decision in 1914 to abandon her artistic ambitions was the crux of her life. More than any other influence, it was her modesty, lack of self-importance and identification with the little things of nature that precluded her from pursuing a career as a painter. It could be argued that these qualities were a form of self-repression, a damaging internalization of contemporary gender hierarchies and assumptions. There is an element of truth in this but it simplifies a more complex story. Certainly constructions of gender in early twentieth-century Britain (and, many would maintain, still today) were severely constraining and oppressive. But to attribute Katherine's failure to become a recognized artist to faults in her character, even if we lay the ultimate blame for these on society, misses two crucial points. Firstly, the problem for Katherine was not art as such, but the public self-assertion that Being an Artist then entailed. In a different time and place, where, rather than being sacralised and mystified as the expression of genius, art was practised unselfconsciously as part of everyday life – in, for example, the world envisaged by Morris' *News from Nowhere* – she would have fared better. Nothing in her character inherently debarred her from artistic creativity: once she had abandoned art as a career goal, she was able to paint freely and with enjoyment. In a sense, the problem for her was the contemporary construction of the artist, rather than of women, although it could be argued that both arose in the context of a society characterized by relations of domination and oppression at every level.

This leads on to a second point. If it was impossible for someone like Katherine to become an artist in early twentieth-century Britain, perhaps the problem lay with the society that permitted only people who were sufficiently assertive, assured and self-promoting to do so. To suggest it was a deficiency in Katherine that she lacked these attributes would devalue much of what she regarded as most estimable in and constitutive of herself: her quietness, sensitivity, gentle and affectionate nature and her special tenderness towards birds, plants and animals. These were also the qualities that made her so much loved by her family. To say that Katherine would have been better off without these characteristics would be tantamount to saying that she should have been a different person. But why should she? Her life was rich and fulfilling in many ways, beyond the common measure, especially in her later years. Other than in its brevity, it is a life more deserving to be celebrated than lamented.

Katherine's deep love of nature and the countryside, and especially her close identification with little birds, allowed her to express and validate the gentle modesty that lay at the root of her character, providing a setting and context in which she could flourish and was free to be herself. This was how she experienced rural landscapes throughout her adult life but in her last years at Titchfield, released at last from the old doubts and fears, her delight in nature blossomed as never before. The impress is still fresh in her notebooks: the swoop of house martins, the misty haze of bluebells, the golden voice of the cuckoo, sunlight glittering on the sea and the scream of returning swifts.

5

Violet Dickinson

Itinerant Craftswoman

Outwardly there are some striking similarities between Violet Dickinson and Katherine Spear Smith. Apart from their gender the most obvious link is that Violet was born on 3 December 1883, only ten months before Katherine. They also came from similarly privileged upper-middle-class backgrounds. The Dickinsons were a few degrees wealthier but the Smiths' income and social position, deriving as it did from professional employment, was more securely established. Both families were deeply committed to the arts although for the Smiths this remained an amateur interest, whereas Violet's father was the well-known and highly regarded art dealer Frank Dickinson, one of the world's leading experts on oriental porcelain. He had a showroom in the West End and was a friend of Lord Kitchener's.[1] This background in the arts decisively shaped Violet's outlook, values, perceptions and the path she took in life. However, as with Katherine, other, less obvious influences were at work too.

Neither Katherine nor Violet married, although children were to play a prominent role in the latter's life. Both women were especially close to a brother; indeed, Violet lived with Cedric (Ced) for most of her adult life. However, Ced was the youngest of the family and it was Violet who protected him rather than the other way round. More importantly, the relationship between Violet and Ced was far more understated and less intense than that between Katherine and Alic. Violet also had two other siblings: Gladys (known as Birdy in the family) and Leslie, both younger than her.

One further resemblance between Violet and Katherine is in the pattern of residential moves progressively further from London. In this, as in other respects such as her wealth, artistic background and setting up household with her brother, Violet is a more extreme case than Katherine, who never moved further than Titchfield (79 miles from London by road), while Violet eventually made her home in Holford, Somerset (166 miles).

Despite their similar background and trajectories, the two women could hardly have been more different in character. Katherine was shy, earnest and

---

[1] Hubert Fox, *Woven from a Stone* (n.p., 1968), chapter 1 [first page]. According to Fox, Dickinson's showrooms were in Wigmore Street, London; however, a death notice stuck into Violet's diary records the address as 104 New Bond Street in 1920. Somerset HC, A/AGV4 (Violet Dickinson Diary, 26 Nov. 1920).

intellectual, while Violet was sociable, hedonistic and lived through her senses, although she read widely and was not without an interest in ideas.[2] Katherine was articulate and emotionally expressive, Violet verbally reticent and averse to effusive feelings, observing with characteristic brevity and emphasis in the back of one of her diaries:

> Don't like demonstrative people![3]

As this perhaps suggests, Violet was confident and assertive: Katherine might have found her rather overbearing. Finally, while Katherine fell back on her family as she grew older, Violet moved away from hers, although, ironically, over time they tended to gravitate back to her. Violet's movement away from London and her family was correlated with an unusual pattern, unique among the diarists considered in this book, of downward social mobility.

Violet shared much with the other diarists in her ruralism, but it was also distinctive in certain ways. For only one of the others, the Whitmanite Johnston, were ideas and ideology such a strong influence. The ideology implicit in Violet's ruralism is more difficult to pin down because there was no single inspiration, but it is an indubitable presence. Perhaps the most important strand was the influence of the Arts and Crafts movement. Behind this lay the aesthetic values of Ruskin and Morris (whose wallpaper graced her childhood home), although the Dickinsons' relationship to this tradition was complex and contradictory, especially in social and political terms.[4]

Unsurprisingly, perhaps, in view of her background, aesthetics and visual beauty played a large part in Violet's affective responses to landscape. Despite this a commitment to a broader sense of ruralism, encompassing production as well as consumption, was central to her life. This broader ruralism derived in the first instance from the family's Arts and Crafts affinities. Subsequently it was developed by experiences of Violet's own – for example, in relation to the 'Peasant Arts' she encountered in Haslemere in 1912, her training at the Midland Dairy and Agricultural College in the same year and subsequent connections with ruralist organizations such as the Women's Institutes, the Women's Land Army, the rural community council movement and various craft guilds in Kent, Sussex and Somerset. Although Violet's connection with rural society and the rural economy was initially slight and detached, and in some ways remained so, she lived her own version of ruralism more fully and comprehensively than any of the other diarists: it came to permeate virtually

---

[2] In these respects Violet more closely resembles Catley, although without his self-consciousness.
[3] Somerset HC, A/AGV4 (Violet Dickinson Diary, 1918, back of diary).
[4] Ruskin: Dickinson Diary, 1 Feb. 1905, 1 Jan. 1940 and 19 Nov. 1944; Morris: Dickinson Diary, 1 Jan. 1940 and 19 Nov. 1944.

every aspect of her life, including work, residence, personal relationships, social networks, leisure activities, values and identity.

The sources for Violet's life are principally her extensive diaries, supplemented by a magazine (the 'IMA') edited by her in childhood, numerous paintings, drawings and photographs, some incorporated in the IMA, and a few letters. The diaries are largely complete from 1899, when she was fifteen, through to a few months before her death in 1953, although there are gaps for 1903–4, 1906 and 1941.[5] There are entries for most days although sometimes she would omit a few days and during uneventful periods occasionally several weeks at a time. It is unclear whether Violet initially expected the diaries to be read by anyone else – perhaps not, as they are neither polished nor consistent and include indiscreet, even occasionally hostile, references to family members. In due course, however, the diaries acquired a subsidiary function as an occasional vector of Violet's relationships with those closest to her. On 2 January 1921, for example, she and Ced read some of her 'old diaries, from 1899', while on 22 October 1942 she read some of her old diaries aloud to her friend Mercy Sholl (later Ede), who 'nearly had hysterics'.[6] Hence we can assume that, at least from 1921, Violet was aware of the possibility of other readers, albeit under conditions of her own choosing. This is, indeed, made explicit in a letter to Mercy Ede dated 15 February 1946, in which Violet thanks Mercy for a drawing:

> The drawing was typical and very good – I shall 'press it' in my diary (which we hope will not be published – with illustrations – until all the celebrities mentioned and libelled therein have 'passed on'!!!)[7]

Most of the diaries are written in pre-formatted volumes but with quite generous space, by no means always filled, for entries. However, the physical form of the diaries did affect what Violet wrote: during the Second World War, when she was unable to obtain pre-printed diaries and had to use notebooks instead, the entries are longer.[8] Qualitatively, however, these wartime diaries are little different. They include more detail of events and names of people she had met but are no more expansive with respect to thoughts and feelings, indicating that the main constraint on the diaries in this regard is not their physical form but Violet's unflagging extroversion.

The IMA, in the main, sheds only indirect light on Violet's life. The first surviving issue of the magazine is from 1903 and the last from 1915; from 1905 there was also a junior version, edited by Birdy, to which Violet contributed frequent illustrations and occasional prose. However, while neither version of

[5] Somerset HC, A/AGV 1-10 (Violet Dickinson Diary; henceforth, Dickinson Diary).
[6] Dickinson Diary, 2 Jan. 1921 and 22 Oct. 1942.
[7] Somerset HC, A/AGV 17 (Letter, Violet Dickinson to Mercy Ede, 15 Feb. 1946).
[8] Dickinson Diary, 1942, front paper.

the IMA tells us much about the day-to-day lives of the Dickinsons, Violet's short stories, anecdotes and editorials reveal dimensions of her character and experience that emerge less clearly from the diaries. The short stories are especially interesting: their free narrative form allowed Violet to give expression, consciously or otherwise, to structures of feeling and wish fulfilment less apparent in the diaries. The anecdotes tell us something about how Violet saw herself and her family and how she wished others to see them. They are often more rounded than comparable accounts in the diaries, filling in more of the emotional atmosphere and perceived implications of the events described, partly because she was *not* writing for herself alone and so felt obliged to explain things that were obvious to her and did not necessarily need to be recorded in the diaries. The editorials are, on the whole, less valuable but do shed some interesting light on the way Violet addressed herself to and interacted with a group of mainly younger readers.

Violet's paintings and drawings, many of which survive, demonstrate that she was an accomplished artist. They include a handful of self-portraits, from one of which a striking, authoritative young woman looks resolutely at the viewer.[9] There are numerous landscapes, seascapes and flower paintings, most revelling in the rich, harmonious colours to which Violet responded so strongly:

> Walked past the head of Luccombe Chine to the Copse – the downs looked too glorious. [I was] sighing for a paintbox.[10]

In some respects, however, it is her drawings and paintings of children and young people that are most expressive, and in conjunction with the written sources, tell us most about Violet's life.

The Dickinsons were enthusiastic photographers, at a time when photography meant elaborate apparatus and a darkroom, and signified (for them at least) wealth, modernity and artistic innovation. The dozens of surviving photographs give a sense of what the family thought was worth looking at, how they wanted to be seen, and, to a limited extent, of the interaction between family members (or, in a photograph showing the parents standing well apart, the lack of this). Finally, Violet's letters to Mercy Ede, dating from the last few years of her life, help to flesh out what had become an important relationship. In the main the letters resemble the wartime diaries, unconstrained by length but similar in tone and content to the main run of the diaries.

---

[9] London Metropolitan Archives, LMA/4292/01/001 (The I.M.A. Double Spring Number, Mar.–Apr. 1903).

[10] Dickinson Diary, 30 Oct. 1909. Compare Dickinson Diary, 14 Oct. 1912: 'the trees down Challock Hill were amazing! – Brown, gold, or red from top to bottom'.

A striking feature of the diaries, letters and to some extent Violet's prose contributions to the IMA is the use of capitals, underlining and exclamation marks. This indicates her emphatic, enthusiastic, extrovert character but also the surprisingly limited range of her verbal register, in contrast to the expressiveness of her artwork, a contrast neatly captured in a brief diary entry for 20 August 1949:

> Wonderful sunset – almost exact replica of Turner's Fighting Temeraire – too lovely for words.[11]

This limited capacity to express her feelings in writing may derive in part from the fact that, like most girls of her class and time, she left school in her early teens. However, in Violet's case this should not be overplayed. She read widely throughout her adult life, including Dickens (avidly), Jane Austen, Elizabeth Gaskell, George Eliot, Tolstoy and other classics, as well as contemporary writers such as Galsworthy, Yeats and T. S. Eliot. She enjoyed intellectual debate and discussion. It seems more likely that the difficulty lay in Violet's access to her own emotions rather than to words – indeed, her letters and wartime diaries show that she could write fluently and copiously but rarely with much introspection or emotional expression.

* * *

Although Violet grew up in an opulent environment, the family's wealth and social position were neither long established nor secure, and this has an important bearing on her life. Frank Dickinson's obituary is rather misleading on this point, claiming that he was the head of a firm established 'as long ago as 1777'.[12] The implication is that the Dickinsons had been art dealers for generations. However, William Dickinson, Frank's father, features as an ironmonger in the 1861 and 1871 censuses; it is only in 1881 that we find him listed as a 'fine art dealer'.[13] A further indication that the family had come up rapidly in the world is that Violet's maternal grandfather, John Almgill, had also been a tradesman – in his case a Soho bridle cutter, not a socially distinguished occupation.[14] But the impression of serenely ascending family fortunes given by the census elides as much as the claim the Dickinson firm was more than a century old. Evidence from the London Gazette reveals that, in 1875, William (now no longer merely an ironmonger but a jeweller and silversmith) and his partner, George Smith, instituted liquidation proceedings under the

---

[11] Dickinson Diary, 20 Aug. 1949.

[12] Somerset HC, A/AGV 16 ('Mr F. Dickinson', newspaper cutting [unprovenanced]).

[13] 1861 England Census, Class: RG 9; Piece: 62; Folio: 15; Page: 26; GSU roll: 542566; 1871 England Census, Class: RG10; Piece: 133; Folio: 17; Page: 26; GSU roll: 823290. On the rise of the London art market in this period see Pamela M. Fletcher and Anne Helmreich, The Rise of the Modern Art Market in London, 1850–1939 (Manchester, 2011).

[14] 1871 England Census, Class: RG10; Piece: 147; Folio: 61; Page: 19; GSU roll: 823294.

Bankruptcy Act, 1869.[15] By the time Violet was born eight years later her father had already done much to restore the family fortunes and remained rich and respected for the rest of his life. But the Dickinsons' restored fortunes were built on foundations unstable even by *nouveau riche* standards: Frank's continuing success in predicting artistic taste and, indeed, his biological survival. It seems likely that the quite disproportionate horror of falling into the ranks of the working class evinced in Violet's diaries and short stories was in part a traumatic echo of the events of 1875, and in part reflected the ongoing fragility of the family's economic base.

Frank seems to have had a close relationship with his children, perhaps especially Violet. According to Hubert Fox, who wrote a short account of Birdy's life, Frank came home from work at 7.30pm and would be greeted enthusiastically by the children. As they grew older he often took them on walks and excursions and played tennis with them.[16] In contrast, by the time Violet's diaries begin, when she and her siblings were in their early teens, Betsey Dickinson appears to have had a semi-detached relationship with them, frequently retiring to her room with minor ailments or to read novels (Marie Corelli was a favourite). She rarely accompanied the rest of the family on their walks, and not always on their holidays either.[17] There are indications that at least some of her illnesses were psychosomatic, and it is suggestive that in spring 1908 she took a 'Rest Cure' at the aptly named Hygeia in Ventnor, by which she was allegedly 'very much benefited'.[18] Presumably it was her family, or at least her domestic situation, from which she felt she needed a rest.

Since Frank was often away on business, travelling to far-flung destinations such as Turkey, Russia, the USA and even Java, the children were left to themselves much of the time when they were not at school.[19] A clannish feeling seems to have developed, not infrequently expressed through minor mischief, especially when, as so often, they were staying away from home: pouring water through ventilation holes, trapping other guests in their rooms by tying string round the door handles, and finding devious ways to disturb their sleep.[20]

Another consequence of the lack of close parental supervision seems to have been that the children developed some peculiar ways of amusing themselves.

---

[15] *London Gazette*, 9 Jul. 1875, p. 3543, col. 1. See also ibid., 6 Jun. 1875, p. 3399, col. 1 and ibid., 1 Oct. 1875, p. 4702, col. 1.
[16] Fox, *Woven from a Stone.*
[17] Dickinson Diary, 11 and 31 Mar. 1899, 9 Mar. 1902 and 26 Aug. 1909.
[18] London Metropolitan Archives, LMA/4292/01/022 (The I.M.A., May–Jun. 1908).
[19] Dickinson Diary, 4 Oct. 1901, 11 Jun. 1902, 27 Apr. 1905, 1 May and 17 Jun. 1907 and 4 Jun. 1909.
[20] LMA/4292/01/010 ('More about Us', The Junior I.M.A., Apr. 1906).

Fox, whose information was derived primarily from Birdy, claims that a favourite pastime of the Dickinson children was to:

> collect snails, kill them in salt and water, and then give them a formal funeral. Boxes of snails lay under wreaths in a toy omnibus and were drawn to the snail cemetery followed by four small children as mourners.[21]

Children's play sometimes reflects events or feelings that disturb them and it seems likely that this somewhat macabre game relates to the anxieties about death manifest in Violet's IMA stories and her childhood and adult diaries.[22] It is noteworthy, for example, that unlike her siblings she did not attend her father's funeral, nor her mother's, her grandmother's or her close friend Kathleen's.[23] The diaries rarely mention serious illnesses by name; we are not told what any of her close relatives died of, and only the sketchiest details of her own illnesses and hospital admissions. She had no ethical objections to hunting or killing animals but a dead mouse lying in the road unsettled her, while in adulthood witnessing the dismemberment of a stag was enough to prevent her from working for the rest of the day.[24]

For much of Violet's childhood the family lived at 4 Newton Grove in Bedford Park (Chiswick). Bedford Park was a model suburb often regarded as a precursor of the garden cities, with ample tree planting, large gardens, houses designed by Norman Shaw and an artistic ambience that attracted interesting residents such as W. B. Yeats (with whom the Dickinsons were acquainted), the publisher Unwin and the acting family the Terrys.[25] Violet attended Bedford Park High School and seems to have done well academically, finishing first in her form in geography, arithmetic and painting in 1899. She and Gladys were taught by, among others, Elizabeth Corbet Yeats, the poet's sister.[26]

---

[21] Fox, *Woven from a Stone*, chapter 1 [first page]. Violet's diary also shows some evidence of an active interest in death – for example she uses semi-Gothic lettering for the words 'Horace Carr died this morning at 5.40. Age 25 years.' Dickinson diary, 25 Apr. 1900.

[22] What the source of these anxieties might have been is a matter for speculation. Her more general fears seem to have been influenced by the combination of a distant mother and a loving but unpredictably absent father, and perhaps this was the root cause of her heightened fear of death too. However it is also possible that she suffered an unrecorded trauma, such as witnessing death at close quarters in early childhood.

[23] Dickinson diary, 1 Dec. 1920, 27 Apr. 1932, 24 Mar. 1924 and 20 Aug. 1947.

[24] Dickinson diary, 2 Apr. 1902; Letter to Mercy Ede, 21 Oct. 1947.

[25] On the early years of Bedford Park see Margaret Jones Bolsterli, *The Early Community at Bedford Park: Corporate Happiness in the First Garden Suburb* (London, 1977).

[26] Dickinson Diary, 9 Mar. 1901. For an interesting account of growing up in Bedford Park that has some parallels to Violet's experiences see Sybil Pearce, *An Edwardian Childhood in Bedford Park* (London, 1977).

The earliest entries in Violet's diary give little indication of her future ruralism – as might be expected, she was more preoccupied with school matters ('I had a good squabble with Eileen'), buying clothes and birthday presents. She acknowledged the 'lovely' view from Box Hill during a family picnic on 17 June 1899 but the lemonade she drank afterwards in Burford Bridge Gardens seems to have made quite as much of an impression. The first indication of a more attentive interest in rural landscapes is in May 1901, when Frank took his daughters on holiday to Minehead and North Devon. Violet enthused about the 'most glorious' cliff walk they went on before breakfast on their first morning there. She admired the red and green rocks, the myriad foxgloves and the smell of the pine woods: '[w]e must have been about ten miles but it was delicious!!!!!!'[27]

In 1901 the family left Bedford Park for reasons that remain unclear, although perhaps in connection with Frank's trip to Russia that year. While Frank searched for a new house, the family lived in hotels in Brighton and St Leonard's and then rented a house in Ventnor. After several months of this peripatetic existence they moved to 12 Ferncroft Avenue in Hampstead, an area with similar literary and artistic connotations to Bedford Park.[28] They were to live at this address for the next ten years. By now Violet had left school and she lived a cultivated life of leisure, painting, taking piano and singing lessons and playing tennis. Apart from its social atmosphere, the great feature of Hampstead from the Dickinsons' perspective was the Heath. Violet frequently walked and sketched there, sometimes with Betsey, sometimes with one or more of her siblings (Frank was presumably at work or abroad much of the time).[29] Hampstead was at that time only a stone's throw from the countryside, such that Violet could go on a '[l]ovely country drive' to Finchley on the top deck of a bus.[30] In August 1902 Violet and Leslie went to stay with friends in Harpenden for a fortnight. Violet made the most of the opportunities, sketching cottages and a cornfield, picnicking outdoors, feeding the chickens and visiting the 'lovely' hamlet of Waters End with its old manor house. There were 'glorious golden beeches' and she, Les and their friends played in the six foot high bracken and 'sprawled about'.[31]

That autumn Violet accepted a request from her friend Lettice Pelham-Clinton to take over the editorship of the IMA. The magazine was to become a major part of her life for the next few years and a study of its contents

---

[27] Dickinson Diary, 30 May 1901. Although Violet's sensibility was primarily visual, she enjoyed the scent of fir trees, heather, bracken and of the country more generally. Dickinson Diary, 8 Aug. 1909 and 28 Feb. 1914.

[28] Frank described the house to Violet, before she had seen it, as 'very picturesque and Bedford Park-y'. Dickinson Diary, 28 Jan. 1902.

[29] Dickinson Diary, 13 Sep. and 25 Oct. 1902.

[30] Dickinson Diary, 18 Jul. 1902.

[31] Dickinson Diary, 2 to 15 Aug. 1902.

provides insight into Violet's character and the ways this informed her rural-ism. Two aspects of the IMA are immediately striking. The first is its title. Although almost always known by its initials, the full title was the 'Invalids Magazine Album'. The emphasis on invalidity warrants some consideration. The IMA's rules stipulated that '[a]ll members must be invalids, or delicate'[32] Violet did have her share of illnesses in her teens: in January 1902 she seems to have had a bout of rheumatic fever, although this does not seem to have recurred in her case, and in November 1905 she had a minor operation, probably a tonsillectomy, after which she was 'very sick and wretched' for a day or two.[33] But there are no indications that she was ill any more often than other young middle-class women. In reality she was far from an invalid – on the contrary, she was notably robust and physically active, as her energetic enjoyment of games, swimming in big waves and frequent walks indicates. Did she really regard herself as an invalid or delicate? One possibility is that the magazine's title had been chosen by Pelham-Clinton and Violet did not want to change it. However, Betsey's behaviour suggests that she may have seen herself as at least a semi-invalid, and perhaps something of this rubbed off on her daughters.[34]

The second very obvious aspect of the IMA is that it was to all intents and purposes a magazine created by girls for themselves. The few male contribu-tors played only a marginal role. Of the twenty recipients of the first issue edited by Violet, for example, eighteen were female. Since the recipients were also the contributors, the balance of the contributions was also overwhelm-ingly female. Violet encouraged 'criticism', by which she meant comments from recipients on the contributions; indeed, a number of blank pages were set aside for this, to be added to by each recipient. These comments, and the collaborative production of the copy for the magazine, generated an ongoing dialogue between the girls who participated. The IMA therefore served to forge, within the context of the magazine, an autonomous community of young women (albeit in this case a virtual one). The desire to create or belong to an autonomous community of this kind, especially an exclusively female one in a rural context, was to be a powerful, recurrent feature of Violet's adult life. Although not herself a Suffragette, Violet had at least one friend who was (Christine Pugh) and was interested in and sympathetic to any effort to create autonomous female organizations and institutions.[35]

---

[32] LMA/4292/01/003 (The I.M.A., Nov.–Dec. 1903).

[33] Dickinson Diary, 2 Jan. 1902 and 11 Nov. 1905.

[34] There may be parallels with the relationship Edwards discerns between female invalidity and enthusiasm for Edith Holden's *The Country Diary of an Edwardian Lady*. Sarah Edwards, 'Private Enterprise: The Country Diary of an Edwardian Lady and Female Fan Communities', *Journal of Popular Culture* 40 (2007), 267.

[35] She was greatly excited by seeing the West End shop windows smashed by the Suffragettes in 1912. Dickinson Diary, 2 Mar. 1912.

In her capacity as editor, Violet was benevolent but firm, bordering on dictatorial. Admittedly, the IMA required careful management. Each issue existed only as a single copy, embodying countless hours of collective artistic labour, so losing it would have been disastrous. There was no way, however, of distributing it to the contributors except by trusting to the postal system, which, remarkably, never seems to have failed. To keep track of the where-abouts of the current issue, Violet required each contributor to send her a postcard on receipt of the magazine and to keep it for no longer than two (occasionally three) days before sending it on to the next member. It was also necessary to insist on a firm copy date, otherwise it would have been impos-sible to keep to the production schedule. Beyond this, there were practical considerations connected with the heavy burden of editorial labour that fell on Violet (for example, photographs should be sent ready for sticking in). On all these points Violet was emphatic, using her accustomed range of capitals, exclamation marks, underlining and stern words.[36] Although this undoubtedly contributed to the impressive quality and regularity of the IMA, Violet's tone and manner also reflected her personality. This is apparent in the more emollient tone of Birdy as editor of the Junior IMA. While Violet always wrote with authority, however, there is also a kindliness in her manner towards the younger readers: 'so work hard, children, and see if you cannot make a fine magazine between you, and we will all help'.[37]

The abundant and accomplished paintings and drawings Violet contributed to the IMA suggest that this was a natural mode of expression for her, more so than writing. She had a sensitive feeling for flowers, for tranquil but often glowing land- and seascapes and for children and young women playing or at rest. Her photographs are less remarkable but underline the leisured, hedonis-tic Dickinson lifestyle – most show seaside scenes, with a few pastoral picnics and rustic buildings.

It is, however, Violet's short stories for the IMA that most reward attention. One of the earliest is 'Una, a Tale for Children', which concerns the misfor-tunes that befall a young woman and her daughter after the death of the father.[38] Economic necessity drives them to live in a poverty-stricken area, where Una (the daughter) falls perilously ill. She is visited by a doctor who, as it turns out, comes from the village where they originally lived. He is 'dreadfully

---

[36] LMA/4292/01/002 and LMA/4292/01/008 (The I.M.A., Sep.–Oct. 1903 and Sep. 1905).

[37] LMA/4292/01/002 and LMA/4292/01/004 (The I.M.A., Sep.–Oct. 1903 and The I.M.A. Christmas Number, Nov.–Dec. 1904).

[38] Some aspects of 'Una', particularly the father's death and the daughter's consequent loss of wealth and status, recall Frances Hodgson Burnett's *A Little Princess*, published in 1905, a year after 'Una' was written (my thanks to Rachael Jones for this link). *The Little Princess* was an expanded version of Burnett's *Sara Crewe: Or, What Happened at Miss Minchin's* (1888), a stage adaptation of which was performed in London under the title *A Little Un-fairy Princess* in 1902.

shocked, to see a lady in such an attic' and promptly whisks them back to their 'own dear village'. This is suggestive in several ways. Illness is prominent, as it was in Betsey's life and in the IMA. The fragility of social position and its dependence on the father is another echo; indeed, a nightmarish fear of falling out of one's 'proper' social sphere and having to live among the working class is what energizes the tale. Implicit in this is an entrenched sense of entitlement, one that is again apparent in Violet's real-life relations with working-class people. Finally, it is telling that the resolution is a return to a village, which functions as a refuge from poverty, illness and, above all, the masses.[39]

'The History of an Umbrella' is a fanciful, first-person narrative of the fortunes of a branch carved into an umbrella handle. The umbrella is cherished by its maker/owner but is stolen by a thief and is thereafter treated just like any other umbrella. Fortunately the original owner sees it for sale and takes it back with him to his country residence. Some of the same themes emerge: hostility to the masses, coupled now with a pro-crafts ethos ('I was not made in a huge factory'); devastating loss of social distinction; the countryside as a refuge. In this story, however, a fear of separation and of outsiders or the unknown comes through more acutely.[40]

The third IMA story that repays analysis is 'Castles in the Air'. Again invalidity is a prominent theme – the protagonist, Paul, is a cripple. He is devoted to a young man, Oliver, who was 'just like a father to him'. Unexpectedly Oliver announces that he is going abroad. Paul is distraught and by means of subterfuge prevents Oliver from embarking on the ship in which he is due to sail. The ship is wrecked and all aboard are drowned, fortuitously including Oliver's wealthy uncle. Oliver is deeply grateful to Paul for inadvertently saving his life and everyone (except the uncle) lives happily ever after.

Although slight and weakly plotted, 'Castles in the Air' is unsettling and, read in the context of Violet's childhood experiences, carries a surprising emotional charge. As in 'Una' and 'The History of an Umbrella', the protagonist suffers from a lack of agency. Perhaps this was ultimately what invalidity signified for Violet. If so, it would seem that, for all her energy, authority and outward confidence, there were aspects of her life over which she felt she had little control. One of these, in childhood at least, may have been her father's frequent, extended and unpredictable absences abroad. Read in this light, there is a terrible pathos in Paul's utter dependence on, and powerlessness to retain, the father-like Oliver. Symbolically perhaps the shipwreck indicates not only the emotional effect on the child of the father figure's departure, but an underlying fear (not unwarranted at a time when long-distance travel was much less safe than today) that a long sea journey might result in his death. The

---

[39] LMA/4292/01/004 (The I.M.A. Christmas Number, Nov.–Dec. 1904).
[40] LMA/4292/01/005 (Junior I.M.A., Apr. 1905).

severely distorting psychological effects of such a situation are apparent in Paul's desperate resort to deception (it is made clear that the journey overseas is of great importance to Oliver, so to prevent it is prospectively a damaging injury to him). There is a contrast here with Violet's two previous IMA stories: on the one hand, for all Paul's panic-inducing sense of powerlessness, he does ultimately act on his own behalf; on the other, the reason he is forced to do so is because the benign *deus ex machina* figures that respectively come to the rescue of Una and the umbrella signally fail to appear in 'Castles in the Air'.[41]

Two other aspects of this story require brief comment. Firstly, there is a sharp separation between an in-group, the people who count, and those who do not. Paul, Oliver and his wife (despite the fact she barely features) count; the uncle and the others on board the ship do not. There is no sense that their demise is to be regretted nor any disquiet that the good fortune of the people who count depends on it. Paul's inner exigencies are too sharp to allow for such regret. This distinction between an all-important in-group and negligible outsiders recurs in various configurations through Violet's life. The second aspect of the story that calls for further comment is the title, or rather the relationship between this and the abundant illustrations. 'Castles in the Air' implies fantasies. The final sentence of the story gestures towards this: Oliver's sudden accession of wealth allows Paul's dream of leaving with him forever to come true. However, this hardly reflects the emotional import of the rest of the story, which concerns the prevention of emotional catastrophe rather than the realization of dreams. The real significance of the title is in relation to the illustrations. Most of these, wrapped elegantly around the text, are characteristically accomplished watercolours of fantasy castles. The main illustration, however, is startling. An entirely naked androgynous figure sweeps high through the air on a swing towards one of the castles of the title. The figure, a copy of Maxfield Parrish's *The Dinky Bird* but with softer and more graceful lines, is painted with a compelling, sensuous tenderness.[42] Violet's mind at the age of twenty-one evidently dwelt on more vivid and intense castles in the air than that ostensible in the text of her story. This is not surprising but there is an unmistakable resemblance between the figure and a few of Violet's other sketches of young women and girls. Her drawings of idle, lounging 'lazy juniors' for the Junior IMA (a humorous attempt to cajole them into contributing more copy) are similarly suffused with tender sensuality, as, years later, is her sketch of munitions workers sleeping on a bus ('girls without hats, in lovely attitudes', in Violet's description).[43] These studies – beautiful, graceful, highly feminized and naturalistic – are informed by the

---

[41] LMA/4292/01/006 (The I.M.A., May–Jun. 1905).
[42] My thanks to Wendy Hawke of the London Metropolitan Archives for drawing my attention to Parrish's original.
[43] LMA/4292/01/009 (Junior I.M.A., Dec. 1905); Dickinson Diary, 11 Jan. 1944.

same aesthetic apparent in most of Violet's other artistic output, notably her flower paintings and landscapes. The implication is that there was a relationship between her sexuality, in both the broad and narrow senses of the term, her artistic sensibility and her responsiveness to nature and land-scape. These connections would indeed prove of crucial significance to Violet in the years ahead.

Meanwhile Violet's cultural education continued, even though she had now left school. She had painting and piano lessons and was elected to the Hampstead Art Society, exhibiting three miniatures at its summer exhibition in 1908.[44] It was a professional necessity for the Dickinsons to keep up with the mainstream of cultivated taste but not to get too far ahead of it. It is therefore unsurprising to find Violet poised between the still influential Ruskin, whose *Seven Lamps of Architecture* she was awarded as a prize in March 1905, and the avant-garde Whistler.[45] Her verdict on an exhibition of the latter's work in 1905 was that 'some [were] absurd, others dainty'.[46] But the Dickinsons would have found nothing to quarrel with in Whistler's advocacy of 'art for art's sake'. They were a world away from Ruskin's moralized aesthetics, although they still respected his authority as an arbiter of taste.

There is also growing evidence of a self-conscious, actively chosen and developed ruralism on Violet's part in her late teens and early twenties. During her recovery from rheumatic fever in 1902, for example, she read *Country Life* while her friend Mrs Dohrman regularly sent her *Country Life in America*.[47] At around this time she also read *Our Village* ('lovely') and some of Emerson's essays.[48] She was enchanted by a house she visited in Chorley Woods: 'Beautiful there – such a pretty little place, with very authentic Voysey houses and all surrounded with hills and woods'.[49] For her twenty-fifth birthday she chose as her present from Les more Emerson essays while Ced, always well attuned to her sensibilities, gave her a 'lovely' edition of Eric Parker's *Highways and Byways in Surrey* (1908) in the year it was first published.[50] All this was in keeping with Frank Dickinson's Arts and Crafts tastes, but he had several other strings to his artistic bow, including contem-porary painting, antique furniture and the oriental porcelain that had made his fame and fortune. In choosing to adopt a ruralist identity, Violet was selectively intensifying one, admittedly prominent, element within the family's wider traditions.

---

[44] Dickinson Diary, 4 Jul. 1907; LMA/4292/01/022 (The I.M.A., May–Jun. 1908).
[45] Dickinson Diary, 1 Feb. 1905.
[46] Dickinson Diary, 2 Mar. 1905.
[47] Dickinson Diary, 17 Jan. 1902, 13 Mar. 1905 and 28 Oct. 1905.
[48] Dickinson Diary, 30 Apr. 1905; 11 Feb. 1907.
[49] Dickinson Diary, 17 May 1907. C. F. A. Voysey (1857–1941) was a highly regarded Arts and Crafts architect and designer.
[50] Dickinson Diary, 3 Dec. 1908.

This increasingly close identification with a broadly Arts and Crafts ruralism was in due course to inform some of Violet's most critical life choices. Yet she was always ambivalent about the anti-capitalist politics of Ruskin, Morris and the 'back-to-the-land' movement that drew inspiration from them. It was not that she shied away from these political aspects. She read not only *Unto This Last* and *News from Nowhere* but also Edward Carpenter's *Towards Democracy* and made extensive notes on Eric Gill, copying out his definition of socialism as 'antipathy to the control of the world by men of business'.[51] She also read other authors with a radical or anti-capitalist turn of mind, including George Gissing, Rabindranath Tagore and Gandhi.[52] C. R. Ashbee's cooperative Guild of Handicrafts intrigued her sufficiently to warrant a journey to Chipping Campden and attentive notes on the Guild's economic arrangements and the influence of Ruskin and Morris.[53] In 1909 she visited Letchworth, admiring the wide grass borders.[54] But figuratively she kept her distance, later referring scathingly to some 'weird people – real garden-cityites'.[55] Really she felt more comfortable in the Tudor village at the Ideal Home Exhibition, about which she enthused unreservedly after a visit in April 1910.[56] Violet's politics, and those of her siblings, remained staunchly Conservative. When they were visited by the socialist Dr Ross in June 1909, the younger Dickinsons set upon him without mercy, and although Violet (unlike Birdy) was never really a political activist, she did canvass for the party in the run-up to the 1923 general election.[57] In the larger scheme of things, these ideological ambiguities reflect the family's economic position as intermediaries between often radical producer-artists and wealthy, conservative consumer-purchasers.[58]

Meanwhile the Dickinsons continued to holiday in picturesque rural locations like North Devon, where they spent another week in spring 1905. Violet's account in the IMA is replete with guidebook tropes: the quaint little villages, the rich colours, the 'sea music' of the waves; farms, cottages, orchards in full bloom and foxgloves everywhere. But there is also a vivid description of an expedition to the Valley of the Rocks, 'round a very narrow and precipitous pathway':

> In places we had to go single file, and hundreds of feet below the waves were dashing on to the rocky beach. I did not enjoy the walk at all, and felt

---

[51] Dickinson Diary, 1918, front papers; 1943, end papers. Violet adorned her notes on Gill with drawings of his children.

[52] Dickinson Diary, 1917 end papers, 1918 and 1940 front papers.

[53] Dickinson Diary, 13 and 13 Oct. 1936 and 19 Nov. 1944.

[54] Dickinson Diary, 8 Jan. 1909.

[55] Dickinson Diary, 17 Jul. 1912.

[56] Dickinson Diary, 23 Apr. 1910.

[57] Dickinson Diary, 30 Jun. 1909 and 23 and 27 Nov. 1923.

[58] One might go further and suggest that in the fluidity and isolation of their social position, their irreligiosity, hedonism and lack of wider social or ethical purpose, the Dickinsons manifested symptoms of Durkheimian anomie.

very giddy. However, I thoroughly enjoyed the wild and rugged beauty of the famous valley (the more so, knowing that we could return by the road!).[59]

Fear of heights is not unusual, although it seems to have been especially pronounced in Violet's case.[60] However, in this instance it was part of a larger pattern. She was afraid of Santa Claus as a child, for example. While this too may not have been unusual, Violet's fear of hearing her sister breathing at night surely was. She also seems to have been afraid of the nocturnal ticking of clocks.[61] Gales terrified her and frequently prevented her from sleeping.[62] During one particularly loud thunderstorm much later in her life, although admittedly when she was on her own, she spent the whole afternoon hiding her head under a rag.[63] Meeting a riderless horse in a lane, again in adulthood, frightened her so much that she attributed the migraine she developed later that day to the shock of the experience.[64] The pattern of disproportionate fear is recurrent and pronounced.

Although the fear elicited by the walk to the Valley of the Rocks and the encounter with the riderless horse in the lane was characteristic, its rural setting was not. Normally Violet was as safe from fear in the countryside as she could be anywhere. Cities were a different matter, especially when she found herself in their working-class quarters:

> [H]ome through Tottenham, which was horrible. Hundreds of children and factory girls.

Dickinsonian normality was quickly restored, however, and Violet's relief is palpable:

> The panoramic view from Muswell Hill was wonderful. At 3 we went to Thresher & Glennys and ordered our spring coats and skirts, blouses and summer dresses. Home about 5.30. Read the life of Mme Vigee le Brun.[65]

What is striking here is how Violet's social and spatial position and her values and attitudes isolate her from the working class. The first sentence of the passage just quoted follows immediately from the last sentence of the

---

[59] LMA/4292/01/006 (The I.M.A., May–Jun. 1905).

[60] Ibid. Earlier on the same holiday she had been unable to look out of the coach window as they drove along a 'dreadful precipice'.

[61] LMA/4292/01/012 (Junior I.M.A., Dec. 1906).

[62] Dickinson Diary, 14 Sep. 1951.

[63] Dickinson Diary, 15 Aug. 1952. This was the night of the Lynmouth catastrophe, but Quarry House lies in an area at very low risk of flooding so Violet's fears would seem to have had little material basis. 'Long Term Flood Risk Information', https://flood-warning -information.service.gov.uk/long-term-flood-risk [accessed 21 Mar. 2017].

[64] Dickinson Diary, 15 May 1949.

[65] Dickinson Diary, 13 Mar. 1907. Thresher and Glenny were (and are) elite London tailors.

preceding excerpt; wrapping her picturesque, ruralist sensibility closely about her insulates Violet from the Tottenham children and factory girls, restoring her equanimity. Evidently they represented some kind of repugnant 'other' to her; even fleeting glimpses from the raised vantage point of a moving car were disagreeable. It was perhaps hardly surprising that someone who shopped at Thresher and Glennys, ordered several new outfits each season and looked to the French painter Louise Élisabeth Vigée Le Brun as a role model felt utterly alienated from the working people of North London.[66] She rarely encountered workers on their own terrain and when she did so her response was typically marked by disdain and discomfort rather than empathy. Until she moved to Somerset, however, complete segregation proved difficult since the two worlds overlapped and (at times) interpenetrated spatially. The same pattern of what she experienced as distasteful and even disturbing exposure to working-class neighbourhoods, rapidly flushed from the mind by plunging gleefully into picturesque rural landscapes, was apparent on a journey to the Lake District in August 1910. On their way up the Dickinsons passed through 'some dreadful places, including Preston and Carnforth', but they soon arrived at their destination, which Violet found 'gloriously wild' and 'just like Switzerland'.[67] She was soon happily absorbed in photographing mountains and waterfalls.[68] It would seem that one of the functions of rural landscapes for Violet was as a screen or curtain that kept disagreeable aspects of reality out of sight and mind.

Even across the Solent on the Isle of Wight, the Dickinsons did not feel entirely safe from the implicit threat of working-class insubordination, as their uncharacteristically aggressive response to what appears to have been a minor instance of childish cheekiness indicates:

> On the way home [from Alum Bay], we stopped for Ced to get out and give a small boy a hiding, who wouldn't move out of the road![69]

This is congruent with Violet's tendency to divide the world into in- and out-groups. She and Ced could show a remarkable indifference to those outside their circle, including, for all the responsiveness to them of which she was capable, towards children. On another occasion, driving through the 'lovely lanes' beyond Godshill in 1907, the Dickinsons 'chased a cow ever so far & it nearly knocked a little boy down'.[70] Here there was no threat, just indifference.

---

[66] Violet and her sisters also habitually shopped at Harrod's, Liberty's and Whiteley's.

[67] The Dickinsons had visited the Bernese Oberland in December 1907. Violet responded conventionally enough, admiring the scenery 'grand every inch of the way – rushing torrent . . . everything covered in snow, pinewoods, brilliant blue sky, and sun shining'. Dickinson Diary, 18 Dec. 1907.

[68] Dickinson Diary, 5 and 6 Aug. 1910.

[69] Dickinson Diary, 19 Jul. 1910.

[70] Dickinson Diary, 19 Jul. 1907.

There was no more compunction two years later, this time in Norfolk, when the Dickinsons found themselves trapped behind a padlocked gate. Rather than attempting to locate the owner, they ordered their chauffeur Harkness (forename not given) to smash the lock.[71]

As the deferential Harkness indicates, when the working class knew their place Violet could feel quite at ease with them, although they never 'counted'. When a tyre burst, for example, it seemed entirely natural to Violet that she should gather 'lovely wildflowers' while Harkness put the patch on.[72] In notable contrast to her cold and shrinking reaction to urban workers and the 'rough' poor, Violet warmed condescendingly to the beaten-down submissiveness of the rural poor, although ideally they merged easily into the picturesque background:

> We came to a log hut, where an old man showed us the path down, and made tea for when we returned. The first cave was a beauty! We went down steep steps to it, and looked right through to the open sea. The water was washing through it, so we could not walk through. Then we had to go back, and down another path, into a little bay, where a boatman was waiting to row visitors round to the caves, as it was high tide. The cliff went sheer up from the sea, and we rowed right underneath it, and round little passages, and then right through the biggest cave. It was like the exhibition, almost too wonderful to be true. We had to row further round to see Swallows, and Sunnyless Caves, and then back. It was very lovely. The old man had made our tea. He was such a dear, he told us how to make Devonshire Cream, and was very friendly, and only wanted 1 ¼ d for each tea!!![73]

This was the poor just as she thought they should be – on hand to minister to tourists' needs, polite, undemanding, self-effacing.

An important feature of Violet's life in her late teens and twenties, one that was instrumental in developing her feeling for rural landscapes, was the Dickinsons' frequent sojourns on the Isle of Wight. The family had been visiting the area round Ventnor since at least August 1901. At some point, probably in 1904 or early 1905, Frank bought St Catherine's House, Niton, and the family spent a considerable part of each year there, including Christmas, Easter and much of the summer. They swam in the sea ('[i]t was rather rough, and awful fun'), clambered over rocks, raced on the beach, played outdoor games like croquet, rounders and tennis, and went on walks and car tours.[74] The diaries convey a sense of rumbustious

---

[71] Dickinson Diary, 10 Apr. 1909.
[72] Dickinson Diary, 30 May 1905.
[73] Dickinson Diary, 2 Jun. 1901.
[74] Violet always found rough seas exhilarating, whether to swim in or look at. Dickinson Diary, 24 Aug. 1910.

physical high spirits. On 25 August 1905 Frank, Violet, Birdy and Ced 'had two long sets of tennis, until it was too dark to play', while on 14 April 1907 '[t]he boys and I played rounders until we could not move!'[75] However, Violet's growing sensitivity to landscape is also apparent. She found the snow-covered St Boniface Down 'so quiet and delicious' on 7 February 1902, and was entranced by a drive through Niton and Whitwell the following day: 'lovely!!!!! The fields + hills so green + peaceful!'[76]

These Isle of Wight holidays became very important to Violet. As early as August 1905 she calls Niton 'home' in her diaries, and she rejoiced in returning there.[77] They got to know the area and found places they liked: Windy Corner, in the undercliff west of St Catherine's Point, was a favourite.[78] Familiarity, compounded with a Dickinsonian sense of entitlement, made the landscape their own. Violet began to refer to the cove below their house as 'our beach', and by 1910 to 'our old glorious walk to Rocken End' (this was just below Windy Corner).[79] They invented family names for some of these places – the 'Wind Blown Meadow', for example, where they spread their picnic rug 'all among the buttercups'.[80] There is a delighted sense of private discovery in Violet's accounts of some of these expeditions, as in May 1909 when they walked down Sack Chute to the shore, along 'little woodland paths lined with primroses, violets'. She thought it 'a Paradise of a place' – indeed it was 'so lovely' that in the afternoon they went there again.[81] This has something in common with the deep absorption Catley found in rural exploration. In Violet's case, however, there is more emphasis, on the one hand, on privacy and, on the other, on collective (familial) experience. This is only superficially paradoxical: rural landscapes provided spaces in which Violet could be together with her in-group while the rest of the world was held at bay. A similar sensibility is apparent in relation to other secluded spots. She was enchanted by The Sheilings, home of their friends the Forbes, reached down a 'wild wooded private lane', and one of her photographs, of Doone Valley, is captioned 'our private waterfall'.[82]

One of Violet's occasional pieces for the IMA, entitled 'The Country in June' and dating from May 1908, conveys a good sense of the spirited

---

[75] Dickinson Diary, 25 Aug. 1905 and 14 Apr. 1907.
[76] Dickinson Diary, 7 and 8 Feb. 1902.
[77] Dickinson Diary, 24 Aug. 1905 and 3 May 1909.
[78] Dickinson Diary, 1 Aug. 1905 and 4 May 1909.
[79] Dickinson Diary, 6 May 1905 and 27 Mar. 1910.
[80] Dickinson diary, 11 May 1909.
[81] Dickinson Diary, 5 May 1909.
[82] Dickinson Diary, 24 Oct. 1908 and Somerset HC A/AGV 12 (undated).

hedonism of these Isle of Wight holidays, and of how this was embedded within the wider landscape:

> It is almost impossible to spend many hours indoors when one is in the country in June – the hedges are never so full of flowers, or the fields of tiny lambs, calves and colts, and the air laden with scent of hay, clover and honeysuckle. Then the first month of bathing has such an attraction, and the craze for tennis has just begun! Gardening, photography, sketching and a thousand other things have to be fitted in – so that by the evening one is so sleepy!![83]

One of the features of their place at Niton that the Dickinsons valued most was the large garden, which overlooked the sea and functioned as an intermediate space between house and countryside. By 1905 Violet had a hammock and spent much time reading in it, sometimes curled up with a kitten.[84] Her diaries mention many of the books she read but rarely give even the most laconic indication of the impression they made on her. One exception was *Mill on the Floss*, which she read aged twenty-three and found 'very amusing', a curious verdict on a notoriously heart-wrenching novel.[85] But this is of a piece with Violet's attitude to literary and intellectual life more generally. She was interested in it and wanted to know about it but does not seem to have let it affect her too deeply. She read Bacon's essays, enjoyed a debate at Westfield College on individuality and happily discussed theosophy, but none of these things seem to have left a lasting impression.[86] An account of a conversation over afternoon tea on 8 May 1905 is indicative of her underlying feeling: 'we had fun talking about Phrenology etc.'.[87]

Although Violet spent so much time in the Isle of Wight, her attitude to landscape in her mid-twenties is perhaps best captured in an account of a holiday in Rye written for the IMA in spring 1908. The little town was 'quaint' and 'very picturesque', 'like walking in a fairy tale'. By the old sea wall 'fishermen in bright coloured jerseys smoke their pipes, and remind one of Dutch pictures'. After dark the organ playing in the church, the moon and stars and distant flashes of a lighthouse created an 'almost theatrical' scene, while nearby Winchelsea was 'the very picture of a place'. The terms 'quaint' and 'picturesque' recur in Violet's landscape description.[88] The aspect of the

[83] LMA/4292/01/022 ('The Editor's Letter', The I.M.A., May–Jun. 1908).

[84] 'I had the hammock all the afternoon for the first time this summer!!!'. Dickinson Diary, 24 Aug. 1910. See also Dickinson Diary, 5 Aug. 1905 and 12 Jul. 1907.

[85] Dickinson Diary, 17 Aug. 1907.

[86] Dickinson Diary, 11 Jan. 1907, 9 Feb. 1907 and 5 Sep. 1915.

[87] Dickinson Diary, 8 May 1905.

[88] For 'quaint', see, for example, Dickinson Diary, 4 Jun. 1901 (Clovelly), 29 Jan. 1902, 24 Aug. 1905, 16 Jun. 1907, 26 Jul. 1907, 24 Oct. 1908, 10 Apr. 1909, 24 Dec. 1926; LMA/4292/01/006 (The I.M.A., May–Jun. 1905) and letter to Mercy Ede dated 27 Oct. 1946, Somerset HC A/AGV 17. Usages of 'picturesque' include Dickinson Diary, 28 Jan. 1902,

landscape that appeals to her is its outward appearance and the extent to which this corresponds to tropes of ancientness, vernacular tradition and rural charm.[89] She has no interest either in the socio-economic life of the places she admires or in the historical processes that produced them. What counts, overtly, is whether somewhere is 'like a picture'.[90] In a sense, the more unreal the landscape the better: one of her highest accolades is 'like fairyland'.[91] The inhabitants of the countryside are regarded in the same light: the jerseys and pipes of the Rye fishermen are more important than their faces, let alone what they might say were Violet to think of talking to them.

The extent to which the reality of country people's lives was subsumed to their picturesque appeal in Violet's eyes is even more obvious in her account of a drive through Dorset in August the following year:

> Pulled up under some lovely fir trees, where I did another sketch. I also took a photo of five gypsy children – lovely, & all in rags & tatters, & brown as oak.[92]

More than any of the other diarists', Violet's relationship to rural landscapes corresponds to what John Urry has called 'the tourist gaze'.[93] This is particularly true in its strongly visual focus, its concern with externals, the lack of interest in historical processes or social structures and above all in the reversal of the notional relationship between representation and reality, whereby reality is valued by reference to pre-existing artistic canons, rather than vice versa. One of the primary consequences of the 'tourist gaze' is often taken to be the marginalization of the rural poor and the trivialization, suppression or denial of their experiences.[94] This is only too apparent in Violet's writing, and in her paintings, which are proverbial 'landscapes without figures' (except, occasionally, for picturesque children). But while Violet's attitudes do on the whole fit the 'tourist gaze' paradigm closely, one or two qualifications are in order. Firstly, the fit was closest when she was in her late teens and twenties. As she matured, other ways of seeing, feeling and being in the landscape grew in her. Secondly, even in her youth aspects of her relationship to landscape did not correspond to the 'tourist gaze'. She responded intensely to non-visual aspects of the landscape, especially smell. She frequently immersed herself *in*

---

10 Apr. 1909, 2 Jun. 1909, 10 Apr. 1912 and 2 Nov. 1915, and letters to Mercy Ede dated 22 and 27 Oct. 1946, Somerset HC A/AGV 17.

[89] Compare Karen Sayer, *Country Cottages: A Cultural History* (Manchester, 2000).

[90] For variants of this expression used in praise of landscape see also Dickinson Diary, 13 and 17 Jun. 1907 (Blenheim Park; the Hog's Back) and 17 Sep. 1908.

[91] For example, Dickinson Diary, 15 May 1907 and 30 Dec. 1908.

[92] Dickinson Diary, 10 Aug. 1909. Earlier that summer she had admired a 'most picturesque gypsy encampment': Dickinson Diary, 2 Jun. 1909.

[93] John Urry, *The Tourist Gaze* (London, 1990).

[94] Newby, *Green and Pleasant Land?*

the landscape rather than merely gazing *at* it, playing in bracken, lying in grass and relishing the buffeting of waves, wind and rain. Thirdly, the touristic aspects of Violet's relationship to landscape cannot be attributed solely, or even primarily, to a pre-existing set of cultural discourses she had absorbed. Certainly she did absorb discursive influences of this kind from her father, through the paintings she saw and from books like *Highways and Byways in Surrey*. Increasingly as she grew older, however, this was not a passive process. She sought out literature, art, people and places that fostered such perspectives because they ministered to needs and preferences that arose from deep psychological sources and from the personal and social circumstances in which she found herself. In large measure, she gazed touristically because it suited her to do so rather than because an external force, be that a cultural abstraction such as a 'discourse' or a more tangible influence such as her father or the Hampstead Art Society, had colonized her mind. Fourthly and finally, although the tourist gaze is undoubtedly distorting and in a sense superficial, the frequent inference that it is merely an idle way to pass time or spend money for people who have too much of both should, in Violet's case at least, be resisted. On the contrary, her touristic consumption of rural landscapes gave her a great deal of pleasure and became a significant part of her identity in youth and early adulthood.

Another developing aspect of Violet's identity was her motherliness. This had been intermittently apparent for years, most obviously in the pages of the Junior IMA, and probably had its origins in her relationship with her siblings. She read to them, played with them, nursed them when they were ill, wrote to Les when he went away to Harrow and always had an especially protective feeling towards Ced.[95] It seems likely that, probably unconsciously and by default, Violet occupied some of the emotional territory Betsey had left vacant, although a degree of motherliness might have been expected anyway in a girl who was the eldest of four siblings. Be that as it may, Violet's motherly feeling became more pronounced in her late twenties. In March 1909 she took seven-year-old Elsa Stuttaford, later to play a major role in her life, for a drive to Elstree, and thought she 'looked sweet in a red riding hood cloak'.[96] Two days later Violet had Doris Barret, a 'lovely little thing', on her lap while playing and singing. Doris 'never moved, but gazed at me, and presently fell sound asleep, & looked too lovely for words', aptly prompting one of Violet's drawings.[97] Two months later Violet played hide-and-seek and danced on the lawn with 'a most amusing, un-shy little girl . . . very cute'.[98] The same feeling spilled over

---

[95] Evident, for example, in a photograph of Frank, Birdy, Violet and Ced sitting on a rock in Somerset HC A/AGV13.
[96] Dickinson Diary, 23 Mar. 1909. Violet had known Elsa since at least 1905.
[97] Dickinson Diary, 25 Mar. 1909.
[98] Dickinson Diary, 7 May 1909.

to adolescent girls such as Megan Rhys, who 'looks a sweet child (she is sixteen) and is most attractive in every way', and is congruent with the 'lazy junior' IMA sketches discussed previously. This way of seeing children was filtered to some extent through Violet's Arts and Crafts sensibility: she thought another girl 'looked very sweet in a Kate Greenaway muslin dress'.[99] However, Violet's feelings towards children had deeper psychological, situational and perhaps age-related roots.

She also had a girlish side herself and was always ready to put herself on the same level as children, taking part in rather than merely organizing games like hide-and-seek. She seems to have found Peter Pan appealing: perhaps a part of her did not want to grow up.[100] In this she may have taken after her mother, who sometimes behaved as if she were one of her children rather than their parent. On 8 May 1909, for example, Betsey, Violet, Birdy and their friend Gertrude went down to the beach at Rocken End and:

> let down our hair, took off our skirts and took photos, madly dancing on the shore.[101]

Two days afterwards, they were:

> very amused by a party of Germans ... they asked 'How long does it last from here to Wroxall' and then we all shrieked with laughter and they all (5 gentlemen) took off their hats as they went out and said 'goodbye' to us. I was glad it was Mother's fault, as she started laughing.[102]

Laughter was an important bonding mechanism for Violet, quite often, as in this example, at the expense of others.[103] It reinforced the distinction between in- and out-groups: 'The people in Woodmans were rediculous [sic] and made us laugh so!'[104] Betsey's proclivity to behave as if she were a girl herself seems to be implicated in this somewhat adolescent conduct.

The IMA was another of Violet's in-groups, and this aspect of it was intensified by the creation of the IMA Fund, 'to help invalids personally known', in 1909. The Fund's income derived largely from sales of paintings and other artwork, the first of which was held, amid great excitement in Ferncroft Avenue on 9 October 1909. It was a financial success and by 1912 the Fund had sufficient resources to pay a doctor to visit a sick baby. Violet's

---

[99] Dickinson Diary, 21 Sep. 1909.
[100] See her photograph of the Peter Pan statue in Kensington Gardens. Dickinson Diary, 1 Dec. 1914.
[101] Dickinson Diary, 8 May 1909.
[102] Dickinson Diary, 10 May 1909.
[103] See also Dickinson Diary, 7 May 1909 and 19 Aug. 1916.
[104] Dickinson Diary, 1 Jul. 1909. The younger Dickinsons gave derogatory nicknames to people they disliked: 'the lunatics' (Dickinson Diary, 8 Jan. 1899) and 'the hooligans' (Dickinson Diary, 31 Mar. 1902), for example.

diary account of her visit to see the baby conveys more horror than compassion:

> Went to see Mrs North's dying baby – a little skeleton – the doctor
> a dreadful, dirty old man.[105]

The 'IMA Fund News' she wrote strikes the same note. She explains that there is 'not much to record this month' before noting that the Fund had given relief to a seriously ill baby, starving in a basement. She then observes baldly that the baby died in a few weeks, before giving news of the 'little cripple' Reggie Bennet. The page on which this is written is beautifully decorated, almost certainly by Violet herself.[106] Evidently it did not occur to her that there was any incongruity between the ornamental presentation and the desperately grim contents. Violet was not an unkind person but her imagination was incapable of leaping across the mental chasm on the far side of which she had placed the working class.

While the baby's death seems to have made little impression on her, 1912 was in other respects a critical year in Violet's life. In April the family stayed in Haslemere, the heart of Arts and Crafts Surrey. Violet had diligently read right through the guidebook beforehand.[107] As was their wont, they travelled by car. The Dickinsons had a *nouveau riche* predilection for up-to-the-minute technology, be that cars, motorbikes, cameras or (later) radios, the flip side of their passion for hand-made vernacular.[108] Both were forms of social capital, markers not only of wealth but of sophisticated, avant-garde taste, distinguishing them from those they regarded as their social inferiors.[109] Violet was delighted when they were told that theirs was the first car to drive up a particular lane.[110] Driving, photography and touristic consumption of the rural vernacular were interwoven:

> [W]e turned left to Elstead, and took photos of the lovely old bridge over the way, and of half-timbered cottages. Then, just over the bridge Birdy took one of old cottage and pear trees in bloom. We then went all through a fine park, full of deer, and past the Georgian house, to Pepper-harrow

---

[105] Dickinson Diary, 16 May 1912.

[106] LMA/4292/01/030 ('I.M.A. Fund News', The I.M.A., 1912).

[107] Dickinson Diary, 7 Apr. 1912.

[108] On the inherent albeit paradoxical co-existence of modern and anti-modern elements within the craft revival, see T. Crook, 'Craft and the Dialogics of Modernity: The Arts and Crafts Movement in Late-Victorian and Edwardian England', *Journal of Modern Craft* 2 (2009), 17–32.

[109] Pierre Bourdieu, *Distinction*, trans. Richard Nice (Cambridge, MA, 1984). Compare also Alex Potts, '"Constable Country" between the Wars', in Raphael Samuel (ed.), *Patriotism: The Making and Unmaking of British National Identity* (London, 1989), 3:160–86.

[110] Dickinson Diary, 12 Apr. 1912.

[Peper Harow] – a lovely old corner, just outside the Park gates, with the church and a fine old farm, backed by fir trees, and a magnificent yew hedge. Birdy took photos – and then we went on to Eashing, where there were some lovely old cottages and she took one, with children at the gate. Then we went to Thursley . . . and saw the murdered sailor's tomb – and took more photos – then straight home.[111]

After lunch the same day Violet, Ced and Birdy walked to Vale Wood Farm. It made a vivid impression on Violet and may indeed have helped to crystallize her vision of the kind of house she would like to live in. Certainly there is a striking resemblance between her description of the interior and that of Heronswood Farm, which she and her father later chose to buy:

We were invited by Mrs Newman to go inside and see the lovely old kitchen, with its enormous open fire, with a great log burning, and huge black caldrons hanging in the chimney! The ceiling was heavy oak beams, and also fine beams in the wall and lovely old lattice window. I took a photo – also of the brick yard at the back, full of milk pans and cans with the dairy maid in the doorway! Her bedroom window – a tiny lattice, not a foot square – in the roof, was the smallest I have ever seen.[112]

The dairy maid is part of a picturesque ensemble, and to Violet the diminutive lattice signified vernacular authenticity rather than insufficient light.

The following day they went into Haslemere itself, visiting St George's Hall, where they:

[S]aw the girls spinning wool, and another weaving at a loom – that was the woollen place – then we went over the road to the Peasants Arts Society weaving house, and saw all their beautiful cloths, towels, bags, and I bought a lovely blue and green apron. Harkness mended a puncture meanwhile. In afternoon, B[irdy], Ced and I walked to Whitwell Hatch, and through woods and meadows and took photos of a lovely haycart and team. After tea we went to Killinghurst Park, on the Chiddingfold Road, where there is a sloping meadow, carpeted with cowslips – and across the drive a wood, full of primroses. I never saw so many cowslips, and we gathered armfuls and basketfuls.[113]

The Peasant Arts Society was the creation of Maude and Joseph King, Ethel and Geoffrey Blount and Greville MacDonald, who between them had a shared vision of reviving what they saw as traditional peasant handcrafts, in their eyes

[111] Dickinson Diary, 9 Apr. 1912. Violet did not suffer from over-refined sensitivity. See, for example, Dickinson Diary, 4 Jul. 1912: 'Enid made us laugh so . . . pretending to hang herself from the hook in our ceiling.'
[112] Dickinson Diary, 9 Apr. 1912.
[113] Dickinson Diary, 10 Apr. 1912.

superior artistically, morally and spiritually to commercial production.[114] The Kings, Blounts and MacDonald believed, as Ruskin had before them, that genuinely beautiful works of art arose from artist-craft workers taking pleasure in creation, rather than making things for the sake of profit. The application of these principles at Haslemere involved the same contradiction that Georgina Boyes identified as foundational to the folk revival in music: locating the folk tradition in the past delegitimized any attempt to depart from the existing canon, thus denying the creative freedom for which folk was most celebrated to contemporary working-class performers and practitioners.[115] Myzelev demonstrates that the anxiety of the Kings and Blounts, who oversaw most of the craft weaving and woodwork in Haslemere, to collect and produce 'genuine' peasant products led them to insist that the local women and girls who worked for them merely copied existing designs (many by Geoffrey Blount) rather than creating their own.[116]

Violet's enthusiasm for the peasant arts undertakings at Haslemere was, however, undiminished by ideological inconsistencies that seem to have passed her by. The day after visiting the Weaving House, the Dickinsons went in search of another of the vernacular crafts for which Haslemere was then celebrated:

> After tea, Mother, Birdy and I rushed all round Haslemere for the genuine 'Stallworthy' pottery, which we hear is now rare, as the potteries are closed, and the Museum has bought some of the last from a little cottage in station road – so we went there first, and bought nearly all the old lady had – some lovely red and orange bowls etc – then to a shop in High St and got some more – and then to Shottermill Post Office. They all have only a few pieces left, so we were just in time, and came home laden.[117]

The contradictions in the Dickinsons' position – celebrating handicraft yet exploiting its producers by cornering the market with ruthless commercial intent – could hardly be more apparent. Yet just as it would be mistaken to belittle Violet's apprehension of rural landscape because it was touristic, so it would be to assume her encounter with Haslemere's Peasant Arts was

---

[114] See the excellent blog 'Peasant Arts: Haslemere', http://peasant-arts.blogspot.co.uk/p/introduction.html [accessed 24 Mar. 2017]. See also A. Myzelev, 'Craft Revival in Haslemere: She, Who Weaves', *Women's History Review* 18 (2009), 597–618.

[115] Georgina Boyes, *The Imagined Village: Culture, Ideology, and the English Folk Revival* (New York, 1993).

[116] Myzelev, 'Craft Revival in Haslemere'.

[117] Dickinson Diary, 12 Apr. 1912. On Stallworthy (Hammer Vale) pottery and its connection with Peasant Arts see G. R. Rolston, *Haslemere 1850–1950* (Farnham, 1964), 48 and Greta Turner, *Shottermill: Its Farms, Families and Mills Part 2 – 1730 to the Early 20th Century* (Headley Down, 2005), 326. I owe these references to the kindness of Lindsay Moreton (Collections Manager, Haslemere Educational Museum).

superficial because she failed to notice its ideological inconsistency. On the contrary, like so much else in this twenty-ninth year of her life, it appears to have had lasting effects. The holiday in Haslemere seems to have been the first time she observed art weaving at close quarters or showed any sustained interest in it. While it cannot be proven that this was why weaving subsequently became so large a part of her life, it seems very likely that the seed of these later developments was planted in Haslemere.

Meanwhile Frank had evidently been giving some thought to what his children should do now that they had finished school. It appears to have been the intention that Leslie should inherit the family business, but occupations needed to be found for the other three. Frank decided to give them a training in agriculture. Ced had already attended courses at the Royal Agricultural College in Cirencester and at Wye College in Kent. Now Frank sent Violet, Birdy and Ced to the Midland Agricultural and Dairy College near Keyworth in Nottinghamshire, which they attended between May and July 1912. Here they learnt the rudiments of farming – one of Violet's principal triumphs being to master the art of butter-making.[118] Following this, Frank bought Little Bower Farm at Molash in Kent for them. Violet and Birdy were to live and work here for seven years.

Violet lost no time putting her newly acquired skills into practice, beginning to churn butter almost as soon as she arrived at Molash.[119] They also kept sheep and campines (hens), which roamed among Little Bower's extensive cherry orchards, idyllically beautiful when in blossom.[120] The purchase of the farm represented in one sense a parting of the ways for the Dickinsons. The farm had in large part been Frank's vision and he often went there. Conversely, there are some indications that his relationship with Betsey, and hers with Violet, was deteriorating. Certainly Betsey came less often and, when she did so, it seems rarely to have been in Frank's company.[121] True to her dislike of demonstrativeness, Violet's diary generally maintained a remarkably even tone towards her relatives but irritation with Betsey crept into it now.[122] At the same time, Molash presaged a pattern of living, in a rural setting with or close to one or more of her siblings, that was to pertain for much of the rest of Violet's life.

Not long after arriving at Molash the Dickinsons helped to set up a local scout group.[123] This reflected Violet's affinity for children, the pleasure she took in organized social activity (with the 'right' sort of people) and the

---

[118]   Dickinson Diary, 23 May 1912.
[119]   Dickinson Diary, 2 Aug. 1912.
[120]   Dickinson Diary, 3 Jan. and 22 Apr. 1913.
[121]   Dickinson Diary, 22 Apr. 1913. Similarly, it was seven months after Violet's arrival in her next home, Heronswood Farm, before Betsey visited. Dickinson Diary, 30 Apr. 1920.
[122]   Dickinson Diary, 25 May 1917.
[123]   Dickinson Diary, 16 Apr. 1913 and 7 Jun. 1914.

family's patriotic Conservatism. In its early days, scouting had a distinctively ruralist ethos, and had links to the network of rural community organizations that developed just before, during and immediately after World War I (the Women's Institutes and the Rural Community Councils, for example).[124] With the declaration of war on 5 August, scouting became a way for the Dickinsons to express their patriotic commitment, in keeping with their ruralism. On the 6th Violet woke Ced at 4.45am, got his breakfast and sent him off with nine scouts to Faversham to guard telegraph poles, run dispatches and otherwise purport to be useful.[125] It was not long, however, before more serious war duties intervened. Ced was admitted to the Royal Naval Air Squadron on 14 November while Leslie had also volunteered.[126] Violet's diary for 13 June is headed 'THE BOYS CALLED ON ACTIVE SERVICE' and by September Ced was in the trenches at Gallipoli.[127]

Despite the war, the rustic idyll continued at the aptly named Little Bower. Violet and Birdy took pupils to teach them about agriculture, providing essential labour for the farm. They continued the IMA for the first two years of the war and there are photos of an IMA tea party and a picnic at Molash.[128] The style of farming at Little Bower certainly corresponded to the 'lighter branches of agriculture' recommended for women farmers at this time.[129] Violet was prepared to work hard, however, and, contrary to assumptions often made about so-called hobby farmers, the idyll not only survived but seems often to have been most vividly experienced when she and the other young women were engaged in demanding physical tasks such as raking hay by hand and even the dirty, exhausting work of loading wheat into a threshing machine, which Violet found 'very picturesque in the half-light with the girls in sunbonnets, baize aprons on blue overalls'.[130] Sheep dipping in the spring proved equally enjoyable and it was typical of the pattern of these Molash years that arduous work and pleasure co-existed. After washing the sheep Violet went for a swim 'among the tadpoles' in the sheep dip and sunbathed afterwards ('lovely!').[131]

[124] On the rural community movement, see Jeremy Burchardt, 'Rethinking the Rural Idyll: The English Rural Community Movement, 1913–26', *Cultural and Social History* 8 (2011), pp. 73–94, esp. pp. 76–9.

[125] Dickinson Diary, 6 Aug. 1914.

[126] Dickinson Diary, 14 Nov. 1914.

[127] Dickinson Diary, 13 Jun. and 2 Sep. 1915.

[128] Dickinson Diary, 1 Dec. 1914.

[129] Nicola Verdon, 'Business and Pleasure: Middle-Class Women's Work and the Professionalization of Farming in England, 1890–1939', *Journal of British Studies* 51 (2012), 393–415. Anne Meredith, 'From Ideals to Reality: The Women's Smallholding Colony at Lingfield, 1920–39', *Agricultural History Review* 54 (2006), 105–21.

[130] Dickinson Diary, 22 Feb. 1915. Hardy makes this task his epitome of harsh, degrading labour for women in *Tess of the D'Urbervilles*.

[131] Dickinson Diary, 19 May 1916. Presumably the sheep dip was a pond.

Leslie was invalided home through illness in autumn 1915 and, at his asking, Violet nursed him in London for a while. There is a sense of triumph and victory in her diary entry for 3 November: 'Leslie returns to Molash from the War!'[132] Evidently there was a dichotomy in her mind between Molash (her rural refuge) and the war (which took place somewhere else). But it was Ced, in Gallipoli, who was in the greatest danger and the strength of Violet's feelings on his safe return breaks through her restricted verbal register:

> 21st February: Ceddy may arrive any day!!![133]

> 22nd February: CEDDY ARRIVED AT Paddington.[134]

> 23rd February: It is a great anxiety over![135]

> 24th February: Terrific snowstorms. Phone – Ceddy answered!!!!![136]

> 26th February: CEDDY CAME HOME. It was beautiful through Perry Wood.[137]

Her joy irradiated the landscape and, the following day, transmuted hardship into celebration:

> 27th February: Eight journeys to feed the sheep through a blinding snow-storm – but it was beautiful.[138]

Sometimes, as on this occasion, landscape seems to have served as a medium through which Violet was able to experience intense emotion she could not otherwise articulate.

Partly because so many men were away fighting, Violet found herself surrounded by women during the war. Her special affinity for and desire to belong to groups of young women had been apparent for years, most obviously in relation to the IMA. But the war greatly magnified it and was crucial in developing the association (never thereafter entirely relinquished) between rural living and female communality. Violet worked with and contributed to the Women's Land Army and the Women's Institutes during the war – indeed, she was a Land Girl herself for a while.[139] But it was with the women who came to work on the farm that she had the closest relationships, notably with Kath, Madge and Florence, who were at Molash from autumn 1915 to August 1916, probably as Land Girls. Working alongside Violet on a day-to-day basis in the secluded, idyllic setting of Little Bower, they came to form another of her

[132] Dickinson Diary, 3 Nov. 1915.
[133] Dickinson Diary, 21 Feb. 1916.
[134] Dickinson Diary, 22 Feb. 1916.
[135] Dickinson Diary, 23 Feb. 1916.
[136] Dickinson Diary, 24 Feb. 1916.
[137] Dickinson Diary, 26 Feb. 1916.
[138] Dickinson Diary, 27 Feb. 1916.
[139] Dickinson Diary, 3, 5 and 30 Jan. 1918.

in-groups. When they left Violet was distraught ('I hate them going!').[140] It is revealing that it was the group she missed more than any single individual:

> I do miss the girls – awfully dull – tried to pretend they'd gone to a lecture at Wye.[141]

The following spring Violet stayed with Kath and Madge on a farm near High Wycombe for several weeks. On the last night Violet recorded that 'Kath came into my bed till 11pm.'[142] Kath returned the visit in August. It is again clear from the diary that the bucolic landscape around Molash not only provided a secluded, private setting in which an unconventional relationship of this kind could flourish, but that the perceived beauty of the landscape was congruent with and flowed into the mutual sensibilities and ethos that connected the young women:

> Kath and I walked up into the wood – lovely springy brushwood – and talked – most Philosophical![143]

After Kath had gone Violet sent a song and photos to her. They stayed the night together in London in January 1918 and the following day went to Harrod's and Selfridge's, where they wore each other's hats. On a few subsequent occasions, Violet was to exchange clothing with women to whom she was passionately attached. It signified a subsuming of identities and suggests something incomplete or not fully realized in her sense of self. Certainly the urge to identify herself with another woman was a powerful one with her.

The freedom and happiness Violet had found working and living together with other young women during the war seems to have liberated her latent sexuality. Passionate as the relationship with Kath was, however, it does not seem to have been exclusive. On her way up to London in February, Violet was entranced by the beautiful hair ('very fascinating') of a WAAC with whom she shared the train compartment. In April she became involved with a young woman named Phil and the same pattern of outdoor liberty and pleasure recurred:

> Gorgeous day. I set everyone to work ... After lunch Phil and I cycled to Perry Woods, where we had 'some' afternoon, in the pulpit and then in the bracken.[144]

Phil seems to have been working at Little Bower and on 22 April Violet recorded in her diary that she '[w]ent in to wake Phil at 5.45, and stayed there till time to get up', while in June she slept with her at Forge Cottage.[145]

[140] Dickinson Diary, 30 Aug. 1916.
[141] Dickinson Diary, 2 Sep. 1916.
[142] Dickinson Diary, 23 May 1917.
[143] Dickinson Diary, 19 Aug. 1917.
[144] Dickinson Diary, 12 Apr. 1918.
[145] Dickinson Diary, 22 Apr. and 10 Jun. 1918.

The end of the war was a relief to Violet but does not seem otherwise to have changed the pattern of her life. What did was Frank's declining health. On 8 May 1919 he went into a nursing home in London. Violet visited him, taking him out for lunch and reading Tolstoy in his room.[146] In some way Frank's ill health seems to have led him to sell Little Bower and buy Heronswood Farm near Rye in its place.[147] While it lacked the spectacular Molash orchards, Heronswood made up for them in its tile-hung, timber-framed vernacular, adjacent oast house and the expansive but intricate rural landscape in which it was set. Violet lost little time in beginning to explore this landscape, delighting in the marshes, woods, blackberries and views.[148] The extensive marshes in particular proved therapeutic in times of tribulation. On 16 January 1920 she learnt that the temporarily absent Ced had developed appendicitis and been (successfully) operated on. The same morning the vet came to shoot her old mare Brownie and unexpectedly announced that the bullock had dropsy and

Figure 5.1   Violet's watercolour of Udimore (near Heronswood) in the snow, 1920
Reproduced by kind permission of the South West Heritage Trust (SHC A/AGV/24)

---

[146] Dickinson Diary, 29 May and 18 Jun. 1919.
[147] Dickinson Diary, 9 Oct. 1919.
[148] Dickinson Diary, 11, 19 and 24 Oct. 1919.

would have to be slaughtered too. After all this, Violet 'walked round [the] marshes to blow it off'.[149] The following day, the carcasses were taken away and afterwards she again went for a walk, presumably for the same reason.[150]

Less than twenty months later Violet had left Heronswood, but two of the events that occurred during the intervening period would shape the rest of her life. The first, and perhaps the most important, was the arrival of Elsa Stuttaford to work as a trainee on the farm on 19 March 1920. Photographs of her at the time show a dapper, confident-looking young woman with an Eton crop, dressed rather mannishly in jacket and trousers.[151] Violet had known her in childhood but does not seem to have seen much of her since then. However, the age difference between them – she was eighteen, Violet thirty-six – suggests that the complication of maternal and erotic feelings apparent in some of the older woman's sketches and diary entries may again have been at work. Setting normative considerations aside, the dual nature of the relationship was liable in the long run to create tensions that might prove difficult to resolve.

In the Edenic Heronswood spring, however, such shadows were far from their minds. It was as if Little Bower had been a dress rehearsal for this. The countryside was not a mere backdrop to the blossoming relationship but (to adapt Wordsworth) 'far more deeply interfused' with it. As with Kath, Madge and Florence at Molash, the relationship developed through working together in the landscape. On 23 March Violet and Elsa called at three local farms in search of broody hens. They had 'no luck, but [a] lovely walk – primroses heavenly'.[152] A similar atmosphere pervades Violet's account of gathering watercress the following month:

> We made the hens comfortable in the bull lodge – then Elsa and I got watercress from the stream by the oast – I went in water boots, but Elsa got the cress. We planted some upstream.[153]

Rich though the pleasures of shared outdoor work were, however, the dominant tone of Violet's Heronswood diary entries is pastoral rather than georgic. As at Molash, but again more intensely, the connection between the landscape, her aesthetic sensibility and the development of a romantic relationship is

---

[149] Dickinson Diary, 16 Jan. 1920.
[150] Dickinson Diary, 17 Jan. 1920.
[151] Photograph, Somerset HC A/AGV 13. Compare Violet's description of Eve Balfour: 'Eton cropped – wearing breeches – just like a man!' (Dickinson Diary, 15 Jan. 1930). Doan argues that masculine attire or appearance sometimes allowed lesbians to recognize each other while passing as women of fashion in the eyes of others. Laura Doan, *Fashioning Sapphism: The Origins of a Modern English Lesbian Culture* (New York, 2001), 120. See also Deborah Cohler, *Citizen, Invert, Queer: Lesbianism and War in Early Twentieth-Century Britain* (Minneapolis, 2010), 155–6.
[152] Dickinson Diary, 23 Mar. 1920.
[153] Dickinson Diary, 10 Apr. 1920.

evident. She and Elsa sketched together in the fields and around the farm and
sallied forth in search of flowers.[154] On 30 April they went up into Coney
Woods and picked broom, campion and bluebells, while a few weeks later:

> Elsa and I went a little way in the Bleriot towards Peasmarsh and then
> walked through woods and along the river – lovely – wildflowers beautiful –
> meadows with ragged robin and honeysuckle and dog roses and elder – also
> foxgloves . . . After lunch we walked to the heronry to see the foxgloves and
> sat there.[155]

What was taking place was a process of mutual exploration and discovery, of
the landscape and of each other. One way this is expressed in the diaries is
through invoking place names that had become resonant for them through
shared experience: Coney Woods, King's Wood, Peasmarsh, the Heronry.[156]
Private places such as The Sheilings, or Steephill Woods near Niton, had
always appealed to Violet. The difference now was the intense present-ness
of being there with Elsa, as on 10 April when 'Elsa and I walked to the ravine
(for 1st time) through Partridge Farm – lovely spot.'[157] In such places, Violet's
diary suggests, she and Elsa experienced the 'contraction of view to one of
absolute locality' that Landry argues can be 'intensely liberating'.[158] The sexual
element of being together in the landscape is less pronounced than it was with
Kath and Phil at Molash, perhaps because it was indissoluble from the larger
emotional whole of this much deeper relationship. Nevertheless, Violet and
Elsa had a powerful urge to be together physically in the landscape that they
had made so much their own:

> In the afternoon, Elsa and I went up into King's Wood, and then lay in the
> bracken till tea time.[159]

The significance of the landscape to their physical relationship is also apparent
in the fact that, weather permitting, they liked to sleep outdoors together.[160]
Through being together in these idyllic private places, Violet and Elsa seem
to have bonded into a single persona, like two previously independent atoms
combining into one molecule. It would not be stretching the analogy too far
to suggest that the landscape was the catalyst for this reaction. Violet had
been looking, consciously or otherwise, for something like this for a long

---

[154] Sketching: Dickinson Diary, 8 Oct. 1920 and 2 Apr. 1921.
[155] Dickinson Diary, 6 Jun. 1920.
[156] Dickinson Diary, 30 Apr., 6 and 27 Jun., 27 Nov. and 3 Dec. 1920.
[157] Dickinson Diary, 10 Apr. 1920.
[158] Landry, *The Invention of the Countryside*, 210.
[159] Dickinson Diary, 27 Jun. 1920.
[160] Dickinson Diary, 27 Jun. 1920. See also Dickinson Diary, 11 Jun. 1920, although on this
occasion they were joined by one of the other girls who worked with them at
Heronswood.

time: a sense of completion, insulating her against the world. The pairing with Elsa was her ultimate in-group. As with previous in-groups, it was in part defined against others:

> We inquired at every ironmongers for 'white lead' – one girl said they had 'lead white' – but that it had no lead in it! Elsa and I got the giggles furiously – then E asked her for 'fish glue' but she hadn't any – so E then asked her if she had any 'gluefish' at which she was furious, and we became quite hysterical.[161]

The second decisive event that occurred while Violet was at Heronswood was the death of her father on 26 November 1920.[162] Violet had always been close to him and she certainly felt the blow: even thirty years later she recorded his birthday ('he would have been 91 today!').[163] At the time, however, she was so absorbed in and sufficed by the relationship with Elsa that she felt the loss less than might have been expected. She showed no symptoms of extreme disturbance, nor were there any drastic voluntary changes in the pattern of her life. Such indications as there were of her grief were typically elliptical and displaced from the text of the diary: a photograph of Frank stuck inside the front cover of the 1920 volume, and inside the back cover, William Allingham's lament 'Four ducks on a pond', often used at funerals. Birdy's reaction was less contained. She borrowed money to go into a farming partnership with a Major Abbot, threw this up within a month, and arrived all of a sudden at Heronswood on her motorbike.[164] Shortly thereafter came '[a]stounding and abominable' letters from her lawyers to the other three, greeted with 'great indignation and also laughter in the camp'.[165] Back at Heronswood in August, Birdy called Elsa, whom she doubtless felt had stolen her sister, an 'impudent pig'. Characteristically but cruelly, Elsa and Violet promptly went off to sketch the pig stys.[166] By the end of the year the relationship between the sisters had broken down completely and it was to be ten years before they met again.[167] Tellingly, Betsey seems to have made no effort to pull the family together in this crisis – none, at any rate, that Violet thought worth recording. She had been drifting away for some time and would henceforth play only a minor role in her eldest daughter's life, to the point where by the early 1930s two years could pass without them meeting.[168]

[161] Dickinson Diary, 14 Mar. 1921.
[162] Dickinson Diary, 26 Nov. 1920.
[163] Dickinson Diary, 10 Feb. 1950.
[164] Dickinson Diary, 3 Dec. 1920 and 9 Apr. 1921.
[165] Dickinson Diary, 23 Jul. 1921.
[166] Dickinson Diary, 17 Aug. 1921.
[167] Dickinson Diary, 13 Jan. 1931.
[168] Dickinson Diary, 13 Jan. 1931.

Heronswood Farm was sold in September 1921 and Violet and Elsa went to live with Elsa's aunt in Stoke-by-Nayland, Suffolk.[169] However, only a few days after arriving, Violet was shocked to be told by her doctor that she had a tumour.[170] Elsa was very upset on the morning of her admission to hospital a fortnight later, and Violet hated leaving her.[171] The operation, evidently successful, was carried out on 28 October but it was nearly a month before she was able to return 'home'.[172] Elsa had also been unwell, possibly with a back complaint, and Violet:

> got on her bed inside the dining room and we talked – and it was lovely to be together again ... [I]n the afternoon ... I tried to sleep but was too excited![173]

The following April the two women moved to the Rectory, Kilve, Somerset, where they had a double room together.[174] Here they kept ducks and geese. After the turmoil of the previous months Violet was overjoyed to be settled with Elsa in their own place in the country. At first Elsa was unable to walk but it was enough to be together. Violet's diary breathes peace and contentment:

> Sat in the garden all afternoon [with Elsa]. I then took Binkie [their dog] down to the shore – heavenly – Welsh coast across the Bristol Channel and Islands – + streams and primroses![175]

By mid-June Elsa could walk again and they began to explore the local countryside: villages and churches, woods and fields, orchids on the cliffs, stag hunting on the hills.[176] On Old Christmas Day, mummers came round, dressed up, with painted faces, and playing tambourines and concertinas ('We gave them cake and money and took photos!').[177] However, happy as she was with Elsa, by January 1923 she had allowed Christine Pugh to move in with them, recreating a community of women in the countryside of the kind that she had found so absorbing at Molash.[178] While the deeper feeling remained, it

---

[169] Dickinson Diary, 28 and 30 Sep. 1921.
[170] Dickinson Diary, 11 Oct. 1921.
[171] Dickinson Diary, 26 Oct. 1921.
[172] Dickinson Diary, 25 Nov. 1921.
[173] Dickinson Diary, 25 Nov. 1921.
[174] Dickinson Diary, 26 Apr. 1922.
[175] Dickinson Diary, 1 May 1922.
[176] Dickinson Diary, 18 Jun. and 8 Sep. 1922 and 17 Jun. 1923.
[177] Dickinson Diary, 8 Jan. 1923. Compare 24 Dec. 1926: 'We heard a quaint morality play broadcast from the little church of St Hilary, Marazion, Cornwall – played by the natives.'
[178] Dickinson Diary, 1 Jan. 1923. The desire to live in a community of peers, rather than with a lover alone, may not be unusual among those whose relationship with their parents has been thwarted in some way. Compare, for example, Richard Holmes, *Shelley: The Pursuit* (London, 1974).

would seem that the first flush of her passion for Elsa was over and her abiding desire to be part of a peer group had reasserted itself. It may have been given added impetus by the splintering of the Dickinson family after her father's death. In these Somerset years Violet often referred to her household as 'the family' (her quotation marks), a feeling that seems to have extended even to the animals they kept.[179]

Although the move to the Quantocks had been a great success, they do not seem to have intended to stay permanently in the Rectory and moved again in June 1924. However, their new home, Higher Pardlestone, was only two miles up the hill, at the top of Pardlestone Lane, halfway to Holford. Christine did not accompany them but they were joined by Leslie for much of the time initially.[180] The move continued the pattern of ever-increasing rural seclusion: while Kilve was quite a large village, there were only four or five other cottages and farms strung out along Pardlestone Lane, which led directly onto the Quantocks only a few hundred yards further on (see cover image). Walking over the hills, usually in company or with her dogs but not infrequently alone, became important to Violet and the diary registers the pleasure she took in the distinctive landscape, raised above and almost out of the surrounding countryside, across which it commanded memorable views:

> Wonderful walk with Mary Witty and Ceddy over the hills – sunny, frosty, rolling fog over the lower country.[181]

The thirteen years Violet spent at Higher Pardlestone, a warm red sandstone cottage tucked away beside the lane in a pretty garden bright with flowers, were among the happiest of her life. The relationship with Elsa gave her deep contentment and, for the first time, she had a stable home in which the person who mattered most to her was permanently resident. This was accompanied by a broadening and deepening of her interest in the countryside. Hitherto, despite her ideological commitment to peasant handicraft and her own personal experience of farming, she had valued the countryside primarily in aesthetic terms, as a visual landscape. Its social life had hardly engaged her attention. To a certain extent her participation in the Women's Land Army, Women's Institute, Guides and Scouts at Molash was an exception, but fostering rural society was not the primary aim of any of these organizations and Violet supported them principally because she wanted to contribute to the war effort and, with respect to the first three, because of her feminist leanings. Now she began to engage with organizations whose raison d'être was to regenerate a rural culture that many feared was melting away in the face of modernity. She and Elsa were particularly drawn to folk dancing and singing.

[179] Dickinson Diary, 29 Dec. 1923.
[180] Dickinson Diary, 23 Jun. 1924.
[181] Dickinson Diary, 13 Jan. 1929.

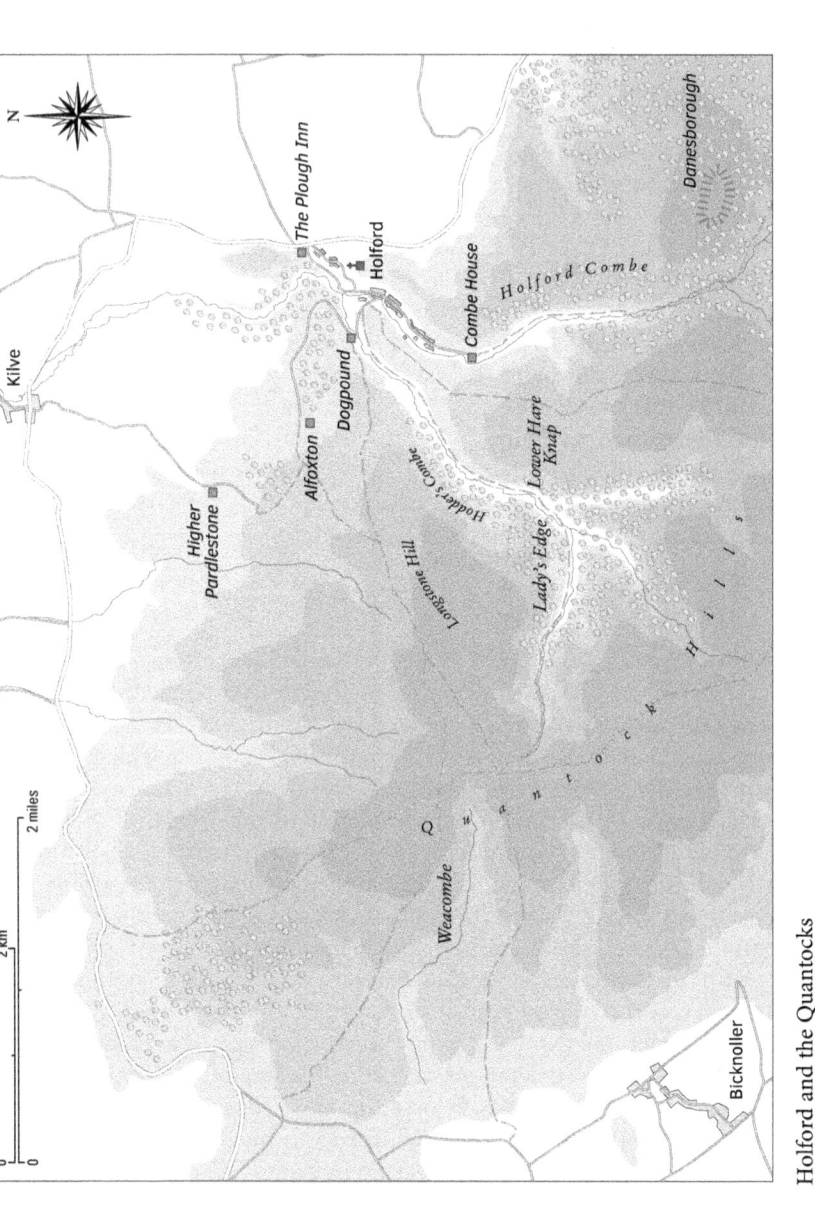

Figure 5.2 Holford and the Quantocks

Violet attended the opening meeting of the Quantock Villages Folk Dancing Society in September 1925 and the following year admired a dance demonstration Joan Sharp (daughter of Cecil) gave at Taunton.[182] Elsa and Violet visited schools to help the children learn country dancing and also taught the local Girl Guides dancing (and nature study).[183] They became involved with the recently formed Somerset Rural Community Council in 1928 while continuing to support the Girl Guides and W. I., the local Holford branch of which they helped to establish.[184] Meanwhile, Elsa became an enthusiastic follower of the Quantock Staghounds.[185] While she was away Violet (who did not ride) went out for long walks across the hills.[186]

There were several reasons for this newfound interest in rural organizations. Violet found she enjoyed the social occasions, especially the dances.[187] The diary entries that describe them are often lengthy and animated, enthusiastically listing the attendees she knew or had spoken to.[188] For someone who preferred not to delve too deeply into her own emotions, but with abundant mental and physical energy, the attractions of these large, lively social gatherings are obvious. Furthermore, it appears that Elsa, a capable and determined organizer, was keen to be involved too. But with respect to the place of the countryside in Violet's life, the larger significance is that she evidently felt secure and settled enough in the Quantocks to put down social roots to a greater extent than she had ever done before.[189]

Leslie was no longer living with them by this time, but in spring 1926 Ced moved into the adjacent cottage, an important step in Violet's reconstitution of a 'family' at Higher Pardlestone.[190] His arrival changed the economic basis of the household. Initially Violet and Elsa had kept poultry but by February 1927 they and Ced had also begun to keep angora rabbits and in due course bees.[191] All three of them took up spinning and weaving, using the fine wool clipped from the rabbits.[192] The following April Major Maurice Fearing Cely-Trevilian, chair of the Somerset Rural Community Council, came to see them to discuss the development of an angora weaving industry in Somerset.

---

[182] Dickinson Diary, 2 Sep. 1925 and 8 Apr. 1926.
[183] Dickinson Diary, 5 Jan. and 6 Feb. 1926.
[184] Dickinson Diary, 23 Nov. and 18 Jun. 1928 and 1 Jan. and 1 Jun. 1927.
[185] Dickinson Diary, 23 Jan. 1925.
[186] Dickinson Diary, 8 Dec. 1925 and 16 Mar. 1926.
[187] Dickinson Diary, 27 Nov. 1926 and 1 and 3 Dec. 1927.
[188] Dickinson Diary, 2 Jul. 1927.
[189] These were very particular social roots, however: in all these years in Somerset there is barely a single mention of a farmer or labourer.
[190] By the late 1930s, however, the cottage seems to have been regarded as Elsa's.
[191] Dickinson Diary, 24 Feb. 1927 and 29 May 1929.
[192] Dickinson Diary, 17 May and 3 Sep. 1928. On hand weaving in the early twentieth century see Tanya Harrod, *The Crafts in Britain in the 20th Century* (New York, 1999), 42–55, 121–3.

Reviving and promoting putatively traditional country crafts was one of the prime concerns of the rural community councils and the Somerset branch was to the fore in this.[193] Cely-Trevilian asked the Higher Pardlestone household to teach spinning and send angora products to a rural industries shop, which was to open in Taunton before Christmas. This duly materialized and there was also an exhibition of Pardlestone angora garments for three days at the Handicraft Exhibition in Taunton the following November.[194]

Meanwhile, Betsey had moved to a house in the area in September 1926, drawn presumably by the presence of two of her children. But other than a motor tour to Matlock Bath in October 1927, she does not seem to have spent much time with them and she returned to London in January 1928.[195] She had never been quite so enthusiastic about the countryside as the other Dickinsons. At long last, however, Violet was reconciled with Birdy and her partner Nora Biddulph (Bay), who moved to Plainsfield in the early 1930s, only a few miles from Higher Pardlestone, and stayed for the rest of her life.[196] For all this, the breach between the sisters was perhaps more papered over than fully healed, and Birdy was much put out after Violet's death in 1953 to discover she had appointed Mercy Ede as her executor.

Between 13 December 1927 and 24 January 1928 Violet was in Minehead Hospital for another unspecified operation (she tells us only that something was 'wrong in [her] right side').[197] The day before her admission she and Elsa went for a long walk together on the hills.[198] Except when in London over New Year, Elsa visited nearly every day. On 22 January she took the recuperating Violet for a drive to Selworthy and something of the latter's relief at having come through the operation successfully and her gladness in being with Elsa again is apparent in her observation that she 'never saw such a unique and beautiful spot' as this.[199]

Three years later it was Elsa's turn to have an operation. Again Violet does not specify the cause but she was very worried and went for a walk up the hill on hearing the news, as she did later that spring on the day Elsa left for a holiday in Italy (possibly to recuperate).[200] Walking served not only to relieve anxiety but also as a way of coming together again after a separation, and two days after Elsa returned from hospital, she and Violet went for a walk

---

[193] Dickinson Diary, 23 Nov. 1928. See also Alan Rogers, *The Most Revolutionary Measure: A History of the Rural Development Commission, 1909–1999* (Salisbury, 1999); Burchardt, 'State and Society'.

[194] Dickinson Diary, 12 Jan. and 20 Nov. 1929.

[195] Dickinson Diary, 20 Sep. 1926, 20 Oct. 1927 and 4 Jan. 1928.

[196] Dickinson Diary, 13 Jan. 1931.

[197] Dickinson Diary, 9 Dec. 1927.

[198] Dickinson Diary, 10 Dec. 1927.

[199] Dickinson Diary, 22 Jan. 1928.

[200] Dickinson Diary, 20 Mar. and 5 May 1931.

together.[201] They did the same (with Ced) two days after Violet's return from a visit to the Guild of Handicrafts in October 1936.[202]

On 20 April 1932 Violet received a letter from Leslie informing her that Betsey was very ill. She and Ced took the train to London, where they saw their mother for the last time.[203] Betsey's death did little, however, to disturb the even tenor of these Higher Pardlestone years, which in economic terms now revolved largely around spinning and weaving.[204] By 1937 Violet's technique had developed to the point where she was awarded a gold star for spinning and silver for weaving at the Women's Institute exhibition in Bath.[205] She and Elsa gave spinning and weaving demonstrations, just as Cely-Trevilian had requested, for example, to the Kilve Women's Guild on 26 January 1933.[206] They took paying pupils, recapitulating not only the economic but also the affective structure at Molash and Heronswood, and further consolidating the substitute family Violet had worked so hard to create in Somerset. One such pupil was Loveday Lewes, who stayed with them for a year in the early 1930s.[207] However, spinning and weaving alone proved insufficient to generate the necessary income and on 2 June 1933 Violet spent the whole day painting a sign that read 'Teas, Fruit and Cream, Coffee, Guests'.[208] It was not long before two strangers arrived to have tea, the first of many who came for refreshment, lodging or, increasingly, out of curiosity to see the weaving.[209] The arrangement worked well, helping the 'Pardlestone Weavers', as they now called themselves, to publicize and sell their work.

However, the peace and contentment Violet had found at Higher Pardlestone was suddenly and unexpectedly shattered in December 1936:

> After dinner I had a terrible shock – E told me, that she didn't want me over in the cottage as P.B. [Pamela Briarley] was the only one who could 'help her'!!! – so I went out to ponder over this.[210]

The following day Elsa came to find Violet and told her she loved Pamela instead. Two days later, Violet wrote in her diary that it had been a 'dreadful week – E still in her room with PB and her cough'. A fortnight later Elsa left

---

[201] Dickinson Diary, 7 and 9 Apr. 1931.
[202] Dickinson Diary, 16 and 18 Oct. 1936.
[203] Dickinson Diary, 27 Apr. 1932.
[204] It cannot be a coincidence that Birdy and Nora became weavers too.
[205] Dickinson Diary, 15 Apr. 1937.
[206] Dickinson Diary, 26 Jan. 1933.
[207] Dickinson Diary, 11 May 1950.
[208] Dickinson Diary, 2 Jun. 1933.
[209] Dickinson Diary, 20 Jun. 1933.
[210] Dickinson Diary, 26 Dec. 1936. This was the sharpest crisis of her life but in seeking to absorb the initial impact by going out for a walk, Violet was responding in the same way as she had to previous severe shocks such as the news of Ced's appendicitis.

Higher Pardlestone to go and live together at 'Sweet Briar', Pamela's cottage in Holford. Elsa left a note but did not speak to Violet in person.[211]

In retrospect, there had been warning signs for some time, but Violet had either not noticed them, or closed her eyes to their implications. As early as 1925, Elsa's delight in hunting had begun to take her away from the older woman. The age difference was part of the problem: while Violet was content with sedate pleasures, Elsa wanted excitement. There are also indications that at times she chafed against Violet's motherliness, although she seems to have remained quite dependent on her until she switched across to Pamela. Perhaps at some level Violet realized that Elsa was restive: in 1931, for example, she seems to have obtained a Dalmatian puppy for her, and they revisited Heronswood (and Little Bower), as if trying to recover past glories.[212]

Once Elsa had made the switch to Pamela, she stuck to her like a limpet. Pamela had two crucial advantages over Violet: firstly, she was fifteen years younger and, secondly, she rode. But like Violet she was older than Elsa, albeit only by two years, and, perhaps more importantly, she shared Violet's outward confidence and assertiveness. In some ways, then, she may have been a like-for-like substitute in Elsa's eyes, while offering attractions Violet could not match. How far the elements that Elsa came to find irksome in the relationship with Violet subsequently replicated themselves with Pamela is difficult to ascertain.

Violet's response to these devastating events was courageous and dignified. Three days after Elsa had left, she gave her an opening to come back, phoning her at Sweet Briar to ask if she would come and help with the accounts. Elsa agreed to do so, but did not come. Violet made no further attempts to persuade her to return. On 13 February Pamela and Elsa arrived at Higher Pardlestone for the first time since they had left, to take Elsa's belongings away – '[a] miserable morning but I suppose satisfactory', as Violet noted. A few days later her friend Kathleen 'cut' Elsa and Pamela when she met them in Bridgwater, an indication of how hurt those who cared about Violet were on her behalf, but 'very silly I think and makes it worse for me' according to Violet. They decided to sell the other cottage now they no longer needed it, which necessitated the 'horrid job' of turning out Elsa's desk. The weather, echoing Violet's mood, was miserably wet and gloomy. On 14 March she had the '[v]ery depressing' job of packaging up Elsa's remaining belongings for the van that came to take them away the following day. The day after that the Dickinsons arranged to rent Quarry House in Holford for three years.[213] As they had decided to sell the cottage, there was no necessity for them to leave Higher Pardlestone: it would seem that Violet simply could not bear to live there any longer. Whether she was subconsciously following Elsa in moving to Holford is open to question.

---

[211] Dickinson Diary, 27 and 28 Dec. 1936 and 12 Jan. 1937.
[212] Dickinson Diary, 29 Sep. and 2 Oct. 1931.
[213] Dickinson Diary, 15 Jan., 13, 15 and 27 Feb. and 4, 14 and 16 Mar. 1937.

That aside, the decision to rent Quarry House proved to be a good one for Violet. In her childhood she had lived a transitory life, moving from place to place. No sooner had she begun to feel at home – in Bedford Park, for example – than they moved somewhere else. Her 1902 diary is telling in this respect. Like most diarists, she wrote her address near the front. But rather than the usual single location, she lists four: Brighton, Haxell's Hotel; St Leonard's, Royal Saxon Hotel; Ventnor, 'Hillside' and Hampstead, 'Westfield'. Although they lived in Hampstead for ten years, Violet spent much of her time at Niton during this period. The destabilization of her sense of home continued with the moves to Molash, Heronswood and Kilve. Higher Pardlestone and Quarry House, by contrast, were genuine, settled homes. The move to Quarry House, of course, was occasioned by loss, and this was part of the groundwork of Violet's feeling about her new home. However, in one respect Quarry House offered something Higher Pardlestone had not. At Pardlestone, Violet, Elsa and Ced had been to a large extent on their own. They do not seem to have had close relations with their few neighbours, who in any case lived some distance away along the lane. Violet seems to have been quite content with this, no doubt because with Elsa, Ced and the animals she had successfully reconstituted a 'family', one indeed that was in many respects more satisfactory than her childhood original. Holford, by contrast, was a community, and one that corresponded almost perfectly to Violet's ideal type (as sketched out, for example, in her short story 'Una'). Set deep within its combe, it looked in on itself rather than out on the world. Quarry House was at the upper, most secluded end of the village, yet close to the nub of this little world, because it adjoined Combe House, residence of the Haymans, who owned much of the village including Quarry House. So although the Dickinsons were moving from an isolated cottage to a village (population 291 in 1951), and thus technically up the settlement hierarchy, in many respects they were also moving into even greater seclusion.[214]

Holford measured up well to Violet's inclinations in other respects too. With its ravine-like glen, rushing streams, steep wooded slopes, thatched cottages and quaint little church, it could not be faulted for picturesque appeal. Moreover, despite its tiny size Holford was proud of its place in literary history, since Coleridge and the Wordsworths had laid the foundations of English Romanticism there while William and Dorothy were living at Alfoxton House. The village was the proverbial face-to-face community where everyone knew each other:

> I walked down the village for some air – amusing to see into lighted
> rooms – Emily Norton reading – Betty and Grandpa Struan putting

[214] GB Historical GIS / University of Portsmouth, Holford AP/CP through time | Population Statistics | Total Population, *A Vision of Britain through Time*. www .visionofbritain.org.uk/unit/10434725/cube/TOT_POP [accessed 6 Apr. 2017].

> children to bed – Mrs Woncott turning out drawers – then watched Harry
> Paul and Ced playing billiards through the window at Garden Reach![215]

Violet's social relationships were arranged in concentric circles. The innermost
circle consisted of herself and, in happier times, Elsa. Outside this were the
other members of whatever her then in-group was: the IMA; Kath, Madge and
Florence at Molash; Ced and the animals at Pardlestone. But she had always
wanted an outer circle, a larger community of people she felt were like her –
hence, in large part, her fond memories of Bedford Park. Yet for all its
attractions, Bedford Park (as Violet noted retrospectively) had not been
securely walled against its urban surroundings: it lay within the shadow of
places like Tottenham. It was only in Holford that Violet finally found her
optimal community. There were no factories or industry: Violet was insulated
from the urban working class by a wide, in practice virtually un-crossable
barrier of countryside. The village itself had a genteel social tone: among Violet
and Ced's acquaintances were doctors, clergymen, retired civil servants and
artists. The few labourers, charwomen and other working people were of
the deferential, subordinate kind Violet liked.[216] Politically, Holford was
thoroughly Conservative; indeed, the whole district was dominated by the
Acland-Hood family with their mansions at St Audries and Fairfield House,
Stogursey. Alexander Fuller-Acland-Hood (Lord St Audries) had been
a prominent Conservative politician and the Hood Arms at Kilve was the
venue for many a Conservative election meeting (occasionally attended by
Violet and Ced).

Well-suited as Holford proved to be to Violet, initially at least the move
did little to ease her pain at the loss of Elsa. Indeed, in August the Dickinsons
seem to have seriously considered the drastic step of relocating to Achill Island,
celebrated for its remoteness and recalcitrance to modernity.[217] That they did
not do so is indicative of how settled they felt in the Quantocks. But it also
owed something to Violet's unassuaged yearning for Elsa, who haunts the
pages of her diary like a ghost that cannot be laid to rest. Inevitably in such
a small, enclosed village, there were frequent mutual encounters. When she
was alone Elsa usually turned tail and fled if she saw Violet coming, but Pamela
was made of sterner stuff:

> Met E and PB – E looks crestfallen and cannot look at me. P looks
> inane.[218]

---

[215] Dickinson Diary, 24 Aug. 1949.
[216] An elderly woman I spoke to in Kilve, who remembered Violet and Ced, remarked that
they were 'gentry' and people like her acknowledged them respectfully when they
encountered them.
[217] Dickinson Diary, 23 Aug. 1937.
[218] Dickinson Diary, 26 Jan. 1938.

Elsa's birthday in August was, Violet noted, 'the first she has had away from us for about 20 years'.[219] The saddest and most unconsciously revealing indication of Violet's pain, and of the nature of her love for Elsa, is a startling Freudian slip in the entry for 29 September:

> Passed VD and Pamela! After tea walked up Hare Knaps.[220]

In February the following year Violet dreamt that she saw Elsa and Pamela parting company. A few days later she penned the eager words 'I think E left PB today.' The day after her hopes rose even higher:

> Lovely day – sunny and warm. Met P alone on Hare Knaps![221]

This, alas, was all too truly a 'castle in the air' and it came tumbling down in April:

> E returned from her 'job' in Devon.[222]

But Violet seems to have confined her emotional tribulation to the privacy of her diary. True to her disavowal of demonstrativeness, she sought to restore civil relations and social decencies with Elsa and Pamela. International affairs, with which she was becoming increasingly concerned, gave her an opportunity:

> PEACE settlement at Munich . . . we heard it on the wireless . . . thrilling. Ceddy went round to Sweet Briar to ask Elsa and PB to make peace also – but all Elsa said was 'You jolly well know what I wrote to you and that's the end.'[223]

Violet was dismayed by the declaration of war on 3 September 1939 but, if she had been sheltered from World War I in Molash, she was still more so from World War II in Holford. The economic basis of the Dickinson household continued to rest principally on weaving and paying guests.[224] As before, war stirred Violet's patriotism, which was congruent both with her Conservatism and her readiness to identify with one group against another. Her diary records the dramatic events of the war with her characteristic exclamation marks and capitals:

> ITALY declared WAR on GERMANY this afternoon![225]

---

[219] Dickinson Diary, 19 Aug. 1937.
[220] Dickinson Diary, 29 Sep. 1937.
[221] Dickinson Diary, 4 Mar. 1938.
[222] Dickinson Diary, 11 Apr. 1938.
[223] Dickinson Diary, 30 Sep. 1938.
[224] Dickinson Diary, 13 Jan. 1942.
[225] Dickinson Diary, 13 Oct. 1943.

The war also provided a kind of external excitement, akin to a sporting contest, which seems to have given Violet a welcome emotional stimulus at a time when she was at a low ebb.

Only a few days after war had been declared Violet helped to form a War Welfare Committee in the village.[226] As at Molash, however, perhaps her main organizational contribution to the war effort was through the Scouts and Guides. Indeed, this had begun even before the war. On 24 August she had attended a Guides meeting at Holford Hut to make arrangements for receiving evacuated children. In April 1940 she was appointed District Captain of the Girl Guides and thereafter often attended Brownies, Guides and Rangers meetings, sometimes leading them herself.[227] One of her favourite activities was organizing trails through the Holford woods and over the lower hills.[228] The Dickinsons sometimes hosted Ranger and Scout meetings at Quarry House, and when the Caldicott School scouts were camping in Hodders Combe, as they did annually, Violet always took care to visit them, on one occasion presenting them with the 'Freedom of Odda's Combe' in the form of a cardboard key purportedly from King Odda, after whom the combe was supposedly named.[229]

However, the most important change brought by the war was the arrival at Alfoxton of Wellington House School, having been evacuated from Kent. In due course, this genteel boy's prep school became a kind of home-from-home for Violet – another of the larger identities into which she subsumed herself and, before long, a peculiarly satisfying and absorbing one. She soon established a professional relationship with the school. By 1943 she was making lino cuts for school Christmas cards; the following year she invigilated for the common entrance examination and began to take art classes.[230] Her affinity for children allowed her to develop good relationships with the boys, many of whom were homesick. She took them out into the woods to gather foxgloves, helped them individually with art and organized craft activities – team kite-making was a great success. Her willingness to come down to their level won their confidence:

> Walked up Hare Knaps – met Nat Smith and Christopher Gimlett alone – so I stayed with them although Christopher didn't want me at first as he said I was 'grown up' – however when I played hide and seek with them among the bracken and branches he was quite pleased.[231]

---

[226] Dickinson Diary, 7 Sep. 1939.

[227] Interwar British Brownies were aged eight to ten, Guides ten to sixteen and Rangers over sixteen. Tammy M. Proctor, *On My Honour: Guides and Scouts in Interwar Britain* (Philadelphia, 2002), 52, 115.

[228] Dickinson Diary, 24 Aug. 1939, 26 Apr. 1940, 14 Feb. 1942, 8 and 29 Mar. 1943 and 18 Mar. 1944.

[229] Dickinson Diary, 2 Aug. 1945.

[230] Dickinson Diary, 1 Dec. 1943 and 28 Feb. and 16 May 1944.

[231] Dickinson Diary, 10 Apr. 1944.

Outdoor play among the bracken featured largely and could provide an occasion for confidences:

> Drawing class at school. Walked them up to the Beeches – Wills told me all about his father and his mother – who follows gliders in her car (she has a German model) – while the other small boys were in ambush in the bracken and kept on rushing out at us with sticks![232]

Violet became fond of many of the boys and would cycle up to school to say goodbye to those who were leaving at the end of term.[233] Her popularity with them reflects the kindness of which she was capable when her fears were in abeyance:

> [O]n sighting me in the distance, Jeremy Huggins said: 'Is it? Is it?'
> 'Is it what?'
> 'Is it the most charming lady coming? Yes it is! Miss Dickinson!'[234]

Fond as she was of the boys, however, it was her relationship with Hubert Riley, the headmaster, that she found most stimulating. They recognized in each other an authority based on position within the school in his case and within the family in hers, and a sense of social and intellectual distinction in comparison to those around them. Holford, for all its virtues, was undeniably an intellectual backwater and she found the lively, light-hearted challenges Hubert flung out at her invigorating and refreshing:

> I walked back to Alfoxton with him, over Hare Knaps, where we had an interesting discussion about whether things really existed, excepting in our own perceptions![235]

Hubert kept her up to date with modern poetry, lending her T. S. Eliot's 'East Coker', 'Burnt Norton' and 'Little Gidding', which must have been much to Violet's ruralist and Conservative tastes.[236] He gave her copies of his own poems for appraisal too, an echo of her old IMA practices and doubtless flattering to her sense of critical acumen.[237]

The relationship also had a flirtatious dimension. He asked her to come over to the school for 'boy and girl' afternoons, induced her to make hop pillows, one for each of them, and joked about marriage:

> Went to school chapel – saw HR [Hubert Riley] – I said 'I hear Holford knows the secret now!' to which he replied 'What secret? That you are

---

[232] Dickinson Diary, 15 Oct. 1945. Compare the closely analogous account for 10 Oct. 1943. ('[T]hey all hid in the bracken and pounced out at us. Dodgson was very chatty – told me all about his family.')
[233] Dickinson Diary, 14 Dec. 1942.
[234] Dickinson Diary, 13 Dec. 1942.
[235] Dickinson Diary, 16 Sep. 1943.
[236] Dickinson Diary, 4 Aug. 1943.
[237] Dickinson Diary, 1943 front papers.

going to marry me?!!!' – 'Well not exactly – I meant that the Americans are coming to Alfoxton'.[238]

This provocative banter gave spice to their intellectual exchanges, as on 19 November 1944 when they had an '[a]musing conversation':

> [H]e said other women were not like me – I said it was a good thing, but a doubtful compliment. We then continued a conversation on subconscious minds . . . HR says we live not in the present – only in eternity – he says we enjoy our bodies – I didn't agree but said we might as well make the most of what delights – if any – they did present . . . he didn't seem sure about this – he asked me if I liked earthy men![239]

This was the only relationship of the kind Violet ever had with a man and seems to have been premised on an assured mutual understanding that it meant nothing. There is no evidence Violet found men physically attractive under any circumstances and the flirtation with Hubert may have provided socially useful cover for her sexuality. Her relationship with Elsa had been no secret, and her friends and acquaintances appear to have accepted it without demur, but the basis for this acceptance seems to have been that the nature of the relationship was not made explicit. It is possible that the unmarried headmaster had similar motivations, although this is pure speculation.

Enjoyable and rewarding as Violet found her exchanges with Hubert, the relationship she formed with another teacher at the school, Mercy Sholl, was more important to her in the long run. Mercy lodged with Violet and Ced at Quarry House for much of the time she was in Holford, thus reconstituting once again the larger 'family' emotional pattern towards which Violet always strove. Mercy's light-hearted vivacity struck a chord with Violet and, as with previous in-group relationships, laughter was a principal bond between them:

> M laughed until she cried . . . already the neighbours say they can hear us laughing![240]

Occasionally one of Violet's in-group relationships with another woman intensified into something beyond this. It seems highly unlikely that Violet's relationship with Mercy was ever a sexual one, but the underlying emotional pattern was recognizably the same as it had been with Kath and Elsa. Just as those two had, Mercy became an alter ego to Violet. On 19 October 1942 Violet crocheted a pair of white bootees for Mercy while reading Dorothy Wordsworth's journals. Mercy at once put them on and paraded about in them looking like a tightrope walker. This was just what Violet had done in her

---

[238] Dickinson Diary, 4 Dec. 1943.
[239] Dickinson Diary, 19 Nov. 1944.
[240] Dickinson Diary, 14 Sep. 1942.

childhood: one Christmas morning, of all her many presents, the one that had delighted her beyond measure was a pair of white-fringed slippers, in which she had spent much of the day pirouetting around the house.[241] Since Mercy knew Violet's diaries, the mirroring may have been mutual, although how far it was conscious is impossible to say. Two years later Mercy became engaged to Jeffrey Ede and shortly thereafter went to supper with friends wearing a silk frock and 'Engagement Ring' of Violet's.[242] This recalls Kath and Violet's exchange of clothes years before. More tentatively one wonders whether Violet may have been influenced by her reading of Dorothy Wordsworth, who famously wore her brother's wedding ring the night before his marriage.[243] After her marriage Mercy took her husband's surname. Whereas Violet had previously referred to her as 'Mercy' in the diary, she now often used her initials: 'ME'.[244]

Even after her marriage Mercy was a frequent visitor to Holford, not least because her brother Ernest was the rector. She made Violet god-mother to her first child and the two women maintained a frequent and animated correspondence when they were apart.[245] On 25 January 1952 Violet sent Mercy something rather more significant than usual:

> Sent off Elsa's old leather coat (over 20 years old!) to Mercy.[246]

In a limited way Mercy had replaced Elsa, although the relationship was much less intense. More important in giving Violet a new centre of interest was her involvement with Wellington House School. But she continued to pine for Elsa throughout the war and beyond. 'Three years ago today, E left us', she recorded on 12 January 1940.[247] Two years later the two women met in public for the first time since 1937, and Violet forced a reply by greeting her.[248] The diary continues to report events in Elsa's life that Violet must have heard third-hand, such as when she got a new job and when she was in bed with a cold.[249] Violet felt Pamela did not look after her properly:

> Saw E and PB in The Plough. E much begrimed – and gnawing water biscuits for her dinner. I think PB might cut her hair![250]

---

[241] LMA/4292/01/012 (The Junior I.M.A., Dec. 1906).
[242] Dickinson Diary, 5 Jul. 1944.
[243] Stephen Gill, *Wordsworth: A Life* (Oxford, 1989), 211.
[244] Dickinson Diary, 14 Sep. 1944.
[245] Dickinson Diary, 22 Sep. 1947.
[246] Dickinson Diary, 25 Jan. 1952.
[247] Dickinson Diary, 12 Jan. 1940.
[248] Dickinson Diary, 17 Feb. 1940.
[249] Dickinson Diary, 15 Oct. 1944 and 18 Jan. 1952.
[250] Dickinson Diary, 3 Oct. 1943.

Although Elsa continued to leap over gates and divert up side paths to avoid encounters, her part-time job at Combe House meant that she was frequently in Violet's sight:

> E very busy hanging out sheets in the orchard – I see her doing it every week!![251]

While Holford protected Violet from the outside world, the quid pro quo of its seclusion was that it was difficult to leave old relationships behind, and deep wounds of the kind Violet had sustained when Elsa left her remained open for longer than they might have otherwise.

As she had been during the First World War, Violet was very frightened by the threat of bombing, despite the fact that in Holford she was at virtually no risk at all.[252] On the one hand, this shows that rural tranquillity was no panacea for deep-rooted psychological fears:

> Awful night of guns and bombs – slept in Ced's room downstairs – no peace till 3am.[253]

On the other, however, the rural environment could provide balm for these fears, even if it could not prevent them:

> Terrible fighting – heard bombs dropping over wireless. After tea, walked up to the beeches – over Pardlestone Hill – heard a Garden Warbler singing.[254]

Although Holford itself was never a target, the Dickinsons could sometimes hear the sound of raids on Bath and other towns to the north. They were outside the range of the air-raid warning sirens but Birdy would phone to let them know when the all clear had been given and, in the stillness of the Holford night, '[t]he quiet and peace afterwards was blissful'.[255] Violet was not the only person who found Holford a refuge. After the Cardiff Blitz the Elphinwell family came to stay at Quarry House for six months. There were other refugees too, for example the Sylvesters, who spent a week in Holford after the traumatic raids on Bath in April 1942.[256]

---

[251] Dickinson Diary, 18 May 1940, 23 Jan. 1944 and 29 Aug. 1947.

[252] Catley's diaries during the Bristol Blitz make an interesting contrast. Although he was directly exposed to heavy bombing over a period of several months, the tone of his diaries is calm. Sleep deprivation, cold and weariness feature prominently but fear does not. BRO, 41419/40 (Catley Diaries, 17 Jan. 1941). See also Dickinson Diary, 12 and 30 Sep. 1917.

[253] Dickinson Diary, 1 Sep. 1940.

[254] Dickinson Diary, 14 May 1940.

[255] Dickinson Diary, 17 May 1943.

[256] Dickinson Diary, 9 Apr. 1943 and 9 May 1942.

Later that year Violet fell ill and her doctor told her she had dysentery.[257] One of the first things she did on her recovery was to go out for a walk over Hare Knaps, behind the house.[258] A week later she felt well enough to go up to the school chapel for the first time for several weeks, where she had a 'most kind welcome from everyone'. She then walked up to the Holford Beeches, where she thought the 'foliage [was] wonderful in the sun'.[259] The pattern recurred in April 1943:

> Although my leg is still not healed, it was such a lovely morning that I walked up Dogpound.[260]

The following day she again went for a walk but only to catch her foot in some paving stones and injure her knee, which had to be put in a splint.[261] Violet was now in her sixties and her health was not as good as it had been. Despite this, walking on the hills was, it would seem, becoming even more important to her. She had, of course, found beauty in rural landscapes for decades but there is a subtle change in tone during the war years in Holford. When she was younger she looked at landscapes with a painter's eye, taking a lively sensory pleasure in colour and 'effects'. Now the beauty she perceived in the landscape is seen with a more inward eye:

> Lovely evening and heavenly views looking up the combe to the channel and across to Wales – unbelievably beautiful.[262]

Most often she walked on Hare Knaps, the heather-clad hill behind Quarry House, or if not on Danesborough, a wooded height the other side of the combe, capped by a prehistoric hill fort commanding grand views, which she seems to have found increasingly rewarding during these Holford years. Another favourite walk was to the Beeches, one of Holford's celebrated features, on the slopes above the village. Two-thirds of the walks recorded in the diaries were now alone. The real proportion may have been higher than this because it seems that she usually took her dog Dusky for a short walk in the evening, rarely mentioned in the diary.[263] Sometimes she went for long walks across the hills, often taking a picnic, although this was usually in company. Whatever the length of the walk, she had a distinct preference for going up rather than walking along the valley bottoms. She did sometimes walk along Butterfly (Holford) Combe or Dogpound Lane but this was often to reach somewhere else.

---

[257] Dickinson Diary, 18 and 30 Oct. 1942.
[258] Dickinson Diary, 7 Nov. 1942.
[259] Dickinson Diary, 15 Nov. 1942.
[260] Dickinson Diary, 2 Apr. 1943.
[261] Dickinson Diary, 3 Apr. 1943.
[262] Dickinson Diary, 3 Aug. 1943. Compare Dickinson Diary, 27 Jun. 1943 and 2 Aug. and 6 Sep. 1944.
[263] Dickinson Diary, 17 May 1943.

Holford's distinctive topography meant that Violet's walks rarely led beyond the bounds of her local world. The village was set at the junction of two deep wooded combes, Butterfly (along which most of the cottages were strung) and Hodders. Two narrow, twisting lanes ran down from here to the main road by The Plough Inn, which formed a sort of gateway to the village, but Violet rarely chose to go that way. In the other direction, the lanes led only to the hills, so there was no through traffic. It was a village that turned its back on the world – even more so during the war given the restrictions on travel. Perpetually criss-crossing the same territory, Violet came to know it intimately. Not only did she choose by preference to stay within it, but inside its bounds she usually followed familiar routes to favoured places, in contrast, for example, to the pleasure Catley and Barmes took in discovering new paths and landscapes. Her diary records hundreds of walks during the years she lived in Holford, characteristically mentioning the people she met, a litany of personal names as familiar as those of the places her walks took her to. Holford's social landscape was as known, contained and secure as its physical one.[264]

Surprisingly perhaps, the arrival of American GIs at Alfoxton a few months before D-Day did little to change this. On the whole the Holford residents were onlookers at rather than participants in their activities, as when Violet watched a bulldozer root up an old tree at one fell swoop, a 'wonderful sight but most pathetic'. Crucially from Violet's perspective, the soldiers seem to have been firmly under the command of their officers and presented no sense of threat:

> Greeted by an American 'black' – lovely musical voice – almost singing! – and with a sweet smile. How unlike the shy, cautious, and almost suspicious British workman!![265]

More important to Violet was her growing friendship with the naturalist Dorothy Long, which quickened her interest in wildflowers, hitherto more aesthetic than botanical. They found rare plants together: elecampane in the Alfoxton shrubbery, Cornish moneywort up Devil's Gallop and wild angelica along the Beeches.[266] Seeing through Dorothy's eyes, Violet noticed things that might otherwise have passed her by:

---

[264] It is revealing in this respect that Violet later drew an analogy between the Holford village community and the 'gracious little acts everyone did' in Elizabeth Gaskell's *Cranford*. Dickinson Diary, 8 Mar. 1949.

[265] Dickinson Diary, 19 Mar. 1944. For all her fear of the working class, Violet seems to have been quite free of racial antipathy, taking, for example, a warm interest in a Jewish refugee who stayed with them before the war. Dickinson Diary, 12 Dec. 1938.

[266] Dickinson Diary, 19, 21 and 22 Sep. 1944.

After lunch we took our tea up Hodders Combe, to look for bog plants, and found several unusual things. It was very beautiful – and we got deeper into the wooded combes, each with its gurgling stream – the banks covered with ferns and mosses and liverworts.[267]

Violet was much excited by the ending of hostilities in 1945 but initially it brought few substantial changes to her life, except that visits to and from friends and the occasional outing became easier. Leslie had married in 1938 and arrived at Quarry House with his wife Pat for a week in June 1945. They, Violet and Ced spent the week cycling to Plainsfield to see Birdy and Bay, down to the sea and walking on the hills.[268] More distinguished visitors were Dr Fisher and his wife Rosamund, who had stayed with them at Higher Pardlestone before the war. Dr Fisher had since become Archbishop of Canterbury. Understandably, Violet felt 'very honoured' – and there was a sense of vindication too, since '[a]s they drove off they met Elsa at the bend – so they must have recognized each other'.[269]

In due course, however, the end of the war brought a signal and unwelcome change: after six and a half years Wellington House School left Alfoxton to return to Kent.[270] Violet's diary for the week before is punctuated with references to last occasions:

Went to school for tea and 'crafts' for the last time.[271]

... went to Alfoxton School Chapel for the last time.[272]

Hubert Riley and the school secretary, Mrs Hill, came over to Quarry House to say goodbye on 4 March and had supper with Ced and Violet: 'we talked to 10pm – then they disappeared for the last time into the darkness of that evening'.[273] Two days later Hubert and the remaining staff left Alfoxton. Undemonstrative Violet might be, but feelings will out and it is difficult to believe it was a coincidence that she fell off her bicycle in the evening and went on to develop a migraine, which recurred the next day.[274] However, there were probably also physical causes for the migraines: there had been at least one previous occurrence and hereafter they troubled her increasingly often.[275]

More positively, the end of the war allowed Violet to visit Leslie and Pat in London. She made directly for the Tate and found an exhibition featuring

---

[267] Dickinson Diary, 17 Sep. 1944.
[268] Dickinson Diary, 12 Jun. 1945. For Violet, unlike Cresswell or Catley, cycling was primarily a means of locomotion rather than apprehending the landscape.
[269] Dickinson Diary, 31 Aug. 1945.
[270] Dickinson Diary, 26 Mar. 1946.
[271] Dickinson Diary, 23 Mar. 1946.
[272] Dickinson Diary, 24 Mar. 1946.
[273] Dickinson Diary, 3 Apr. 1946.
[274] Dickinson Diary, 5 and 6 Apr. 1946.
[275] Dickinson Diary, 11 Apr. 1945.

works by Cezanne, Picasso, Matisse, Nash and Piper 'very thrilling'. She revisited her old stamping ground of Hampstead Heath, but there was also a commercial purpose to this London trip. She had supper with Mr Macmillan, chairman of Fourth City Building Society, who had previously commissioned a poster from her. Two days later she visited their offices – 'my posters in [the] window and all over the walls everywhere in various colours!'.[276] The upshot was another commission, of a cottage, which Violet began painting in August.[277] This was a useful addition to the Quarry House finances, although sales of woven goods were going well, amounting that month to a very respectable £180.[278] Holford's rural location was critical to their income in these years. The surrounding landscape provided Violet with subject matter for her posters and for the linocuts and pastels she also made and sold. She and Ced harvested natural materials for dyeing and, more importantly in financial terms, the perception of handloom weaving as a traditional country craft was crucial to sales. Similarly, the landscape in which Quarry House was set was an essential part of its attraction for the paying guests who came to stay (as it had been at Pardlestone).

Another benefit of the end of the war was that holidays became more feasible. In October Violet and Ced went to Brixham and her diary and letters to Mercy gush enthusiasm for the 'magnificent scenery' along the coast, in terms that recall the old Isle of Wight days: 'one would never tire of the views – if only my eyes would let me draw and paint more I should be doing it all day – and night'.[279] In January 1947 she and Ced, with Birdy and Bay, revisited Engelberg (Switzerland) in search of snow, but found more in Holford on their return:

> Had to dig our way out of the door. Every tree, twig and wire coated in ice – wonderful sight. I spent afternoon taking photos – up to my knees in snow.[280]

Unfortunately, however, Violet's health was deteriorating. She was suffering from intermittent migraines and had persistent eye trouble and a general sense of debility in May, frequently and quite uncharacteristically staying in bed for all or part of the day. It is a sign of how important her walks had become to her that she continued to go out whenever she could, as on the 15th, when despite the fact that her head was 'still queer' she walked up to the Beeches, or on the 18th, when after sleeping in the afternoon she went a little way up Danesborough.[281] In July her doctor diagnosed anaemia and put her on iron tablets but when she had still not improved two months later he told her, much

---

[276] Dickinson Diary, 15 and 17 May 1946.
[277] Dickinson Diary, 21 Aug. 1946.
[278] Dickinson Diary, 26 Aug. 1946.
[279] Dickinson Diary, 26 Oct. 1946 and letter to Mercy Ede, 30 Oct. 1946, A/AGV 17.
[280] Dickinson Diary, 9 Jan. and 6 Mar. 1947.
[281] Dickinson Diary, 13, 14, 15, 17 and 18 May 1947.

to her chagrin, that her feelings were 'mental!!!! – the usual excuse of artistic temperament etc!!!!'.[282]

Perhaps the highlight of 1947 was her holiday in Kent at Dorothy Long's. They found all manner of rare orchids, watched birds, looked at Dorothy's flower photographs and went to a folk-dance party at Saltwood. Although Violet's respect for Dorothy's scholarly severity maintained a certain distance between them, there is a faint hint of previous relationships with women in Violet's entry for 8 June when she 'walked ... with Miss Long – arm in arm!'.[283] After leaving Dorothy Violet made her way to Wellington House School, now back at Westgate-on-Sea on the other side of Kent. She was welcomed warmly by Hubert Riley and other old acquaintances and later that summer there was a return visit to Holford.[284]

Early 1948 found Violet in a calm but contemplative mood, with a sense of things passing. On 10 February, she noted that it was 'Father's birthday (he would have been 89 today) – he died 28 years ago'. Perhaps to mark the occasion, she went on a longer walk than usual, up Dogpound Lane, down through Falk's Wood into Hodder's Combe, and up again over Hare Knaps before returning home. She enjoyed the lovely views in the frost and sunshine and after lunch gathered snowdrops, primroses and violets to send to Leslie.[285] A few weeks later she walked up to the Firs and down Hodder's Combe through the wood, thinking of 'all the processions we had had to the Caldicott Scout Camp – by day and night'.[286] Three days later Ernest Sholl called round to discuss his upcoming wedding, a subject which no doubt gave Violet pause for thought. After tea she walked to the top of Danesborough:

> [L]ovely views and layers of hills to Dunkery, Porlock etc – patches of sunlight and shadow – Wales and mountains very clear – it seems queer to think those views had been there – just the same – for thousands or millions of years – while humans come + go + are forgotten so soon – makes one feel very small.[287]

If this seems melancholy, it also suggests that Violet's deep dwelling in the stable security of Holford may have allowed her to shed some of the defensive and disfiguring Dickinsonian sense of entitlement so evident in her earlier years.[288] There are other indications too that, despite her intermittent ill health, many of Violet's anxieties and fears had begun to drop away in this

---

[282] Dickinson Diary, 5 and 23 Jul. and 3 Sep. 1947.
[283] Dickinson Diary, 8 Jun. 1947.
[284] Dickinson Diary, 10 and 11 Jun. and 3 Aug. 1947.
[285] Dickinson Diary, 10 Feb. 1948.
[286] Dickinson Diary, 27 Mar. 1948.
[287] Dickinson Diary, 30 Mar. 1948.
[288] Compare her response to seeing one of the new National Health Service opticians in 1949: 'forms to fill in – felt nobody – which of course I am!'. Dickinson Diary, 7 Jun. 1949.

period. Classical music, to which she listened frequently on the radio these days, could bring the same kind of peace as the contemplation of landscape:

> Louis Kentner playing Mozart's Coronation piano concerto ... very lovely – so gentle and unworried![289]

Photographs from the time bear out this serenity. One, for example, shows Violet smiling and relaxed as she enters the house holding a bunch of flowers. She is dressed in down-to-earth clothes and the smile seems natural and unforced (see Figure 5.3).[290]

This peace of mind, while in part arising from the Holford landscape, also allowed Violet to enjoy it more fully than ever before:

> Before supper, I walked up the hill through wood and round the old strawberry field – the cuckoo was calling – + lovely birdsongs – the birch trees ... with deep yellow red catkins hanging in cascades with a pearly full moon showing through them in a misty blue sky – too lovely for words. The beech buds, not yet burst, were touched with the sun.[291]

Fortunately for Violet, not all the wartime connections disappeared straight-away. The Hodders Combe Scout camps, for example, continued:

> Ann Lovett [various other girls] and I walked to Hodders Combe over the hills to the Scout camp – lovely moon and perfect calm – beautiful sight – enjoyed it – singing – dancing – magnificent fire – cocoa and cake – walked home at midnight over Hare Knaps. Ann wore my skiing suit! They were all Guides and are all aged 18![292]

There were also revivals of pre-war organizations and activities, including the Somerset Guild of Craftsmen, of which Violet and Ced were made honorary life members in 1950, and the Rural Community Council.[293] However, her health continued to deteriorate and in February 1949 she began to experience an unpleasant sensation she described as 'heart bumping', which gave her much trouble.[294] She felt very tired and was afflicted with further migraines.[295] On doctor's orders she stayed in all day on 16 March, which, for someone who usually preferred energetic activity to introspection, was unsurprisingly 'very boring'.[296]

One consolation was the interesting visitors who continued to come their way. One of these was Ann Lovett's father, another bishop, who spent the

---

[289] Dickinson Diary, 13 Jan. 1948. For her growing appreciation of classical music see also Dickinson Diary, 25 Oct. 1947 and 20 Mar. and 3 Sep. 1948.
[290] A/AGV 13.
[291] Dickinson Diary, 20 Apr. 1948.
[292] Dickinson Diary, 3 Aug. 1949.
[293] Dickinson Diary, 15 May and 16 Aug. 1948 and 13 Aug. 1950.
[294] Dickinson Diary, 12 and 17 Feb. 1949.
[295] Dickinson Diary, 15 and 28 Mar. 1949.
[296] Dickinson Diary, 16 Mar. 1949.

Figure 5.3   Violet outside Quarry House
Reproduced by kind permission of the South West Heritage Trust (SHC A/AGV/15)

evening with them on 16 August. He discoursed in grand clerical manner but on subjects that appealed to his hosts:

> [H]e asked whether we realized that only humans create with their hands and are never so happy as when creating etc etc – we also talked of the beauty of birds, butterflies and flowers and the wonder of them.[297]

[297] Dickinson Diary, 16 Aug. 1949.

This was music to the Dickinsons' Arts and Crafts ears and to Violet's increasing absorption in the Holford landscape. A more unusual visitor was a machine spinner from Rochdale, but surprisingly he read from the same script:

> His idea is that after the next war (atomic) the industrial cities will be wiped out and the remaining population will have to go back to primitive ways to exist – grow their food, <u>hand spin and weave</u> etc!!![298]

Another consolation was watching the deer that sometimes came down from the hill and could be seen from the Quarry House windows:

> After supper I saw a <u>large stag in the orchard</u> eating apples – we watched it for ½ hour in the lovely setting – and while Cyril Smith was playing Liszt's piano concerto![299]

The red deer had come to have a special meaning for Violet since she moved to Holford. In the autumn she walked up the hills hoping to hear stags belling and in the spring she looked for their cast antlers.[300] She frequently mentions the 'Stags' Soiling Pool' (mud bath) and deer tracks and traces in her diaries:

> After lunch I walked up Hare Knaps – saw many traces & sleeping places & hair of red deer in the bracken.[301]

They were part of what endowed the area with its distinctive local character and in that regard Violet valued them in much the same way as she had the Stogursey Mummers. But there was more to it than that. Part of it was her old artistic sensibility:

> Watched a herd of deer on the skyline from the kitchen window – lovely sight – 6 or 8 against a lemon sky + tracery of leafless trees.[302]

But she had never watched anything in her youth with the almost reverent attention she gave to the deer in Holford:

> I watched 14 deer in the orchard from 8 o'clock till dark – lovely sight, as they gracefully pulled down young branches and nibbled leaves just unfurling.[303]

Characteristic of Violet's vivid descriptions of deer, especially in these post-war years, is a sense of separation. Heedless of her gaze, they were a vision of beauty sufficient unto themselves. Like distant views and classical music, they

---

[298] Dickinson Diary, 26 Aug. 1949.
[299] Dickinson Diary, 27 Aug. 1949.
[300] Dickinson Diary, 24 Oct. 1937, 27 Sep. 1944 and 23 Mar. 1938.
[301] Dickinson Diary, 30 Apr. and 29 Sep. 1944 and 13 Feb. 1946.
[302] Dickinson Diary, 16 Apr. 1948.
[303] Dickinson Diary, 30 Apr. 1951.

suffused her mind with serenity. Although she was quite free of any striving at such times, looked at in a certain light this was a not insignificant human achievement. To enjoy things in their own right, without seeking to possess or assimilate them to herself, was not something she had shown much capacity for in her younger days. While it owed something to age, this change is also further testimony to the soothing effect of her long dwelling in the Holford landscape.

The aspect of the deer that distinguished them from views and music was their living wildness. The parallels and contrasts between their lives and Violet's were pronounced. They inhabited the same landscape and their paths continually crossed hers:

> Walked up Dogpound to the Beeches – saw stags with hinds – a few yards away – then walking home over Hare Knaps, 2 hinds bounded through the bracken beside me.[304]

Yet although they were at times almost within touching distance, they were always the other side of an impassable gulf of wildness. As she tramped the Holford hills on her many solitary walks in the years after Elsa left her, Violet carried her sorrow with her. There was a part of her life that had come to an end, a loss that was not to be made good. The deer, by contrast, bounding away over the bracken or arching their graceful necks in the orchard, were wild and free, unburdened by human sorrow.[305] Watching them may at some level have allowed Violet to experience the loss her undemonstrativeness precluded her from verbalizing, and perhaps even to find a measure of consolation and acceptance. Certainly in a larger sense her inveterate walking over the Holford hills was part of an unarticulated process of coming to terms with loss.[306]

To many of Violet's neighbours deer primarily signified hunting. Violet's relationship to the hunt was ambivalent. She was not one to set herself against any group she belonged to, so it is unsurprising that she did not overtly oppose hunting. Indeed, she recognized it as an authentic part of Quantock tradition and to that extent legitimate and even welcome. She was appalled, however, that children were allowed to watch the kill and the gory details of the hunt horrified her:

> We had a 'kill' in Combe House orchard last week – they cut it up outside our garden gate! – and after all the horrible details Mrs [illegible] finally drove off with 'it' in the back of her car!!! – crowds of people – no work that afternoon – I felt quite sick![307]

---

[304] Dickinson Diary, 7 Dec. 1947.

[305] Deer 'bounding through the bracken' is a recurrent phrase in Violet's diaries. See, for example, Dickinson Diary, 18 Sep. 1944.

[306] Compare Mark Christopher Allister, *Refiguring the Map of Sorrow: Nature Writing and Autobiography* (Charlottesville, 2001).

[307] Dickinson Diary, 10 Jan. 1949; Letter to Mercy Ede, 21 Oct. 1947.

Many followed the hunt on foot but, for all its local significance, Violet was not one of these. There is a sense that, underneath, she found deer hunting abhorrent and, had her social circumstances allowed, she would have turned her back on it.

Weaving continued to be a core activity at Quarry House and, now the war was over, the Dickinsons again took pupils. At least two of these, Dagma Henrikson and Anna-Karin Alfredsson, came from Scandinavia, where the rural crafts and ethnographic movement was more developed than in England.[308] Meanwhile Violet and Ced continued to attend and, it would seem, sometimes lead, weaving classes at Watchet.[309] Violet's account of a busy day in August 1950 gives a good impression of her life at this time:

> Leslie, Ced and Pat went to Old Forge [Plainsfield] for a day's wool dyeing
> so I was home alone – started by having migraine
> 8 customers before lunch – tried sitting in the garden afterwards but first the butcher 2nd the fishmonger 3rd postman – then Mercy with Sarah and Katherine in the pram!!! We had tea in the garden.
> Mrs Lee Smith called with raspberries – then Mr Cooper arrived with 8 Scouts!!!
> Then I cooked supper and the others got back 7.30 – some day – !!
> My ribs are v painful.[310]

As the number of customers suggests, Violet and Ced were becoming quite well known locally and, among those with interests in the crafts, further afield too. Violet featured in the local press ('Spinning in the sun, Miss V. Dickinson of Holford, Somerset, keeps an old craft in the public eye') and they were visited by the landscape gardener and weaver Doris Ogilvie, by a friend of the potter Bernard Leach, and, on a day when more than fifty people came to see the weaving, by Christopher Heal of the well-known London design business.[311] Violet continued to paint as well and had a notable success when her pastel of the carpenter's shed at Alfoxton was one of fifty-one selected out of thousands submitted to tour the country as part of the mobile Festival of Britain exhibition.[312]

However, although she and Ced were enjoying increasing recognition, Violet's health continued to deteriorate and on 29 October 1952 she made what was to prove the last entry in her diaries. She was subsequently admitted to the Mount Royal Nursing Home in Minehead, from where she continued to correspond with Mercy. On 1 May the following year she wrote that she had very painful pleurisy, asthma and skin trouble. But she was in good spirits,

---

[308] Dickinson Diary, 5 May and 21 Sep. 1950.
[309] Dickinson Diary, 28 Sep. 1950 and 5 Apr. 1951.
[310] Dickinson Diary, 3 Aug. 1950.
[311] Dickinson Diary, 21 Aug. 1951 and 22 May and 1 Aug. 1952.
[312] Dickinson Diary, 27 Mar. and 24 Jun. 1951.

taking particular pleasure in the 'glorious views from my windows and excellent food'.[313] This, however, was her final letter to Mercy. She died on
10 July 1953.[314]

* * *

Violet's flight to successively more remote rural refuges was, in the last
analysis, an attempt to escape from herself. This does not sound promising
but there may not have been a realistic alternative. She showed no interest
whatsoever in consciously confronting her fears – indeed, one of her most
consistent traits was her lifelong determination to avoid outright emotional
'demonstrativeness'. She had many strategies for doing so: merging her identity with another woman's, sinking it in an in-group, laughter, extrovert
socialization and, not least, sheer stoicism. Even if she had wanted to face the
anxieties and insecurities that afflicted her head on, it is doubtful whether she
had the cognitive or linguistic tools to do so. Her powers of emotional self-
expression were severely restricted, at least in writing, and since her letters,
especially, often seem close to speech, it is difficult to believe that she would
have been able to go much beyond this orally. But surprisingly perhaps,
Violet's withdrawal to the countryside did not in the end trap her in an
emotional cul-de-sac. On the contrary, there are clear indications that her
long dwelling in the stable, secure and thoroughly known physical and social
landscape of Holford helped to ease some of the fears that had previously
constrained her, allowing her to achieve a genuine degree of serenity and more
inner freedom than in her younger days. It would appear that, unconsciously
no doubt, this was a case of retreating in order to better advance.

---

[313] Somerset HC, A/AGV19 (Letter, Violet Dickinson to Mercy Ede, 1 May 1953).
[314] England & Wales, National Probate Calendar (Index of Wills and Administrations),
1858–1966, 1973–95, 1953, 865.

Restorers

Withdrawing to the countryside was to all intents and purposes a one-way street (or lane perhaps?) for Spear Smith and Dickinson. While the general practitioner John Johnston and probation officer/lay preacher Bert Bissell also found rural landscapes therapeutic, there was a fundamental difference. They turned to the countryside in large part to strengthen and energize them in their life's purpose, which both men saw as lying in the city – in Johnston's case, serving his mainly working-class patients in industrial Bolton, and, in Bissell's, bringing the word of God to the often wayward youth of Dudley. Johnston's Whitmanite faith in nature and Bissell's Methodism were the expressions, in each case, of deep inner conviction, on which the two men depended for their optimism and capacity to rise to the demanding requirements of their occupations. The inevitable knocks and reverses of life at times dimmed this certitude or even threatened to extinguish it altogether. Going out into the countryside played a vital role for both men in allowing them to refurbish and restore the framework of their beliefs. In other respects, however, they related to rural landscapes quite differently.

6

Dr John Johnston

Bolton Doctor

Born in 1852, John Johnston lived for virtually the whole of his life in northern Britain. He grew up in the Scottish country town of Annan, within sight of England a few miles away across the Solway Firth. His father, William, was a successful builder, highly respected among his neighbours and a pillar of the community. John, the eldest of three children, was very close to both parents. He revered his father's uprightness and integrity, noting in adulthood that he regarded him as one of the 'tripod of men' on whose character and ideals he built his own value system (the others were his Bolton friend J. W. Wallace and the poet Walt Whitman). When confronted with a difficult decision in adult life, John often found himself asking the question his father used to put to him in childhood: 'But is it right, John?' His father's seriousness and depth of character went hand in hand with an unswerving although at times stern love. John's mother, Ellen, was no less devout but a milder and gentler person, devoted to her children and perhaps above all to her eldest son.[1]

This powerful home background seems to have propelled John forward academically. He won prize after prize at school and went up to the University of Edinburgh to study medicine in 1868 at the age of sixteen. Here he continued to study hard and, after qualifying, was appointed house surgeon at the Birmingham Children's Hospital. Two years later the opportunity to obtain a good practice in Bolton arose and, after some deliberation, John decided to take this up, influenced no doubt by the greater proximity to Annan. His marriage to Margaret (Maggie) Beddows in 1878 brought him great contentment. The relationship proved stable and enduring and, although Maggie does not seem to have played a large part in John's intellectual life, she ran the household smoothly and efficiently, helped John with bookkeeping and, above all, provided him with a secure emotional haven. John worked extremely hard and, partly as a result, his practice grew in a gratifying way. The Johnstons' income rose from £187 in 1888 to £1,200 in 1901. This allowed them to move to a larger house in suburban Bolton in 1899 and out of Bolton altogether to Lostock in 1902. Thereafter Johnston worked as Bolton's public vaccinator and as an ambulance class instructor until the First World War,

[1] BAHC, ZJO/1/29 (Johnston Diary, [summer 1898]).

when he became a surgeon at Queen Mary's Military Hospital in Whalley twenty miles across the moors to the north. In 1917 he was appointed medical officer at Townleys Hospital back in Bolton, retiring two years later. He died in 1927.[2]

Johnston was no more typical of the northern relationship to the country-side than any other northerner, but the fact that he came from the north is important and affected the character of his ruralism in several ways. His Scottish origins mattered to him and provide an opportunity to assess how far English landscapes may have had different meanings for someone raised the other side of the border. Living and working in a northern industrial town like Bolton for so many years, however, had a more profound influence on his ruralism. There are interesting parallels and contrasts with Hallam, who lived for most of his life in a factory town too. Apart from his northernness, Johnston also differed from the other diarists in that he was (or became) a professional. Harold Perkin wrote influentially about the 'rise of professional society' in modern Britain and Johnston is a good example of a man who made his way from a less exalted background to achieve professional qualifications and the income, security and status that went with them.[3] He was the only one of the eight diarists who was university educated, paradoxically since he was born earlier than any of the other diarists, at a time when studying for a degree was rare. This affected his ruralism in many respects, not least its literary tone and mode of expression.

The Character of Johnston's Ruralism

'[L]ove of nature ... has done more to enrich my enjoyment of life than any other influence', Johnston declared in a memoir of his early years written in 1886 when he was thirty-four.[4] Other influences, notably family and perhaps disposition, contributed profoundly to Johnston's enjoyment of life but his diaries provide abundant evidence to confirm that a love of nature was indeed absolutely central to him. Throughout his life he went out into the countryside frequently and was an attentive observer of the natural world. He noticed small details, for example that buttercups in bright spring sunshine look 'burnished and polished inside', that unfledged nestlings resemble 'miniature Saurians' and that rushes have 'white cellular pith like solidified froth'.[5] His command of

---

[2] BAHC, ZJO/4/1–3 (John Johnston Memoir). See Paul Salveson, 'Loving Comrades: Lancashire's Links to Walt Whitman', *Walt Whitman Quarterly Review* 14 (1996), 63. See also the biographical sketch on the Bolton Archives and History Centre Whitman Collection webpage. www.boltonlams.co.uk/archives/walt-whitman-collection [accessed 29 Oct. 2018].

[3] Harold Perkin, *The Rise of Professional Society: Britain since 1880* (London, 1990).

[4] BAHC, ZJO/4/3 (Johnston Memoir).

[5] BAHC, Johnston Diary, ZJO/1/9 (22 May 1890) and ZJO/1/4 (16 and 17 Jun. 1889).

language allowed him to register his observations with impressive precision and immediacy, as in this description of a stormy day on the Isle of Man:

> What a magnificent morning is this ... the entire rock-bound coast is whitened by a continuous line of breakers which are now rolling rolling in and dashing themselves to sunlit spray against the rocks with a roar and a boom like thunder – and as they advance and retreat they curl, foam, churn, seethe, boil, hiss, and leap as if they in their mad fury were trying to rend the rock ramparts and uproot the Island from its foundations.[6]

Knowledge and Emotion

Despite his powers of observation, Johnston was no scientific naturalist. He was unable to identify or misidentified many species, including some of the most common. On one occasion he was struck by two small birds 'singing their minor strains with a pleasing repetition of gently falling notes beginning high on the scale and coming down through all the gradations of tone down to the bottom'. This is a sensitive and accurate description of the song of the willow warbler, one of the commonest summer visitors to Britain. Johnston's diary entry reveals his uncertainty: initially he thought the birds were finches but this is crossed out and replaced by tits, later also deleted and replaced with a blank.[7] Other common birds that Johnston seems to have misidentified include a crow 'cawing as he sails slowly overhead' (surely a rook, the soft 'caw' of which is quite different from the harsh 'kraak' of a crow) and swallows 'darting wheeling and screaming overhead in pursuit of the insects' (a good description of the rapid twisting flight and screeching call of the common swift but not of the graceful swooping arcs and subdued twittering of the swallow). 'Oh how ignorant I am about Bird Life', he repined, modestly and accurately.[8] Yet this did not induce him to undertake a serious study of ornithology: evidently he had little of either the collector or the classifier in him. He exemplifies Bellanca's characterization of late nineteenth-century amateur natural history as concerned primarily with spiritual experience and insight, a response in her view to the professionalization of scientific natural history, which left amateurs unable to keep up. She cites Gissing's *The Private Papers of Henry Ryecroft*, in which the protagonist experiences a kind of spiritual rebirth through being in

---

[6] BAHC, ZJO/1/33 (Johnston Diary, 16 Sep. 1906).

[7] BAHC, ZJO/1/9 (Johnston Diary, 26 May 1890). Compare Alan Davies and Ruth Miller, *The Joy of Birdwatching: For Those Who Love Seeing Birds in the Wild* (Chichester, 2015). 'A Willow Warbler ... has a charming, floaty song which works its way gently down the scale.'

[8] BAHC, Johnston Diary ZJO/1/30 (26 Jul. 1898) and ZJO/1/4 (16 and 17 Jun. 1889). For the distinction between rook/crow and swallow/swift calls see the British Trust for Ornithology's video guides. www.bto.org/about-birds/bird-id/bto-bird-id-corvids and www.bto.org/about-birds/bird-id/bto-bird-id-hirundines-and-swift [both accessed 28 Nov. 2022].

the countryside, noting that Ryecroft's 'sense of awe arises almost entirely from aesthetic and quasi-religious responses, in contrast to the awe expressed by diarists like Emily Shore and George Eliot that was knowledge-inspired as well as aesthetic and spiritual'.[9] However, as Johnston's diary amply testifies, the inference that those whose response to nature was primarily aesthetic or spiritual rather than scientific observed it less closely should be avoided. The contrast lay in the motivation rather than the quality of the attention.

The Natural and the Human

Nature meant so much to Johnston that one might anticipate he sought in nature a refuge from or antithesis to the human and that the landscapes he most cherished would be those that appeared least touched by human hands. This, however, was not the case. Crops, livestock, farm buildings and agricultural processes feature frequently in his diary and he wrote with empathy and respect of farming people. He was grateful to a 'farmer's kind wife' who offered him shelter from a rainstorm and enjoyed talking to farmers, while noting wryly their different and sometimes more utilitarian landscape sensibilities. On a visit back to Dumfriesshire he met a Mr Frood, 'a splendid specimen of a Scottish yeoman – tall well built handsome his frank rubicund face fairly beams with good nature and honesty'. Johnston pointed out the beauty of the golden-yellow wild mustard growing among the crops. He was intrigued and pleased by Frood's direct and outspoken response: 'it may be beautiful but we joost hate it'. Frood explained that the mustard impoverished the soil, spoilt the crop and was difficult to separate from the harvested grain.[10]

Historical and Geographical Dimensions

While Johnston loved nature and empathized with the farming community, he showed little interest in other aspects of the rural landscape. He praised the village of Witherslack in Westmorland as a 'quaint old time place' but, as the casual and faintly patronizing tone suggests, architecture meant little to him: cathedrals, abbeys and churches, castles and mansions, even picturesque cottages, are conspicuous by their absence in his voluminous writings. Unlike most of the other diarists, his interest in the countryside was distinctly ahistorical. In part this may be because he was born slightly earlier, at a time when 'the countryside' was still an emerging cultural phenomenon. But this did not stop contemporaries of Johnston, such as Hardy, Hudson or Morris, from celebrating the rural past. Johnston's Scottishness is another possible

---

[9] Bellanca, *Daybooks*, 231. Compare the analogous contrast between Richard Cresswell's scientific interest in plants and his daughter's aesthetic and emotional responses.

[10] BAHC, ZJO/1/4 (Johnston Diary, 14–21 Jun. 1889).

explanation. Perhaps the history embedded in English rural landscapes meant little to him because he did not feel it to be *his* history. He showed no more enthusiasm, however, for the historical traces legible in the Scottish landscape. A rare exception to his usual indifference to historic buildings sheds some light on the puzzle. Peel Castle on the Isle of Man was a:

> hoary picturesque ruin ... clean-cut against the sky of soft grey looking the embodiment of majesty and speaking eloquently of the past and its tragedy to the present and its contrasted commonplaceness – but to my mind productive of infinitely greater happiness to its people – the common people – the people upon whom depends all that is best and noblest in this nation of ours.[11]

Johnston's primary ideological commitment was his belief in the power and beneficence of nature, which he saw as a universal, perpetually self-renewing life force. Understood in this way, nature had no history and Johnston preferred to immerse himself in it and look cheerfully to the future rather than dwell on the human-induced tragedy of the past.

The geographical boundaries of Johnston's countryside were more accommodating. Despite his hatred of the urban, he was always ready to appreciate rural elements within Bolton. Radcliffe Road in the suburb of Darcy Lever was a great favourite: Johnston relished its fine display of cherry, hawthorn, lilac, laburnum and rhododendron blossom.[12] After moving out of central Bolton in 1899 he was able to satisfy some of his longing to surround himself with the sights and sounds of nature by turning to gardening.[13] In this respect there is a parallel with Hallam, whose garden, in later years, similarly assumed some of the functions previously fulfilled by the countryside. However, whereas this helped to reconcile Hallam to his previously detested home town of Swindon, Johnston never softened towards Bolton, perhaps in part because his gardens at 'Annandale' and 'Sunnybrae' were successive steps in a conscious quest for a more rural environment:

> It is sweet to get back to our dear little house at Lostock – our little countrified home. But alas I must not stay here long – for, my work calls me to busy Bolton.[14]

Some aspects of Johnston's ruralism were indeed equally or even more fully realized in his gardens than in the open country. In the first place, because

---

[11] BAHC, ZJO/1/33 (Johnston Diary, 24 Jul. 1911).

[12] BAHC, ZJO/1/20 (Johnston Diary, 26 May 1892).

[13] BAHC, ZJO/1/30 (Johnston Diary, 30 May 1899).

[14] BAHC, ZJO/1/32 (Johnston Diary, 8 Dec. 1902). If anything Johnston's detestation of Bolton increased as he grew older, especially after his appointment at the grim workhouse hospital of Townleys in 1917. See BAHC, ZJO/1/49 (Johnston Diary, 12 Nov. and 20 Dec. 1918).

Johnston believed there was a single spirit animating nature, of which a flower, bird, tree or for that matter hill or waterfall was merely an expression, there was a sense in which all manifestations of nature, great or small, were equal. This was one reason he was less inclined to celebrate landscapes for their sublimity than many of his contemporaries. A garden, from this point of view, was as wonderful as a mountain. Secondly, the key distinction for Johnston was not between the natural and the human, but the natural and the artificial. Nature in his eyes encompassed activities that he perceived to be in harmony with it, such as gardening and agriculture, just as it did children, farmers and adults whose souls were open, he believed, to its benign influence. Thirdly, Johnston often emphasized that he had planted many of the flowers in his gardens himself:

> What a joy is my garden to me! And what unalloyed delight to roam about and watch the growth and blooming of the flowers many of which I have myself planted and tended.[15]

A list of thirty-one different flower species follows this quotation. The fact that he had 'planted and tended' these flowers evidently gave them a special value to him. For a man who felt so much affinity with the young it must have been hard that his marriage proved childless; perhaps growing and caring for flowers provided some degree of compensation. Finally, Johnston's love of nature was deeply bound up with his close personal relationships, domesticity and love of home. The garden at Sunnybrae signified and partook of the happiness that grew on him living there with Maggie as the years went by.

Rurality and National Identity

Given the strength of the nexus between national identity and representations of landscape in literature, art and even music in late nineteenth-century Britain, one might expect that Johnston's response to the English countryside would be powerfully shaped by his Scottishness. On the whole, however, this was not the case. In common with many emigrants, Johnston's sense of his own nationality was multiple, or at least elastic. Occasionally he thought of himself as a 'Britisher' (16 June 1889) although his tendency to use Scots words at moments of heightened emotion and his deep-seated attachment to Annan suggest that any such Britishness may have been a veneer. The thinness of Johnston's British identity, however, may reflect a wider failure of Britishness to put down cultural roots, despite the efforts of generations of propagandists from James Thomson to Rudyard Kipling and beyond. Strikingly, Johnston appears to have been quite at ease with Englishness as an identity, appropriating it unselfconsciously when he wanted to. It would seem that there was little if any tension or contradiction between his Scottish

---

[15] BAHC, ZJO/1/32 (Johnston Diary, 4 Sep. 1904).

and English selves.[16] No doubt this reflected his happy childhood in Scotland and successful professional career in England. However, the more important point is that national identity did not occupy a prominent place in his consciousness. He rarely used the adjectives 'English', 'Scottish' or 'British' except in the context of weather, which is sometimes 'English':

> [A] characteristically typical English spring day.[17]

> Oh what is there more delightful than an English June? The crown of all the year![18]

Hallam and Spear Smith also connected weather with national identity (but hardly ever with landscape), in language almost identical to Johnston's.[19] Perhaps weather seemed more generic and universal – the same blue sky, cumulus clouds and sunshine could be seen anywhere in England. Landscape, by contrast, is always specific and particular, irreducibly place-bound and therefore resistant to assimilation, although Readman shows that in published discourse regional landscape identities could contribute to rather than conflict with wider understandings of Englishness.[20]

Johnston's Scottish ancestry seems to have had little influence on the affective significance English landscapes held for him. There was no holding back in his joyful response to the countryside when in England rather than Scotland, no sense of something withheld because these were not quite *his* landscapes. Compare the two following diary entries:

> This was one of the most enjoyable walks I ever had in all my life. The evening was simply perfect and the country is looking more lovely than I ever remember seeing it. The vegetation has come on apace and the wealth of foliage and of blossom is simply phenomenal – the hawthorn trees are fairly weighed down with their abundance of lovely bloom and look as if they had been snowed on – the laburnums bend beneath their wealth of tossing tassels and look like fountains dripping with liquid gold – the lilacs too have an unusual amount of purple blossom – the rhododendrons are a glory with their rich display of red and white – the mountain ash with its beautiful blossom is a charm to the eye – some of the fields and many of the slopes as

---

[16] On the elision of Scottish, English and British identities see Readman, *Storied Ground*, 19, 47–8, 52–89.

[17] BAHC, ZJO/1/20 (Johnston Diary, 21 Mar. 1892).

[18] BAHC, ZJO/1/20 (Johnston Diary, 1 Jun. 1892). See also BAHC, ZJO/1/33, 6 Jul. 1906.

[19] Golinski demonstrates that in the eighteenth century the mild, variable and rainy English climate was linked to national identity through the perceived moderation of both. Conversely the three diarists associated only the warmest, sunniest spring and summer days with Englishness (never autumn or winter). Does this indicate a shift in representations of English climate? J. Golinski, *British Weather and the Climate of Enlightenment* (Chicago, 2007), 57–8.

[20] Readman, *Storied Ground*, 16–21.

well as the woods are <u>blued</u> over with wild hyacinths (such a luxuriance of
these as I never saw anywhere before) while others are <u>yellowed</u> with buttercups, daisies and red and white clover (such a rich harmony of colour –
yellow, white and red, all among the green) – the golden gorse on the slopes
and rock cliffs are aflame with gorgeous yellow.[21]

* * *

In the morning M[aggie] and I took a walk up the right bank of the river. It
was as glorious a June day as ever dawned out of the heavens and the
whole riverside and surrounding country was one blaze of gorgeous
colour. Such a wealth of may blossom I never remember – for the hedges
and bushes were simply weighed down with their burden of lovely
blossom which almost hid the green and looked just like freshly fallen
snow at a distance. The so called 'Whin Bush' was a beautiful picture and
the great hedge near the Howes Pool was a mass of perfect bloom . . .
   Above the watermill the wealth of blossom was added to by great
masses of bloom and laburnum – 'the fountain-like laburnums dripping
showers of gold' – and the view up the river from the top of the bank near
the Cemetery wall was most entrancing.[22]

The first of these passages is an account of a walk from Rivington Lane to
Adlington in Lancashire while the setting for the second is Annanwater in
Dumfriesshire. Yet the word-painting is from the same palette: glorious weather,
a wealth of blossom so profuse it looked like snow, gorse and laburnum,
loveliness beyond anything recalled. It would be impossible without contextual
knowledge to say which passage referred to England and which to Scotland.

It is true that Johnston had a special affection for the landscape of Annandale. In
the brief memoir he wrote in 1884 he declared that 'a more beautiful river than the
Annan I have yet to look upon', although this must be set against the statement
quoted earlier in this chapter that the (Lancashire) countryside was looking 'more
lovely than I ever remember it' on his walk round Rivington. It would be reading
against the grain to look for consistency in Johnston's many declamations of this
kind – they were expressions of the strong feeling of a moment, temporarily
eclipsing other scenes and memories. The object of his present contemplation,
whether that was the outward landscape or the inward one of memory, always
tended to trump less immediate recollections. His love of Annan and its countryside was, in any case, due not to its Scottishness but to its deep associations with his
childhood. He had little to say about Scottish landscapes other than those round
Annan, and when he wrote about Annan the connection with childhood was
almost always explicit.[23] Cognitively, Johnston's dissociation of landscape and
national identity reflected his Whitmanite understanding of nature as the universal

[21] BAHC, ZJO/1/20 (Johnston Diary, 3 Jun. 1892).
[22] BAHC, ZJO/1/29 (Johnston Diary, 10 Jun. 1898).
[23] BAHC, ZJO/4/4 (Johnston Memoir).

benign life force, which could not possibly be contained within or altered by artificial lines on a map. At a deeper, affective level, his response to rural landscapes ministered to more powerful needs than those his sense of nationhood engaged.

The Seasons

Warm sunny weather in spring and early summer never failed to delight Johnston. He appreciated the rich colours of autumn too but unlike poets such as Thomson, Coleridge, Keats and Hardy he took no pleasure in equinoctial storms, leaf fall or the decline of the year.[24] The crisp freshness of frosty winter nights was more to his taste:

> It was a glorious starlit night – the snow lay thick on the ground there was a keen frost and as we tramped along the crisp crackling roadway beneath the brilliant starry sky we conversed on things which lay nearest our hearts.[25]

Snowfall, especially overnight, had a special attraction because of the way it could lend enchantment to otherwise dull or even disagreeable landscapes. Sometimes it enthused him into poetry, as in 'Two Winter Pictures':

> *Morning*
> This morn our Lane is 'passing-wondrous fair' –
> For angel-down-like snow has fallen everywhere,
> Mantling the landscape and the ebon trees,
> As with a heaven-sent robe of beauty rare.

> *Afternoon*
> Behold a wondrous transformation scene!
> The snow has gone – the fields again are green –
> The trees have doffed their ermine garmenture,
> And Earth appears where Fairyland has been.[26]

The extraordinary effect snow can have on landscape is a poetic commonplace, celebrated in much-anthologized verses by Bridges, Frost and others. Johnston's poem has two more unusual features. Firstly, it enacts a double transformation – 'ebon trees' are mantled with their snowy 'robe of beauty rare' but by the afternoon have 'doffed their ermine garmenture'. Secondly, and more remarkably, textual and contextual evidence suggests that for Johnston the second change carried a weightier emotional charge. Few poets celebrate thaws but for Johnston this one constituted a 'wondrous

---

[24] For Johnson's appreciation of autumn colours see BAHC, ZJO/1/31 (Johnston Diary, 4 Nov. 1900 and 19 Oct. 1902).

[25] BAHC, ZJO/1/19 (Johnston Diary, 18 Feb. 1892).

[26] BAHC, ZJO/5/1 (Johnston Cuttings Book, 17 Feb. 1904).

transformation'.[27] The poem ends affirmatively with the green of Earth (implicitly pointing towards spring) rather than the white of Fairyland. Johnston's stance is a deeply realist and humanist one: Fairyland is beautiful but insubstantial; the natural world, there all around us every day for those with eyes to see, is every bit as beautiful as the dream.

Landscape Types

Differences between individuals in their preference for particular landscape types remain largely unexplored in historical contexts. What Johnston looked for above all in landscapes was that they should be animated, pulsing with light, colour, movement and life. Hence he loved deciduous woods on sunny days in spring, meadows strewn with flowers, rivers and streams. He cherished the sea too, familiar with it as he was from his Annan childhood. He regarded it as a living part of nature and responded enthusiastically to its ceaseless movement and vivifying effect on the senses:

> I was out betimes for a ramble along the magnificent sands to the edge of the slowly incoming tide and inexpressibly sweet to me was the sight of the curling white-crested waves advancing and retreating upon the yellow sand, the fresh breezy smell and the hoarse and incessant roar of the heaving ocean.[28]

Conversely, empty, monochrome, seemingly dormant landscapes, however natural, rarely appealed to him. This helps to explain some otherwise puzzling features of his landscape preferences. The landscape type for which south Lancashire was best known was moorland. Bolton itself was more favourably placed for accessing the moors than most Lancashire towns, only three miles from the lower slopes of Winter Hill (456 m), the highest point of the West Pennine Moors. But although, as Harvey Taylor has shown, generations of Bolton millworkers made these hills their own, not least through a celebrated mass trespass on Winter Hill in 1896, Johnston rarely chose to visit the moors.[29] Equally striking is his lack of affinity for mountains. The geographical poles of Johnston's life were Bolton and Annan. It was probably not coincidental that his favourite holiday spot was Grange-over-Sands, roughly halfway between the two. Grange lay at the southern end of the Lake District, then as now the most revered of English landscapes and the spiritual home of Romanticism. Johnston admired Wordsworth and was much moved by a visit to Grasmere. Mountains were central to Romantic visions of landscape and to what Nicolson termed 'the aesthetics of the infinite' and, for all these

---

[27] Edward Thomas' 'Thaw' was composed just over a decade after Johnston's poem.
[28] BAHC, ZJO/1/22 (Johnston Diary, 10 Jul. 1892).
[29] Taylor, *A Claim on the Countryside*, 45–8, 49–50, 120.

reasons, one might have expected them to appeal especially to Johnston, who indubitably understood nature as a portal to an infinite world of noumenal truth.[30] Yet he showed little enthusiasm for them. Occasionally he climbed one of the lower heights, seemingly for the sake of the view, but he rarely mentions mountains admiringly, and then typically for their beautiful rather than sublime qualities, or because the particular mountain had strong personal associations:

> As we drove through Clarencefield village we had Auld Criffel in full view and right beautiful did he look wreathed in a purple mist his outline being clean cut against the clear blue sky while on either side of him was the undulating horizon line of distant hills.[31]

Criffel is a mountain in Galloway and, although only 570 metres high, it has sufficient prominence to dominate the surrounding area. It was visible in the distance from Annan so formed part of the backdrop of Johnston's childhood. Here it is Criffel's familiarity that counts for most – hence the affectionate Scots adjective 'Auld' and the personification ('on either side of him'). He also celebrates the mountain's beauty. But sublime elements such as power, might, awe and terror are notably absent.

Nature as Johnston apprehended and loved it, then, was very different from the mighty but often stern force that appealed to English neo-Romantics like Leslie Stephen. Nor is there any hint of post-Darwinian disillusionment: there was no place in his conception of it for 'the survival of the fittest'. Unlike Jefferies, Williamson or, later, Hughes, Johnston had no interest in ferocity or predation. One of the few occasions on which he acknowledged this aspect of nature is instructive:

> From Ruthwell we went to Hayberry Mill where we spent the evening wandering about the fields looking at the stock and the crops. A day or two previous to our visit Mr Graham sen[io]r had found that a partridge which had built its nest on the same spot for several years in succession had been killed off the nest and eaten by a fox. I saw the nest in which were four bonny brown eggs quite cold and near it some scattered feathers and a leg and foot – the remnants of the poor little martyred partridge. I brought the eggs and the leg home with me – mementos of that bird tragedy.[32]

Johnston empathizes strongly, not to say anthropomorphically, with the partridge. It is the loyalty of the bird to its home and the pathos of its demise that stirs his feelings: the cunning and ruthlessness of the fox evoke no response at all.

---

[30] Marjorie Hope Nicolson, *Mountain Gloom and Mountain Glory: The Development of the Aesthetics of the Infinite* (Ithaca, NY, 1959).

[31] BAHC, ZJO/1/4 (Johnston Diary, 16 Jun. 1889).

[32] BAHC, ZJO/1/4 (Johnston Diary, 16 Jun. 1889).

The Benevolence of Nature

The words Johnston used to describe his sensations in the countryside underline this: 'sweetly peaceful', 'restful', 'soothing', 'salutary', 'blissful content',
'happiness', 'serenity', 'spirit-healing beneficence', 'beauty', 'joyous delight'.
What Johnston found and cherished in nature was mildness not wildness:

> Save for the occasional matin-song of a wren and the now and again
> fluting of a blackbird and the rustle of the breeze through the trees the
> silence is unbroken and the Great Spirit of Nature whispers her message of
> Love – that 'God's in His heaven' (and earth) and 'all's right with the
> world'.[33]

Like his near-contemporary Kropotkin, whom, however, he does not seem to
have known, Johnston was more impressed by the evidence of 'mutual aid'
than of competition within nature, noting, for example, how flowers 'invited
the insects to partake of their honey'.[34] He had a special tenderness for quiet,
undemonstrative things – grass, leaves, insects and small birds – referring to
them in a companionable, affectionate way. A bird, for example, is 'my little
songster friend'.[35] He writes about and sometimes addresses birds, animals
and insects with friendly egalitarianism:

> [T]he bees and butterflies are now enjoying their nectar – sipping. One
> great yellow bodied fellow is humming from flower to flower and weigh-
> ing down the delicate petals with his heavy, bulky body.[36]

Descriptions like this testify to Johnston's recognition of and pleasure in the
existence of other living things in their own right. Often, as in Spear Smith's
case, identification with animals is based on a perceived similarity of some
kind. The pleasure Johnston took in this bee, conversely, arose from the bee
doing its own thing in its own way, without reference to him. The same feeling
is evident in his description of a chaffinch:

> [H]e has just alighted on the grass within a few feet of me – such
> a beautiful fellow he is! With barred wings and bright, beady eyes. But
> a moment does he stay – a single movement of mine and he is off in terror
> at the great black thing sitting on a basket in the sun, and wasting its time
> staring and scratching at white paper instead of enjoying the life of a bird
> in the trees and the sunlit air.[37]

For all his empathetic recognition of the chaffinch's distrust, Johnston characteristically situated himself physically and figuratively as part of the natural world,

---

[33] BAHC, ZJO/1/33 (Johnston Diary, 23 Sep. 1906).
[34] BAHC, ZJO/1/4 (Johnston Diary, 16 Jun. 1889).
[35] BAHC, ZJO/1/4 (Johnston Diary, 17 Jun. 1889).
[36] BAHC, ZJO/1/33 (Johnston Diary, 12 Aug. 1906).
[37] BAHC, ZJO/1/33 (Johnston Diary, 5 Aug. 1906).

a very different positioning from the separate, possessing 'male gaze' critiqued by recent scholarship.[38] Caught in the rain while out cycling on 26 May 1892, he took shelter in an outhouse, absorbing the sounds around him:

> As I sat there alone I heard the rain pattering on the roof and dripping from the eaves, a cow was audibly munching her cud through the wall, pigeons were cooing in the dovecot, ducks were uttering their quiet quacking sounds from beneath an upturned farm cart where some fowls were huddling and a lark, undeterred by the rain, was carolling in the dull grey sky.[39]

During his first two decades in Bolton Johnston was moving sharply to the left, from Liberal Unionism to the Independent Labour Party. His non-hierarchical, comradely sense of nature went hand in hand with this increasingly democratic and socialist politics. Sitting in Raikes Wood in Bolton on 24 May 1893, he noted that 'robins are singing all around me and filling the air with melody': nature as collective action for the common good.[40]

Modes of Being in the Countryside

Reading in the Countryside

Johnston often took a book with him when went out into the country. He had that special intimacy with his favourite writers that comes with reflection and re-reading. To many who live so much with books, their physical form becomes important as well as their words and meaning. Johnston was no exception: he referred to the books he brought with him on these occasions as his 'companions', almost the adult equivalent of a child carrying a doll.[41] Reading, talking to friends and being in the countryside were cognate activities for him: in each case he sought to achieve a sense of connection, with the author, his friend and nature respectively. As might be expected, it brought him particular pleasure when he was able to bring all three together:

> This latter reading [of passages from Goethe's *Wilhelm Meister* mentioned by Carlyle] was given out of doors on the rustic bridge over a tiny brook in Rivington and very impressive and memorable was the scene during the reading.
>
> JWW [Johnston's friend James Wallace] sat down on the ground his back against the red painted gate, the rest of us distributing ourselves on and near the railings of the bridge as Wallace read the fine passages aloud to which we all listened with absorbing interest at the same time drinking

---

[38] For example, A. Pritchard and N. J. Morgan, 'Privileging the Male Gaze: Gendered Tourism Landscapes', *Annals of Tourism Research* 27 (2000), 884–905.

[39] BAHC, ZJO/1/20 (Johnston Diary, 26 May 1892).

[40] BAHC, ZJO/1/22 (Johnston Diary, 24 May 1893).

[41] BAHC, ZJO/1/4 (Johnston Diary, 9 and 14–21 Jun. 1889); BAHC, ZJO/1/9 (Johnston Diary, 22 May 1890); BAHC, ZJO/1/22 (Johnston Diary, 5 Jul. 1892 and 9 May 1893).

in the sweet influences of that lovely scene – the brooklet flowing silently [inserted: a water rat once disturbed that silence] beneath us and bearing on its bosom a few stray flower blossoms and tiny bubbles – the tangle of ferns, nettles, grasses and long lily-like leaves which lined its banks or grew from its bed – the grey farm buildings – the beautiful undulating pastoral landscape – the noble Pike half veiled in mist – the cloudless blue sky – the low lying sun setting like a golden glowing disc and reflected in the smooth surface of the brook whose waters it visibly tinged pink – the bees hummed (and the midges bit!) and the fragrantly sweet air all contributed to our enjoyment of that hour when we listened to the beautiful reading of our dearly loved friend and master.[42]

Wallace frequently read to Johnston, both when they were with their other friends (the 'Eagle Street College', as they called themselves with reference to Wallace's address) and when they were alone. Usually the book would be by one of the well-known nineteenth-century nature writers – Wordsworth, Thoreau, Emerson, Whitman or Carpenter.

In choosing to read or to be read to so often outdoors, Johnston knew that he was observing one of Whitman's emphatic injunctions. Having discovered a first edition of *Leaves of Grass* in an Annan newspaper office, he 'carried it away' to nearby Milnfield Wood, sat down among the trees and:

[R]ead the first printed words of my grand old hero. And what more fitting place could they be read in? For is it not one of his intimations that we are to take these 'Leaves' and 'read them in the open air and every season of every year of your life'?[43]

It would be easy to infer that it was through Whitman's influence that Johnston developed his habit of reading outdoors. In fact it was a prominent feature of his childhood and continued while he was an undergraduate in Edinburgh.[44] His invocation of Whitman was a retrospective rationalization of a practice established decades previously.

Reading and the Making of Johnston's Ruralism

As his lifelong relationship with books suggests, literary influences played an important part in shaping Johnston's ruralism. Defining that part, however, requires care. The most straightforward aspect is the way his writing and

---

[42] BAHC, ZJO/1/22 (Johnston Diary, 22 Jul. 1892). The 'Pike' is Rivington Pike, a prominent local landmark.

[43] BAHC, ZJO/1/4 (Johnston Diary, 19 Jun. 1889).

[44] BAHC, ZJO/4/2 (Johnston Memoir). Reading outdoors is a somewhat neglected historical subject. See E. J. Scholl, 'Taking Reading Outdoors', *Reading Today* 20 (2003), 12, and Belden C. Lane, 'Backpacking with the Saints: The Risk Taking Character of Wilderness Reading', *Spiritus: A Journal of Christian Spirituality* 8 (2008), 23–43.

phraseology is coloured by the books he read. It is difficult, for example, not to hear Shelley's 'To a Skylark' close behind this passage:

> Dear little bird! What a heartful of happiness you must have to be able to utter so joyously and continuously. Sing on blithe little warbler and teach us all the lesson that we are meant to be happy while we stay here.[45]

Similarly, it seems likely that Wordsworth's 'Highland Lass/Reaping and singing' was in Johnston's mind when he described:

> Two lusty Scotch reapers mowing the long sweet scented grass and clover by hand stooping down and swinging the long curved bladed scythe with such graceful sweeps. I could not help admiring the picturesqueness of their figures as they strode along and cleared a broad path through the tall grass.[46]

As this passage suggests, Johnston was familiar with the language of landscape aesthetics that had evolved since the eighteenth century. A visit to Dolgellau in mid-Wales wrought him to express himself in the familiar clichés of the well-educated tourist:

> [A] most charmingly Romantic ravine . . . a brawling torrent tumbles and dashes over and between huge grey moss-grown boulders and fallen tree trunks amid a profusion of ferns and mosses trees and wildflowers all intermingled in wild picturesque confusion and discord and yet perfect harmony.[47]

Almost identical passages could be found in hundreds of nineteenth-century travellers' diaries, letters and memoirs. Yet although Johnston could hardly help seeing nature to some extent through this prism, the careless way he throws terms such as 'Picturesque' and 'Romantic' into his description, making no distinction between them, indicates that he was not much interested in the aesthetic theories of his day.[48] Picturesque archetypes such as ruins and rocks rarely make an appearance in Johnston's numerous and lengthy descriptions of rural landscape. Romantic apprehensions of nature were so variously inflected that it is difficult to generalize but the boisterous delight in the power of nature characteristic of foundational works of English Romanticism such as

---

[45] BAHC, ZJO/1/4 (Johnston Diary, 17 Jun. 1889). Years later, on a walk near Rivington, Johnston asked Wallace to recite Shelley's 'sublime poem' when they saw larks in the sky. Wallace purported not to be able to remember it so Johnston recited the first few lines to get him started. BAHC, ZJO/1/32 (Johnston Diary, 22 Apr. 1904).

[46] BAHC, ZJO/1/4 (Johnston Diary, 19 Jun. 1889).

[47] BAHC, ZJO/1/6 (Johnston Diary, Aug. 1889 [n.d.]).

[48] As Readman observes, despite the efforts of theorists such as Uvedale Price and Richard Payne Knight, 'a vague and capacious pictorialism remained the order of the day' throughout the nineteenth century and beyond. Readman, *Storied Ground*, 98. See also *Storied Ground*, 257.

Wordsworth's 'Lines Composed a Few Miles above Tintern Abbey' or
Coleridge's 'Kubla Khan' is also almost entirely absent in Johnston. This corresponds to a difference in positioning in relation to nature. The Picturesque
established the 'view' as the dominant mode of landscape perception.
Although Romanticism encompassed a wider range of postures, the popularity
of views increased exponentially during the nineteenth century as travel, tourism
and the guidebooks and postcards that promoted them reached new audiences.
Johnston quite literally stood (or more often sat) apart from this, placing himself
within nature rather than gazing upon it from a distant vantage point. His
version of nature was gentle and nurturing rather than wild and passionate. It
is revealing that he chose to end his description of the 'charmingly Romantic
ravine' at Dolgellau by emphasizing the 'perfect harmony' of nature rather than
its 'wild picturesque confusion'.

How far Johnston's reading shaped his immediate apprehension of nature as
well as the way he expressed this in writing is more difficult to say. Sometimes,
certainly, the perception preceded the literary connection. His initial description of wasps and bees at Dormont Grange lacked any literary references but in
a later revision to the entry he inserted the phrase 'the ships of the flowers as
Jefferies calls them'. In some respects, of course, the question of whether his
reading shaped his perceptions and dispositions, or was shaped by them, is
a false dichotomy: each shaped the other. What can be said is that because he
was such an intellectual man, read so widely, and thought with and through the
books he read, Johnston was more influenced by his reading than any of the
other diarists in this book, even the highly literary Catley. In words he quoted
from one of the writers he most admired, Emerson, Johnston sought to 'hitch
[his] wagon to a star', in his case principally Whitman.[49] However, many of his
strongest and most recurrent impulses, including those that had the most
decisive influence on his life course such as his desire to protect the weak
and his deep loyalty to family and friends, do not bear any obvious relation to
his reading preferences and seem to have predated them. On the whole it
would seem that Johnston's character and family background shaped the
broad outlines of his values and commitments. These informed his literary
preferences, which in turn refined and developed his values and commitments,
within the established structure of his adult character.

Johnston's *weltanschauung* was, nevertheless, very important to him. It
provided him with something analogous to, although not necessarily
a substitute for, religion – a frame of reference for interpreting the world
and guiding his actions. Not everyone needs a frame of reference equally much.
There is little indication that Dickinson or Cresswell (for all her Anglican

---

[49] Whitman, however, was important to Johnston as much as a personally known comrade
as for his ideas. 'Dear Walt! How glad I am to have known you!' BAHC, ZJO/1/22
(Johnston Diary, 26 Mar. 1893).

orthodoxy) drew on a defined value system in making the decisions, large and small, that shaped their lives. For others, including Bissell and Spear Smith as well as Johnston, an explicit frame of reference was central. Seeing nature through Whitman's eyes gave it a deeper and more coherent meaning for Johnston, even though this built on extensive foundations laid down since childhood.

Writing in the Countryside

If Johnston's enthusiasm for reading in the open air was unusual, still more so was his habit of writing in the midst of nature. Writing, in common with other forms of representation, is usually regarded as at least one step removed from experience. Many critics have been suspicious of it for this reason, regarding it as cerebral and abstract in contrast to more fully embodied modes of being. In Johnston's case, however, writing played a much richer, indeed in many respects constitutive, role. Uniquely among the diarists I have looked at, Johnston frequently wrote in real time, as he experienced. This was, indeed, characteristically the case when he wrote in the open air.[50] On these occasions the distinction between representation and experience, language and life, collapses as each flows into the other. The experience is immanent in the writing:

> I write this note in Raikes Wood where I have escaped for an hours solitary communion with nature. What a difference is perceptible since I was here last (Apr 23rd). The trees are now adorned with their lovely green leaves upon which the afternoon sun is shining and casting beautiful dappled shadow patterns which change with every movement of the branches but always beautiful to me. I am sitting upon a sloping bank facing the brook which flows lazily along. All around and overhead are the lovely greens in infinite and charming variety of the new leaves some in shadow some in bright gleaming sunshine others in half sunlight and shadow but all dancing up and down in the gentle zephyr of this gloriously perfect Spring day – a day to make glad the hearts of all men. To my left a grand thrush is discoursing his melodious music for my benefit and asking me all sorts of questions such as 'What are you doing?' 'What are you doing?' 'I see you, I see you, I see you.' 'Wait a bit, wait a bit, wait a bit.' 'Who are you? Who are you?' . . .
>
> I think I will stop writing and lie down 'abstracted' and listen to the 'beautiful tales of things and the reasons of things'.
>
> [In a different style of handwriting] I was roused from my reverie by a fresh arrival in the woodland choir – a splendid blackbird which perched . . . upon the topmost branches.[51]

---

[50] For example, the entry titled 'Written in Raikes Wood': BAHC, ZJO/1/22 (Johnston Diary, 18 May 1893). Smith sometimes wrote in the open air too, on the common at Fittleworth or under Titchfield Lodge's medlar tree, but with less immediacy.

[51] BAHC, ZJO/1/11 (Johnston Diary, 12 May 1891) (spelling as in the original).

It is not only the use of the present tense: it is that the experience happens while, and even perhaps because, Johnston writes. The act of writing precipitates his awareness of the 'beautiful dappled shadow patterns which change with every movement of the branches but always beautiful to me'. Perhaps he might not notice them were he not writing. As his pen moves across the page he becomes aware that he wants to 'lie down "abstracted" and listen' to the sounds of nature. For a while Johnston's experience closes off to us while he does so and, when we pick up the thread again, it is retrospective and lacks the same immediacy.

In open-air passages like this Johnston's diary often prefigures or even initiates the action it describes – the usual relationship between event and (subsequent) diary entry is reversed. Despite the immense weight of meaning that he attached to nature, he is refreshingly honest about its discomforts: 'a lark was singing a few minutes ago and the midges are biting me most objectionably so I think I'll have a smoke to stop them'. The irritation the midges are causing breaks through the crust of his consciousness in mid-sentence, and as he writes the decision to have a smoke comes to him.[52]

Just as Johnston's diary coalesces experience and representation, it persistently undermines the material separation between observer and observed. Nature literally wraps itself around him while he records it. 'A bramble trawls its slender green stem across my feet and the long grasses ... are nodding their heads right over my book as I write.'[53] It is as if nature flows into Johnston's diary through his body. How far this happened spontaneously and how far he was conscious of wanting to dissolve the distinctions between nature, experience and writing is difficult to say. Certainly the drive to do so was very strong, as the numerous leaves, pressed flowers and other natural objects contained in the diaries indicate.[54] He was, again in the most literal sense, bringing nature inside his 'book of the self'. This extra-textual material can be regarded as a form of bottled experience, sometimes going beyond what writing is capable of expressing.[55] Annie Pickersgill's forget-me-not is a case in point:

> Visited Annie Pickersgill who for the last 3 months has been slowly sinking into consumption which is now rapidly taking her towards the valley of the shadow. She is a tall graceful girl of 18 yrs with beautiful blue eyes and

[52] BAHC, ZJO/1/22 (Johnston Diary, 7 Jun. 1892). Compare BAHC, ZJO/1/9 (Johnston Diary, 26 May 1890): 'I have just had to shift my seat as I saw a few ants crawling over my book (prevention is better than cure).'

[53] BAHC, ZJO/1/9 (Johnston Diary, 26 May 1890).

[54] For example, a sprig of heather inserted in the 1902 volume of Johnston's diary, BAHC, ZJO/1/32.

[55] On extra-textual material in diaries see Lejeune, On Diary, 39–40. See also Huff, 'Reading As Re-vision', 517–18.

a characteristic pink and white complexion and has borne her affliction with heroic patience. As usual in such cases she was very despondent at the beginning of the illness but is now very hopeful and says she is getting better a little every day. Poor thing! She will never be better in this world. This morning I was greatly touched by my visit to her.[56]

While Annie spoke about her hopes for the future, with only a faint undertone of anxiety, Johnston struggled to reconcile honesty with compassion, and tried to avoid meeting the eyes of Annie's stricken family. Knowing his fondness for flowers, Annie gave him a forget-me-not before he left. Perhaps at some level she was more aware of the real situation than she acknowledged. Johnston was deeply affected. He took the flower home with him, pressed it and stuck it into his diary, where it remains to this day, mute and faded but carrying an undiminished emotional charge.

Walking and Loafing

While Johnston took great pleasure in the episodic manifestations of nature he found in the course of his medical rounds – a thrush singing as he cycled home from an early-morning call to Darcy Lever, snow falling at night on the cobbled streets of Bolton – he longed to immerse himself more comprehensively in it. This was difficult in late nineteenth-century Bolton but Johnston found his own rural haven in Raikes Wood, between Bolton itself and Darcy Lever. He went there frequently when he had a spare hour or two, referring to it as 'my little rural retreat' and 'this dear little wood'.[57]

Johnston's modes of engagement with landscape in Raikes Wood and elsewhere prompt questions about the range of spatial practices in the countryside. Walking and lines in the landscape have been the subject of a great deal of stimulating and imaginative research, writing and artistic practice over the past few decades. Much of this has foregrounded the relationship between walking, landscape and identity. John Wylie, for example, argued in a reflection on a day's walking along the South-West Coast Path that 'multiple and varied' configurations of self and landscape emerge from the 'performative *milieu*' of walking along a path.[58] Dunham draws attention to the ways in which 'Kilvert's movements through the countryside (and his vivid descriptions of encounters with landscape and figures) supported not only his deliberate construction of an idealized "self", but a series of "other", more surprising and sometimes disturbing, identities.'[59] Repeated walking through

[56] BAHC, ZJO/1/22 (Johnston Diary, 26 Jun. 1892).

[57] BAHC, ZJO/1/22 (Johnston Diary, 7 and 21 Jun. 1892).

[58] J. Wylie, 'A Single Day's Walking: Narrating Self and Landscape on the South West Coast Path', *Transactions of the Institute of British Geographers* 30 (2005), 234–47.

[59] Philip Dunham, '"An Angel-Satyr Walks These Hills": Landscape and Identity in Kilvert's Diary', in P. S. Barnwell and Marilyn Palmer (eds.), *Post-medieval Landscapes* (Macclesfield, 2007), 169–84, at 171.

deeply known local landscapes enabled Kilvert to develop and experience these identities and to express them in writing.

Rural landscapes were every bit as important to the formation and expression of Johnston's identity as Dunham suggests they were for Kilvert. But walking was less important for Johnston than 'loafing'. He took this term from Whitman, who used it in two well-known lines of 'The Song of Myself' and occasionally in essays and other writing. For Whitman, loafing seems to refer to any form of unpurposive outdoor relaxation but Johnston applied the word in a much more specific context, to a landscape practice that appears to have been of his own devising.[60] The core feature of loafing in Johnston's sense was sitting or occasionally standing quietly, typically in a wood, field or garden, absorbing the influences around him. Crucially, loafing did not involve movement, or, more precisely, it reversed the relationship between subject and landscape in this respect. Sitting on a tree stump in a wood, Johnston was almost entirely still. But, as his diary entries emphasize, the landscape was in lively motion round him:

> I write this note at 4pm in a wood just behind the Great Lever vicarage. The sunbeams are dancing on the grass and glinting thro the green leaves which are gently swaying to the fresh breeze. Overhead there is the airy music of the rustling leaves and as I look up I get glimpses of blue sky with sailing white cloudlets between them . . . all round the brown sparrows are gently chirruping and hopping about on the bushes.[61]

After moving to 'Annandale' in 1899 and especially 'Sunnybrae' in 1902, Johnston often chose to loaf in his own garden. He wrote numerous 'Garden Notes' at Sunnybrae, recognizably continuous with his old Raikes Wood notes, but more standardized and consistent in style and form. Johnston had in effect developed his own literary micro genre, albeit one that nodded respectfully to Whitman and drew also on Emerson and Thoreau's sensibilities and values. As with the Raikes Wood notes, the emphasis is on immediacy and direct observation, leading to emotional and spiritual transcendence:

> The cows are leisurely feeding in the field just over the wall – my canary is singing oh so sweetly in the kitchen window – a thistledown has just lighted on the grass plot and oh there sails along a big dragonfly – the very first I have ever seen here and such a handsome fellow! With his big club shaped body and his widespread gauzy wings he flies and floats in the air like a small bird – in fact at first sight I thought he was a bird . . . Overall

---

[60] For Whitman's use of 'loafing' see 'From the Desk of a Schoolmaster' (Sundown Papers, 5), *Long-Island Democrat*, 24 November 1840; 'Some Hints to Apprentices and Youth' (editorial); 'Loafing in the Woods', Walt Whitman, *Prose Works* (Philadelphia, 1892).

[61] BAHC, ZJO/1/9 (Johnston Diary, 26 May 1890) (spelling as in the original).

there broods the spirit of peace and beauty – a holy calm betokening the sacred presence which pervades all nature.[62]

Johnston continued to loaf in the countryside as well as his garden even after moving to Sunnybrae in 1902, both around Lostock and when he was away from home, wherever he could find a secluded spot encompassed by nature, among the sand dunes at St Anne's, in the woods of Shap Wells near Penrith, or on the cliffs above Peel, which became a holiday home-from-home for John and Maggie in the early years of the twentieth century.

Cycling

Johnston enjoyed walking, especially with friends, but, loafing apart, cycling was his preferred mode of being in the countryside. Cycling has a mixed character and Johnston relished it for many reasons, not all intrinsically related to nature or the countryside. Like Cresswell, he was delighted to discover it and found it physically exhilarating. This intense embodiment was, however, in part dependent upon cultural influences Johnston had absorbed, in the first instance through his medical training and reading and secondly from Whitman:

> I do not know any experience to compare with cycling in its tranquilising effect upon the mind and heart. In half an hour after starting – and I go at a very moderate pace – the blood becomes oxygenated and the 'humours' stagnant in the liver and internal organs are stirred and swept out of the system . . . the man is not the same as he was . . . his vital energy is renewed and with this comes a different feeling towards external nature . . . everything seems _good_ and he himself feels at peace with all men and with the whole scheme of the universe.
>
> It seems to me that this is because he is then in a more healthy frame of mind than he was before and being so he is in a condition to be more _en rapport_ with eternal nature for as Whitman says 'only health puts us _en rapport_ with the universe'.[63]

As the reference to 'eternal nature' and the quotation from Whitman indicate, the somatic pleasures and perceived benefits of cycling merged into Johnston's wider values and outlook on life. Hence in practice he almost always chose to cycle in rural environments, relishing the fresh air, colourful flowers and trees, the birdsong, and the sense of unconfined space, which resonated with the physical freedom of movement:

> In afternoon I had a delightful ride on my cycle up and down the lanes of Great Lever. As I pedalled along I noted the meadows and fields all radiant

---

[62] BAHC, ZJO/1/32 (Johnston Diary, 4 Sep. 1904).
[63] BAHC, ZJO/1/20 (Johnston Diary, 26 May 1892).

with golden dandelions and white-petalled daisies and heard the songs of
the lark and the scream of the swallow overhead, all around being bathed in
a restful soothing peace which entered into my heart and made me happy.[64]

Immersive Ruralism

As this and many similar passages suggest, Johnston's apprehension of the
countryside was physical and multisensory. 'What better could anyone wish
for than a bouquet of sweet-smelling clover', he declared on 9 June 1889. He
revelled in the lush scent of new-mown hayfields and the 'delicious fresh
breeziness' of a morning when the air 'tasted so sweet and fragrant'.[65] Just as
Johnston's writing breaks down the boundaries between experience and representation, so in this passage he seeks to dissolve the distinction between the
senses, eliding touch, smell and taste. He enjoyed gathering fruit and berries,
recalling how he and his friends used to pick and eat 'brummles' (blackberries)
which 'hung in very tempting clusters' in the lanes around Annan in his
childhood. He was equally alert and receptive to sound:

> [T]he all-pervading silence is unbroken save at intervals by the call of
> a passing bird – a plover has just gone by calling 'pee-wit, pee-wit',
> a pigeon has cloven the air with its sharp, whip-like wing sound – the low
> of a distant cow, the call of a chanticleer, the coo of a turtle dove, the
> occasional bark of a far-away dog, the chatter of the russet-coated sparrows.[66]

Even where the primary sensation was visual Johnston often uses a non-visual
metaphor to express it, eliding the senses again: 'I stayed there a long time
drinking in the rich beauty of the sight.'[67]

Opportunities and Constraints

As a professional man, Johnston had a little more control over his time than
employees such as Hallam, Bissell, Barmes and Catley. He was able, as they
were not, to find an hour or two during the working day to steal away to Raikes
Wood or some other 'rural refuge' and he could also take more frequent
holidays. However, in practice, Johnston's surgery hours were difficult to
change once established and constrained both the timing and character of
his rural encounters. Visits to Raikes Wood had to be fitted in between
afternoon surgery, which might end at 3.15pm, and tea at 5pm. If Johnston

---

[64] BAHC, ZJO/1/20 (Johnston Diary, 26 May 1892).
[65] BAHC, ZJO/1/4 (Johnston Diary, 9 Jun. 1889). Compare BAHC, ZJO/1/33 (Johnston
Diary, 22 Jul. 1906): 'how sweet is the odour of the new mown hay as I turn over and
snuffle into its crackling flower besprinkled aromatic grasses'.
[66] BAHC, ZJO/1/33, (Johnston Diary, 12 Aug. 1906).
[67] BAHC, ZJO/1/20 (Johnston Diary, 1 Jun. 1892).

had visits to make in the afternoon, there might not be time for loafing.[68] More ambitious excursions to Rivington and beyond were out of the question, except on summer evenings if he had no calls to make. Unlike Catley, Johnston was not inclined to go out in foul weather and tended to return home if it began to rain. Conversely, a 'truly glorious day' like 24 March 1893 was likely to tempt him out – this was indeed his first visit to Raikes Wood since 'the fall of the leaves' the previous year.

Explaining Johnston's Ruralism

Childhood Origins

Johnston's ruralism was rich, diverse and sustained. To account for it, the many strands of which it was woven must be related carefully to the other dimensions, events and circumstances of his life. As so often with Johnston, it makes sense to begin in Annan. His friend Willie Graham's house, 'The Moat', seems to have become a sort of second home to him: its gardens offered scope not only for reading and studying but also endless opportunities for play, and he and Willie made the most of this, especially on Saturdays, the one free day of the week in Presbyterian Annan:

> Saturdays at the Moat were red letter days to me. These we spent either in roaming thro' the extensive grounds, birdsnesting – not harrying them for that we abhorred – or climbing the trees in the orchard, playing croquet or cricket or enjoying ourselves as boys only can about the stables and hayloft. To us boys the Moat was a veritable Paradise and many were the happy hours we spent among its delights to which I had always free entrée.[69]

Another school friend was John Irving Pool, son of Mr Pool of Staythrowes Farm. It was a great treat to be invited to spend Saturday there:

> Besides the farm with all its attractions there was a splendid threshing mill driven by horsepower and <u>such</u> a barn and stackyard![70]

Although his father did not farm himself, Annan was a small town in a country district and Johnston spent much of his time in and around farms as a boy. The affinity he felt for the agricultural world in adult life should be understood in this light. He seems to have been allowed almost complete freedom to explore Annan's rural surroundings. Above all, he cherished the Annanwater, which meandered past the grassy Holme, under the red arches of Robert Stevenson's sandstone bridge, over the long, slanting weir and down to the Solway Firth two

---

[68] BAHC, ZJO/1/22 (Johnston Diary, 7 Jun. 1892). 'I have finished my work till 6pm.'
[69] BAHC, ZJO/4/2 (Johnston Memoir).
[70] BAHC, ZJO/4/2 (Johnston Memoir).

miles below the town. The unpublished memoir Johnston wrote in 1886 recalls
this aspect of his childhood rapturously:

> Here is the pond in which we bathed; there is the greensward of the holm
> upon which we used to run races to dry ourselves after our bathe like wild
> Indians, fly kites and play at 'knifery'. Here are the shallows in which
> I waded and in which we fished, there is the wood in which we bird-nested
> and there are the hazel trees from which we gathered nuts and cut
> whistles. There is the grassy bank where we gathered primroses and violets
> in spring or reclined at our ease, book in hand, eagerly following the
> adventures of Robinson Crusoe or 'Guy Mannering' or Redgauntlet or the
> heroes of Fennimore Cooper, Ballantyne, Crockett or Maryatt.[71]

That Johnston wrote this memoir when living in Bolton, separated in time and
space from his Annan childhood, influences the selection of material he presents
and its emotional tone. However, there is no reason to doubt that the events he
describes actually occurred. The passage just quoted is remarkable on several
counts. It reveals the rich diversity of ways in which he and his friends engaged
with the river and the landscape through which it passed: they waded, swam,
fished, explored, climbed, gathered and read. Linked to this, it demonstrates how
childhood landscapes can become intimately known through repeated, multiform
engagement with them. Ironically, the bounded, familiar character of such childhood landscapes offers rich opportunities for exploration and discovery.[72]
Johnston and his friends ran races across the holm 'like wild Indians' and the
books they read echoed and reinforced this sense of excitement and adventure.
There was a complementarity between exploring material and literary landscapes,
one that was to persist throughout Johnston's life, and Defoe, Scott, Fennimore
Cooper and the like doubtless fired the imagination more vividly through being
read in the children's own landscape of adventure.

Although Annan was in many respects a provincial backwater, the town was
conscious of its history and did not lack local pride. The school was
a distinguished one, numbering Carlyle and the celebrated albeit controversial
preacher Edward Irving among its recent alumni. The influence of both was
still felt in the town while Johnston was growing up, in the earnest and intense
atmosphere of religious and moral seriousness. This was to become increasingly important to him as he grew older but in his boyhood it was Annan's less
rarefied although perhaps no less vigorous popular culture that appealed, the
jewel in the crown of which was the annual Annan Fair. As was so often the
case in small country towns and villages, the fair generated tremendous
excitement – farmworkers and others came in from miles around, festivities
went on long after dark and, reflecting the vivid impression it made on him as
a child, he devoted several pages of his memoir to describing it.

[71] BAHC, ZJO/4/4 (Johnston Memoir).
[72] This theme is explored in more depth in Burchardt, 'Far Away and Close to Home'.

Johnston's happy childhood laid the foundations of his adult ruralism. Memories typically have a powerful spatial component and any happy childhood is likely to foster positive associations with the landscape types in which it unfolds, but the rural landscapes of Annandale were, in Johnston's view at least, especially conducive to youthful freedom and enjoyment: 'fortunate indeed is the town with such a river [as the Annan] and fortunate indeed is the boy or girl who has spent his or her childhood by its banks'.[73] Less fortunate, perhaps, was the doctor separated from these banks by professional exigencies. Like Hallam, Johnston was an exile of the Industrial Revolution. Just as Hallam had to leave his beloved Lockinge because agriculture was in decline and the nearest employment he could find was in Swindon, so Johnston had to leave Annan because it was in grimy but booming 'Worktown' (as the Mass Observers were to christen Bolton decades afterwards) that he found a good professional opening. At the simplest level, going out into the countryside allowed him to reconnect with his childhood. It is probably not accidental that he liked to use Scots words such as 'glen' to describe features of the English countryside (e.g. Sunday, 9 June 1889; Monday, 26 May 1890). He empathized with those, human or animal, who were loyal to their customary home, attempting to persuade Wallace that it could only be because of their overpowering desire to return to 'the old home of their ancestors' that swallows returned annually from the warmth and plenty of Africa to breed in Britain.[74]

The adult Johnston's vivid and happy memories of his own early years fostered a passionate protectiveness and compassion towards children, tinged sometimes with sentimentality, that has much in common with his empathy for the small things of nature:

> I had to speak rather sharply to one of my female patients today about frightening her children with my name . . . I love little children dearly and I cannot bear the thought of them being frightened at me.[75]

His tendency to lapse into Scots vocabulary when writing about children, birds and animals ('bonnie wee lambies') underlines the link with his own childhood.[76] This readiness to identify with children allowed him to engage with them on their own level, as his gleeful account of an episode during a holiday in North Wales indicates:

> Yesterday afternoon I enjoyed as much as any for I was a boy again! Would you believe it? I actually assisted to build a sand castle! There are

[73] BAHC, ZJO/4/3 (Johnston Memoir).
[74] BAHC, ZJO/1/22 (Johnston Diary, 5 Jul. 1892).
[75] BAHC, ZJO/1/20 (Johnston Diary, 26 May 1892). For other instances of Johnston's tenderness towards children see BAHC, ZJO/1/31 (12 Aug. 1902), BAHC, ZJO/1/33 (17 Jun. 1906), BAHC, ZJO/1/35 (20 Jun. 1914) and BAHC, ZJO/1/37 (Feb. 1917).
[76] BAHC, ZJO/1/22 (Johnston Diary, 18 Mar. 1893).

two splendid little chaps staying at our hotel who were delighted at my
offer to go with them and dig.[77]

Johnston's perception of childhood as pure and innocent resonated with and
amplified his ruralism. It particularly delighted him to see children among fields
and flowers:

> The meadows by the waterside opposite the moat were carpeted by butter-
> cups and intermingled daisies until nothing but a golden yellow was to be
> seen. In the middle of one stood two little children with red and blue frocks
> wh[ich] made strikingly beautiful patches of colour among the yellow.[78]

This might call Allingham or Greenaway to mind, but it was Wordsworth's vision
of rural childhood to which Johnston responded most strongly. He and Maggie
visited Grasmere in 1890 and, with some difficulty, he persuaded a curly-haired
local girl named Christina to read 'We Are Seven' at the poet's grave.[79] Not content
with this, he proceeded to Dove Cottage, where he read the same poem to the
family, of seven children, then in residence. Johnston's attitude to childhood can
therefore be situated in a cultural context but it would be a mistake to see it as
deriving from this context. Rather Johnston's own childhood experiences and
emotional needs predisposed him towards, and were in turn given expression by,
texts such as Wordsworth's poem. Personal experience and social circumstances
underpinned the uptake of a cultural idiom in this instance, rather than the other
way round.

University Experiences

Johnston's experiences as a medical student in Edinburgh amplified his ruralism. He greatly enjoyed Professor Balfour's lectures on botany given in the
Edinburgh Botanic Gardens at 8am during the summer session. These lectures
and the beauty of the Gardens deepened his interest in plants and crystalized
his love of nature into consciousness:

> To sit with our text books beneath the shade of those splendid trees on
> a summer's afternoon or evening or to ramble among the groves of
> foliage-lined walks or within luxurious Palm Houses and Conservatories
> in which grew the flora of almost every country in the world was indeed
> a charming way of studying Botany and of inspiring us with a love of
> nature and all her works – a love which has never ceased to deepen in me.

---

[77] He also helped children with their sand buildings years later on the Isle of Man: BAHC,
ZJO/1/33, (Johnston Diary, 24 Jul. 1911).

[78] BAHC, ZJO/1/29 (Johnston Diary, 10 Jun. 1898).

[79] 'We Are Seven', one of the defining Romantic statements of the 'child of nature' trope, is
a dialogue between a 'rational' adult narrator who attempts to persuade a child that she has
only four siblings since two lie in the churchyard. The child remains serenely obdurate.

Even more enjoyable were the Saturday excursions in search of specimens. These ranged surprisingly far across the Scottish countryside, through the Lothians, Fife and even Inverness-shire. The young men collected plants in vascula and, on their return, sorted, dried and pressed them in their herbaria.[80]

Illness and Recovery

Johnston was evidently flourishing at Edinburgh, reconciling academic success with personal happiness as effortlessly as he seems to have done as a schoolboy. But his progress was rudely interrupted by a severe illness in October 1871. For a long time his life 'hung trembling in the balance'. His family took him back home to Annan and nursed him devotedly:

> Often in the dead of night did I hear the sound of my dear good father's voice in the adjoining room, as he wrestled on his knees in prayer ... Never can I sufficiently express my sense of obligation to my parents and sister for all their loving care in ministering to me and in endeavouring to mitigate my suffering; for not only was I reduced by the fever and diarrhaea [sic] but I endured a considerable amount of severe pain, the great exhauster of nerve energy and I think no pain is more depressing than pain in the abdomen the seat of the great central sympathetic nervous system ... No one who has not experienced it can form any idea of the condition of helplessness [and] dependence to which the strongest man can be reduced in a short time by such a fever as typhoid.[81]

Johnston's illness and convalescence lasted for several months and set back his medical studies by a whole year. However, by 1886 he looked back on it in positive terms:

> The experience has been most valuable to me and the lessons learned from it have been of incalculable benefit to me. If there is one thing more than another which a medical man should be full of it is sympathy and loving kindness and I know of no better teacher of this than personal experience.[82]

The illness also marked a new stage in Johnston's relationship to nature and the countryside. Throughout his protracted illness he was confined to bed, reduced to staring at the pattern on the wallpaper, longing for the evening during the day and for the morning during his often-sleepless nights. When he began to recover he developed a passionate craving to look at the sky and the natural world outside. As soon as he was well enough his father carried him to a chair facing the window and, even fifteen years later, that first look outside

---

[80] BAHC, ZJO/4/3 (Johnston Memoir).
[81] BAHC, ZJO/4/4 (Johnston Memoir). Years afterwards Johnson concluded that the illness had in fact been appendicitis.
[82] BAHC, ZJO/4/3 (Johnston Memoir).

was imprinted on his memory: the flying clouds, the garden with its hedges and gooseberry bushes now all black and leafless, and the familiar landscape with Criffel in the distance. This first view was 'a joy unspeakable and its influence was tonic and restorative – as nature ever is to her children jaded with work, distressed by grief, or worn by illness'. Here, for the first time, nature played what was to become one of its central roles in Johnston's life: to restore his optimism, cheerfulness and faith in life.[83]

As his recovery proceeded he was allowed to go outside. Supported on either side by his mother and sister, he walked very slowly as far as the bridge. It was a cold but sunny day and he stood for a long time 'gazing with delight upon the long sweeping sinuous curves of the smoothly-flowing river and upon the beautiful landscape every feature of which I had been familiar with from childhood'. This outing was an overwhelming experience, surpassing even his first view from the window. From then on, he went out every day, anticipating the outing eagerly and seeming 'literally to feed upon the fresh air and sunshine'.[84] Complex but powerful emotional forces were at work in him. On the one hand, rural landscapes had become associated with freedom and escape from oppressive confinement, a linkage that was to play a major role in his later life. Undoubtedly he experienced the beauty of the countryside with exceptional intensity while he was convalescing, and this seems to have carried over into his subsequent apprehension of nature. He was also, even at this early date, recapitulating his childhood:

> My favourite walk being the bank of our beautiful river indulging in fond retrospective thoughts of the happy days of childhood spent there. In those daily walks I seemed to renew my youth as I regained my strength and they did a great deal towards instilling that love of outside nature which has been an unfailing source of pleasure to me.[85]

In his adult life the role of the countryside as a gateway through which he could return to Annan and childhood was to be crucial to him.

Nature and God

Marsh's suggestion that nature served as a substitute for God among many of the 'Back to the Land' enthusiasts she studied also applies to some extent to Johnston.[86] Having at length recovered from his illness, he returned to Edinburgh to complete his studies in October 1872. At some point thereafter he underwent a textbook example of a late Victorian crisis of faith and of the energetic exploration of alternative spiritualities that often succeeded it.

---

[83] BAHC, ZJO/4/3 (Johnston Memoir).
[84] BAHC, ZJO/4/4 (Johnston Memoir).
[85] BAHC, ZJO/4/4 (Johnston Memoir).
[86] Jan Marsh, *Back to the Land: The Pastoral Impulse in England, 1880–1914* (London, 1982), 5, 35.

Although he remained reticent about this, the imprint of the experience is clear. In the aftermath of his father's death in 1898 Johnston declared that his 'rebellion' was 'quelled now for ever' and that all the doubts which had 'assailed my faith' were dissipated.[87] It is hardly surprising that Johnston suffered a spiritual crisis as a young man. He was caught between two powerful forces – his father's rock-like Scots Presbyterianism and the rapid adoption by the late nineteenth-century medical profession of science as a source of intellectual authority and professional identity.[88] A man as intelligent, widely read and interested in the intellectual currents of his day could hardly ignore the profound challenge to biblical authority posed by geological uniformitarianism, evolutionary theory and textual and historical criticism of scripture. There was almost certainly a generational element in Johnston's 'rebellion' too. As Frank Turner persuasively argues, crises of faith were often a reaction against stifling religious pressures within intensely evangelical families and were 'part and parcel of the normal and necessary achievement of personal independence and autonomy of a child from a family'.[89] The relationship between William Johnston and his elder son matches this description precisely.

Like so many intellectually minded late Victorians, it was the perceived loss of existential and ethical meaning that most exercised Johnston – the universe as a vast blank. He turned to writers like Carlyle, Ruskin and Arnold, with their urgent but non-theistic moral charge, emerging in each case from a powerful heritage of evangelical Protestantism the literal coordinates of which no longer appeared tenable. Ruskin looked to nature as a source of truth and moral insight, and this seems to have proved an attractive philosophy for someone as attached to trees, flowers and the countryside as Johnston. At this time Johnston's reading also included works by other writers who were challenging the boundaries of traditional religion, seeking to detach faith from biblical literalism or attempting to develop entirely new ethical frameworks. In January 1888 he was reading George MacDonald's *Robert Falconer*, which explored a young man's spiritual struggles, and J. R. Seeley's anonymously published *Ecce Homo*, regarded as daring and scandalous in its time because it presented Christ in human terms.[90] He was strongly drawn to Jefferies, a writer whose contemporary influence has not received the attention it deserves from

---

[87] BAHC, ZJO/1/30 (Johnston Diary, 7 Jul. 1898). However, his father's death did not lead him all the way back to the Christian fold but rather to pantheism and a belief in spiritual immortality.

[88] On the adoption of science by doctors as a means of establishing their professional credentials and authority see Christopher Lawrence, *Medicine in the Making of Modern Britain, 1700–1920* (London, 2006).

[89] Frank M. Turner, 'The Victorian Crisis of Faith and the Faith That Was Lost', in Richard J. Helmstadter and Bernard Lightman (eds.), *Victorian Faith in Crisis: Essays on Continuity and Change in Nineteenth-Century Religious Belief* (London, 1990), 21.

[90] BAHC, ZJO/1/1 (Johnston Diary, 29 Jan. 1888).

recent scholarship.[91] Jefferies' intensely emotional nature mysticism seemed to offer a source of meaning and a basis for ethics in a world in which the historicity of the Bible and the divinity of Christ could no longer be taken for granted. However, the writer who addressed Johnston's needs most compellingly in the long run was Whitman. Johnston and Wallace read and discussed *Leaves of Grass* unflaggingly and, as Harry Cocks has shown, developed their own understanding of it centred on a dogma-free spirituality, loving comradeship and a belief that in some sense the soul was immortal.[92] Ultimately what Whitman offered them was an immanentist world view in which nature, understood as benign, harmonious and all-reconciling, had replaced God. At a more personal level, Whitman served as an alternative father figure for Johnston, allowing him to establish a degree of distance from William without having to reject entirely the affective, cognitive and ethical structures that had sustained him in childhood.

Anti-urbanism and Anti-industrialism

Literary and intellectual influences therefore played a significant role in Johnston's adoption of a conscious, ideological ruralism, although experiences in childhood and as a student undoubtedly predisposed him towards writers who looked to nature to resolve spiritual doubts. However, a theoretical commitment to ruralism does not go very far to explaining why Johnston chose to spend so much time in the countryside as an adult. He could just as well have sat in his study and contemplated nature from there, as Leslie Stephen allegedly did.[93] Johnston's adult love of nature and the countryside needs to be contextualized in relation to his environmental, professional, social and personal circumstances as well as cultural discourse and past experience. In particular, his antipathy to Bolton is pivotal. 'Never shall I forget the feeling of utter loneliness and desolation that came over me as I stood on the platform of Bolton Station for the first time early one morning in June 1876', he wrote in his memoir, appropriately entitled 'How I Came to Bolton'.[94] Certainly Bolton could hardly have been more different from Annan. Whereas Annan was a small market town with a gently subsiding population (4,570 in 1851; 4,309 in 1901), Bolton was a large, rapidly growing industrial borough (population 114,712 in 1851; 257,587 in 1901).[95] Annan's

---

[91] Jan Marsh, writing in 1982, was, however, well aware of his significance, observing that *The Story of My Heart* became 'a key text of the age'. Marsh, *Back to the Land*, 36.

[92] Harry Cocks, 'Calamus in Bolton: Spirituality and Homosexual Desire in Late Victorian England', *Gender & History* 13 (2001), 191–223.

[93] Marsh, *Back to the Land*, 37.

[94] BAHC, ZJO/4/1 (Johnston Memoir).

[95] These figures are for Annan Burgh and Bolton Poor Law Union respectively. GB Historical GIS / University of Portsmouth, Annan Burgh through time | Population Statistics | Total Population, A Vision of Britain through Time. www.visionofbritain.org.uk/unit/10357767/

primary economic function was as a service centre for its rural hinterland. The only local industry of note was shipbuilding and this was in decline due to the silting up of the lower reaches of the Annanwater. Bolton, conversely, was overwhelmingly dominated by two industries, cotton textiles and mining. In 1881, textiles accounted for 64 per cent of female and 27 per cent of male employment in Bolton Poor Law Union, and mining for another 25 per cent of male employment.[96] These fundamental socio-economic differences were reflected in the contrasting townscapes of the two communities. Bolton could be discerned from miles away by the pall of smoke hanging over the town. Its myriad chimneys clustered close together and gave the town a distinctive silhouette, although by 1876 the clock tower of the new town hall, completed only three years before at a cost of £167,000, rose majestically above them. Despite this impressive testimony to civic pride, Bolton remained a dirty and overcrowded town. Much of the housing was back to back, many families lived in cellars, drainage and sanitation were inadequate and the River Croal was polluted with sewage, cinders and the effluent of factories, foundries and bleach works. The public health and social consequences were predictable – crime and alcoholism were rife, while a survey in 1850 found that there were more brothels than places of worship.[97] Annan, by contrast, was a dignified, well-built town, clean, airy and firmly in the grip of a small elite of local worthies.

Even in Raikes Wood, Bolton was never far from the fringes of Johnston's consciousness. The nearby bleach works frequently obtruded: 'alas that eyesore . . . is keeping up a perpetual noise and one of its big chimneys belching forth volumes of hideous black smoke and polluting what wd be blue sky but for it and such as it'.[98] To get away from such disfigurement altogether, he had to go further into the country, as when he visited a friend in Ilkley in 1902:

> 'Tis a great delight to me to escape from Bolton to this invigorating hill-land and to ramble over its windswept moors and through its shady woods and its tinkling dells.[99]

cube/TOT_POP [accessed 30 Jul. 2014]. GB Historical GIS / University of Portsmouth, Bolton PLU/RegD through time | Population Statistics | Total Population, A Vision of Britain through Time. www.visionofbritain.org.uk/unit/10030160/cube/TOT_POP [accessed 30 Jul. 2014]. Bolton Union included a number of other smaller settlements; the Metropolitan Borough had a population of 168,215 in 1901. GB Historical GIS / University of Portsmouth, Bolton MB/CB through time | Population Statistics | Total Population, *A Vision of Britain through Time*. www.visionofbritain.org.uk/unit/10003179/cube/TOT_POP [accessed 30 Jul. 2014].

96 GB Historical GIS / University of Portsmouth, Bolton PLU/RegD through time | Industry Statistics | Occupation data classified into the 24 1881 Orders, plus sex, *A Vision of Britain through Time*. www.visionofbritain.org.uk/unit/10030160/cube/OCC_ORDER1881 [accessed 30 Jul. 2014].

97 Raymond Hargreaves, *Victorian Years: Bolton 1850–1860* (Bolton, 1985), 9, 16, 5.

98 BAHC, ZJO/1/22 (Johnston Diary, 24 Mar. 1893).

99 BAHC, ZJO/1/31 (Johnston Diary, 12 Oct. 1902).

An uncompromisingly forthright diary entry written on his way back to Bolton from several idyllic days at Dormont Grange distils Johnston's loathing of Bolton and the way this fed his ruralism:

> A glorious Sunday morning – a <u>Sun</u>-day in reality it proved to be such a day as makes one feel glad to be a Britisher for when we have a summer it is very delightful indeed. At least it is to me who am cooped up most part of the year in a big town with which I grow more and more dissatisfied the older I grow. Town life seems to be such an unnatural mode of Existence and to anyone who has a love of the open air the trees, grass and flowers it is intolerable. Now I have always loved the country and that love seems to have developed into a passion for I am never so happy as when in it. In fact I feel an entirely different being so great is the effect of pure air and sunshine upon me. And I am certain I shall never be satisfied until I can live in it altogether. As I write (at Chorley station) I feel an inexpressible repugnance to return to the grime and impurity of Bolton after spending such a week as I have . . .
>
> I say this in spite of the fact that I have been successful in Bolton in my profession far beyond my expectations and deserts, but after being there for over 13 years my heart's desire is to get away from it to the pure delights of nature.
>
> After all it is not an unnatural desire for was I not born and brought up in a little country place and are not my earliest and most lasting remembrances all of country pleasures, green fields, the beautiful river, the seashore, boating, fishing . . . the day spent at farmhouses in the hayfields among the waving corn and barley the wildflowers and fruits and the pretty birds.
>
> But I fear I must continue to sigh for these a while longer as my work lies in Bolton where I must earnestly buckle to once more and do my duty like a true man. Here I am in sight of Rivington Pike and soon the chimneys and smoke of Bolton will greet me.[100]

Professional Burdens

Johnston also cherished the countryside as an escape from his professional trials and tribulations, of which there were many. He found his lack of control over his working life particularly hard to endure, exemplified by the night work he so detested:

> [I]n spite of the generally accepted idea that 'a Dr gets used to being called up at night' I invariably answer that summons with reluctance. I wonder if the man exists who can get up at 2am without a protest, or a mild grumble

---

[100] BAHC, ZJO/1/4 (Johnston Diary, 16 Jun. 1889). Compare BAHC, ZJO/1/31 (Johnston Diary, 29 Aug. 1902): 'Oh what a blessed relief it is to me to escape even for an hour or two from the ugliness the impurity the noise and the altogether <u>unnaturalness</u> of the town to this little haven [Sunnybrae] of beauty, peace and rest!'

at being disturbed. I don't think it is in human nature to be roused out of the first sleep and be compelled to go out and yet feel perfectly good tempered about it. And yet a Dr is expected not only to do this but to go with alacrity whenever called on, to take a deep interest in the case and to make believe that so far from being a trouble it is a positive pleasure to him to lose his night's sleep!

A Dr does not get accustomed to night work. At least I don't. In fact the older I get the more do I dislike it – I protest against it – tho not of course in the patient's hearing. More especially when I find that the night call is generally unnecessary and might easily have been avoided by a little pre-thought on the part of the patient or friends. But the Drs comfort or convenience is the last thought in their minds.[101]

Johnston worked long hours with few intermissions. A typical day began at 8am with a cold shower followed by breakfast at 8.30. He saw patients until 9.15 or 9.20 and then set out on his first round of visits in Great Bolton. After calling at home for messages at 10.30, he resumed his round, finishing up in the working-class suburb of Darcy Lever, where he had many patients. He returned home for dinner at 1pm, saw patients and dispensed between 2 and 3 and then went out on foot to finish his list of calls. After tea at 5 he consulted from 6 often until nearly 9, after which he sometimes had to make evening calls. Supper was at 9.30 and bed at 10.30 or 11.[102] Worse still were the night-time midwifery cases, as on Tuesday, 24 May 1892:

> Since yesterday I have had a notable experience. One of my midwifery cases – Mrs S. – proving very tedious I was compelled to remain with her all night – and a tough job I had. The birth after a long and painful struggle, occurred at 2.10am and from that time till 4am I was engaged in a desperate fight with haemorrhage which continued intermittently all that time and finding that it continued to be uncontrollable and fearing for the patient's life I sent for Dr Mallett who came promptly and with whose valuable assistance the haemorrhage was got under [control]. But the patient could not be left till nearly 6 am by which time I was completely 'pumped' physically, to say nothing of the nervous exhaustion due to the anxiety and worry about the case. I then came home and got a couple of hours sleep but had to be up again at 8.30 to resume my ordinary work feeling about as 'half-baked' as ever I did in my life. The patient I am glad to say is now doing well and the baby is alive and well.[103]

Six days later Johnston had what he called 'rather a crowded sort of day', beginning with a midwifery case at 1.20am, continuing with two further births, 30 or 40 visits and concluding only at 11.30pm.[104]

---

[101] BAHC, ZJO/1/1 (Johnston Diary, 29 Jan. 1888).
[102] BAHC, ZJO/1/1 (Johnston Diary, 29 Jan. 1888).
[103] BAHC, ZJO/1/20 (Johnston Diary, 24 May 1892).
[104] BAHC, ZJO/1/20 (Johnston Diary, 30 May 1892).

Outbreaks of epidemic disease imposed an even heavier workload on him. During the 1891 flu he recorded that he had had '9 days of the hardest work' in his life, dispensing for up to eighty patients in a single day, and at one point coming down with 'a touch of influenza' himself.[105] Over and above the ever-present risk of infection to which his profession exposed him, Johnston also encountered less obvious but equally lethal dangers. On one occasion, for example, he was chased out of a house to which he had been called by an insane poker-wielding maniac threatening to kill him.[106] On the whole, however, it was not so much the physical rigours and risks of medical work that irked him but the emotional vexations. It required 'constant vigilance' to keep his practice together: while doctors had made great strides in establishing a professional monopoly on medical care by the time he qualified from Edinburgh, this did little to reduce competition *within* the profession. In the early 1890s many of his long-standing patients in Darcy Lever deserted him, won over by the unscrupulous wiles of a Dr Brodie, who 'went about in a blustering, bumptious manner, telling folks the most marvellous tales of himself and his wonderful abilities and the extraordinary cures he had made'.[107] Worse still was the ingratitude of patients, a theme Johnston returned to frequently. He lamented that patients who had hung on his every word while ill were often tardy, even resentful, about paying their bills once they had recovered. Many of the most trying difficulties arose from the contradictions inherent in private medical practice. He wanted to help his patients but depended for his living on making them pay. He admired the 'honesty . . . integrity . . . and uprightness of life' of many of the Darcy Lever villagers but could not always emulate this himself because he would lose his patients if he told them their complaints were more imaginary than real and they should not have called him during the night for trivial causes.[108] These dilemmas became more acute during the 1890s as Johnston moved to the left. Should he be open about his increasingly socialist convictions? This seemed the only honest and dignified course of action. But he would almost certainly lose many of his middle-class patients, whom he had been using to cross-subsidize those too poor to pay. In order to maintain what he regarded as an acceptable income, he would have to discontinue this, defeating one of his principal purposes.

Johnston's rural havens provided a refuge from these professional tribulations. He seized a brief window of opportunity to go to Raikes Wood after being 'kept very busy' for ten days during the influenza epidemic, for example, and then again after a further draining week.[109] Another of his visits to the wood followed a taxing midwifery case which 'fairly took it out of me'.[110]

[105]   BAHC, ZJO/1/11 (Johnston Diary, 9 Jun. 1891).
[106]   BAHC, ZJO/1/29 (Johnston Diary, 21 Jun. 1898).
[107]   BAHC, ZJO/1/20 (Johnston Diary, 2 Apr. 1892).
[108]   BAHC, ZJO/1/20 (Johnston Diary, 2 Apr. 1892).
[109]   BAHC, ZJO/1/11 (Johnston Diary, 12 May and 9 Jun. 1891).
[110]   BAHC, ZJO/1/22 (Johnston Diary, 21 Aug. 1892).

Sitting in such a place he was secure from interruption – patients could not come and harass him since they did not know he was there. It is evident from his descriptions of these occasions, mostly written *in situ*, that the contrasting surroundings also helped him regain his peace of mind. There was little in a wood that was likely to provoke associations with medical anxieties – no consulting rooms, clamorous or suffering patients, drugs, surgical implements, medical literature or any of the other paraphernalia of his professional life. Associations are in the mind, and had Johnston's anxieties been sufficiently intense it is unlikely that removing himself from the environments in which they arose would have been sufficient to quell them, even temporarily. However, the less the overlap between the refuge environment and that in which the anxieties arise, the easier it is likely to be to turn thoughts into different channels. This must always to some extent involve an act of will, one that in Johnston's case presumably became easier through force of habit – the regular sequence of walking into the wood, finding a place to sit, getting out and opening his diary. Later in life, the garden at Sunnybrae, with its flowers, birds and view of distant hills, met many of the same needs:

> What a blessed relief it is for me to escape from the turmoil of Bolton and medical practice there to this! Truly 'tis a haven of refuge and I and my dear M are at one in our thorough appreciation of the Blessing that has come into our lives.[111]

Indeed, wherever his work took him, Johnston seems to have sought out a 'sequestered nook' to escape its pressures. Even under the highly regulated regime of Queen Mary's Military Hospital he found a 'quiet and restful spot' by the side of a tiny streamlet meandering through the meadows, providing a 'welcome change from the turmoil of the red-bricked hospital'.[112]

Problem-Solving

Johnston could have taken advantage of the freedom from disturbance and the mental calm he found in the countryside as a programmatic opportunity to solve some of the many practical, emotional and ethical difficulties that arose in the course of his life. In the main he eschewed the instrumentality of this approach, preferring to allow nature to take complete possession of his mind so that he was wholly absorbed in and taken up by the influences of the place and the moment. However, sometimes his thoughts turned of their own volition to problems that preoccupied him. Sitting outdoors on his mother's birthday, for example, he began as usual with close observation of the scene before him, noticing how the haymakers held their rakes in different ways, and a two-horse rake in the same

---

[111] BAHC, ZJO/1/31 (Johnston Diary, 4 Jun. 1902).
[112] BAHC, ZJO/1/40 (Johnston Diary, 25 Jun. 1916).

field. His attention then shifted away from the external scene and thoughts about his mother arose – how much he owed to her love and self-sacrifice, her deafness and the way this isolated her, followed by fears that he had not repaid her sufficiently for all that she had done for him. This led to a resolution to go to see her before long, which he put into practice soon afterwards.[113]

Restorative Ruralism

More important to Johnston was the restorative function of the countryside at an affective rather than a conscious cognitive level. Being in the countryside allowed him to shrug off the vexations, disappointments and anxieties of daily life and typically he came back from visits to Raikes Wood or other rural landscapes cheered, refreshed and reinvigorated. His 1889 Dormont Grange holiday had, he concluded on his return, been 'a week of pure and unalloyed delight and has been a splendid restorative to my mind and body jaded with my town life and professional work'.[114] Out for a walk with Wallace near Rivington a few years later on a 'simply perfect' summer evening, he was delighted by the bright colours and sheer abundance of the vegetation and the 'soul-refreshing greenness' of the grass.[115] So pronounced was this restorative effect that Johnston even heard it in the sounds of nature, recording on another occasion in Raikes Wood that 'a couple of sparrows are telling me to "cheer-up! cheer-up" as plainly as they can speak'.[116] Nature was among other things a form of spiritual medicine for Johnston – just as he cured others, nature cured him. On one of his return visits to Annan he wandered up the Annanwater as far as the disused quarry of Galabank where:

> Alone and entirely secluded from human observation I spent two good hours. I had not even a book of any kind with me and sitting down upon an old tree root with no other company but the birds ... Oh it was such a quiet haven of rest and I could feel the subtle influence of nature penetrating me filling my soul with its benignant medicinal virtue and much did I regret having to leave it and return to the town.[117]

This restorative, medicinal function of nature seems to have remained a constant feature of Johnston's adult life – an undated 1916 diary entry about a walk that cheered his depressed spirits is, for example, headed 'A Woodland Siesta – the Vis Medicatrix Naturae' ('the healing power of nature', a phrase attributed to Hippocrates).[118]

---

[113] BAHC, ZJO/1/22 (Johnston Diary, 21 Jun. 1892).
[114] BAHC, ZJO/1/4 (Johnston Diary, 14–21 Jun. 1889).
[115] BAHC, ZJO/1/22 (Johnston Diary, 3 Jun. 1892).
[116] BAHC, ZJO/1/22 (Johnston Diary, 7 Jun. 1892).
[117] BAHC, ZJO/1/4 (Johnston Diary, 17 Jun. 1889).
[118] BAHC, ZJO/1/40 (Johnston Diary, undated [summer 1916]).

A closer look at Johnston's loafing narratives helps to explicate the restorative effect of the countryside on him. Although they are temporally and spatially highly specific, they typically progress through regular affective stages. The first of these is the fixing of location (often given as a title, for example 'In Raikes Wood' or 'A Garden Note'). This is followed by the fixing of time, season and weather – '[i]t is 8pm and a lovely summer's evening'.[119] The third stage is usually an emphasis on Johnston being 'alone, quite alone'. The fourth stage, much the lengthiest, consists of detailed, close multisensory observation of the landscape around him. The final stage expresses the thoughts and feelings that have arisen in him while he has been loafing. All these elements are present in his diary entry for 6 July 1906:

An Early Morning Scene: Hay Harvesting

This morning I was awake [sic] by an unusual sound in the field over my garden wall – the sound of the mowing machine. Soon I was out and into the garden and mounting the wall. I looked at the picturesque scene. Here are some of its elements:-

A morning of perfect tranquillity – not a breath of air stirring, the trees motionless in their every twig and leaf – a grey haze filling the sky and a slight mist overhanging the field where the fine team, driven by the man uncoated with up-rolled shirt sleeves, were tramping through the long grass and dragging the great mower whose whirring knives were swathing it down like the waves of a grassy sea – and how responsive were the horses to the driver's slightest touch and word! 'Way!', 'Gee up!', 'Steady there, Rose!', 'Back!', 'Wo!', 'Stand up!' etc.

And out in the field beyond – the lowing of cattle just being driven through the gate – the fluting of a blackbird and the vociferous, oft-repeated musical phrasings of our grand-voiced thrush from the tops of the sycamore – the warble of a tiny wren in the hedgerow and of a chaffinch nearby – overhead the swallows darting and screaming on the hunt for breakfast – and over all the serenity, the peace, the beauty and the alluring charm of an English summer's morn.

Long and long did I stand gazing at the lovely scene drinking in its spirit – so refreshing, so revivifying to the human soul attuned to its message![120]

Loafing was above all a spiritual exercise for Johnston, with close affinities to meditation, involving as it did intense concentration on something outside himself. His complete absorption in the specificities of location, time, weather and season relates to suggestions that modern experience has become increasingly detached from these verities.[121] Some researchers go further, arguing that

---

[119] BAHC, ZJO/1/30 (Johnston Diary, 26 Jul. 1898).
[120] BAHC, ZJO/1/33 (Johnston Diary, 6 Jul. 1906).
[121] Landry, *The Invention of the Countryside*; Richard Mabey, *Nature Cure* (London, 2005).

our collective alienation from nature has exposed us to 'Nature Deficit Disorder', a view with which Johnston would almost certainly have sympathized.[122]

Solitude and Communion

Solitude was essential to Johnston when he was loafing:

> I am sitting upon a sandhill on the sea shore, south from St Anne's, half buried amid the long dried grass which covers the sandhills as far as the eye can reach upon either side as well as in front and behind ... With sandhill, grass and shore, gull and lark, sea and sky and sun I am absolutely alone – and very soothing it is to sit here 'far from the madding crowd'.[123]

Yet one of loafing's prime functions was achieving a sense of complete together-ness and communion with those he loved, especially after the death of his parents in 1898. This is perhaps less paradoxical than it sounds. It was only when he was able to exclude distracting social or psychic intrusions that he could reach deeply enough into himself to experience this profound sense of unity:

> I ... am now sitting in the shade of the summer house, alone, absolutely alone except for my pussy cat which slumbers at my feet. And yet I am not alone – for am I not surrounded by the spirits of my dear friends – gone indeed from my mortal vision, but surely not gone from me? Amid the hush and stillness of this glorious morning I am conscious of a nearness of their personal presences – Father, Mother and uncles, aunts, friends many – which seem to hallow the place and make it sacred.[124]

For Johnston, as for most of the other diarists, the countryside was also a crucial site for the creation, development and sustenance of relationships in a more direct sense. To be out in the countryside with another person, or group of people, with whom he felt wholly at one could be as rich, satisfying and profound an experi-ence as to sit alone in a wood. Just as rural solitude enabled his 'best self' to live, so being out in the fields and woods, on the hills or by the sea, with someone he cared deeply about enabled Johnston to achieve a complete togetherness with them that was difficult or impossible to attain in an urban context. This is particularly obvious in relation to the two people whom in adult life he perhaps loved most – Maggie and James Wallace. His walks with Maggie were infrequent but

---

[122] Richard Louv, *Last Child in the Woods: Saving Our Children from Nature-Deficit Disorder* (New York, 2005); Andrew Biro, *Denaturalizing Ecological Politics: Alienation from Nature from Rousseau to the Frankfurt School and Beyond* (Toronto, 2005).

[123] BAHC, ZJO/1/34 (Johnston Diary, 10 Apr. 1909). Compare the very similar entry for 24 May 1902: BAHC, ZJO/1/31.

[124] BAHC, ZJO/1/33 (Johnston Diary, 2 Sep. 1906). Compare another 'Garden Note', for 25 Sep. 1904, BAHC, ZJO/1//32: 'a feeling of quiet restfulness and peace possesses my soul ... I ponder and send out loving thoughts to my loved ones – my friends'.

much cherished. They seem to have taken place more often when the two were on holiday – perhaps the pattern of their daily life in Bolton did not provide many opportunities for spending time outdoors together. On 3 June 1890 they were staying at Grange-over-Sands and climbed Yewbarrow Crag together, where they 'enjoyed an hour's "confab" and the delightful prospect from that commanding rock ... the fine fresh breeze blowing on our faces the glorious stretch of sea and land spread before us'. Later that day they went for another 'delightful walk' and had a 'nice talk about literature and the delights of nature'.[125] What emerges from Johnston's diary but is difficult to capture in quotations is the gladness and buoyant sense of freedom that being together in the countryside seems to have released in Johnston and Maggie. It was similar with Wallace although the shared happiness with Maggie had a more tender quality whereas exuberance was the keynote with Wallace:

> We were in exuberant spirits – and as we strode along the lark carolled and soared heavenwards, the robins and thrushes and blackbirds sang their vesper hymns in the woods and from the hedges and we sang aloud our joy of heart too.
> Of course we talked but so enjoyable was it I seem to have little recollection of what it was all about.[126]

Comradeship

Comradeship was, as Cocks perceptively argues, the glue that held the Eagle Street College together. He draws attention to the depth, strength and durability of the friendship between College members and above all between Wallace and Johnston. College meetings, initially at Wallace's Eagle Street house, defined the group but for Wallace and Johnston, tête à tête walks in the countryside were at least as formative. '[M]uch did I enjoy that delightful walk and that sweet talk with my dear dear friend and comrade', Johnston noted in his diary after one such occasion.[127] These walks became increasingly frequent and enriching after Wallace moved out to Adlington, in a verdant valley at the foot of Rivington Pike. The two men's mutual delight in the landscape confirmed the congruence of their sensibilities and drew them still closer together:

> When we were passing a tiny brook I said: 'Listen to that brook! It seems to be talking. I wonder what it is saying?'

[125] BAHC, ZJO/1/9 (Johnston Diary, 3 Jun. 1890).
[126] BAHC, ZJO/1/20 (Johnston Diary, 3 Jun. 1892).
[127] BAHC, ZJO/1/19 (Johnston Diary, 18 Feb. 1892). See also, for example, BAHC, ZJO/1/32 (Johnston Diary, 22 and 30 Apr. 1904).

Figure 6.1   James Wallace (seated) with John Johnston on 5 June 1921
Reproduced by kind permission of Bolton Library and Museum Services (BAHC,
ZWN/11/2/15)

JWW: 'If you <u>could</u> tell, you w[oul]d be a greater poet than Walt [Whitman]. It says
         different things to different people and to each one it says something different.'
JJ: 'What does it say to you?'
JWW: 'I don't know.'

> And then he quoted from Jean Paul Richter. The exact words I did not
> catch. But it was to this effect 'Oh my immortal soul! Thou discernest
> things wh[ich] I never have and never shall see.'[128]

[128]   BAHC, ZJO/1/22 (Johnston Diary, 4 Jul. 1892).

In Wallace and Johnston's eyes the comradeship they experienced on their walks extended to and encompassed the whole of nature, including, in principle, the rest of humanity. However, it was much easier to feel in harmony with humanity generally than particularly and the two men had ambivalent feelings about encountering other people when they were out in the countryside. They would have liked to share the profound truths and way of seeing they believed they had discovered but the obtruding presence of discordant elements threatened to puncture the experience of universal harmony they sought:

> Going along the road we passed two or three couples whereon he said 'There's quite a crowd here! We must have this altered.'

JJ: 'But if you find this country so enjoyable and if nature speaks to you such beautiful things and is so beautiful herself why sh[oul]d you object to others coming to enjoy it too?'
JWW: 'Well, if you don't <u>know</u> why, I can't tell you.'
JJ: 'Is it because you think that nature will not speak to them unless they, too, come alone?'
JWW: 'Why, yes! Something like that!'[129]

Conversely, Johnston was keen to share the rural landscapes and places he loved with those to whom he felt close. He and Maggie went on walks with College member Fred Wild and his wife, and he was even prepared to take Wild and other close friends such as Edward Carpenter ('a dear good fellow') to Raikes Wood.

Nature's Profusion

A long-established tradition discerns beneath the many cultural layers of humanity's relationship to landscape a tragic kernel – the knowledge of our inescapable mortality, for which we seek consolation in the apparent permanence of landscape. 'Et in Arcadia ego' – even in Arcadia there is death.[130] In Johnston's case this was initially rather muted, although as the years passed the countryside became charged with meanings in relation to the deaths, anticipated or actual, of those he loved. Even then, however, he continued to associate nature overwhelmingly with life and joy rather than death and suffering. This vision of nature was as arbitrary and partial as its red-in-tooth-and-claw Tennysonian inverse: he was drawn to and actively sought out those aspects of nature that

---

[129] BAHC, ZJO/1/22 (Johnston Diary, 5 Jul. 1892).
[130] 'I [death] am present even in Arcadia.' On the ambiguities of this phrase, which seems first to have been used in Guercino's eponymous painting, circa 1618–22, see Erwin Panofsky, 'Et in Arcadia Ego: On the Conception of Transience in Poussin and Watteau', in R. Klibansky and H. J. Paton (eds.), *Philosophy and History: Essays Presented to Ernst Cassirer* (Oxford, 1936) 223–54. See also Schama, *Landscape and Memory*, 517–25.

were consonant with his own prior conception of it, notably sunshine and flowers. He wrote, for example, of 'a dozen celandines all open wide to the sun ... sending a beam of hope and joy into my heart'.[131] Even in the absence of sunshine, flowers rarely failed to lift his spirits; phrases such as 'gather the flowers of happiness' recur in the diaries. It gave him special pleasure to see flowers in great drifts, a compelling manifestation in his eyes of nature's inexhaustible profusion and abundance, as on a journey north from Bolton in 1889:

> The country through which we passed [on the train] was in all the luxuriance of its summer beauty – one remarkable feature being the immense number of marguerites which fairly carpeted the sides of the railway completely whitening the pass as if it had been snowed on. I never remember seeing such a profusion of this beautiful daisy.[132]

Therapeutic Ruralism

Johnston was a compassionate man, sometimes wrenchingly affected by the suffering of his patients. One example among many was the brush maker William H-:

> He told me a good deal of his life-history which is pathetically sad. He has been ill for some months. This kept gradually worsening until now he is dropsical in legs and altogether hopelessly consumptive – wasted to a shadow.[133]

Whether by chance or design, Johnston went for a cycle ride round the roads of Great Lever that afternoon and was much cheered by the freedom of movement, flowers and birdsong.

Another regular patient was a 'Mr B'. Visiting him on 20 May 1892, Johnston found him 'slowly going downhill – but oh so patient so very patient was the dear old man'. Evidently much moved, he went straight out into a patch of wood near Mr B's house in Sharples, rather than waiting for the next convenient opportunity to get to Raikes Wood, and wrote a Nature Note infused with unwonted gravity.[134] There seems little doubt that what he had just experienced deepened his response to the landscape on this occasion. Equally, the beauty and tranquillity of the scene facilitated the full

---

[131] BAHC, ZJO/1/20 (Johnston Diary, 2 Apr. 1892). Compare BAHC, ZJO/1/4 (Johnston Diary, 14–21 Jun. 1889): 'The day turned out to be gloriously fine the sunlight streaming down in all his power and filling the Earth with happiness and life', prompting him to write a poem.

[132] BAHC, ZJO/1/4 (Johnston Diary, 14–21 Jun. 1889).

[133] BAHC, ZJO/1/20 (Johnston Diary, 24 May 1892).

[134] BAHC, ZJO/1/20 (Johnston Diary, 20 May 1892).

development and expression of his feeling, which a jarring environment or one more subject to interruptions might not have done.

A more complex example followed from the visit of W. Hibbs, a travel companion of Johnston's and occasional member of the College, on 20 June 1914. Hibbs had come to consult Johnston professionally – he was suffering from a brain haemorrhage that had affected his speech, memory and intellectual powers. Johnston's diary entry for the day in question begins as a Garden Note:

> A sweet evening after a hot day. I am sitting in the summer house now embowered in honeysuckle and clematis, the graceful tendrils of which are entwined round the stems and swaying into the doorway . . . Beyond the garden is the grey mist enshrouding the distant hills, over which is the sunset sky . . . Over the wall in the field to the right the haymakers are busy stacking the surplus of their season's fine crop and the sound of the voices of children float over on the breeze as they romp and play among the hay and on the great rick.

This, however, leads into an account of the consultation with Hibbs:

> Alas that I have been witness of another picture – a human picture – a picture of pathos and sadness.

After a detailed description of Hibbs' pitiful condition Johnston reflects on the implications for himself:

> To such a condition may any of us be reduced by a tiny clot of blood upon our brain. I have a premonition that I shall one day have an apoplectic seizure and become a poor, paralysed, helpless thing . . . An intimation from the King of Terrors that I too am on the open road of the universe – the Road which ends in the Dark Valley which each one must enter and traverse alone, alone alone![135]

This is all the more striking for the infrequency with which Johnston expresses concerns about his own mortality in the diaries.[136] It would seem that the peace of mind induced by loafing in the summer house and writing the Garden Note enabled him to access his feelings about the consultation with Hibbs and articulate the deeper fears that lay behind them.

A fourth example of the way Johnston's landscape practices helped him to express and to some extent process distressing experiences is his response to the outbreak of the First World War. He was called upon to assess the fitness to serve of a large number of Bolton army volunteers and found it a trying task, taking

---

[135] BAHC, ZJO/1/35 (Johnston Diary, 20 Jun. 1914).
[136] One other example is the diary entry for 19 Sep. 1900, BAHC, ZJO/1/31, following the death of his Aunt Frances.

a secret pleasure in rejecting recruits while feeling sorry at disappointing them so bitterly. Afterwards he wrote a Garden Note:

> It is a beautiful morning with intermittent sunshine and a fine fresh breeze wh[ich] sways the trees still in full leaf, till they sigh and rustle like the incoming tide breaking upon the pebbly beach at Peel … And here I sit alone – thinking reminiscing (oh how much does one seem to do this as one grows older!) pondering over many things – friends, problems, experiences etc – and over all my thoughts is the terrible one of that European horror of war – of men – Christians all – massacring each other at the bidding of rulers. And for what a Phantom?[137]

So fundamental and various were the functions nature and the countryside played in Johnston's life that he was understandably discomposed when circumstances prevented him from getting out. On one occasion, reduced to desperate measures by the persistent rain that prevented him going for a cycle ride, he tried Bolton's fêted Turkish baths instead but this unfortunately left him with a bad headache.[138] Worst of all was the gloom of winter. It is true that he appreciated snow, frosty nights and winter sunrises and sunsets.[139] But it was too cold to loaf and even his walks and cycle rides were few and far between after October and before March. The difficulty was that, alone among the diarists, he had developed a form of ruralism that depended on signs of life, growth and plenitude, which became increasingly scarce as the nights drew in. Moreover, as he grew older he became ever more attached to sunshine and warmth. It seems likely that the suspension of his ruralist activities was one of the main reasons Johnston was often low-spirited in mid-winter.[140] His diaries register his delight at the first day of the year warm enough to sit outside again.[141]

Mortality and Loss

Johnston's devotion to his parents came at a price: he was haunted by their anticipated mortality. Reflecting on his mother's ageing in Raikes Wood, he found a parallel to it in the change of the seasons: 'each day is shorter than its predecessor and brings us nearer to the time of sadness, and death'. However, rather than seeking consolation for this in the apparent eternity of the natural

---

[137] BAHC, ZJO/1/35 (Johnston Diary, 23 Aug. 1914).
[138] BAHC, ZJO/1/22 (Johnston Diary, 4 Jul. 1892).
[139] BAHC, ZJO/1/33 (Johnston Diary, 22 Nov. 1911).
[140] See for example BAHC, ZJO/1/49 (Johnston Diary, 20 Dec. 1918). This was probably one of the motivations of his holidays to Morocco in February 1903 and Egypt in February 1905. BAHC, ZJO/1/32 (undated note at end of 1903 entries) and BAHC, ZJO/2/4–6.
[141] BAHC, ZJO/1/33 (Johnston Diary, 23 Apr. 1913).

world, Johnston wrapped the present more vividly around him, stepping into the moment rather than out of time:

> But my visit to this dear little wood has heartened me and I feel inclined to exclaim 'Not yet! Not yet that time of gloom! Look around you and see those fields shining in the glorious sun and listen to those woodland choristers – go it my black-robed golden beaked little friend up there – for I dearly love to hear you! – trilling for . . . gladness of soul and wanting me to be glad too and to enjoy the sweet summer joys and all their joys while they last too! I <u>will</u> give myself up to them and I will get all the joy and gladness I can out of them.[142]

So determined was Johnston to recruit nature onto his side in the struggle of life-in-the-present against death-in-the-future that he folded a sycamore or elm leaf into this page of his diary, as if it were a charm or elixir against the looming shadows ahead.[143]

The dreaded time came in 1898. By May William's health had deteriorated to the point that Johnston brought him, with difficulty, back to Bolton. He was quite helpless and his son and daughter-in-law had to do everything for him. Johnston had to be up many hours each night attending him, which he found a 'terrible trial' on top of his regular work as a doctor. But far worse was the 'beclouding' of his father's true self:

> His interest in the world is nil hardly anything concerns him but his physical wants and necessities.
> And oh what a heart-rending spectacle all this is for me![144]

In early June they took him back to Annan. William's health was collapsing rapidly and by the 9th he was delirious, having to be restrained physically from getting up in the night again and again. Johnston's account is piercing:

> And here let me make a confession! I am afraid that now and again my patience was tried <u>beyond</u> its power of endurance and I fear I may have yielded to the provoking irritation at times and perhaps been less gentle with him than I ought to have been.
> After he had got to sleep I was tortured with that thought and made myself quite ill with it.
> If my self-accusing is right may God forgive me!

---

[142] BAHC, ZJO/1/22 (Johnston Diary, 21 Jun. 1892). Compare BAHC, ZJO/1/33 (Johnston Diary, 24 Jun. 1906): 'And now we have passed the zenith of the year! Three days ago the sun passed his meridian and commenced his slow but certain journey downward to winter's darkest day! But now is the joy time of the year – and a real joy time should we make of it.'

[143] BAHC, ZJO/1/22 (Johnston Diary, 21 Jun. 1892).

[144] BAHC, ZJO/1/29 (Johnston Diary, 19 May 1898).

In the morning, though no longer delirious, William was very weak and tearful, crying at the least thing. But his son had to return to Bolton:

> It cut me to the heart to have to leave him and the thought of him is scarcely ever absent from my mind.

Before he and Maggie left, however, they went for a walk along the Annanwater. There could have been no better balm for his distempered spirit. The sun shone, the sky was blue, every bush and tree seemed to be festooned with blossom and the meadows were swathed in golden-yellow buttercups. As they continued their walk:

> A beautiful collie – Roy was his name some children told us – followed us and as we sat on the bank Roy nestling up to my dear M as if he had known her all his life the peace and serenity and beauty of that lovely scene entered my soul and I felt that somehow despite their present untoward appearances everything must 'work together for good to them that love the Lord'.[145]

What is particularly striking here is how, as Johnston experiences it, the landscape links and creates unity between people and the life around them, connecting him to Maggie at a time he might otherwise have felt separated from her by the grim, intense experience he was undergoing; Maggie to the collie Roy, all three of them to the children who know Roy's name, and ultimately everything to the universal good.

William died not long afterwards. A few days later Johnston went to sit in the cemetery and wrote an entry in his diary sitting on the curbstone around his father's grave. The idiom is that of Raikes Wood and the Garden Notes. What had begun as a self-conscious personal practice had become, it would seem, sufficiently deep-rooted that he could turn to it even in the extremity of his father's death. Just as in Raikes Wood, he began by attempting to attune himself to nature: the murmuring of the Annanwater; the gentle breeze; cattle lowing; 'wee birds' twittering. While he sat there, attending closely to the sounds around him, he became, according to the account in his diary, increasingly conscious of his father's 'presence'.[146] Nature had become a portal to the spirit world, to unity with his now-dead father, just as previously it had enabled him to achieve a state of oneness with Maggie or his College friends.

He responded to Ellen's death a few weeks later in a similar way.[147] Back in Bolton his garden became an important site of memory. Sitting there peacefully a year later brought thoughts of 'my poor dear departed ones'.[148] In 1902 the anniversary of his mother's death fell on a Sunday, so he was able to spend

[145] BAHC, ZJO/1/29 (Johnston Diary, 10 Jun. 1898).
[146] BAHC, ZJO/1/30 (Johnston Diary, 26 Jul. 1898).
[147] BAHC, ZJO/1/30 (Johnston Diary, 4 Aug. 1898).
[148] BAHC, ZJO/1/30 (Johnston Diary, 30 May 1899).

most of it in the garden, bringing 'thoughts, thoughts, thoughts too deep too sacred for expression but very sweet and precious despite their sadness'.[149] Places connected with his parents now became vital conduits for Johnston as it was there that he felt most conscious of their continuing 'presence'. Walking with Maggie in the grounds of Shap Wells Hotel, which he had often visited with them, he felt the wood was like a 'vast cathedral'. The following day he spent mainly alone:

> As I wander about this place I am vividly conscious of the presence of my father who seems to sanctify it and fill it with a strange and deep seated joy.[150]

As might be expected, it was at Annan, to which he continued to return frequently, that he felt the connection with his parents most strongly. A poem he wrote on a visit in August the following year sums up the way in which Annan, its river and the sense of home, security and love they held were now more deeply than ever embedded in the core of his being:

> Though Eastward, though Westward, afar may I stray –
> Nor distance, nor time can e'er sever
> My hert frae its sanctuary – Annan the fair,
> And its beautiful, soul-gladdening river.[151]

Johnston's happy childhood in Annan was one of the foundations of his ruralism but before 1898 his accounts of countryside walks, rides and loafing only infrequently invoke Annan. Thereafter, however, thoughts of Annan often emerged in relation to and found expression through being in the countryside. A particularly poignant occasion was the consecration of a new cemetery at Queen Mary's Hospital in Whalley:

> While the service . . . was proceeding, the birds sang the breezes blew and the sun shone upon the scene which was backed by noble Pendle Hill along whose steep sides of green the sun-shadows slowly travelled. The fields arrayed in their tricolour of white daisies, golden buttercups and emerald grass . . .
>
> As we stood there a Midland train passed on its way to Scotland – and the sight of it took my thoughts to Annan and Home and the quiet little God's acre where lie all that was mortal of my dear good father and mother in sound of the music of Annan water.
>
> After the ceremony I spent an hour in the fields and in the woodland dells where little fragrant wild roses are now flinging out their sprays of pink and white high into the air from the hawthorn hedges.[152]

---

[149] BAHC, ZJO/1/32 (Johnston Diary, 3 Aug. 1902).
[150] BAHC, ZJO/1/31 (Johnston Diary, 16 Aug. 1902).
[151] BAHC, ZJO/1/32 (Poem dated 10 Aug. 1903).
[152] BAHC, ZJO/1/40 (Johnston Diary, 29 Jun. 1916).

The Coming of Night

A less obvious effect on Johnston's ruralism of the death of his parents, and the growing consciousness of mortality and aging this prompted, was a new responsiveness to the coming of night and the turning of the year:

> A wee birdie has been chirruping near me but he has now ceased and softly so softly silently descends the veil of Night upon the world.[153]

There is a breathless, rapt quality to Johnston's descriptions of nightfall after 1898:

> The only sounds are the soft splash of the tiny wavelets upon the beach far below, the boom of the homing bees, the call of swiftly flying seagulls, the occasional evensong of a robin and the voices of the children playing in the far-off town – not a breath of air is stirring – deeper and deeper glows the sky until at the horizon it is red-gold. Then slowly slowly does it fade – the evening star appears in the glow – others follow – gradually does the darkness deepen – then out rush the stars seemingly all at once – and it is night.[154]

Watching night descend on a similar occasion a few years later impressed Johnston with 'the air of serenity and peace and rest which broods over the scene like a holy presence'.[155] As this suggests, while the broad outlines of Johnston's ruralism remained largely unchanged by his parents' deaths, there is a greater tenderness, reverence and spiritual awe in his descriptions of rural landscapes and natural phenomena:

> Soon came the moon lifting her golden rim from the edge of the horizon and slowly raising her great disc ... Up and up rose this great glowing plate into the sky of soft grey, lighting the darkling world with its effulgent beams until it hung in serene majesty of loveliness – Queen of the Night – Luna Regina, Majestica, Imperialis.[156]

This new sensibility did not displace the sensual, embodied delight in nature so evident in Johnston's younger days. Rather, it seems to have added an extra layer to it:

> After a week of bitter East wind drying up everything and making people feel miserable this morning broke benignant – the wind gone, the sun shining out bright and warm, the sky blue, the birds singing – the cuckoo

---

[153] BAHC, ZJO/1/31 (Johnston Diary, 7 Oct. 1902). On Johnston's awareness of his ageing see BAHC, ZJO/1/32 (Johnston Diary, 25 Sep. 1904).

[154] BAHC, ZJO/1/33 (Johnston Diary, 17 Sep. 1906).

[155] BAHC, ZJO/1/33 (Johnston Diary, 22 Jul. 1911). Compare BAHC, ZJO/1/31 (Johnston Diary, 7 Sep. 1902): 'over all there broods a spirit of peace and rest and holy joy'.

[156] BAHC, ZJO/1/40 (Johnston Diary, 5 Jun. 1916).

again calling – and the world adorned in all its summer loveliness and charm, speaking of peace and joy and hope and love.

Sitting alone here in the summer house – my dear M[aggie] has gone to church – how beautiful is the prospect, how serene ... the air is soft and voluptuous – the sun is warm and bright and in my heart is a sweet and holy calm and a serene happiness – as if the day had been made specially for me.[157]

The links between Johnston's intensified awareness of the passing of things, his feelings about Annan and his perceptions of landscape emerge with particular clarity in an account of a walk he undertook with his friend Lieutenant Mitchell while working at Queen Mary's in 1916:

> As we wandered on in the sunset we revelled in the beauty through which we passed, and noting the changes that were slowly creeping over the countryside. Two weeks ago the hawthorn was at its acme of loveliness – the hedges being white with the summer snow which now lay scattered over the fields thro which we passed. And the thought that came uppermost was that of the transitoriness of things in the order of nature ... At the end of our walk we sat down by the river – [I] was again reminded of my beloved Annanwater.[158]

Pantheism

The most significant change in Johnston's ruralism brought about by the death of his parents, however, was that it crystallized his latent pantheism, previously manifest only in generalized, even evasive, intimations. It is telling that this seems to have come to him while writing a Nature Note sitting on a rock above the Annanwater. After describing how a cow came down to drink and hearing children prattling in the local dialect familiar from his childhood, Johnston observed that the beauty of the scene:

> seems to sink deeply into me – to interpenetrate my very being. I have a vivid sense of the one unity the oneness of the universe and of the essential unity of myself with my surroundings – that these rocks trees flowers birds and the flowing river are a part of me – that I am one with them and that we are all equally divine all manifestations of the spiritual the only real and permanent world. Here surely does one feel not only in touch with but a veritable part of the infinite.[159]

---

[157] BAHC, ZJO/1/32 (Johnston Diary, 12 Jun. 1904). A week earlier Johnston had relished a 'blissful day of sunshine ... filling the Earth with sensuous beauty and my heart with joy unspeakable'. See also BAHC, ZJO/1/31 (Johnston Diary, 13 Apr. 1902) when the beauty of the sunset and 'larks in great numbers soaring and singing skyward' filled his heart 'with a great gladness and peace'.

[158] BAHC, ZJO/1/40 (Johnston Diary, 25 Jun. 1916).

[159] BAHC, ZJO/1/31 (Johnston Diary, 12 Aug. 1902).

The intellectual origins of Johnston's pantheism lie in the first instance in Richard Maurice Bucke's theory of 'cosmic consciousness', itself diffusely informed by Emerson and Whitman's transcendentalist faith in nature and by Carpenter's idealist speculations. Bucke's claim that the entire universe was alive attracted much attention from the Eagle Street College.[160] Johnston also discussed the possibility that matter was 'but congealed spirit' directly with Carpenter.[161] But how far the evolution of Johnston's deeper-lying convictions is attributable to the influence of these ideas is much less clear. As we have seen, the groundwork of his love of nature was laid in childhood and youth, before he had encountered any of them. When in early adulthood this developed into a vague belief in a universal benign spirit at work within nature, the decisive influence, rather than the impact of new ideas, was Johnston's need to reject his father's narrow and intellectually outdated Presbyterianism while retaining some kind of spiritual and ethical framework. Furthermore, although he was familiar with Whitman, Bucke and Carpenter's ideas from the 1880s, it was only after the death of his parents that he became committed to a definite belief in spiritual immortality in a pantheistic universe. Again this was driven by emotional pressure – the need to narrow the affective gap between him and his father by explicitly acknowledging a divine order in the universe, and to allow him to believe in his parents' continuing spiritual existence – rather than by any new intellectual influences.

Johnston's pantheism represented a firm repudiation of his earlier dalliance with atheism but in other respects it was an extension and development of much that was already implicit in his thought, practices and sensibility. It was also congruent with his democratic socialist politics and his deep-seated belief in comradeship. So it is perhaps unsurprising that it proved enduring. A note in his 1916 diary, written while he was working at Queen Mary's, restates Johnston's faith with great clarity, while indicating how it was sustained by, and underpinned belief in, the therapeutic and restorative functions of nature:

> Feeling depressed and out of spirits one afternoon – for I may here confess that there are many things and conditions here to <u>down</u> me – that life here is not all 'sweet milk' – I wandered out alone through the top gate crossed the road climbed the fence and entered the little wood. Making my way through the tangle wood I walked to the far side where I saw two young fillies careering round and round a field at top gallop and chasing the poor cows. Round and round they galloped and galloped as if from sheer love of the exercise and delight in their youth and super abundant energy.
>
> Then I sat down upon the stump of a tree and absorbed the sweet and sanative influences of the place – the pure air, the beauty of the young

---

[160] On Bucke see S. E. D. Shortt, 'Bucke, Richard Maurice', in *Dictionary of Canadian Biography*. Vol. 13 (Toronto, 2003). www.biographi.ca/en/bio/bucke_richard_maurice_13E .html [accessed 29 Sep. 2018].

[161] BAHC, ZJO/1/32 (Johnston Diary, 1–2 Nov. 1902).

greenery outbursting in emerald tufts upon the trees, the fresh green of the grass, and above all the spirit healing beneficence wh[ich] seemed to be poured into my depressed spirit.

As I sat there . . . I felt how true it is that there is no consolation like that of nature – no sympathy like that of woods & fields & hills – the sympathy that comes from life – the life that comes into us when we live near to nature and realize that all nature is <u>alive</u> – that our life is but a part of the universal life wh[ich] works in all things.[162]

* * *

For all his happy childhood, loving family, staunch friends and strength of character, Johnston, like the rest of us, was exposed to doubts and fears, shocks and setbacks, practical, professional and affective reverses. These disrupted his equanimity, threatening to fragment the unified framework of consciousness and convictions on which his self-belief rested. In quiet green spots like the little wood next to the horse field, he was free of the clash and conflict with other wills, perceptions and circumstances from which these disintegrating pressures arose. Alone or in the real or imagined presence of people he held dear, he could reconnect to the deepest certainties of his being, the ultimately perhaps commutable assurances of the benignity of nature, his rootedness in Annan with its 'soul-gladdening river' and his parents' enduring and inextinguishable love.[163]

[162] BAHC, ZJO/1/40 (Johnston Diary, undated entry [Spring/Summer 1916]).
[163] BAHC, ZJO/1/32 (Poem dated 10 Aug. 1903).

7

Bert Bissell

Dudley Probation Officer

'Left for Scotland, for Glasgow & Oban, feeling that God was calling me there & that I should have some thrilling religious experiences there', wrote Bert Bissell in his diary on 12 August 1932.[1] Bert's confidence that a reaffirmation and deepening of his Christian faith would ensue informed not only this first visit to the West Highlands but every one of his rural excursions and holidays. Given his highly purposive and specific approach, it is perhaps unsurprising that over time Bert developed a far stronger affinity than any of the other diarists for a single landscape type – mountains, in his case, above all Ben Nevis.

Bert was born on 9 January 1902 at Goole in the East Riding of Yorkshire. His father, the Reverend Joseph Benjamin (Ben) Bissell, was a Primitive Methodist minister whose roots were in Halesowen in the Black Country. Ben's family had been Primitive Methodists for generations, on the whole neither poor nor prosperous.[2] He married Charlotte Allen, a church school teacher and daughter of a policeman, in Burslem on 17 July 1894. As was standard for Primitive Methodist ministers, Ben was expected to move around the circuits at quite frequent intervals.[3] The family lived successively in Quinton (Birmingham), Talke (Staffordshire), Dawley (Shropshire), Darlaston (Staffordshire) and Coventry (Warwickshire).[4] Bert was the third of five brothers, and, partly no doubt because of the family's frequent relocations, was sent to a Methodist boarding school, Bourne College in Birmingham. From there he won a scholarship to Bablake School in Coventry, then on its way to becoming a Direct Grant grammar school and one of the more distinguished educational establishments in the West Midlands. Bert boarded here from 1915 to 1918. He continued to impress academically, rising to second and then first in the class, and excelled on the sports field, especially at football and cricket (he was given a trial

---

[1] Dudley Archives and Local History Centre [DALHC], DBIS1/1 (Bissell Diaries, 12 Aug. 1932).
[2] Don Bissell and Barry Weetman, *Bert Bissell: God's Mountaineer* (Peterborough, 1997), 7.
[3] Primitive Methodists, following the pattern established by the Wesleyans, grouped their chapels into local circuits and ministers were normally appointed to these rather than to chapels as such. Delia Garratt, 'Primitive Methodist Circuits in the English–Welsh Borderland', *Rural History* 14 (2003), 39, 44–6.
[4] Bissell and Weetman, *Bert Bissell*, 9.

by Warwickshire County Cricket Club). He became head prefect of the 'Indoor' (boarding) school and began to take a pastoral interest in the other boys, drawing doubtless on the model provided by his father. Wartime circumstances also served to bring out Bert's care for the boys who were, in a sense, in his charge: he had to comfort some whose fathers had been killed while serving in the armed forces.[5]

At this time a proud future of academic and sporting success seemed to beckon. Bert had ambitions of becoming a teacher. However, he was struck down by the 'Spanish' influenza epidemic of 1918 and was seriously ill for several months. Although he returned briefly to Bablake, he was unable to complete his education and had to leave before sitting his final exams. Much debilitated, he had to forgo his sporting hopes too. It was necessary to do something to earn a living so he decided to set up a credit clothing and footwear business in Coventry. He had some success with this, partly because his popularity and connections with Bablake teachers, scholars and their families provided him with a ready-made market.[6] He was initially unenthusiastic about his parents' move to Brierley Hill near Stourbridge in 1921: he continued to live in Coventry and seems to have invested his hopes more in his nascent clothing business than his father's Bent Street chapel. However, once Bert began to teach at the chapel Sunday School, his empathy for 'lads' and young men, one of his defining and lifelong characteristics, soon began to come through: 'God put a spark of love in my heart for them', he explained afterwards. He built on the Sunday School by establishing a young men's 'class' (the Methodist term for a congregation).[7]

Bert could not have known it but his parents' move to Dudley in 1925 was to prove critical to his future. He was still living in Coventry but had been spending weekends in Brierley Hill. Now he had to decide whether to continue with the young men's class, in which he had invested much time and effort and to which he felt committed. The difficulty was that he would no longer have a base in Brierley Hill and would have to divide his time between three places, in an era when travel was expensive and generally slow. In the end his decision was made when he was approached to lead the Vicar Street (Dudley) Bible class by two of its stewards in August 1925. Having accepted this offer, Bert threw his prodigious energies into 'winning lads for Christ' in Dudley. He began an extensive programme of door-to-door visiting and, remarkably, the class grew from just five men in 1925 to more than three hundred just four years later. In 1930 he felt 'called by God' to give up his business in Coventry and move in with his parents in Dudley. This was a brave decision since it meant foregoing his regular income for an uncertain future, but reflected his deepening

---

[5] Ibid., 15, 17–19.
[6] David Monkton and Alan Wedge (eds.), *Bert Bissell Remembered: An Anthology* (Alsager, 2001), 13.
[7] Bissell and Weetman, *Bert Bissell*, 20–1.

commitment to Vicar Street. His mother, a woman of staunch religious faith, accepted with good grace. The family achieved a measure of economic security, although hardly prosperity, when Bert was appointed lay pastor of Vicar Street Methodist Church at a salary of 30s per week the following year.[8]

In 1928 Ben fell into the grip of a severe depressive illness that led to frequent hospitalization and home care. We have little direct evidence of the effect on Bert of the sudden and unexpected decline in his hitherto dynamic father, but it must have been considerable. Bert had in several respects followed in his footsteps: most importantly in becoming a pastor, but also in his energetic proselytization, his determination and his willingness to use unconventional methods to promote the gospel.[9] It seems likely that one of the reasons Bert moved to Dudley was to help his mother care for his father and to support her emotionally. Ben died three years later. His son recorded in his diary:

> At 8AM in morning dad passed away and went to receive his eternal reward. Now out of much suffering and pain. Very sad day in my history.[10]

From then until the end of her life, Bert lived with Charlotte. This further strengthened their already close relationship – she cared for him at times of illness and acted as his housekeeper.[11] The powerful bond with his mother helps to explain why Bert never married, although his intense dedication to what he saw as God's work, which the diaries show filled almost every waking minute at least from 1930 onwards, may have done even more to keep him single.[12] The Vicar Street class quickly generated a range of associated activities and organizations. Bert could see that the Sunday class meeting itself did not fully cater for the needs of all those he hoped to reach, and also that smaller, less formal gatherings could act as feeders to the main class meeting. So he instituted the Fireside Club, a Monday evening social gathering mainly aimed at the younger 'lads', the group meeting (Fridays), the Vicar Street Mission Band, which represented the class in municipal celebrations, processions and other events and served to publicize the class' work, and the League of Youth, less closely tied to Vicar Street and aimed at boys who, for one reason or another, were not initially attracted to a church-based organization.[13]

[8] Ibid., 22–3, 32.
[9] It is intriguing that Bert, unlike his father, never became an ordained minister. This was probably partly because he soon became a salaried probation officer, but also because of his very special relationship with Vicar Street and with the town of Dudley. As a circuit minister he would have had to forgo this. For the energy and unconventional methods Ben Bissell brought to his preaching see ibid., 29.
[10] DALHC, DBIS1/1 (Bissell Diaries, 17 Feb. 1931).
[11] Bissell and Weetman, *Bert Bissell*, 15.
[12] DALHC, DBIS1/1–56 (Bissell Diaries).
[13] Monkton and Wedge (eds.), *Bert Bissell Remembered*, 19; Bissell and Weetman, *Bert Bissell*, 27, 45–8.

The 'Black Country', of which Dudley was often regarded as the capital, deserved its name. For much of Bert's life the town was dominated by heavy industry, notably chain-making and mining. In the early twentieth century Hingley's Netherton Works was among the largest and best-known marine chain makers in the world, responsible for forging the chains and anchors of the *Titanic*, the *Mauretania* and other famous ships. Like most towns dependent on heavy industry, however, Dudley was blighted by unemployment in the interwar period and from the 1970s onwards. Vicar Street itself was set in an impoverished, densely packed area of working-class housing and many of the families Bert knew were desperately poor. Trouble with the police and convictions for minor theft were not uncommon. Bert saw it as his duty, and indeed as a God-given opportunity, to do everything he could to help. He was a frequent visitor to Winson Green prison and became well known to the Dudley magistrates. This led, in 1933, to his appointment as part-time probation officer for Dudley.[14] The work was perfectly suited to his convictions and personal qualities. He wrote in his diary, with characteristic emphasis:

> An eventful week in my life, an unofficial appointment of Probation Officer for Dudley. A great opportunity for service given me by God. I must always remember it is a divine appointment – a divine trust – that no matter how weak or stubborn they are God's children and that he cares for them as much as the King. I must be kind, tenderhearted and forgiving & patient.[15]

Bert's absolute dedication and his unshakeable conviction that every single one of his probationers, no matter how unpromising, was capable of redemption, allowed him to achieve remarkable results. In 1935, for example, not one of his eighty-six cases broke the terms of their probation, 'a really marvellous record . . . surely God is with me, calling me to some fresh endeavour – fresh faith', as he wrote on 1 January 1936.[16] His success won him the offer of a full-time appointment in 1937. This made little difference to the hours he worked, which had far exceeded those he was contracted for from the start, but he felt obliged to give up his work as lay pastor at Vicar Street on the grounds that it was not possible to undertake two jobs if one of them was a full-time appointment. However, he remained deeply committed to Vicar Street and, while his brother Ernest now became the lay pastor of the class, no one was in any doubt that Bert remained its unofficial leader.[17]

For the next thirty years Bert continued to work as Dudley probation officer and to support and foster the Vicar Street class and its associated groups. He reached retirement age in 1967 and had to give up probation work, reluctantly since he felt he was in his prime. He needed an outlet for his seemingly

---

[14] Bissell and Weetman, *Bert Bissell*, 61–4.
[15] DALHC, DBIS1/2 (Bissell Diaries, 29–30 Apr. 1933).
[16] DALHC, DBIS1/7 (Bissell Diaries, 1 Jan. 1936).
[17] Bissell and Weetman, *Bert Bissell*, 67.

inexhaustible energies and found it in the cause of world peace. In his eyes this was best done by creating ties of friendship between communities. He was an early practitioner of town twinning, establishing an enduring link between Dudley and Fort William in Scotland. This was later extended to Hiroshima, a controversial initiative at the time because many in Dudley felt strongly about the Japanese treatment of British POWs during the Second World War. Despite his advancing years, he also visited a number of other countries in his efforts to promote peace and reconciliation and was a pioneer of race relations work back at home in the West Midlands, welcoming many Afro-Caribbean and Indian 'lads' to his groups and classes.[18]

Charlotte died in 1954, a severe blow to Bert, who was unwell for weeks during and after her final illness.[19] Nevertheless the pattern of his life was well established and his work as a probation officer and in connection with the Vicar Street class offered tremendous rewards. Despite the successive deaths of his brothers, he could write after being introduced to the Queen in 1972:

> [L]ife is like a fairy story at times. Mine has been marvellous – all due to my wonderful Lord, who has guided me and blest me all my life and allowed me to work at Vicar Street.[20]

This sense of achievement and fulfilment was boosted by the many honours bestowed on Bert in recognition of what he had done at Vicar Street, in the probation service and for world peace: an MBE as early as 1959, the Freedom of the Borough of Dudley in 1981, the World Methodist Peace Award in 1987 and the Rotary International Medal in 1989.[21] Bert took an open, unselfconscious pride in these marks of civic and international esteem. It also gave him great satisfaction that, quite remarkably, at least eighteen of his protégés went on to become ordained ministers, while well over a hundred served as lay preachers at some time in their lives.[22] Of the young men Bert befriended, it was perhaps Inderjit Bhogal who had the most distinguished career within organized religion. But Bert did not live to see his inauguration as President of the Methodist Conference in 2001. Although he remained fit and active until well into his nineties, he fell and broke his hip in 1998 and died at Nethercrest Nursing Home in Dudley later that year.[23]

* * *

[18] Monkton and Wedge (eds.), *Bert Bissell Remembered*, 46–7, 49, 54; Bissell and Weetman, *Bert Bissell*, 41–2, 93–7.
[19] DALHC, DBIS1/29 (Bissell Diaries, 26 Mar. 1954ff.).
[20] DALHC, DBIS1/47 (Bissell Diaries, 30 May 1972).
[21] Monkton and Wedge (eds.), *Bert Bissell Remembered*, 10.
[22] Bissell and Weetman, *Bert Bissell*, 50; Monkton and Wedge (eds.), *Bert Bissell Remembered*, 76.
[23] Monkton and Wedge (eds.), *Bert Bissell Remembered*, 10, 54.

From his childhood onward, the countryside played an important part in Bert's life. His early years were spent in semi-rural environments: Quinton and Talke were large villages rather than towns. But they were set in a landscape of collieries, brickworks and pot-kilns as well as farms, so the social coordinates of the countryside Bert knew in his childhood were very different from the more purely agricultural, landowner-dominated landscape in which, for example, Hallam and Cresswell grew up. This was probably one of the reasons Bert's attitude to working-class, industrial England was so much more positive than theirs and may also help to explain his indifference to 'south country' thatched cottages, manor houses and quaint villages.

Bert was particularly fond of his uncle and aunt's farm at Frankley, near Halesowen, which he often visited, continuing to do so in adulthood. When his uncle was forced to give it up in 1939, Bert noted sorrowfully:

> Today I went to Frankley to see uncle Joe who was a little better. All were sorrowful over the impending departure from the farm. What changes life brings – it is sad indeed to think of leaving the old farm, the ducks the geese, the horses & live elsewhere.[24]

It seems likely that this early familiarity with agriculture and farm animals was one of the sources of Bert's lifelong enjoyment of country scenes and life. At least as important, however, were the Primitive Methodist camp meetings at Mow Cop, a steep, rocky hill in Staffordshire commanding an extensive view of the Cheshire plain. The hill and the village of the same name have a notable place in Primitive Methodist history: it was here that Hugh Bourne held the first camp meeting on 31 May 1807 and here that he and William Clowes joined together to form the Primitive Methodist Church in 1811.[25] Many subsequent camp meetings were held there, including a spectacular centenary meeting featuring eighty speakers and an estimated one hundred thousand participants in 1907.[26] Bert attended several camp meetings at Mow Cop in his childhood and the vivid scene can hardly have failed to make an impression on his imagination: the 'castle' (actually an eighteenth-century folly) crowning the summit of the hill, rising up dramatically above the surrounding landscape; the huge crowds; and the excitement and intensity of the meetings, which sometimes lasted for several days.[27]

As an adult Bert often went on rural walks or cycle rides, occasionally on his own but much more often with one of his groups of young men – the Vicar Street Cycle Club, for example. His favoured local destinations were the hills

[24] DALHC, DBIS1/14 (Bissell Diaries, 8 Apr. 1939).
[25] G. C. Boase, 'Bourne, Hugh (1772–1852)', rev. W. J. Johnson. In *Oxford Dictionary of National Biography*, Oxford, 2004; online ed., May 2006. www.oxforddnb.com/view/article/3005 [accessed 3 Jan. 2013].
[26] 'Mow Cop Interactive: A Past & Present Look at Mow Cop'. Primitive Methodist Movement. www.mowcop.info/htm/church/primitive2.htm [accessed 3 Jan. 2013].
[27] Bissell and Weetman, *Bert Bissell*, 10–11.

and beauty spots of the Black Country: the Rowley, Clent and Lickey Hills, Frankley, Enville, Kinver, Prestwood and Arley. As with Johnston, but unlike the other diarists, these walks and rides were strictly seasonal: Bert rarely went out into the countryside before April or after September. Summer was also the season when he normally took his holidays. The seasonality of Bert's ruralism was partly due to its character: most of the time he had some of his 'lads' with him and he knew they were more likely to enjoy themselves in better weather. Like Johnston, and for related albeit distinct reasons, he saw nature as a benign force and may have preferred to encounter it in its more smiling moods.

At least from 1930, when the diaries begin, Bert took his holidays almost exclusively in the mountains. His attitude was not in the least nationalistic. The scenery of the Scottish Highlands, Switzerland or Germany was just as good in his eyes, or indeed better, than that of England. He wrote on one occasion of 'the charm of the English country lane' and again of the 'lovely English countryside' but such references were rare and, as the rather tepid and conventional language indicates, a long way from the spiritual intensity that characterized his encounters with the Welsh, Scottish and European mountains. Over time he became progressively more ambitious in the ranges he

Figure 7.1   Bert on a mountain expedition
Reproduced by kind permission of Dudley Archives and Local History Service (DALHC, BIS/2/43)

sought out. In 1931 it was Snowdonia, in 1932 and 1933 the Highlands, in 1934 Switzerland and in 1935 the Bavarian Alps. Among the mountains he climbed in the Alps were the Zugspitze (2,962 m) and the Mönch (4,107 m). He began to undertake trips with some of his lads on the less demanding of these climbs, tackling Snowdon with them for the first time in 1935.[28]

Increasingly, however, his love of mountains centred on Ben Nevis and the surrounding area. He was with a party of lads from Dudley in 1945 when victory against Japan was declared. Feeling that the ending of the war was a momentous event that should be celebrated appropriately, Bert took his party up the mountain and constructed a peace cairn on the summit. This marked an important stage in the development of Bert's sense of Ben Nevis as, in his words, a 'holy mountain', fused in his mind with the cause of world peace. He and his followers placed a plaque on the cairn celebrating the bond between Dudley and Fort William and reaching out a symbolic hand of friendship to 'the youth of every nation in the world'. Subsequently he was instrumental in placing many other inscribed stone tablets on the cairn, linking different organizations and places to each other. The most important of these to him was the Hiroshima stone, added in 1968.[29]

Convinced that mountains brought people closer to God and that climbing them could contribute to harmony within and between nations, Bert began a series of international peace climbs in bitterly divided places including South Africa and Ireland (where he climbed on both sides of the border). He visited Japan in 1972 to foster the links of friendship between Dudley, Fort William and Hiroshima. Ben Nevis, however, remained his spiritual lodestar. He continued to make annual visits, eventually climbing the mountain a remarkable 107 times.[30]

Bert's unremitting determination to scale summits, whether geographical, spiritual or, in his school days, academic and sporting, might suggest that he was fiercely competitive and wracked with emotional tension. This could hardly have been further from the case. On the contrary, his character and convictions had an extraordinarily monolithic quality, grounded in his stable, loving family background and obdurately resilient Christian faith. There is virtually no evidence of inner conflict or indeed development in his diary, to the point where an entry from the 1930s could be exchanged with one from the 1970s with respect to tone, style, values and outlook without looking out of place. There was little outward change either: he lived in Selbourne Road for the rest of his life after moving there at the age of twenty-eight and was the guiding spirit of the Vicar Street class throughout that time. He prayed every

[28] DALHC, DBIS1/1–20, passim.
[29] Monkton and Wedge (eds.), *Bert Bissell Remembered*, 41–9; Bissell and Weetman, *Bert Bissell*, 91–7.
[30] Bissell and Weetman, *Bert Bissell*, 98–106.

morning, then typically went out on a round of visits, preaching and meetings, returning home in the evening, writing up his diary and praying again before bed. Everything he did was integrated into this encompassing religious framework. Even his occasional attendance at sporting events and his annual holidays had a spiritual meaning: competitive team sport exemplified the strenuous effort and fellowship that underpinned Christian commitment while holidays offered spiritual refreshment and renewal.

If Bert's life was so stable and free of emotional tension, how can we make sense of his inveterate determination to pit himself against the mountains? There can be very few others who have climbed Ben Nevis more than a hundred times and few also who have reached the summit in the tenth decade of their life.[31] Part of the answer may be metabolic: Bert had extraordinary physical energy and it was probably satisfying and perhaps even necessary to him to expend it. In Dudley he tramped the pavements often almost from morning to nightfall, visiting errant lads and families in trouble. He thought nothing of cycling and walking long distances – when still living in Coventry he used regularly to walk the thirty miles between Brierley Hill and Coventry. When he arrived at a holiday destination he would often rush straight up the nearest mountain, as on the first morning of his holiday at Barmouth in 1936:

> The morning was wet. Away I went over the mountains after having breakfast with Cecil Thomas at the Ceylon Café. Away I walked over the 500 yards trudge to Cader Idris. The walk was through Arthog and right away over the mountains and through the passes . . . Climbed Cader Idris in heavy rain – quite a stiff climb and lonely and dangerous in the mist.[32]

Even more precipitate was his ascent of Snowdon on 10 June 1935:

> I went to Snowdon, 10 o'clock, all along coast, Colwyn Bay, Llandudno, Llanfairfechan, Penmaenmawr, Bangor, Menai Bridge, Carnaervon, Llanberis arrived 12.30. Rushed up mountain in 1 ¾ hours.[33]

There are, however, many other ways to expend physical energy – organized sport, for example. The apparent contradiction between Bert's almost

---

[31] Bissell and Weetman, *Bert Bissell*, 110; Monkton and Wedge (eds.), *Bert Bissell Remembered*, 47.

[32] DALHC, DBIS1/7 (Bissell Diaries, 15 Aug. 1936). Bert's accounts of his ascents are laconic, emphasizing the heights of mountains (often recorded) and arduousness of climbs rather than (for example) views from summits. This approximates to the 'immersive' mountaineering tradition dominant in the late nineteenth and early twentieth centuries, foregrounding the physical and technical rather than emotional aspects of mountaineering. Alan McNee, '"Cold Stony Reality': Subjectivity and Experience in Victorian Mountaineering', *Dandelion Journal: Postgraduate Arts Journal & Research Network* 2 (2011). https://doi.org/10.16995/ddl.252.

[33] DALHC, DBIS1/5 (Bissell Diaries, 10 Jun. 1935).

compulsive drive to climb mountains and the serenity and stability of his character can better be explained with reference to his powerful conviction that he would succeed in any endeavour he undertook. This applied across the different facets of his life and was so deeply ingrained that he was well-nigh unable to accept evidence to the contrary, as on the occasion he took some of his lads to see Sir Douglas Bader in London. The legendary fighter ace was not at home but Bert took his lads by taxi to Bader's office in the Civil Aviation building, only to be denied admission since they had no prior appointment. Bert, however, refused to leave and eventually Bader gave in.[34] An even more striking example is the peace message Bert wanted the USSR to include with its first moon mission. According to Don Bissell and Barry Weetman, it was impossible to convince Bert that the Russians had turned down his request: 'He went on believing that [his message was] encapsulated within that first rocket probe to the face of the moon.'[35]

Bert, then, evidently felt an overriding inner assurance of success. In this light, it seems likely that his need to reach the summit of mountains gave rise to little or no anxiety because he was not open to the possibility of failure. Attaining the summit of the mountain was an expression and joyous confirmation of what he knew already, rather as his first visit to Scotland duly yielded the 'thrilling religious experiences' that he had anticipated beforehand. The rare occasions when he was forced to turn back before summiting were, as might be expected, difficult for him. His tendency was to recast them as heroic failures, emphasizing the extremity of the weather conditions that had defeated him and his lads, but this was not entirely satisfactory.[36]

***

To understand why mountains were so important to Bert, we should start where he always did: with the Bible. He would undoubtedly have been familiar with every one of the many scriptural references to them.[37] Noah's Ark came to rest on the mountains of Ararat, according to Genesis, while God appeared to Moses on Sinai and gave him the Ten Commandments.[38] Moses did not live to enter the Promised Land but saw it spread out before him from Pisgah, one of the

---

[34] Steve Walker, 'Wouldn't Take "No" for an Answer', in Monkton and Wedge (eds.), *Bert Bissell Remembered*, 54–5.

[35] Bissell and Weetman, *Bert Bissell*, 99–100.

[36] DALHC, DBIS1/7 (Bissell Diaries, 2 Jun. 1936).

[37] Jon Mathieu argues that mountains were not generally sacralized before the eighteenth century. However, his claim that the place of mountains in the Bible is ambivalent rests on the slight foundation of a reference to Josiah 40:4 ('Every valley shall be exalted, and every hill made low'), which in any case does not seem incompatible with a conviction that mountains have a spiritual significance. Jon Mathieu, 'The Sacralization of Mountains in Europe during the Modern Age', *Mountain Research and Development* 26 (2006), 343–9.

[38] Genesis 8:4; Exodus 19–32.

peaks of Mount Nebo.[39] Joshua built an altar on Mount Ebal and offered his people a choice: to obey God and enjoy his blessings (represented by the wooded Mount Gerizim nearby) or to disobey him and be cursed – symbolized by the bare, rocky heights of Mount Ebal.[40] King Saul and his son Jonathan made their last stand against the Philistines on Mount Gilboa and were killed there.[41] Mount Zion, one of the hills of Jerusalem, was the site of the City of David and became a synonym for Jerusalem, the people of Israel and the heavenly city.[42] Elijah challenged the prophets of Baal to a contest on Mount Carmel.[43] Mountains were equally critical in the New Testament. When the devil tempted Jesus in the wilderness he took him up to a 'very high mountain' and showed him all the kingdoms of the world.[44] The longest piece of teaching by Jesus recorded in the New Testament is the Sermon on the Mount (location not specified in the Bible), in which many of the central tenets of Christianity are set out.[45] The Transfiguration, in which Jesus appeared before his disciples in divine form, took place after he had led them up a high mountain, sometimes identified with Mount Hermon.[46] Perhaps the most resonant of all biblical heights, however, was the Mount of Olives overlooking Jerusalem. Here David passed when fleeing from his son Absalom's rebellion, Solomon built an altar and Ezekiel saw God's glory leaving Jerusalem. Zechariah prophesied that God would stand on the Mount of Olives on Judgement Day and that the Mount would split in two. Jesus wept over the fate of Jerusalem from the Mount before his triumphal entry into the city. According to Matthew, he taught and prophesied to his disciples on the Mount and went there on the night of his betrayal. The Garden of Gethsemane, where he prayed with his disciples on the night before his arrest (the Agony in the Garden), is on the lower slopes of the Mount, while the Ascension (when Jesus was taken up to heaven) also occurred on the Mount, according to the account in Acts.[47]

Mountains and other high places were therefore deeply imbued with historical and symbolic meaning within the Christian tradition. They were sites of significant spiritual events and, especially, intermediate locations between earth and heaven, where God often became manifest to prophets, disciples and other believers (Sinai, the 'high mountain' of the Transfiguration, the Mount of Olives). They were a setting for spiritual struggle and triumph over

---

[39] Deuteronomy 34:1.
[40] Joshua 8:30, 33.
[41] 1 Samuel 28:4, 31:1, 8; 2 Samuel 1, 21:12; 1 Chronicles 10:1, 8.
[42] 2 Samuel 5:6–7, 9–10.
[43] 1 Kings 18:19–46; 2 Kings 2:25, 4:25.
[44] Matthew 4:8.
[45] Matthew 4:23–5.
[46] Matthew 17:1.
[47] 2 Samuel 15:30; 2 Kings 23:13; Ezekiel 11:23; Zechariah 14:4; Matthew 21:1, 24–6; Luke 19:29, 21:37, 41–4, 22:39, Acts 1:9–12.

evil (Mount Ebal, Mount Carmel, the temptation in the desert). Mountains also enabled believers to ascend both physically and spiritually closer to heaven and were places from which a view of paradise might be obtained (Pisgah, Zion, the Ascension).

Nonconformists, in particular Methodists and Primitive Methodists, were perhaps more conscious of these associations and meanings than Anglicans at this time, due to their greater emphasis on the Bible as a source of authority and their interest in and respect for the Old Testament. Mountains as metaphors for spiritual struggle and the immediate presence of God spoke to the strong messianic and millennial strands within the Methodist Connexion. It was no doubt for these reasons that Mount Zion was one of the most popular names for Methodist chapels. The Primitives took the biblical emphasis on mountains even further, incorporating it in their traditions and mode of worship. Outdoor camp meetings, often on high places, became one of the defining features of Primitive Methodism and Mow Cop its spiritual home, in contrast to Wesleyanism's more domesticated urban roots in Bristol and London.[48]

In addition to the biblical and denominational meanings attached specifically to mountains, landscape and the natural world also had a range of more general spiritual meanings in late nineteenth- and early twentieth-century Britain. The intellectual heyday of natural theology – the attempt to deduce the existence of God from reason and experience – may been long past by the time Bert was born, but it had a long afterlife in the pervasive and often intense absorption of genteel Victorians in natural history, a mode of perceiving nature whose imprint can still be discerned far into the twentieth century. Bert shared this tradition's conviction that the beauty and harmony of nature was proof of God's existence and goodness, and the scale and majesty of mountains of his grandeur and power. But he was at a wide remove from its reverent concern to study God's 'book of nature' in detail, carefully discriminating between species.[49] While seeing beautiful flowers or rare fauna gave him great pleasure, there are few references to the names of plants or animals in his diaries. Cresswell, no professional botanist either, typically recorded more than fifty distinct plant, bird, insect or animal species in a year of diary entries, whereas Bert's entries, of a similar length and frequency, average only about five a year and never use scientific names. He refers only to familiar species such as primroses and daffodils, using generic terms for anything more unusual.[50] Walking in the Grampians, for example, Bert noted that he had seen '[a] hawk, deer, roedeer'. Although he was able to identify the roe deer, the hawk could be any of at least seven small-to-medium-sized birds of prey that

[48] Methodist Central Hall opened in 1912.
[49] Barber, *The Heyday of Natural History*.
[50] DALHC, DBIS1/14 (Bissell Diaries, 17 Apr. 1939).

bred in the Highlands at this date, while the generic 'deer', although probably red deer, could have been fallow or one of the other introduced species.[51]

Perhaps the main reason Bert had so little interest in identification is that it depends on the discrimination of differences. This is the mark of an intellectual disposition and, despite his success at school, Bert was anything but intellectual. He seems largely to have eschewed theology and the theoretical and evidential challenges to Christianity posed by geology, natural selection and historical criticism of the Bible did not trouble him. Books of any kind other than scripture are rarely mentioned in his diaries. He tended to see the world clearly but broadly, taking things at face value rather than musing on their underlying significance: a man of action rather than thought. In response to seeing *Modern Times*, in which Chaplin uses comedy to pose searching questions about exactly the kind of industrial mass production that employed so many of the people Bert knew in Dudley, and to which critics have devoted pages of analysis, he wrote only a single sentence in his diary: 'Went to see Charlie Chaplin in "Modern Times", quite a good picture, creates roars of laughter, only had to pay 6d.'[52]

The symbolic charge carried by biblical mountains, the traditions of Primitive Methodism and the continuing sway of natural theology at a popular level provided the cognitive framework underpinning Bert's feeling about the countryside, nature and mountains. But they do not explain why, in contrast to many other Primitive Methodists equally influenced by natural theology and aware of the significance accorded to mountains in the Bible, he embraced this framework so wholeheartedly. Doing so requires, on the one hand, a recognition that Bert's conscious choices and actions were almost always motivated by his determination to 'win lads for Jesus' and, on the other, that, like all of us, he was powerfully affected by more private, spontaneous and perhaps involuntary emotions and responses.

The overcrowded, noisy, grimy and in some respects squalid environment in which Bert's young men lived gave the natural theology tradition a particular relevance to his ministry. For many of them even the local West Midlands countryside had been a closed book before meeting him and the expeditions he organized once or twice a year to Snowdonia, the Cairngorms or Fort William introduced them to landscape grandeur far beyond anything most of them had known. The shared effort and exposure to danger involved in climbing mountains also offered exceptional potential to forge what Bert described as Christian fellowship. He summarized the goals of his Scottish expeditions as follows:

> [W]hen I take my parties to Scotland – it is the Lord's work.= The aim and objective = To win lads for Jesus as they behold the glories of the hills and

[51] DALHC, DBIS1/2 (Bissell Diaries, 19 Aug. 1933).
[52] DALHC, DBIS1/7 (Bissell Diaries, 24 Aug. 1936).

> the majesty of His creation and also the beauty of His love and the
> fellowship of the holiday group at Fort William.[53]

This otherwise apt assessment, however, omits one of Bert's most important aims – to demonstrate, literally and metaphorically, that anyone could reach the summit so long as they were prepared to make the unremitting effort required to do so. The implications extended far into the everyday lives of his lads: success in overcoming temptation or previous moral failure (as in the case of his probationers), patience in enduring illness or emotional trials, determination to find work and hold down a job, discovering the energy and determination to achieve academic or sporting success. The peaks to which Bert led expeditions therefore had to meet three criteria: they must be as high as possible, they must involve arduous ascents but they must nevertheless be attainable by young men with no previous climbing experience. This goes a long way to explaining why Bert preferred to take his lads to Ben Nevis rather than any other summit even though it had no special place in Christian tradition and was no more beautiful than hundreds of other mountains in Scotland or elsewhere:

> The climbing of Ben Nevis. We climb the highest – or shall do if it is God's
> will. May this be an indication that we shall want to climb the highest –
> spiritually & morally.[54]

Bert's love of Ben Nevis and its district also, however, had more personal dimensions. He had close friends in Fort William among the civic authorities, the mountain rescue team and the Duncansburgh church community. Religion was still a dominant social and cultural force in Fort William, as across much of rural Scotland, and he wrote approvingly of 'a grand Sunday in the Highlands', consisting of little other than a succession of services.[55] He set up a young people's exchange between Dudley and Fort William and the return visit to Dudley became one of the highlights of his year. He was awarded the Freedom of Lochaber (the administrative district encompassing Fort William) in 1991, the same year in which a civic ceremony was held in Dudley to name his house 'Ben Nevis'. It was wholly appropriate that he should be buried in the Glen Nevis cemetery at the foot of his beloved mountain. Fort William had become, as he wrote in his diary in 1978, his 'second home'.[56]

Bert wrote about 'mighty Ben Nevis' with increasing awe as his feeling for the mountain deepened. It was, as he confided to his diary on 12 August 1966, a 'Sacred Mountain'; leading his lads to the summit was 'the annual

---

[53] DALHC, DBIS1/53 (Bissell Diaries, 26 Jul. 1978).
[54] DALHC, DBIS1/20 (Bissell Diaries, 8 Jun. 1945).
[55] DALHC, DBIS1/26 (Bissell Diaries, 9–23 Aug. 1951).
[56] DALHC, DBIS1/53 (Bissell Diaries, 2 Jul. 1978).

pilgrimage'.[57] He was fully conscious of the scriptural antecedents, to which he often referred. God seemed closer and his 'guidance' more palpable in and around Ben Nevis: <u>'God always reveals himself powerfully whenever anything from Fort William is concerned'</u>, he noted on 25 May 1957. In 1963 he wrote of 'the Miracle of Ben Nevis ... That word acts like magic "Ben Nevis" ... Wonders will never cease on Ben Nevis'.[58]

It would be easy to attribute this special 'magic' to personal identification but formulating the issue in this way runs the risk of distortion. For some of the diarists, notably Spear Smith and Catley, identity was certainly a central issue. Both were acutely self-conscious, worked energetically to construct a stable and satisfying sense of identity, and found this elusive. Bert, however, was quite the opposite. Ben Nevis did not serve to prop up a fragile sense of self in his case and still less was it a projection of narcissistic grandiosity. Nor did it represent escapist alienation from his everyday surroundings. If Fort William was Bert's second home, Dudley was his first, thoroughly urban as it was, and he cared deeply about the town and its people.

Nevertheless, even Bert experienced failure at times and, unsurprisingly in view of his outlook and expectations, he found it difficult to deal with. In August 1935, for example, he took some of his lads to Barmouth, hoping to persuade them to climb Cader Idris and infuse them with the wonder of the mountains, but things did not go according to plan:

> After a very wet night the storm was still raging in the morning – I got out and fetched wood and made a fire and some of the lads had breakfast. The tents were flooded, the lads spirits were down to zero and many wanted to go back so I advised all of them to go. In a few moments their bags were packed and off they went to the station. The camp which had been the scene of so many happy events was deserted ... It had been a glorious time with the lads and Ernie and myself felt very lonely after their departure.[59]

A few days later he made a quite uncharacteristically downbeat entry in his diary: 'Returned from Barmouth feeling sad over non-success at camp.'[60] There were other failures too: sometimes gales or snow prevented him from reaching the summit of a mountain; sometimes his probationers let him down; there were times (not many of them) when he failed to persuade somebody to do something on which he had set his heart.[61] More serious blows included the

---

[57] DALHC, DBIS1/41 (Bissell Diaries, 12 and 16 Aug. 1966).
[58] DALHC, DBIS1/32 and 1/38 (Bissell Diaries, 25 May 1957 and 1 Jul. 1963).
[59] DALHC, DBIS1/5 (Bissell Diaries, 19 Aug. 1935).
[60] DALHC, DBIS1/5 (Bissell Diaries, 21 Aug. 1935).
[61] He failed to reach the summit of Snowdon with the League of Youth on 2 June 1936. He heard the news that, for the first time, one of his probationers had re-offended on 13 May 1936 (DALHC, DBIS1/7). He failed to persuade the Soviet Union to carry a capsule including a peace message with their moon probe in 1959. Bissell and Weetman, *Bert Bissell*, 99.

collapse of the Dudley branch of the League of Youth during the Second World War, the opening of a strip club adjacent to the Vicar Street chapel, illnesses (especially as he got older) and the loss of family and friends, above all the death of his mother in 1954. Occasionally it is possible to discern from the diaries how shocks such as these could, despite his remarkable buoyancy, inner integration and strength of conviction, open cracks through which doubts and discouragement crept in. Perhaps the most fundamental and vital of the many things mountains, and Ben Nevis especially, did for him was to restore his inner equilibrium – his faith in himself, in life and in God – the overwhelming conviction that everything was divinely ordained for the best.

A good example of the way mountains could restore and replenish Bert's optimism is the events of June 1975. He had been feeling unwell and, most uncharacteristically, found himself wishing that he did not have to go on his annual Scottish holiday, normally the highlight of his year. Things got worse en route: in Glasgow he was further dispirited to see 'three teenage girls mocking shamefully an old man testifying to Jesus – a very sad affair'. However, north of Glasgow matters began to improve, as his diary entry, written up subsequently, reveals:

> Already I was beginning to feel better, it is amazing how tonic like the Scottish Holidays are to me. The great scenery, the tonic air, the kindness of everyone, the happy memories that return – the anticipation of things to come. All those things inspire me. The day was hot but the charming scenery was more heavenly than ever and the mountains and the mist provided me with really new scenes of Scotland. So I thank God for the healing powers of mountains, moorland, mists and valleys & heaths etc. It all acted like magic.[62]

Whereas other aspects of his mountain experiences were enhanced by or even dependent upon the presence of others, the restorative 'magic' mountains and sometimes other rural landscapes could bring was most powerful when the only things present to Bert were his own mind, nature and God. Even a country walk in the environs of Dudley could affect him deeply under such circumstances:

> Lovely outing in country. Clent Church. Stillness of evening, Birds singing. Be still and know that I am God: convincing experience.[63]

Nevertheless his profoundest experiences of this kind came on the rare occasions when he was completely alone in the mountains:

> Lovely weather – went to Lochnagar alone – a beautiful day with God – saw golden eagle – took compass and map – best day.[64]

---

[62] DALHC, DBIS1/50 (Bissell Diaries, 26 Jun. 1975).
[63] DALHC, DBIS1/1 (Bissell Diaries, 14 Apr. 1931).
[64] DALHC, DBIS1/2 (Bissell Diaries, 19 Aug. 1931).

Very <u>misty</u> and cold, all alone with God [on Snowdon]. Had a wonderful conversation with Him over look and see that the Lord is good. Wonderful spiritual experience. Thanks be to God![65]

Bert's diary offers little extended reflection on what landscape meant to him. A rare exception is the entry for 21 June 1945, which distils what he felt when he was 'alone with God' in the mountains:

The Strength of the Hills. The hills are unchanging – 'Before the Hills in Order Stood'. We recognize in this the unalterability of the heart of God. We have allowed the changefulness of our moods to be transferred to our conceptions of God.

To be amongst the hills for a time is to have one's ears filled with the music of running water.

Dependence is proclaimed by every spring – dependence upon God – the more truly religious a man is the readier will he be to bow his heart in thankfulness. The millions in the valley depend upon it.

To lie sprawling on a sunny hillside, a treasure of wildflowers in one's hand – watch the clouds go sailing by it is easy to believe in God.

So to the Hills we must go for meditation – for strength – for joy – for worship – to be near the living God. Our Maker – our Redeemer – our Friend.[66]

The restorative function of being 'amongst the hills' is very apparent here: their 'strength' calls us back from 'the changefulness of our moods' (implying doubt and wavering faith) to a recognition of the 'unalterability of the heart of God'. The mountains reaffirm Bert's core apprehension of things, his fundamental orientation towards the world, expressed through his Christian faith. A central element of this is a sense of harmony ('to have one's ears filled with the music of running water'): that everything ultimately works together for the good. That sense of harmony is bound up with a benign, pervasive experience of beauty ('a treasure of wildflowers in one's hand') and, above all, of peace: in Bert's account he (or the subject) is completely still ('sprawling on a sunny hillside') while the clouds move serenely past him.[67] This is the same transcendent yet entirely calm spiritual experience registered in Bert's accounts of climbing Lochnagar and Snowdon alone, and was one of the fundamental touchstones of his life.

As with Johnston's loafing, what Bert found in the mountains was a reflection of something that was in him already, but that was subject to disruption and even temporary obscuration down in the 'valley' (Dudley, society, the world). It is difficult to trace this astonishingly irrepressible optimism to its source. Bert

[65] DALHC, DBIS1/5 (Bissell Diaries, 10 Jun. 1935).
[66] DALHC, DBIS1/20 (Bissell Diaries, 21 Jun. 1945).
[67] Johnston was often similarly still amidst a moving landscape when loafing in Raikes Wood.

would have said that it came from God. Whatever view we take of this, there can be little doubt that his childhood experiences provided a crucial foundation. It may have been from his father, who was as determined as Bert to achieve the highest possible within his sphere, that Bert's powerful drive to get to the literal and metaphorical summit derived. Had that been Bert's only inheritance from his parents, an unhappy and anxious life, beset by a constant fear that he would fall short and that he needed to achieve more, might have been in prospect. What balanced Bert's drive to reach the top was his assurance that he would succeed and that God's love would not fail even in the improbable event that he did not. This is most obviously attributable to aspects of his home background that made it a stable and happy one, as well as a launch pad to achievement: the strength of his parents' marriage, the close, affectionate relationship with his brothers, especially Ernie, and, above all perhaps, his mother's unquestioning devotion. His happy childhood was profoundly formative and even determining: indeed, affectively at least, he never really left home. Certainly he chose to stay within the powerful family habitus rather than seeking to challenge or extend it. One way of looking at his adult life is as an ongoing attempt to recreate and share with others the conditions of his childhood: bringing people to God replicated his father's life work, his unusual decision to move back to his parents' house was a decision to stay within the bosom of the family rather than break away from it, and his lifelong dedication to realizing Christian fellowship among his lads can be seen as an extension of the powerful experience of fraternity that growing up with four brothers had given him. Underpinning everything was his deep conviction that all would be well and his efforts would be crowned with success. Attaining mountain summits confirmed this, strengthening his inner certainty, filling him with joy and inspiring him with the wish to bring these experiences to others.

Explorers

Intense personal encounters with landscape perhaps mattered more to Sadie Barmes and Fred Catley than to any of the other diarists: their ruralism was marked by an energetic, active desire to explore and to discover for themselves. Yet the motivations that led them in this direction were quite different. For all his eager pursuit of fresh experience, pleasure in finding new paths and encompassing interest in every aspect of the countryside, Fred's ruralism was rooted in a need for stability and security, whereas the delight Sadie took in exploring rural landscapes was part of a passionate educational quest for knowledge, understanding and personal growth.

8

Sadie Barmes

London Clerk

Sadie Barmes was born in 1907, five years after Bert Bissell, into a family roughly on the same social and probably income level. Bert's father was a nonconformist minister and his mother a teacher while Sadie's father was a greengrocer. Both Sadie and Bert lived on the fringes of major conurbations for most of their lives: the West Midlands in his case, London in hers. Unlike Bert, however, Sadie was Jewish. It would be doing her a disservice to assess her diaries through this prism alone since her ethnicity was only one of many influences on her. Nevertheless, it is helpful to situate her life in relation to the wider history of British Jewry, especially in the interwar years, the period to which her surviving diaries belong. This was an era of flux but also to some extent of stabilization for British Jews after the fissures created in the Jewish community by the mass migrations from Eastern Europe from the 1880s to the early 1900s. The wealthy leaders of Anglo-Jewry, families such as the Rothschild banking dynasty, had for decades pursued a strategy of cultural Anglicization. By adopting the political and social values of the British elite and assimilating to them in terms of language, customs and dress while retaining their religion and communal organizations, these leading Jews sought to carve out a secure, low-profile niche for the Jewish community within British society. They had some success in doing so, as is evident in the progressive removal of civil disabilities through the nineteenth century, culminating in full civic equality in 1890 and in the acceptance of Benjamin Disraeli, a baptized Jew, as prime minister in 1874.[1] Whether opting for full-scale assimilation like Disraeli or cultural Anglicization while retaining their Jewish faith, as did most of the members of families such as the Rothschilds, Montefiores, Salomonses and Montagus, wealthy Jews were on the whole well integrated into the upper ranks of British society by the late nineteenth century.

However, the arrival of tens of thousands of mainly Yiddish-speaking Russian and Eastern European Jews in Britain from 1880 onwards disrupted this equilibrium. The immigrants were mostly poor, often desperately so, and were in no position to conform to the standards of genteel respectability

---

[1] Michael Clark, *Albion and Jerusalem: The Anglo-Jewish Community in the Post-Emancipation Era 1858–1887* (Oxford, 2009). See also Tony Kushner, *Anglo-Jewry since 1066: Place, Locality and Memory* (Oxford, 2013); David Cesarani, *The Making of Modern Anglo-Jewry* (Oxford, 1990).

enjoined by the Anglo-Jewish establishment.[2] Nor did they necessarily wish to conform: they brought with them their own values and perspectives and a small but active minority had adopted anarchism, socialism or communism. The fact that most of the immigrants settled initially in the East End of London, a vast, overpopulated slum onto which many of the most lurid fears of respectable society had been projected since the 1880s, only made matters worse.[3] Many established British Jews, often more or less comfortably integrated into Gentile society, reacted with dismay, fearing that the immigrants would be seen as a burden on society, as culturally alien and as politically dangerous, and that long-resident British Jews would be tarred with the same brush.

By the 1920s some of these tensions were receding. The rate at which Jewish immigrants were arriving in Britain had slowed to a trickle following the Aliens Act of 1905 and there was a strong outmigration of Jews away from the traditional areas of settlement in the East End of London towards the suburbs, especially areas such as Hackney, Hendon and Golders Green. It has been argued that at the same time young Jews were moving away from the values of their parents and adopting non-Jewish habits, customs and values. This was different from earlier assimilation because it was generational rather than associated with upward social mobility, and from Anglicization because it represented a reaction against, or at least a distancing from, the established institutions of organized British Jewry.[4]

In an interesting article David Dee suggests that membership of left-wing outdoor organizations was a major route whereby young Jews could 'wander' away from their family and cultural backgrounds if they wished to do so.[5] To a certain extent Sadie fits this pattern. During the 1930s she went on several holidays with International Tramping Tours and other left-wing organizations.[6] It was through a holiday arranged with the Social Democratic Workers' Party of Austria that she met Robert Wunderer, to whom she became transiently engaged, although there does not seem to have been a distinctive outdoor element in this case. Later it was on a walk organized by the communist

---

[2] David Cesarani, 'A Funny Thing Happened on the Way to the Suburbs: Social Change in Anglo-Jewry between the Wars, 1914–1945', *Jewish Culture and History* 1 (1998), 6.

[3] For cultural fears in relation to the East End see Judith R. Walkowitz, *City of Dreadful Delight Narratives of Sexual Danger in Late-Victorian London* (Chicago, 1992). See also Seth Koven, *Slumming: Sexual and Social Politics in Victorian England* (Princeton, 2006); Kellow Chesney, *The Victorian Underworld* (London, 1973); Sarah Wise, *The Blackest Streets: The Life and Death of a Victorian Slum* (London, 2009).

[4] Cesarani, 'A Funny Thing Happened', especially 6–10.

[5] David Dee, '"Wandering Jews"? British Jewry, Outdoor Recreation and the Far-Left, 1900–1939', *Labor History* 55 (2014), 563–79.

[6] International Tramping Tours was a pacifist travel organization co-founded by the Quaker socialists Margaret and Frank Happold. See Christine Collette, *The International Faith: Labour's Attitude to European Socialism, 1918–1939* (London, 1998), 102; Douglas George Hope, *Thomas Arthur Leonard and the Co-operative Holidays Association: Joy in Widest Commonalty Spread* (Newcastle upon Tyne, 2017), 106.

newspaper the *Daily Worker* that she met her future husband Alfred Attfield.
Neither of these men was Jewish so one could reasonably argue that holidays and
rambles organized by left-wing organizations led Sadie away from her Jewish
roots. However, this simplifies a complex story. In the first place, Sadie's family
were quite Anglicized to begin with. Lewisham was not one of the traditional
areas of Jewish settlement. Sadie's father changed his name from Moses to the
progressively more English Morris, Maurice and then Charles Maurice; he did
not wear the kippah. Sadie attended an Anglican primary school,
a nondenominational secondary school and a conventional Guide group rather
than one of the specifically Jewish troops.[7] She was, therefore, thoroughly
assimilated long before she became involved with left-wing outdoor groups.
Dee argues that many young Jews joined such groups more because of their
interest in leisure than out of political enthusiasm but in Sadie's case it was the
other way round.[8] She joined the Labour Party in 1926 and the Independent
Labour Party (ILP) in 1930 but it seems only to have been in 1932 that she went
on her first holiday with International Tramping Tours.[9] Furthermore, in
moving to the radical left, she ran the risk of undermining relationships with
her many politically centrist or conservative Gentile friends. For Sadie, then,
political engagement preceded rather than followed membership of left-wing
outdoor groups and, while it may have distanced her from her parents' values, it
also took her away from mainstream norms and social networks into which she
had previously been well integrated.

A more decisive influence on Sadie's ruralism and, for that matter, on other
aspects of her life, was the size and structure of her family. She had no fewer
than eight siblings, all brothers, and remained close to them throughout her
life, even the two who emigrated to Australia. Gregariousness was one of her
most pronounced traits – Sadie loved to be and, as the photographs in the
diaries bear witness, usually was in the middle of things. This can hardly be
unrelated to the large and happy family in which she grew up. It may also be
relevant that Sadie was the seventh of nine children: tentative evidence from
sibling studies suggests children lower down the birth order may be more
radical, open to change and willing to venture further from family norms.[10]

---

[7] The information in this paragraph is taken from 'Sarah Sadie Attfield 14th May 1907–
22nd October 2004', Funeral Commemoration Speech by John Attfield, Delivered at
Lewisham Crematorium, 18 Dec. 2004, in author's personal possession. A photograph on
the third slide shows Moses (Morris) Barmes bare-headed. For Jewish Guide groups see
Tammy M. Proctor, '(Uni)Forming Youth: Girl Guides and Boy Scouts in Britain, 1908–
39', *History Workshop Journal* 45 (1998), 114.

[8] Dee, 'Wandering Jews?', 565.

[9] 'Sarah Sadie Attfield 14th May 1907–22nd October 2004'.

[10] Gad Saad, Tripat Gill and Rajan Nataraajan, 'Are Laterborns More Innovative and
Nonconforming Consumers Than Firstborns? A Darwinian Perspective', *Journal of Business
Research* 58 (2005), 902–9.

One of the things Guide camps and other group holidays offered Sadie was a chance to get away from her family while reconstituting what was, functionally, a temporary new family of her own choosing around her.

Education was another major influence. Although she later described herself as an 'ardent royalist' in her teens, Sadie was evidently much impressed by the headmistress at her school, Sydenham County Secondary, who was a Labour supporter. Labour had an increasing presence in Lewisham between the wars, partly because of the development of London County Council's Downham estate (1924–30) and partly because of the energetic efforts of local organizers, led by the redoubtable Herbert Morrison, leader of London County Council, who took Lewisham East from the Conservatives in 1945.[11] Sadie's enthusiasm for education also affected her life in a range of less tangible ways. She read avidly and participated eagerly in further education after leaving school. Camping and holidays were not primarily educational but they were congruent with Sadie's passion for learning. They gave her opportunities to apply her book-learnt knowledge of nature, art and architecture to real-life settings, enabled her to widen her outlook by meeting interesting people with different backgrounds and perspectives, provided secluded time and space in which she could formulate her own ideas and values, and offered plentiful scope for discussing these with friends her own age who were trying to do the same. From her mid-twenties, however, Sadie's intense desire to learn and absorb new experiences may to some extent have led her away from the countryside. The artistic and architectural wealth of France, above all the Louvre, Versailles and Chartres, fascinated her. Inevitably, in this phase of her life, foreign places seemed more exciting than England and, although she did not lose her love for the English countryside, it no longer exercised the same pull over her. The Alps, however, filled her with wonder and it was perhaps not so much that she was turning away from the rural as turning away from home in these years.[12]

The Girl Guides is another important context in understanding the place of the countryside in Sadie's life. The First World War and its aftermath were a crucial period in the development of Guiding. Prior to the war the Guides had been a minor organization – indeed, they had been established only in 1909.[13] Baden-Powell had not originally anticipated that girls would be attracted to scouting and was dismayed to find that unofficial female and mixed scout troops were springing up all over Britain. It was to stop this and channel what he saw as misdirected excitement into more seemly outlets that he agreed to the creation of the Girl Guides. At first the Guides grew slowly, not

---

[11] Tom Jeffery, 'The Suburban Nation: Politics and Class in Lewisham', in D. Feldman and G. S. Jones (eds.), *Metropolis: Histories and Representations of London since 1800* (London, 1989).

[12] Barmes Diaries (esp. 26 Jul. to 9 Aug. 1930 and 15–31 Aug. 1931).

[13] Richard A. Voeltz, 'The Antidote to "Khaki Fever"? The Expansion of the British Girl Guides during the First World War', *Journal of Contemporary History* 27 (1992), 627–38.

least it would seem due to the caution and conservatism of Baden-Powell's sister Agnes, who was concerned to restrict them to the narrow range of decorous activities she regarded as suitable for girls. However, after Baden-Powell married Olave St Clair Soames in 1912, he passed responsibility for the Guides over to his wife. Olave was more attuned to the yearning for adventure and excitement among many girls and did much to shape the subtle, complex and fluid mixture of discipline and freedom, conformity and rebelliousness that characterized the Guides and played such a large part in their success and durability.[14]

Partly because of this flexibility, Guiding proved remarkably adaptable across the spectrum of class, religious, ethnic and regional differences in Britain. Nevertheless, the more prosperous outer suburbs were its heartland and Lewisham itself had among the highest Guide membership densities of any London borough.[15] In many ways, joining the Guides was the natural course for Sadie to take. It was another step on the road to assimilation – this was what other Lewisham girls of her age and social background did. However, it may have had an additional appeal to Sadie because, for all her sociability, she had no sisters. As she grew into her teens this may have become increasingly important for her.

The main sources for Sadie's life are her diaries and the supplementary information supplied by her son John. The diaries differ from those used elsewhere in this book in several respects. Firstly, they are still in private hands. I have only seen digital photographs of them. Secondly, they cover only one aspect and only just over a decade of Sadie's life – her camps and holidays between circa 1920 and 1932. Thirdly, most of the diary is explicitly retrospective, on internal evidence probably dating from circa 1930, although at least one of the preceding sections was copied from a diary written at the time of the events described. The retrospective part of the diary has some of the limitations but also some of the advantages of memoirs. Like a good memoir, it offers 'digested' experience – the passage of time enabled Sadie to write in a more considered and reflective manner than most diarists are able to achieve. Conversely, there is less detail and immediacy; more may have been forgotten or screened out. Fourthly, while all the camps described in the diary were rural, many of the holidays were predominantly urban. Sadie's diary is therefore less weighted towards the countryside than any of the others assessed in this book. That granted, it should be said that, even when Sadie is on holiday in an urban setting, her love of nature and the rural frequently comes through. Fifthly, an interesting feature of the diaries is that as Sadie grew older, she often took her

---

[14] On the early history of Guiding see Tammy M. Proctor, *Scouting for Girls: A Century of Girl Guides and Girl Scouts* (Santa Barbara, 2009). See also Rose Kerr, *The Story of the Girl Guides 1908–1938* (London, 1976); Proctor, *On My Honour*.
[15] Proctor, '(Uni)Forming Youth', 112.

holidays abroad, offering a useful point of comparison with the other predominantly English diaries.

A valuable feature of Sadie's diaries is that they are lavishly illustrated by photographs, some presumably taken by Sadie, others, featuring her, by one or other of her fellow campers. For the earlier parts of the diary these photographs are in a sense the principal source since Sadie uses them to prompt her memories. This tends to mean that, for the earlier camps, the diaries consist of a series of punctuated 'spots of time' related to the photographs. Since the photographs are likely to represent highlights from the camps, this probably means that some of the more mundane or even unhappy phases of camp life are overlooked in these earlier diaries, although on the whole the tone of the early diaries is similar to the later, contemporary diaries. The photographs also show things that do not emerge so clearly in the text, such as Sadie's expression, her positioning in relation to other campers, what she was wearing and the landscape in the background.

Sadie's decision to devote a diary exclusively to camps and holidays is interesting. She regarded camps as a form of holiday and sometimes explicitly refers to them as such. Evidently she thought holidays were both distinctive and important, more worthy of being recorded and preserved than other uses of time. The interwar years were a critical period in the development and definition of the concept of the holiday in Britain and Sadie's diaries need to be seen in this context.[16]

The first holiday recorded in the diary, and Sadie's first Guide camp, was at Baynards Park in Surrey. Writing up her diary several years later, Sadie could not remember whether the camp had been in 1920, 1921 or 1922. What comes across vividly, however, is her delight in being out in the countryside, pleasure in roughing it away from domestic comforts and intense engagement with the other campers. Her first recollection was of '[h]ow we walked through the estate along a tree shaded roadway, past the charcoal burner's hut'.[17] Charcoal burning had become, in this period, an emblematic rural craft, paradigmatically alien to and threatened by modernity. It features notably in Arthur Ransome's almost exactly contemporary *Swallows and Amazons* (1930) and *Swallowdale* (1931), where the charcoal burners are equated with savages yet turn out, in the latter book, to possess curative knowledge that saves the youthful 'civilized' protagonists from disaster.[18]

On the way to the Baynards Park camp Sadie's Guide troop was overtaken by a storm. They sheltered from the rain under a leaf (evidently a large one if

[16] John K. Walton, 'Tourism and Holidays in Britain between the Wars: Approaches and Opportunities', in Helen Pussard and Robert Snape (eds.), *Recording Leisure Lives: Histories, Archives and Memories of Leisure in 20th Century Britain* (Eastbourne, 2009).

[17] Barmes Diaries, 2 (n.d.).

[18] Hazel Sheeky Bird, *Class, Leisure and National Identity in British Children's Literature, 1918–1950* (Basingstoke, 2014).

the text is to be taken literally) and 'sang an accompaniment to its splatter', the first of many occasions on which Sadie and her companions were to sing to keep up their spirits in the face of adverse weather and threatening natural conditions.[19] There was a fine balance here – too much adversity might have broken the campers' spirits or, probably not in Surrey but certainly on some of Sadie's later Alpine adventures, even proved fatal but short of this, adversity was an exhilarating liberation from the padded prison of urban 'mod cons'. Discomfort and a frisson of danger also rapidly developed the comradeship that Sadie valued perhaps more than anything else in her experience of camping.[20]

A marked feature of these camps, in common with those of many other early twentieth-century youth organizations, was their emphasis on nature and rurality.[21] At Baynards Sadie recalled climbing on her friend Doris Carter's back to decorate the Guide leaders' windowsills with dog roses and meadowsweet. Rambling was the order of the day and gave a delightful sense of freedom ('[w]e ran our own activities'). The human and the natural were intertwined in Sadie's sense of the rural: along with the flowers and trees, she photographed the Elizabethan mansion to which the park belonged, admiring the Tudor roses on the door handles. Her verdict was that '[w]e left after a week of glorious adventure, fully determined to prove the joys of camping on all possible occasions'.[22] Although this is a retrospective judgement, Sadie's enthusiastic embrace of camping over the following decade suggests that it is probably close to what she felt at the time.

Sadie's next Guide camp was at Chailey in East Sussex in 1922 or 1923, when she was fifteen or sixteen. It seems to be rare for young children to appreciate landscape: Ruskin was typically precocious in admiring the view from Friar's Crag at the age of five. Sadie was following a much more normal pattern in discovering this form of beauty in her mid-teens: '[t]here's a common nearby with a distant windmill against the skyline a vivid picture'. She learnt the difference between heather, bell heather and 'erica' (presumably cross-leaved heath, *Erica tetralix*) and watched the white pigeons in the church courtyard while she waited there during the service.[23] While she never forgot her Jewish

---

[19] Barmes Diaries, 2 (n.d.). This was in accordance with the eighth of Baden-Powell's original Guide Laws: 'A Guide smiles and sings under all difficulties.' World Association of Girl Guides and Girl Scouts, 'The Original Promise and Law'. www .wagggs.org/en/about-us/our-history/original-promise-and-law [accessed 12 Dec. 2018].

[20] On Guiding and adventure see Sian Edwards, *Youth Movements, Citizenship and the English Countryside: Creating Good Citizens, 1930–1960* (Cham, 2017), 107–17.

[21] Edwards, *Youth Movements*.

[22] Barmes Diaries, 6 (n.d.).

[23] Barmes Diaries 7 (n.d.). The Guide Promise was sufficiently generic with respect to God that it posed little obstacle to Jewish membership, although there were greater barriers to non-Judaeo-Christian faiths. Proctor, *On My Honour*, 141–2.

ancestry, there is little indication in the diaries that it gave rise to a sense of exclusion, as this calm, peaceful memory suggests.

In 1924 Sadie went on a 'post-matriculation' holiday to Bletchingley, also in Surrey. Although it was not a Guide camp, she justified its inclusion in her diary on the grounds that she and her school mates 'lived the life glorious', a telling assessment of what this kind of collective camping meant to her in her youth.[24] For the next two years no camps are recorded in the diary, perhaps because, having left school, she was searching for secure employment. She found this in 1926 when she entered service with London County Council (LCC), working as a clerk in County Hall, and later in the LCC's schools' health service, where she continued until 1965, when she was transferred to Lewisham Borough Council. By 1926, then, Sadie had achieved a degree of economic independence and stability and it is probably no accident that the next record of a camping holiday dates from the following year.[25] This was another Guide camp, although she was now a Ranger (i.e. a member of the senior section of the Guides). The camp was at Storrington in Sussex, where she also camped in 1928, 1929 and 1930. Novelty was an important part of the attraction of holidays to Sadie – the excitement of arriving in a new place – but the Storrington camps show that successively revisiting somewhere familiar could foster deeper feelings:

> Storrington Whitsun camps have seemed one long serial of happy weekends – each joined to the last so that, when I arrive at the old Pulborough Station & watch the familiar fields and shadowy downs pass along our road, & catch my first glimpse of Chanctonbury Ring, standing out on a far corner of the hills, the intervening months seem to fade & pass so that this year's camp seems but a continuation of the last & each year brings a longer weekend.[26]

This sense of a familiar, beloved rural landscape – a 'home-from-home' – recurs in the diaries on which this book draws. Johnston's Raikes Wood, Catley's Chew valley and Bissell's Ben Nevis are examples. A characteristic, perhaps defining, feature of such landscapes is that they partake of the familiarity, comfort and security of home while being immune from the trials, conflicts and demands that are, at least to some extent, an inevitable part of home life.

The Storrington camps seem to have expanded Sadie's horizons both literally and figuratively. There is a new intensity and vividness of feeling in her response to landscape, mainly no doubt due to her growing maturity but owing much also to the scale and sweep of the South Downs and, initially at least,

---

[24] Barmes Diaries 9 (n.d.).
[25] 'Sarah Sadie Attfield 14th May 1907–22nd October 2004'.
[26] Barmes Diaries 11–12 (n.d.).

perhaps to the resumption of a cherished activity after a lengthy interruption. The 1927 Storrington camp was Sadie's first time under canvas:

> I shall never forget that first morning's awakening in my airy palace of green canvass bathed in greeny golden light, to the song of lark & chaffinch & rustles of wing in the silver birches nearby. That first view of sweeping downs – velvety & green, sun swept & shaded.[27]

The spiritual centre of this landscape was Chanctonbury Ring, a place that has powerfully focused the emotional responses of countless visitors over the years. In the words of the Sussex historian Peter Brandon '[t]he grand landmark of Chanctonbury Ring acquired a mystical and symbolic force without equal in southern England'.[28] This is amply borne out in Janet Pennington's history of the Ring in which she demonstrates that it was held in special affection not only by well-known writers and composers such as Francis Kilvert, Wilfrid Scawen Blunt, Hilaire Belloc, Eleanor Farjeon, John Galsworthy, Philip Gosse and John Ireland, but also by untold numbers of less celebrated people, especially those with a Sussex provenance.[29] Such was the response it evoked from Sadie that, despite her atheism, she found herself drawing on religious metaphors in her description:

> And, always, our pilgrimage to Chanctonbury Ring. A wondrous pilgrim's way through beech woods, still in their glory of delicate spring green, full of faery lights & shadows, dancing shadows at our feet & drifting light overhead. The grey restful tree trunks ever strike a deep cathedral note in the chime of dancing joy bells of spring. Then the swift walk on velvety turf to the top of the downs, bare & swelling, beauty unadorned – to the Ring itself. Then, & then only, a consummate reward, to seek the beauties of her view around. Oh – the joy of that distant flash of sea, with its shadowed ships & pursuing smoke.[30]

However, while the feelings described here are certainly metaphysical and perhaps spiritual, they are not intrinsically theistic. Sadie always strongly resented any implication that her atheism impeded her emotional, spiritual or aesthetic responses, as when she politely but firmly explained to a missionary that she was at least as capable of appreciating beauty as the next person despite not being a Christian.[31]

From about this time Sadie's accounts of her camps become increasingly embodied. But as her ecstatic description of climbing Chanctonbury Ring demonstrates, this physicality was a gateway to spiritual experience, not an

---

[27] Barmes Diaries 11 (n.d.).
[28] Brandon, *The Discovery of Sussex*, 31.
[29] Janet Pennington, *Chanctonbury Ring: The Story of a Sussex Landmark* (Steyning, 2011), 13, 93–114.
[30] Barmes Diaries 12 (n.d.).
[31] Barmes Diaries 19–20 (n.d.).

alternative to it; or rather, the two were one and the same thing. The words 'dancing' and 'joy' recur in this and other similar passages in the diaries. The physicality could be sensuous – walking over velvety turf, the bare and swelling downs – but it could also be strenuous:

> And those well remembered hikes over the downs. Long days of back aching climb to those glorious heights, of exciting meals cooked in magic copses, of weary, happy shiftings back to camp.[32]

Here the ache seems a ticket of entry to the glory, just as the weariness is of the happiness. This asceticism closely resembles that Melanie Tebbutt describes in relation to G. H. B. Ward, the leading figure in the Sheffield Clarion Ramblers. Tebbutt argues that the strenuous asceticism Ward espoused was related to a particular ideal of manliness.[33] This may well be so but Sadie's diary suggests it could also function in a less gendered way. The implicit rejection of passive consumerism and materialism may be more pertinent in this context.

Next year at Liss in Hampshire Sadie met up again with the 'old jolly crowd of Rangers'. Her recently discovered delight in rural landscapes and being in nature was much in evidence:

> [W]e had a glorious site is Miss Shorter's chestnut woods – & camp fires under beech trees, lit by the setting sun, on a hill darkclad by trees & lightened by the songs of birds. We had delightful hikes through woods & heather-clad hillsides with lovely views of the downs – & dear Chanctonbury Ring.[34]

From 1929 onwards, however, Sadie's holidays more often took her abroad. She was spreading her wings as she grew older, more independent and more confident.[35] In August 1929 she went to Dieppe, still with the Guides. This represented an extension, rather than a rejection, of her previous (and continuing) holidays in the English countryside. On the train to Newhaven she enjoyed the 'setting sun cut off by gentle Surrey hills, &, then, moon bathed trees and fields', quite in the old manner. In Dieppe she had fewer opportunities to get out into the countryside but relished it when she did:

> This morning we went for the most glorious ride ever – we visited the Phare D'Ailly – an awfully well constructed affair ... with wonderful lights of glass prisms ...
>
> The drive was beautiful, the countryside very lovely. There were the typical Poplar-lined avenues, beech copses & honeysuckle-crowned

---

[32] Barmes Diaries 13 (n.d.).

[33] Melanie Tebbutt, 'Rambling and Manly Identity in Derbyshire's Dark Peak, 1880s–1920s', *Historical Journal* 49 (2006), 1125–53.

[34] Barmes Diaries 17 (n.d.).

[35] The 'widening circles' of Sadie' life in this period recall D. H. Lawrence's Ursula Brangwen (*The Rainbow*, 1915).

hedgerows – & near the lighthouse was a lovely stretch of common & I had a topping talk on route with Miss Shortt.[36]

Sadie evidently valued the countryside around Dieppe in part for what she perceived as its distinctively French qualities.[37] She seems to have been more conscious of its Frenchness than she was of the Englishness of the English countryside. This is perhaps hardly surprising – France represented an unfamiliar other so Sadie was primed to notice the ways in which it was different. She took much the same pleasure, however, in discovering and registering the characteristic features of regional landscapes in England: the heather-clad Surrey hills, the smooth turf and bare heights of the South Downs, weatherboarded farm buildings in Kent. Although the external objects that engaged her attention in each setting contrasted, the internal quality of the experiences hardly differed. This is reflected in her use of the same adjectival palette to express her responses to English and French rural landscapes – 'very lovely', 'glorious', 'beautiful', 'wondrous', 'delightful' – and emphasis in both cases on vivid colours, exhilarating views and intense sensation.

Two other aspects of the Dieppe holiday also proved compelling for Sadie: the sea and the town's historic buildings. Seascapes are not landscapes, except in the loosest and most encompassing usage, but land features in many seascapes and vice versa. Historically and etymologically the words 'seaside' and 'countryside' are close cousins. 'Seaside' came first: it was already widely current by the 1780s, and may have influenced the emergence of 'countryside' a few decades later.[38] By the second half of the nineteenth century each had become powerfully associated with leisure, an association that was to some extent implicit from the start, insofar as each was 'over there' – not part of the space through which the observer moved in the course of his or her regular business. Beyond these basic similarities, which made both available as places of escape from the hegemony of the urban and the artificial, countryside and seaside also shared some more specific features. Both, in certain guises, could instantiate what Nicolson in her pioneering study of the cultural history of mountains referred to as 'the aesthetics of the infinite'.[39] This inexhaustibility is very apparent in Sadie's rapturous descriptions of watching the sea, 'an untiring pastime'. On arriving in Dieppe one of the first things she and her friends did was to go off 'to the far plage – & gazed & gazed at the sea. Oh, the colouring was too wonderful for words – blues & greens – such as we never see

---

[36] Barmes Diaries, 16 Aug. 1929.
[37] Compare the entry for 18 Aug. 1929: 'After tea we rode to Criel thro' rather lovely country – quite different from that of home no hedges & copses – occasional stretches of woodland – but mainly huge fields. I did enjoy the ride.' See also the following day: 'lovely ride – thro' typical French country, large open fields, copses of beech, avenues of poplars & occasional thatched cottages'.
[38] Oxford English Dictionary, 'Sea-Side | Seaside, N.' (Oxford).
[39] Nicolson, *Mountain Gloom*.

reproduced nowadays – I've only seen them on the ancient tile work at the B. M. [British Museum]'. Later in the week she watched the sea 'ever changing, restless & almost intolerably deep in hue'.[40] As these quotations suggest, it was not only the infinitude but also the beauty of the sea, and especially its colours, that entranced Sadie.[41]

Like Chanctonbury Ring the sea had a powerful aura that gave a journey to it a crescendo rhythm:

> After tea Lily & I walked to Pourville. We found a delightful lane, then a bit of road, then another lane, & finally – the sea. It seemed to burst on our vision like a sea of silver – a glory of sun-bathed, sparkling waves – & beyond, interminable stretches of blue, ridden by foam-flecked sea horses. It was one of those scenes one hopes to keep to keep forever, 'to burst upon that inward eye which is the bliss of solitude'.[42]

Yet there were also differences. Although Sadie enjoyed swimming in the sea, it did not offer her the ecstatic freedom of movement that dancing on the grass or under the trees could. Nor was there the same sense of being immersed in nature, even becoming part of it, which she experienced on some of her rural camps. Perhaps, too, for all the beauty and wonder of the sea, there was something austere and unapproachable about it.[43] Contrast her first sight of English countryside on returning home:

> Somewhere round 4pm we sighted England – gleaming white like icebergs – smoothly rounded snowy cliffs – & soon we were able to distinguish the country beyond – long rolling hills, corn clad & girdled by belts of trees & hedges – oh lovely. Perhaps, after all, it is not so hard to come home again.[44]

This endorses Readman's perceptive observation that the focus of the strongest affective responses to the White Cliffs of Dover was what lay inland rather than out to sea: the sheltering domesticity of the countryside, not imperial visions of Britannia ruling the waves.[45] As with most of the other diarists, it was rare for Sadie to feel patriotic emotion in relation to landscape. She did so on this

---

[40] Barmes Diaries, 12 Aug. 1929.

[41] She found both aspects in the mountains too: a year later in the French Alps she was thrilled not only by the view from a summit, extending 'range beyond range', but also by the 'marvellous green and blue effects' of an ice grotto and the waters of a rushing stream 'sometimes . . . green, sometimes blue, sometimes grey – & always foam-flecked in white'. Barmes Diaries, 26 Jul. to 9 Aug. 1930.

[42] Barmes Diaries, 16 Aug. 1929. The quotation is from Wordsworth's 'I Wandered Lonely As a Cloud'.

[43] Compare Cresswell, The North Cornish Coast, 35: 'there must be awe mixed with our admiration' [of the sea].

[44] Barmes Diaries, 25 Aug. 1929.

[45] Readman, Storied Ground, 45, 49.

occasion because she was seeing it through the temporarily defamiliarized eyes of the returning traveller. Her lack of interest in, or even awareness of, the Englishness of English landscapes at other times is indicative of how thoroughly and unselfconsciously English she felt.[46]

Like the sea, historic buildings appealed to Sadie for reasons that in some respects paralleled but in others differed from her love of nature and the countryside. Beauty was the most obvious link: the language in which she describes medieval churches, the sea and mountain landscapes are at times interchangeable. The 'very lovely' colouring of the nave of St Jacques, for example, was 'a greenish, greyish like tint', while the colours of the rose window were 'very pure and deep'.[47] Age mattered too: of the many buildings Sadie enthused about in her diaries, the most recent was the Palace of Versailles (seventeenth and eighteenth centuries).[48] She loved churches and cathedrals, castles, cottages, farm buildings and windmills. While rural landscapes were not, perhaps, old in quite the same sense, both, in Sadie's eyes, were antithetical to the modern. Sadie does not mention the National Trust in her camping diaries but her conclusion, on seeing a Norman church shortly after arriving back in England from Dieppe, that France 'hasn't' all the age & beauty' is reminiscent of the Trust's remit to preserve places of 'Historic Interest or Natural Beauty'.[49] Buildings also appealed to Sadie's more intellectual side, her interest in art and history. Associations with Joan of Arc permeate her account of medieval Rouen, while in the cathedral ('a most lovely building inside and out') she enjoyed the contrast between Gothic and Renaissance styles in the tombs of the two cardinals.[50] Conversely, the countryside gave her more physical and emotional scope and freedom.

Sadie was moving to the left politically during these years, continuing the journey she began at Sydenham County Secondary. She joined the Labour Party in 1926, canvassing voters in Forest Hill and even speaking on street corners. In April 1929 she read Philip Snowden's *Socialism and Syndicalism* and wrote in the record she kept of books she had read '[f]inished my conversion!' Shortly afterwards she joined the Independent Labour Party, where she mixed with luminaries such as George Bernard Shaw and Jimmie Maxton, the Clydebank MP. By circa 1937, in common with many young Jews, she had

---

[46] In contrast, say, to Nikolaus Pevsner, whose 1955 Reith Lectures on 'The Englishness of English Art' could surely only have been penned by someone for whom England was an adopted country. 'The Reith Lectures: Nikolaus Pevsner: The Englishness of English Art: 1955'. BBC Online. www.bbc.co.uk/programmes/p00h9llv [accessed 22 Sep. 2015].

[47] Barmes Diaries, 14 Aug. 1930.

[48] She found the Arc de Triomphe 'most impressive' but her account of it is otherwise cool, without the effusiveness of her descriptions of Gothic cathedrals. Barmes Diaries, 28 Jul. 1930.

[49] Barmes Diaries, 24 Aug. 1929.

[50] Barmes Diaries, 19 Aug. 1929.

Figure 8.1   Sadie (far right) on camp at Storrington, *c*.1928
Reproduced by kind permission of John Attfield

become a member of the Communist Party, in her case apparently under the
influence of Harry Pollitt.[51] On the face of it there is little indication of this
trajectory in her camping diaries – no record of political activities or even
discussions, no political reflections and no indication that her choice of
destination was influenced by her strengthening political convictions. It is
true that she and her friends abandoned a plan to go to Germany in summer
1931 because of the political and financial turbulence there but this was for
the sake of prudence rather than in protest at the growing strength of the
Nazi Party ('there was shooting all night in Cologne').[52]

However, at a deeper level there are interesting connections between Sadie's
camping and her political values. The experience of camping was an intensely
communal one for her. This was probably true for most young campers but
especially so for Sadie. In virtually every photograph she is at or near the centre
of the group, typically with an arm around or pressed up close against one or
more of the other campers (see Figure 8.1). She took a full and active part in
camp life, entering enthusiastically into the collective experience. Except when
describing uniquely individual perceptions – the impression a cathedral or
mountain made on her, for example – she habitually used the first-person

[51] 'Sarah Sadie Attfield 14th May 1907–22nd October 2004'.
[52] Barmes Diaries, 15 Aug. 1931.

plural in her camp diaries. She hiked, cooked, cleaned, pitched tent, shared discomforts, played games, danced, sung and shed the last-night tears with her companions.[53] These camps, whether with the Guides or other groups, approximated to temporary communes. Virtually everything was shared: accommodation, food, tasks and pleasures. Private property was effectively non-existent for the duration of the camp. Even the clothes were interchangeable on a Guide camp since everyone wore uniform.[54] There was an expectation that everyone would contribute and work together for the common good. Historians such as Gillis and Springhall argue that uniformed youth movements such as the Scouts and Guides inculcated an ideology of imperialism, although more recent scholarship has tended to emphasize the complex and often contradictory ideological and political currents and practices within Scouting and Guiding.[55] In Sadie's case the Guide promise to serve God and love King and Country seems to have made little impression. As we have seen, Guide camps were, among other things, an occasion on which she could develop her sceptical, unorthodox ideas about religion. The communitarian practice of Guide camps evidently influenced her much more than their establishment ideology. Although they sprang from different sources, the powerful collective, service-oriented and internationalist elements of Guiding and Scouting were more consonant with the values of the left than has perhaps been recognized. Certainly, in Sadie's case, Guide camps seem to have provided fertile soil for the growth of an existing socialist seed.

What appears to have been the last of Sadie's Storrington camps took place at Whitsun in 1930. It was not, on the whole, especially memorable, partly because it was small and partly because 'Clarkie', who had shared many previous camps with Sadie, was not there. But there was one 'never to be forgotten delight', best described in Sadie's own words:

> Peggy, Phyllis, Doris Lake & I went to the sanctuary bathing pool – deep hidden in rhododendron & birch bushes, overshadowed by soaring pines ... where the beauty within the pool matched that without. We swam and played in the water or lay quiet to watch birds & insects skim its

---

[53] Barmes Diaries, 24 Aug. 1929. On camp chores and communality see Edwards, *Youth Movements*, 213–14.

[54] Guides could be fiercely proud of their badges and some Guides owned accessories or uniform components cut from more expensive cloth than others. Proctor, '(Uni)Forming Youth'. However, the main point of uniform was to create a shared sense of collective identity and to suppress individual differences. Interestingly Sadie never mentions badges nor uniform differences, although she does record passing her '1st class hike'. Barmes Diaries, Whitsun, 1930.

[55] John Springhall, *Youth, Empire and Society: British Youth Movements, 1883–1940* (London, 1977); John Gillis, 'Conformity and Rebellion: Contrasting Styles of English and German Youth, 1900–33', *History of Education Quarterly* 13 (1973), 254. For a more nuanced view see Allen Warren, 'Sir Robert Baden-Powell, the Scout Movement and Citizen Training in Great Britain, 1900–1920', *English Historical Review* 101 (1986), 376–98.

surface – where broken flowers lay like drifting butterflies – whilst all about us beauty danced in the hot haze of the sun.

And then we danced on the soft white sand among the bushes. Light, fantastic, weird & wild, each according to her mood – & all clad only in bathing costumes – free of convention, free of self – only expressing by movement the joy & glory of the day.

I hold that, indeed, one of the happiest memories of my life.[56]

This was not the first time Sadie had played in a pool with her companions – in 1927 they had spent 'happy hours' paddling in a dew pond on the downs 'or lying by the side watching the swallows dip across its surface'.[57] She swam frequently in the sea while in Dieppe, and seems to have danced whenever she could. Dancing by moonlight in pyjamas was a recurrent feature of Sadie's Guide camps and on one pouring wet lunchtime she and her friends again donned bathing costumes and danced round preparing dinner while the others stayed in the tents.[58] What these occasions have in common is a sense of joyful physical freedom and release from constraint. Pyjamas and bathing costumes restricted the body less than clothes; materially and symbolically, they were only one step from nudity. There is an implicit erotic element here but, at least in the case of the most richly described occasion, at the Sanctuary Bathing Pool, this was subsumed in an encompassing experience of unity, in which the boundaries between physical and spiritual, self and other, human and natural dissolved. The birds, insects, flowers, butterflies and girls swoop and skim alike and the beauty that dances in the hot haze of the sun embraces subject and object, perceived and perceiver. In many respects this distils the essence of the 'life glorious' that drew Sadie back time after time to these rural camps. She sought and seems often to have found a prelapsarian, Edenic quality of undividedness, one that perfectly corresponded to her nascent political ideals. There seems little doubt that the liberatory and communitarian experiences of group camping helped to make Sadie a socialist, although it may partly have been because she already sought freedom and communion that she was so drawn to camping.

In July 1930 Sadie visited the Alps for the first time, staying with a party of English Guides in a chalet at Les Houches near Chamonix. As we have seen, the cultural history of mountains has an extensive historiography. Sadie's response to her first encounter with the Alps in some respects recapitulates familiar 'sublime' tropes such as awe, wonder and a sense of danger, although this does not make her responses any less authentic. They walked across a glacier, wearing special non-slip climbing socks bought at a shop in Les Boissons:

---

[56] Barmes Diaries, Whitsun 1930.
[57] Barmes Diaries, 13 (n.d.).
[58] Barmes Diaries, 21 Aug. 1930.

> We . . . began our climb across the ice by negotiating a steep ladder – &
> then steps cut in an almost sheer ice cliff. Walking across was fairly easy, as
> the socks prevented slipping – but going down the other side was awful.
> No one felt safe till all were down & there were 30 of us to go – one at
> a time, clutching the guide's hand for dear life – sheer drop of 100 ft & only
> a few steps cut in slippery ice to help us.[59]

Two days later Sadie's group went for a five-hour mountain climb, crossing
snowfields and bare slippery rocks edged by precipices. 'I must admit I was
scared in places, tho' I enjoyed the experience immensely', she confided to her
diary afterwards. On the way back they were overtaken by a thunderstorm and
were soon 'soaked through and singing hard to hide our fears' as they slithered
and slipped on the wet stones underfoot while lightening flashed and thunder
rolled around them.[60]

Like many a traveller before and after she was dazzled by the Alpenglow:

> In the evening, too, we fed on beauty – for the Mt Blanc range was perfect,
> grey & white & green against the clear blue sky – a sky almost impossibly
> blue, shading to steel, then slaty blue as the evening drew in. And, as the
> sun sank, the colours took a wonderful pinkish flush – which passed
> across & at last left the whiteness of the snow almost too intense.[61]

As this suggests, beauty was more than a pleasure for Sadie – it was an appetite,
perhaps even a need, one that was most frequently and fully met in the
encounter with nature and rural landscapes. When the time came to leave
she wrapped it closely round her, storing it in her memory for leaner times like
a squirrel caching nuts for the winter:

> One last look at the loveliness we leave. Near towering, rugged heights –
> afar snow-clad peaks . . . distance embowered in an azure haze . . . Sadness
> & beauty close intertwined – how in the deeper distance those dear heights
> tower into threatening blackness. Oh – in all your moods be forever with
> me – let me see thee always when beauty seems most far.[62]

Sadie had no more difficulty loving landscapes than she did people. She
embraced both warmly, referring to 'our mountain' and 'our lake' ('One bright
spot was the moonlight on our lake outside Aix – lovely.').[63] Indeed, the two
were not really distinct. Her love of landscapes such as those round Storrington
or Les Houches partly arose from the experiences she had shared with her
fellow campers in these landscapes. Conversely, the countryside provided an
opportunity to live out a shared communal life in which the barriers of social
convention and private property were temporarily set aside.

[59] Barmes Diaries, 31 Jul. 1930.
[60] Barmes Diaries, 2 Aug. 1930.
[61] Barmes Diaries, 1 Aug. 1930.
[62] Barmes Diaries, 8 Aug. 1930.
[63] Barmes Diaries, 8 Aug. 1930.

While the Alps made a profound impression on her, in most respects her response to them was not fundamentally dissimilar to the way she related to the English countryside. Rather than mountain landscapes striking her as wholly distinctive, for example, she felt they were a scaled-up version of familiar English landscapes: 'the harebells & stonecrop, & pinks & rockroses are lovely vegetation similar to ours but more profuse – bilberries, strawberries & raspberries very plentiful'.[64] Just as congruent human elements like rural crafts and venerable buildings were part of her sense of what constituted the English countryside, so in the Alps she 'loved, too, the valleys & chalets, churches & cottages, & hilltop chateaux'.[65]

Only just over a week after returning from Les Houches, Sadie was off on camp again. Tatsfield on the slopes of Surrey's North Downs might have seemed rather tame after the Alps, but this was the first time she had been an officer responsible for running a Guide camp so it was a momentous experience: 'I spent years preparing for camp & had much worry in anticipation – but it was worth anything.' As quartermaster she took great pride in her store tent and in ensuring the Guides under her care were well fed. The sense of responsibility for the 'kiddies' brought out a new, motherly side to Sadie's character that was to develop strongly in later years:

> [W]e were thrilled to death to be officers in camp ... & the girls were so appreciative of everything. I did not realise they were so fond of me before ... I used to tuck them in & kiss them goodnight – & feel quite motherly. Wood & Peggy said they'd never met keener or more cheerful & enthusiastic guides.

One night one of her fellow officers thought she heard people in the lane adjacent to their campsite and, their minds full of tales of tramps and horse thieves, they stayed up watching for them. It was a false alarm but they were rewarded by a gloriously starry night. The next evening three Scouts they had met turned up together with a lone camper whom Sadie took to the store tent and fed. They had great fun dancing and after the children were in bed sat up with the Scouts over coffee and cigarettes till midnight. As always, the last day of the camp brought sadness but overall it had been 'a glorious week'.[66]

Early the next year she visited friends at Chelmondiston in Suffolk, where she walked alone in the beautiful park, saw a kingfisher, and 'danced by the river when no one was by'. At Whitsun she was at Tatsfield, and again in July, but on each occasion only for the weekend. The summer camp that year was at Falfield in Gloucestershire. It was hard work because the 'kiddies' were all very young and could not do much on their own account. But Sadie thought the Cotswold

[64] Barmes Diaries, 30 Jul. 1930.
[65] Barmes Diaries, 4 Aug. 1930.
[66] Barmes Diaries, 16–24 Aug. 1930.

countryside 'very lovely', especially the lanes and the 'splendid' hills. On the second day they had a hay fight and in the evening sang loudly in a tent to keep up their spirits during a tremendous thunderstorm. On the whole, however, it was not as rewarding as the previous year's camp in Surrey. Sadie seems to have had little support – 'it was like being a lone officer'. Without a group of companions her own age she missed the comradeship camp usually provided and she had to work so hard that there was little if any of the carefree joy she had so often found on rural camps before. This seems to have been Sadie's last Guide camp. Certainly it had been a deflating experience but Sadie was moving away from the Guides for other reasons too. As she grew older she sought wider horizons and greater excitement. Her French holidays had given her a taste for the Continent. Although she had enjoyed being a camp officer at Tatsfield, Sadie primarily wanted comradely relationships with her peers on camp – looking after 'kiddies' was satisfying in another way but it was not a substitute. Her developing political interests and commitments also pointed in a different direction – increasingly she wanted to spend time with friends who shared her political values, not something she could achieve through the Guides.[67]

In August, accordingly, she went to Paris, Chartres and Rouen with three friends. She admired the splendours of Versailles, especially the magnificent vistas, the lawns, canals and Marie Antoinette's rustic Hameau. In Paris she discovered new beauties in Nôtre Dame, detested the Eiffel Tower and enjoyed the Louvre, preferring the 'delicate trees & landscapes' of Corot to the fleshiness of Rubens. Chartres Cathedral entranced her: 'the best cathedral in France and the cream of Gothic architecture'. Back in Paris they revisited Versailles on one of the rare Sundays that the fountains were in full play – an 'absolutely superb' sight. They took in a visit to 'dear familiar Rouen', picnicking in the hills above the Seine, before taking the train to Dieppe and hence by ferry back to England.[68] The following Easter she walked with a large group of friends from Gravesend to Canterbury, 'through lovely bits of Kent by the Medway'. They stayed at youth hostels, some more satisfactory than others, and were, according to Sadie, 'a very jolly party', a claim her photos substantiate. Although this was a walking holiday rather than a camp, with adult friends not Guides, the rural landscapes they passed through appealed to Sadie in very much the old way. There are photographs of trees and rivers, weatherboarded farm buildings, cottage interiors, cows in an orchard and the group resting for lunch after a hard morning's tramp. Beyond Charing they walked through beautiful beech and pine woods bathed in drifting mist, an eerie but memorable experience. Most of the group went home after arriving at Canterbury but Sadie and two friends took the bus to Folkestone and walked on along the

---

[67] Barmes Diaries, 1931 (passim).
[68] Barmes Diaries, 15–30 Aug. 1931.

clifftop to Dover, sheltering from a rainstorm in a galvanized iron shed and making tea in a dixie.[69]

That summer (1932) Sadie went on what seems to have been the first of a number of Continental holidays with the left-wing outdoor organization International Tramping Tours (ITT). On this occasion they went to the Vosges. We do not have a diary as such from this holiday, only some photographs and a one-page article Sadie wrote for ITT's magazine. After an opening flavoured with a characteristic hint of irony ('[t]he perfect holiday – well, perhaps we may not reach that height'), the article highlights elements very similar to those she had found so rewarding on Guide camps: beauty, peace, pleasant company, old towns and villages with picturesque houses and a vista leading towards a majestic cathedral. She reserved her most vivid prose for intense experiences of nature and landscape: '[c]an you imagine day-long tramps through forests, black depths of pine or grey-green drifts of beech, walking along paths softly carpeted by moss, or beech leaves long dead, in some places in gloom so deep as to conjure up all your childhood's memories of goblins and dwarfs?' Still more magical was watching the sun rise and set at Le Hohneck:

> where, high above the surrounding hills, you may watch the sunset … with purple shadows in the east and a flaming west, while, on the near mountains, clouds lie like drifting snow. And in the morning you may awake to a world of colourful mists, 'dream shadow dim'. And watch the colours deepen and fade; first on the hill tops as the sun sweeps the mist away, then in the distance, where the mist gathers into a soft background to the deep-shadowed hills.

Among the photographs from this holiday are several of pine woods and one each of the sunrise and sunset at Le Hohneck. The latter, on the last page of the diary, emanate mystery and atmosphere. Evidently Sadie still regarded natural beauty as a means of accessing spiritual experience.[70]

After 1932 no further written record of Sadie's camping and walking holidays appears to exist but a memoir written by her son provides a brief outline of later events. The 1930s were an active period for her – she took evening classes at Goldsmith's College and then, from 1933, at the London School of Economics. In 1934 she was promoted to administrative grade in the London County Council Health Department, having passed an internal promotion exam. She read widely, went to the theatre and concerts, and developed her political interests. One of her closest friends during this period was Edith King, a fellow member of the ILP who later married the distinguished peace campaigner and anti-racist Fenner Brockway. The mid-1930s were overshadowed by the death of her mother, Kate, in 1933 and the illness of her

---

[69] Barmes Diaries, 1932 (passim). A dixie is a large iron cooking pot.
[70] Barmes Diaries, 1932 (passim).

father, whose care occupied much of her time until his death in 1938. However, this did not prevent Sadie from going abroad. In 1934 she visited Austria on the invitation of the Austrian Social Democratic Party and fell in love with Robert Wunderer, the son of the chief oboist in the Vienna Philharmonic Orchestra. They became engaged in 1935 but the relationship broke down the following year. In 1937 Sadie visited the USSR and became engaged to Fred Hess, the purser of the Russian ship that took her back home. She visited him in Leningrad again in April 1939 but was dissuaded from immediate marriage by one of Fred's friends, a government official who explained to her that, if she got married in the Soviet Union, she would find it difficult to leave. War intervened and Sadie lost contact with Fred.[71]

During the war Sadie worked in the administrative department at Dulwich Hospital and then in the hospital staffing department, coincidentally based during the war at Sydenham County Secondary School. She joined the Women's Royal Naval Service in 1943, serving first in Southampton and then in Liverpool. This was a political act from Sadie's point of view: she was passionately committed to fighting Nazism and wanted to contribute directly to the war effort.[72]

Sadie's love of nature and the countryside continued although now often coupled with her political interests: it was no accident that the August bank holiday ramble on which she met Alfred was a *Daily Worker* event. From 1943 the two of them lived together in Camberwell Grove, marrying in 1950 soon after John's birth. A photograph shows Sadie and Alfred with friends and their dog Sally on a rural walk in the late 1940s. They are seated on the grass under the spreading branches of what looks like an oak.[73]

In 1965 Sadie was transferred to Lewisham Council's schools service, working at New Cross Town Hall for the next three years until her retirement. The family moved from Sydenham to Chelford Road in Bromley the following year. Sadie remained politically active with the Communist Party, the Co-operative Movement, the Pensioners' Campaign, the peace movement and anti-racism campaigns. Every year she took a holiday abroad with friends, attending seminars organized by the Sonnenberg Association for world peace in the Harz mountains in Germany several times and visiting her brother Mark in Australia in 1986 at the age of seventy-nine. Alfred, who was fifteen years older than her, died in 1983. Even in the 1990s, when Sadie was in her eighties, she remained politically active in the Lewisham Pensioners Forum. She continued to live on her own until 2002, when she and John decided she should live with him and his wife in Germany, where she enjoyed a period of better health and good care before dying, at the age of ninety-seven, in October 2004.[74]

---

[71] 'Sarah Sadie Attfield 14th May 1907–22nd October 2004'.
[72] 'Sarah Sadie Attfield 14th May 1907–22nd October 2004'.
[73] 'Sarah Sadie Attfield 14th May 1907–22nd October 2004'.
[74] 'Sarah Sadie Attfield 14th May 1907–22nd October 2004'.

* * *

Although the most obvious respect in which Sadie differed from the other diarists was her Jewishness, as we have seen this does not appear to have had much bearing on her feeling for the countryside. There was rather little self-conscious Englishness in her attitude to rural landscapes but this was also true of the Gentile diarists. Similarly, her delight in the Alps and French Gothic architecture was quite typical for educated Englishmen and women of her day and could have come straight from the pages of Ruskin (whom, however, she never mentions). On the whole it seems unlikely that her participation in outdoor activities and organizations contributed much to her assimilation since she had been highly assimilated from childhood and it is not clear that she felt a need to be any more fully assimilated than she was. She does not seem to have felt any lack of acceptance and never hid her Jewish background, of which she was proud, but nor did she feel any need to parade it.[75] There is no mention of anti-Semitism in the diaries and the rare occasions on which she had to miss out for religious reasons, as when the other Guides in her troop went to church, are described in tranquil terms, without resentment. Perhaps, having already made one cultural transition, Sadie was more open to new ideas and influences than most English Gentiles but beyond that it is difficult to discern a specifically Jewish contribution to her ruralism, although other aspects of her life, including her political trajectory, may have been more directly influenced by her ethnicity.

More unquestionably pertinent to Sadie's ruralism as represented in the diaries is her age at the time of the events described: she was between her early teens and mid-twenties. The Guide camps that feature so prominently were a very important staging post on her journey to adulthood, giving her a taste of independence and fostering her personal growth in many other respects too. Later she was ready for something more challenging so she graduated to adventurous holidays on the Continent while continuing to walk and take short breaks in rural England. Although historians have devoted much attention to exploring the ways in which girls and young women were socialized into gender roles by religious, educational and social organizations, in Sadie's case more striking is how important group camps were in the development of her own individual outlook, perspectives and values.[76] This was partly because they provided a setting for encounters with a wide range of people, including some who were unlike any she had met in Lewisham. Sadie drank this up

[75] On finishing Israel Zangwill's *Children of the Ghetto* in June 1929, Sadie noted: 'Jews in London – "The Lane" etc – people, places & customs I know & love – made me strongly pro-semitic – I hadn't realized before how much of it all is in me.' John Attfield, personal communication (email), 6 Nov. 2020.

[76] On self-development and the active agency of Guides see Edwards, *Youth Movements*, 211–12, 259–60.

eagerly, fascinated by people like Miss Schaffter, 'who has most wonderful photographic studies of her cats', and her nephew the Persian missionary.[77] She had long discussions with friends, companions and chance acquaintances about ideas and religion, expounding her theory of a universal mind 'to which we return and from which we came' to Clarkie on the Liss camp in 1928, for example.[78] These discussions were informed by Sadie's reading: friends claimed that she always had a volume of poetry with her when on camp. Perhaps even more important than talking and reading, however, was thinking. The rural camps (more than the urban holidays) gave her the solitude and space to think her own thoughts in a free setting. Our environment influences what we think in myriad subtle ways – in escaping from her familiar home environment she also escaped to a certain extent the pull and sway of familiar home assumptions.

Sadie was far from alone in finding these aspects of the Guide camps rewarding.[79] Nor was she alone in relishing the warmth, merriment and camaraderie they could generate. The intensity with which this communal dimension appealed to her joyous, extrovert character was perhaps more unusual, however. For Sadie camping was not just a means of forming relationships with particular individuals, but of becoming one with the whole group. It was almost as if, at first no doubt unconsciously, she was seeking to establish an alternative value system within these self-contained rural spaces. Guide and Scout camps were never intended to be more than the most moderate of rural utopias but the situational elements they shared with the strongly rural tradition of radical communities and communes in Britain could at times create surprising parallels.[80]

The rural setting of most of the Guide camps mattered not only because it contrasted with and was separate from the everyday urban context in which Sadie's life and that of her peers unfolded, but for other reasons too. Beauty was vitally significant to Sadie in her teens and twenties and the countryside was one of the principal places she found it. Initially her responses to landscape were perhaps somewhat derivative, seen through a Picturesque and Romantic lens, although the later sections of her diary show that she was becoming increasingly independent and assured in her aesthetic judgements. The Storrington camp of 1927 seems to have been a turning point, while three years later the grandeur of the Alps made an overwhelming impression:

---

[77] Barmes Diaries, 18–20 (n.d.).
[78] Barmes Diaries, 17–18 (n.d.).
[79] Edwards, *Youth Movements*.
[80] On the strength of the nexus between alternative communities in nineteenth- and twentieth-century Britain and the countryside see Dennis Hardy, *Alternative Communities in Nineteenth-Century England* (London, 1979) and Chris Coates, *Utopia Britannica: British Utopian Experiments, 1325–1945* (London, 2001).

Figure 8.2   Sadie (centre) wearing her long hair loose in the countryside, *c*.1932
Reproduced by kind permission of John Attfield

> Mist in the valley when I awoke at 6.30 ... and much rain all morning,
> punctuated with burning sunshine. I love the way the clouds roll back and
> forth across the mountains.[81]

Bound up with Sadie's responsiveness to nature was her capacity to become
wholly absorbed in a particular place and moment, an experience that Landry
suggests is perhaps most richly instantiated by riding to hounds.[82] Sadie,
however, had no need to hunt to achieve this kind of epiphany – she found
it through the heat of campfire flames on her face in a dark copse, the ceaseless
movement and changing colours of the sea, the gleaming snows of Mont Blanc.
As this indicates, although Sadie was fully alive to the visual beauty of the
countryside, she also enjoyed it with and through her other senses: the sound
of cow bells, the scent of fresh hay. At times the sensory pleasure of being in

---

[81] Barmes Diaries, 3 Aug. 1930.
[82] Landry, *The Invention of the Countryside*.

nature could rise to a kind of transcendence in which Sadie became wholly at one with her environment and lost any separate consciousness of self. This was often accompanied by dancing and sometimes singing.

The delight Sadie took in the physical freedom of being in the countryside echoes Marsh's account of Edward Carpenter and his fellow devotees of the Simple Life in *Back to the Land*.[83] Like them Sadie found the countryside a liberating escape from constraints. In the same way as the enthusiasts for 'rational dress' she loved to wear light, simple clothing such as pyjamas and bathing suits that left her body free to move. She also liked to wear her long hair loose, as a photograph of her with a group of rambling friends, possibly in the Vosges, shows (see Fig. 8.2). But I have found no evidence of direct influence, nor in view of her educational context, the social circles she moved in and the books we know she read does it seem likely.[84] Probably the parallels owe more to similar circumstances and motivations. Most of the Simple Lifers, like Sadie, were young, intellectually minded and free of responsibilities, a freedom that in turn owed something to rising living standards and a more benign demographic regime. In Marsh's view the Simple Lifers were reacting against Victorian 'stuffiness' as well as the materialism of their own times. After another four decades of research historians are now more chary of the stereotype of Victorian repression but there is little doubt that many young people, certainly including Sadie, felt they were breathing a freer atmosphere in the early twentieth century. When free-spirited young people find themselves with a group of like-minded peers in the countryside, away from society's oversight and from spatial confinement, it is perhaps not surprising if they revel in their physical freedom, even if the cultural and ideological contexts differ significantly.

As Sadie got older she gravitated away from the Guides but the wider adult outdoor movement became increasingly important to her. She stayed in youth hostels and went on Continental tours with International Tramping Tours and rambles organized by the *Daily Worker*. There are links here with our final diarist, Fred Catley, who also enjoyed collective rambling and hostelling and, like Sadie, cherished the group friendships and the opportunities to meet young people of the opposite sex that went with it. On the whole, however, at least during the period for which we have the diaries, the organized outdoor movement was much less central to Sadie than to Fred.

Sadie was one of the least ruralist of the eight diarists: education, political commitment and above all family mattered more to her. Even so, the countryside played a very important role in her life. Although she turned to it not out

---

[83] Marsh, *Back to the Land*.

[84] She did know George Borrow's *Lavengro* (1851) and *The Romany Rye* (1857), as well as other classics of post-Romantic tramping literature such as Patrick MacGill's *Children of the Dead End* (1914) but this would not have taken her very far in the Simple Life direction. Personal communication (email) from John Attfield, 6 Nov. 2020.

of need, to make good some previous hurt or shore up a threatened part of herself, she had an active, urgent desire for what she knew it could offer. This overlapped with the rewards yielded by some of her other activities and interests, notably foreign travel, architecture and the sea. Nevertheless, the countryside gave her much that she might not have been to find, at least in such full measure, from any alternative source. Above all, it was a natural space in which she could discover herself and unite with others.

9

Fred Catley

Bristol Bookseller

The subject of this final chapter, Fred Catley, although among the most prolific of the eight diarists, was in some ways also the most elusive. He was born in Bristol on 14 June 1911, the third child of Charlotte Elizabeth (*née* Everitt) and Joseph Catley. His mother, born in 1876, was five years older than her husband, whom she had married in 1904. Their first child, Will, was born two years later and Gladys followed in 1907. Joseph, a thoughtful and comparatively well-educated man, was a clerk at Britton's boot factory in Kingswood. The Catleys were Methodists and were embedded in a number of local Methodist social networks but, according to Fred, his father was 'more socialist than Methodist' in outlook. Joseph was passionately committed to a vision of agrarian independence, influenced it would seem by the land reform campaigns of the late nineteenth century and perhaps by earlier traditions of agrarian radicalism. However, his utopian visions were brutally terminated by the First World War – he was killed near Arras on 27 August 1917. This was, in many respects, the determining event of Fred's life, although (or, indeed, partly because) he was only six at the time. Looking back in 1989, at the age of seventy-eight, Fred wrote that 'as a war-widow with pension and small allowances for three children and 12/6 from Britton's, [my mother] was at least no worse off after the War, but the loss to us all was more than I can ever know' – an assessment that, as regards him personally at least, is corroborated in numerous ways by his diaries.[1]

Fred was deprived of his remaining parent in March 1931 when Charlotte succumbed to flu, leaving him in a denuded household consisting of just himself, Will and Gladys.[2] He was the only one of the diarists to be orphaned before the age of twenty. The other unusual feature is that he worked not only for the same employer, George's Bookshop in Bristol,

---

[1] Fred Catley, Danny Price, Cynthia Floyd et al., *Something about Bristol: Memories of Life in the City from the 1920's to Today* (Bristol, 1989), 4–5.

[2] According to Fred, Will was 'considered' to be 'mentally handicapped' and the family received an allowance in relation to this. But since Will read widely, wrote poetry and was regarded by Fred as a telling critic of his work, the learning disability, if there was one, cannot have been severe. Bristol Archives [BA], 41419/22,25,36 (Fred Catley Diaries, 9 Nov. 1932, 1 Jan. 1934 and 5 May 1938).

43

for his entire forty-eight-year career (1928–76), but in the very same building.[3] Outwardly, the diarist with whom Fred had most in common was Bert Bissell: both were white-collar workers who grew up on the fringes of large provincial cities in lower middle-class Methodist families. However, their characters and values were in drastic contrast. Fred was a highly cultured, rather hedonistic atheist, open-minded, introspective and self-critical, whereas Bissell, as we have seen, read little apart from scripture and was ascetic, unwavering in his faith, unselfconscious and virtually immune to self-doubt. Even the one deep concern the two men shared, their commitment to world peace, sprang from different sources – personal experience for Fred, religion for Bissell. These differences were reflected in their ruralism: Bissell's narrow but powerful, focused almost exclusively on mountains, Fred's catholic and comprehensive.

There is a closer and more revealing parallel between the ways Fred and Katherine Spear Smith related to landscape, despite their very different social backgrounds (not to mention genders). Both were acutely preoccupied with establishing and defining their identities, in a more energized and self-reflexive way than the other diarists, and for each the countryside played a crucial role in this process. In both cases their adopted rural identities were instrumental, and pivotal, to their professional ambitions as, respectively, writer and painter. A further marked, albeit ironic, parallel is that neither achieved more than exiguous success in achieving these professional goals. Here the parallels begin to break down, however. The failure of Spear Smith's ambitions to become a painter entailed a major psychological crisis, whereas Fred's quest for literary recognition simply faded into the background. Temperamentally, the two were profoundly different: Spear Smith was far more idealistic and high-minded and more appears to have been at stake in her ruralism.

On the whole, indeed, the diarist whose ruralism had most in common with Fred's was Barmes. Both explored the countryside eagerly, delighted in discoveries they made for themselves while doing so and had an open, inclusive attitude to different landscape types and elements. Each took pleasure in the constructed as well as natural features of the places they visited, particularly admiring ancient buildings. A major motivation for their countryside expeditions and outings was to find deeper meanings and experiences than they expected to encounter in their daily urban lives. However, Barmes was more outgoing and self-confident: rural camps and holidays were part of a wider process of educational development and personal and political growth for her, whereas this was true only in a qualified sense for Fred.

---

[3] Catley, Price, Floyd et al., *Something about Bristol*, 53.

The Diaries, Journals and Poems

The main sources for Fred's life are in the Bristol Record Office. The memoir he contributed to the edited compendium *Something about Bristol* extends only to a few paragraphs and, while offering interesting observations about his childhood, must be treated with caution given that it was written almost three-quarters of a century after the events it describes. There is also his mother's diary but this is scarcely longer and consists mainly of a record of expenditure.[4] More illuminating are Fred's poems, mainly written in the 1930s.[5] Their contents can sometimes be linked to events and episodes that feature in his diaries, which are by far the most important source for his life. These cover a thirty-eight-year period, from 1925, when he was fourteen, to 1963, when he was fifty-two, and are exceptionally full and continuous. Fred made a distinction between 'journals' and 'diaries': the journals are more expansive, with some entries running to thirty or more pages for a single day, whereas the diaries were written in preformatted pocketbooks that limited the length of entry to eight or ten lines. In his late teens and early twenties Fred wrote journals; in his late twenties he wrote co-extensive journals and diaries; in his thirties and early forties he tended to write either a journal or a diary for a given year; and from then onwards until the sequence ends, he kept only diaries. Both diaries and journals describe day-to-day events but only the journals reveal much about Fred's thoughts, feelings and reactions. This means we know little about Fred's childhood or the last forty-one years of his life but we can reconstruct, often in great detail, what he was doing on a daily basis for much of the intervening period, including his walks, cycle rides and other visits to the countryside. However, our understanding of the affective significance of the countryside for him is skewed towards his youth and early middle age, when he was still keeping journals.

Whereas some diaries, such as Cresswell's, appear to have been written for their author's eyes alone, Fred's diaries and journals are a more complex case.[6] He was the most literary, albeit not the most intellectual, of the diarists considered in this book, and his diaries contain long lists of books read – forty-eight of them in 1943, for example. Among these were several well-known rural diaries including those by Gilbert White, Parson Woodforde, Dorothy Wordsworth, Francis Kilvert and W. N. P. Barbellion.[7] Surprisingly, however, the imprint of canonical literature on Fred's diaries (although not on his poetry) appears to have been slight. A more potent influence on them may

---

[4] BA, 41419/69 (Charlotte Catley Diary).
[5] BA, 41419/70 ('A Collection of Poems Written by F. J. Catley').
[6] For the sake of brevity, henceforth I use 'diary' to encompass diaries and journals except where I make an explicit distinction between the two.
[7] Fred bought White's *The Natural History of Selborne* on 7 Dec. 1926 (BA, 41419/3). He began reading Barbellion on 1 Oct. 1932 (BA, 41419/25).

have been his friendship with Norman Bright. During the 1930s the two young men often met up on Brandon Hill, a park in the centre of Bristol, during Fred's lunch hour, and each sometimes read the other extracts from his journal.[8] It may well have been under this influence that Fred, at an uncertain date, copied out his 1925 and part of his 1926 diaries in a new volume titled 'A Twentieth-Century Journal'.[9] This journal is glossed with explanatory notes in square brackets, obviously intended for a reader. The implication is that Fred did not think his diaries were suitable for publication in their original form but that if appropriately edited they might be published or, at least read, by others. There is no indication that Fred ever did attempt to publish his diaries and he did not complete his 'Twentieth-Century Journal'. However, it is probably not an accident that the diaries eventually found their way into a record office.

How far Fred's intermittent expectation, or hope, that his diaries might eventually find readers affects their value as a source for understanding his ruralism is difficult to say. He was in any case highly self-conscious so even if he had intended to keep the diaries private, he would still have had an implied reader looking over his shoulder much of the time. One might perhaps expect that this would induce him to suppress, consciously or otherwise, information that cast him in a poor light. This may have been the case, although Fred repeatedly castigates himself for laziness and sometimes for other discreditable traits such as envy, volatility, susceptibility, lack of punctuality and, in at least one instance, dishonesty. Evidently the utility of the diary form as a tool of self-analysis and improvement counteracted the temptation to present a wholly sanitized version of the self. But perhaps a more powerful counterweight was the vividness with which Fred recalled his experiences, especially in the journals. At times he appears to be reliving rather than merely retelling the events of the day, often describing where he went and what he did in remark-able, almost compulsive, detail. Under this influence the diaries tend to shed what literary pretensions they have and become a more direct and unadorned record of experience.

Childhood and Schooldays

Fred reminisced glowingly about his rural upbringing in *Something about Bristol*:

> I was born in a house which no longer exists, in country which has long since disappeared – on June 14th, 1911, a hot summer, at 1 Cuckoo Lane, St George ... The lanes were narrow and rough, with hedges and elm trees ... I remember stone stiles and fields and footpaths ...

---

[8] See especially BA, 41419/22 (Fred Catley Diaries, 1932, passim).
[9] BA, 41419/9 ('A Twentieth-Century Journal').

The great change came when a new road was driven through between
school and church ... For a time we still had country round us. The life of
the fields – little owls, swallows, cuckoos, warblers, haymaking – ebbed
away as new houses were built.

   ... [a]las! the newcomers succeeded in having [the road name] altered
to 'Kingsway Avenue'. Goodbye, Cuckoo Lane! I'm glad I was born
there.[10]

However the nostalgic tone calls into question how faithful a rendering of
childhood experience this is. The earliest contemporary evidence that points in
the same direction is the botany notebook Fred began in 1923 at the age of
twelve.

   The diaries themselves commence in 1925 and allow a much fuller reconstruction of Fred's circumstances and the development of his ruralism. At this
point he was a pupil at Queen Elizabeth's Hospital (QEH), one of Bristol's
leading grammar schools. He had missed much of his first year at the school
through 'nerves and illness' but since then had done well, taking second place
overall in his form in 1925.[11] He excelled in English, recording on 2 February
that he had been asked to read out his essay on 'A Christmas Story' to the class
('Best. Mark 9/10. V.G.').[12] Some of the lessons were enjoyable – learning
about submarines in physics, for example, while on 26 March 1926 he had
a 'fine' history lesson.[13] There were the usual schoolboy troubles with baffling
assignments, peers and punishments: on 26 February 1926 he had 'rotten
algebra problems', while the previous June he had been cut on the head
when another boy threw a pencil case and the day afterwards had '6 unseen
from Mr Evans' for talking.[14] But on the whole he flourished academically and
does not seem to have been short of friends.

   Whether or not Fred had been influenced by growing up with the 'life of the
fields' around him, the diaries leave no room for doubt that his ruralism was
well established by the time he was fourteen. The Catleys lived in Kingswood,
on the north-west side of Bristol, and he often went on walks with his friend
Cliff Trew to Willsbridge weir and Hanham Woods.[15] Fred had also begun to
read about nature and the countryside, sending away to the GWR for their free
booklet on 'Cornwall and Its Wild Life', and on 11 April started to compose
'Poems of Nature in the Countryside', consisting mainly, it would seem, of
verses in praise of flowers such as moschatel, marsh marigold and
honeysuckle.[16] On 8 July he noted that he was learning to ride a bike, an

[10] Catley, Price, Floyd et al., *Something about Bristol*, 4–5.
[11] BA, 41419/9 ('A Twentieth-Century Journal'), 16 Nov. 1925; BA, 41419/2.
[12] BA, 41419/2, 2 Feb. 1925.
[13] BA, 41419/2, 23 Feb. 1925; BA, 41419/3, 26 Mar. 1926.
[14] BA, 41419/3, 26 Feb. 1926; BA, 41419/2, 23 and 24 Jun. 1925.
[15] BA, 41419/2–3, passim.
[16] BA, 41419/2, 11 and 15 Apr. 1925.

important development given how much cycling was to matter to him in years to come.[17] Later that month he went out for a long walk with his friends Cliff and Dick, along the Chew valley to Chewton Keynsham, Burnett and Compton Dando.[18] This is the first mention of an area that was to become of core emotional significance to him (see Figure 9.2). Despite the shorter days and colder weather, his rural expeditions continued in the autumn and winter.[19] By now he could cycle proficiently, riding to Stockwood and Queen Charlton with his school friend McGill on 11 October. He repeated the excursion on foot with Cliff a few weeks later, praising Queen Charlton as a 'very pretty, old fashioned village'. A fortnight later his essay on 'A Country Church' made such an impression on his teacher that he asked Fred to take it to the headmaster.[20]

Even at this age Fred provides an interesting example of the ways in which different rural-related pastimes can relate to each other. It would be easy to label him as a cyclist, a walker or a member of the 'outdoor movement' but in fact he was all these things and many more, forming an interconnected pattern. Botany is a case in point. He regarded it as his 'own special private study' and frequently noted flowers he had seen on his walks.[21] This sometimes informed his indoor leisure, as on the evening of 29 May 1926, which he spent identifying a flower he had found at Burnett the previous Tuesday (it turned out to be hound's-tongue). Later that summer he bought a *Botanist's Pocket Book* from George's.[22] As we have seen, his botanical interests also shaped his poetry and, although the heyday of Victorian pteridomania was long past, he collected ferns from the countryside and was much put out when some workmen 'nearly ruined them'.[23]

Fred's rural interests were congenial to his 'elders and betters' – not only his family but chapel and school too. The new minister at the local Methodist chapel, a Mr Barry, preached a 'beautiful and interesting' sermon on the text 'God planted a garden', quoting from Wordsworth, for the Flower Service on 16 May.[24] In the summer Fred went on a chapel charabanc tour to Tintern and Chepstow.[25] That October the school gave his essays on 'A Deserted Village' and 'Woods in Autumn' nine marks out of ten.[26] But, unbeknownst perhaps to these worthies,

---

[17] BA, 41419/2, 8 Jul. 1925.
[18] BA, 41419/2, 28 Jul. 1925.
[19] For example on 11 Oct., 2 Nov. and 31 Dec. 1925. BA, 41419/2.
[20] BA, 41419/2, 11 Oct., 2 Nov. and 13 Dec. 1925.
[21] BA, 41419/4, 20 Apr. 1927.
[22] BA, 41419/3, 29 May, 26 Jul. 1926.
[23] BA, 41419/3, 23 Apr. 1926. He also collected lichens. BA, 41419/3, 9 Oct. 1926.
[24] BA, 41419/3, 16 May 1926. Barry preached another 'magnificent' sermon on Wordsworth for the next year's Flower Service. BA, 41419/5, 14 May 1926. On the Flower Service, a distinctively Methodist institution, see S. J. D. Green, *Religion in the Age of Decline: Organisation and Experience in Industrial Yorkshire, 1870–1920* (Cambridge, 1996), 334.
[25] BA, 41419/3, 14 Aug. 1926.
[26] BA, 41419/3, 25 and 28 Oct. 1925. The school also encouraged Wordsworth: BA, 41419/5, 6 May 1927.

the countryside also provided Fred with opportunities to engage in minor acts of defiance and misdemeanour. He was never shy of trespassing: back in April he had climbed over a wall into 'Hales' Field' and picked the lock of the milking shed.[27] Like many children of his time and before, he went birds' nesting.[28]

The following year continued much the same. He became more interested in birds, putting suet out for the blue tits in January.[29] Later in the year he was pleased to discover a dunnock's nest in the garden. He watched it closely and on 27 April was able to report that two nestlings had hatched.[30] He read Wordsworth, although with less enjoyment than he had anticipated, and other classic ruralists including Borrow, Ruskin, Mitford, Hudson, Edward Thomas and Thoreau.[31] His favourite author, however, was Jefferies, whose *The Open Air* he had been given as a school prize the previous October. It was, he enthused, '[t]he most delightful book I have ever yet read'.[32] During 1927 he read Jefferies' *Wild Life in a Southern County, Pageant of Summer, The Story of My Heart* and *Field and Hedgerow*, as well as Thomas' *The Life of Richard Jefferies*.[33] Fred identified closely and enduringly with Jefferies – twenty years later he still found his work 'very enjoyable'.[34] Part of the appeal was undoubtedly Jefferies' vast and encompassing knowledge of the countryside. Yet, while admiring their writing, Fred did not respond in the same way to Cobbett or Hudson, who are at least Jefferies' equal in this respect. What distinguishes Jefferies' ruralism is that it becomes a vehicle for self-discovery and gives expression to an intense, at times embattled, individualism. These aspects emerge most compellingly in his spiritual autobiography *The Story of My Heart*, a book that made a deep impression on Fred, whose ruralism it paralleled in several respects. Jefferies also seems to have helped Fred in his difficult relationship with Methodism. Although still enmeshed in Methodist social institutions and traditions, Fred with his wide reading, open-mindedness and self-conscious modernity found the rigidity and anti-intellectualism of some currents of Methodism increasingly irksome:

> At B.C. [Bourne Chapel] in the afternoon Dr Rendle Short spoke, and actually showed some sparks of humour: a man I greatly dislike, a brilliantly clever surgeon, a typical Methodist: grey-haired, a repulsively hard and over-bearing face, an incisive Bristolian accent. Hard, narrow-minded, pharisaic, says his face.[35]

[27] BA, 41419/3, 24 Apr. 1926.
[28] BA, 41419/3, 12 Apr. 1926.
[29] BA, 41419/4, 14 Jan. 1927.
[30] BA, 41419/4, 12 and 27 Apr. 1927; see also 5 May and 10 Jun. 1927.
[31] BA, 41419/4, 21 Feb. 1927 (Wordsworth and Borrow); BA, 41419/5, 4, 5, 7 Jun. (Mitford), 7 Jul. (Hudson and Thomas), 1, 7 Sep. and end-of-year summary (Thoreau).
[32] BA, 41419/3, 1 Dec. 1926.
[33] BA, 41419/4, 7 Jan. 1927; BA, 41419/5, 4, 5 Jun. and 5 Jul. 1927.
[34] BA, 41419/47, 10 Jan. 1947.
[35] BA, 41419/22, 4 Dec. 1932.

In Fred's eyes Jefferies represented the antithesis of this:

> At Bible-class in the afternoon, when Mr and Mrs Breddy sang duets (very
> poor Sankey-ish sort of stuff) and Mr Rodway, in addition to inflicting on
> us a similar solo, gave a most abominable address, a wildly impractical and
> absurd exhortation to prepare for the Second Coming and hurry to save
> our souls, with an attempt at wholesale conversion to wind up! I think the
> man is a fool and a religious maniac. I longed for the fresh air and beauty
> of Richard Jefferies. I wonder how many of these ranters have read 'The
> Story of My Heart'.[36]

Another aspect of Jefferies that surely resonated is his sense of oppression, of
being forced by circumstances to undertake 'wearisome work' in a town when
with his whole heart and soul he wanted to be out in the countryside.[37] Fred
drew more sustenance from school, and later from work, than he was usually
willing to admit, but he always bridled at the lack of freedom:

> I was reading 'Modern Poetry of Springtime' in 'John O' London's
> Weekly' today. The poetry was extremely beautiful; and when I read
> such literature and think of the country at this time, a great longing
> wells up within me, to leave this dull routine, this school and city life,
> and go out into the great wide country spaces, out where violets and
> primroses are springing up; I cannot express my longing, and yet my
> thankfulness that such things are is still more unspeakable. Oh! for
> a World where nought but Beauty lived![38]

This yearning may have been magnified by the intensifying academic pressure
as Fred neared the end of his school career – a week beforehand, for example,
he had described that afternoon's geography exam as 'simply atrocious – really
tragic!'[39]

Discovering the Chew Valley

Despite the constraints he was under, Fred continued to go out frequently into
the countryside, sometimes with his family, more often with Cliff. An especially rewarding and perhaps consequential excursion was to Publow and
Stanton Drew in the Chew valley, partially reprising a 'very excellent time'
with Gladys the previous year.[40] On this occasion the party was larger, consisting of Charlotte, Will and a family friend as well as Fred and Gladys. As before,
they took the train to Pensford, then walked across the fields. Publow, with its
stone, half-timbered and thatched cottages, delighted Fred, who described it as

[36] BA, 41419/16, 6 Jul. 1930.
[37] Richard Jefferies, *The Story of My Heart* (1883; London, 1946 ed.), esp. 15, 37.
[38] BA, 41419/4, 14 Mar. 1927.
[39] BA, 41419/4, 7 Mar. 1927.
[40] BA, 41419/4, 6 Apr. 1926.

'exceedingly beautiful', praising the church with its ornate Somerset tower as 'a gem of architecture'.[41] It was, however, the wildlife that pleased him most:

> The ornithology of this district is exceptionally interesting. Simply strolling about the district, I noted today several birds which I have never noticed before ... There were jackdaws at Publow church; I noticed a water-ousel on the Chew at Publow, and coots, moorhens, nuthatches, sedge warblers, robins, wrens etc ... I should very much like to reside here where I might study the Ornithology, Zoology and especially the Botany of this portion of the Chew valley.[42]

This was not, as it might seem, a passing fancy. Fred's affinity with the lower Chew valley strengthened and deepened over the years, and in 1945 he fulfilled his wish of eighteen years before by moving to Woollard, the next village downstream from Publow.

A clue to the powerful appeal of the Chew valley can be gleaned from Fred's account of another visit a month later, this time with Cliff:

> When we reached Burnett, the quaint little village which I know so well, we stopped at the tiny church and entered it ... Of all churches I love this the most. Though very small ... and not strikingly beautiful (such as Publow Church, for example) there is a charming peace, a venerable quiet very marked here; though this scarcely explains my preference, since all country churches are so. Its smallness is one thing I love; the age of the building, the tablets, and the tombs also. The small organ takes my fancy; the stained glass windows please me; and, perhaps the chief thing, it is the country church which I know best, and have had time to learn to love.[43]

It was precisely its familiarity that made Burnett church so cherished by Fred. This helps to explain one of the most strongly marked features of Fred's ruralism: the prevalence and emotional significance of repeated visits. The same pattern is apparent in several of the other diarists but none of them carried it as far, developed it as fully or drew as much sustenance from it as Fred. It is true that he gradually widened his range over the years and in due course developed a warm appreciation for further-flung landscapes such as the Quantocks, Exmoor, the Wiltshire downs and north Hertfordshire, but more often he chose to revisit areas he already knew intimately. A kind of emotional stratigraphy was at work: each visit laid down another layer of meaning, so that there was a sense in which, on subsequent visits, he re-experienced all his previous visits too, just as Barmes tells us she did on her annual Storrington camps.[44] This was especially

---

[41] BA, 41419/4, 19 Apr. 1927.

[42] BA, 41419/4, 19 Apr. 1927. A water ousel is a dipper.

[43] BA, 41419/4, 14 May 1927.

[44] Similarly, it always pleased Fred when one landscape echoed another he had enjoyed, as when some 'silky willows' near home reminded him of the Lea valley in Hertfordshire. BA, 41419/34, 19 Sep. 1937.

compelling when Fred had engaged with and acted in the landscape when he had been there before, rather than simply passing through it:

> From the church, we followed for a short distance the lane towards Compton Dando; then, lifting our bikes over the wall into the field, we placed them under the hedge. This is the field where last year we made our first personal acquaintance with the lapwings, and it adjoins the wood and tiny stream, in which and by which we lit a fire last year, made tea, and thoroughly enjoyed ourselves.[45]

Fred often recapitulated previous visits in his diary like this, using it as a tool to embed the past in the present.[46]

'Fragrant Memories'

A few weeks after revisiting the lapwing field, he and Cliff took the opportunity of the Whitsun holiday to go trespassing again, this time in the Willsbridge woods:

> Since the woods are really private, one scarcely meets anyone there; they are very extensive, thick and by far the finest woods I know. The Spiked Star of Bethlehem (a very rare plant except in this neighbourhood) grows in great profusion here.[47]

Leaving the woods, they made their way across the fields, breathing in the 'delicious' smell of new-mown grass, to 'quaint old' Court Farm, where they watched the numerous swallows, admiring their wonderfully quick performances on the wing and the beautiful blue shade of their plumage.[48]

Once term began Fred's life continued much as before: hard work and 'appalling' exams in uncongenial subjects at school; much music; visits to George's and the reference library and rural excursions when possible. The summer proved exceptionally wet, but he managed some enjoyable outings, including at least five to the Chew valley ('glorious', 'exquisitely lovely' and 'beautiful') and a brief but exhilarating holiday in Bournemouth. He began to gather together and read his father's diaries, intending to find all his papers and make a complete collection. Ominously, Fred noted that 'Ma has not been particularly well lately' on 5 September but he does not seem to have had any inkling of how serious this was to prove. Certainly it did not stop the Catleys

---

[45] BA, 41419/4, 14 May 1927. Tea almost always featured prominently on the Catleys' rural excursions; asking a farmer for milk was a familiar ritual.

[46] See, for example, BA, 41419/4, 10 Apr. 1927, 41419/20, 10 Aug. 1931, 41419/28, 23 Aug. 1934 and 41419/34, 1 Aug. 1937.

[47] BA, 41419/5, 9 Jun. 1927.

[48] BA, 41419/5, 9 Jun. 1927.

going blackberrying a few days later.[49] Looking back on the holiday, Fred felt that it was the best he had yet had:

> The bicycle made a great difference, and each holiday I try to see more of Nature or Art – in short, Beauty in any form – than I have formerly, thus making my holiday happier and progressing towards my ideal. This holiday will leave fragrant memories of the lanes and by-ways and old-fashioned villages with their sweet old churches in North Somerset, my own district; of the Bournemouth pines, and sea, and people; and of the sunshine, and shadow, and rain of this fitful summer. So I can go thus back to the drudgery, the hard work – almost slavery it will be during this last year – of the institution which, as far as the work is concerned, I in great part loathe and hate – Q.E.H.[50]

Reading and Rurality

When he was unable to escape from Bristol altogether Fred's favoured place of refuge at this time was George's. He uses intriguingly similar language to describe the bookshop as for many of his rural excursions:

> There is nothing more delightful for sheer pleasure than this place. How we love to delve among their immense stores of books; there is something adventurous in it; we discover some fresh shelf which we have never explored, or some new books for our edification.[51]

Fred's immersion in George's was to prove as lasting as his devotion to the countryside, so it is worth reflecting on the parallels between reading and rurality in his life. Both offered rich, in practice limitless, scope for exploration; allowed him to formulate his tastes and preferences unhindered; offered quietness and peace; and insulated him from uncongenial surroundings and circumstances. As well as ministering to the same needs in some respects, Fred's reading and his ruralism also fed off each other directly. A good example is his investigation of the Wansdyke, a linear earthwork of ancient but uncertain origins part of which runs through the Chew valley, in autumn 1927. He had encountered it on one of his expeditions the previous year and now decided to spend a free afternoon in the library making notes on it. As he explained, 'since I know and love the district dealt with so well, I spent a most enthralling time'.[52] A week later he had another free afternoon and promptly

---

[49] BA, 41419/5, 3 Aug. to 9 Sep. 1927.
[50] BA, 41419/5, 12 Sep. 1927. Ten years later Fred's anger still burnt brightly: BA, 41419/34, 9 Feb. 1937.
[51] BA, 41419/4, 4 Jun. 1927.
[52] BA, 41419/5, 13 Sep. 1927. The book he read was Albany Major and Edward Burrow's *The Mystery of the Wansdyke* (Cheltenham, 1926).

rode to Stantonbury, looking superb in its autumn colours, to trace the line of the Wansdyke as well as he could.[53]

Unlike several of the other diarists, Fred rarely read in the countryside, although in later years when he was working at George's he might take a book with him to Brandon Hill or the Avon Gorge during his lunch hour:

> It was a superbly warm May day, so at lunch time I rode up to the Downs just off the Prom and, wheeling the bike over the grass, went a short way down into the steep woods above the Avon Gorge and there sat on a rock and ate my dinner. I had Sturt's 'A Small Boy in the 60s' with me, but did not read much, as I was so absorbed in the beauty of the day, the gorge and the woods. The trees are in their first green.[54]

Although they were mutually sustaining activities that fulfilled similar functions for him, it seems that the sensory immediacy of being in the countryside sometimes left little scope for reading.

Fred was confined to bed with chickenpox for much of the following January but on the 25th was well enough to take his bike out and made for Stanton Prior, the far side of Burnett Hill.[55] This took him past the 'exceptionally beautiful' fir trees at its crest ('I love that little clump of trees very dearly').[56] Probably, having been cooped up indoors with a disagreeable illness for so long, he was keen to make contact with the landscapes that meant most to him.[57] However, the relationship between familiarity and novelty was a complex one. A few weeks later he and Cliff found a quiet side road to Norton Malreward, 'new ground to us, and very delightful', on the north side of the Chew valley.[58] Such references to the pleasure of discovering new ground are common and chime with the trope of exploration that unites Fred's reading and his rural excursions. But with respect to the excursions, the crucial point is that this was new ground within a known landscape. Fred was getting the best of both worlds: the excitement of novelty, in this context, served to make the familiar even more deeply known.[59]

A question mark, however, increasingly hung over the secure stability of his life as winter gave way to spring. His last term at QEH was approaching and he would need to find a job. On 15 May one of his teachers, Mr Smallpage, astutely suggested that librarianship might suit him.[60] It turned out that there was

[53] BA, 41419/6, 20 Oct. 1927.
[54] BA, 41419/25, 2 May 1934.
[55] BA, 41419/6, 25 Jan. 1928.
[56] BA, 41419/4, 14 May 1927.
[57] There is a faint echo here of Johnston's delight in rediscovering the countryside after his recovery from a far more serious illness.
[58] BA, 41419/6, 21 Feb. 1928.
[59] Compare BA, 41419/25, 7 Oct. 1933, when Fred discovered an interesting new road but noted in his diary that 'it was the old well-known roads I was gladdest to see again'.
[60] BA, 41419/7, 15 May 1928.

a vacancy at Bristol University library and on 15 June Fred and another QEH leaver were interviewed for the post. The other boy got the job. Fred was bitterly disappointed. Other positions were hard to come by – there were no vacancies at the *Bristol Times and Mirror* nor at the city archives, although in desperation Mr Smallpage took him to the latter for an interview in case a vacancy should arise.[61] Term ended (28 July) with Fred still jobless.

The Particularity of Landscape Experience

But these anxieties did not dampen Fred's enthusiasm for exploring the countryside around Bristol. Among several memorable excursions over the summer, perhaps the one that reveals most about the significance of rural landscapes to him in his late teens was another visit to the lapwing field by the Compton Dando lane. What comes through most clearly is the intense specificity. He is at pains not only to describe the landscape but to identify exactly where they went and what they did there. So detailed are the text and accompanying sketch map that it is possible to follow in Fred's footsteps to within a few metres:

> We picnicked at the spot marked x. Will and I followed the top hedge, wandered about in the field testing the echo from the wood (after I had crossed the two gates at the top of the orchard, into the little side lane, and then returned again to Will) ... We eventually came out into the lane from Burnett to Compton Dando, but turned off into the little side-lane, which I knew to be blind, and very wild.
>
> We followed it to its end, down past the great orchard, and returning we crossed the hedge into the orchard to look at what we thought might be barrows but apparently are not.
>
> Eventually, coming on up the lane, we crossed the two gates into the field (at the corner of the orchard) and met Ma and Gladys. We strolled down to the stream and up to the spring, and then out to the lane again, and thus to Burnett.[62]

It matters to Fred to pinpoint in which angle of the wood they had their picnic, how far along the lane they went, where they crossed the hedge and gates and that they went down to the stream before going back up to the spring. So detailed, almost reverent, is the account that it is easy to forget that at one level what he is describing is nothing more than walking about in a field and its immediate vicinity. Evidently, then, these minor actions held a significance for him that transcended their apparent inconsequence.

At this point it is useful to make a distinction between Fred's first-order experiences and his subsequent rendering of them in the diary. This is not a distinction much emphasized in the preceding chapters because my concern

---

[61] BA, 41419/7, 16, 20 Jul. 1928.
[62] BA, 41419/7, 6 Aug. 1928.

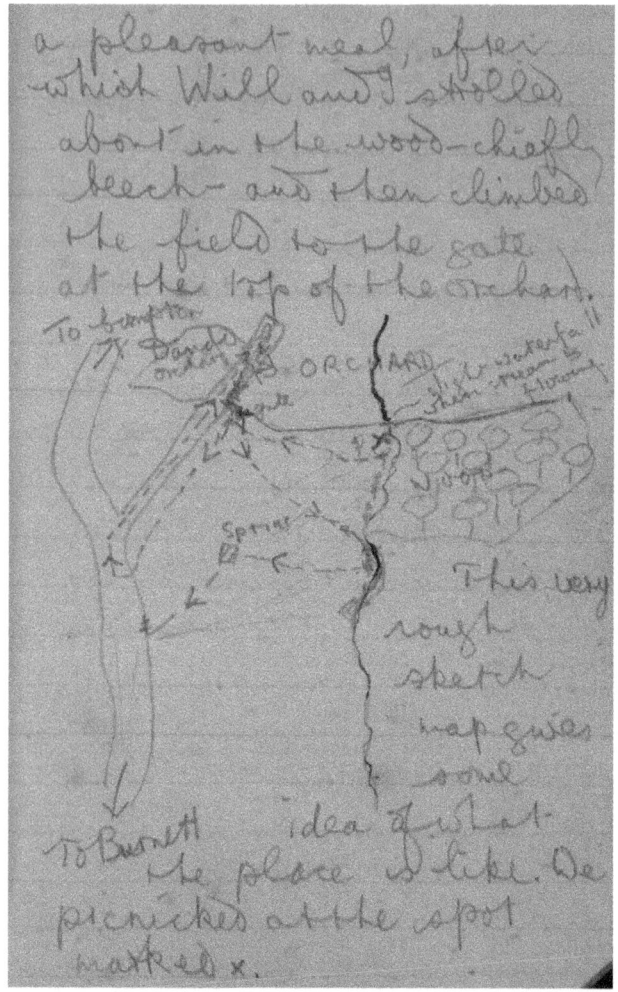

Figure 9.1   Map of the lapwing field by the Compton Dando lane
Reproduced by kind permission of Leonora Mullen and Bristol Archives. BA, 41419/7,
6 Aug. 1928

throughout is with experience rather than representation. But sometimes, as
here, representation itself partly constitutes experience, or at least develops and
extends it.[63] In this instance Fred's first-order experiences were of picnicking in
a secluded, sheltered spot by the stream bed, then wandering round the wood,
lane, orchard and field with Will, meeting up with their mother and sister again

---

[63] Compare Johnston's Raikes Wood notes, which, however, were written in real time, to
intensify the present, rather than retrospectively, to intensify the past.

and making their way back to Burnett. There is a sense of being encompassed by and absorbed in the landscape – although the scale was in fact tiny, it makes the opposite impression on Fred: the orchard is 'immense', the wood a 'great' one, the lane 'very wild'. Recollecting this afterwards, what he seems to have wanted to do is to articulate and crystallize his experiences. It is as if the immediacy and vividness of the experiences at the time had overloaded his capacity to process them and only by being replayed in his mind afterwards can they be fully apprehended. This helps to explain the detail of Fred's account: he must specify an experience as precisely and completely as possible to isolate its particular nature – what made it this rather than that. Recapitulating his experience of the day's landscapes in his diary also allowed Fred to fix them, converting them from evanescent impressions to permanent storage in a kind of external memory. Diary writing therefore not only told the imaginary reader about what Fred had been doing, thinking and feeling on his rural excursions, but itself constituted an important way of furthering and deepening those experiences.

'Deep Draughts of Beauty'

Two days later the Catleys took a charabanc tour to Minehead. Fred was disappointed by Nether Stowey, despite its literary distinction, but entranced by the Quantocks:

> I have never seen anything more splendidly grand and lovely than the great heath-clad heights of Quantock. Their vivid beauty defies description.[64]

Both conventional framing and a filtering, gauging individual sensibility are at work here. As Fred's critical response to Nether Stowey indicates, he was quite ready to question received opinion. Yet his enthusiasm for the Quantocks, the highest hills he had yet been among, was shaped by Romantic expectations of mountain grandeur, while his assertion that their beauty 'defies description' was, as Lydia Wevers has shown, a characteristic trope of Romantic travellers.[65]

Hardly had they left the Quantocks than they were on the road from Watchet to Minehead. Fred was seventeen and had just left school, and his bright, expansive cast of mind illuminates his continuing account of this memorable expedition, one superlative quickly outstripping the next:

> Surely this road ... is one of the most perfect stretches of road in the world; the beauty of this district, with its hills and glorious views and lovely villages, is matchless.[66]

---

[64] BA, 41419/7, 8 Aug. 1928.
[65] Lydia Wevers, 'The Pleasure of Walking', *New Zealand Journal of History* 38 (2004), 45. Fred uses the trope quite often, for example in relation to Cheddar Gorge (BA, 41419/10, 1 Apr. 1929) and the view from Green Down (BA, 41419/10, 2 Apr. 1929).
[66] BA, 41419/7, 8 Aug. 1928.

They had lunch on the beach at Minehead, walked up North Hill to a farmhouse for milk and climbed the church tower, guided by two girls who, Fred felt, had the 'freshness of moor and sea and the West about them'.[67] High Town, with its thatched cottages and steps, was 'surely one of the loveliest places in England'. Looking back on the day, Fred felt that it had marked an epoch in his life:

> This day will always be significant to me. Never before have I received such deep draughts of beauty and inspiration as I received from the loveliness of the Quantocks and the district thence to Minehead. The weather was glorious and the views superb. My feelings on returning were almost indescribable; regret for the beauty of the day so quickly fled, hope that I might visit it all again before very long, and the strange sweet feeling of having drunk deeply of Life and worshipped at the shrine of Beauty.[68]

Three days later he and Gladys went to stay with Uncle Will in London. Fred was unimpressed by the 'much-vaunted' beauty of the Thames valley and dismayed by the last thirty miles into London, an 'endless suburb . . . without the poetry either of country or city'.[69] Revealingly, on their return journey his enthusiasm for the landscape revived as they neared home: '[H]ow strongly I felt the thrill of approaching my own West country again!'[70]

Precarious Employment

Back in Bristol the search for work went on. There was a possibility of obtaining a place at Northern Assurance but Fred hated commerce and dreaded the thought of having to work there.[71] More cheering were cycle rides to Clevedon and Maes Knoll with Cliff on 3 and 18 September. The Swiss valley at Clevedon with its 'quiet air of peace and loveliness' in the mellow evening sunlight was a 'spiritual experience not to be described' while the view from the ridge above Tickenham was 'surely one of the loveliest in Somerset'. Conversely, the great hill fort of Maes Knoll had a 'sort of lonely awfulness (not chilling but inspiring)' about it, and he was sorry to have to descend into the everyday world again.[72]

On 22 September Fred received a letter from the headmaster of QEH, who told him that there was a vacancy at George's bookshop 'of all places'. Four days later Fred was interviewed by Mr George himself and his appointment

[67] BA, 41419/7, 8 Aug. 1928.
[68] BA, 41419/7, 8 Aug. 1928.
[69] BA, 41419/7, 11 Aug. 1928.
[70] BA, 41419/8, 18 Aug. 1928.
[71] BA, 41419/8, 24 Aug. 1928.
[72] BA, 41419/8, 3 and 18 Sep. 1928.

was confirmed on the 29th. He started at George's on 1 October, initially spending much of his time in the basement putting catalogues in envelopes.[73] Perhaps because full-time employment constrained his opportunities to do so, he did not go out into the countryside as much as in previous autumns. But as the year drew to a close he looked back on some of the vivid experiences of the summer, writing a long description of the Chew above Keynsham for a *Bristol Observer* competition.[74]

Music had always been important to Fred and he was delighted when his mother (perhaps assisted by his wages) bought a piano for him on 5 February 1929. Thereafter he practised frequently. A less welcome development was the disturbing news that the bookshop was about to change hands, which might mean redundancies.[75] However, the improving weather enabled Fred to return to the Chew valley the day after the change of ownership was confirmed (8/9 March). He cycled as far as the cricket ground near Stockwood with McGill and then continued alone in the warm spring sunshine to Norton Malreward, where he cooled off in the 'delightfully secluded' churchyard. Everything smelt delectably fresh and damp due to the recent thaw and he was pleased to find a few violets and two snowdrops in bloom:

> I should have loved to have remained in this wonderful green sanctuary, this sweet-smelling churchyard where every minute 'absorbs the soul and fills it with beauty'.[76]

This account inscribes a complex mix of influences. It is difficult not to connect Fred's desire to remain in a 'green sanctuary' with his precarious employment situation, and this is perhaps the most important element. The immediacy and force of his sensory response to rural landscapes is also in evidence, as it was later that day when he paused on the bridge at Stanton Drew to 'breathe in the freshness of the stream'.[77] Yet the objects of Fred's attention and his disposition in the churchyard were shaped too by cultural practices and paradigms. His family, the chapel, Bristol museum and the school encouraged an interest in wildflowers, while the quotation comes from Jefferies, whose way of seeing and feeling was doubtless also with Fred in the churchyard.[78]

---

[73] BA, 41419/8, 22, 26 and 29 Sep. and 1, 2 and 3 Oct. 1928.

[74] BA, 41419/8, 30 Nov., 1 and 2 Dec. 1928.

[75] BA, 41419/10, 5 and 29 Feb. 1929.

[76] BA, 41419/10, 9 Mar. 1929.

[77] He described another stream encountered that day as 'very musical'. As with most of the other diarists considered in this book, Fred's experience of rural landscapes was richly multisensory. BA, 41419/10, 9 Mar. 1929.

[78] Richard Jefferies, *The Life of the Fields* (Cambridge, 2010), here p. 64.

'The Real Mendip Spirit'

This was the first of many excursions that spring, mainly to the Chew and beyond to the Mendips.[79] Fred seems not to have minded much whom he went with – sometimes his companion was Basil Payne, a colleague from George's, sometimes Cliff and sometimes his family. Where possible Fred went by bike but family expeditions were by bus and foot. Perhaps the most memorable of these outings was with Cliff on 1 April. The main feature was the terrible north-westerly wind, so strong that at one point Cliff dismounted even though they were going along the level, while Fred struggled on at less than walking pace. It rained almost incessantly the whole morning and well before midday the two young men must have been wet through, exhausted and, one would have thought, thoroughly dispirited. Quite the contrary, however, in Fred's case at least – he revelled in the gale and the sodden landscape:

> Here [on the top of Mendip], with the fierce gale and the grey rain and greyer sky, and endless olive-brown downs with a few woods and farms fading back into the greyness of the rain, there was the real Mendip spirit, wild and awe-inspiring and very beautiful.[80]

What was it about the Mendips, on this and many subsequent occasions, that appealed so powerfully to him? A crucial characteristic they shared with the Chew valley was that they were comparatively uncelebrated. Unlike, for example, Cheddar Gorge, the Cotswolds or the Thames, they were culturally uncolonized: he could discover them for himself. As he criss-crossed these landscapes on foot and by bike he came to know them intimately; events, impressions and experiences accumulated, and the places where they occurred were gradually woven into the fabric of his being. Yet in another way the affective meaning of Chew and Mendip was vitally different. The Chew valley was close to home – just over the hill from Bristol – invisible, separate but, for all that, next door. It was a gentle, welcoming landscape, bright with flowers in spring and the scene of many a family picnic. The Mendips offered something more challenging, with their steep climbs, exposure to the elements and long, bare lines. He preferred to write about them in the singular, as 'Mendip', implying a single essence rather than loose plurality. Many times, high on the plateau, he was transported with a kind of exuberant delight in

---

[79] A ride with Basil Payne along '[a] road without traffic, high and lonely' on 30 March was the first time he had been on top of the Mendips except once or twice in a bus or charabanc. BA, 41419/10, 30 Mar. 1929 and 41419/14, 31 Dec. 1929.

[80] BA, 41419/10, 1 Apr. 1929.

the landscape. Seeking to express this afterwards, Fred typically used adjectives such as 'pure', 'real' or 'full':

> Up here it was pure Mendip – the long grey walls and rolling down with green fir-copses and behind us a great stretch of gorse and fern. We were about 800 feet up.[81]

Despite his ruralism, Fred sometimes found conventionally picturesque landscapes too sweet for his palate. Of the fêted Castle Combe valley he wrote:

> This is supremely lovely country – almost too lovely: it could cloy in time, with its rich woods and valleys, old houses and streams.[82]

He disliked the Cotswolds for similar reasons. They were too romantic: Painswick, for example, was 'painfully neat rather than beautiful – a prim place'. What he wanted, he explained, was something 'wild ... naked [and] primitive' – exactly the qualities he found in the 'high and lonely' Mendips.[83] Unadorned and free from superficial prettiness, the Mendips evidently brought Fred closer to what he considered the roots of his being. Above all, perhaps, he found in them an experience of authenticity. It is difficult to pin this down to specific cultural influences: existentialism was barely inchoate in the early 1930s and Fred does not seem to have read proto-existentialist thinkers such as Kierkegaard or Nietzsche (let alone Heidegger). A diffuse home-grown Romanticism may be more to the point. Perhaps he had *Wuthering Heights* somewhere in mind: Fred thought it 'glow[ed] from beginning to end with a sort of dark fire'. Jefferies' quest for 'soul-life' may also be relevant and, in a more general way, the English nature-writing tradition in which Fred was steeped.[84]

Landscape, Loss and Identity

The profound significance of landscapes such as the Mendips and the Chew valley to him, does not, however, seem to have exposed Fred to loss of the kind Spear Smith suffered through her devotion to Lee Common or the elm trees outside Titchfield Lodge. It was not that Fred's landscapes mattered less to him, but they mattered in a different way, as an episode on 28 April reveals:

> We rode ... along the delightful Chew valley Compton Dando road. I was angered and surprised to see that road widening operations on that delightful bit of narrow road at the corner near the wood ... have entirely

---

[81] BA, 41419/10, 2 Apr. 1929. Compare also BA, 41419/25, 5 May 1934 ('a grand unspoiled road, giving you the full Mendip flavour').
[82] BA, 41419/25, 21 Apr. 1934.
[83] BA, 41419/24, 25 Aug. 1933 and 41419/10, 30 Mar. 1929.
[84] BA, 41419/20, 25 Nov. 1931.

destroyed one of the thick, beautiful hedges that used to have its bank
thick with hart's tongue fern and primroses, and has left a horrible red
bank with iron railings. Oh! the blindness of rural district Councils![85]

Where Spear Smith would have been acutely hurt, Fred is angry. Moreover, the
note of humour in this more robust response suggests his equanimity has not
been much disturbed, an impression confirmed by the next sentence, which
extolls the 'charming country' and admirable views around Hunstrete.[86]

The difference is partly a matter of scale. Spear Smith's landscapes tended to
be less extensive and more intimate than Fred's – a common or a copse rather
than a valley or range of hills. Commons could be converted to golf courses and
copses cut down but however unenlightened the local authority, it could hardly
mar the whole Chew valley, still less the Mendips. The contrast in scale is itself
attributable, in part, to the speed with which the two respectively moved through
the landscape: Spear Smith slowly, on foot, Fred more rapidly, on his bike. Yet
these contrasts should not be overdrawn since Fred walked too, and frequently
dismounted even when he cycled. Just as she had her elms, he had his clump of
fir trees on Burnett Hill.[87] The crucial difference lay deeper, in the way rural
landscapes contributed to each diarist's identity. Spear Smith projected her
emotions and her sense of self into the landscape. In woods, trees, flowers and
birds she found a reflection of her own quietness, modesty and sensitivity, even
beauty perhaps. Landscape and nature became a kind of external soul. Spear
Smith may not have worn her heart upon her sleeve but she gave it to her 'little
bird friends', and suffered with them. The countryside affirmed Fred's sense of
self in a quite different way. He did not seek his own qualities in the landscape –
whereas Spear Smith's self-image is readily apparent in her descriptions of the
Grass of Parnassus she drew in the Highlands or the little church in the fir wood,
comparable accounts in Fred's diaries yield few clues to his perceived identity.
Neither the negative nor the more positive traits (cheerfulness, independent-
mindedness) he attributes to himself can be discerned in his landscape descriptions. Indeed Fred was in general much less concerned with his character and
emotions than Spear Smith was with hers. Rather it was through enabling him to

---

[85] BA, 41419/10, 28 Apr. 1929.

[86] BA, 41419/10, 28 Apr. 1929. Compare also their contrasting responses to the destruction
of, respectively, the nests of a dunnock and a long-tailed tit: Fred's regretful but phleg-
matic, Katherine's traumatized. BA, 41419/38, 5 May 1939; Nature Notebooks, 21
Apr. 1912.

[87] Fred in fact wrote a poem about the felling of an elm tree but it ends on a characteristically
optimistic note: he notices that the lost beauty has opened a 'new world' to his sight,
allowing him to see a line of poplars and three delicate birches. 'A Collection of Poems
Written by F. J. Catley', BA, 41419/70. Being able to see the 'sunset [redden] in a broad
expanse of sky' where her elms had been, conversely, did little to mitigate Smith's 'great
sadness' that they had been cut down. HRO, 19M99/2/11 (Smith Nature Notebooks, 23
Feb. 1917).

formulate and articulate his values (at least his aesthetic ones), his likes and dislikes, that the Chew valley, the Mendips and the other landscapes he cherished contributed so much to his sense of self. Rural landscapes helped both Fred and Spear Smith know themselves, then – but different aspects of themselves. For Fred landscape was a touchstone of his preferences, of his personal values and commitments. The mode in question was an assessing, evaluating, at least partly intellectual one. Subject and object remained separate: what counted in the end about the hedge along the Compton Dando road was not its continued existence but the fact that his response to its beauty on previous occasions had sharpened his awareness of what he liked. The removal of the hedge, although regrettable, could not take this away. The implication is that Fred's identity was more cerebral and externally directed than Spear Smith's: he experienced himself through coming to know what he liked, she through coming to know what she felt.

This assessing and evaluating mode was not just a matter of registering preferences. It also at times involved a fine discrimination of the quality and character of different landscapes, a comparative placing and ordering:

> [W]e went up through Hodder's Combe, to my mind the most beautiful of all this side of the Quantocks once the houses at the bottom have been passed. It increases in loveliness as one ascends. We bore westwards by Lady's Edge, most perfect way of all, with its little stream and still woods.[88]

Fred's ability to identify and specify what he regarded as the most beautiful landscapes of particular types was founded on extensive knowledge. It constituted a kind of mastery, an expert ability to read the landscape, strengthening his belief in his own powers.

Exploration

Among the principal sources of this knowledge was the relaxed but satisfying practice Fred referred to as 'exploring', as when he and Cliff ventured into the Devil's Punch Bowl, one of the largest swallet holes in the Mendips:

> It is a huge circular hollow, almost a perfect hemisphere, thick with brushwood and its rim very green and beautiful with a few young firs. Bluebells were thick at the top. We descended the very steep slope into this mysterious and rather awe-inspiring place, down into the dark-green and rather damp depths. Cliff and I (rather vandalistically, perhaps!) carved our names on a tree.[89]

---

[88] BA, 41418/20, 11 Aug. 1931.

[89] BA, 41419/10, 20 May 1929. Fred used the word 'exploring', or cognate terms, frequently to describe this kind of activity: BA 41419/16, 10 Jun. 1930; 41419/20, 10 Aug. 1931; 41419/25, 3 Apr. 1934; and 41419/47, 24 Aug. 1947.

Whether Cliff's presence encouraged Fred – not a great respecter of property at the best of times – to cut his name in the bark is unclear.[90] The act of doing so, however, reprehensible as it may be, is not mere vandalism, any more than it was when Hallam subjected Lockinge church tower to the same treatment: it signifies a desire literally to inscribe yourself into the landscape – even, perhaps, to transcend in that way the division between self and world. Indeed 'exploration' and the practices associated with it epitomize the open-ended, two-way flow between people and landscape of Ingold's dwelling perspective. But with its connotations of intrusion and colonization, the word also raises questions about Fred's relationship with those who lived in these places. While Fred's landscapes, unlike Spear Smith's, were predominantly social rather than private, this was because they were shared with other 'explorers' – his family, friends, ramblers and cyclists. His relationship with the inhabitants of the countryside was more remote. A bike ride with Basil Payne on 11 May 1929 elucidates this. The two young men had stopped for refreshment at the Colliers Arms in Bishop Sutton:

> In the bar parlour were a little group of rustics, whose quaint talk concerning cider not only amused us but reminded us strongly of Hardy and Walter Raymond.[91]

Fred's interactions with rural workers were not usually so patronizing but he had few points of contact with them: buying milk, asking for tea and, on occasion, staying the night in a farmhouse. On all the many occasions he entered fields or woods he hardly ever met a farmer. He professed to feel more at ease with 'rough working-class people' than their polite middle-class counterparts, and this may have been so, but the cultural gulf was wide.[92]

There was, however, a twist in the tale: many among Fred's acquaintance, including the Catleys themselves, were only one generation removed from the land. Less than a month after the encounter in the Colliers Arms, Basil led Fred to a 'romantic little combe' near Chewton Mendip, with a couple of cottages and the ruins of another one, in which it transpired Basil's father had been born.[93]

---

[90] Lack of respect for property: making no effort to repair a drystone wall he damaged in the Mendips, for example. BA, 41419/28, 24 Aug. 1934.

[91] BA, 41419/10, 11 May 1929. Walter Raymond (1852–1931) was a Somerset novelist often, in his time, compared to Thomas Hardy: 'Walter Raymond', *Somerset History: Capturing the Heritage of Somerset*. www.somersethistory.co.uk/walter-raymond [accessed 18 Apr. 2016]. On regional stereotypes in fiction see Snell, ed., *The Regional Novel*, 36–8.

[92] BA, 41419/25, 22 Apr. 1934. Compare Tom Jeffery's claim that university-educated 'yak yaks' were much more likely to elicit hostile reactions from lower-middle-class observers than was the working class. Tom Jeffery, 'A Place in the Nation: The Lower Middle Class in England', in Rudy Koshar (ed.), *Splintered Classes: Politics and the Lower Middle Class in Interwar Europe* (New York, 1990), 71.

[93] BA, 41419/10, 20 May 1929. Fred later attributed it largely to Basil's influence that 1929 had been 'first and foremost a Somerset year'. BA, 41419/14, 31 Dec. 1929.

Fred's own paternal grandparents had lived in Holcombe, near Bath, and, passing by on a cycling tour in April 1934, Fred hoped to find their cottage again, but in vain because he failed to recognize it.[94] From this point of view, these rural excursions were a kind of return, but one that could never be completed because it was a return to a past that no longer existed. There is an echo of a wider class history of dispossession and displacement from the land here, a history experienced by Hallam in the previous generation at first hand.

The 'Armchair Countryside'

The winter of 1929–30 proved exceptionally wet, with extensive floods across the Somerset Levels. Fred had to content himself with vicarious ruralism. He bought S. E. Winbolt's *Somerset* and read it at Gladys's in the dinner hour, pronouncing its 'magnificent photos' a 'treat'. At home he was absorbed in *Unknown Somerset* while later in the year he bought J. L. W. Page's *An Exploration of Exmoor and the Hill Country of West Somerset* and read J. W. Gough's 'fascinating' *The Mines of Mendip*. Fred is an excellent example of someone who enjoyed the 'armchair countryside', to adopt Bunce's useful phrase.[95] In his case this was not confined to literature. He also enjoyed paintings and drawings of rural landscapes, even, despite his impecuniousness, buying a sketch of Marshfield by his friend Harold Stone.[96] He had a 'delightful' time at the Clifton Arts Club exhibition during one dinner hour; not coincidentally, three Chew valley landscapes pleased him most ('Pensford', 'Elms, Compton Dando' and 'The Ford, Chew Stoke').[97] Ruralist music too appealed, again especially when it pertained to his own stamping ground – a performance of W. H. Reed's *Two Somerset Idylls* and Gustav Holst's *A Somerset Rhapsody* was much to his taste.[98] The relationship between the armchair countryside and outdoor enjoyment of rural landscapes continued to be mutually constitutive. Two days after buying the sketch from Harold Stone he went on a bike ride through Marshfield while a holiday in Dorset led him back to William Barnes:

> What I most remember about this day is my delighted reading of Barnes' Dorset dialect poems. I got a little selection of them back in February, read a few and then almost forgot it. Now, coming back fresh from Dorset, I remembered them again ... Today I took them with me and read and read, and delivered some aloud to Will, being unable to contain my appreciation. The best of them have such perfect simplicity, such

---

[94] BA, 41419/25, 4 Apr. 1934.
[95] Michael F. Bunce, *The Countryside Ideal: Anglo-American Images of Landscape* (Abingdon, 1994), 37–76.
[96] BA, 41419/24, 7 Sep. 1933.
[97] BA, 41419/10, 17 May 1929.
[98] BA, 41419/42, 26 Jan. 1942.

a felicity of words, that they call up the country more vividly than any
other poems except Edward Thomas's.[99]

A limitation of the armchair countryside was that its pleasures were essentially private, Fred's advocacy of Barnes notwithstanding. Conversely, the
more embodied the experience of the countryside, the more it could become
collective. A family outing to Weston-super-Mare on 10 June 1930 exemplifies this. After a bracing walk along the shore at Anchor Head, Will, Gladys
and Fred went exploring in the nearby woods. Fred was particularly keen to
see Worlebury Camp although the guidebooks he had consulted maintained
that it was private.[100] They made their way up a steep path, struggled through
some trees and came out on a tremendous pile of limestone fragments, which
they then realized was in fact a section of the hill fort's ramparts. Fred briefly
lost Will and Gladys but, after whistling and shouting, they were reunited and
walked round the ramparts. They were rewarded by 'one of those heart-
stirring views of which Somerset can show so many, far more, surely, than
any other county in England' and felt 'supremely pleased with everything and
well repaid for our climb'.[101] The shared physical and emotional experience
of clambering up the hill, pushing through the trees, discovering the camp in
defiance of guidebooks and property rights, losing and finding each other,
and the view as the reward for their efforts had brought the three of them
together, in a way analogous to the Christian fellowship Bissell's expeditions
to Ben Nevis aimed to foster, or the shared hardships of Barmes's Guide
camps.

Bridge and Valley

Later that month Fred got a new bike. He was keen to try it out and, predictably, his first major expedition was through the Chew valley:

> I took the Burnett road ... and then struck the lovely side road through
> the Chew valley. I stopped for a few minutes in that delightful spot on the
> bridge over the weir beyond Chewton House, and then went on through
> charming little Chewton Keynsham. This road is one of my favourites,
> and it is not much marred even where they widened it last year near
> Woolscombe Bottom, for the new bank is rapidly becoming overgrown.
> Indeed the whole road, right from here to Publow is a gem, just a beautiful
> lane but with a splendid surface.

[99] Marshfield: BA, 41419/24, 9 Sep. 1933. Barnes: BA, 41419/31, 20 Jun. 1936. Compare also
BA, 41419/34, 4–11 Apr. 1937, when Fred 'looked at Isle of Wight maps and guides,
enjoying the anticipation almost as much as I shall the holiday'.

[100] Fred noted that 'camp-hunting' was one of their favourite pastimes, consistent with
Landry's claim that hunting metaphors often underpin rural leisure practices. Landry,
The Invention of the Countryside.

[101] BA, 41419/16, 10 Jun. 1930.

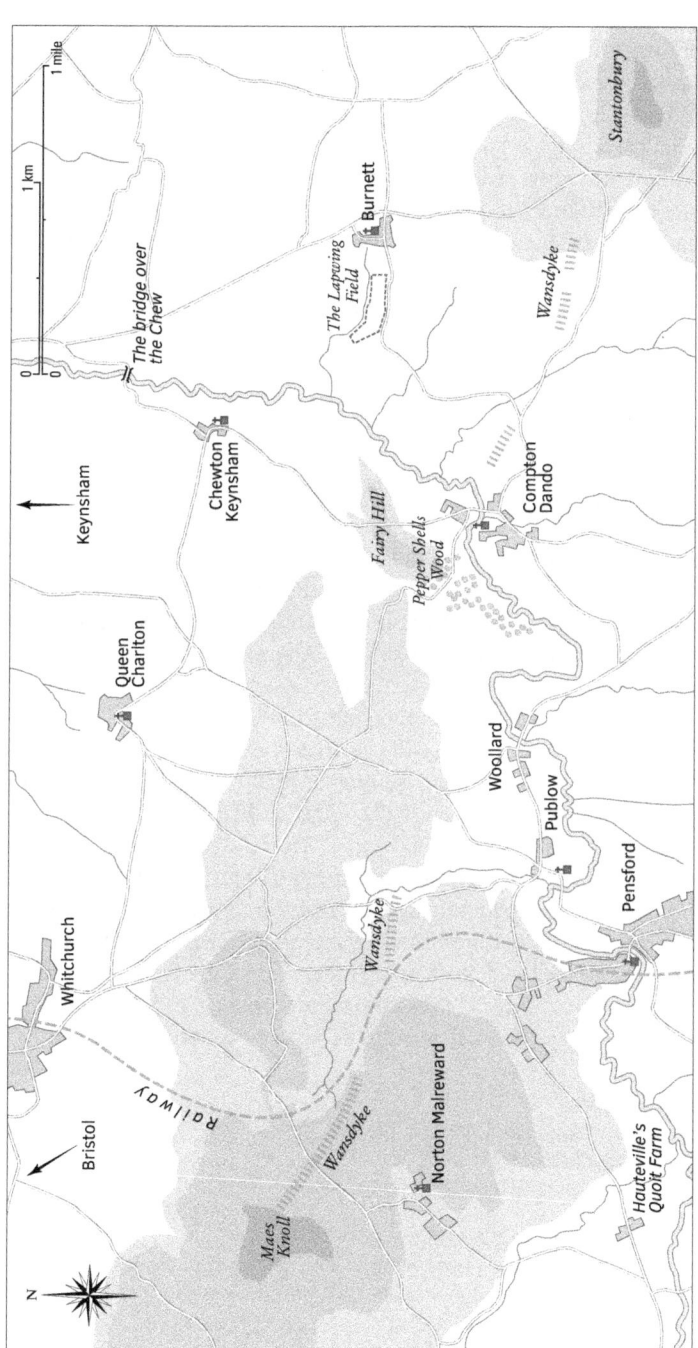

Figure 9.2 The Chew valley

> I successfully negotiated Fairy Hill and ran down into Compton Dando,
> then on to Wollard, through absolutely flawless country.[102]

Fred often mentions the bridge over the weir by Chewton Keynsham.[103] It was
a ritual for him to pause there, contemplate the scene and pay his respects to
a place that evidently had a special meaning to him, one he never explains but
which we can tentatively reconstruct. Firstly then, the bridge was the gateway
to the Chew valley, his holy of holies. There can be little doubt that it was
powerfully charged with liminal significance. Perhaps, in pausing there, he cast
off his quotidian self, rather in the way that people sometimes change clothes
when they come home from work or school. There is a parallel with the diary of
Jane Holmes, which recounts the author's girlhood play experiences in a patch
of south Wiltshire countryside she and her half-sister called 'Arcadia', reached
by crossing a bridge they named 'the Gateway to Paradise'.[104]

Secondly, gazing into the water from a bridge was (as it doubtless remains)
a widespread spatial practice – compare Hallam, for example:

> Stayed in Hungerford some time watching the trout in the beautiful clear
> stream the Kennet which is like crystal.[105]

It seems unlikely that a discursive explanation, literary or otherwise, can
account for the two men's similar behaviour in this instance. More probable
is a combination of unconscious imitation of friends or relatives whom each
had seen doing the same, and the opportunities inherent in the situation. The
continuous flow of transparent water seems to prompt contemplation, partly
no doubt because it is such an obvious metaphor for life.

Perhaps the core of the appeal of the bridge over the weir to Fred, however,
was that it represented the concentrated quintessence of what mattered most to
him in landscapes such as the Chew valley or the Mendips. Affectively it
belonged, in his eyes at least, uniquely to him.[106] The bridge was not a famous
landmark, so when he first noticed its beauty, it felt like his own discovery. He
had come to appreciate it in the first flush of his passion for the countryside and
since then had crossed it many times, most of them memorably happy ones. It
was part of the landscape he loved most, and while it was secure from any taint of
Bristol, it was also close to home. This relationship to home was vitally important. Real, day-to-day homes can never quite be all they should: the world too

---

[102] BA, 41419/16, 5 Jul. 1930.

[103] See also, for example, BA, 41419/4, 15 Apr. 1927.

[104] Jane Holmes, *Footloose in South Wiltshire* (Gloucester, 2007). The origins and implications of Holmes' remarkably rich childhood toponomy are explored in Burchardt, 'Far
Away and Close to Home'.

[105] Hallam Diaries, BRO D/EX 1415/2, 30 Apr. 1892.

[106] Anything that he felt to be his Fred prized greatly. Compare, for example, his enthusiasm
for Edmond Holmes' *The Tragedy of Education*: 'this book has a spiritual flame about it.
It is <u>mine</u>.' BA, 41419/25, 22 Apr. 1934.

often intrudes, bringing in its unwelcome baggage of pressures, worries and unwanted circumstances. For Fred the Chew bridge and the valley beyond were a veritable home-from-home, an ideal transposition into which the world could not follow him. It was no accident that he eventually moved there, but perhaps also no accident that the move did not last: in making it his real home, he inadvertently let the world in with him.

The joyful sense of reunion Fred felt on returning to places such as this bridge, the fir clump, the lapwing field or, on a larger scale, the Mendip plateau arose from his feeling that they were his in this special way. Any landscape, or indeed skyscape, whose beauty he had discovered for himself and from which he had been separated for a while could prompt it:

> But when I got home, just at midnight, I found no mist there ... and Sirius, that pearl, that flower, that loveliest of lovely things, shooting its rose and clear green rays in the eastern sky. After so many months, I saw it with intense joy.[107]

Left Alone

By the end of the year (1930) Fred was involved in a relationship with Joan Barton, a young woman who shared his literary interests. Although he had been drawn to several girls his own age and younger before, this seems to have been the first time anything mutual developed. Fred was undeterred by Charlotte's disapproval, recording with some satisfaction that he had 'asserted [his] independence' by going over to Joan's against his mother's wishes.[108] But the friction proved painful when Charlotte's health deteriorated in March 1931. She had been suffering from respiratory problems for some time and an attack of flu proved too much for her. On the 10th she could hardly breathe or speak and just after noon the following day Fred received a phone call at work to come home immediately. He rushed back to find a 'terrible change': 'her face was yellow and colourless, her mouth gasping and her eyes drawn'. Unable to speak and hardly conscious, she died shortly after 1pm. He was unsure whether she had known him.[109]

Fred's diary gives only occasional glimpses of his underlying state of mind over the ensuing days and weeks. One of the most telling came the day before the funeral, a Sunday:

> Did not go out all day. Reading Maupassant in French: somehow I could read that, though not English when I tried.[110]

---

[107] BA, 41419/24, 15 Nov. 1933.
[108] BA, 41419/18, 28 and 29 Nov. 1930 and 3 Mar. 1931.
[109] BA, 41419/18, 11 Mar. 1931.
[110] BA, 41419/18, 15 Mar. 1931.

He went back to work on Tuesday but on his return found the house 'very lonely, with everyone gone and a great emptiness'.[111]

Later in the year he wrote a poem that perhaps speaks for some of the diary's silences:

The Pool

I could not think that she had died
Till I wandered to the quiet pool
Over which, heads together, we leaned
And looked on its surface, clear and cool;

I could not think that she had died
Till I saw, mirrored therein, a head,
Unknown its pale face, glassy its eyes:
- And all the trees shrieked 'She is dead!'[112]

This registers how difficult he had found it to come to terms with his feelings, and the role landscape played in helping him begin to do so, albeit in guarded terms: his mother is not explicitly identified with the 'she' of the poem and, in a further protective dissociation, nor is Fred with the 'pale face'. A poem is always a literary transfiguration rather than a direct record of experience but other evidence also implies that Fred found it hard to acknowledge his mother's death or recognize its effects on him. In contrast to his father, she is barely mentioned in his subsequent diaries, and when she is, Fred seems anxious to change the subject. On 25 October 1931, for example, Fred recorded that he had 'met Mr Strange, and he was chattering about Mother and the War and other gloomy subjects'.[113]

Initially the blow that had befallen Fred drew Joan closer to him but this did not last: as early as 4 April he noted that there was '[s]till a slight coldness with Joan, which I made worse by a misplaced remark'.[114] Their relationship, initially intense – Fred later referred to it as 'brief and violent' – seems to have cooled over the year, at least on Joan's side.[115] By mid-October they had reached the point where she felt called upon to write a 'long and sensible, reasonable' letter setting out the position between them.[116] This was not promising and although Fred was delighted with her Christmas present (Edward Thomas's *Collected Poems*) the relationship seems to have faded into arm's-length friendship early the following year.[117]

---

[111] BA, 41419/18, 17 Mar. 1931.
[112] 'A Collection of Poems Written by F. J. Catley', BA, 41419/70.
[113] BA, 41419/20, 25 Oct. 1931.
[114] BA, 41419/18, 4 Apr. 1931.
[115] BA, 41419/40, 1941 introductory remarks.
[116] BA, 41419/20, 13 Oct. 1931.
[117] BA, 41419/20, 24 Dec. 1931.

Concerned, perhaps, for their orphaned cousins, Nellie and Katie came down from London for a week during the summer and they all went off to Watchet. Most days they walked over Exmoor or the Quantocks. Fred drank in Exmoor's beauty avidly – the view inland from Selworthy Beacon, across a vast stretch of country mottled with pale sunshine and cloud shadow, was 'far lovelier than could possibly be imagined'.[118] Although he may have loved the Chew valley more, only the Mendips and, later, the South Wiltshire downs filled him with awe in the same way as Exmoor's 'boundless yet beautiful monotony'.[119]

Navigation and Leadership

The other notable feature of this holiday was Fred's newfound role as leader. He knew the hills better and was a far more experienced navigator than his companions. When they 'seemed to be getting rather lost' after walking up Cloutsham Water, and the other four were resigning themselves to a night in the open, Fred led them up a steep path that his sense of direction told him ought to bring them out near Webber's Post. Presently they emerged onto the moor by some fir trees and there it was, within a few yards of them.[120] Three days later Fred again took the lead, planning their entire walk from Porlock Weir to Oare and the Chalk Water.[121]

In years to come Fred was to reprise this leadership role many times, often with larger, non-family groups. On the weekend of 25/26 March 1939 he was with a party of more than thirty young people at Hutton Youth Hostel (Somerset). One of the group had an uncle at nearby Rackley Farm but no-one seemed to know how to get there, 'not even the owner of the uncle'. So Fred led the group down the side of the hill till they came in sight of the farm.[122] Navigational prowess and knowledge of the countryside enabled him to break out of the social diffidence that had held him back and gain the respect of his peers, especially in the heyday of the Youth Hostels Association (YHA) in the 1930s and 1940s.

Literary Endeavours

As summer 1931 passed into autumn Fred began a new short story, 'This Came', about a man, his wife and cancer, 'a theme ... which interests me frightfully'. Later that month he suddenly realized that it was really a novel.

---

[118] BA, 41419/20, 10 Aug. 1931. Compare Dickinson's similar response.
[119] BA, 41419/20, 13 Aug. 1931.
[120] BA, 41419/20, 10 Aug. 1931.
[121] BA, 41419/20, 13 Aug. 1931.
[122] BA, 41419/38, 26 Mar. 1939.

Incidents and characters ran wild in his mind while in the bath and he went to bed much excited about it. He worked at it on and off for much of the next two years. But like the guide to the Mendips he wrote in 1934, and most of his poetry, it was never published.[123] Since neither book manuscript survives, it is impossible to assess how far this was due to limitations in the works themselves, or whether Fred was disadvantaged by his lowly social origins and lack of connections. However, his diaries show that he could write vividly and, whatever the merits of 'This Came', it is difficult to imagine that the Mendip book can have lacked interest given Fred's vast knowledge of and intense emotional engagement with the subject. The poems are a different matter since fifty or so are preserved in the Bristol Record Office. About half a dozen appear to have been published in leading poetry or countryside journals such as *John O'London's Weekly*, *The Adelphi*, *The Field* and *Country Life*, which shows that Fred's background was not an insuperable barrier to his literary ambitions. Many of them are accomplished but few are entirely persuasive. Fred felt this himself:

> I spent most of the evening on a new poem 'The Enchantment'. Quite pleasing, and yet disappointing, as always, damn it![124]

It is difficult to pinpoint the problem. Fred was a close observer of the countryside and could turn an effective phrase – 'green electric fire' to describe the returning life-force of spring, for example. However, many of the poems are derivative: too often Thomas or occasionally Hardy can be heard speaking through them. More seriously, the underlying thought is frequently platitudinous and perhaps because of this the poems rarely end on a convincing note. The title and first stanza of 'The Sword' raise expectations that a new observation about nature, darkness or war will be forthcoming but in the final verse it emerges that the 'sword' is no more than a shaft of sunlight reflecting from a glasshouse, carrying no symbolic charge at all.[125]

Bounty, Beauty and Ugliness

There was more satisfaction in the family tradition of self-provisioning, which went all the way back to Joseph's dream of agrarian independence. He had been a great gardener, keeping careful records of what he grew. Charlotte had maintained this tradition, specializing in fruit-picking and jam-making. The back of her diary lists quantities of blackcurrants, loganberries and other fruit, with the date of each year's first picking.[126] Deprived of their mother, Will,

---

[123] BA, 41419/25, 13 Apr. 1934.
[124] BA, 41419/20, 22 Nov. 1931.
[125] 'A Collection of Poems Written by F. J. Catley', BA, 41419/70.
[126] Diary of Charlotte Elizabeth Catley, BA, 41419/69.

Gladys and Fred seem to have thrown themselves into harvesting blackberries and elderberries with particular energy. They found 'an abundance of splendid fruit' at Pipley Bottom, a favourite haunt, and when they got home set about making jam. It had been a 'most successful and enjoyable expedition', and they repeated it many times subsequently, even after the war when they were no longer living together.[127] Like making tea, picnicking, exploring and carving your name in a tree, harvesting wild food is a way of acting in and becoming part of the landscape, rather than merely observing it.

Whether because of the superlative weather or because time and his recent experiences had changed him, Fred responded to the beauty of the countryside with unprecedented intensity that autumn. As so often before, the Chew brought this new feeling into focus:

> Everywhere the country had been beautiful but the Chew valley was lovelier than I have ever before known it. It was still deep green – the elms in particular were only just beginning to be touched with yellow, a bough here and there, and the dark green was the richer for it – while the soft autumnal amber sunshine lay in pools on the road under the trees. Somehow everything was more beautiful today ... The next turning on the left is at Bromley, and leads past a row of blatantly white-and-red new houses ... to come out at this place, where there is a colliery and the country is just pretty, from the green beauty of which Chew Magna and the little river are the 'fons et origo' is something of a shock. But the road to Stanton Drew, which I now took, plunges once more into the river valley where the old magic reasserts itself.[128]

As the disparaging reference to Bromley indicates, however, he was at the same time becoming more antipathetic to urban modernity, to the point where this becomes one of the dominant notes of his diary for the following year (1932). On 1 October he had had to leave a parcel at Barton Hill and found 'that place of slums, gasometers and dirty women ... even more depressing than usual in the rain'.[129] Fred's growing dislike of Bristol forms an interesting counterpoint to Hallam's gradual rapprochement with Swindon. Both men developed an affection for their respective local areas, based on a kind of home feeling. But whereas for Hallam this eventually encompassed Swindon's urban core, Fred projected it onto the adjacent countryside: in ascending scale the Chew valley, Somerset and the West Country. Admittedly, Bristol was not quite as bad as 'disgusting', 'pretentious', 'never-ending' Bournemouth:

> It made me shudder to look inland and see the great level jumble of houses, chimneys and pines, without a single striking feature.

---

[127] BA, 41419/20, 19 Sep. 1931; BA, 41419/24, 16 Sep. 1934; BA, 41419/34, 11 Sep. 1937; BA, 41419/47, 21 and 22 Sep. 1947; BA, 41419/59, 25 Sep. 1955.
[128] BA, 41419/20, 10 Oct. 1931.
[129] BA, 41419/22, 1 Oct. 1932. The misogyny is uncharacteristic.

But he attributed his preference to the fact that, despite its size, green hills were always visible from Bristol, so the grudging concession turns out to be merely a restatement of his ruralism.[130]

Fred's growing hostility to urban environments gave his ruralism a more conscious and sharply defined ideological edge:

> The Frome and the stream that joins it at Moorend were full and noisy. Frome is a delightful shallow rapid stream here under the alders and willows – what a contrast to its corpse-like stillness in the slums of Bristol![131]

Yet even in the early 1930s, when his anti-urbanism was at its peak, his feelings about cities were not as pervasively negative as this might suggest. He was excited when Nellie and Katie suggested they might take him to Paris, and for all his dismay at London's sprawling suburbs, he greatly enjoyed its art galleries and found the city 'dazzling, brilliantly attractive' in the dark.[132] Indeed, the hard anonymous glitter of urban streets at night had an appeal for him almost anywhere, even in Bristol.[133] Most of the time, however, he seems to have lived in and moved through his home town without any very strong feeling about it either way. Since it formed the almost constant backdrop to his daily life, this was virtually inevitable. It has often been argued, by scholars such as Bunce and Lowe for example, that ruralism is an expression of anti-urbanism but this can hardly be so in Fred's case.[134] His enthusiasm for, absorption in and close identification with the countryside long predated his vehemently anti-urban period in the 1930s and was quite out of proportion to the mild dislike of Bristol that characterized his feelings most of the time before and after this phase.

Fred's attitude to commerce underwent a somewhat parallel evolution. He had never liked it – when set an essay on 'Buying and Selling' at QEH he had written about a country marketplace, 'thus "wangling" a nasty subject'.[135] But as with his anti-urbanism, his anti-commercialism came more sharply into focus in the early 1930s. Returning home on 5 November 1932 he 'was sorry to come to the electric lights of Keynsham, and worst of all that disgusting red FRY shouting to sky and country from their Somerdale factory'.[136] He was far from alone in feeling that there was a profound incompatibility between

---

[130] BA, 41419/24, 23 Aug. 1933.

[131] BA, 41419/34, 6 Feb. 1937.

[132] BA, 41419/20, 13 Oct. and 18 Aug. 1931.

[133] BA, 41419/20, 18 Oct. 1931.

[134] Bunce, *The Countryside Ideal*; Lowe, 'The Rural Idyll Defended'.

[135] BA, 41419/4, 25 Feb. 1927.

[136] BA, 41419/22, 5 Nov. 1932. The construction of Fry's chocolate factory between 1921 and 1933 drastically altered the landscape around Keynsham. By 1929 more than five hundred thousand square feet of floor space had been built and by 1934 the factory had over three thousand employees. In 1932 the large 'FRY' sign was on the south end of 'B' block. 'Remembering Somerdale', *Around Keynsham & Saltford Past & Present: Journal of the Keynsham & Saltford Local History Society* 10 (2010), 16, 18.

advertising and the countryside. Roadside advertisements had been the subject of legislation as early as 1925 and were one of the principal concerns of the CPRE in its early days. Shell-Mex attempted to ingratiate itself with the public by removing eighteen thousand signs in 1929.[137] The objection to advertisements seems to have been partly on account of their prominence and visibility, qualities intrinsic to their function. However, to Fred and many others, there was a more fundamental conflict. Commercial advertising is unavoidably materialistic, seeking to persuade some people to consume so that other people can make money. A taint of insincerity, even perhaps dishonesty, hangs about it: the advertiser neither knows nor cares whether it is in the interests of the target consumer to buy their product. To someone like Fred, for whom the countryside represented purity, truth and beauty, advertising in the countryside was necessarily anathema.[138]

A third element of Fred's growing alienation in the early 1930s was his situation at work. He had never been well paid: he started on a wage of only fifteen shillings a week and after more than twelve years still earned no more than three pounds per week before deductions.[139] This put him on a lower wage than many factory workers and well below the normal range of lower middle-class incomes.[140] He resented this: when given a five-shilling rise he 'did not feel grateful in the slightest' while a previous rise had been 'very much overdue'.[141] On another occasion he was so piqued to receive only a 2/6 rise that it gave him a bad headache.[142] Furthermore, although George's was an extremely congenial environment, the work itself was dull and repetitive. There is a single entry in his diary for the penultimate week of 1933: 'This week being one of unvaried work, every day resembling every other day, there is not much to be noted.'[143] Partly no doubt because he did not enjoy it, he was liable to be late for work, provoking a sharp reprimand from one of the directors.[144] But the worst aspect of work, at this stage of his life at least, was quite simply that it confined him and kept him from doing what he wanted. Work, like school before it, was a form of imprisonment:

> It was too cruel to have to spend a day like this in a shop. It was as though December were making a special effort to prove that Winter can not only

---

[137] Dennis Norman Jeans, 'Planning and the Myth of the English Countryside in the Interwar Period', *Rural History* 1 (1990), 254–5.

[138] On objections to rural advertising see Readman, 'Landscape Preservation', 61–83.

[139] BA, 41419/40, 29 Jan. 1941.

[140] According to Tom Jeffery, skilled workers could expect to earn four to five pounds a week and the core of the lower middle class between two hundred and fifty and five hundred pounds a year in the 1930s. Jeffery, 'A Place in the Nation', 74.

[141] BA, 41419/40, 29 Jan. 1941; BA, 41419/24, 15 Sep. 1933.

[142] BA, 41419/38, 23 Feb. 1939.

[143] BA, 41419/24, 18 to 23 Dec. 1933.

[144] BA, 41419/24, 27 Sep. 1933.

equal but surpass the other seasons in beauty. The unfailing sunshine was
delicious: the air was clear, cold, invigorating. Out in the country the quiet
innumerable tree, field and hill colours must have been lovely beyond all
words. I wanted to be out in a wood.[145]

The alienation Fred was experiencing so acutely was accompanied by a marked
shift to the political left. On 5 October 1932 Will went to a communist meeting at
St Michael's Hall; Fred would have gone too had it started later. Meanwhile he had
been reading Morris's *News from Nowhere* and Murry's *Necessity of Communism*,
which he finished on 30 October.[146] Only three days afterwards came one of his
most damning and ideologically inflected outbursts against urbanism:

> I rode along the New Cut and home through Barton Hill. Never have I felt
> so strongly before the inhumanity of the things Man constructs for
> himself – the dark buildings and blazing lights of the city, monster cranes
> by the river, chemical works. The drizzle soaked steadily down.[147]

Such sweeping, systematic and outspoken antipathy to the urban and commercial goes beyond anything Fred had written previously. Back in 1927, for
example, he had expressed horror at the squalid district Cliff Trew lived in
and declared he could 'never stand a city life' but there is little sense of urbanism
as a historically specific social formation potentially amenable to change.[148] He
probably owed this new perspective to Morris and Murry. It is unlikely to have
been an accident he was reading these authors in the early 1930s: their condemnation of industrial capitalism chimed not only with his existing experiences and
intimations but also with the wider climate of the times. The Wall Street Crash
and its aftermath, including the collapse of the Labour government in 1931, led
to a sharp upturn in Communist Party membership in Britain.[149]

Fred's diatribes against Bristol, commerce and capitalism in late 1932 are
juxtaposed with an intense apprehension of the beauty of individual trees and
appropriation of them to his own identity. He refers to 'my great elm' and 'my
false acacia', and subsequently 'my own birch-tree' and '[m]y beautiful golden
little poplars'.[150] On 8 October, in the Chew valley, he was:

> engaged noticing the autumnal colours of the country – three elms near
> the river at Somerdale, two tinged and one wholly yellow: the bryony, field
> maple and hawthorn colouring the hedges around Stockwood; some elms

---

[145] BA, 41419/22, 1 Dec. 1932. Compare BA, 41419/34, 6 Feb. 1937: 'Far too lovely
a morning to be spent in a shop . . . I longed for freedom.'
[146] BA, 41419/22, 5 Oct. 1932; John Middleton Murry, 1932.
[147] BA, 41419/22, 2 Nov. 1932. Plainly the weather influenced Fred's perceptions but this
was hardly the first gloomy autumn evening he had known in Bristol.
[148] BA, 41419/4, 12 Apr. 1927.
[149] Andrew Thorpe, 'The Membership of the Communist Party of Great Britain, 1920–
1945', *Historical Journal* 43 (2000), 781.
[150] BA, 41419/22, 13 Oct. 1932; BA, 41419/36, 31 Mar. and 1 Apr. 1938.

near Whitchurch crowned with brilliant yellow, blossoming bright as golden-rod, a most lovely fulfilment; a far-away russet horse-chestnut, solitary in a field near Stanton Drew; and again, as I returned from Chew, a little hedge-elm one clear flame of yellow, virginally pure and unspotted.[151]

At twenty-one, Fred's capacity to appreciate beauty, and to articulate his appreciation, was developing. This was related to the evaluating and assessing mode that allowed him to identify Hodder's Combe as 'the most beautiful of all this side of the Quantocks', although the temporal and spatial scales were quite different. The beauty of the little hedge-elm existed as a one-dimensional point in time and space, a single moment of concentrated aesthetic experience, whereas Fred's apprehension of Hodder's Combe was a more cerebral composite of many perspectives and occasions. Both were 'his' but it may have been easier to imagine that the beauty he perceived at the micro scale of the first was his alone.

Fred's end-of-year summary for 1932 concluded that it had been a great year for reading and that he had advanced a good deal intellectually. 'My Utopia becomes clearer', he pronounced – a revealing choice of words since it echoes the title of his father's political testimony. Practically, however, he felt that he was very much where he had been a year ago.[152]

Sea and Downs

The following year saw little change in Fred's circumstances either at work or at home. It was mainly notable for the summer holiday in Lyme Regis and some memorable excursions later that summer and autumn. Lyme appealed to Fred partly because of the contrast between its sparkling blue sea and the 'mudcoloured streak' of the Bristol Channel.[153] He also admired the town, harbour and cliffs. The most compelling attraction, however, was the 'glow and freedom of human life on the beach'. He was enchanted with the beauty of young girls, 'children with breasts just budding', and by one inadequately covered girl in particular, aged he later 'saw with surprise' no more than thirteen or fourteen.[154] The diaries record several occasions when Fred took an interest in adolescent and in at least one instance even younger girls, and he does not seem to have felt there was anything improper or questionable about this. He appears to have been unconscious of or to have repressed the indubitably sexual character of these feelings. Certainly his diary indicates that he regarded his

---

[151] BA, 41419/22, 8 Oct. 1932.
[152] BA, 41419/22, 31 Dec. 1932.
[153] BA, 41419/24, 20 Aug. 1933.
[154] BA, 41419/24, 16 Aug. 1933.

responsiveness to the beauty of early teenage girls as of a piece with his appreciation of other kinds of beauty, in landscape, music or literature for example. It seems likely that Fred had something in common with John Ruskin and Francis Kilvert in this respect. Each revered purity as an aesthetic and moral value, and imputed it both to nature and childhood. Yet in a painful and disturbing irony, the same structure of feeling also channelled, perhaps indeed generated, strong sexual impulses in all three men, impulses which however remained unacknowledged and unenacted. In Fred's case the feeling was connected to a profound, devastating sense of loss. Of two girls he had been drawn to at Lyme, he later wrote:

> I never saw them again, though I searched the faces of the people for the rest of the week. Never to see people again, never again – to think this is one of the most stabbing of thoughts.[155]

The core of this feeling cannot have been displaced grief for his mother, since he had felt the same desolating emotion two years before she died in relation to a little girl he had seen acting in a pantomime. Probably it derived in some way from his own childhood – perhaps, like so much else in his life, it was obscurely related to the traumatic loss of his father.[156]

As usual Fred took every opportunity to get out into the countryside that summer. A charabanc tour to Dorset on 22 August proved unexpectedly compelling, in ways that cast light on central aspects of what the countryside meant to him. Although the rain fell unbrokenly on the way back, the long ride over the uplands from Shaftesbury to Warminster, his first close view of the South Wiltshire downs, was unforgettable:

> Nothing I have ever seen, not Exmoor itself, impressed me so much as these vast bare heights, stretching away on every side in the damp greyness of the evening, with Great Ridge Wood on the near horizon to the east. It was one of those things which seem, when one looks back upon them, to be so perfect and impalpable that one can scarcely believe in their existence outside the imagination. I find this often happens with tracts of country: not only afterwards, when I see them in memory, but even when I am actually looking at them . . . I do not mean so much that they seem unreal, for at such moments reality seems closer than at any other time, and the things the realest of all things; but that they seem to be on a different plane of existence, a plane nearer truth. At such times I am, and am aware I am, most alive: and yet my own existence has nothing to do with the essential truth of the thing before me. It is not that I transmute these things, but these things that transmute me.[157]

---

[155] BA, 41419/24, 16 Aug. 1933.
[156] BA, 41419/14, 15 Feb. 1929.
[157] BA, 41419/24, 22 Aug. 1933.

Fred's sculptural feeling for the broad sweep of hills, for landscape in large masses, form rather than detail, was culturally somewhat precocious. According to Peter Howard, it was only during what he terms the 'Formal Period' (1950–80) that chalk downland became artistically fashionable. It is true that avant-garde pioneers like John Piper and Paul Nash had already discovered an affinity between the 'hard, flowing outlines' of the downs and modernist abstraction before the Second World War, but abstract art did not appeal to Fred, and in any case Nash's *Equivalents for the Megaliths*, the best-known expression of this sensibility, dates only from 1935.[158] H. J. Massingham's *English Downland* (1936) also postdates the charabanc ride across the downs, and although Fred may have been familiar with some of his earlier books and articles, he shows few signs of Massingham's interest in the nexus between downland and prehistory. The most probable literary influence is Hudson's *A Shepherd's Life* (1910), which Fred knew well. Hudson, however, was more interested in the farming, people and wildlife of the downs than in the landscape as such; nor can his influence easily explain how the Wiltshire downs came to be connected with Exmoor and the Mendips in Fred's mind. His feeling for these spare, sweeping landscapes, then, can be linked to wider developments in artistic and literary taste, but does not seem to have been closely derivative from them.

Landscape, Selfhood and Sensation

The significance of Fred's account of the charabanc ride from Shaftesbury to Warminster, however, resides more in what it tells us about how he experienced landscape than why he preferred one form of it to another. His poem 'Mendip Landscape', written the same year, provides an illuminating comparison, construing the relationship between self and landscape in very similar terms:

> And then – myself. If I were happy or sad
> I cannot say. That day's myself being dead
> - If ever it existed – will not rise
> From a shut sepulchre, a covered bed.

> Myself. Yes, there were horses, stony earth
> Larches and beech, grey walls and whitish sand
> A sky that spit thin intermittent rain
> At the worn melancholy of this land.

> But I. I cannot think it. These alone
> Existed on that day. There was no I.
> It was an empty vessel brought away
> These undulating hills, this heavy sky.[159]

---

[158] Howard, *Landscapes*, 173, 76.
[159] 'A Collection of Poems Written by F. J. Catley', BA, 41419/70.

Fred figures himself as an 'empty vessel', passively transmuted by the landscape. So vivid, immediate and overwhelming is the experience that it completely possesses him, leaving no room for self-consciousness. Hence the paradox that he is 'most alive' when he has ceased to be aware of himself at all.[160] What he is describing could be understood as a form of mysticism, a secular version of religious transcendence. It bears comparison with Buddhist and Taoist practices, and perhaps strands of Christian mysticism, that seek to overcome the separation between self and world (or God). Fred's experience of the South Wiltshire downs and Mendips, however, does not seem to have required the support of any validating theological or philosophical framework.[161]

What enabled landscape to affect Fred so powerfully? A clue can be found in another poem, 'The Rain Unlocks the Scent', probably written about the same time:

> The rain unlocks the scent
> Of July afternoon
> After hot weeks of drought;
> And wakens soon
>
> That other rain which comes
> To bless the prisoned mind
> And free perfumes as fresh,
> As pure and kind
>
> As honeysuckle and hay,
> Clover and meadow-sweet.
> I touch the living grass
> And feel the summer heat.
>
> And know that happiness,
> Drenching the senses five,
> Which, making all things one,
> Might bring the very dead alive.[162]

This touches on many of the central aspects of Fred's experience of rural landscapes. It stands in a long line of poetry and prose that heralds the

---

[160] This perhaps instantiates Dutcher and colleagues' concept of connectivity with nature, involving the 'dissolution of boundaries and a sense of a shared or common essence between the self, nature, and others', which the authors see as the basis of environmental values. Daniel D. Dutcher, James C. Finley, A. E. Luloff and Janet Buttolph Johnston, 'Connectivity with Nature As a Measure of Environmental Values', *Environment and Behavior* 39 (2007), 474–93.

[161] By the late 1930s, however, Fred was aware of Buddhism and Taoism, both of which he discussed with Will on walks in 1937. BA, 41419/34, 21 Aug. and 2 Oct. 1937.

[162] 'A Collection of Poems Written by F. J. Catley', BA, 41419/70. On histories of scent see Mark S. R. Jenner, 'Follow Your Nose? Smell, Smelling, and Their Histories', *American Historical Review* 116 (2011), 335–51.

countryside as a mental and spiritual escape from a deadening, prison-like city, of which the opening lines of Wordsworth's *Prelude* and Keats' 'To One Who Has Been Long in City Pent' are perhaps the best-known examples. Jefferies may also have been in Fred's mind. As we have seen, Fred felt intermittently 'prisoned' first by school and later by work and Bristol. More interesting, however, is a second aspect of the poem, what it identifies as the source of the spiritual rain that frees the oppressed mind from bondage. It is direct sensation – the scent of honeysuckle, hay, clover and meadow-sweet, the touch of the grass and the feel of the summer heat. This rich multisensory experience describes Fred's actual encounters with the countryside well. Of course, not every moment was like this but his diaries repeatedly invoke smell, taste, touch and sound as well as vision:

> I cannot have too much of the young living green of trees at this time
> of year. The woods on the other side of the river are a lovely sight …
> Another delightful thing during the last two days has been the cutting of
> the grass on Christ Church green and by the Mansion House. The fresh
> scent is as good as a drink of pure water.[163]

Landscape was not alone in affecting Fred's senses so vibrantly. He relished food ('[t]he divinest tripe and onions for dinner!'), warm baths and of course music.[164] It is indicative of the richness of his sensory experience that when something pleased him intensely he characteristically expressed this with a metaphor pertaining to a different sense. Reading Proust enveloped him in a 'delicious mist' while a bright September day was 'sweet as a ripe apple'.[165] Johnston, seeking to attune himself as closely as possible to nature, sometimes used this idiom too, but it was rare among the other diarists.

The Swiss psychologist Carl Jung hypothesized four distinct psychological functions: thinking, feeling, sensing and intuition. Jung believed that, in some individuals, one or other of these functions predominated. While Jung's theory of personality types has received limited empirical support, Fred is a textbook example of an individual who experienced and related to the world primarily through sensation, to the partial and sometimes even complete exclusion of alternative modes of apprehension (such as Jung's other three psychological functions).[166] The consciousness of such a person might be entirely filled with the object of sensation – landscape, food or music, for instance – just as Fred

---

[163] BA, 41419/38, 4 May 1939. See also the Chew valley ride on 9 Mar. 1929 described earlier in this chapter: BA, 41419/10.

[164] Food: BA, 41419/25, 12 Jan. 1934 and 41419/34, 17 Jan. 1936; baths and music: BA, 41419/24, 18 Nov. 1933.

[165] BA, 41419/24, 14 and 15 Sep. 1933. On the difficulty of expressing sensory experience see Martin Jay, 'In the Realm of the Senses: An Introduction', *American Historical Review*, 116 (2011), 307–15, at 309.

[166] Carl Jung, *Collected Works of C. G. Jung*. Vol. 6. 2nd ed. (Princeton, 1971), 3–7.

describes his response to the South Wiltshire downs and the Mendips. It is not surprising that when he came across John Cowper Powys's *In Defence of Sensuality* at George's, he thought it looked 'close enough to my own mind and happiness to be of value to me', later concluding that it 'makes plain the root of my own happiness'.[167]

There is no better example of his capacity to be totally absorbed in the moment than the boat trip he took with his friend Haynes (from George's) on 26 August 1933. The plan was to 'adventure' up the Avon from Bath. They set off soon after 11.30 and went joyfully upstream. The sun beat down on the shining green river, which they had entirely to themselves except for a few fishermen and children bathing. Then they came to an immense willow lying right across the stream and had some difficulty getting through – 'an exciting procedure'. At Warleigh Ford they had lunch on an island, to reach which they had to cross a crude suspension bridge, a few narrow boards strung up with wire, 'like walking across a swaying rope'.

Negotiating the channel that by-passed the weir above the island proved challenging. The channel, a mere green groove, was so shallow and sandy as to be nearly impassable. It was far too narrow to allow rowing but fortunately some bathers gave them a hand and after about half-an-hour's continuous labour they were able to row off up the river. This stretch, which few seemed to penetrate, must, Fred afterwards opined, be the finest on the whole river:

> The valley here is surpassingly beautiful, the river ineffably calm and quiet, here and there greensurfaced with reeds, waterlilies and weed, but as wide and clear an expanse of water as any on the Avon from Conham upwards. Slowly and pleasantly we moved up the river and passed under the 18th century aqueduct.[168]

Some children told them that this was as far as they could go, so they got out and went for a walk along the canal, its motionless water so thick with weed that it closed up again immediately when they threw in a large stone. They came to a track, which they followed till at last they caught a glimpse of Bradford-on-Avon. By now wet with sweat and exhausted with dust and heat, they cut down to Avoncliff in search of tea, which they eventually found at 'Mrs Ricketts up on the Tump'. Never, Fred assured readers of his diary, was tea enjoyed more.

Back at Limpley Stoke, they rowed away, floating easily down the river. The evening was 'the quintessence of the day, a white flower opening after heat'. Reaching the rowing station about 9 o'clock, they cycled back to Keynsham,

---

[167] BA, 41419/34, 10 and 13 Sep. 1937.
[168] This was the Dundas Aqueduct at Limpley Stoke.

where they parted. It had been a superb day, one of those 'one remembers and remembers, thinking "How happy I was then" ... A river is a magical place'.[169]

So vividly could Fred experience rural landscapes that, as on the Avon or a few days before in South Wiltshire, they could seem dream-like and hallucinatory but, at the same time, 'the realest of all things'. Although he read little philosophy, there was an implicit idealism in his view of the world. Behind the day-to-day world of appearances, he seems to have felt, lay something more real and numinous (although this intimation never hardened into a formal belief). Blackberrying that autumn in Pipley Bottom with Will and Gladys, he felt this with particular force. As so often with his most transcendent landscape experiences, it came to him through the gateway of the senses, as we have seen a perhaps unusually wide one in his case:

> We settled down near the stream for tea. It is a little runnel not much more than a yard wide, embowered in alders, always running swiftly with small sounding waterfalls here and there. At one I bathed my hands, breathing a faint but definite perfume of peppermint. The valley was quiet as thought. There was a certain tall thin elm at a distance, whose head was clear against the sky. I looked at it again and again: the tree was reality, another facet of eternal truth and beauty.[170]

Rural Renewal

On New Year's Eve Fred reflected in his usual way on the year that was drawing to a close. Although it had been an agreeable one, he was little closer to his goal of 'freeing [him]self': escaping, perhaps by means of literary success, from having to live in a town and the perceived drudgery of working at George's. He had written far less than he should have done but had enjoyed the:

> unemotional acquaintances with people like Haynes, with the mutual music and book-talk and those halcyon times on the river ... As with most years, the greatest pleasure has been in being in the open air, walking, cycling or (for the first time, this year) rowing. I develop if I do not advance.[171]

Despite the apparent equanimity of this assessment, Fred's sense that he was stagnating became increasingly oppressive in the early months of 1934. The year started badly when Will did not like his latest composition, 'Hillscape, with Figure of Man', which he had finished with some satisfaction

---

[169] BA, 41419/24, 26 Aug. 1933.
[170] BA, 41419/24, 16 Sep. 1933.
[171] BA, 41419/24, 31 Dec. 1933.

the previous evening. Thursday, 4 January was '[a]nother flat day' and ten days later things were even worse:

> I stayed home in the evening and did some half-hearted typing. Bad, bad, bad ... A bad day, my mind sluggish. I am incredibly lazy. A little writing in the evening.[172]

Fred suffered acutely from the age-old conflict between the desire to remain comfortable and a sense that he ought to achieve something. He was in the throes of trying to finish 'This Came' and not finding it easy:

> 'This Came' has got behind during the last fortnight, and though I am near the end I can go no quicker, for I am no more certain of these last three or four thousand words than I was of the whole fifty thousand when I began it two and a half years ago. I dug up my old diaries and notes for some help. It weighs me down. All the time, year after year, my cry is 'Flow fast my tears that I have nothing, nothing done.' That is and always has been my feeling. Not just the things I want to do, but nothing – no washing up, no gardening, no helping with housework: not just no writing, no harmony, no piano-practice, no study. Alack![173]

Thinking of his favourite spots in the countryside gave him some consolation. The 6th of February was '[a]t last a real Spring day ... I think there must be a few violets at Norton Malreward now, and perhaps here and there a celandine'. However, only when he was able to get out in person on 3 March did the gloom that had enveloped him since the start of the year finally lift. There is an exuberant sense of rebounding joy, as if the stream of life within him had been frozen and now began to flow again:

> March weather in its perfect bloom. I cleaned the bike and set off for a ride about quarter to four in the afternoon. There was one of those magnificent royal south-west winds, full of life abounding, that invigorate and fill the day without being too great a hindrance to riding. On such a day it was inevitable that I should make for the Chew ... I reached Keynsham by four o'clock and went on to Chewton, still lying unchanged in its valley as though the earth had just created it. It is as natural as a tree. I stopped a moment on the bridge to look at the water, the trees, the rookery and the framed glimpse of Chewton. Then I rode on to Fairy Hill, where I left Jacob [his bicycle] by the roadside and climbed to the field above, where the line of wind beaten hawthorns runs along the edge of the hill towards the river. Here I got the full glory and richness of the wind and the whole green hollow of the country before me, Compton Dando below, Marksbury against the sky line and Burnett away to my left on the hillside. I walked about in ecstasy, unwilling to break the enchantment.[174]

[172] BA, 41419/25, 4 Jan. 1934.
[173] BA, 41419/25, 26 Feb. 1934.
[174] BA, 41419/25, 3 Mar. 1934.

The breeze is a familiar Romantic metaphor for the renewal of spiritual life, as in the opening lines of *The Prelude*, Coleridge's *The Eolian Harp* and *Dejection* or Shelley's *Ode to the West Wind*. How far the Romantics were in the back of Fred's mind when he wrote this passage is difficult to say. A more definite influence was the embodied experience of cycling. Fred felt the wind directly on his face and hands, in his nostrils and in the ache of his leg muscles as he pushed against it. As on previous occasions, sensory apprehension transmuted into spiritual experience. It is telling that Fred dismounted: he wanted to be as fully in the landscape as possible, to become part of it ('I walked about in ecstasy'). Climbing the hill also allowed him to see the whole of his beloved valley spread out below him. Its beauty and antiquity offered an Edenic reconciliation between the human and the natural – Chewton is 'as natural as a tree' and lies 'unchanged in its valley as though the earth had just created it'. This was the regeneration Fred had been needing after his despondency in Bristol, and it had immediate consequences:

> In the evening I wrote well and truly at 'This Came'. All but finished.[175]

Avoiding Change

Three days later he heard that Marie Fudge, from Bourne Chapel where he played the organ, was to be married and that she would like him to play at her wedding. He had admired her from afar for some time, and received the news with mixed feelings:

> Last night's surprise still disturbs me and will disturb me for a long time. The excitement has given place to romantic melancholy, quite genuine and lasting (I write this some days later). I do not want change ... Have I extracted as much as I might have done out of nearly four years' acquaintanceship with her, who was at once the loveliest and the merriest of all? Simply as an observer, that is. I do not want to be more intimate.[176]

Fred's observation that he did not want change was astute. It echoes his end-of-year summary for 1933, in which he had noted that the 'delightful undisturbing connections' with 'unemotional acquaintances' like Haynes had been one of the happiest things. With this in mind, the facts that he continued to live with his brother and sister for so many years, that he stayed in the same job for his entire career, that his relationships with women rarely went beyond friendship and that his favourite places tended to be those with which he was most familiar take on new significance. At some level, consciously or otherwise, he took care to avoid change, and was usually successful in doing so. What the root cause was is difficult to say, although his family

---

[175] BA, 41419/25, 3 Mar. 1934.
[176] BA, 41419/25, 7 Mar. 1934.

background must have contributed. His mother seems to have been a diffident, perhaps even timid, person, whose example probably did little to encourage adventure in her children. Joseph appears to have been more spirited: certainly he was capable of enthusiasm and had independent, passionately held convictions. His death may, then, have been a double blow to his children, not only through the direct emotional injury it inflicted but by depriving them of qualities Charlotte may not have been in a position to replace. Her death when Fred was still not twenty undoubtedly had a drastic effect on her children, although by this time their characters were largely formed and, in Fred's case at least, his antipathy to change already well established. However, with Charlotte gone, the family drew in on itself and it is probably not an accident that neither Will nor Gladys married (at least during the period of Fred's diaries) nor that the three siblings continued to live together until Fred's wedding, by which time Will was thirty-nine and Gladys thirty-eight.

This casts Fred's ruralism in a quite different light. His accounts of excursions to landscapes such as the Chew, the Mendips, Exmoor or the Wiltshire downs are often charged with such spiritual and emotional significance that it is natural to assume they must have wrought major changes in his life. But this was not necessarily the case – perhaps, indeed, quite the opposite. Fred, as he himself recognized, was extremely labile on a day-to-day basis, given to fits of sudden enthusiasm for particular authors, ideas or individuals, and prone to express himself in superlatives. This was partly a consequence of his intense sensory responsiveness, which left little room for anything other than the immediate experience. However, his superficial volatility belied a deeper, less obvious but much more consequential stability. It was, paradoxically, partly because Fred's experiences of rural landscapes were often so encompassing at a physical, sensory level that they did so little to change him. Too little of his own thoughts, beliefs, values and convictions remained present for there to be anything for the sensory experience to interact with. As he wrote so revealingly in 'Mendip Landscape', he was an 'empty vessel' into which the landscape poured itself. Afterwards, he could not believe he had been present at all, and in a sense perhaps this was true. His account of his response to the South Wiltshire downs reinforces the point: 'my own existence has nothing to do with the essential truth of the thing before me'. An empty vessel is unaffected by the content poured into it when it is poured back out. Hence, for all the drama and intensity of these encounters with landscape, he went back home unchanged, except perhaps in a temporary sense, as when his ecstatic enjoyment of the south-west wind on Fairy Hill lifted his spirits and enabled him to complete 'This Came'.

This does not mean that Fred's engagement with rural landscapes was unimportant – far from it. The experiences were exceptionally rich in themselves, among the most rewarding and satisfying of his life. Spiritual experiences of this kind do not necessarily need to have further consequences: they may be an end in themselves, and Fred, something of an epicurean, certainly considered them so. More fundamentally, the countryside was profoundly important in enabling him to avoid change: it was one of the most important and enduring sources of stability in his life. Rather like George's bookshop, it was a place where nothing very much was likely to happen. To a large extent Fred was in control when he was in the countryside, much more so than if he had chosen to spend his leisure time in ways that promoted encounters with other people, in dance halls perhaps, at football matches or even drinking in the pub. His preference for repeat visits and known landscapes reduced the risk of unwelcome events still further. At a deeper level, the Chew valley functioned as an emotional anchor and haven, a place that was always there, that was preeminently his and where he always felt at home. To a lesser extent other cherished landscapes such as Pipley Bottom or the high Mendips served the same function. Such places were guarantors of stability: they would not fail him however he might be buffeted and beset by difficulties in his day-to-day life in Bristol.

Collective Ruralism

As Fred said, however, he developed if he did not advance. Within a pattern of remarkable overall stability, less fundamental aspects changed. From the mid-1930s, for example, he showed a growing inclination towards collective enjoyment of the countryside in large groups of people his own age. Family excursions into the countryside were a longstanding Catley tradition, and sometimes Fred had brought a friend or two along with him. But after Charlotte died the generational composition of these expeditions altered. That is unsurprising, given that there were no older relatives in Bristol to whom the Catley siblings were close. A less predictable consequence of Charlotte's death seems to have been that the Catleys, Fred especially, increasingly went out into the countryside in much larger parties than before. During the loosely organized family outings of his childhood and youth, he had often left the others behind to go exploring with Will or whichever friend he had brought with him, but many of these larger group outings in the mid-1930s and 1940s were more cohesive.

One of the consequences of these shifts seems to have been a greater emphasis on youthful light-heartedness and high spirits. On 2 April 1934 the Catleys took Rose Payne (Basil's sister) and the three Wadham girls out on a walk over Charmy Down near Bath. After a 'splendid' scramble up the hill they had the wide airy down almost to themselves. They linked arms in a long string and swung along singing ('One of my finest days for years', Fred commented afterwards). The diary frequently mentions collective singing on walks at this time.[177]

It was in this year that Fred joined the recently formed YHA, greatly facilitating his newfound desire for collective company in the countryside. It also made it much easier for him to undertake ambitious cycling and walking tours at weekends and during the holidays. Previously his expeditions had mainly been limited to a single day or, when he was on holiday, to a single base. Nevertheless, the YHA marked a development rather than a radical break in Fred's ruralism. His desire to associate with other young people in the countryside predated his membership of the YHA by several years – it is first apparent, in fact, on the Exmoor holiday with Nellie and Katie in 1931. He had even begun to go hostelling before becoming fully involved with the YHA: in the early 1930s quite a number of farms refurbished outbuildings or attics as accommodation for walkers and cyclists. Temple House Farm near Doulting, where Fred stayed in August 1934, was one such place. Among his fellow guests on that occasion was a 'bright and amusing' young cycle tourist from Manchester who walked with him for a couple of miles the following morning before they parted 'very amicably'. The long periods of solitude between such meetings enhanced Fred's enjoyment of them:

> Near Masbury station I met two other walkers, two men. We hailed each other with great pleasure and stopped to talk for a few minutes. They were the first I had seen, and I the first they had seen, for a long time.[178]

This was followed by a long walk on his own through a wood, thickly overgrown with ash and hazel, along a path almost stopped up by brambles, nettles and long, wet grass, just the kind of exploring he most relished.[179]

Rural Contentment

After the public and private turmoil of the previous half decade, Fred's life seems to have settled into a steadier pattern in the mid-1930s, with a secure job, a stable home, ample undemanding friendships and plenty of scope to pursue his interests and pleasures, although the underlying personal difficulties had receded rather than been resolved. When he was out in the countryside a sense of peace and contentment often spread through him in these years, especially if he was on his own, enclosed by trees, walls, weather or darkness. Caught in the rain at Queen Charlton on 5 May 1934, he found an open barn and 'spent a delicious twenty minutes by that perfect village green, with its cross and

---

[177] BA, 41419/25, 2 Apr. 1934. See also, for example, BA, 41419/20, 10 and 11 Aug. 1931.
[178] BA, 41419/28, 24 Aug. 1934.
[179] Compare Fred's description of Asham Wood: 'I long to explore it ... a huge tawny wild wood, forest-like ... a gypsy-ish scrubby place.' BA, 41419/25, 3 and 14 Apr. 1934.

circling houses in the evening light'.[180] A few months later, rain again forced him to seek shelter, this time under a tiny beech tree ('my green roof'):

> Here I sat very happily for a time, with a low wall, a field and beyond that a wood, behind me, and in front a plantation of little conifers.[181]

Nothing brought inner calm to Fred more completely, however, than a hard day's walk through remote country. On 23 August 1934 he hiked, accompanied some of the way by Will, from Temple House Farm to Bruton, returning via West Cranmore:

> There is an extreme quiet about this country and this evening particularly so. Vale Farm seemed deserted. We crossed the stream and climbed a rough lane to the very lovely eastern corner of Westcombe, which also seemed deserted, unbelievably quiet. The lane from here to Lower Alham, after passing a huge empty building and a farm, degenerated into the rough green sort of track we love and brought us among trees to a ford and the ancient mill house ... This was good walking.[182]

Fred had a little room to himself at the farm, the bed placed such that you saw a beautiful view of the 'dim white hills' before you went to sleep, and again when you woke in the morning. On returning from his walk, Fred:

> drew myself some water and with great satisfaction went upstairs to my cell and, in the dusk changing to moonlit night, washed hands and face and feet. It had been a great walk – 25 miles – and after I had washed I felt very much at peace. I went downstairs and heated myself my baked beans.[183]

But, as ever, there was a price to be paid. This experience of serenity measured the distance between the life he actually lived and the one he would freely have chosen:

> I was sorry to be back in Bristol and wished for my bare monastic cell at Doulting.[184]

Methodist Nuisances

Fred and his siblings had contemplated moving house for years without doing much about it. Now, spurred on by his discontent with Bristol, they set to in earnest.[185] He would have preferred to have 'uprooted entirely and taken to

---

[180] BA, 41419/25, 5 May 1934.

[181] BA, 41419/28, 22 Aug. 1934.

[182] BA, 41419/28, 23 Aug. 1934. The quietness of the countryside was partly due to agricultural depression and depopulation. Fred's unawareness of this gauges his separation from the inhabitants of 'his' landscapes.

[183] BA, 41419/28, 23 Aug. 1934.

[184] BA, 41419/28, 24 Aug. 1934.

[185] BA, 41419/33, 16–25 Jan. 1936.

a country life' but that seemed impossible as things stood, so he was prepared to settle for 'a pleasant suburb a little nearer my work', preferably Horfield, where there was a common that would never be built on. They would get a more modern, convenient house and it would free him from 'all my present ties, my Bible Class and Organ and choir and concert party and all other Methodist nuisances'.[186]

But Fred's unhappiness had deeper causes than living in the wrong house or 'Methodist nuisances'. Perhaps the most serious problem was an absence of purpose or direction, underpinned by a deep lack of orientation and grounding. His rejection of Methodism was, if anything, a symptom of this. He flitted from one value system to the next. As a teenager he had been a Christian but gradually lost his faith. He then developed an intense admiration for Jefferies but this was a personal identification that did little to provide him with a wider sense of purpose. His brief dalliance with communism in the early 1930s did not last: he was voting Liberal by 1950 and subsequently developed Conservative sympathies.[187] The contrast with Bissell's lifelong, unwavering Christian faith or Johnston's consistent evolution from Liberal Unionism to ethical socialism, every step informed by thought and experience, could hardly be greater. A similar lack of grounding is evident in Fred's literary tastes. In October 1932 he pronounced Morris's optimistic, idealistic News from Nowhere the 'sanest, clearest book I have read for years' but only two months later he confessed to an 'idolatrous admiration' for the pessimistic, cynical Guy de Maupassant.

Pacifism

There was, however, one conviction that Fred held to consistently, and acted on despite the fact that it exposed him to opprobrium and potentially more serious consequences: pacifism. This was apparent as early as 1933, long before it became clear that another European war was likely, when Fred heard Alderman Mapps speak on disarmament, and discussed pacifism with his friend Parson Deeks. In 1936 he was influenced by Aldous Huxley's pamphlet on pacifism and an address by Fred Hocking on the same subject, both of which he judged 'excellent'. The following January he was inspired by a big peace meeting in Bristol at which Vera Brittain and Siegfried Sassoon spoke.[188] On 2 September 1939, the day before war was declared, he wrote in his diary that he was determined to resist conscription and in the event did so, registering as a conscientious objector on 15 June 1940. He opposed the bombing of German cities, denouncing (albeit privately) Churchill's 'bloodthirsty barbaric

---

[186] BA, 41419/31, 22 Jan. 1936.
[187] BA, 41419/54, 23 Feb. 1950 and 41419/61, 3 Nov. 1956.
[188] BA, 41419/34, 13 Jan. 1937.

speech of revenge' on 14 July 1941.[189] While many of his other attitudes changed after the war, Fred's pacifism did not: he was uncompromisingly hostile to the British invasion of Suez and believed it had precipitated the Soviet invasion of Hungary.

The reason Fred was so steadfast in his pacifism was surely that, unlike his other political views, it came from the heart rather than the head. It was his protest against the world for depriving him of his father. Fred acknowledged that he could barely remember him: what he felt so acutely was the loss of what he imagined Joseph would have provided, rather than of the relationship as it was. This comes through most powerfully in relation to his father's values. At some level, Fred knew he was missing something indispensable in that area, and tried to recapture it by assembling and reading his father's 'literary remains'. Among these, the most important was a pencil manuscript entitled 'My Utopia'. Joseph's idea, 'the idea which dominated his life', was to free himself from 'wage slavery' by tilling the soil, keeping fowls and gradually building up a smallholding. But no literary testament, however eloquent, could give Fred as much as he was looking for, and, after reading it on 1 March 1936, he lamented:

> It almost makes one weep to see a man like this being cut off suddenly, enjoying life because of his absorbing purpose and then being killed in a lunatic war without reaching anything. If only he'd come back![190]

His father's death, pacifism and war were the subjects of Fred's longest and most deeply felt poem, 'Two Pendants to War'. There are several typescript copies in the Bristol Record Office file of Fred's poems; one of these is the last item in the folder. It appears to have been Fred who arranged them in their current order, so this is probably indicative of the poem's significance to him. It recounts his father's last moments:

> My father
> Was killed but would not kill.
> He was an idealist, something of a poet,
> Something of a coward also, if you wish,
> Seeing he shrank from taking another's life.
> Nevertheless, to salve his patriotic conscience,
> He left wife, children; left
> His meagre clerkship at thirty shillings a week,
> Became a soldier, infantry private in Flanders.

[189] Churchill declared in this speech that it was 'time that the Germans should be made to suffer in their own Homeland and cities something of the torment that they have, twice in our lifetime, let loose upon their neighbours and upon the world'. 'Do your worst; we'll do our best.' www.nationalchurchillmuseum.org/do-your-worst-well-do-our-best.html [accessed 30 Nov. 2022].

[190] BA, 41419/31, 1 Mar. 1936.

> Finally, running with a message, he was shot . . .
> And now, my words, you should sing,
> For this is the biography of a disinterested man
> Who deserved a better elegy than this.
> Yet say (my love unspoken)
> Say that I honour him that he would not kill.

The poem points out that Fred and his contemporaries are the 'sons of a murdered generation/And of a generation of murderers', and with this in mind, repeatedly asks 'What am I? What are we?'. No answer is forthcoming, and the poem ends on an indeterminate note with a prayer to the 'terrible yet unmalignant Nothingness' to send an answer to 'this riddle of non-selfknowledge'.[191] Ironically, in suggesting links between his uncertainty about who he was, his childhood bereavement and his pacifist convictions, Fred demonstrates remarkable insight into himself.

Whatever else his ruralism might give him, it could not make good a loss on this scale. However, it could and did provide comfort and consolation for more minor inflictions. On 17 May 1936 he had a tooth extracted but it snapped again and again during the surgery and, in the end, the dentist had to leave one root in. 'It was just HELL', Fred explained afterwards. 'One of the worst half-hours of my life.' It reveals something of the soothing power the countryside had for him, even by proxy, that when he got home he chose to read a classic work of rural fiction, Adrian Bell's *The Cherry Tree*, to take his mind off the pain.[192] During another visit to the dentist he drew solace from the bright green of new leaves visible through the window.[193] After recovering from an unpleasant chest infection ('[t]hree days I would prefer to forget'), the first book he felt well enough to read was *Living in the Country*, while studying maps of the New Forest preparatory to a holiday enabled him to put a trying day at the shop behind him.[194]

The countryside (although perhaps not its armchair substitute) could also help him work through practical and emotional problems. On 4 August 1936 Will and Gladys quarrelled in the morning, as a result of which she was silent and listless all afternoon. In this gloomy, oppressive atmosphere the Catleys set off for their projected evening walk. But the magnificence of the view from Lansdown, extending as they followed the edge round from the Westbury White Horse to Stourton Tower, the Mendips and then a glimpse of the sea and the Welsh mountains, restored Fred's spirits. It was, he wrote afterwards, a walk that gave the mind a chance to breathe: 'What an eagle place, what glory!'[195] The following evening, though tired, he had 'such a desire for a sight

[191] 'Two Pendants to War', BA, 41419/70 ('A Collection of Poems Written by F. J. Catley').
[192] BA, 41419/31, 17 May 1936.
[193] BA, 41419/38, 18 Apr. 1939.
[194] BA, 41419/40, 1 Feb. 1941 and 41419/38, 20 Jul. 1939.
[195] BA, 41419/31, 4 Aug. 1936. Compare BA, 41419/34, 10 Jul. 1937: 'My river afternoon had effected a change of mood in me, and I now felt happy.'

of wide bare downs to unclog the mind' that he toiled all the way out through the city and beyond to Dodington Ash, over twenty miles there and back.[196] On other occasions he used rural walking in a more cerebral way to think through practical problems.[197] When the Catleys were informed that Will's allowance was to be reduced from one pound to 13/6 per week, for example, Fred went out to consider this in the Clifton woods.[198]

Sheep and Cows

The year 1936 seems to have been a tipping point in the conflict within Fred between his desire, on the one hand, to achieve something, principally in the literary sphere, and on the other, to wrap himself in the comfort of his home, secure job and rewarding pastimes. At the start of the year, not for the first time, he had been unhappy and restless, anxious to drive himself on. Twelve months later he felt quite differently, observing in his end-of-year summary:

> I seem to have ceased to worry much about 'advancing' and to trust rather to the inevitability of change. Perhaps that is one way of being happy.[199]

This echoes a poem Fred wrote the same year, 'Nursery Rhyme', in which he contrasts sheep, high on the metaphorical hill, who 'Cry and will not be still', with the wise cows down in the vale, who are too placid and content to 'Fear, struggle or cry'.[200] In years to come the bleating of the struggling sheep could still sometimes be heard in Fred but bovine wisdom increasingly predominated.

Calm enjoyment of the countryside, untroubled by doubts and fears, is indeed the dominant note of the 1937 diary. After a long walk around Brockley and Burrington Combes with Norman Bright, he felt '[g]reatly at peace with myself'. Another walk, this time with Will, imbued him deeply with the beauty of the countryside near Siston:

> I could have sat and looked and looked at these fields, with the course of the stream marked by alders, the hill in the distance with the copse of elms above the Syston road on its flank and a smaller clump crowning it near Blue Lodge. The pattern of fields and black copses, bright larch plant-ations, farm on the hill and farm in the valley by the winding line of the stream's course – this I found entirely satisfying.[201]

---

[196] BA, 41419/31, 5 Aug. 1936.
[197] Rebecca Solnit surmises that the mind, like the feet, 'works at about three miles an hour'. Rebecca Solnit, *Wanderlust: A History of Walking* (London, 2001), 10.
[198] BA, 41419/36, 5 May 1938.
[199] BA, 41419/31, Dec. 1936 [no date].
[200] 'Nursery Rhyme', BA, 41419/70 ('A Collection of Poems Written by F. J. Catley').
[201] BA, 41419/34, 18 Apr. 1937. Compare also similar responses on 1 Aug. and 3 Sep. 1937, BA, 41419/34.

This is an eminently aesthetic response, comparable to the pleasure an accomplished musical or artistic composition can yield. As with anything that focuses the mind's attention wholly on a benign external object, the experience was a restful one, as several of the other diarists also found when contemplating rural landscapes.

The one fly in the ointment was an acute attack in early summer of what Fred referred to as 'that fever in the blood, febris sexualis'.[202] Fred traced this to a charabanc outing on 12 May, when he had slipped his arm round a Miss Gibbs, who seems to have worked at George's. But there was, he recognized, more to it than this. At twenty-six, he felt that the best half of his youth had gone without having done 'any of the things a young man ought to do – never danced, played tennis, made love, kissed, and so on'.[203] Contrary to his hopes, his Isle of Wight holiday in June only inflamed him further: everywhere he looked there seemed to be young women in bathing costumes or lovers disporting themselves on grassy banks.[204]

More therapeutic, and indeed the highlight of the year, was the long cycling tour he took to East Anglia later that summer. Barely had he got through Bath before his spirits began to rise: he relished the 'superb solidity' of the hills, houses and even trees of 'this magnificent stone country'. But as ever it was the elemental austerity of the 'mind-expanding' South Wiltshire downs that stirred him most:

> [H]uge fields stretched in sweeping lines to the pale swell of the downs, that carried the eye westward past Urchfont Hill. Nothing on earth seems more beautiful to me than these chalk downs. I could renounce all my home country for them.[205]

He continued into Hampshire and Surrey but as he drew closer to London, heavy traffic and ugly, haphazard modern development ('a bastard thing, neither country, town, nor suburb') shocked and bewildered him, much as similar scenes had done on the way to Uncle Will's in 1928.[206] It was only when he reached north Hertfordshire that things improved, the more so because here he was among 'broad, noble' chalk downs again:

> No country ever appealed to me more than this clean, wide country of stubble-fields and thatched and timbered houses. I did not feel the lack of high country, for these low hills have sufficient sweep to suggest height.[207]

---

[202] BA, 41419/34, 11 Jun. 1937.
[203] BA, 41419/34, 11 Jun. 1937.
[204] BA, 41419/34, 12–19 Jun. 1937.
[205] BA, 41419/44, 28 Aug. 1937.
[206] BA, 41419/34, 3 Sep. 1937.
[207] BA, 41419/34, 31 Aug. and 1 Sep. 1937.

By the time he reached the North Sea at Dovercourt he had almost forgotten Miss Gibbs and 'febris sexualis'.[208]

Fred followed a more northerly route on the long journey home, through High Wycombe, Wallingford and Wantage. This allowed him to take in Liddington Castle, scene of some of most vivid experiences described in Jefferies' *The Story of My Heart*:

> When I saw the ramparts of the camp close above me, I left the bike and, for Richard Jefferies' sake, climbed the steep field to the earthworks. A pilgrimage I have often made in thought. Thistledown blew in clouds along the fosse. I walked all round the rampart in the wind, very happy to be where I had so often hoped to be.[209]

Over to Clifton

The search for a new home had continued intermittently since early the previous year: they were under no immediate pressure to move and it proved difficult to find a satisfactory place they could afford. It was only on 15 November 1937 that the Catleys eventually relocated, to a large flat on the top floor of 16 Canynge Road, Clifton, nearer both to Fred's work and the countryside, with fine views of the downs, the Avon Gorge and Leigh Woods.[210] The move seems to have worked well for all three of the young Catleys. Partly because attractive green space was now virtually on his doorstep, Fred went out even more often, typically with one or both of his siblings or a friend. At this stage of his life he had a marked preference for walking in company. It is true that many of his most exhilarating experiences took place when he was alone in the landscape. But he was also prone to anxiety, as his account of a walk in the country the other side of the suspension bridge candidly acknowledged: 'As usual, a continuous worried monologue went on inside me.'[211] Perhaps walking with others helped to assuage this.

Wartime Autumn

Like most of the diarists, Fred was usually far more affected by private than public events. However, as summer 1938 gave way to autumn the shadow of war began to loom ominously.[212] Monday, 26 September, a beautiful day of summer-like warmth, was spoiled by 'nerve-wracking' war fear. The

---

[208] BA, 41419/34, 2 Sep. 1937.

[209] BA, 41419/34, 4 Sep. 1937.

[210] BA, 41419/34, 5 and 15 Nov. 1937.

[211] BA, 41419/42, 12 Dec. 1942. This was, however, at a difficult point in his relationship with the woman who became his wife.

[212] The first mention of fear of war over Czechoslovakia in Fred's diary is on 14 September 1938. BA, 41419/36, 14 Sep. 1938.

following day was even worse, dark and drizzly, '[a]ltogether one of the blackest of days, with hardly any hope anywhere'. By Thursday, plunged into impotent despair at the crassness of humanity, Fred was considering emigration, although the following day news of the Munich agreement brought uneasy reassurance.[213] This was shattered by Germany's annexation of the Sudetenland on 15 March 1939.[214]

Fred's pervasive anxiety about international affairs did not impede and may indeed have contributed to his growing involvement with the YHA. This was centred on the weekends that he now began to spend at hostels. A typical example was 17–18 December 1938, when he cycled via Chewton Mendip and Wells to the hostel in Street. There was what Fred described as a 'good party' – twenty-eight in all. They played games, pausing only for supper, till after midnight. Then they went out for a walk along the ridge to Butleigh before going to bed about 2am. In the morning the whole group walked to the Hood monument, then after lunch went their separate ways, Fred riding home with one of the other hostellers.

These large YHA groups did have some drawbacks, notably that they virtually precluded the intense experiences Fred often had when alone or with one or two chosen companions in the countryside. However, in the main the YHA weekends supplemented rather than replaced his existing walks and rides, offering him reliable access to the collective ruralism he had been drawn to since his mother's death. As well as games, singing and dancing were common and he seems to have found the easy, undemanding conviviality appealing. There was little danger of the kind of interpersonal intimacy he preferred to avoid: these large gatherings dissolved the individual in the mass. Significantly, he often used the word 'crowd' to describe them. He usually mentioned the numbers present: the more the merrier. At Dursley on 28 October 1939, for example, there was 'a good crowd ... about 12 men and 10 girls'.[215] In effect, the YHA provided him with a ready-made group of friends, brought together not only by their temporary inhabitation of a shared space but by their membership of the YHA and participation in its ethos. This formed a bond outside the hostel too: when a young man with a rucksack at Wookey Hole asked him whether he was going up to the hostel at Ebbor Farm, Fred was 'pleased to be recognized as a Y.H.A.-ite'.[216] There was a sense of connection with people who would otherwise have remained strangers, an overcoming of the normal social barriers. This is perhaps why Fred often drew attention to the far-flung places other hostellers had come from, as on 3 September 1938 when there was a 'pleasant crowd' at Hutton Youth

[213] BA, 41419/36, 26–30 Sep. 1938.
[214] BA, 41419/38, 15 Mar. 1939.
[215] BA, 41419/38, 28 Oct. 1939.
[216] BA, 41419/28, 24 Aug. 1934.

Hostel, '[t]wo from London, several Yorkshire men, two Welsh and one from Dudley'.[217]

Although Fred was reluctant to be drawn into emotional entanglements, it had been a long time since his brief albeit intense 'friendship' with Joan Barton, and part of the appeal of the YHA was undoubtedly that it gave him an opportunity to meet unattached young women:

> The one good thing about walking with a party is that you can change your companion so easily: after walking with nice little plump Helen – a nurse at the General Hospital – I could change to Lionel . . . and then to Cicely – my favourite of them all – or to another Helen . . . and her small thin friend Lavinia, commonly called 'Weed'.[218]

This is the first, not altogether prepossessing, mention in the diaries of the woman who became Fred's wife. Initially he showed no special interest in her: the group was more important to him than the individuals within it and, even with respect to those, Lavinia would not at this point have been his preferred companion.

All of this, however, was cut across by the outbreak of war on 3 September. Fred was despondent:

> I think we are criminally wrong, if not so much as Germany. I am sick of the world's madness and ours in particular.[219]

His diary entries for the last few months of 1939 juxtapose despair at international affairs and fear of the consequences war might bring with radiant descriptions of the autumnal beauty of the countryside. On 7 October he and Gladys cycled through the 'deep beautiful lanes' to Lower Failand in warm afternoon sunshine to pick blackberries. The 21st was a 'most lovely afternoon' but perhaps the climax of the season came the following day:

> Thick mist in the morning. Lovely the russet and yellow edge of the Downs above the invisible chasm of the Gorge (like looking into a grey waveless sea); lovely the leaves fallen.[220]

Two days later he wrote a poem titled 'Wartime Autumn'.[221] It is evident from the elegiac tone the poem shares with the preceding diary entries that the grim political and military context had heightened Fred's responsiveness to the landscape. No longer could its tranquillity be taken for granted, yet never before had it been so valuable as a refuge from the 'horror and madness' he perceived around him.[222]

---

[217] BA, 41419/36, 3 Sep. 1938.
[218] BA, 41419/38, 26 Mar. 1939.
[219] BA, 41419/38, 3 Sep. 1939.
[220] BA, 41419/38, 22 Oct. 1939.
[221] BA, 41419/38, 24 Oct. 1939.
[222] BA, 41419/38, 30 Nov. 1939.

Initially, however, there was little change in his outward circumstances. He continued to work at George's, practice piano and write poems. These typically arose from his walks, at this point mainly in the Avon Gorge or across the suspension bridge in Leigh Woods. His bike rides also continued, as did his still frequently ruralist reading. Now that he was press secretary of the local YHA, he attended committee meetings and spent quite a bit of time writing up minutes or notes in the evenings. He listened to the radio, read the papers and *Peace News*, attended Peace Pledge Union meetings, worried about the war and worked with Will and Gladys on the allotment that they had taken.[223] At a personal level he had become involved with Jeanne Burnett, whom he seems first to have met at Dursley Youth Hostel on 28 October 1939.[224] He spent a happy weekend with her and 'the others' at Croscombe hostel on 9– 10 March 1940 but, as ever in his case, the course of true love did not run smooth. By the end of the month he was '[d]ecidedly in the doldrums', thinking constantly of the weekend at Croscombe.[225] His misery was compounded by the news that Jeanne had gone to the cinema and was intending to meet up with his old school friend Viv Steer. Viv, however, was more interested in someone else.[226]

Conscientious Objection

Fred registered as a conscientious objector during a holiday in Devon in June 1940. The diary he was using during this holiday was a pre-formatted pocketbook with limited space for entries, and he reduced the size of his handwriting to squeeze in more words, filling spaces in the margins and wherever he could. However, private matters retained their ascendancy over his mind. The eager words almost all relate to what he saw and did on his walks: the 'most delicious cold water' at a cottage, the 'splendid' rocks of Watcombe, charcoal burners in the Teign gorge, a perfect cream tea at Clifford Farm. One such entry, for Monday the 10th, ends with the laconic postscript 'Norway gone. Italy in the war'. Even in the midst of a global conflict Fred was unwilling to allow international affairs to distract him from what he really cared about.[227]

His tribunal came up on 26 September. He stood his ground, despite an attempt at browbeating and interruption by an air-raid warning, and to his immense relief was exempted from conscription on condition that he remained in his present employment and did part-time humanitarian

---

[223] BA, 41419/39, 8–14 Apr. 1940. This was a typical wartime week for Fred, during which all the activities mentioned occurred at least once.
[224] BA, 41419/38, 28 Oct. and 25 Nov. 1939.
[225] BA, 41419/39, 9–10 and 18–23 Mar. 1940.
[226] BA, 41419/39, 6 Jun. 1940.
[227] BA, 41419/39, 8–16 Jun. 1940.

work.[228] Within this pattern of continuity in his occupational, social and private life, there were, however, inevitably some shifts in emphasis. Looking back on his experiences of the war to date on 31 December, he felt that the most important effect on him had been to bring him closer to the YHA and his friends there, above all the 'lovely and loveable' Jeanne, though he was unsure whether he could be of any value to someone so 'bright and beautiful and independent'. Regarding his personal development, the important thing about 1941 was that it would be his thirtieth year:

> Shall I feel a failure if it produces nothing of greater value than previous years have done? The truth is, I often feel a miserable failure now: yet there is always hope. I am one who submits rather than strives, but I must strike the right balance between quiescence and action if this year is to be memorable, happily memorable, in my personal life. That it may be grimly memorable in other ways I do not overlook. The bombs are waiting for us.[229]

They were indeed. On 3 January the sirens sounded and this time it was a real raid with flares, fires and high explosives. They sheltered in the basement, turning out to see what was going on at intervals.[230] A nearby house caught fire and Fred went to see if he could help. Without any affectation of heroism, he endured the Bristol Blitz with courage and composure. It was the broken sleep and discomfort he minded most, exacerbated by the severe winter and his overnight fire-watching duties.[231] After another heavy raid on the 17th, when they had had to get up and dress in the freezing cold and go down to the basement again, Fred wrote that he 'hated life today: hated the aftermath of the night, hated the bitter cold, the miserable discomfort of the shop and my own feebleness'.[232] During this difficult period he sought refuge when he could by crossing the suspension bridge to the 'peaceful and remote-seeming' rural haven of Bower Ashton.[233]

Living Unmoved

The war did surprisingly little to disrupt Fred's countryside outings. The high point of his relationship with Jeanne came on one such occasion, 4 May 1941. They had spent the previous night with the usual YHA crowd at Batheaston

---

[228] BA, 41419/39, 26 Sep. 1940.
[229] BA, 41419/40, 31 Dec. 1940.
[230] Unlike many Bristol families, the Catleys did not 'flit' to the countryside or shelter in the Portway tunnel overnight, perhaps because Clifton was less heavily bombed than the docks and city centre.
[231] BA, 41419/40, 27 Jun. and 26 Oct. 1940.
[232] BA, 41419/40, 17 Jan. 1941.
[233] BA, 41419/40, 11 Jan. and 8 Feb. 1941.

hostel. The weather was wonderful and in the morning, nine of them went for
a walk over Bathampton Down and on to the sloping field above the aqueduct
at Limpley Stoke. Here they settled down to eat lunch and sunbathe. Fred lay
next to Jeanne, while arguing about communism with his friend Arthur:

> Like most communists, he has the gift of the gab and certainly had the
> advantage of me. But I had the advantage of Jeanne's dear body beside me,
> and as I argued I sometimes stroked her leg or fondled her small foot or
> touched her knee or soft thigh, and when I stretched out beside her, her
> arm might be against my cheek, or I would open my eyes to see the curve
> of her breast under her thin blouse, or the fair down under her arm-pits
> when she stretched her arms above her head, or the fine golden hair on her
> arm stretched across her body. My heart melted with tenderness. I could
> have done anything for her: I could not speak to her without feeling
> a special gentleness in my voice.[234]

Borne up on this flood tide of emotion, Fred pressed his suit with Jeanne. She
seems to have responded ambivalently and he wrote to her on the 22nd, asking
for clarification. Two days later she replied, telling him that she only wanted to
be friends. It was a repeat of the denouement of his relationship with Joan Barton
ten years before. Fred was distraught: '[m]y only relief throughout this week-end
was music – my piano, Chopin, Beethoven, Brahms'.[235] But his YHA social
nexus and the beauty of the countryside with which it was interwoven soon
brought more lasting consolation. On Saturday the 31st, he cycled to Wookey
Hole youth hostel, where he was delighted to find one of the Helens, Weed and
two other friends. The following day he rode to Wells, Glastonbury, along the
beautiful Polden ridge road and on through the Quantocks to Brendon hostel on
Exmoor. After supper he walked down the stream towards Watersmeet:

> The loveliness of the day and the country and of this evening gave me real
> peace of mind, and I was happy, thinking of my friends, of Weed and
> Jeanne.[236]

By the end of the year Weed had displaced Jeanne in Fred's affections. She
seems to have been a teacher but beyond this Fred's diaries tell us little about
her background, commitments or character, although they do tell us a great
deal about their relationship. Initially things seem to have gone well. He made
a good start to 1942 by writing 'lovingly' to her in the small hours of 1 January;
it was '[t]he happiest of New Year's Days', although he added with a hint of
foreboding that he hoped its promise was not a false one. Three days later he
went for a walk on his own in Leigh Woods, gleams of winter sun on the bare
trees and bracken. As so often, a vivid experience of landscape bore fruit in

---

[234] BA, 41419/40, 4 May 1941. As ever, sensation affected Fred more powerfully than ideas.
[235] BA, 41419/40, 22 and 24 May 1941.
[236] BA, 41419/40, 1 Jun. 1941.

a poem.[237] This one, 'Walking in the Silent Woods', completed the following day, is especially revealing:

> Walking the silent woods,
> Thinking of one I loved, of others I loved,
> Through whom I lived, from whom came joy or pain
> To shake the meaning out of tranquillity,
> I strove to put away uncertainty
> And teach the changing heart to live unmoved
> And never lose its quietness again.
>
> Walking the silent woods,
> Seeing fingers of sunlight touch the fern,
> Watching the sombre trees wake to the light,
> I saw the wish was foolishness. I knew
> That certainly as April would prove true
> To these bare woods, so would my season turn
> And inward lovelier Spring transform my sight.[238]

The poem makes explicit Fred's desire to 'live unmoved', and the way in which the quiet of the countryside ministered to this. But it also registers Fred's responsiveness to the life he perceived in nature, and the power this had to revive his latent optimism. His forthcoming marriage to Weed expressed both aspects of his personality. In the context of his profound aversion to emotional risk, the decision to marry her was a brave, forward-looking one but, as it transpired, the marriage proved rather like a hermit crab's change of shells: swapping one secure home for another that gave even better protection.

This, however, lay in the future and there were difficulties aplenty to negotiate before he got there. Even knowing what to call her was far from straightforward. As he began to think of her more seriously, Fred's diary abandons the undignified 'Weed' progressively for 'Wd.', then Lavinia (but she disavowed this name), 'L.', 'L.E.' and finally 'E.' (for Elizabeth).[239] The main flashpoint in their relationship was her incorrigible dilatoriness about answering his letters. Fred was, of course, exceptionally literary and capable of writing 'pages and pages' to her in a single evening, and she may simply not have known what to say in reply. As Fred noted perceptively, 'I send her more than she can cope with and am hurt at the lack of response.'[240] It was certainly far from a meeting of minds. In reaching out beyond his safe emotional base, Fred was exposing himself to injury and rejection, and needed frequent reassurance.

---

[237] Compare 'The Ravens', inspired by a walk in the Avon Gorge with Will (BA, 41419/38, 29 Jan. 1939) and 'Dry Leaves', arising from a walk along a green lane leading to Tucking Mills (BA, 41419/25, 3 Mar. 1934).

[238] 'A Collection of Poems Written by F. J. Catley', BA, 41419/70.

[239] BA, 41419/42, passim.

[240] BA, 41419/42, 3 Oct. and 1 Dec. 1942.

Marriage

Much the same pattern continued through 1943 and it is not altogether surprising that, in the early months of 1944, Fred became briefly involved with another woman. Perhaps this prompted Elizabeth to give him more compelling proofs of commitment than hitherto but in view of the almost incessant worry she had caused him, it remains difficult to understand why, shortly afterwards, he agreed to become her husband. Nevertheless, on 18 May they put down a deposit for a house in Woollard and six days later were married at the Bristol Register Office, leaving thence for a honeymoon on Exmoor.[241] There was, alas, no immediate alchemy in the wedding. Elizabeth went away, possibly for a holiday, in late August. Fred had supplied her with stamped postcards, envelopes and writing paper and she had apparently suggested she might write every day. He received not a word from her, however, and by the evening of 30 August felt '[t]horoughly and bitterly tired and unhappy'. The following day he had still heard nothing and wrote furiously in his diary, '[w]hat is one to do with such a woman?'.[242] Yet, as before, her physical presence dissipated these miseries. On 17 September he recorded:

> E home at the end of the afternoon, very loving, both of us happy to be together again.[243]

Perhaps for financial reasons, it was not until 29 March the following year that they were able to move into their new home at Woollard.[244] This was a decisive step because it signified not only the dissolution of the old Catley household that had served Fred's need for stability well for so many years but also the fulfilment of his long-held dream of living in the countryside, and not only the countryside but the Chew valley withal. There are signs that the move revived Fred's boyhood desire to study the ornithology and natural history of the Chew, not that this had ever entirely gone away. On 8 and 9 April he recorded the arrival of willow warblers and on the 18th a cuckoo at Publow.[245] He revisited his familiar haunts with Elizabeth, walking with her up the Chew through Chewton Keynsham and so to Woollard ('[a] lovely walk'), as if seeking to connect his new home with the old emotional pattern.[246] Consciously or otherwise, he also carried over many of the old Catley traditions into his new life. His father would have approved of the apples, pears, plums, red and black currants, gooseberries and potatoes they grew in the garden while Will and Gladys would have felt at home on, and indeed

[241] BA, 41419/45, 18 and 25 May 1944.
[242] BA, 41419/45, 30 and 31 May 1944.
[243] BA, 41419/45, 17 Sep. 1944.
[244] BA, 41419/46, 29 Mar. 1945.
[245] BA, 41419/46, 8, 9 and 18 Apr. 1945.
[246] BA, 41419/46, 11 Mar. 1945.

sometimes participated in, the gathering expeditions.[247] Will visited for the first time on 5 May and thereafter came at least monthly; Gladys visited rather less often.[248]

There were still occasional quarrels with Elizabeth. These persisted throughout the period of their married life recorded in the diaries. She was never entirely reliable and seems to have felt no compunction about taking her feelings out on Fred.[249] Will seems to have been one source of tension. On 21 December 1959 Fred and Elizabeth met him in Park Street. On hearing that he would have the following Saturday and Sunday off work, Fred:

> asked him to come out to us for the two days, staying the night, as he has nowhere else to go. When I got home in the evening I found E. in a savagely morose mood, almost refusing to speak at all. A miserable evening. I guessed that the reason was Will's coming next week-end. How w'd she like two days in a single room with a gas fire?[250]

Domesticity

But these quarrels were infrequent and soon made up – even on this occasion, one of the worst, Elizabeth relented before they went to bed the following evening.[251] The protracted misery of 1942–3 was a thing of the past. Evidently it had really been driven by the anxieties her absence gave rise to in Fred and, now that he was actually living with her, these fears fell away. The overriding impression to which the diaries of the late 1940s and 1950s give rise is of contented domesticity. There are many references to warm and happy fireside evenings 'chez nous' and Fred usually seems to have been very glad to see his wife when he came home, especially if it had been a busy, tiring day at the shop. Sometimes he refers to her as 'dear E.', and he bought her flowers and booked a theatre performance for their wedding anniversary.[252] Although he was only thirty-two when they married, the question of children does not seem to have troubled them, and by the late 1950s their domestic life had taken on some of the ambience of a settled elderly couple. They listened to the radio and drank Horlicks in the evening, and brought each other cups of tea in bed on Sunday mornings.[253]

One day was, indeed, becoming very much like another. On weekdays Fred left home about 8.30, waited for a variable length of time for a lift into Bristol and was routinely late for work. George's seems to have been busier than

---

[247] BA, 41419/46, 12 Mar. and 16 Apr. 1945.
[248] BA, 41419/46, 5 May 1945.
[249] See, for example, BA, 41419/47, 21 May 1947 and 41419/54, 30 Jan. and 23 Feb. 1950.
[250] BA, 41419/64, 21 Dec. 1959.
[251] BA, 41419/64, 22 Dec. 1959.
[252] BA, 41419/47, 2 Jan., 8 Feb., 3 May and 13 Dec. 1947; BA, 41419/64, 25 May 1959.
[253] BA, 41419/62, 22 Aug. 1957; BA, 41419/53, 13 Nov. 1949.

before and he was often tired by the time he came home. On spring and summer evenings he worked in the garden – there are frequent references to mowing the lawn and chopping 'stick' (firewood) – and he dug, planted, weeded and harvested according to season. After tea he would listen to the radio and perhaps play the piano, attend to YHA matters or write a little.[254] Weekends were similar but they had more time for gardening and usually went for a walk or occasionally a cycle ride. After getting back from work on Saturdays Fred had lunch and then often a doze; on Sundays they had a lie-in.[255]

The settled domesticity of the Woollard years encouraged but also expressed a significant change in Fred's social position. With two incomes, no children and the economy buoyant, the Catley finances prospered. In the 1930s Fred was in many respects a classic exemplar of the marginal lower middle-class: underpaid, resentful of this, forced to live a more Spartan existence than he would have liked, and politically radical. By the 1950s he was living in a different, securely middle-class world. One of the most obvious signs was the ever more far-flung and expensive holidays that he and Elizabeth began to take. Their first foreign holiday was in 1950, to Provence; subsequent holidays took them to Austria, Switzerland and Spain.[256] Back at home, 'mod cons' were making their appearance. Their purchase of a hoover occasioned great excitement and Fred spent most of the next morning hard at work with it, following which he put together the new lawnmower and cut the grass.[257] Fred gave Elizabeth a pair of brass candlesticks for her birthday in 1950, a far cry from his delight eighteen years earlier when Joan Barton had given him Thomas's poems for Christmas. It was not long before they were employing an occasional gardener.[258] Elizabeth played tennis and Fred listened to *Any Questions?* on the radio.[259] They were evidently building up substantial cash reserves, invested in the Bristol & West Building Society and Premium Bonds, and on 11 March 1952 purchased 87 Temple Street, Keynsham for rent, letting it out to the sitting tenants.[260] He had become quite senior at George's and owned shares worth at least £415 in the bookshop by July 1960.[261]

---

[254] Almost all these activities occurred, for example, on 4 Mar. 1950, a Saturday typical of this period. BA, 41419/54.

[255] See, for example, BA, 41419/49, 13 Nov. 1949.

[256] Fred had, however, toured Belgium, Luxemburg, the Netherlands and Germany for ten days with Viv Steer in 1939. BA, 41419/38, 26 May to 4 Jun. 1939. For the Catleys' post-war holidays see BA, 41419/46–68, 1945–63, passim.

[257] BA, 41419/54, 14 and 15 Apr. 1950.

[258] BA, 41419/54, 14 Jun. 1950.

[259] BA, 41419/47, 12 Aug. 1947 and 41419/68, 12 Apr. 1963.

[260] BA, 41419/64, 16 Dec. 1959, 41419/68, 12 Feb. 1963 and 41419/56, 11 Mar. 1952. Ironically, Fred had gained experience in assessing properties through his YHA work since there was a constant need for new hostels at this period.

[261] BA, 41419/56, 27 Aug. 1956 and 41419/65, 6 Jul. 1960.

Nature and Culture

These pervasive changes had a substantial bearing on Fred's ruralism. The attractions of his own hearth and garden reduced his incentive to go out and he had less time to do so: the long journey back from work discouraged evening expeditions while the garden required much upkeep at weekends. It is unsurprising, therefore, that, other than when they went to stay at youth hostels, as they still did once in a while, almost all their outings were short, local walks. It was as if Fred's world had contracted to the horizon of the Chew valley. Whereas his youthful diary entries often read like litanies of settlements, as ambitious excursions take him from one village to the next, now the names that recur are on a more intimate scale: lanes, small woods, farms and hills. Perhaps Elizabeth was a less accomplished walker (as she certainly was cyclist) than he. But there also seems to have been a desire to stay close to home, within the confines of their charmed valley. Whatever the motivation, the effect as they criss-crossed the local landscape was to weave it together in a pattern centred on their cottage at Woollard. Learning and using the colourful, highly localized place names of their home range, and associating them with distinct functions, was an important part of this: Pigsmoor for 'stick', Green Lane for blackberries, Smallbrook Lane for Snowdrops, Lord's Wood for Daffodils, Peppershells for Bee Orchids. The firewood, fruit, mushrooms and flowers they gathered from such places connected the landscape still more directly with their home, literally bringing the countryside into it. Before he lived there, it had been vital for Fred that the Chew valley, hidden behind Dundry Hill and guarded by the bridge at the entrance to the valley, was separate from his real home in Bristol. Now, however, his instinct seems to have been the opposite, seeking to draw cottage and landscape together as closely as possible.

The fullest expression of this impulse was in relation to flowers, in which Fred became more absorbed while living at Woollard than he had been since his early teens, partly perhaps because the contraction in scale of his landscape encounters had refocused his attention on small things. Not only did they plant their garden and adorn their house with local wildflowers, but Fred began writing a book about them, *Flowers in a Village*, hoping with poignant resignation that it would 'prove less barren than the others'.[262] The title elides the natural and the human in two ways: it balances the implicitly natural 'flowers' with the indubitably human 'village' and, in preferring 'flowers' to 'wildflowers', it includes garden flowers as a middle term between the natural and the human. Furthermore, the village in question encompasses Fred's own house and garden. *Flowers in a Village* therefore brings together house, garden, village and countryside, extending and formalizing the effort to integrate

---

[262] BA, 41419/56, 17 Feb. 1952.

nature and culture evident in many of Fred's other activities during these Woollard years.

It was not to last, however: the temperate bliss of the Catleys' Chew valley idyll was terminated rather abruptly by developments in the summer of 1956. Following the death of a previous director, it became apparent that Fred might be invited to step into his shoes (4 June).[263] Six weeks later Fred and Elizabeth were arguing about whether they should move three miles over the hill to the Bristol suburb of Whitchurch.[264] It is not clear who was on which side but it would be surprising if Fred had favoured the idea. Nevertheless the move eventually went ahead.[265] Fred seems to have been prepared to stand his ground with his wife when he really cared about something, as with Will staying for Christmas in 1959, so there is a puzzle here. There are a number of possibilities. One is that it was an implicit condition of accepting the directorship that Fred would no longer be late for work and the inadequate public transport from Woollard made this impossible to achieve without moving (or learning to drive and buying a car, which he does not seem to have considered). A second is that the inconvenience of the journey into Bristol had simply become too great. A third possibility is the lure of a more modern, convenient and well-serviced house: for all the charm of its location, the cottage at Woollard was deficient in this regard.[266] What does seem clear is that the Chew no longer had as powerful a hold on Fred as in days gone by: living there for over a decade, although rewarding in many respects, had deprived the valley of some of its special magic.

Affluenza

The formal offer of the directorship came on 27 August. Fred's feelings were ambivalent – previous hints had left him '[d]epressed, tired, bitter' – but he accepted it.[267] The conflict in his feelings was really one between his old and new selves. His old self, like his lodestar Richard Jefferies, resented any infringement on his freedom, hated institutions, despised pecuniary motives and wanted to be out in the open air. His new, embourgeoised self had developed a taste for material consumption, acquisition and, to read between the lines in the diary, social status. In the event, his fears that the directorship might prove emotionally burdensome, even perhaps spiritually deadening, turned out to be only too well-founded. He had always been

---

[263] BA, 41419/61, 4 Jun. 1956.

[264] BA, 41419/61, 18 and 21 Jul. 1956.

[265] BA, 41419/62, 7 Jan. 1957.

[266] They had had to spend a whole day cleaning up after a burst pipe on 20 May 1956, came back from holiday on 25 August to find the lights had failed and rain had got into the back bedroom and had further burst pipes on 24 November and 4 December. BA, 41419/61.

[267] BA, 41419/61, 23 Jul. 1956.

prone to anxiety and the directorship exacerbated this. By summer 1957 there are already more frequent references to being 'very tired' and unwell, often explicitly in the context of work. On 9 August, for example, he had a 'very trying' day at the shop: they were short-staffed for a visit from the Ward Lock representative, and Fred had to stay till nearly 7pm clearing up.[268] Over the next few years matters got progressively worse. There were troubles with the accounts and concerns about embezzlement, challenging behaviour from an insolent employee and on 6 February 1959 Fred found himself in the unpleasant position of having to sack one of his fellow workers.[269] Many days at work are described as 'really worrying', 'busy and very trying' or the like.[270] Fred's health suffered – he was often 'rheumaticky' and developed chronic bowel problems.[271] A brief diary entry for 2 April sums up the situation:

> At home in the evening. Worried – 'business worries' – I lost my soul for money when, against my will, I became a director of George's.[272]

To the extent to which the move from Woollard was a consequence of Fred's change of status, there is perhaps some truth in this, although it is unclear who Fred felt had prevailed on him to accept the directorship (presumably either Elizabeth or the management of George's). It must also be recognized that becoming a director was only one further step along a road that had already taken him far from his high-minded, anti-materialist youth.

Walking was neither so easy nor so appealing from Whitchurch as it had been from Woollard – they now had the city on three sides of them and several roads on the other. To get to attractive country it was necessary to have transport. Fred began cycling a bit more again but Elizabeth was less keen. A presumably unanticipated effect of their move was therefore that they no longer went out together so often, although there was no obvious deterioration in their relationship. Fred's rides were strongly routinized: almost always he cycled to the post office at Gilda for the newspapers, then continued, with minor variations, on the short but hilly round along Norton Lane and back over Maes Knoll. There are indications that routine and regularity were becoming a more important part of his ruralism in other respects too: he was disappointed, for example, not to see a dipper in a place he had seen one before on 17 August 1963.[273] But there is little evidence of the weaving together of home and landscape that had been such an important feature of the Woollard years. Flowers continued to matter to him – he was pleased to see

[268] BA, 41419/62, 6 and 9 Aug. 1957.
[269] BA, 41419/64, 6 and 16 Feb. and 28 Apr. 1959.
[270] BA, 41419/64, 21, 23 and 31 Jan. 1959.
[271] BA, 41419/64, 6 and 27 Feb. 1959.
[272] BA, 41419/64, 2 Apr. 1959.
[273] BA, 41419/68, 17 Aug. 1963.

some cheddar pinks in the eponymous gorge on 7 June 1959, impressed by the
alpine flora on their holiday in Davos later that year and took much pleasure in
the profusion of flowers he and Elizabeth had planted in their garden.[274]
However, presumably because the countryside was now so much less accessible on foot, they rarely brought flowers or other natural produce back home.

Fred still enjoyed the countryside but his experience of it was becoming more
passive. There is more emphasis on views and little evidence of the active
participation in the landscape so characteristic of his youth. Even gathering
now appears to be a thing of the past. Car trips with friends begin to feature
occasionally and Fred's dwindling ruralism becomes gradually more distant,
transient and consumerist.[275] On their frequent holidays he and Elizabeth spent
much time ambling around whichever town they were visiting, buying souvenirs, staying in for the evening at their hotel talking to other guests, playing
games or reading detective fiction and, especially, eating and drinking. Fred had
always enjoyed food but it does not feature largely in his pre-war diaries. In
contrast, a not untypical late 1950s holiday entry is 3 April 1959, which finds
room in its thirty-three lines for the details of four meals.[276] The post-war Fred
was often scathing about the quality of food and coffee served in the cafés and
hotels he patronized: he had always been an attentive, discriminating critic but in
his younger days this pertained to landscape rather than gastronomy.

Another indication of the waning intensity of Fred's ruralism is that he now
had much less to say. His pre-war journals give the impression of a necessary
outpouring of vivid experience. But the journals give way to preformatted pocket
diaries from 1954, other than his 1956 journal, which he gave up in early April:
evidently Fred's experiences no longer clamoured for expression. There were
occasional exceptions – his obsession with a young woman named Liz in late
1963, for example ('it still gets you even in the 50's!').[277] However, the prose in
which he registers countryside outings is almost invariably now low-key and
matter-of-fact. Where there is an indication of his emotional response, this usually
consists simply of the word 'lovely'. On 23 August 1957, for example, Fred and
Elizabeth were on holiday in North Wales and had a 'lovely walk, by stream, wood
and glade, with lovely distant views of both waterfalls' on the Rhaeadr Fawr.[278]
This implies a calm, contented apprehension of rural landscapes, consistent with
the settled suburban domesticity on which Fred's life was now centred. In
comparison to the urgency of his pre-war ruralism, it is like an intense youthful
love affair that has subsided into placid middle-aged affection. With this in mind

[274] BA, 41419/64, 7 Jun., 8 Aug. and 26 Apr. 1959.
[275] Car trips: BA, 41419/64, 7 Jun., 29 Aug. and 1 Nov. 1959 and 41419/68, 6 Apr., 20 Oct.
and 24 Nov. 1963.
[276] BA, 41419/64, 3 Apr. 1959.
[277] BA, 41419/68, 29 Sep. 1963. Fred's mind was much eased by a long conversation with
'dear E.' about Liz on 3 Oct. 1963: BA, 41419/68.
[278] BA, 41419/62, 23 Aug. 1957.

it is perhaps not surprising that, on the rare occasions Fred's landscape descriptions from these years rise to eloquence, there is often a connection with the past. On 30 March 1959 they caught a bus to East Harptree, walked to Chewton Mendip and picked white violets and primroses – an area and activity familiar to Fred from childhood. Fred noted how Chew Lake looked like a blue estuary in the sun.[279] This sense of revisiting strengthens over the following years. He spent much time re-reading his old diaries and reviewing his relationship with Norman Bright.[280] On 3 July 1960 he went on a ride through Norton Malreward, Stanton Drew and other old haunts, and was filled with '[n]ostalgic delight at the stone buildings and cattle smell of [Hauteville's] Quoit Farm'.[281] It is as if he was seeking to catch an echo of the more urgent impressions of earlier days.

The last entry in Fred's diary is for 31 December 1963. He was fifty-two and had forty years still to live, years about which we know next to nothing due to the lack of evidence in the public domain. The year 1963 has no special significance in his life, so this chapter has an essentially arbitrary ending. It is fitting that the final entry in the diary describes a 'pleasant' bike ride through Queen Charlton into the Chew valley at Keynsham. Ironically, however, the purpose of this ride was to collect rent from 87 Temple Street.[282] The profound continuity in Fred's life is evident but so is the way familiar places and practices had acquired new meanings in the radically changed context of his post-war years. The countryside was still a source of pleasure and even stability for him, but increasingly through retrospect – rarely now did it provide the ecstatic sensory experiences of his youth.

Perhaps the fundamental problem was that, for all it had given him, his ruralism was evidently unable to make good the lack of grounding and orientation from which he had suffered all his life. When he was young this had mattered less. He may not have known what he believed in or where he was going, but it was liberating and life-affirming to react against the institutions and circumstances that constrained him. As he got older, however, the fire of youth burnt lower and his comfort-loving side, what he referred to as his 'laziness', began to predominate. His marriage met one of his prime needs, for stability and security, but it did so in a way that enhanced the temptations to take his ease at home. These temptations were further magnified by the time period in which Fred's married life fell: the affluent post-war years. In a remarkably short span of years, Fred became incorporated into a commercial, consumerist system he had previously rejected and, with neither youth nor an underlying sense of purpose to sustain him, went too gently into a fitfully embittered night of comfortable stagnation.

---

[279] BA, 41419/64, 30 Mar. 1959.
[280] Reading old diaries: BA, 41419/64, 1 Dec. 1959 and 41419/68, 5 May 1963. Norman Bright: BA 41419/65, 17 Jul. 1960.
[281] BA, 41419/65, 3 Jul. 1960.
[282] BA, 41419/68, 31 Dec. 1963.

CONCLUSION

Towards a Deep History of Landscape

Beneath its outward contours and the ways these have been represented in public discourse, landscape has a deep, private history that is still largely unwritten. This is the history of its affective meanings and significance to the individuals who lived in, worked upon or passed through it. The deep history of landscape is inaccessible compared to its already well-worked material and cultural history, yet it holds the key to understanding why landscape meant so much to so many people in the past. It should therefore be central to how historians think about landscape, even though it is elusive and difficult to reconstruct. *Lifescapes* has attempted to tunnel down into this deep history through eight short landscape biographies, each of which explores the changing place of landscape in the subject's life. While the method is potentially applicable to landscape in any historic time or place, to give the book coherence (and remain within my own area of research expertise), I have focused on English rural landscapes between circa 1870 and circa 1960.

For each of the individuals considered here rural landscape was much more than just a backdrop or incidental 'scenery': it was a deeply integrated part of the wider pattern of their lives. Examining how they used, thought and felt about the landscapes they dwelt in and moved through illuminates fundamental aspects of their characters, circumstances and efforts to accommodate the one to the other. Their affective relationships to landscape also bear the imprint of major life events such as migration, courtship, unemployment, social mobility and the death of family and friends. Furthermore, as well as reflecting other aspects of their lives, the affective meanings with which individuals endowed landscapes could become an active, constitutive influence in their own right. It was in large part through quiet contemplation of rural landscapes that Johnston came to terms with the death of his parents, while Spear Smith's exhilarating encounters with flowers, birds, woods and the sea helped her to put her failed artistic ambitions behind her.

As this suggests, landscape played a dynamic, ongoing and indeed enduring role in the lives examined here. Often, the experience of landscape has been represented as if it consisted of discrete moments, profound, mundane or somewhere in between, connected perhaps with how others have experienced or represented the landscape in question, but not part of a continuing flow of personal life. The dominance of landscape painting in representations of the countryside and the normative convention of the view are influential cases in point.[1] A landscape painting presents itself as a single moment of experience, although it is of course constructed through time and the 'moment' it represents is an illusory, even impossible, one. Similarly, a view, whether indicated on a map, engraved on a hilltop plaque, or reproduced in a photograph, is predicated on the notion of a single, special (even epiphanic) moment of experience – hence best-selling books with titles like *England's 100 Best Views*.[2] For the eight diarists, however, landscape did not consist of a few isolated moments of experience. On the contrary, for several of them rural landscapes in various guises were of central significance throughout their recorded lives – not merely landscapes but lifescapes.

Rural landscapes also figured prominently in the lives of millions of other Englishmen and women between the late nineteenth century and the mid-twentieth, more so in some cases than others of course, just as there was a gradation among the individuals studied here between the ultra-ruralist Fred Catley and the more moderate Sadie Barmes. Undoubtedly the eight diarists were towards the ruralist end of the spectrum but it would be surprising if the traits, patterns and motivations identified in this study did not also apply in some degree to the much larger group of those with a more diffuse interest in the countryside. That, however, must await further research. The remaining pages of this book draw together the evidence presented in the preceding chapters, seeking firstly to explain popular ruralism, secondly to summarize its more salient characteristics and thirdly to highlight some of its wider implications.

Explaining Popular Ruralism

The Seeds of Popular Ruralism

What initially drew the subjects of this book to the countryside? Five of them grew up in rural or semi-rural areas, and for two this was a powerful influence. Johnston spent his childhood in the quiet Dumfriesshire market town of Annan, playing on the banks of the Annanwater and around the local farms. Hallam's early years in the small Berkshire village of Lockinge are less well documented, but as young men he and his friends roamed extensively across the local fields, woods and downs. For both Johnston and Hallam these

---

[1] On the dominance of landscape painting in representations of the countryside see Newby, *Green and Pleasant Land?*, 15–18; On views see also Bunce, *The Countryside Ideal*.

[2] Simon Jenkins, *England's 100 Best Views* (London, 2013). See also, among numerous examples, Julia Bradbury, *Unforgettable Walks: Best Walks with a View* (London, 2016) and David Corfield, *Roads with a View: England's Greatest Views and How to Find Them by Road* (Dorchester, 2010).

experiences were formative and lasting. Catley too had a rural upbringing and wrote nostalgically about it in old age but, although the imprint of growing up in or on the fringes of the countryside is discernible in the diaries he wrote while still actually living there, his ruralism sprang primarily from other sources. Much the same might be said of Bissell: childhood residence in the industrial villages of Talke and Quinton can hardly account for his subsequent love of mountains, while periodic visits to his uncle's farm in Frankley almost certainly contributed more to the low-key affection for agricultural landscapes he retained as an adult. Cresswell's childhood diaries, if she kept any, do not survive, so it is difficult to assess the significance rural landscapes held for her at this stage of her life, but the indications are that she found Teignmouth, her small Devon hometown, rather dull.[3] The three remaining diarists grew up in urban areas. A country childhood could, then, contribute powerfully to but was neither a necessary nor a sufficient foundation for lifelong ruralism.

More important than where someone lived were their family traditions. Fathers seem to have been particularly influential in this respect.[4] Frank Dickinson was a discriminating Arts and Crafts collector; it was no accident that three of his four children became craft weavers in adulthood. Alic and Katherine Spear Smith increasingly entered into their father Walter's enthusiasm for mountain climbing and landscape painting as they grew older. Yet parental and wider family traditions were never adopted wholesale – they were invariably transmuted, combined with other influences or reflected in different idioms. Cresswell eschewed her father's gardening, fungi collecting and landscape painting interests, but her love of wildflowers and rural excursions was connected with them. Catley did not share his father's back-to-the-land dream of smallholding self-sufficiency but he was an assiduous harvester of wild food and moved to the countryside when he could afford to do so, where he took much time and trouble over his garden. In some cases family traditions became diluted in the second generation. The Smith parents cherished the sea but, although their daughter identified with her forebear Captain Spear in childhood, as she grew older she found land- rather than seascapes most appealing.[5] Conversely, a family tradition that had been subsidiary in one generation could develop more strongly in the next. This was certainly the case for the younger Dickinson siblings, for whom the countryside became central in a way it had

---

[3] 'It's a dismal hole, and gets worse': Diaries, 18 Feb. 1916, DRO 4686M/F53.

[4] On fatherhood in the long nineteenth century see Trev Lynn Broughton and Helen Rogers (eds.), *Gender and Fatherhood in the Nineteenth Century* (Basingstoke, 2007). See also Laura King, 'Hidden Fathers? The Significance of Fatherhood in Mid-Twentieth-Century Britain', *Contemporary British History* 26 (2012), 25–46; Margareth Lanzinger, 'Introduction: The Power of the Fathers', *The History of the Family* 17 (2012), 279–83.

[5] On the powerful nexus between the sea and British identities see Brian Lavery, 'The Sea and British National Identity', *Mariner's Mirror* 95 (2009), 141–8 and Readman, *Storied Ground*, 25.

not been to their father, for all his Arts and Crafts sympathies, let alone their bel monde mother. In short, family traditions could undoubtedly predispose towards the development of strong affective responses to landscape in adult-hood but there was nothing automatic or deterministic about this.

Much the same might be said about education and reading, which contrib-uted in varying degrees to the ruralist interests of each of the diarists, not only through what they learnt but sometimes where they learnt it. Johnston recorded the pleasure he took in reading outdoors in a school friend's garden, and as a medical student enjoyed lectures in Edinburgh's botanic gardens and plant-collecting trips in the Highlands.[6] After graduating he fell under the influence of a succession of nature writers before becoming a disciple of Walt Whitman. Hallam's love of his native Berkshire was deepened by 'topograph-ical and antiquarian reading'.[7] Spear Smith read Wordsworth and Ruskin, which shaped and amplified the meanings she found in the countryside.[8] Her training as an artist at King's College London also affected her responses to rural landscapes, allowing her to see them (especially their colours) more observantly and vividly. Barmes was rarely without a volume of poetry in her pocket and her taste for writers such as Keats presumably filtered through into what she felt and saw in the countryside, although beyond the occasional quotation it left little imprint in her diaries. A more definite influence was her membership of the Girl Guides. The ideological and discursive underpin-nings of Guiding and Scouting included nature study and natural history as well as a more diffuse 'outdoor' muscular Christianity.[9] Catley's school, Queen Elizabeth House in Bristol, set its pupils essays on Wordsworth, whom one of the preachers at his chapel also extolled. His reading, as eclectic in adulthood as might be expected of someone who spent his entire working life in a bookshop, included a rich vein of ruralist literature, notably Jefferies.

Many recent studies of landscape have placed almost exclusive emphasis on cultural vectors of this kind. Yet people do not respond equally and consistently, or sometimes even at all, to the discursive influences put in their way (as any but the most inspired or self-deluding university teacher must rapidly discover). It was not only the subjects of this book, but all their contemporaries, who grew up in a culture, and particularly a literary tradition, pervaded with pastoral and Romantic influences.[10] No-one could escape this

---

[6] On the history of botanic gardens see John Prest, *The Garden of Eden: The Botanic Garden and the Recreation of Paradise* (New Haven, 1990). On botanic gardens and medical education see Clare Hickman, 'Curiosity and Instruction: British and Irish Botanic Gardens and Their Audiences, 1760–1800', *Environment and History* 24 (2018), 59–80.

[7] Hallam Diaries, BRO D/EX 1415/30.

[8] On Wordsworth's influence see Stephen Gill, *Wordsworth and the Victorians* (Oxford, 1998).

[9] Edwards, *Youth Movements*.

[10] Christopher Hilliard, 'Modernism and the Common Writer', *Historical Journal* 48 (2005), 769–87, at 771. See also Gill, *Wordsworth and the Victorians*.

and the more highly educated someone was, the more their exposure to such influences. Yet while the eight diarists were far from unique in the intensity and extent of their ruralism, they were certainly towards the upper end of the scale. Explaining why they responded so much more strongly to discursive influences than many others equally exposed to them is difficult without invoking non-discursive factors. Nor should we assume that people's interests and values are primarily shaped by, for example, the books they read, rather than the other way round. People tend to read books that are congruent with their existing outlook (and the same applies in some degree to other cultural representations they encounter). 'Books only teach you what you bring to them', Maggie Johnston observed to her husband, a view that is perhaps as tenable as its chicken-and-egg opposite.[11] Certainly Johnston, Hallam and Catley, whose diaries begin in or refer extensively to their childhoods, had already developed pronounced ruralist interests before they read much ruralist literature. It was because of these established ruralist tastes that writers like Whitman and Jefferies appealed, more than the other way round.

Indeed, as Georgina Boyes argued in her study of the folk revival, it is a serious mistake to assume non-elite men and women are uncreative and can only recycle existing cultural representations.[12] Not only can and do they choose between these, they also adapt, modify and extend them, as Bissell did in combining scriptural mountain metaphors with Romantic tropes and his own hopes and exigencies to formulate his concept of 'the miracle of Ben Nevis', whereby anything connected with the 'sacred mountain' was touched by a kind of blessing. Nor did the protagonists of this book confine themselves to working within established ideas and patterns of behaviour. On the contrary, they were richly innovative in their landscape practices. Johnston developed a remarkable mode of sedentary meditation that fused nature, writing and self-realization, first in Raikes Wood and later in other rural settings. Cresswell named her church-and-countryside exploration 'gëorgoepiscoping', taking the word from her fellow Devonian Coleridge. But the fact she found it necessary to adopt such an obscure term shows how unusual her practice was, nor indeed was there much in what she did that Coleridge would have recognized.[13] The deep layering of personal experience, folklore, landscape history and archaeology registered in Hallam's accounts of his explorations of the Lockinge downs has no real parallel among the published rural writers of his time. Catley effectively invented a new region, the Chew valley, creating his own highly personal landscape practices as he explored it. There were many of these, among them the ritual of pausing to gaze at the water flowing beneath

---

[11] Johnston Diary, 3 Jun. 1890, BAHC.

[12] Boyes, *The Imagined Village*.

[13] On Coleridge's use of 'gëorgoepiscoping' see M. E. Sandford and R. Watters, *Thomas Poole and His Friends* (Bridgwater, 1996), 256.

the bridge over the Chew before entering the valley and, after he moved to the Chew village of Woollard, locating, bringing home and planting wildflowers to connect home and countryside.

As some of these examples suggest, the material properties of landscape are crucial. They shape and constrain cultural representations – the Fens have never been celebrated for their rugged coastline, nor Cornwall for chalk downs.[14] More than this, the material properties of a landscape directly affect the 'fit' between it and the individual's life situation and circumstances, independently of how it is figured discursively. It mattered to Johnston as a child that the River Annan was shallow enough to wade in and had wide, grassy, accessible banks because this enabled him to play in and beside it. If the river had been deep and inaccessible, he would not have been able to do so, however it had been represented. Similarly for Cresswell the abundance of wildflowers in the meadows round Exeter greatly facilitated the flower gathering and arranging that was such an important part of her life – this would scarcely have been feasible had she lived in Whitechapel. The physical arduousness of climbing mountains and the fact that it was not possible to go further upwards than the summit was crucial to Bissell because the collective experience of exhaustion and attainment contributed directly (and not only through scriptural and Romantic representations) to the Christian fellowship he hoped to foster.[15]

Nevertheless, just as people are to a greater or lesser extent discriminating and selective in the discursive elements they adopt, so they are in finding landscapes with the material properties they want. Spear Smith spent much time in woods, not because she lived in unusually woody places, but because her shy, retiring personality valued seclusion. Nor was it accidental that the energetic, even combative, Cresswell chose to cycle up so many hills. In understanding what landscapes mean to people and why they value them, it is indispensable to consider the ways life situations and circumstances, and the needs and preferences that arise from these, resonate with the material and cultural properties of particular landscapes, and shape responses to them. In general terms, affective landscapes reflect the societies from which they emerge. This is equally true of material and cultural landscapes. But whereas dominant power structures, interests, ideologies and representations are

---

[14] Compare Readman, *Storied Ground*, 50. '[T]o function as any sort of widely recognisable landmark a landscape needs to be visually memorable.'

[15] In this respect I am in sympathy with proponents of James and Eleanor Gibson's concept of affordances as 'properties of the environment that are both objectively real *and* psychologically significant', although in my view the psychological significance of an affordance is variable because it is mediated through the distinctive psychological characteristics of the individual in question. See Catharine Ward Thompson, 'Landscape Perception and Environmental Psychology', in Howard et al. (eds.), *The Routledge Companion to Landscape Studies*, 20.

directly reflected in material and cultural landscapes, affective landscapes are in many respects better considered as *inverse* images of the societies that produce them. People project onto landscapes, or seek to find in them, the qualities, opportunities and experiences they miss in their day-to-day lives. This means that affective landscapes can be read as an index of the tensions and contradictions within a particular society, and the constraints and limitations it differentially imposes on its members.

On the other hand, however, it also allows landscape to mediate between the self and the world, helping individuals to find ways of adapting to their circumstances, reducing social friction and hence contributing to the sustainability of a given social configuration. When Cresswell was gëorgoepiscoping through rural Devon, or Johnston sitting in Raikes Wood, each left behind their primary social settings (home, workplace, community or whatever). Of course, they brought aspects of these settings with them, but many obligations, pressures and problems had been placed at one remove – Cresswell's insufferable relatives, Johnston's ungrateful patients. When they returned, each was, even if only very slightly, a changed person – perhaps a little more optimistic, refreshed, better able to resume life in their everyday social context. On his way back to the tribulations of medical practice in Bolton from an idyllic week in the countryside, Johnston resolved that he would 'earnestly buckle to once more and do my duty like a true man'.[16] Cresswell likewise, driven to distraction by her ailing and querulous mother, escaped for two exhilarating days to the Quantocks and, on coming home, promptly finished the book she had been struggling with for weeks.[17]

Patterns of Response

If affective landscapes are reflections (or inverse images) of the societies that give rise to them, we should expect them to be no less diverse than those societies. It would, therefore, be a mistake to look for any singular 'meaning' of landscape, even within a defined historical context. At the same time, to a certain extent each society might be expected to generate its own distinctive pattern of responses to landscape. The present study can claim only to have identified some of the more prominent strands of this pattern as it pertained to late nineteenth- and early twentieth-century England. I have used four of these strands as the organizing principle for *Lifescapes*, grouping its subjects under the headings of Adherers, Withdrawers, Restorers and Explorers. Adherers were drawn to rural landscapes because these offered, or could be construed as offering, a guarantee of continuity and durability. A characteristic feature of Adherers was deep attachments in their personal lives, which left them

---

[16] Johnston Diary, 16 Jun. 1889.
[17] Cresswell Diaries, 12 Sep. 1903.

exceptionally exposed and vulnerable to change. Rural landscapes, they hoped, were places where 'things will go onward the same', bulwarks against the ceaseless attack of time.[18] Withdrawers were more concerned to escape from perceived dangers in the present than to maintain their connection to a cherished past. Hence they valued the countryside primarily as a refuge, somewhere they could shelter from what they experienced as potentially overwhelming external pressures and threats. Restorers had a more optimistic and confident relationship to landscape. For them landscape was neither something to hold on to nor retreat into but a place where they could reconnect with the deepest certainties of their being. Accordingly, the landscapes that appealed most strongly to Restorers were typically quiet and often remote or unpeopled landscapes such as mountain tops – but equally private gardens. In these places Restorers were able to process disruptive or disturbing influences and regain their equanimity and sense of ethical rootedness. Finally, Explorers had perhaps the most open relationship to landscape. For them it offered above all scope for discovery, sometimes intense emotional experiences and encounters, and the growth of self-knowledge.

Each of these categories corresponds to a core feature of the ruralism of two of the subjects of this book. Hallam and Cresswell were Adherers, Dickinson and Spear Smith Withdrawers, Johnston and Bissell Restorers and Barmes and Catley Explorers. However, the four categories are neither mutually exclusive nor exhaustive. Johnston had some Adherers characteristics, for example, just as Spear Smith showed Explorer traits at times, while Adherer and Withdrawer elements are discernible in Catley. Furthermore, affective landscapes played many subsidiary roles in each diarist's life. Some of these might have gained prominence if I had had time to research other lives in comparable depth, and further, hitherto unidentified, roles would undoubtedly have emerged. The four categories that structure this book are intended to draw attention to pronounced clusters within the spectrum of psychological characteristics that, in my view, lie at the root of affective responses to landscape, but it is these characteristics rather than the clusters abstracted from them that have explanatory primacy. A fully specified deep history of landscape would indeed approximate to an inventory of the predominant psychological characteristics of the society under investigation, insofar as these expressed themselves in relation to landscape.[19] It is inconceivable that we could ever in practice attain such a radically ambitious goal. But the starting point for any serious inquiry into the past is a recognition that the holy grail of comprehensive historical

---

[18] Thomas Hardy, 'In Time of "The Breaking of Nations"', first published in the *Saturday Review*, 19 Jan. 1916.

[19] Compare Erich Fromm's concept of social character, developed in *Escape from Freedom* (New York, 1941), 275–96. See also Walter A. Jensen, 'Erich Fromm's Contributions to Sociological Theory' (PhD, Western Michigan University, 2015), 59–172.

knowledge will always remain out of reach; and thankfully that has not yet stopped us trying to make progress towards it.[20]

Adherers

The descriptive and explanatory value of the categories outlined above is really only demonstrable in detail, for which readers are referred to the eight preceding biographical chapters, but is briefly recapitulated here. For Adherers like Hallam the temporal dimension of the landscape was fundamental. He recorded local customs and traditions, collected flints, copied inscriptions and, despite his plebeian origins, became a leading light in the admittedly small world of Berkshire local history. He felt a passionate loyalty to his home village of Lockinge, to the adjacent downs and to the county of Berkshire.[21] This reflected his happy childhood and the patronage of the dominant local landowner, Lord Wantage. The tenacity and force of Hallam's feelings contributed to an unusual strength of character, and a lasting, devoted marriage, but he suffered for it, most devastatingly following his mother's death when he was only sixteen. Never safe from these acute emotional risks, Hallam turned to the countryside as an embodiment and even guarantee of continuity. This was congruent with his Conservative politics and dedication to the aristocracy, to whom he looked to defend the social and physical coordinates of the countryside of his childhood. Preservation and conservation were his watchwords and nothing delighted him more than to see a manor house carefully maintained or respectfully restored.

Cresswell too poured out her feelings unstintingly, to her servant Mary, her publisher Prescott Row, and her numerous cats. Above all, however, it was her father, the Reverend Richard Cresswell, to whom she was devoted, and his death when she was twenty had as profound an effect on her as Hallam's loss of his mother did on him. Even fifty-six years later she wrote on the anniversary of Richard's death of 'the dismals of this hateful day' and all her major adult projects were directly connected to him, notably through a persistent and powerful identification with Devon clergymen. The first in a series of guidebooks she wrote was about Dartmoor, a special place for the two of them since her childhood. She then commenced a remarkably ambitious survey of all the Anglican churches in Devon, which took her up hill and down dale into every corner of the county over a period of several decades. After completing this she soon began what she referred to as her 'magnum opus' – a history of Devon clergymen. Just as Hallam did, she cherished the traces of the past in the

---

[20] As Readman observes, the past can never be known in its entirety but we can 'fail better' as historians. P. Readman, 'Walking, and Knowing the Past: Antiquaries, Pedestrianism and Historical Practice in Modern Britain', *History* https://doi.org/10.1111/1468-229X.13184, 23.

[21] Compare Keith D. M. Snell, *Parish and Belonging: Community, Identity and Welfare in England and Wales, 1700–1950* (Cambridge, 2006).

countryside, which offered her a shelter from and antidote to change. 'The country never changes, except when it is built on', she observed with satisfaction, if doubtful accuracy.[22] While Cresswell's fear of change may have been exacerbated by franchise reform, which as a Conservative she opposed, by falling church attendance and by the travails of the aristocracy, her diaries show little concern with these issues, which were in any case less acutely felt in Devon than more urbanized areas.[23] As with Hallam, the core of her ruralism was a passionate craving for stability and continuity in the people and things she loved.

Adherer characteristics are also apparent, if less fully developed, in some of the other diarists, most obviously Johnston and Catley. Johnston did not suffer an early bereavement but professional exigencies forced him to leave Annan when he was sixteen, first to study in Edinburgh and subsequently obtain a medical practice in Bolton. He felt the separation from his parents keenly and, as they aged, became preoccupied by their anticipated mortality. Immersing himself in nature, especially where there was a river, lake or flowery meadow to remind him of his childhood, reassured him that he carried their love within him and that nothing could take it away. For all this, there are significant respects in which Johnston's ruralism does not match the Adherer profile. He had little interest in the human dimension of the landscape, still less in its history. The central Adherer concern with generational continuity, woven into the landscape through centuries of life and labour, was almost completely absent too. Partly, perhaps, because of this he felt no attachment to the social and political structures associated with the historic continuity of the landscape. Indeed, far from being a Conservative, Johnston became increasingly committed to radical political change.

Catley's ruralism also served to protect him from change, and made a vital contribution to his security. This can again be related to the death of a parent: Joseph Catley was killed at the Battle of Arras in 1917, when Fred was only six. The immediate consequence was to plunge the family into financial anxiety. It also drew in on itself: Fred and his siblings continued to live at home until he was in his early thirties. Their mother Charlotte was a self-effacing woman, evidently quite unable to fill the gap left by her husband's death. In later years Fred could hardly recall his father and spent much of his adult life metaphorically searching for him. Places like the Chew valley or Pipley Bottom were emotional anchors, enduring and reliable in a way he had learnt human relationships might not be. But in other respects, Fred was no Adherer. While fond of his brother, he was not a man of deep attachments and his

[22] Cresswell Diary, 28 Mar. 1928.
[23] For the comparative slowness of socio-economic change in early twentieth-century Devon see Brassley, Burchardt and Thompson (eds.), *The English Countryside between the Wars*.

ruralism lacked the strongly historical, even archaeological, character so apparent in Hallam and Cresswell. Throughout the period when his ruralism was at its height, he was, like Johnston, sharply anti-Conservative.

Hallam, Cresswell, Johnston and Catley each therefore showed Adherer characteristics but to varying degrees and in different forms. This can be related to their contrasting life histories and circumstances, especially differences in the timing and nature of parental bereavement. Hallam and Cresswell, in whom the Adherer characteristics were strongest, lost beloved parents when they were old enough to have formed genuine, reliable relationships with them based on mutual knowledge. For both it was the guarantee of historical continuity they read into the rural landscape that gave them security. The enemy they feared was external change. This was true for Johnston too, but his ruralism was notably present-centric. It was through contemplating nature's ceaseless activity and perpetual self-renewal that he was able to tap into the roots of his own security. Perhaps this was related to the fact that, during the years his ruralism developed, his parents were still alive. Catley, in the bleakest position of the four, looked to rural landscapes for a more pervasive security. Unlike Hallam and Cresswell, whose fear was only of external change, Catley feared any kind of change, including that generated from within. The often 'unbelievably quiet' countryside he preferred to frequent helped him avoid disturbing emotional encounters that might prompt change of this kind. For Catley, therefore, rural landscapes offered security at the price of stifling development. This was in part because they were a substitute for a security he had never had, whereas for Hallam, Cresswell and eventually Johnston, they were a means of holding on to a real source of security of which life had partially deprived them.

Withdrawers

Withdrawers were preoccupied with more immediate problems than Adherers – they looked to rural landscapes as a refuge from things they found frightening, threatening or disagreeable. This aspect of rural landscapes connects with Prospect-Refuge Theory, the model of landscape experience originally developed by Jay Appleton, which construes landscape preferences socio-biologically as deriving from evolutionary pressures in the early human African savannah.[24] However, for Appleton, refuge landscapes were one pole of a binary model whereas the diaries and life writing sources I have studied suggest a much richer spectrum of landscape responses.[25]

[24] Jay Appleton, *The Experience of Landscape*. Revised ed. (Chichester, 1996).
[25] My sources also suggest that prospects were usually part of an ongoing flow of landscape experience rather than an isolated element in their own right, notwithstanding the undoubted centrality of views in representations of the countryside.

Dickinson is a paradigmatic example of a Withdrawer. One of the primary reasons she was so strongly drawn to the countryside is that it offered her shelter from things she was frightened of and a screen to keep them out of sight. Among these were illness, which (not unreasonably given the high urban mortality rates of nineteenth-century Britain) she associated with towns; the terror of falling into poverty, and the associated loss of social distinction, epitomized by urban slums; an acute fear of strangers; dread of the urban working class; and a horror of death and violence, exacerbated by fears of bombing during both world wars.[26] Seeking to escape these existential threats, real and perceived, Dickinson retreated successively further into the country-side, from Hampstead to Kent, Sussex and then Somerset, ultimately with better results than might have been anticipated.

Dickinson's near contemporary Spear Smith shared some of her fears, although less acutely. She too shrank from 'common people' and from the horror of war, although in her case the pressure of feeling that she ought to achieve something was a more urgent problem.[27] Since she hoped initially to become a painter, this pressure manifested itself in self-doubt and misery during her artistic training and a sharp dislike of more assertive female 'career artists'.[28] Like Dickinson, Spear Smith retreated to the countryside. In her case this was a figurative as well as a literal retreat. As an escape route from art, Spear Smith recast herself as a 'lover of nature'. This was accompanied by a geographical retreat that was a milder echo of Dickinson's – from Dulwich to Rickmansworth and finally Titchfield in Hampshire.

None of the other protagonists of this book exhibited the characteristic Withdrawer pattern of progressive rural retreat, but several of them used the countryside as a temporary refuge, primarily from workplace, urban or indus-trial environments they found irksome or oppressive. Hallam, for example, was the epitome of proletarian alienation: forced to leave his rural childhood home and work in a giant industrial complex, oppressed by the factory bell, night work, industrial injuries, the threat of unemployment, heat, cold and sheer boredom, and miserable at being cut off from his rural roots. Hatred of his work and Swindon was one of the reasons he so often cycled out to the Marlborough Downs and took his family on rural walks. It was similar with Johnston. As a general practitioner, he had a greater measure of control over his labour than Hallam but his diaries nevertheless bear compelling witness to the trials of his professional life: ungrateful patients, overdue bills, long hours and night calls, unscrupulous quacks, worrying cases and patients whose

---

[26] On high rates of urban mortality in nineteenth-century Britain see S. Szreter and A. Hardy, 'Urban Fertility and Mortality Patterns', in M. Daunton (ed.), *The Cambridge Urban History of Britain* (Cambridge, 2001), 629–72.

[27] The quoted phrase is from HRO, 19M99/1/2a (Smith Diary, 14 Jul. 1906).

[28] Compare Marsh, 'Resolve to Be a Great Paintress'.

suffering he could do little to relieve. When he could find time to do so, he sought respite from these and other sources of distress and anxiety by retreating to one of his favoured rural enclaves, where he would lick his wounds and compose himself while quietly watching the plants, insects, birds and sky. Catley too sometimes took refuge in the countryside from tribulations such as the pressure of exams in his last year at school or worries about losing his job when George's bookshop came under new ownership.

Restorers

It was primarily as a site of ethical renewal and regeneration that Johnston and his fellow restorer Bissell valued the countryside, however. For both a consciously articulated ethical frame of reference played a crucial role in this process: discursive influences made a more pronounced contribution to their ruralism than for the other diarists. Johnston revered the ideas and person of Walt Whitman and was also impressed by the theory of cosmic consciousness advanced by Whitman's doctor R. M. Bucke.[29] Before falling under Whitman's sway he had been an admirer of a succession of other nature writers, notably Emerson, Thoreau, Carpenter and Jefferies.[30] The imprint of these influences on him was substantial, for example in his belief in the universal power of nature, in nature as the ultimate ethical foundation, in its inexhaustibility and unfailingness, and in its superiority to human institutions and social conventions. Other, non-discursive influences also contributed, however. His rural childhood provided a crucial base layer, leaving happy memories of reading in Willie Graham's garden, playing in and around Staythrowes and other local farms, and richly imaginative childhood games on the banks of the Annanwater. The experience of confinement indoors during a long, life-threatening illness while he was a medical student also fed powerfully into his perception of and beliefs about nature and the countryside. Out of these mixed influences Johnston constructed his own personal ideology of nature. The force that drove him to do so was what could be construed as an archetypical late Victorian crisis of faith – an urgent need for new ethical

---

[29] S. E. D. Shortt, 'Bucke, Richard Maurice', in *Dictionary of Canadian Biography*. Vol. 13 (Toronto, 2003). www.biographi.ca/en/bio/bucke_richard_maurice_13E.html [accessed 29 Sep. 2018]. On Whitman's influence in England, and specifically Bolton, see Michael Robertson, 'Worshipping Walt: Lancashire's Whitman Disciples', *History Today* 54 (2004), 46; Paul Salveson, *With Walt Whitman in Bolton: Spirituality, Sex and Socialism in a Northern Mill Town*. 2nd ed. (Huddersfield, 2008); Salveson, 'Loving Comrades'; Kirsten Harris, *Walt Whitman and British Socialism* (London, 2016); Carolyn Masel, 'Poet of Comrades: Walt Whitman and the Bolton Whitman Fellowship', in Janet Beer and Bridget Bennett (eds.), *Special Relationships: Anglo-American Affinities and Antagonisms* (Manchester, 2018), 110–38.

[30] On the influence of American nature writers in Britain see Mark Bevir, 'British Socialism and American Romanticism', *English Historical Review* 110 (1995), 878–901.

foundations, independent of his father's fervent Protestantism but retaining as much as possible of its ethical power.[31] He is the only one of the diarists who clearly fits the pattern identified by Marsh of substituting nature for lost religious faith, although it might be argued that what mattered in Johnston and his father was not so much the specific coordinates of their belief systems as the underlying ethical energy and seriousness that informed them.[32]

As this perhaps suggests, when Johnston was sitting in Raikes Wood, on the beach at St Anne's, above the Ramsey cliffs or in his beautiful garden at Lostock, underneath the conscious ideological retrieval and refurbishment less conscious processes of restoration were at work. The attributes of the rural or naturalistic environments in which he placed himself on these occasions were pivotal to this: quietness, solitude and freedom from disturbance, contributing to a sense of harmony between self and world, with nothing jarring or intrusive and no imposition of unwanted demands. Undoubtedly Johnston was also affected at this deep unconscious level by the resemblance between the places where he chose to contemplate nature and the rural landscapes of his Annan childhood. In such environments and circumstances, doubts, fears, shocks and reverses gradually dropped away, and his optimistic character and deep-seated faith in himself and life reasserted themselves. Because he often recorded these occasions in notes written in real time, it is possible to trace this quite closely in his diary entries. The typical format of these entries is an initial focus on close, detailed external observation of his immediate environment. This is followed by a middle section in which Johnston articulates some current trouble or woe, usually of a piercing nature such as his fear that he had not been a truly gentle and patient nurse while looking after his ailing father. The final section of the note reflects on this and restores Johnston's equanimity, albeit at the price of acknowledging and accepting the sorrow articulated earlier.[33]

The parallels between Johnston and Bissell with respect to the restorative power of rural landscapes are close. In Bissell's case too there was what could be considered a large discursive superstructure – his Methodist faith – but again this was underpinned by an optimistic, confident character and a staunch, loving family background.[34] From this arose his deep conviction that all would be well and that his efforts, in whatever direction he extended

---

[31] Compare Turner, 'The Victorian Crisis of Faith'.

[32] Marsh, *Back to the Land*.

[33] A characteristic example of Johnston's nature notes is appended to his diary entry for 12 May 1891, ZJO 1/11, BAHC.

[34] On twentieth-century British Methodism see David William Bebbington and David Ceri Jones, *Evangelicalism and Fundamentalism in the United Kingdom during the Twentieth Century* (Oxford, 2013). See also Clive D. Field, 'Fun, Faith and Fellowship: British Methodism and Tourism in the Twentieth Century', *Journal of Tourism History* 7 (2015), 75–99.

them, would be successful. It was challenging for him when things failed to work according to this template – when, for example, one of the probationers he had trusted lapsed into their old ways or his hopes of involving the Soviet leadership in a modest peace initiative were dashed. Being in the countryside helped to restore his temporarily tarnished optimism. Even a pleasant walk amid spring sunshine and flowers could have a positive effect but it was mountains he found most restorative. Attaining a mountain summit confirmed his belief that there was a benign order in the universe under which his endeavours would prosper, suffusing him with quiet exhilaration, strengthening his inner certainty and inspiring him with the wish to bring these experiences to others.

Powerful and profound as were the restorative processes Johnston and Bissell experienced in rural landscapes, to a certain extent they involved a reassertion of self *against* the world. Bissell seems to have been, in the long run, almost impervious to change in his fundamental world view and understanding of life, so it would not be unfair to suggest that his mountain restorations involved a pushing back against, even ejection of, aspects of experience that contradicted his world view. Johnston was more accommodating. While the function of his 'nature notes' was still primarily to restore pre-existing inner certainties, he was more willing and able than Bissell to allow himself to be affected and changed by life, especially as he grew older. When he was young, immersion in the teeming immediacy of nature's 'now' was his primary response to fears of looming future darkness. As the years passed, however, plunging joyfully back into the fullness of an active life no longer seemed a sufficient answer. His nature notes dwell more on the literal and metaphorical coming of night, with a rapt and tender closeness of observation. Experience and his awareness of the passage of time, in his own life and the lives of those he loved, had wrought a change in him. Perhaps, too, he no longer felt as much physical energy and vigour as in his youth. In any case, sitting quietly in rural landscapes (especially in twilight and darkness) was the crucial vector of this process.

Explorers

Johnston, then, had a certain openness to new experiences. However, on the whole, like Bissell, he knew what he was going to find when he set off to the countryside. By contrast, for Explorers like Catley and Barmes, the countryside could be the site of unexpected encounters and new discoveries. In Catley's case this was largely an intellectual process. Countless walks and bike rides taught him to know the rural landscapes to the south and east of Bristol intimately. Because he knew them so well, and because he felt free of social pressures or anxieties when he was out in the countryside, he was able to formulate his own tastes and preferences unhindered – this church rather than that, this path rather than the other, this overgrown wood, that place to picnic, this little combe rather than its more celebrated neighbour. Through knowing what he liked, he came to know his own values better, and his growing discrimination gave him a sense of expertise and mastery that strengthened his social assurance and allowed him to walk taller in company. At a deeper emotional level, however, Catley's intense involvement with the countryside shielded him from change rather than fostering development, so he does not fit as unambiguously into the Explorer category as the other diarists do into the primary categories to which I have assigned them.

Barmes, on the other hand, could hardly have been more of an Explorer. For her being in the countryside was a means of personal discovery, development and fulfilment. As a young woman she had an active, urgent desire for beauty, nature and meaning. The many Guide camps she attended, and later her more adventurous holidays on the continent with groups like International Tramping Tours, were a rite of passage and a vital stage in growing up. They brought her companionship, laughter, adventure, a degree of independence and freedom from many of the constraints of home and school. More than this, however, they helped her develop her own outlook, perspective and values. They provided a setting for new encounters with places and people, leading to long discussions with friends but also, at times, to solitude, space and freedom to think for herself. It was perhaps mainly through these camps that Barmes developed a deeper feeling for the natural world and they were formative in the growth of her ideas about religion, freedom and selfhood. Her fellow guides played an essential part in this, as sounding boards, adversaries and providers of new ideas, so the process of self-discovery was also a process of discovering others. These and other intense shared experiences brought Barmes powerfully together with her outdoor companions. Much of this was to do with her age and being with other young people in a relatively unfamiliar and unsupervised environment, but the rural setting mattered. It provided more privacy and seclusion, more space and freedom, and a sense of being somewhere different and unfamiliar.[35] Encountering the natural world with its strange and perhaps more vivid sensory impressions was important too.

Elements of Explorer ruralism are also apparent in some of Spear Smith's encounters with landscape. Diffident in company, she was at her happiest and freest in quiet, unfrequented countryside – Lee Common, the Wendover beech woods, the copse at Titchfield. Such places allowed her to express and validate her modesty and gentleness through observation of and response to unobtrusive landscape features. Being in and moving through the landscape could be a process of self-discovery too. The misty mountain vistas of the Lake District stirred youthful hopes and longings, even if at other times her devotion to nature could act as a dreamy substitute for achieving them. Often the most

---

[35] On the opportunities the countryside provided for children's play see Colin Ward, *The Child in the Country* (London, 1988).

telling realizations arose from entirely serendipitous encounters: the harsh, unyielding mountains of Snowdonia confronting her with the painful truth that she did not have it in her to conquer the artistic heights she had been striving to climb, the Wild Arum in the Chilterns teaching her that beauty depended on an environment in which it could flourish, the thrilling sight of Ben Nevis as the train came round the curve, releasing a great pent-up surge of longing to be free from the inner constraints that had weighed her down for years.

Other Dimensions of Landscape Experience

The four major patterns of affective landscape relationships outlined above draw attention to the most prominent and pervasive features of the landscape experience of the subjects of this study, and to important similarities and contrasts between them. They should not, however, be allowed to obscure the fundamentally multifaceted character of each individual's landscape experience. Moreover, some aspects of landscape experience were common to many or most of the diarists without being centrally significant to any of them.

Therapy   One such aspect was the huge variety of therapeutic possibilities, physical, affective and cognitive, offered by rural landscapes.[36] When she was older and suffering from poor circulation, for example, Dickinson sometimes went for walks to warm herself up. She also used walks to allay worries, absorb emotional shocks and, it would seem, as an act of remembrance. Spear Smith too walked therapeutically. On one occasion, singing German Lieder had left her 'much troubled', so she went for a stroll and felt 'so much better' on her return.[37] A few years later she wrote to her brother that she had had a 'lovely walk this morning' and could think much better in the open air.[38] Catley used a range of landscape practices for conscious therapeutic and problem-solving purposes. When the household finances were threatened by a projected reduction in his brother's allowance, he went for a walk to work out what to do. After being rejected by his prospective girlfriend Jeanne, he sought consolation by cycling to the distant Exmoor hills, where he found the beauty of the landscape soothing. When he was unsettled, he often sought the tranquillity of remote farms and hostels in the Mendips, where he would stay overnight before returning to his unsatisfactory day-to-day life in Bristol. Even the 'armchair

---

[36] For a review of the extensive literature on nature and ecotherapy see L. S. Franco, D. F. Shanahan and R. A. Fuller, 'A Review of the Benefits of Nature Experiences: More Than Meets the Eye', *International Journal of Environmental Research and Public Health* 14 (2017), 864.

[37] Smith Diary, 4 Jun. 1912.

[38] Letter, Katherine Spear Smith to Alic Smith, 6 Jan. 1915, PA SMA 1 29, New College (Oxford) Archives.

countryside' could prove therapeutic for him: following a hellish dental appointment he recovered at home by reading Adrian Bell's *The Cherry Tree*.[39] Similarly after a nasty chest infection, the first book he felt well enough to read was *Living in the Country*.[40]

Freedom   It is often assumed that what people seek in the countryside above all is freedom.[41] This was a major, persistent motivation for only one of the diarists (Cresswell), but it mattered to several of the others. Barmes always seems to have felt a sense of liberation from bodily constraint when out in the countryside: her rural camp and holiday diaries are replete with accounts of dancing, singing, wearing light, simple clothing and exuberant physical self-expression. Although of a later generation, she had much in common with the devotees of the Simple Life described in *Back to the Land*.[42] Evidently, and unsurprisingly, Barmes felt less free to behave in this way in an urban setting. Ruralism as a reaction against physical constraint was also a pronounced feature of a critical phase of Johnston's life. During the illness that nearly killed him in his youth he was rigorously confined indoors. Until he began to recover he had been unable even to see out, and he describes his first glimpse of the local mountain, Criffel, from the window of his sick chamber with vivid intensity. When he was well enough to leave the house for the first time he made his way, supported by his parents, down to the bridge over the Annanwater and, as he recovered, began to re-explore the Annan countryside of his childhood with passionate eagerness. The powerful experiences of these months seem to have established an equation between rural landscapes and freedom from oppressive circumstances, and also taught him to regard the countryside as a gateway back to his childhood, associations that persisted through his long years as a Bolton general practitioner.

The more severe constraints, however, were usually social or psychological rather than physical. Cresswell loved the countryside not only because she felt it 'never changes' but also because it gave her freedom to do what she wanted. At one level, this can be understood in relation to the circumstances of her adult life – the drudgery of looking after her ailing mother, the frustration of having dull, unenterprising relatives outstaying their welcome, vexatious servants. Her response to these and many other irksome situations was to leap on her bicycle and make for 'the wilds'. She was hardly unique, however, in being constrained by external circumstances. The intensity of her urge for freedom is better attributed to character than circumstances – indeed, it was apparent even in her childhood. She was, as her father's diaries reveal, a much-indulged

---

[39] Bunce, *The Countryside Ideal*.
[40] BRO, 41419/31, 17 May 1936 and 41419/40, 1 Feb. 1941.
[41] Thomas, *Man and the Natural World*, 268.
[42] Marsh, *Back to the Land*.

youngest child, extremely fond of having her own way. The freedom Cresswell sought in remote parts of rural Devon was the counterpart of the 'wilds' within her. That said, rural Devon gave her a real, not just metaphorical, experience of freedom because she was genuinely at greater liberty to do what she liked in the privacy of the countryside than under watching eyes and social constraints at home or outdoors in Exeter.

Identity   For some of the diarists the countryside was an important source of identity. Being a rural artist-craftswoman gradually became central to Dickinson's sense of who she was; the news that she and Ced had been made honorary life members of the Somerset Guild of Craftsmen warranted four exclamation marks in her diary.[43] It was Catley and Spear Smith, however, who invested most energy in developing self-conscious landscape-related identities. During Catley's youth and early adulthood his need to assert his individuality and identity was paramount. The rural landscapes he most valued at this time were those he felt to be 'his'. This was a large part of why he was drawn to less iconic landscapes that had not yet been culturally colonized. The landscapes that appealed most to him were those he perceived as authentic and unadorned and to which he felt he could relate directly without cultural intermediaries. Landscapes such as the Chew valley, the Mendips, Exmoor and the South Wiltshire downs became assertions of himself. The more withdrawn parts of some of these landscapes became homes-from-home, places where he felt free to be himself, where he could do as he wanted, and which he knew thoroughly and intimately. Cresswell shared this home-from-home feeling with Catley, although for her it applied principally at the scale of a county (rural Devon) and corresponded to an ambivalence about her real homes, successively in Teignmouth, Dawlish and Exeter. Conversely, she was much less preoccupied with her identity than Catley was with his.

   To a greater extent than any of the other diarists, Spear Smith's ruralism was focused on observing and recording flora and fauna. Encouraged by her brother, she constructed a persona as a 'lover of nature'. This expressed itself in practice through a close identification with the little things of nature (songbirds and their nests, the more delicate flowers, secluded copses), an identification that helped shore up her in some ways fragile sense of self. But the 'sensitive' persona she built up on this basis hindered her from developing social relationships and made it more difficult for her to forge a successful artistic career. Hence although nature, the countryside and specific rural landscapes could readily be incorporated into personal identities, when this happened in a self-conscious, artificial way, the outcome could be problematic and its sustainability questionable.

---

[43] Dickinson Diary, 13 Aug. 1950, Somerset Heritage Centre, A/AGV/9.

Social Opportunities   While in Spear Smith's case an intense identification with the countryside proved isolating, for the other diarists rural landscapes were an important, even vital, source of relatedness and connection. The tight mesh of norms defining acceptable conduct in settled areas lifted and loosened out in the open country. Relationships were less hemmed in by external constraints and there was more scope for them to unfold in response to their internal dynamics. Hallam, for example, used walks, rides and sometimes fishing or bathing expeditions to develop friendships with young men his own age like the Whittles in Lockinge or Austin in Swindon. He courted his wife-to-be, Sophie Hawkins, mainly by walking over the Lockinge downs with her. Cresswell took friends on flower-collecting expeditions and her relatives on bike rides, although sometimes with counterproductive results (sister-in-law rode too slowly).[44] There are fragmentary indications that she may have conducted an abortive rural courtship with the mysterious 'H' and, more certainly, she greatly enjoyed country car tours with acquaintances like Mr Warren and Evelyn Worthington in her old age. Dickinson invariably used walking as a means of cementing her most valued friendships and had an interesting practice of almost immediately going out on a walk with a returning friend whom she had not seen for some time.[45] The countryside also offered her unique sexual opportunities. For a closet lesbian in the early twentieth century privacy and discretion were essential, and Dickinson seems not to have felt confident of this in urban settings. Barmes and Catley too valued the group friendships, camaraderie and, sometimes, romantic opportunities that could arise through being together with their peers in the countryside. Catley's navigational prowess allowed him to take a leadership role on walks, bypassing the social diffidence he otherwise suffered from.

Communion   Rural landscapes could also foster a much deeper sense of human connection, one for which the best word is perhaps 'communion'. This was why Johnston was so keen to take his dear friend Wallace on rural walks at any opportunity. Out in the countryside they were at much less risk of interruption than they would have been back in Bolton and could take unfettered delight in being together, rejoicing in their shared Whitmanite ideology and drawing each other's attention to interesting plants, animals and topographical features. Landscape was equally important to Bissell as a medium for deep human connection. 'Christian fellowship' with the young men he led up Ben Nevis had profound spiritual implications in his eyes: he regarded it as a kind of outdoor communion between those present and God. The comradely sisterhood Dickinson found so enriching and enthralling, derived from living

---

[44] Cresswell Diaries, 15 May 1919.

[45] On walking and friendship see T. Edensor, 'Walking in the British Countryside: Reflexivity, Embodied Practices and Ways to Escape', *Body & Society* 6 (2000), 89–91.

and working alongside other young women in an agricultural setting, was also, in the human sense, a form of communion, although Bissell might not have recognized it as such (Johnston probably would have). She first became aware of it, arising it would seem spontaneously from the situation, while working at Molash in Kent alongside members of the Women's Land Army. Rural seclusion freed the women from masculine oversight and they revelled, almost in an outlaw spirit, in the liberty of the woods and fields. Dickinson's hedonism merged with a genuine recognition that farming, if it was to succeed, required hard work, in a neo-Georgic intermingling of agricultural labour and collective pleasure.[46] A shared ruralist ethos united the young women ideologically while also encouraging a responsiveness to beauty that morphed readily into sexuality. Hence it was in the bucolic landscapes of Molash (Kent), Heronswood (Sussex) and Holford (Somerset) that Dickinson formed passionate attachments, one of which became the deepest and perhaps most consequential relationship of her life.

Meaning   The conviction that our lives have a meaning beyond mere animal existence was vitally important to many of the diarists, often expressing itself in social or political activism. Bissell is perhaps the clearest example. War, violence and racism were, as he saw it, the three most terrible scourges of the twentieth century. They were in profound contradiction to his constitutive religious faith. He devoted much of the latter part of his adult life to working for peace, focusing particularly on the nuclear arms race, apartheid and sectarian conflict in Northern Ireland. Mountains were the principal resource he drew on to achieve this.[47] He saw them as symbols of peace, partly because their significance in several major religious traditions gave them ecumenical potential, partly because they were international, in the sense that there were high peaks across the world, and partly because he believed the effort to surmount these peaks was or could be a shared human endeavour. He sought to activate what he saw as these intrinsic properties of mountains not only through his peace climbs but by promoting international exchanges of mountain-related gifts and encouraging the placement of plaques invoking world peace on summits around the world.

Rural landscapes also played important roles for several of the other diarists in creating meaning and enabling them to live in accordance with this. The camps, group walks and international tours she went on helped Barmes develop her socialist values and put them into practice, allowing her to distance

---

[46] On twentieth-century Georgic see Jeffrey Mathes McCarthy, *Green Modernism: Nature and the English Novel, 1900 to 1930* (New York, 2015) and Bullard (ed.), *A History of English Georgic Writing*.

[47] On Methodist peace-making in mid twentieth-century Britain see Michael Hughes, 'Methodism, Peace and War, 1932–45', *Bulletin of the John Rylands Library* 85 (2003), 147–67.

herself from antithetical influences such as advertising, commerce and the press, set aside social conventions and live communally in close proximity to the natural world.[48] Dickinson's outlook was different, although there was a point of contact in her conviction of the superiority of natural materials and folk art to commercial production. Nevertheless, during the long years she lived in the Quantocks, Dickinson remade her life to make it consonant with her beliefs more thoroughly than any of the other diarists. While she was ethically reticent, and it could be argued that her principles were more artistic than ethical, there is nevertheless an impressive consistency. From her source of income (primarily handloom weaving, using natural dye materials she gathered herself) to her leisure activities (folk dancing) to the organizations she joined (craft guilds), everything formed part of a single pattern, one deeply embedded in and dependent on the social landscape and ecology of the Quantocks.

Absorption in the Moment   A conscious sense of meaning and purpose may be one way to achieve a satisfying relationship between self and world. But there are other less cerebral routes to the same goal. One of these is becoming so absorbed in a particular time and place that all consciousness of anything else is lost. Spear Smith and Johnston seem to have felt this at times in their ecstatic response to nature (especially in spring sunshine), and Dickinson in the early stages of her relationship with Elsa Stuttaford. But it was the two Explorers, Catley and Barmes, who experienced it to the fullest degree. The impression landscapes like the Mendips or the South Wiltshire downs made on Catley was so immediate and overwhelming that he figured himself afterwards as an empty vessel into which they had been poured. Ironically, the completeness with which these experiences took possession of him left him unchanged when they receded but, for all that, they were among the most intense and cherished of his life. Barmes's responses to rural landscapes had something in common with this in that they were often aesthetic and certainly intense. She wrote vividly about them: a camp fire in a dark copse, the sea 'restless & almost intolerably deep in hue', moonlight on an alpine lake. Especially when dancing in the open air, her delight in the somatic freedom she found in the natural world could induce an ecstatic state of transcendent union with her companions and the environment around them.

Acceptance   Rural landscapes could also prove instrumental in reconciling self and world in a more profound and lasting way. Dickinson was oppressed by many difficulties, chief among them debilitating emotional fears, family conflict and the breakdown of her relationship with Stuttaford, which caused

---

[48] On early green socialism in Britain see Peter Gould, *Early Green Politics: Back to Nature, Back to the Land, and Socialism in Britain* (Brighton, 1988).

her deep and lasting pain. Her long dwelling in the stable, safe and thoroughly known physical and social landscape of Holford gave her some of the security she had lacked earlier in life, allowing her to develop a quiet appreciation of the beauty of things quite separate from herself. Time and deep immersion in the Holford combes and hills eventually softened her sadness at the loss of Elsa, bestowing a degree of emotional serenity and more inner freedom than when she was younger.

Cresswell experienced something similar. Her childhood was happier than Dickinson's, leaving her less burdened by emotional constraints and limitations, but her father's death brought it to a devastating conclusion, reverberating down the years. A further difficulty was her need to have her own way, which put a strain on many of her relationships. In youth and early adulthood Cresswell engaged extremely actively with rural landscapes but as she grew older she became more sedentary, especially in the warmer months. She spent many hours sitting on quiet hillsides, listening to the larks, watching butterflies or gazing at bluebells. The diary entries that record these occasions breathe serenity and suggest that, as for Dickinson, protracted dwelling in peaceful natural environments had wrought, or at least facilitated, an easing of inner pressures and soothed long-standing pain.[49] Quiet solitude among flowers and birdsong was also a prominent feature of Smith's recovery from acute mental crisis at Titchfield, exemplified in her remarkable nature notebook entry for 26 April 1916. After much tribulation she had by this time renounced her hopes of becoming an artist, or indeed achieving outward distinction of any kind at all, but the pervasive beauty and sense of oneness with nature she experienced among the primroses and sunlight of a local copse enabled her to acknowledge and accept her pain, leaving her at peace with herself.[50] For Hallam, quasi-rural havens such as Swindon's Town Gardens played a comparable role, helping him come to terms with his perceived urban exile and, in due course, his wife's death.

The Flow of Life   Hallam's diaries of earlier years show that he had achieved another kind of relatedness to the world which, if perhaps less transcendentally serene, connected him more closely with the wider flow of public life. His extended accounts of exploring the Lockinge countryside evince three simultaneous levels of experience, each apprehended with remarkable vividness – the present, there immediately around him; his childhood memories of the place where he was, themselves often multi-layered; and the local history and traditions relating to it that had been recounted to him or that he had found out for himself. Thus being in the landscape was intensely personal but at the same time supra-personal for Hallam, embedding his own life history in his

---

[49] Compare the experiences described in Allister, *Refiguring the Map of Sorrow*.
[50] HRO, 19M99/2/9 (Smith Nature Notebooks, 26 Apr. 1916).

community's through collective local knowledge. It was a remarkable, if quite unselfconscious, reconciliation of apparent antinomies, bringing together past and present, human and natural, self and world in a single experience.

Perhaps the closest approach to Hallam's lived understanding of the Lockinge landscape in contemporary published work is a passage from W. H. Hudson's *A Shepherd's Life* (1910). Hudson writes as an outsider – literally looking down on the village from above – and can only attempt to imagine what Hallam knew from within. But in this account of the Vale of the Wylie, bestrewn with traces of prehistory, he sketches the outlines of a comparably encompassing landscape sensibility:

> Up here on the turf, even with the lark singing his shrill music in the blue heavens, you are with the prehistoric dead, yourself for the time one of that innumerable, unsubstantial multitude, invisible in the sun, so that the sheep travelling as they graze, and the shepherd following them, pass through their ranks without suspecting their presence. And from that elevation you look down upon the life of to-day – the visible life, so brief in the individual, which, like the swift silver stream beneath, yet flows on continuously from age to age and for ever.
>
> All this [is] not in the conscious mind when we are in the vale or when we are looking down on it from above: the mind is occupied with nothing but visible nature . . . But if one is familiar with the vale; if one has looked with interest and been deeply impressed with the signs and memorials of past life and of antiquity everywhere present and forming part of the scene, something of it and of all that it represents remains in the subconscious mind to give a significance and feeling to the scene, which affects us here more than in most places.[51]

In the countryside, Hudson, like Hallam, felt himself to be amidst nature and history. Non-human life and the traces of past lives were all around. Yet, in the benign context of the English countryside, they exerted no pressure and presented no threat. This made it easier to feel at one with an ongoing flow of organic life than it might have been in settings – such as most urban ones – where the resistant otherness of living people was harder to escape, except by closing the door on them.

Explaining Popular Ruralism: Summary

How can we account for the patterns of response to and engagement with rural landscapes described above? The most powerful and persistent influence seems to have been character structures and dispositions formed in childhood and youth.[52] Subsequent circumstances could intensify or weaken the affective

[51] W. H. Hudson, *Impressions of the South Wiltshire Downs*. 2nd ed. (London, 1910), 114–15.
[52] This emphasis on the formative influence of childhood is consistent with the tripartite model of landscape aesthetics developed by Steven Bourassa: Steven C. Bourassa, 'A Paradigm for Landscape Aesthetics', *Environment and Behavior* 22 (1990), 787–812. See also Thompson, 'Landscape Perception and Environmental Psychology', 30.

response to landscapes, or bring different aspects to the fore, but on closer examination were less decisive than they sometimes appear to be. The passionate need for freedom that informed Cresswell's ruralism long predated the restrictions she encountered as a woman trying to make her own way in the world and the unwelcome burden of looking after her elderly mother. Similarly, Dickinson's flight to the countryside should not be attributed to the threat of war, illness or class-based violence, to which she was no more exposed than other women of her time and social position. As with Cresswell's need for freedom, Dickinson's excessive fears originated in her childhood: with her withdrawn, hypochondriac mother, unpredictably absent father and the traumatic bankruptcy the family had suffered in recent memory. Hallam exemplifies the same pattern. At first glance it would be natural to attribute his ruralism to his detestation of Swindon and the GWR Works but in fact it was already well established before he left Lockinge, where the deep attachments to people and place that underpinned it were laid down. With Johnston likewise, it was not only or even mainly due to the rigours of his work or the grime of Bolton that he resorted to the countryside, or the best nearby substitute he could find for it. On the contrary, the roots of his ruralism can very clearly be traced to his happy childhood in and around Annan, to the loving but ethically strenuous home he grew up in and to his need to establish his independence from while remaining connected to this. These and other experiences deriving from his childhood established the strong affinity he felt for rural landscapes and the structures of feeling that enabled him to draw so effectively on them for restorative purposes. The same can be said of the other diarists: although social and cultural influences and circumstances arising in adulthood could intensify their ruralism or give it new applications, its groundwork lay far back in the circumstances of their childhood and youth, especially in family structures, dynamics and events, the effect of these on character and disposition and, sometimes, the topographical context in which these influences played out.

If it was indeed psychological structures and patterns of response formed mainly in the first two decades of life that largely shaped the affective significance of landscapes, many conventional explanations for the popularity of the countryside in the late nineteenth and early twentieth centuries are open to question. Urbanization, industrialization, class differentiation and war may have been less significant in this respect than sometimes assumed, unless it can be shown that they had marked effects on the nature of family life. War, so often placed at the centre of narratives of social change in twentieth-century Britain, had surprisingly limited effects on most of the diarists.[53] All of them lived through at least one of the two world wars but only Catley's life was

---

[53] A widely read recent history of twentieth-century Britain explains that 'we think the Second World War was a watershed in the twentieth century': Julie-Marie Strange,

indubitably transformed by this, through the death of his father near Arras in 1917. In countries where the effects of the two world wars were traumatic for a higher proportion of the population, as across much of Continental Europe during the Second World War, the relationship between war and the affective significance of landscapes may well have been different.[54]

Just as the evidence presented in this book places a question mark over the significance of 'big events' in explaining the affective relationship between people and landscape, so it does over cultural change. As we have seen, the eight diarists drew freely on a diverse range of rural representations, adopting and adapting elements selectively according to their exigencies, while ignoring or rejecting other elements. Furthermore, they were creative and innovative in developing new landscape practices where the existing cultural repertoire did not meet their requirements. So it is perhaps unsurprising that the changing representation of the countryside in media such as publishing or landscape painting appears not to have affected the everyday meanings of rural landscape as decisively as deeper-seated, more personal influences. For example, historians such as Alun Howkins and Martin Wiener devoted much attention to analysing the cultural rise of the 'South Country' – the shift in ruralist sensibilities from the Romantic celebration of rugged northern peaks to the late Victorian/Edwardian idealization of the pastoral landscapes associated with southern England.[55] There is ample evidence of this in poetry and landscape painting.[56] Ironically, however, the only diarist whose landscape tastes fit the 'South Country' mould well is the Scottish Johnston, and in his case not because he had been influenced by poets like Tennyson or painters like Constable, but because his vision of nature was a gentle, benign one with no room for Romantic extremity. The other diarists all responded passionately to mountains (Dickinson, Spear Smith, Bissell, Barmes) or wild moorland (Cresswell, Catley), except for Hallam who rarely ventured far from home so hardly saw any non-'South Country' landscape.

Often linked to the rise of the 'South Country' is the nexus between the countryside and English national identity that, many historians believe, developed in this period. I would not wish to question the strength of this connection at the level of published discourse: many studies bear witness to it, although its nature and implications continue to be debated.[57] However, the

---

Francesca Carnevali and Paul Johnson, *Twentieth-Century Britain: Economic, Cultural and Social Change*. 2nd ed. (Harlow, 2007), 3.

[54] Schama, *Landscape and Memory*, 120–34.

[55] Howkins, 'The Discovery of Rural England', 62–88. Wiener, *English Culture and the Decline of the Industrial Spirit*, 41–2; Calder, *The Myth of the Blitz*, 180–208.

[56] David Gervais, *Literary Englands: Versions of 'Englishness' in Modern Writing* (Cambridge, 1993), chapter 1. See also Louis James, 'Landscape in Nineteenth-Century Literature', in G. E. Mingay (ed.), *The Rural Idyll* (London, 1989).

[57] Readman, *Storied Ground*; Matless, *Landscape and Englishness*; Mandler, 'Against "Englishness"'; Miller, 'Urban Dreams and Rural Realities: Land and Landscape in English

conventional historiographical assumption that national identity was central to popular *experience* of the countryside is another matter altogether. Rural landscapes carried intense associations and meanings for each of the people studied in this book but patriotism did not figure prominently among these. Most of the time it was too abstract, too remote from the pressing concerns of personal life. It was only in special (notably liminal) circumstances that it came, fleetingly, to the fore. One example is Cresswell's night walk along the North Devon cliffs, looking at the lighthouses flashing all the way along the Bristol Channel, 'tireless guardians of England's coast'.[58] Another corresponds to a more familiar cultural trope – Barmes's joyful response to sighting the 'snowy cliffs' and 'long rolling hills' of Kent as she returned by ferry from France.[59] England's territorial identity was so closely associated with its island-ness in this period that it is hardly surprising the coast could elicit strong patriotic responses, especially in circumstances that drew attention to its liminality.[60] However, once the coast was out of sight, Englishness was usually out of mind. Whether they were one side of a national border or the other made little discernible difference to how the eight diarists responded to rural landscapes. It is impossible without contextual information to tell Johnston's lush descriptions of English and Scottish riverside meadows apart. Cresswell exulted in exploring Bavarian valleys in much the same way she did the 'wilds' of her own country. She consoled herself on her tearful departure from Oberammergau by reflecting that 'the mountains on which we rambled are unchangeable', effectively the same thought as her later observation that '[t]he [English] country never changes except when it is built on'.[61] It is true that she disliked the Italian landscape but this, as she confessed, was because her 'heart [was] in Devon'.[62] She felt equally 'an exile' in Cumberland and had little time for Cornwall either.[63] Spear Smith's dreamy vistas of Fairfield (England), the Llanberis Pass (Wales) and the Great Glen (Scotland) stirred similar hopes and longings, while Dickinson thought the English Lakes 'just like Switzerland'.[64]

Culture, 1920–1945', *Rural History* 6 (1995), 4–37; Patrick Wright, *On Living in an Old Country: The National Past in Contemporary Britain* (London, 1985); Howkins, 'The Discovery of Rural England'; Wiener, *English Culture and the Decline of the Industrial Spirit*.

[58] Cresswell, *Barnstaple*, 39. Mais was similarly fascinated by the lighthouses of the Bristol Channel. Robson, *An Unrepentant Englishman*, 23–4.

[59] Barmes Diary, 25 Aug. 1929. On responses of homeward-bound Englishmen and women to the White Cliffs of Dover see Readman, *Storied Ground*, 25–51, especially 38–40.

[60] Brian Lavery, *The Island Nation: A History of Britain and the Sea* (London, 2005); Ken Lunn and Ann Day, 'Britain As Island: National Identity and the Sea', in Helen Brocklehurst and Robert Phillips (eds.), *History, Nationhood and the Question of Britain* (Basingstoke, 2004). See also Readman, *Storied Ground*, 25, 32–4, 38–9.

[61] Cresswell, *A Retrospect*, 62; Cresswell Diaries, 28 Mar. 1928.

[62] Cresswell Diaries, 4 Nov. 1925.

[63] Cresswell Diaries, 26 Jun. 1922 and 26 Aug. 1919.

[64] Dickinson Diaries, 18 Dec. 1907.

Bissell's ascents of the Zugspitze (Germany), Mönch (Switzerland) or Cader Idris (Wales) were exhilarating, but essentially interchangeable, spiritual experiences. Barmes thought the alpine flora 'similar to ours, but more profuse', while her numinous descriptions of Chanctonbury Ring (Sussex) and Les Houches (Chamonix) are closely comparable.[65] Undoubtedly landscape was central to English national identity in this period, but the same does not hold true in reverse, at least affectively. Perhaps people simply did not think about national identity very often. Certainly it was not a major part of their experience of landscape, either on a day-to-day level or in relation to its deeper meanings and functions in their lives.

The same could be said of the 'moral geographies' that Matless, Brace and others have argued were projected onto rural spatial practices during this period.[66] While these are amply present in published writing about the countryside, their imprint at the level of experience was slight, at least in the case of the individuals considered here. Trespass for private pleasure (rather than as a political act), driving carelessly, picnicking anywhere and everywhere, knocking down walls and frightening the cattle feature in the diaries studied without a trace of guilt or discomfort, while there are few or no indications of the moralistic concern to regulate behaviour in the countryside that Matless has described as a dominant and dominating ruralist discourse in the first half of the twentieth century.[67] Perhaps when people were in the public eye these discourses may have had more purchase over their behaviour but when they were in private or with intimate companions, many other motivations and influences seem to have made themselves felt.

Does the Experience of Landscape Have a History?

If neither public events nor cultural change had as much influence over the private experience of landscape as has often been imagined, it is not unreasonable to ask whether the experience of landscape can be said to have a history in the conventional sense. The evidence this book presents does indeed suggest that fundamental, even timeless, aspects of life play a decisive role in the experience of landscape – the death of people we love, deep-seated emotional fears, resistance to constraint. It seems quite possible that wherever secure, stable, socially and environmentally sheltered landscapes like the Holford hills have existed, there will have been people like Dickinson for

---

[65] Barmes Diary, 30 Jul. 1930.

[66] Matless, *Landscape and Englishness*; Catherine Brace, 'A Pleasure Ground for the Noisy Herds? Incompatible Encounters with the Cotswolds and England, 1900–1950', *Rural History* 11 (2000), 75–94.

[67] D. Matless, 'Visual Culture and Geographical Citizenship: England in the 1940s', *Journal of Historical Geography* 22 (1996), 424–39.

whom they provided sanctuary, whatever the discursive context. However, even if, as argued here, the dominant influences on the experience of landscape were psychological, it would be quite mistaken to infer that the experience of landscape has no significant history, since individual psychology is profoundly affected by family structures, relationships and behavioural norms, which plainly do have a history. It is possible to make tentative connections between three of the four major patterns of response to landscape identified in *Lifescapes* and this wider history. There is a close link between Adherer ruralism, for example, and loss of a parent in childhood or youth. All three of the subjects of this book who suffered this (Cresswell, Hallam and Catley) had pronounced Adherer characteristics. None of the other five did so except Johnston, separated from his parents in his youth, and haunted by a fear of their demise. An inverse correlation between Adherer ruralism and parental life expectancy, which rose rapidly in the late nineteenth and early twentieth centuries, could therefore be anticipated.[68] It is probably not an accident, then, that Adherer traits are prominent in three of the four earliest-born diarists, but only in Catley among the four latest-born – and since he lost his father at the age of six, he is in a sense the exception that proves the rule.

Connecting Withdrawer ruralism with historical change is more difficult because its genesis is less clear. Dickinson's Withdrawer traits were linked to insufficient parental care and attention, but Spear Smith's to overprotectiveness and a lengthy childhood separation from her brother. Both lacked a stable home for a significant part of their childhoods: Dickinson because her parents moved frequently, preferring at times to rent or even live in hotels than buy a permanent home, and Spear Smith because her parents moved to-and-fro between India and England, and after returning to England sent her and Alic on extended visits to relatives. More research is needed before it is possible to confirm how common Withdrawer ruralism was, whether there were changes in its incidence and, if there were, how far this can be connected with wider patterns of demographic or familial change.

Restorer ruralism may have a more specific historical context, although as ever the narrow basis for generalization must be kept in mind. Both Johnston and Bissell were powerfully influenced by Protestant nonconformity, even if Johnston subsequently lost his faith, and it could be argued that this was the source of their deep-seated ethical assurance (while acknowledging that the strong, loving families in which each grew up is an at least equally compelling explanation). Some historians argue that Britain remained a broadly Christian society until the 1960s but church attendance, at least in the Protestant

---

[68] Clare Griffiths and Anita Brock, 'Twentieth Century Mortality Trends in England and Wales', *Health Statistics Quarterly* 18 (2003), 5–17.

churches, began to decline much earlier.[69] As the long tradition of Protestant nonconformity faded, and with it perhaps the moral energies it had once generated, did Restorer ruralism fade too?

Conversely, there are indications that Explorer ruralism may have become more prevalent in the late nineteenth and early twentieth centuries. On the whole, rural landscapes mattered more in relation to identity, self-discovery and self-development to the later-born subjects of this book. None of the diarists born before 1885 showed much concern with these issues whereas they were pressing preoccupations for Spear Smith, born 1885, Catley, born 1911 and to a lesser extent Barmes, born 1907. It seems possible, then, that the self-reflexive possibilities of rural landscape experience were more highly valued in the later part of the period. It has sometimes been claimed – albeit more often by sociologists than historians – that 'modernity' was characterized by greater individualism, self-consciousness and reflexive self-management.[70] While this remains unproven, it is beyond doubt that most English people were better educated and had more leisure time than their predecessors a century before and so had a wider range of conceptual and linguistic tools at their disposal, and more time for reading, writing, self-expression and self-development.[71] For people like this rural landscapes would have offered rich opportunities, in much the same way as they did for Barmes and Catley. This suggests that Explorer ruralism may have been a central mode of popular landscape experience in mid-twentieth-century England, and perhaps beyond.

How Much Progress towards a Deep History of Landscape Has Lifescapes Made?

Having sketched some of the potential connections between the conclusions of this book and wider demographic and social changes, it may be useful to review the progress *Lifescapes* has made towards a deep history of landscape in modern England. The first step in opening up a recalcitrant, seemingly inaccessible area of history is always to develop a suitable methodology. My initial intention was to adopt a quantitative approach, attempting to identify and record key dimensions of the rural landscape interactions (such as the frequency, length and location of walks and bike rides) of as many people as feasible, preferably on a rigorous statistical basis. While I still think there is much scope for further quantitative historical research on the outward aspects of rural leisure and landscape practices, it gradually became apparent that the

---

[69] Callum G. Brown, *The Death of Christian Britain: Understanding Secularisation, 1800–2000* (London, 2000); Hugh McLeod, *Religion and Society in England, 1850–1914* (Basingstoke, 1996). Robin Gill, *The Empty Church Revisited* (London, 2017), 110–68.

[70] For a useful summary of this debate see Simon Duncan, 'The World We Have Made? Individualisation and Personal Life in the 1950s', *Sociological Review* 59 (2011), 242–65.

[71] Hinton, *Seven Lives*, 23.

fragmentary and incommensurate nature of the source material bearing on the more inward aspects which most interested me did not readily lend itself to statistical analysis. I also became increasingly aware, on the one hand, of how subtle, complex and varied the affective meanings of landscape can be and, on the other, of how rarely we make them explicit, even to ourselves. The only hope of retrieving something so obscure and intangible seemed to be through intensive biographical research.[72] Locating suitable source material proved to be one of the most difficult and time-consuming elements of the project, given that I wanted not only to catch the traces of these evanescent impressions and responses but also to contextualize them as comprehensively as possible in relation to other facets of the individual's life. Nevertheless, after much searching of diary bibliographies, life writing resources and online catalogues, many emails to archivists and follow-up visits to record offices, and with valuable help from my former PhD student Sue Clifford, I was eventually able to find ample source material for my purposes.

I then needed to develop a method of assimilating and analysing this copious material. A certain amount of selection was possible, for example in diaries where successive entries seemed to have little or no relevance to landscape. However, I came to the conclusion that, at least for the individuals under study, almost all aspects of their lives were bound up in some degree with the affective significance of landscapes to them, so an unduly selective approach would carry heavy interpretative costs. By contrast, allowing myself to become as fully absorbed as possible in the source material proved highly effective and rewarding. For each of the diarists I was able to identify a rich and varied range of landscape interactions; to trace the development of these interactions across decades, and, in some cases, almost entire lifetimes; to show how these landscape interactions responded to other developments in the individual's life, for example in relation to education, employment, housing, place of residence, religion, politics and relationships; to assess how far different life stages were associated with their own distinct modes of relating to rural landscapes; and to identify many of the core meanings and functions of landscape in the lives of the eight individuals. The upshot was that it proved possible to reconstruct the place of landscape in their lives in far more depth and detail than I had anticipated. However, it should be acknowledged that the method is not a quick one – on the contrary, it depends on deep immersion in extremely rich and extensive source material, requiring many years of study.

Furthermore, even after the personal landscapes of the individuals concerned have been reconstructed in this way, what we obtain is a kind of

---

[72] In this respect my arguments align with calls for a 'biographical turn' in History. See Renders, Haan and Harmsma, eds., *The Biographical Turn*; D. R. Meister, 'The Biographical Turn and the Case for Historical Biography', *History Compass* 16 (2018), 16:e12436. https://doi.org/10.1111/hic3.12436.

collective landscape *biography* rather than the deep *history* of landscape that this book set out to develop: a few boreholes into an otherwise unknown stratum. Is this as far as a deep history approach can take us? Does the biographical method on which it depends inevitably yield results that are too irreducibly particular to be usable in constructing a wider history of landscape experience? To go beyond this, to make the transition from deep biographies to a deep history, common factors in the landscape experiences of the individuals studied must be found. The most fundamental common factor I have been able to identify is that for each of the diarists, deep-seated psychological characteristics best explain the affective significance of landscape. Beyond this, it proved possible to develop a rough typology of affective relationships to rural landscapes in this period (the Adherer–Withdrawer–Restorer–Explorer framework). This typology, however, is tentative and incomplete: much additional research will be required to achieve anything like a comprehensive and authoritative account of affective landscapes in modern Britain. Moreover, it is difficult to envisage a short-cut method to identifying the underlying psychological coordinates of an individual's relationship to landscape. Nevertheless, *Lifescapes* has demonstrated that sources exist which, suitably analysed, can give historians some purchase on this, so the research agenda implied, although time-consuming, is not impossible. Only thus, indeed, can we hope to take the measure of the extraordinarily diverse, and sometimes extraordinarily profound, ways in which landscape mattered to people in the past.

A second test of how much progress *Lifescapes* has made towards the deep history envisaged is how far it has been possible to connect it with a wider established history. This is a challenging proposition, not only because the typology of relationships to affective landscapes developed in this book remains provisional, but also because the causes of the patterns are complex and, in some cases, unclear (as for Withdrawers). Despite this, it has been possible to associate three of the four major patterns observed with long-term demographic and social changes, in particular increasing adult life expectancy, the decline of nonconformity and the rise of education and leisure. It seems likely that some of the subsidiary patterns identified in *Lifescapes* were also connected with wider changes of this kind. No sooner were Bissell and Barmes out in the countryside with others, for example, than they began to build relationships, seeking to foster a warm group camaraderie that embraced all those present. Indeed, there was nothing either valued more about rural landscapes than their scope to catalyse intra-group union in this way. He was an apolitical Methodist who read almost nothing apart from the Bible whereas she was a Jewish socialist with a passion for education, so the social and cultural influences bearing on them were very different and can hardly explain the similarity in their behaviour. What perhaps can is the one obvious thing they had in common. This was that they had unusually many siblings –

Bissell was one of five, Barmes one of nine – with whom each had close and affectionate relationships. On their rural walks, camps and climbs they may have been trying, consciously or otherwise, to recreate an affective pattern that they found comfortable, familiar and rewarding. Did other people from large, happy families also find this kind of group camaraderie especially appealing? If so, the fall in completed family size during the second half of the twentieth century may well have contributed to the decline in collective rural leisure practices (such as youth hostelling) that took place over the same period.

Many other psychological patterns are of course also strongly influenced by family structures and relationships, which have a clear and now reasonably well-understood history.[73] Further research should be able to link this much more extensively with the historical experience of landscape if, as *Lifescapes* argues, differential psychological structures play a decisive role in forming our affective relationship with it. However, doing so is contingent on establishing a more comprehensive and secure typology of affective landscape relationships than has been possible here, so it must be admitted that this dimension of the deep history of landscape remains comparatively undeveloped.

The Characteristics of Popular Ruralism

Walking and Other Modes of Landscape Encounter

In addition to its main concern with explaining popular ruralism *Lifescapes* has yielded a serendipitous harvest of perspectives on its character. It has become clear, for example, that walking, despite the emphasis placed on it, was only one among a much wider range of rural spatial practices. We may have underestimated how energetically people interacted with the landscape: few simply passed through. Dickinson is a good example – as well as walking she enjoyed playing, even as an adult, in bracken and woods, foraging, gathering and harvesting, crawling in search of flowers, lying in long grass, being buffeted by the wind and swinging in her hammock.[74] She also picnicked, sketched, photographed and went on car tours. Other modes of engaging with the landscape recurrent in the eight diaries include not only recognized leisure pursuits like cycling, boating, swimming, fishing, camping and hostelling but also more informal and intimate activities such as exploring, cooking, dancing, singing, sitting, reading and writing. Each had its own distinct ambience and

---

[73] Robert Woods, *The Demography of Victorian England and Wales* (Cambridge, 2000); For the twentieth century see Pooley and Turnbull, 'Counterurbanization'; Joanne Bailey, 'The History of Mum and Dad: Recent Historical Research on Parenting in England from the 16th to 20th Centuries', *History Compass* 12 (2014), 489–507; Paul Atkinson et al., 'Patterns of Infant Mortality in Rural England and Wales, 1850–1910', *Economic History Review* 70 (2017), 1268–90.

[74] Crawling in search of flowers: Dickinson Diary, 22 Sep. 1944.

implications, serving different purposes and yielding different satisfactions. Without question, walking was the central mode of landscape experience, but an exclusive focus on it at the expense of other modes, many of them more fully embodied, intense and absorbing, distorts our understanding.[75]

Collecting and Connecting

One such mode, gathering, was especially prevalent and rich in meaning. Blackberrying features regularly in the Catley, Cresswell, Dickinson, Johnston and Hallam diaries, as does flower-picking in the first four. Hallam was more interested in foraging for wild food such as raspberries, watercress and mushrooms, possibly reflecting his working-class origins. Johnston went nut-gathering as a child and used to cut pieces of wood to carve into whistles from hazel trees. Catley and his siblings collected 'stick', mushrooms, whortle-berries and elderberries, the last of which they made into jelly.[76] But it was Dickinson whose gathering was most persistent and varied. Among the plants and materials she collected from the countryside were 'armfuls and basketfuls' of cowslips; primroses, foxgloves, heather, bracken and catkins; blackberries, bilberries, chestnuts and watercress; lichens and larch bark for dyeing wool; firewood; decorative twigs, moss, stones and coloured leaves; and even sand and grit for a rock garden.[77]

The diarists had many motivations for gathering. Simple appetite and the pleasure of taste was especially important for children: Johnston wrote vividly about the 'brummles' (blackberries) that 'hung in very tempting clusters' in the lanes around Annan when he was a boy. For some, including Catley and Hallam in their childhood and youth, gathering served to relieve pressure on straitened family budgets. Those like Dickinson and Cresswell with seemingly unlimited physical energy enjoyed the activity and purpose that gathering gave to their outings. Free food provided relief from the oppressive ubiquity of the cash nexus in modern Britain; gathering also confirmed the plenitude of nature, which mattered particularly to Cresswell and Johnston, in the latter case partly because it spoke to his Whitmanite ideology.[78]

Above all, however, gathering was a means of connecting. Almost invariably it was a collective activity, binding those undertaking it together in a shared objective: Hallam with the Whittle brothers up on the downs, and with Sophie during their courtship and marriage; Cresswell with her close friend Mary Alban; Dickinson with lovers, companions and pupils, and Catley with his

---

[75] For a valuable recent study of walking in a historical context see Bryant, Burns and Readman, *Walking Histories*.

[76] BA, 41419/24, 18 and 21 Aug. 1933; BA, 41419/33, 15 and 16 Aug. 1936.

[77] See, for example, Dickinson Diary, 14 Oct. 1912: 'Coming back we . . . gathered glorious beech and maple leaves and bracken.'

[78] Richard Mabey and Marjorie Blamey, *Food for Free* (London, 1972).

siblings. Gathering could connect people across spatial and temporal barriers too. Dickinson sent snowdrops and violets to her brother Leslie, and Cresswell heather to her niece Clarice, both far away in London. Gathering was a constitutive family tradition for the Catleys and after their mother's death, Fred, Will and Gladys used it as a way of holding on to each other and shoring up their diminished sense of family. In Fred's case, and perhaps for the others, it was one more of his attempts to connect across the years to his father, for whom self-sufficient growing and harvesting had been a central value.

Among the many kinds of connection gathering afforded, the most fundamental perhaps was between the human and the natural. Rather than just perceiving or transiting the landscape, gatherers participated in it, getting grazed, stung, pricked and berry-stained, aligning themselves with the animals and birds that feed on and use for nests and shelters the same materials. For several of the diarists, the converse – taking the country into the city, or nature indoors – was of prime importance too. Wildflowers brought into Exeter, whether by the flower-seller William Burnett, country girls in town for the day or she herself, gave Cresswell special delight. Catley's efforts to erase the boundary between the wild and the domestic reached their apogee after he moved to the countryside in 1945. He took pleasure in discovering the distinctive spots where particular species or natural resources were to be found, brought them back assiduously to his house and garden and wrote a book, *Flowers in a Village*, that even in its title insists on the harmony between nature and culture in rural life.

Scale and the Experience of Rural Landscapes

Although there has been some interesting research on how people travel through landscape, especially the implications of moving at different speeds, less attention has been paid to the remarkable contrasts in the scale at which landscape was experienced, a feature that emerges clearly from this study.[79] At one end of the spectrum was Spear Smith, for whom the largest important landscape feature was a single mountain, common, copse or row of trees, but who primarily valued micro-scale features such as flowers or birds' nests. For Hallam, Lockinge and its countryside mattered most, although he later developed a secondary county-level affinity for Berkshire. Cresswell, whose ruralism had so much in common with Hallam's, also identified with landscape at a county level. Few landscape features outside Devon had any lasting significance for her but everything within Devon mattered. Dickinson hardly cared where her landscapes were, but very much about their seclusion. After arriving

---

[79] Una Brogan, 'Two-Wheeled Sensibility: Sensory Engagement with Place in British, American and French Cycling Narratives, 1880–1914', *Cahiers Victoriens et Edouardiens* 83 (2016).

in the Quantocks, the boundedness, apparent separateness and increasingly deep familiarity of the hills and combes around Holford became vitally important to her – a territory defined geomorphically and by the range of her daily walks rather than administratively. Catley energetically identified and explored new territories for himself, each of which had different connotations and functions. The most important was his Chew valley home-from-home – separate enough from Bristol that he felt shielded from what he experienced as his oppressive school and later work environments, but close enough to be easy of access. Other territories, defined in relation to what he considered their distinctive landscape characteristics, served other functions but all shared the crucial feature that they were 'his'. Bissell's feeling about landscape, as about nature, was generalizing and undiscriminating until he developed his special relationship with Ben Nevis and the Fort William area. He was the only one of the eight for whom the landscape he most cherished was at such a distance from his home and the only one for whom it was in another country. This suggests that the very different scales at which people experienced and valued rural landscapes depended principally on how these landscapes functioned in their lives, although the way they were accessed mattered too: Spear Smith and Hallam, whose primary landscape identifications were perhaps on the smallest scale, almost always walked, whereas Catley, with his more far-flung allegiances, often cycled.

Private and Social Landscapes

The scale at which landscape was apprehended relates to the extent to which it had a social dimension. Spear Smith's landscapes were essentially private, shared only with her brother. Other people could be an almost unbearable intrusion on landscapes that at times became extensions of herself, infused with her own delicate sensibility. Catley's landscapes were social in that he frequently chose to explore them in the company of others – his brother Will, youth hostelling companions, various not-quite girlfriends. This social dimension mattered to him and entered into the quality and nature of the landscape experience. Nevertheless, the people he was with were invariably visitors too: he remained as cut off from the people who lived and worked on the landscapes he passed through as was Spear Smith. Conversely, the landscape Hallam most valued, the countryside around Lockinge, was genuinely communal. As the son of a farmworker, he knew it as a working and living as well as leisure space – not only on his own immediate account but also through his family, friends and acquaintances and through his ample knowledge of local history and folklore.

Vision and the 'Tourist Gaze'

Although there is a real sense in which someone like Hallam experienced landscape more authentically than those who were merely visitors, *Lifescapes* suggests that the so-called tourist gaze, epitomized by Dickinson, should not too quickly be dismissed as superficial.[80] While Dickinson could indeed be astoundingly unaware of the lives and needs of the residents of the 'quaint' country cottages she eagerly photographed, she was also, of all the subjects of this book, the one whose ruralism eventually pervaded and structured her life most comprehensively. Moreover, the aspects of rurality that came to matter so deeply to her – among them vernacular architecture, rural crafts and folk tradition – cannot be separated from the 'tourist gaze' that informed her photography and rural car touring.

The scholarly critique of the tourist gaze derives in part from a wider suspicion of purely visual modes of apprehension, which are often regarded as detached, disembodied, separating and superficial.[81] Yet all the subjects of this book, even Dickinson, experienced rural landscapes in richly multisensory ways, through smell, taste, touch and hearing as well as sight.[82] While scholars may well be justified in critiquing the *representation* of the countryside as overwhelmingly visual, the everyday *experience* of rural landscapes seems to have been anything but.[83]

Town and Country

The 'tourist gaze', as it applies to the countryside, is paradigmatically the idealizing gaze of an urban observer. This, it is often assumed, actually reflects experience in, and attitudes to, the city rather than the country.[84] Hence pro-ruralism is frequently equated with anti-urbanism, and the second is taken to explain the first.[85] This is linked to a way of understanding the so-called rural idyll that construes it as a reaction to or at least a consequence of the Industrial Revolution, an approach characteristic of the influential currents of scholarship deriving from Raymond Williams's *The Country and the City*.[86] As an interpretation of literary and high

---

[80] On the tourist gaze see Urry, *The Tourist Gaze*. For a more lenient view see Readman, *Storied Ground*, 261–2.

[81] M. B. Kearnes, 'Seeing Is Believing Is Knowing: Towards a Critique of Pure Vision', *Australian Geographical Studies* 38 (2000), 332–6. See also Michael S. Carolan, 'More-Than-Representational Knowledge/s of the Countryside: How We Think As Bodies', *Sociologia Ruralis* 48 (2008), 408–22.

[82] Compare Martin Phillips, 'Baroque Rurality in an English Village', *Journal of Rural Studies* 33 (2014), 56–70; Isis Brook, 'Aesthetic Appreciation of Landscape', in Howard et al. (eds.), *The Routledge Companion to Landscape Studies* (London, 2018), 43–4.

[83] This has been recognized for years by archaeologists and medieval/early modern landscape historians influenced by phenomenology but less so perhaps by modernists.

[84] Miller, 'Urban Dreams and Rural Realities'.

[85] Thomas, *Man and the Natural World*, 268; Lowe, 'The Rural Idyll Defended', 113; Bunce, *The Countryside Ideal*, 11.

[86] Wiener, *English Culture and the Decline of the Industrial Spirit*; Howkins, 'The Discovery of Rural England'; Miller, 'Urban Dreams and Rural Realities'; Tim Cloudsley,

cultural attitudes to the countryside, this has proved fertile, illuminating and in many respects compelling. However, the evidence on which this book is based suggests that anti-urbanism was less central to popular experience of the countryside: none of the diarists were drawn to rural landscapes primarily by anti-urbanism (or anti-industrialism). Perhaps, on reflection, this is not surprising. Many writers and artists felt a responsibility to address the wider issues of their times, of which, in the nineteenth and early twentieth centuries, urbanization and industrialization were probably the prime examples. But as revisionist research on the Industrial Revolution has demonstrated, for most people, things changed slowly.[87] As ever, personal considerations dominated everyday life – food, health, relationships, income and expenditure, housing, work. Few of these would have been obviously linked to urbanization and industrialization in most people's minds, even housing and work. People who grew up in a town, or had worked from the outset in a factory or mine, probably took this largely for granted. Catley, Bristol born and bred, is a good example: his diaries show that most of the time he went about his hometown without taking much notice of it one way or the other. Only during the early 1930s, when he was discontented with himself, his work and his personal relationships, and was under the influence of left-wing political thought, are there sharp comments in his diaries on the ugliness of Bristol's slums and factories. People who moved to an urban area from a rural background or into factory work from other employment may have experienced things differently, and it is interesting that the two most anti-urban diarists, Johnston and Hallam, both had rural childhoods.

The urban landscapes that inspired the strongest dislike were usually associated with heavy industry – the factory smoke and bleach works effluent so detested by Johnston in Bolton, the 'dreadful places, including Preston and Carnforth' that Dickinson passed through on a journey to the Lake District, the 'monster cranes by the river, chemical works' Catley railed against in Bristol.[88] While only Hallam, of the people studied in this book, worked in a factory, his hatred of it certainly contributed to his ruralist disposition. But this is also a reminder that, even in the nineteenth century, only a minority of people were employed in the industrial sector.[89] Most others had no more than incidental contact with factories or industry and it is difficult to believe that this can have affected them sufficiently to account for the scale of ruralism in the period.

'Romanticism and the Industrial Revolution in Britain', *History of European Ideas* 12 (1990), 611–35. For an assessment of the influence of *The Country and the City* see Gerald M. MacLean, Donna Landry and Joseph Ward, *The Country and the City Revisited: England and the Politics of Culture, 1550–1850* (Cambridge, 1999).

[87] Emma Griffin, *A Short History of the British Industrial Revolution* (Basingstoke, 2010), 144–61.

[88] Catley Diaries, BRO, 41419/22, 2 Nov. 1932.

[89] William D. Rubinstein, *Capitalism, Culture and Decline in Britain, 1750–1990* (London, 1993), 24.

Even Hallam and Johnston loved the country long before they learnt to hate towns: it would be more true to say that their anti-urbanism was due to their pro-ruralism than the other way round.

If anti-urbanism and anti-industrialism were relatively minor causes of ruralism, this would help to explain why rural landscapes continued to be cherished throughout the twentieth century and, at least if we can judge by the membership figures of leading rural conservation organizations like the National Trust and the RSPB, remain so at the time of writing.[90] Polluted towns have been cleaned up and industry has declined precipitously but the countryside shows no signs of becoming less popular.[91]

The comparatively subdued place of anti-urbanism in the affective signifi-cance of rural landscapes may also shed light on the failure of the garden city movement to transform settlement patterns and society in the way its foun-der, Ebenezer Howard, anticipated.[92] Howard construed town and country as antithetical poles that needed to be synthesized – hence his concept of 'town-country', or the garden city, which was supposed to combine the best of the two.[93] But Howard presupposed that people have a single, stable preference. That was true for some of those studied here – Johnston, Hallam and Catley, for example – whose preference was unambiguously for the countryside. Others, however, felt no contradiction in enjoying both countryside and town: it was possible to be enthusiastically pro-urban while also being enthusiastically pro-rural.[94] Barmes, with her passionate delight in the medieval towns of northern France but also in the South Downs and the Alps, is a good example. Bissell, awe-struck though he was by Ben Nevis, felt thoroughly at home in Dudley and identified strongly with the town. But of all the diarists it was Cresswell whose ruralism was most starkly incompatible with Howard's vision. Although she loved her hometown of Exeter deeply, she fled frequently from it to the remotest 'wilds' of the Devon countryside. This dialectical drive towards both company and solitude

---

[90] Membership of the National Trust passed 5 million in 2017. www.nationaltrust.org.uk/news/membership-reaches-five-million [accessed 14 Oct. 2018]. The RSPB had 1.2 million members in 2017–18. www.rspb.org.uk/globalassets/downloads/documents/abouttherspb/annual-review-archive/annual-review-17-18.pdf, page 3 [accessed 14 Oct. 2018].

[91] A Countryside Agency survey found that more than half the UK population would like to live in the countryside, for example (c.1998): Peter Webber, *The U.K.* (Cheltenham, 1998), 24.

[92] On the garden city movement see Stephen Ward, *The Peaceful Path: Building Garden Cities and New Towns* (Hatfield, 2016); Peter Hall and Colin Ward, *Sociable Cities: The Legacy of Ebenezer Howard* (Chichester, 1998); Standish Meacham, *Regaining Paradise: Englishness and the Early Garden City Movement* (New Haven, 1998).

[93] Ebenezer Howard, *Garden Cities of Tomorrow: Being the Second Edition of 'Tomorrow: A Peaceful Path to Real Reform'* (London, 1902), 15–19.

[94] Compare Readman's plausible suggestion that the cultural resonance of the Thames owed much to the way it linked rural to urban, past to present. Readman, *Storied Ground*, 251–2, 242–3.

reflected a division within her own nature, between powerful needs for freedom and authority, the wilds and home. Despite their apparent incompatibility, each depended on the satisfaction of the other for its continuing fulfilment. Exeter would have become stifling had she not been able to escape to places like Dartmoor; conversely, were it not for the affective security and existential rootedness she found in Exeter, Dartmoor might always have seemed as cold and empty of meaning as it did on 13 September 1935, shortly after the death of her servant and intimate companion Mary Kitto.[95] Much of the value Cresswell found in town and country was therefore contingent on their separateness; 'town-country' would have been anathema to her, and anyone like her.

Cresswell's case underlines that town and country are states of mind rather than fixed spatial categories. What is regarded as 'rural' sometimes plays vital roles in the psychic economy of individuals, and people will make use of the best 'rural' that is in practice available to them. This is the explanation for the apparently disproportionate value attached to sometimes tiny areas of undeveloped land in the middle of urban areas. Johnston's Raikes Wood, Catley's Brandon Hill, Hallam's Town Gardens and (in her childhood) Dickinson's Hampstead Heath are examples. Such *rus in urbe* places can have an affective, functional significance quite out of proportion to their apparent landscape value, even though they are often quickly relinquished when a 'better' rural becomes available. Johnston no longer visited Raikes Wood, which had once meant so much to him, after moving from Bolton to his 'little countrified home' in Lostock.

The Countryside and Nature

These indications that there was a hierarchy of rural places, with those that were furthest from urban areas being preferred, might seem to suggest that a major motivation for the diarists' ruralism was to get away from other people into 'nature'. But many of the most vital functions of the countryside for the diarists were social rather than anti-social, in the sense that they were about creating, maintaining or strengthening connections with other people rather than turning away from them. In some instances the connections which people sought to maintain through landscape were with the past, as with Hallam's devotion to Lockinge and Cresswell's to her father's Devon. From this perspective 'nature' in the narrow sense, exclusive of human life, was not enough. The limitation of the non-human natural world was that it does not have a meaningful history: at the level of perception, nature is perennially the same (dinosaurs notwithstanding). The nearest thing to a past that nature has is the seasons, which mattered greatly to most of the people considered in this book.

[95] Cresswell Diary, 13 Sep. 1935.

However, while the cyclicity of the seasons is a powerful guarantor of continuity, the seasons erase the past too: the annual cycle of rebirth is also an annual cycle of death. It is telling that each of the diarists most passionately concerned to maintain the connection with the past in their personal lives cared deeply about the historic element of the countryside as well. What many of them held most dear was the continuity of life, uniting the human and the non-human in a richly integrated ongoing pattern: the human in the natural, rather than a version of either that excluded the other. Landscapes whose human and natural elements could be perceived as springing from a deep common root were therefore especially cherished, like Chewton Keynsham as Catley saw it one day in March 1934, 'lying unchanged in its valley as though the earth had just created it'.[96]

Gender, Class and Age

The landscape biographies that form the core of *Lifescapes* indicate that gender, class and age affected how the countryside was experienced, but at least in relation to class and gender, less than might have been expected.[97] Cresswell (middle-class female) had more in common with Hallam (working-class male) in her ruralism than either did with any of the other diarists, and Johnston (university-educated Scottish doctor) likewise with Bissell (lower middle-class English probation officer). Nature and the countryside were vitally important to Spear Smith (upper-middle-class female) and Catley (lower-middle-class male) in the construction of their respective identities. Conversely, Johnston and Catley, both well-educated non-conformists who lost their faith, were almost the antithesis of each other in their ruralism. It is true that of the eight diarists studied both the Withdrawers (Dickinson and Spear Smith) were female and both the Restorers (Johnston and Bissell) male. There may be a significant gender pattern here, although possibly more so in relation to Restorers than Withdrawers, since Dickinson's brother Ced was every bit as much a Withdrawer as she and had a very similar life trajectory. Undoubtedly, gender did affect the experience of rural landscapes, in a wide range of temporally and spatially contingent ways. For the eight diarists considered here, however, these effects were not pronounced at the level of deep experience. If, at least for the time and place under study, there was more that united than divided the sexes in relation to the fundamental meanings landscape held for them, it may be necessary to look at a greater number of cases than has been possible in this book for the gender differences that certainly were there to emerge clearly.

---

[96] BA, 41419/25, 3 Mar. 1934.

[97] Contrast Hinton, *Seven Lives*, 164: 'The most systematic contrast between the life experiences of the mass observers lay across the fault line of gender.'

Class differences are even less marked than gender contrasts, except in relation to transport. For example, it was partly due to their upper-middle-class backgrounds that Dickinson and Spear Smith made little use of public transport to access the countryside. Car touring was an important mode of rural landscape encounter for Dickinson as early as the 1890s whereas the working-class Hallam had to wait until the 1940s before he could do likewise, and then in someone else's car. The imprint of the considerable wealth, status and occupational differences between the subjects of this book on the deeper meanings landscape held for them is less easily discerned, although it should be kept in mind that only one of them (Hallam) was unambiguously working class – further research into working-class affective landscapes might reveal more distinct class-based patterns. The same applies *a fortiori* to ethnicity, given that I was unable to find diaries written by people of colour that met the study criteria and that it is difficult to trace Barmes's Jewishness in her ruralism.

Age had rather more obvious effects.[98] Unsurprisingly, rural excursions seem to have been most frequent in youth and early adulthood, when maximum physical capacity coincided with minimum commitments. However, there are few signs that interest in the countryside diminished with age (Catley is a partial exception). What did change were the modes of engaging with rural landscapes. In childhood, play, exploration and gathering seem to have been particularly significant. In youth, exploration continued to be an important mode, but intense sensory immersion seems to have been especially important for some. Young adulthood was often characterized by long walks, usually with friends, and bike rides. For five of the eight diarists there was little change as they entered middle age, but only one of these five married. A more typical example of middle-aged ruralism may have been William Hallam, for whom children initially brought a drastic reduction in rural outings. But these resumed in the form of short walks and picnics as the children became more mobile. In old age most of the diarists enjoyed sitting quietly in the landscape, especially in sunny weather. This could bring sensory experiences no less rewarding than, although different from, those of youth, and, at its best, a rare serenity. However, in the main the deeper motivations of, and satisfactions deriving from, rural landscape encounters changed less than the modes of accessing and moving (or not moving) through them.

---

[98] Compare Elizabeth Ewan and Janay Nugent, 'Introduction: Adding Age and Generation As a Category of Historical Analysis', in Elizabeth Ewan and Janay Nugent (eds.), *Children and Youth in Premodern Scotland* (Martlesham, 2015). See also 'Chronological Age: A Useful Category of Historical Analysis', AHR Roundtable, *American Historical Review* 125 (2020), 371–486.

Wider Implications

Historiographical Bearings

The apparently limited capacity of some of our core explanatory categories to account for the character of, and changes in, the experience of landscape in late nineteenth- and early twentieth-century England warrants further reflection. The integrity of any academic discipline, history included, can be maintained only if its key organizing concepts are subject to continual challenge and interrogation. Just as physicists are constantly hoping to find 'new physics' that cannot be explained within the framework of the standard model, so historians should be looking for 'new history' – evidence that problematizes and calls into question our dominant interpretative paradigms and that suggests new lines of inquiry which may ultimately lead to better paradigms.[99] Taking a deep history approach to the experience of landscape offers some intriguing glimpses of potential 'new history', in particular through unearthing evidence that implicates enduring psychological patterns formed in childhood and youth, and the demographic and familial structures that bear on these, as key explanatory factors affecting attitudes, values and behaviour, in contrast to discursive influences, 'big events' such as the world wars, and even staple categories of historical explanation such as class, gender and national identity (at least as independent variables; class and gender are of course among the influences that shape psycho-social experience in childhood).

The wider inference may be to endorse the cultural turn's rejection of the socio-economic determinism of vulgar Marxist accounts, but to raise a question mark over its replacement of this with what has at times threatened to become an equally rigid, and arguably even less plausible, cultural determinism.[100] It would indeed be quite mistaken, in the light of the evidence presented in this study, to attempt to read directly across from someone's class or gender to their affective relationship to landscape. But this would not be due to cross-cutting discursive influences. On the contrary, the sources on which this study are based suggest little correlation between discursive influences and affective relationships to landscape. Johnston and Catley were both great admirers of Jefferies, for example, but the ways they engaged with rural landscapes and the meanings these landscapes held for them were drastically different. Bissell and Catley's childhood home and community environments were dominated by Methodism, yet again their adult ruralism differed in almost every particular. Rather, the evidence presented in this book seems to me to indicate, many of the most powerful determinants of individuals' lives can only be captured at a fine scale of resolution. Very broad categories such as

---

[99] Joseph D. Lykken, 'Beyond the Standard Model', arXiv preprint arXiv:1005.1676 (2010).
[100] Compare Geoff Eley, 'Dilemmas and Challenges of Social History since the 1960s: What Comes after the Cultural Turn?', *South African Historical Journal* 60 (2008), 310–22.

class and gender do of course have some explanatory power, but they will often be too coarse-grained to be of much heuristic value. The early death of a parent had much more influence on Hallam, Cresswell and Catley's respective relationships to rural landscape, for example, than their class or gender did directly. Indirectly, however, socio-economic changes such as improved economic security and rising adult life expectancy were critical, because they were major influences on the contrasting psychological circumstances that this book argues were the principal first-order cause of differing affective relationships to landscape.

The Achilles' heel of cultural accounts has always been their difficulty in explaining change. If discourse is entirely unconstrained by non-discursive factors, there is no obvious reason why a particular discourse, if it is sufficiently powerful, pervasive and well-established, should ever give way to another.[101] To avoid this danger of circularity, discursive dogs endlessly chasing their own representational tails, it is difficult at some point to avoid invoking non-discursive constraints. A good example is Stedman-Jones' 'The Language of Chartism', one of the foundational statements of the cultural turn. Stedman-Jones argues that Chartism's language of popular exclusion from an aristocratic state became implausible once Sir Robert Peel abandoned protectionism and repealed the Corn Laws.[102] But if one non-discursive event of this kind can drive discursive change, it is difficult to see why others should not too. In relation to the cultural history of landscape, perhaps a deep history approach may in due course offer a way out of this impasse. As we have seen, the eight diarists were selective and discriminating in their response to representations of English rural landscapes, adopting some while filtering out others. They did so, to a large extent, on the basis of how far these representations spoke to the underlying psychological patterns that *Lifescapes* argues were at the root of affective responses to landscape. A better understanding of the subtle shifts and fluctuations of these psychological patterns over time might help to explain why particular landscape discourses waxed and waned. It would be premature to attempt to do so on the basis of the provisional typology developed in *Lifescapes* but I can see no reason why further research should not be able to extend and strengthen this, allowing more secure and persuasive connections with a wider social and cultural history to be made. If, for example, such research were to confirm the suggestion mooted in Chapter 3 that Adherer ruralism was especially prevalent in the last two or three decades

---

[101] William M. Reddy, *The Navigation of Feeling: A Framework for the History of the Emotions* (Cambridge 2001), xi.

[102] Gareth Stedman Jones, 'The Language of Chartism', in James Epstein and Dorothy Thompson (eds.), *The Chartist Experience: Studies in Working-Class Radicalism and Culture, 1830–60* (London, 1982).

of the nineteenth century, this would open up a new line of explanation for the rise of preservationist discourses and organizations during that period.

The Possibilities and Limits of Ruralism

The eight individuals studied in this book invested great hopes in landscape. Were they right in thinking that it can sustain and perhaps even transform our lives? Coleridge, retreating from his youthful ideals, warned sternly against such heady beliefs:

> I may not hope from outward forms to win
> The passion and the life, whose fountains are within.[103]

With this in mind, turning to nature or the countryside in search of answers to our problems could be seen as an evasion, an illusion, even an emotional cul-de-sac. Undoubtedly it was sometimes a form of emotional retreat. This was very clearly the case for Dickinson and Spear Smith. While Dickinson certainly felt safer in Holford than she would have done in Hampstead during the Second World War, even in deepest Somerset she continued to suffer from terrible anxiety and dread about bombing.[104] Moving from one place to another could not necessarily extirpate deep-rooted psychological fears. Similarly with Spear Smith, there are questions about the extent to which drawing back into the countryside and becoming a 'lover of nature' replaced social relationships rather than giving her a more secure base from which to develop them. Nevertheless, an initial emotional retreat seems to have enabled both women to achieve a long-term advance. After finally abandoning her artistic ambitions Spear Smith found contentment, peace of mind and at times glowing happiness in exploring the flora and fauna of the fields, woods and marshes near her Titchfield home. Dickinson had in many respects a more difficult background to contend with and also suffered devastating rejection when her lover of many years suddenly walked out on her. Nevertheless the protective cocoon provided by the intimate, closed and known landscape of Holford seems to have helped her to achieve a greater degree of emotional security and acceptance over time. By contrast, Catley's rich, diverse engagement with rural landscapes, seemingly much bolder and more outward-looking than Spear Smith's or Dickinson's, failed to sustain him as he grew older, partly perhaps because, for all its apparent sophistication, its core function was really to enable him to avoid change.

---

[103] Samuel Taylor Coleridge, 'Dejection: An Ode', in *The Poetical Works of Samuel Taylor Coleridge: With Life* (Edinburgh, 1881), 510–13.

[104] The aphorism 'Et in Arcadia, Ego' ('Even in Arcadia, I [death] am present') could have been coined for her).

The evidence suggests, then, that rural landscapes could sometimes provide an environment favourable towards personal development and the resolution of apparently intractable emotional difficulties. But there was no magic in the countryside: whether it proved a way forward or a diversion from the real issues depended on the use the individual in question chose or was able to make of it. Equally, the countryside was just one way, used by some people, of achieving or attempting to achieve these inner goals. There were undoubtedly other arenas, activities and practices that offered a comparable or perhaps even wider range of affordances.[105] It would be interesting to identify some of these alternative practices. For example, the pastimes and leisure activities of the individual diarists may have had overlapping functions and these could be investigated. Reading mattered greatly to Johnston, Hallam, Barmes and Catley, who was also very fond of music, as was Spear Smith.[106] Local history and antiquities fascinated Hallam, Cresswell and to a lesser extent Catley.[107] These areas of activity may have connected to some of the same patterns and achieved some of the same purposes as rural landscapes. To take one example, music, like the countryside, may have allowed Catley to experience intense sensations that nevertheless left him unchanged after they receded, and therefore did not entail any emotional risk. It also seems likely that there were other, quite unconnected activities and practices that achieved broadly similar purposes but which appealed to people to whom it did not occur or who could not or did not want to meet them through rural landscapes. There might have been many reasons for this. Over and above distance, time and transport costs, there must have been numerous material, cultural, familial and psychological barriers which in practice limited the affective availability of rural landscapes. Both the functionally parallel practices to affective engagement with rural landscapes and the barriers to such engagement deserve further research.

Beyond Ruralism

Is it possible to imagine a future in which rural landscapes were affectively redundant because the difficulties that people had once turned to them in the hope of escaping or resolving no longer existed? On the whole this seems

---

[105] The concept of landscape affordances is reviewed in H. Heft, 'Affordances and the Perception of Landscape: An Inquiry into Environmental Perception and Aesthetics', in C. Ward Thompson, P. Aspinall and S. Bell (eds.), *Open Space: People Space 2: Innovative Approaches to Researching Landscape and Health* (Abingdon, 2010).

[106] On the history of reading see Jonathan Rose, *The Intellectual Life of the British Working Classes* (New Haven, 2002). On amateur music see Dave Russell, *Popular Music in England: 1840–1914. A Social History* (Manchester, 1987); and Paula Gillett, *Musical Women in England, 1870–1914: Encroaching on All Man's Privileges* (Basingstoke, 2000).

[107] For cultures of local history see Alan J. Kidd, 'Between Antiquary and Academic: Local History in the Nineteenth Century', in R. C. Richardson (ed.), *The Changing Face of English Local History* (Aldershot, 2000).

unlikely, since many of them are deep-seated, enduring human problems. Cresswell's devotion to rural Devon, for example, was a displaced form of devotion to (and grief for) her father. A future in which we do not suffer when the people we love die is hard to imagine and might not even be desirable. However, the uses people make of landscape are also a social barometer. Many of the difficulties the diarists turned to the countryside for relief from were social or political in origin and might not arise in a society better adapted to its members' needs: Hallam's hatred of his deadening factory employment; the lack of social care for Cresswell's mother; the damage the competitive, status-conscious world of professional art inflicted on Spear Smith; the acute anxieties Dickinson's nouveau-riche isolation generated in her; the conflict between Johnston's principles and the exigencies of private medical practice; Barmes's desire to live in a cooperative society based on sharing, so different from the one she actually inhabited; Catley's father being 'cut off suddenly ... in a lunatic war without reaching anything', in the words of his son, suffering the lifelong consequences. Even Bissell's ruralism had a significant sociogenic component at one remove, since among its primary motivations was to redeem young men from the poverty, crime and misery of industrial Dudley. Hence it is possible to imagine that some existing functions of affective landscapes might become less pressing were we able to create between us a less isolating, divided and insecure society than the one we live in today.

AFTERWORD

The Politics of Landscape Experience

When I began writing this book the best part of two decades ago, I hoped to find a single explanation for popular ruralism. It was a disappointment to discover that rural landscapes fitted into each of the diarists' lives in a different way. However, on consideration I realized that hidden beneath this apparently multi-causal explanation was the mono-causal explanation I had been seeking. What the diarists looked for and what they took from the landscapes they were drawn to corresponded in each case to the distinctive assemblage of their psychological characteristics, refracted through the circumstances in which they found themselves. Since none of them had the same mix of characteristics or circumstances, it is unsurprising that landscape figured differently in each of their lives. Certainly there were some commonalities, and I have tried to draw attention to the most prominent of these through the Adherer–Withdrawer–Restorer–Explorer framework. But even within each of these categories there were wide differences in landscape experience. Of all the diarists, Cresswell and Hallam had most in common in the way they related to rural landscapes. Yet many elements of Cresswell's ruralism, including the irrepressible need to be free of social constraints that played such a large part in it, found little echo in Hallam, and this was equally true the other way round.

Scholars have made many value judgements, sometimes explicit, more often implicit, about different modes of relating to landscape. The 'tourist gaze' has been critiqued for its superficiality, as has the so-called rural idyll, the aesthetic of the Picturesque and the modernizing tidiness of 'planner–preservationists'. Some ways of apprehending landscape have been seen as superior to (perhaps because more authentic than) others. That may be a persuasive critique where mere 'attitudes' to landscape are concerned – half-baked ideas picked up from somewhere else, informed by no great depth of feeling or conviction. As I read and thought about the eight diaries, however, I became increasingly reluctant to make such judgements: for each of the diarists rural landscapes had, I found, been vectors of deeply felt hopes, fears, commitments and needs. This was true even for Dickinson, in whose relationship to landscape the much-anathematized tourist gaze played a significant part. But although Dickinson's understanding of and respect for the rag-wearing gypsy children or Sussex fishermen she photo-graphed was rudimentary and insufficient, the motives and pressures that informed her ruralism went no less deep than they did for the other diarists. Moreover, for each of the diarists, many of the motives that fed their ruralism were quite unconscious. It makes no more sense to praise or blame these motives (or the combined pattern they form) than to applaud someone for their age, height, gender or any other unchosen attribute. To be a Restorer like Bissell was not in any meaningful sense a better way to relate to landscape than to be a Withdrawer like Spear Smith. Each was an authentic reflection and expression of the diarist's character and circumstances, equally valid in its own right.

I began to wonder if the same might apply to other aspects of the diarists' experience – politics, for example. This mattered greatly to several of them, but (unlike landscape) not to all. Spear Smith was more concerned to hide from society than to change it, Bissell sternly repressed whatever political convictions he may have had to avoid alienating any of his congregation, Dickinson's politics were more a matter of fear than conviction and, except in one particular, Catley's politics expressed transient attitudes rather than a deeper orientation towards life. But Hallam and Cresswell's Conservatism, Johnston's ethical socialism, Barmes's Communism and Catley's pacifism were expressions of aspects of their respective characters and experiences that were fundamental in the same way their orientation towards landscape was. Their political views were far from being merely the result of propaganda, false consciousness or illusion. To take Hallam and Barmes, perhaps the most extreme examples: Hallam's almost feudal Conservatism expressed his deep-seated loyalties, profound gratitude to his patron Lord Wantage, and powerful need for continuity. Barmes's Communism sprang every bit as much from the roots of her being: her warm, joyous nature, generosity, gregariousness and the need to unite and share with others that these qualities prompted. If Hallam had not adhered staunchly to Conservatism (as he understood it), or if Barmes had not poured her spirit into Communism (again, as she understood it), each would have been less true to essential aspects of themselves; in D H Lawrence's idiom, a part of them would have remained 'unborn'.

There is a real and important sense, then, in which we should celebrate Hallam and Cresswell's Conservatism, Barmes's Communism, Johnston's socialism and Catley's pacifism. This seems to me a profoundly challenging conclusion to anyone with strong political convictions. At first glance it leads to a complete impasse: if all deeply held convictions are in principle equally valid, agreement seems impossible and we are left in an unhappy limbo of never-ending conflict. Certainly this line of thought implies a vastly different approach to political discussion than the superficial debate-style point-scoring currently prevalent in politics and the media. If deeply held political convictions express profound life experiences, fragments of a larger truth unseen, then attempting to gainsay them by rational argument is not only utterly futile but a loss to ourselves, because we are closing our eyes to life truths others have experienced and we perhaps have not.

This implies a much longer, more respectful conversation, founded on a desire to understand rather than persuade. We need to hear each other's truths, search for progressively fuller and more satisfactory ways of reconciling and integrating these, and seek to develop political institutions and processes that foster rather than thwart this more inclusive conception of democracy: a politics of patient listening rather than assertive telling. In the light of this I have refrained from my original intention of concluding in the same way as many of the works of history that have most inspired me, by linking the evidence I have presented to an explicit statement of my own political convictions. It seems to me that this would be out of keeping with the spirit of respect for each of the diarists, and every reader, which has been my guiding light. What I have tried to do instead in this book is to take a step back, into the realm of values from which political convictions grow, seeking to instantiate the more patient, listening mode from which it is at least conceivable that understanding, perhaps even agreement, might eventually develop. However, although I leave it to you, the reader, to draw your own political conclusions should you think them warranted, two things seem clear. The first is that any depth of mattering the preceding chapters inscribe arises from the common humanity we share with each of the diarists. The second is that the foundation of this book is a historiographical ethics of equal respect and care. Few would argue with this in a historical context, but whatever the other political implications of *Lifescapes* for different readers, we cannot be justified in withholding from present lives what we so obviously owe to those in the past.

SELECT BIBLIOGRAPHY

Primary Sources

Author's Personal Possession. Diaries of Sadie Attfield (née Barmes, 1920–32).

Berkshire Record Office. Diaries, Manuscripts and Other Papers of William Henry Hallam. D/EX 1415/ 1–63 (1886–1952).

Bolton Archives History Centre. The John Johnston Papers. ZJO/1/1–49 (1887–1918).

Bristol Archives. Diaries and Journals of F. J. Catley, 41419/2–68 (1925–63).

Devon Heritage Centre. Diaries of Beatrix F. Cresswell, 4686 M/F/36–77 (1898–9, 1901–40).

Dudley Archives and Local History Centre. Personal Records of Mr Bert Bissell. DBIS 1–56 (1930–81).

Hampshire Record Office. Papers of Katherine Spear Smith. Journals and Commonplace Books, 19M99/1 (1901–14). Nature Diaries, 19M99/2 (1901–19).

London Metropolitan Archives. The Invalids Magazine Album, LMA/4292/01 (1903–15).

New College, Oxford, Archives. Papers of Alic Halford Smith. PA/SMA 1/12–29 (1890–1919, 1954).

Somerset Heritage Centre. Dickinson of Holford, 1899–1990. Diaries [of Violet Dickinson], A\AGV/1–10 (1899–1902, 1905, 1907–52).

Secondary Sources

Appleton, Jay. *The Experience of Landscape*. Revised ed. Chichester, 1996.

Bellanca, Mary Ellen. *Daybooks of Discovery: Nature Diaries in Britain, 1770–1870*. Charlottesville, 2007.

Bunce, Michael. *The Countryside Ideal: Anglo-American Images of Landscape*. Abingdon, 1994.

Hinton, James. *Nine Wartime Lives*. Oxford, 2010.

    Seven Lives from Mass Observation: Britain in the Late Twentieth Century. Oxford, 2016.

Howard, Peter. *Landscapes: The Artists' Vision*. London, 1991.

Howard, Peter, Ian Thompson, Emma Waterton and Mick Atha, eds. *The Routledge Companion to Landscape Studies*. 2nd ed. London, 2018.

Ingold, Tim. *The Perception of the Environment: Essays on Livelihood, Dwelling and Skill.* London, 2000.

Landry, Donna E. *The Invention of the Countryside: Hunting, Walking, and Ecology in English Literature, 1671–1831.* Basingstoke, 2001.

Lejeune, Philippe. *On Diary.* Honolulu, 2009.

Macfarlane, Robert. *The Old Ways: A Journey on Foot.* London, 2012.

Marsh, Jan. *Back to the Land: The Pastoral Impulse in England, 1880–1914.* London, 1982.

Matless, David. *Landscape and Englishness.* London, 1998.

Readman, Paul. *Storied Ground: Landscape and the Shaping of English National Identity.* Cambridge, 2018.

Schama, Simon. *Landscape and Memory.* London, 1996.

Taylor, Harvey. *A Claim on the Countryside: A History of the British Outdoor Movement.* Edinburgh, 1997.

Thomas, Keith. *Man and the Natural World: Changing Attitudes in England 1500–1800.* Harmondsworth, 1984.

Walker, Helen J. 'The Outdoor Movement in England and Wales, 1900–1939'. University of Sussex, PhD, 1987.

Whyte, Nicola. 'Senses of Place, Senses of Time: Landscape History from a British Perspective'. *Landscape Research* 40, 8 (2015): 925–38.

Williams, Raymond. *The Country and the City.* London, 1973.

INDEX